Kaplan Publishing are constantly finding new difference to your studies and our exciting or offer something different to students looking

C000039605

This book comes with free MyKaplan online r study anytime, anywhere. **This free online resource is not sold separately and is included in the price of the book.**

Having purchased this book, you have access to the following online study materials:

CONTENT	ACCA (including FBT, FMA, FFA)		FIA (excluding FBT, FMA, FFA)	
	Text	Kit	Text	Kit
Electronic version of the book	✓	✓	✓	✓
Check Your Understanding Test with instant answers	✓			
Material updates	✓	✓	✓	✓
Latest official ACCA exam questions*		✓		
Extra question assistance using the signpost icon**		✓		
Timed questions with an online tutor debrief using clock icon***		✓		
Interim assessment including questions and answers	✓		✓	
Technical answers	✓	✓	✓	✓

* Excludes BT, MA, FA, FBT, FMA, FFA; for all other papers includes a selection of questions, as released by ACCA
** For ACCA SBL, SBR, AFM, APM, ATX, AAA only
*** Excludes BT, MA, FA, LW, FBT, FMA and FFA

How to access your online resources

Kaplan Financial students will already have a MyKaplan account and these extra resources will be available to you online. You do not need to register again, as this process was completed when you enrolled. If you are having problems accessing online materials, please ask your course administrator.

If you are not studying with Kaplan and did not purchase your book via a Kaplan website, to unlock your extra online resources please go to www.mykaplan.co.uk/addabook (even if you have set up an account and registered books previously). You will then need to enter the ISBN number (on the title page and back cover) and the unique pass key number contained in the scratch panel below to gain access. You will also be required to enter additional information during this process to set up or confirm your account details.

If you purchased through the Kaplan Publishing website you will automatically receive an e-mail invitation to MyKaplan. Please register your details using this email to gain access to your content. If you do not receive the e-mail or book content, please contact Kaplan Publishing.

Your Code and Information

This code can only be used once for the registration of one book online. This registration and your online content will expire when the final sittings for the examinations covered by this book have taken place. Please allow one hour from the time you submit your book details for us to process your request.

Please scratch the film to access your unique code.

Please be aware that this code is case-sensitive and you will need to include the dashes within the passcode, but not when entering the ISBN.

KAPLAN

PUBLISHING

ACCA

Strategic Professional – Options

Advanced Taxation (ATX-UK) (Finance Act 2021)

EXAM KIT

For June 2022 to March 2023 examination sittings

PUBLISHING

British Library Cataloguing-in-Publication Data

A catalogue record for this book is available from the British Library.

Published by:

Kaplan Publishing UK

Unit 2 The Business Centre

Molly Millar's Lane

Wokingham

Berkshire

RG41 2QZ

ISBN: 978-1-78740-895-1

Acknowledgements

These materials are reviewed by the ACCA examining team. The objective of the review is to ensure that the material properly covers the syllabus and study guide outcomes, used by the examining team in setting the exams, in the appropriate breadth and depth. The review does not ensure that every eventuality, combination or application of examinable topics is addressed by the ACCA Approved Content. Nor does the review comprise a detailed technical check of the content as the Approved Content Provider has its own quality assurance processes in place in this respect.

The past ACCA examination questions are the copyright of the Association of Chartered Certified Accountants. The original answers to the questions from June 1994 onwards were produced by the ACCA and have been adapted by Kaplan Publishing.

CONTENTS

Section

Versions of some questions in this Exam Kit may also be available on the ACCA Practice Platform on the ACCA website. They are a very useful reference, in particular to attempt using ACCA's exam software. However, you should be aware that ACCA will decide when those questions will be amended for syllabus changes or replaced, so they may differ slightly from the versions in this Exam Kit.

Key features in this edition

In addition to providing a wide ranging bank of real past exam questions, we have also included in this edition:

- An analysis of all of the recently published examination questions.

- Exam specific information and advice on exam technique.

- Our recommended approach to make your revision for this particular subject as effective as possible.

  This includes step by step guidance on how best to use our Kaplan material (study text, pocket notes and exam kit) at this stage in your studies.

- An increased number of enhanced tutorial answers packed with specific key answer tips, technical tutorial notes and exam technique tips from our experienced tutors.

- Complementary online resources including full tutor debriefs and question assistance to point you in the right direction when you get stuck.

You will find a wealth of other resources to help you with your studies on the following sites:

www.mykaplan.co.uk

www.accaglobal.com/en/student.html

Quality and accuracy are of the utmost importance to us so if you spot an error in any of our products, please send an email to mykaplanreporting@kaplan.com with full details, or follow the link to the feedback form in MyKaplan.

Our Quality Co-ordinator will work with our technical team to verify the error and take action to ensure it is corrected in future editions.

INDEX TO QUESTIONS AND ANSWERS

INTRODUCTION

The style of the ATX exam questions has changed over the years and significant changes have had to be made to questions in light of the legislative changes in recent Finance Acts.

Accordingly, many of the old ACCA questions within this kit have been adapted to reflect the new style of exam and the new rules. Therefore, some questions may not be worth 35, 25 or 20 marks. If changed in any way from the original version, this is indicated in the end column of the index below with the mark *(A)*.

Also included are the marking schemes for past ACCA real examination questions to assist you in understanding where marks are earned and the amount of time to spend on particular tasks. Note that if a question has been changed from the original version, it will have also been necessary to change the original ACCA marking scheme. Therefore if a question is marked as adapted (A) you should assume that this also applies to the marking scheme.

Note that the majority of the questions within the kit are past ACCA exam questions, the more recent questions are labelled as such in the index.

KEY TO THE INDEX

ANSWER ENHANCEMENTS

We have added the following enhancements to the answers in this exam kit:

Key answer tips

All answers include key answer tips to help your understanding of each question.

Tutorial note

All answers include more tutorial notes to explain some of the technical points in more detail.

Top tutor tips

For selected questions, we 'walk through the answer' giving guidance on how to approach the questions with helpful 'tips from a top tutor', together with technical tutor notes.

These answers are indicated with the 'footsteps' icon in the index.

ONLINE ENHANCEMENTS

 Question debrief

For selected questions, we recommend that they are to be completed in full exam conditions (i.e. properly timed in a closed book environment).

In addition to the ACCA's technical answer, enhanced with key answer tips and tutorial notes in this exam kit, online you can find an answer debrief by a top tutor that:

- works through the question in full
- points out how to approach the question
- how to ensure that the easy marks are obtained as quickly as possible, and
- emphasises how to tackle exam questions and exam technique.
- These questions are indicated with the 'clock' icon in the index.

 Online question assistance

Have you ever looked at a question and not known where to start, or got stuck part way through?

For selected questions, we have produced 'Online question assistance' offering different levels of guidance, such as:

- ensuring that you understand the question requirements fully, highlighting key terms and the meaning of the verbs used
- how to read the question proactively, with knowledge of the requirements, to identify the topic areas covered
- assessing the detailed content of the question body, pointing out key information and explaining why it is important
- help in devising a plan of attack.

With this assistance, you should then be able to attempt your answer confident that you know what is expected of you.

These questions are indicated with the 'signpost' icon in the index.

Online question enhancements and answer debriefs will be available on MyKaplan at:

www.mykaplan.co.uk

TAXATION OF INDIVIDUALS

TAXATION OF CORPORATE BUSINESSES

ANALYSIS OF PAST EXAMS

The table below summarises the key topics that have been tested in recent examinations.

Key:

Q   The question references are to the number of the question in this edition of the exam kit.

✓   Refers to questions which have not been included in the kit due to similarity to other recent questions.

	Sept 2018	Dec 2018	Mar/Jun 2019	Sept/Dec 2019	Mar 2020	Sept/Dec 2020	Mar/Jun 2021
IHT							
Lifetime gifts	Q53, ✓	Q36	Q37	Q46	✓, Q54	Q23, Q80	Q47
Death estate							
Diminution in value				Q46			
BPR/APR	✓		Q37	Q46			Q6
Gift with reservation					Q54		Q6
Quick succession relief							
Consequences of lifetime giving		Q36					Q47
Overseas aspects	Q53					Q23	Q47
Trusts							
CGT							
Basic computations	Q53	Q36		Q21, Q22	✓, Q79		
Leases							Q63
Shares		Q36	Q37, Q13		✓	Q23	
Reorganisations					✓		
Capital gains tax reliefs:							
Incorporation relief	✓			Q21	Q79	Q23	
Rollover relief	✓, Q76					Q15	
BADR	✓	Q36	Q37		Q79		
Gift holdover relief	✓		Q37	Q46	Q79		
PRR/letting relief		Q5					Q6
Planning	Q53	Q36					
Overseas aspects				Q46	✓	Q23	Q47
Income Tax							
Personal tax computations	Q53	Q5	Q37	Q21, Q22	Q14, Q54		Q47
Redundancy payments							
Share options and share incentives		Q5	Q37, Q13				Q6
Employment benefits		Q5	Q37, Q61			Q62	Q63
Employed v self employed							
Property business profits					Q54		
Overseas aspects of income				Q46	✓	Q23	Q47
NICs	✓		Q37, Q61	Q21, Q22	Q14	Q23	Q63

	Sept 2018	Dec 2018	Mar/Jun 2019	Sept/Dec 2019	Mar 2020	Sept/Dec 2020	Mar/Jun 2021
Self-employed Income							
– Opening year rules			Q13		Q14		Q24
– Change a/c date							
– Closing year rules						Q23	
– Capital allowances							Q24
– Trading losses	✓		Q13	Q21, Q22		Q15	
– Partnerships			Q13	Q22			
Badges of trade							
Self-assessment							
Employee v partner				Q22			
Corporation Tax							
Anti-avoidance – trading losses							
Loss relief			Q77	Q21	Q79		
Loan relationships				Q78			
Research and development			Q61		Q79		
Intangible assets				Q78	Q79		Q24
Transfer pricing				Q78			
Close companies	✓			Q21		Q62	Q63
Purchase of own shares							
Personal service company							
Groups	Q76	✓	Q77	Q78			
Consortium relief					Q79	Q80	
Capital gains implications including rollover	Q76, ✓	✓					Q63
Pre entry cap loss							
Substantial shareholding exemption	Q76			Q78			
Overseas Aspects		✓	Q77		Q79	Q80	
Extraction of profits (salary vs. dividend)	✓						
Liquidation							Q24
Administration		✓				Q62	
Sole trade v company				Q21			
Financial planning							
Investments	Q53				Q14		
Pensions		Q5			Q54		
EIS/SEIS/VCT	Q53				Q14		
Stamp Duty/SDLT	Q76						
VAT							
Registration/deregistration	✓		Q61		Q14	Q15	
Schemes				Q21			
Partial exemption							
Capital goods scheme		✓		Q22			
Groups			Q77				
Land and buildings	Q76	✓		Q22		Q80	Q24
Transfer of going concern	Q76						
Overseas aspects					Q79		
Ethical issues	Q76	✓	Q77	Q21	✓	Q80	Q47

EXAM TECHNIQUE

- We recommend that you spend **15 minutes reading the questions** at the beginning of the exam:
  - read the questions and examination requirements carefully, and
  - begin planning your answers.

  See the Exam Specific Information for advice on how to use this time for this exam.

- If 15 minutes are spent reading the exam, this leaves three hours to attempt the questions.

- **Divide the time** you spend on questions in proportion to the marks on offer:
  - one suggestion for this examination is to allocate 1.8 minutes to each mark available (180 minutes/100 marks), so a 20 mark question should be completed in approximately 36 minutes. If you plan to spend more or less time than 15 minutes reading the exam, your time allocation per mark will be different
  - within that, try to allow time at the end of each question to review your answer and address any obvious issues.

  Whatever happens, always keep your eye on the clock and **do not over run on any part of any question!**

- If you **get completely stuck** with a question:
  - make a note of the question, and
  - **return to it later.**

- A date assumption will be given at the start of each question. You should pay careful attention to this date and the timing of events noted in the scenario in relation to it. Some events may have already happened, whereas others may be planned for the future. For events which have already occurred reliefs may still be able to be claimed, but you need to consider if the relevant claim date has already passed. For future events there could be tax planning implications that could be discussed.

- Stick to the question and **tailor your answer** to what you are asked.
  - Pay particular attention to the verbs in the question.
  - Try to apply your comments to the scenario where possible.

- If you do not understand what a question is asking, **state your assumptions**.

  Even if you do not answer in precisely the way the examining team hoped, you should be given some credit, if your assumptions are reasonable.

- You should do everything you can to make things easy for the marker.

  Make sure your answers use headings so it is easy for the marker to follow what you're doing.

- **Written questions**:

  Your answer should have:
  - a clear structure
  - a brief introduction, a main section and a conclusion.

  Be concise. It is better to write a little about a lot of different points than a great deal about one or two points.

  You will have the choice of producing your answer using a word processor or spreadsheet. For answers that are mostly written you may find the word processor most useful.

- **Computations**:

  It is essential to include all your workings in your answers and ensure that they are clearly labelled.

  Although computations may be prepared using standard formats, you should always think about whether there is an easier way to arrive at the answer by working in the margin, say.

  You may find the spreadsheet function most useful for detailed computations.

- **Reports, memos and other documents**:

  Some questions ask you to present your answer in the form of a report, a memo, a letter or other document.

  Make sure that you use the correct format – there could be easy marks to gain here.

- **Scratch pad**:

  You will be able to make notes in the scratch pad to help with your planning. Please be aware that anything in the scratch pad will not be seen by the marker, and will therefore not score any marks. If you are sitting your exam via remote invigilation then you will not be permitted to use scrap paper, so the scratch pad will be the only way to carry out your planning. The scratch pad is available in the ACCA Practice Platform for you to practise using.

- **Requirements**:

  It is good practice to copy and paste the question requirements into your answer space. These can then be used as headings for your answer to ensure you are tailoring your answer to what the question has asked for.

EXAM SPECIFIC INFORMATION

THE EXAM

FORMAT OF THE EXAM

Number of marks

Section A: Two compulsory case-study questions:

Question 1	35
Question 2	25

There will be five ethics marks and four professional skills marks in this section.

Section B: Two compulsory 20 mark questions,
covering both business and personal tax issues

40 marks in total
_____
100
_____

Total time allowed: 3 hours and 15 minutes.

Note that:

- From March 2020, strategic professional exams have become available by computer based examination. This has now been rolled out to all markets so you will sit your exam as a CBE.

- Candidates will be expected to undertake both calculation and narrative work. The questions will be scenario based and may involve consideration of more than one tax, some elements of planning and the interaction of taxes.

- Every ATX exam will include an ethical component for five marks in section A. The questions on ethics will be confined to the following areas:

    - prospective clients

    - conflicts of interest

    - disclosure of information to HM Revenue & Customs

    - money laundering

    - tax irregularities

    - tax avoidance

    - tax evasion.

- Apart from the above, any subject may be tested anywhere in the exam for any number of marks.

- The exam will not just test ATX knowledge: TX knowledge is still highly examinable, but will be tested in a more advanced way.

- The requirements of a section A question may be presented in one of two different ways:
  - in full in the requirement exhibit, or
  - a brief overview can be provided in the requirement exhibit with further detail in other exhibits in the CBE.

PASS MARK

The pass mark for all ACCA Qualification examinations is 50%.

SUGGESTED APPROACH TO THIS EXAM

The ATX examination will be 3 hours and 15 minutes long, with no separate time allocated for reading and planning. However, reading and planning are crucial elements of your examination technique and it is important that you allocate time in the examination to this.

Spend time reading the examination questions carefully. As stated earlier, we recommend that 15 minutes should be spent reading the questions.

There is no choice of questions in the exam, but there is a decision to be made regarding the order in which you should attempt the questions.

Therefore, in relation to ATX, we recommend that you take the following approach with your reading and planning:

- **Skim through the whole exam**, assessing the level of difficulty of each question.

- **Note** in the scratch pad **the amount of time you should spend on each part.** Do this for each part of every question.

- **Decide the order** in which you think you will attempt each question:

  This is a personal choice and you have time on the revision phase to try out different approaches, for example, if you sit mock exams.

  A common approach is to tackle the question you think is the easiest and you are most comfortable with first.

  Others may prefer to tackle the longest questions first, or conversely leave them to the last.

  Psychologists believe that you usually perform at your best on the second and third question you attempt, once you have settled into the exam, so not tackling the bigger Section A questions first may be advisable.

  It is usual however that students tackle their least favourite topic and/or the most difficult question in their opinion last.

  Whatever your approach, you must make sure that you leave enough time to attempt all questions fully and be very strict with yourself in timing each question.

- **For each question** in turn, read the requirements and then the detail of the question carefully.

  Always read the requirement first as this enables you to **focus on the detail of the question with the specific task in mind**.

  For computational questions:

  Highlight key numbers/information and key words in the question, or use the scratch pad or answer space to make notes to yourself to remember key points in your answer. Remember that any notes made in the scratch pad will not be seen by the marker and so will not score marks.

  For written questions:

  Take notice of the format required (e.g. letter, memo, notes) and identify the recipient of the answer. You need to do this to judge the level of sophistication required in your answer and whether the use of a formal reply or informal bullet points would be satisfactory.

  Plan your beginning, middle and end and the key areas to be addressed and your use of titles and sub-titles to enhance your answer.

  For all questions:

  Spot the easy marks to be gained in a question and parts which can be performed independently of the rest of the question. For example, tax payment dates, ethical issues, laying out the answer in the correct format etc.

  Make sure that you do these parts first when you tackle the question.

  Don't go overboard in terms of planning time on any one question – you need a good measure of the whole exam and a plan for all of the questions at the end of the 15 minutes.

  By covering all questions you can often help yourself as you may find that facts in one question may remind you of things you should put into your answer relating to a different question.

- With your plan of attack in mind, **start answering your chosen question** with your plan to hand, as soon as you are ready to start.

 Always keep your eye on the clock and do not over run on any part of any question!

DETAILED SYLLABUS

The detailed syllabus and study guide written by the ACCA can be found at:

www.**acca**global.com/en/student.html

KAPLAN'S RECOMMENDED REVISION APPROACH

QUESTION PRACTICE IS THE KEY TO SUCCESS

Success in professional examinations relies upon you acquiring a firm grasp of the required knowledge at the tuition phase. In order to be able to do the questions, knowledge is essential.

However, the difference between success and failure often hinges on your exam technique on the day and making the most of the revision phase of your studies.

The **Kaplan study text** is the starting point, designed to provide the underpinning knowledge to tackle all questions. However, in the revision phase, poring over text books is not the answer.

Kaplan online knowledge checks help you consolidate your knowledge and understanding and are a useful tool to check whether you can remember key topic areas.

Kaplan pocket notes are designed to help you quickly revise a topic area, however you then need to practise questions. There is a need to progress to full exam standard questions as soon as possible, and to tie your exam technique and technical knowledge together.

The importance of question practice cannot be over-emphasised.

The recommended approach below is designed by expert tutors in the field, in conjunction with their knowledge of the examining team and their recent real exams.

The approach taken for the applied skills level exams is to revise by topic area. However, with the strategic professional exams, a multi topic approach is required to answer the scenario based questions.

It is very important that you familiarise yourself with the layout and functionality of the exam. You can do this by practising past exam questions which have been released in the ACCA practice platform. This enables you to attempt the questions in the real exam format and then self-mark them using detailed marking guides. More information on the practice platform and how to access it can be found at the following link:

https://www.accaglobal.com/gb/en/student/exam-entry-and-administration/computer-based-exams/strategic-professional-cbes/cbe-practice-platform.html

You need to practise as many questions as possible in the time you have left.

OUR AIM

Our aim is to get you to the stage where you can attempt exam standard questions confidently, to time, in a closed book environment, with no supplementary help (i.e. to simulate the real examination experience).

Practising your exam technique on real past examination questions, in timed conditions, is also vitally important for you to assess your progress and identify areas of weakness that may need more attention in the final run up to the examination.

In order to achieve this we recognise that initially you may feel the need to practise some questions with open book help and exceed the required time.

The approach below shows you which questions you should use to build up to coping with exam standard question practice, and references to the sources of information available should you need to revisit a topic area in more detail.

Remember that in the real examination, all you have to do is:

- attempt all questions required by the exam

- only spend the allotted time on each question, and

- get them at least 50% right!

Try and practise this approach on every question you attempt from now to the real exam.

EXAMINER COMMENTS

We have included the examiner's comments to the specific new syllabus examination questions in this kit for you to see the main pitfalls that students fall into with regard to technical content.

However, too many times in the general section of the report, the examiner comments that students had failed due to:

- 'misallocation of time'

- 'running out of time' and

- showing signs of 'spending too much time on an earlier question and clearly rushing the answer to a subsequent question'.

Good exam technique is vital.

STRATEGIC PROFESSIONAL CBE

From March 2020, ACCA introduced Strategic Professional computer based examinations (CBE) in selected locations. Strategic Professional CBE has now been extended to all locations and the paper-based exam is no longer available.

This Exam Kit is appropriate for CBE exams. It is essential that students become familiar with the CBE environment as part of their exam preparation. CBE versions of some past exam papers can be attempted on the ACCA practice platform. Moreover, the response areas in those past exam papers can be used when attempting questions from this Exam Kit. The more familiar you are with the CBE platform, the easier you will find your real CBE exam. For additional support please refer to the ACCA Global website.

THE KAPLAN ATX REVISION PLAN

Stage 1: Assess areas of strengths and weaknesses

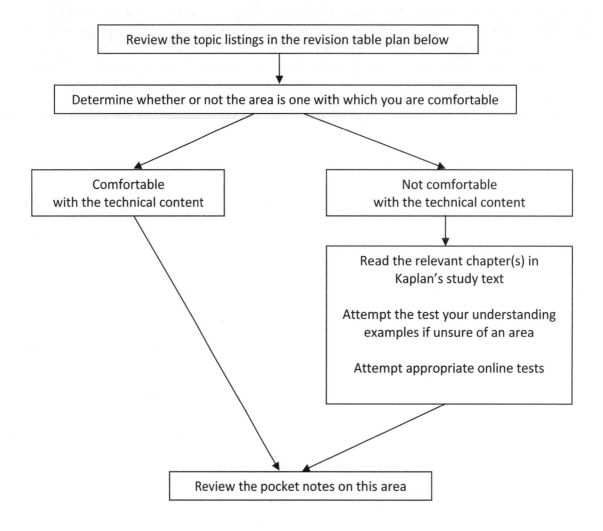

Stage 2: Practise questions

Follow the order of revision of topics as recommended in the revision table plan below and attempt the questions in the order suggested.

Try to avoid referring to text books and notes and the model answer until you have completed your attempt.

Try to answer the question in the allotted time.

Review your attempt with the model answer and assess how much of the answer you achieved in the allocated exam time.

KAPLAN PUBLISHING

Fill in the self-assessment box below and decide on your best course of action.

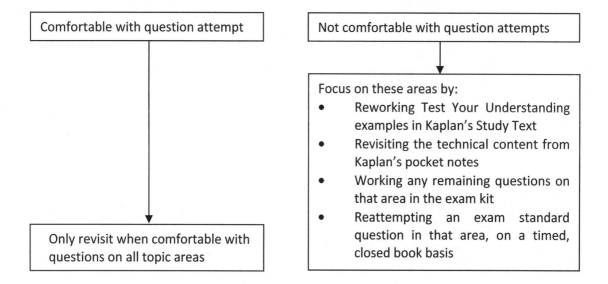

| Comfortable with question attempt | Not comfortable with question attempts |

Focus on these areas by:
- Reworking Test Your Understanding examples in Kaplan's Study Text
- Revisiting the technical content from Kaplan's pocket notes
- Working any remaining questions on that area in the exam kit
- Reattempting an exam standard question in that area, on a timed, closed book basis

Only revisit when comfortable with questions on all topic areas

Note that:

 The 'footsteps questions' give guidance on exam techniques and how you should have approached the question.

 The 'signpost questions' offer online question assistance to help you to attempt your question confidently and know what is expected of you.

 The 'clock questions' have an online debrief where a tutor talks you through the exam technique and approach to that question and works the question in full.

Stage 3: Final pre-exam revision

We recommend that you **attempt at least one three hour and 15 minute mock examination** containing a set of previously unseen exam standard questions.

It is important that you get a feel for the breadth of coverage of a real exam without advance knowledge of the topic areas covered – just as you will expect to see on the real exam day.

Ideally this mock should be sat in timed, closed book, real exam conditions and could be

- a mock examination offered by your tuition provider, and/or

- a practise exam released on the ACCA practice platform.

KAPLAN'S DETAILED REVISION PLAN

Very few of the recent ATX exam questions focus on just one area of tax.

This is especially true of the big scenario questions, which often test several different areas.

This revision plan aims to lead you through a selection of the best questions, broadly grouped by the areas covered, and will ensure that you revise all of the key topics.

It is especially important that you practise the more recent questions, as the examining team has its own particular style.

Familiarisation with this style of questions will help to make sure that you are as well-prepared as possible for the real exam.

Topic	Study Text Chapter	Pocket notes Chapter	Questions to attempt	Tutor guidance	Date attempted	Self-assessment
Corporation tax	Corporation tax is often an area that students struggle with, but in recent exams has regularly formed the basis of one of the compulsory scenario questions. For this reason, it would be a good idea to start by revising corporation tax to ensure that you have enough time to cover it thoroughly.					
Losses, anti-avoidance re trading losses c/f;	3	1	Q64 Daube Group	The corporation tax scenario questions will often involve a group of companies; VAT is a regular feature too.		
Losses and gains groups;	4	2	Q74 Harrow Tan Ltd	Use your Kaplan pocket notes to make sure that you are happy with all the different group definitions and implications before attempting these questions. You must also learn the reliefs available for the various types of losses, as it is easy to get these confused.		
Substantial shareholding exemption;	2	1				
Pre entry capital losses; Capital loss restriction;	4	2		Rollover relief is the only capital gains relief available to companies, making it a highly examinable area.		
Rollover relief;	9	6		VAT on land and buildings is a favourite area, and regularly features in questions.		
VAT: Land and buildings and overseas aspects;	26, 27	3, 18		Don't worry if you find these questions hard – the scenario questions will get easier with practice. There are walkthrough answers to help you if you get stuck.		
Ethics	14	10				

Topic	Study Text Chapter	Pocket notes Chapter	Questions to attempt	Tutor guidance	Date attempted	Self-assessment
				Note that stamp duty and ethics often represent easy marks in this type of question.		
Substantial shareholding exemption;	2	1	Q78 Kitz Ltd	Another excellent scenario question. Having attempted the previous two questions, you should start to find these easier as you become familiar with the style of question and the areas that are frequently tested.		
Degrouping charges;	4	2				
Transfer pricing;	2	1				
Loan relationships;	2	1				
Intangible fixed assets	2	1				
Sale of shares versus sale of assets;	4	2	Q76 Grand Ltd Group	This big scenario question covers disposal of a subsidiary through sale of its shares or assets. Look at the mark allocations here to gauge how much you need to write.		
Substantial shareholding exemption;	2	1		Transfer of going concern is something that is often tested with a transfer of trade and assets, so ensure you learn the conditions and be prepared to apply them to the scenario.		
Degrouping charges;	4	2		The question has some easy marks for stamp duty land tax and ethics, so ensure you allocate your time so that you can pick these up.		
Stamp duty land tax;	6	7				
VAT: Transfer of going concern;	26	18				
Ethics	14	10				

Topic	Study Text Chapter	Pocket notes Chapter	Questions to attempt	Tutor guidance	Date attempted	Self-assessment
Further issues: Research and development;	2	1	Q75 Set Ltd Group, Q80 REP Ltd	Before attempting Q75, use your Kaplan pocket notes to make sure that you learn the rules governing the following:		
Overseas aspects: Controlled foreign companies (CFCs);	5	3		– enhanced relief available to companies for R&D expenditure, and		
CT instalments;	1	1		– the conditions and possible exemptions for CFCs.		
VAT: Land and buildings and overseas aspects;	26, 27	3, 18		There are also marks here again for group loss reliefs and VAT.		
Ethics	14	10		Then attempt Q80, which is another big scenario question covering many of the same areas – with some inheritance tax thrown in at the end!		
Test question			Q71 Hahn Ltd Group	Now try attempting this question under exam conditions. If you spend 15 minutes reading and planning at the start of the exam, you have 1.8 minutes per mark, so 63 minutes in total.		

Topic	Study Text Chapter	Pocket notes Chapter	Questions to attempt	Tutor guidance	Date attempted	Self-assessment
The Capital taxes	The key capital taxes are capital gains tax and inheritance tax. Inheritance tax often features as part of both a compulsory question and an optional question, often linked with capital gains tax.					
Inheritance tax basics; Income tax basics; Trusts	10–12 16 13	8 11 9	Q26 Alex Q29 Surfe	Q26 is a good question to start with, covering the basic calculations and includes a straightforward income tax computation in part (a), and a written section on trusts. Trusts often feature as a small written section. Q29 also has a section on trusts and some basic inheritance tax computations, as well as some slightly trickier calculations. Related property and the transfer of a spouse's unused nil rate band are regularly tested, so make sure that you are happy with these.		
Inheritance tax: further computations; Business property relief (BPR); Admin	10–11 11 12	8 8 8	Q28 Kepler	This question includes popular complications: the diminution in value principle and BPR. BPR features in nearly every exam, so you must learn the conditions in detail. Also use your Kaplan pocket notes to make sure that you learn the payment dates for inheritance tax, particularly payment by instalment.		

Topic	Study Text Chapter	Pocket notes Chapter	Questions to attempt	Tutor guidance	Date attempted	Self-assessment
Inheritance tax versus capital gains tax; Agricultural property relief; BPR; Gift holdover relief, Private residence relief; Planning	12 11 11 9 9 12	8 8 8 6 6 15	Q25 Joan Ark Q35 Sabrina and Adam (a) Q33 Cada	The examining team often test both the inheritance tax and capital gains tax implications of lifetime gifts, and there are many questions on this area. Q25 is not in current exam style, but is a great question as it covers most of the calculations and reliefs available for both IHT and CGT. Before attempting this question, make sure that you revise the CGT reliefs thoroughly, and try not to get IHT and CGT confused! Note that part (ii) of this question, on the advantages of lifetime gifts, is very general. You will probably have to apply this knowledge in an exam question, and just pick out the points which are relevant. Have a go at Q35 (a), a real past exam question from section B of the exam. This question covers IHT and CGT with reliefs. Then try Q33, another section B question.		
Test question			Q32 Pescara	Try answering this one under exam conditions.		

Topic	Study Text Chapter	Pocket notes Chapter	Questions to attempt	Tutor guidance	Date attempted	Self-assessment
Income tax				Income tax is not likely to be tested on its own at ATX, but will often feature as part of a bigger question.		
				For many of the questions set at this level, the examining team will not require you to do a whole income tax computation, but rather to start part way through.		
				For example, you may have to calculate just the tax on some extra income, working in the margin.		
				Be prepared to write about employment benefits as well as doing calculations.		
Employment income; Private residence relief; Letting relief; Pensions; Share options	17 9 19 17	12 6 13 12	Q5 Demeter	This question is split into four requirements which are all independent of one another and can be attempted in any order. The first three requirements all cover TX knowledge, so you should find these straight forward if you have revised this well. Be careful in parts (b) and (c) as you need to ensure you have both explanations and calculations in order to score well. Part (c)(ii) covers share option plans. As this is one of the few new areas of employment income at ATX it is frequently tested.		
Company share option plan; Share incentive plan; Private residence relief; Letting relief; Gift with reservation	17 17 9 12	12 12 6 8	Q6 Yacon Ltd and Daikon	The first part of this question covers two tax-advantaged share schemes: the CSOP and SIP. Share schemes are frequently tested, as they are not examined at TX. The last part of the question covers another topic that often features in the ATX exam: gifts with reservation of benefit for inheritance tax. Make sure that you are able to identify these and explain the consequences.		

Topic	Study Text Chapter	Pocket notes Chapter	Questions to attempt	Tutor guidance	Date attempted	Self-assessment
Personal financial planning	You may be asked to advise on suitable investment products in the exam, particularly tax efficient forms of investment. Again, this is not likely to form the basis of a whole question, but will generally be combined with other areas.					
Self-employment Income tax and NIC; Choice of year end date; Voluntary VAT registration; Enterprise investment scheme and EIS reinvestment relief	21 21 26 18 9	16 16 18 10 6	Q14 Tomas and Ines	This question is made up of four parts which focus on self-employment aspects, VAT and the enterprise investment scheme (EIS). Use your Kaplan pocket notes to revise the conditions for EIS before attempting this question – you need a good knowledge of the rules.		
Pensions	19	13	Q49 Stella and Maris	This question tests all aspects of pensions and so is a good one to practise to get back up to speed. Although pensions were covered at TX, they still feature quite often at ATX.		
Test question			Q39 Poblano	Try attempting this question to exam time.		
Overseas aspects of personal tax	Overseas aspects for individuals are very popular in the exam, often appearing in section B questions but also sometimes in the section A scenario questions. Before attempting these questions, use your Kaplan pocket notes to revise the definitions of residence and domicile, and make sure that you can explain how a person's status affects the way they are taxed.					
Overseas aspects: Inheritance tax; Residence tests; Capital gains tax	12 20 20	14 14 14	Q44 Noah and Dan	This is a good test of your knowledge of the rules regarding domicile, deemed domicile and the implications for inheritance tax, together with computations. This question also covers some of the residence tests, which regularly feature in the exam.		

Topic	Study Text Chapter	Pocket notes Chapter	Questions to attempt	Tutor guidance	Date attempted	Self-assessment
Capital gains tax: overseas aspects	20	14	Q45 Max	This is a great question to revise the temporary absence rules for CGT, with IHT and CGT for lifetime gifts too. It contains a both words and numbers, and you must apply the rules to the scenario to score well.		
Income tax overseas aspects	20	14	Q47 Fiona (c)	Part (c) of this question covers the remittance basis for income tax. This is often tested, so make sure that you learn the rules.		
Test question			Q46 Emma	Try attempting this excellent scenario question, covering various aspects of overseas personal tax, to exam time.		
Business scenarios				There are lots of business scenarios for the examining team to test, and because of the many aspects of tax that apply, these often feature as big section A questions. Much of the knowledge required is basic TX knowledge, but you must make sure you keep this knowledge up to date.		
Commencement of trade with basic income tax; NICs; IHT re lifetime gift; EIS relief	21 10 18	16 8 10	Q50 Pippin	This is a scenario involving calculating the additional finance needed for an individual to start a business as a sole trader. There are many easy marks available for basic knowledge – the hard part is finding the relevant information and structuring your answer.		
Change of accounting date and choice of year end	21	16	Q8 Piquet and Buraco (a)	This question requires careful thought about the impact of a change in year end on an individual's overlap profits.		

Topic	Study Text Chapter	Pocket notes Chapter	Questions to attempt	Tutor guidance	Date attempted	Self-assessment
Cessation of trade; IHT related property	22 11	16 8	Q11 Juanita	The first part of Q11 requires you to calculate the reduction in IHT if a gift had been made as a lifetime gift instead of at death. This tests one of the new areas at ATX which is related property, though there are still plenty of marks for brought forward knowledge from TX. The second part of the question is looking at comparing post tax income from two potential cessation dates. This tests mostly brought forward knowledge but with higher skills aspects as you are expected to work in the margin and think about what taxes would be suffered.		
Test question			Q9 Ray and Shanira	This is a good question on changing business scenarios, which also tests VAT registration and husband and wife planning!		
Incorporation; CGT: Incorporation relief, SBAs, Business asset disposal relief	22 9 9	16 6 6	Q16 Stanley Beech (a)	Incorporation is a popular scenario as there are many different tax implications. This question cover some of these areas, particularly the CGT aspects with some planning points.		
Test question			Q18 Ziti	Try attempting this question to exam time.		
Qualifying interest payments; Partnerships; Basis periods; Redundancy; Income tax computation	16 23 21 17 16	11 16 16 12 11	Q10 Amy and Bex	This section B question is mainly made up of areas which are within the TX syllabus, such as partnership profit allocation and opening year rules. Redundancy payments are very common in the exam so make sure you revise these before attempting this question.		

Topic	Study Text Chapter	Pocket notes Chapter	Questions to attempt	Tutor guidance	Date attempted	Self-assessment
Test question			Q38 Nucleus Resources	Try attempting this question to exam time.		
Family companies and planning scenarios	The following are also common scenarios that you need to be familiar with, although areas such as IR35, purchase of own shares and liquidations tend to only come up every few sittings in the exam.					
Business structure: unincorporated versus company; Loss reliefs; VAT registration	21, 2 3 26	16, 1 1 18	Q17 Desiree	Before attempting this question, you may want to use your Kaplan pocket notes to revise loss reliefs and the opening year assessment rules for individuals. Try not to confuse unincorporated businesses (individuals) and companies: the computations for individuals are all based around the tax year, whereas companies are taxed based on their chargeable accounting period.		
Extraction of funds from a company	24	17	Q16 Stanley Beech (b)	Extraction of funds from a company is an area you should be familiar with, but this question illustrates how the examining team likes to test common topics in a less obvious way.		
IR35	24	17	Q48 Monisha and Horner (b)	You may want to revisit the test your understandings covering the calculation of deemed direct payments under IR35 before attempting this question.		
Purchase of own shares	24	17	Q60 Traiste Ltd	Make sure you learn the conditions for purchase of own shares before you do this question. Part (c) illustrates another way that the examining team can test extraction of funds from a company.		

Topic	Study Text Chapter	Pocket notes Chapter	Questions to attempt	Tutor guidance	Date attempted	Self-assessment
Close companies; VAT: Partial exemption	24 26	17 18	Q56 Nocturne Ltd	Close companies are a fairly regular feature in the exam. Make sure that you know the definition and the tax consequences. This question also covers VAT for partially exempt businesses, which is another area that you need to be happy with.		
Liquidations	8, 24	5, 17	Q24 Joe (a)	Liquidations are not tested regularly, but are fairly straightforward and mainly involve consideration of the difference in tax treatment between dividends and capital gains.		

Note that not all of the questions are referred to in the programme above.

We have recommended an approach to build up from the basic to exam standard questions where possible.

The remaining questions are available in the kit for extra practice for those who require more questions on some areas.

TAX RATES AND ALLOWANCES

Throughout this exam kit:

1   You should assume that the tax rates and allowances for the tax year 2021/22 and for the financial year to 31 March 2022 will continue to apply for the foreseeable future unless you are instructed otherwise.

2   Calculations and workings need only to be made to the nearest £.

3   All apportionments should be made to the nearest month.

4   All workings should be shown.

Income tax

		Normal rates	Dividend rates
Basic rate	£1 – £37,700	20%	7.5%
Higher rate	£37,701 – £150,000	40%	32.5%
Additional rate	£150,001 and above	45%	38.1%
Savings income nil rate band	– Basic rate taxpayers		£1,000
	– Higher rate taxpayers		£500
Dividend nil rate band			£2,000

A starting rate of 0% applies to savings income where it falls within the first £5,000 of taxable income.

Personal allowance

Personal allowance	£12,570
Transferable amount	£1,260
Income limit	£100,000

Where adjusted net income is £125,140 or more, the personal allowance is reduced to zero.

Residence status

Days in UK	Previously resident	Not previously resident
Less than 16	Automatically not resident	Automatically not resident
16 to 45	Resident if 4 UK ties (or more)	Automatically not resident
46 to 90	Resident if 3 UK ties (or more)	Resident if 4 UK ties
91 to 120	Resident if 2 UK ties (or more)	Resident if 3 UK ties (or more)
121 to 182	Resident if 1 UK tie (or more)	Resident if 2 UK ties (or more)
183 or more	Automatically resident	Automatically resident

Remittance basis charge

UK resident for:	Charge
Seven out of the last nine years	£30,000
12 out of the last 14 years	£60,000

Car benefit percentage

The relevant base level of CO_2 emissions is 55 grams per kilometre.

The percentage rates applying to petrol-powered motor cars (and diesel-powered motor cars meeting the RDE2 standard) with CO_2 emissions up to this level are:

51 grams to 54 grams per kilometre	14%
55 grams per kilometre	15%

The percentage for electric-powered motor cars with zero CO_2 emissions is 1%.

For hybrid-electric motor cars with CO_2 emissions between 1 and 50 grams per kilometre, the electric range of a motor car is relevant:

Electric range

130 miles or more	1%
70 to 129 miles	4%
40 to 69 miles	7%
30 to 39 miles	11%
Less than 30 miles	13%

Car fuel benefit

The base figure for calculating the car fuel benefit is £24,600.

Company van benefits

The company van benefit scale charge is £3,500, and the van fuel benefit is £669. Vans producing zero emissions have a 0% benefit.

Individual savings accounts (ISAs)

The overall investment limit is £20,000.

Property income

Basic rate restriction applies to 100% of finance costs relating to residential properties.

Pension scheme limits

Annual allowance	£40,000
Minimum allowance	£4,000
Threshold income limit	£200,000
Income limit	£240,000
Lifetime allowance	£1,073,100

The maximum contribution that can qualify for tax relief without any earnings is £3,600.

Approved mileage allowances: cars

Up to 10,000 miles	45p
Over 10,000 miles	25p

Capital allowances: rates of allowance

Plant and machinery

Main pool	18%
Special rate pool	6%

Motor cars

New cars with zero CO_2 emissions	100%
CO_2 emissions between 1 and 50 grams per kilometre	18%
CO_2 emissions over 50 grams per kilometre	6%

Annual investment allowance

Rate of allowance	100%
Expenditure limit	£1,000,000

Enhanced capital allowances for companies

Main pool super deduction	130%
Special rate pool first year allowance	50%

Structures and buildings allowance

Straight-line allowance	3%

Cash basis accounting

Revenue limit	£150,000

Cap on income tax reliefs

Unless otherwise restricted, reliefs are capped at the higher of £50,000 or 25% of income.

Corporation tax

Rate of tax – Financial year 2021	19%
– Financial year 2020	19%
– Financial year 2019	19%
Profit threshold	£1,500,000

Value added tax (VAT)

Standard rate	20%
Registration limit	£85,000
Deregistration limit	£83,000

Inheritance tax: nil rate bands and tax rates

Nil rate band		£325,000
Residence nil rate band		£175,000
Rate of tax on excess	– Lifetime rate	20%
	– Death rate	40%

Inheritance tax: Taper relief

Years before death	**Percentage reduction**
More than 3 but less than 4 years	20%
More than 4 but less than 5 years	40%
More than 5 but less than 6 years	60%
More than 6 but less than 7 years	80%

Capital gains tax: tax rates

	Normal rates	**Residential property**
Lower rate	10%	18%
Higher rate	20%	28%
Annual exempt amount		£12,300

Capital gains tax: business asset disposal relief and investors' relief

Lifetime limit – business asset disposal relief	£1,000,000
– investors' relief	£10,000,000
Rate of tax	10%

National insurance contributions

Class 1 Employee	£1 – £9,568 per year	Nil
	£9,569 – £50,270 per year	12%
	£50,271 and above per year	2%
Class 1 Employer	£1 – £8,840 per year	Nil
	£8,841 and above per year	13.8%
	Employment allowance	£4,000
Class 1A		13.8%
Class 2	£3.05 per week	
	Small profits threshold	£6,515
Class 4	£1 – £9,568 per year	Nil
	£9,569 – £50,270 per year	9%
	£50,271 and above per year	2%

Rates of interest (assumed)

Official rate of interest	2.00%
Rate of interest on underpaid tax	2.60%
Rate of interest on overpaid tax	0.50%

Standard penalties for errors

Taxpayer behaviour	Maximum penalty	Minimum penalty – unprompted disclosure	Minimum penalty – prompted disclosure
Deliberate and concealed	100%	30%	50%
Deliberate but not concealed	70%	20%	35%
Careless	30%	0%	15%

Stamp duty land tax on non-residential properties

Up to £150,000	0%
£150,001 – £250,000	2%
£250,001 and above	5%

Stamp duty

Shares	0.5%

TIME LIMITS AND ELECTION DATES

Income tax

Election/claim	Time limit	For 2021/22
Agree the amount of trading losses to carry forward	4 years from the end of the tax year in which the loss arose	5 April 2026
Current and prior year set-off of trading losses against total income (and chargeable gains)	12 months from 31 January following the end of the tax year in which the loss arose	31 January 2024
Three year carry back of trading losses in the opening years	12 months from 31 January following the end of the tax year in which the loss arose	31 January 2024
Three year carry back of terminal trading losses in the closing years	4 years from the end of the last tax year of trading	5 April 2026
Set-off of loss on the disposal of unquoted trading company shares against income	12 months from 31 January following the end of the tax year in which the loss arose	31 January 2024
Transfer of assets eligible for capital allowances between connected parties at TWDV	2 years from the date of sale	

National Insurance Contributions

Election/claim	Time limit	For 2021/22
Class 1 primary and secondary – pay days	17 days after the end of each tax month under PAYE system (14 days if not paid electronically)	22nd of each month
Class 1 A NIC – pay day	22 July following end of tax year (19 July if not paid electronically)	22 July 2022
Class 2 NICs – pay days	Paid under self-assessment with balancing payment	31 January 2023
Class 4 NICs – pay days	Paid under self-assessment with income tax	

Capital gains tax

Election/claim	Time limit	For 2021/22
Replacement of business asset relief for individuals (Rollover relief)	4 years from the end of the tax year: – in which the disposal occurred or – the replacement asset was acquired whichever is later	5 April 2026 for 2021/22 sale or acquisition (if later event)
Holdover relief of gain on the gift of a business asset (Gift holdover relief)	4 years from the end of the tax year in which the disposal occurred	5 April 2026
Disapplication of incorporation relief	2 years from the 31 January following the end of the tax year in which the business is transferred	31 January 2025
	If sell all shares by 5 April following tax year of incorporation: Time limit 12 months earlier than normal claim date	31 January 2024
EIS reinvestment relief	5 years from 31 January following the end of the tax year in which the disposal occurred	31 January 2028
Business assets disposal relief and investors' relief	12 months from 31 January following the end of the tax year in which the disposal occurred	31 January 2024
Determination of private residence	2 years from the acquisition of the second property	

Self-assessment – individuals

Election/claim	Time limit	For 2021/22
Pay days for income tax and class 4 NIC	1st instalment: 31 January in the tax year	31 January 2022
	2nd instalment: 31 July following the end of tax year	31 July 2022
	Balancing payment: 31 January following the end of tax year	31 January 2023
Pay day for CGT (not UK residential property) and class 2 NIC	31 January following the end of tax year	31 January 2023
Pay day for CGT on UK residential property disposals	Within 30 days of the disposal	

Self-assessment – individuals

Election/claim	Time limit	For 2021/22
Filing dates If notice to file issued by 31 October following end of tax year	Paper return: 31 October following end of tax year Electronic return: 31 January following end of tax year	31 October 2022 31 January 2023
If notice to file issued after 31 October following end of tax year	3 months from the date of issue of the notice to file	
Retention of records Business records	5 years from 31 January following end of the tax year	31 January 2028
Personal records	12 months from 31 January following end of the tax year	31 January 2024
HMRC right of repair	9 months from date the return was filed	
Taxpayers right to amend a return	12 months from 31 January following end of the tax year	31 January 2024
Error or mistake claim	4 years from the end of the tax year	5 April 2026
HMRC can open an enquiry	12 months from submission of the return	
HMRC can raise a discovery assessment – No careless or deliberate behaviour	4 years from the end of the tax year	5 April 2026
– Tax lost due to careless behaviour	6 years from the end of the tax year	5 April 2028
– Tax lost due to deliberate behaviour	20 years from the end of the tax year	5 April 2042
Taxpayers right of appeal against an assessment	30 days from the assessment – appeal in writing	

Inheritance tax

Election/claim	Time limit	For 2021/22
Lifetime IHT on CLTs – pay day	Gift before 1 October in tax year: Following 30 April Gift on/after 1 October in tax year: 6 months after the end of the month of the gift	30 April 2022
Death IHT : on lifetime gifts within seven years of death (CLTs and PETs) and on the estate value	6 months after the end of the month of death	
Deed of variation	2 years from the date of death – in writing	
Transfer of unused nil rate band to spouse or civil partner	2 years from the date of the second death	

Corporation tax

Election/claim	Time limit
Replacement of business asset relief for companies (Rollover relief)	4 years from the end of the accounting period: – in which the disposal occurred or – the replacement asset was acquired whichever is later
Set-off of brought forward losses against total profits (income and gains)	2 years from the end of the accounting period in which the loss is relieved
Current year set-off of trading losses against total profits (income and gains), and 12 month carry back of trading losses against total profits (income and gains)	2 years from the end of the accounting period in which the loss arose
Surrender of current period and brought forward losses to other group companies (group relief and consortium relief)	2 years after the claimant company's accounting period
Election for transfer of capital gain or loss to another company within the gains group	2 years from the end of the accounting period in which the disposal occurred by the company actually making the disposal

Self-assessment – companies

Election/claim	Time limit
Pay day for small and medium companies	9 months and one day after the end of the accounting period
Pay day for large companies	Instalments due on 14th day of: – Seventh, Tenth, Thirteenth, and Sixteenth month **after the start** of the accounting period
Filing dates	Later of: – 12 months from the end of the accounting period – 3 months form the issue of a notice to deliver a corporation tax return
Companies error or mistake claim	4 years from the end of the accounting period
HMRC can open an enquiry	12 months from the actual submission of the return
Retention of records	6 years from the end of the accounting period

Value added tax

Election/claim	Time limit
Compulsory registration Historic test: – Notify HMRC	30 days from end of the month in which the threshold was exceeded
– Charge VAT	Beginning of the month, one month after the month in which the threshold was exceeded
Future test: – Notify HMRC	30 days from the date it is anticipated that the threshold will be exceeded
– Charge VAT	the date it is anticipated that the threshold will be exceeded (i.e. the beginning of the 30 day period)
Compulsory deregistration	30 days from cessation
Filing of VAT return and payment of VAT	End of month following the return period

Section 1

PRACTICE QUESTIONS

TAXATION OF INDIVIDUALS

EMPLOYMENT

1   MORICE AND BABEEN PLC (ADAPTED) *Walk in the footsteps of a top tutor*

You should assume that today's date is 6 April 2022.

Morice is the finance director of Babeen plc. Babeen plc is a non-close quoted trading company. Morice wants to provide information to the company's employees on a proposed Save As You Earn (SAYE) share option scheme, a medical care scheme and payments to employees for driving their own cars on business journeys. Morice also requires advice on the capital gains tax implications of a sale of shares.

The following information has been obtained from a telephone conversation with Morice.

Proposed SAYE scheme rules:

– Employees will invest in the scheme for five years.

– The scheme will permit monthly investments of between £5 and £750.

– The scheme will be open to all employees and directors who are at least 21 years old and have worked full-time for the company for at least three years.

– The share options granted under the scheme will enable employees to purchase shares for £2.48 each.

Detailed explanations, with supporting calculations, requested by Morice:

– Whether or not each of the proposed rules will be acceptable for a SAYE scheme.

– The tax and national insurance liabilities for the employee in the illustrative example below in respect of the grant and exercise of the share options, the receipt of the bonus and the sale of the shares on the assumption that the scheme referred to meets all of the HMRC conditions.

Illustrative example – SAYE scheme that meets HMRC conditions:

- The share options will be granted on 1 January 2023 to purchase shares at £2.48 each.
- The employee will invest £250 each month for five years.
- The amount invested will be used to exercise share options.
- The share options will be exercised on 31 December 2027 and the shares will be sold on the same day.
- The employee's interest in the employing company will be less than 1%.
- A share in the employing company will be worth: £3.00 on 1 January 2023
  £4.00 on 31 December 2027

Medical care scheme:

- Babeen plc is to offer free private health insurance to its employees.
- The health insurance will cost the company £470 annually per employee.
- The insurance would cost each employee £590 if they were to purchase it personally.
- Employees who decline the offer will be able to borrow up to £12,500 from Babeen plc to pay for medical treatment.
- The loans will be interest-free and repayable over four years.

Payments to employees for driving their own cars on business journeys:

- For each mile driven – 36 pence.
- For each mile driven whilst carrying a passenger – an additional 3 pence.

Sale of shares in Wind Ltd:

- Morice subscribed for 3,500 £1 ordinary shares in Wind Ltd at par in April 2017.
- Wind Ltd is a UK manufacturing company and is not a qualifying company under the enterprise investment scheme or seed enterprise investment scheme.
- Morice sold all of his shares in Wind Ltd in August 2021 for £150,000.
- Morice is a higher rate taxpayer and has made no other disposals during the tax year 2021/22.

Required:

(a) Prepare the DETAILED explanations, with supporting calculations, as requested by Morice in respect of the proposed SAYE scheme.   **(10 marks)**

(b) Explain the income tax and national insurance implications for the employees of Babeen plc of:

(i)   the medical care scheme   **(3 marks)**

(ii)   the payments for driving their own cars on business journeys.   **(4 marks)**

(c) Calculate the capital gains tax payable by Morice on the sale of the Wind Ltd shares and explain the rate of tax that has been used.   **(3 marks)**

You should assume that the rates and allowances for the tax year 2021/22 apply throughout this question.

(Total: 20 marks)

2 HYSSOP LTD *Walk in the footsteps of a top tutor*

You should assume that today's date is 1 April 2022.

Hyssop Ltd wishes to provide assistance with home to work travel costs for Corin, who is an employee, and also requires advice on the corporation tax implications of the purchase of a short lease and the value added tax (VAT) implications of the sale of a warehouse.

Hyssop Ltd:

– Is a UK resident trading company.
– Prepares accounts to 31 December each year.
– Is registered for VAT.
– Leased a factory on 1 February 2022.

Corin:

– Is resident and domiciled in the UK.
– Is an employee of Hyssop Ltd, who works only at the company's head office.
– Earns an annual salary of £55,000 from Hyssop Ltd and has no other source of income.

Hyssop Ltd – assistance with home to work travel costs:

– Hyssop Ltd is considering two alternatives to provide assistance with Corin's home to work travel costs.

Alternative 1 – provision of a motorcycle:

– Hyssop Ltd will provide Corin with a leased motorcycle for travelling from home to work.
– Provision of the leased motorcycle, including fuel, will cost Hyssop Ltd £3,160 per annum. This will give rise to an annual taxable benefit of £3,160 for Corin.
– Corin will incur no additional travel or parking costs in respect of his home to work travel.

Alternative 2 – payment towards the cost of driving and provision of parking place:

– Hyssop Ltd will reimburse Corin for the cost of driving his own car to work up to an amount of £2,240 each year.
– Corin estimates that his annual cost for driving from home to work is £2,820.
– Additionally, Hyssop Ltd will pay AB Parking Ltd £920 per year for a car parking space for Corin near the head office.

Acquisition of a factory:

– Hyssop Ltd acquired a 40-year lease on a factory on 1 February 2022 for which it paid a premium of £260,000.
– The factory is used in Hyssop Ltd's trade.

Disposal of a warehouse:

- Hyssop Ltd has agreed to sell a warehouse on 31 December 2022 for £315,000, which will give rise to a chargeable gain of £16,520.
- Hyssop Ltd had purchased the warehouse when it was newly constructed on 1 January 2019 for £270,000 (excluding VAT).
- The warehouse was used by Hyssop Ltd in its trade until 31 December 2021, since when it has been rented to an unconnected party.
- Until 1 January 2022, Hyssop Ltd made only standard-rated supplies for VAT purposes.
- Hyssop Ltd has not opted to tax the warehouse for VAT purposes.
- The capital goods scheme for VAT applies to the warehouse.

Required:

Note: You should ignore value added tax (VAT) for parts (a) and (b).

(a) Explain, with the aid of calculations, which of the two alternatives for providing financial assistance for home to work travel is most cost efficient for:

    (i)   **Corin.**   **(5 marks)**

    (ii)   **Hyssop Ltd.**   **(3 marks)**

(b) Explain, with the aid of calculations, the corporation tax implications for Hyssop Ltd of the acquisition of the leasehold premises on 1 February 2022, in relation to the company's tax adjusted trading profits for the year ended 31 December 2022 and its ability to roll over the gain on the sale of the warehouse.   **(8 marks)**

(c) Explain, with the aid of calculations, the VAT implications of the disposal of the warehouse on 31 December 2022.   **(4 marks)**

                                                (Total: 20 marks)

3   METHLEY LTD (ADAPTED) *Walk in the footsteps of a top tutor*

You should assume that today's date is 6 April 2022.

Your firm has been asked to provide advice to Methley Ltd, a close company, in respect of the provision of share incentives, a motor car and an interest-free loan to employees. A non-UK domiciled employee also requires advice in relation to the remittance basis.

Methley Ltd:

- Is a UK resident trading company which is a close company.

Simon – share incentives:

- Simon is a director of Methley Ltd and owns 20% of its ordinary shares.
- Methley Ltd intends to provide Simon with shares worth £25,000, in the form of either free shares or share options.
- The free shares would be issued in June 2023.
- The share options would be issued under a tax advantaged company share option scheme (CSOP) in June 2023 and Simon would exercise the options in October 2027.
- In either case, Simon will sell the shares in December 2029.
- Simon is a higher rate taxpayer.

Chris:

– Is employed by Methley Ltd and owns 10% of its ordinary shares.

– Has been offered the sole use of a company motor car or, alternatively, a loan to enable him to purchase the same motor car himself.

– Receives a salary from the company of £60,000 and receives dividends of £2,000 each year.

Chris – alternative 1 – company motor car:

– Methley Ltd would purchase the motor car on 1 October 2022 for £9,600, which is £800 less than the list price.

– The motor car would immediately be made available to Chris exclusively for his private use.

– The motor car has CO_2 emissions of 76 grams per kilometre and is diesel powered. The car meets the RDE2 standard.

– Chris would contribute £700 per year towards the private use of the motor car. Chris pays for all of his diesel himself.

– Methley Ltd would give the motor car to Chris after three years, when its market value is expected to be £6,300.

Chris – alternative 2 – loan:

– Methley Ltd would provide Chris with an interest-free loan of £9,600 on 1 October 2022.

– The loan would be written off in three years' time.

Yara – non-UK domiciled employee:

– Is currently resident in the UK but domiciled in the country of Setubia.

– Became UK resident when she was employed by Methley Ltd on 1 April 2014.

– Receives an annual salary from Methley Ltd of £82,000 and has no other UK source of income.

– Receives rental income from an unfurnished residential property in Setubia.

Yara – overseas rental income:

– The gross annual rental income from the overseas property is £24,000.

– Yara only remits £10,000 of this income to the UK each year.

– Yara has previously claimed the remittance basis each tax year.

Required:

(a) Compare and contrast the tax implications of both the acquisition and disposal of the shares in Methley Ltd if Simon acquires the shares through a tax advantaged company share option scheme (CSOP) or, alternatively, as an award of shares.

Note: You are not required to comment on any national insurance contributions implications. **(7 marks)**

(b) Prepare calculations to determine which of the two proposed benefits (the company motor car or the loan) will result in the lower overall income tax cost for Chris.

(6 marks)

(c) Advise Yara whether or not it would be beneficial for her to claim the remittance basis in the tax year 2021/22, and calculate the increase, if any, in her income tax liability for the tax year 2021/22 compared to that of previous years, assuming that she chooses the most tax beneficial course of action.

Note: You are not required to consider the potential availability of double taxation relief (DTR). **(7 marks)**

(Total: 20 marks)

4 DAMIANA PLC *Walk in the footsteps of a top tutor*

You should assume that today's date is 1 August 2022.

Luiza, the finance director of Damiana plc, requires advice on the corporation tax treatment of the company's expenditure on research and development (R&D) and the consequences of the late filing of its recent corporation tax returns. Luiza also wishes to know the tax implications for her of two alternative ways of acquiring shares in Damiana plc.

Damiana plc:

– Is a UK resident quoted trading company.

Damiana plc – R&D expenditure:

– Damiana plc is a large company for the purpose of tax relief for R&D expenditure.
– During the year ending 31 March 2023, Damiana plc will incur expenditure on qualifying R&D of £169,000.
– Damiana plc will have taxable total profits, before any deduction in respect of R&D expenditure, of £1,675,000 in the year ending 31 March 2023.

Damiana plc – late filing of corporation tax returns:

– Damiana plc prepared accounts for the 18-month period ended 31 March 2021.
– The corporation tax returns for this period were filed on 15 July 2022.
– All previous corporation tax returns have been filed on time.

Luiza:

–   Is employed as the finance director of Damiana plc, earning a gross annual salary of £165,000.

–   Has no other source of taxable income.

–   Has been offered two alternative ways to acquire ordinary shares in Damiana plc.

–   In either case she will sell these shares on 10 November 2025 when their market value is expected to be £32.70 per share.

–   Uses her annual exempt amount for capital gains tax purposes each year.

Acquisition of Damiana plc shares – alternative 1:

–   Damiana plc will transfer 5,000 ordinary shares (a 1% holding) to Luiza on 1 November 2022 for which Luiza will pay £1 per share.

–   The market value of these shares on 1 November 2022 is expected to be £24.50 per share.

–   Damiana plc does not expect to pay a dividend in the foreseeable future.

Acquisition of Damiana plc shares – alternative 2:

–   Damiana plc will grant options over 5,000 ordinary shares to Luiza on 1 November 2022 under its newly established enterprise management incentive (EMI) scheme.

–   The exercise price of these options will be £23.00 per share.

–   Luiza will exercise the options on 2 November 2025.

Required:

(a)   **Explain, with supporting calculations, the tax relief available for the research and development (R&D) expenditure incurred by Damiana plc in the year ending 31 March 2023, and the amount of corporation tax which will be saved as a result of claiming this relief.** **(5 marks)**

(b)   **Identify the accounting periods for which corporation tax returns were required from Damiana plc in respect of the 18-month period ended 31 March 2021. State the due date(s) for filing the returns in each case, and the implications for Damiana plc in respect of their late filing.** **(3 marks)**

(c)   **Explain the tax implications for Luiza if she acquires 5,000 ordinary shares in Damiana plc alternatively, (1) by means of a transfer on 1 November 2022, or (2) as a result of exercising the share options on 2 November 2025. On the assumption that she sells the shares as planned on 10 November 2025, calculate Luiza's net increase in wealth under each alternative.** **(12 marks)**

(Total: 20 marks)

5   DEMETER

You should assume that today's date is 5 December 2022.

Demeter has recently taken up a new employment and is seeking advice on the tax treatment of certain components of his remuneration package, and the relief(s) available to reduce the chargeable gain on the sale of his house.

Demeter:

–   Is UK resident and domiciled.

–   Commenced employment with Poseidon Ltd on 1 December 2022.

–   Will have no source of income, other than from Poseidon Ltd, in all relevant future tax years.

–   Will be a higher rate taxpayer in all relevant future tax years.

–   Has relocated to London, from Manchester, a city around 200 miles north of London, to take up this employment.

Remuneration package from Poseidon Ltd:

–   Demeter will receive an annual salary of £130,000.

–   On 1 December 2022, Poseidon Ltd made a one-off lump sum payment of £20,000 to Demeter as an inducement to take up employment with the company.

–   Poseidon Ltd paid Demeter £5,000 towards his costs of relocating to London. The company is also paying him £1,500 each month for four months from 1 December 2022 towards renting accommodation in London until he purchases a new house on 1 April 2023.

–   On 1 December 2022, Demeter was granted share options in Poseidon Ltd's non-tax advantaged share option scheme.

–   From 6 April 2023, Demeter will participate in Poseidon Ltd's occupational pension scheme.

Relocation to London:

–   Demeter incurred costs in relation to his relocation to London of £6,000. This amount includes estate agent fees of £2,800 in connection with the sale of his house in Manchester on 31 October 2022.

–   Demeter signed a four-month lease for a flat in London from 1 December 2022 at a monthly rental of £1,700.

House in Manchester:

–   Demeter purchased the house on 1 May 2009 and lived in it as his main residence.

–   Demeter let the top floor of the house (comprising 30% of the total house) to tenants from 1 May 2011 to 31 October 2022. The tenants did not share Demeter's living accommodation or take meals with him.

–   Demeter continued to occupy the remainder of the house as his main residence until 31 October 2022, when the entire house was sold.

–   The sale gave rise to a gain, before any reliefs, of £94,000.

–   Demeter did not own any other house throughout the period from 1 May 2009 to 31 October 2022.

Demeter – pension contributions:

– Demeter has made tax-allowable contributions of £40,000 (gross) to a personal pension plan for the last five tax years and will continue to do so in future tax years.

– From the tax year 2023/24, Poseidon Ltd will contribute an amount equal to 10% of Demeter's annual salary to its occupational pension scheme.

– Demeter will make no contributions to Poseidon Ltd's occupational pension scheme.

Poseidon Ltd's share option scheme:

– On 1 December 2022, Poseidon Ltd granted Demeter options over 3,000 shares in its non-tax advantaged share option scheme at a 5% discount on the market value of the shares on that date.

– The market value of Poseidon Ltd shares on 1 December 2022 was £4.20 per share.

– Demeter will exercise the options on 6 April 2028, and immediately sell the shares.

– Poseidon Ltd believes that the market value of its shares on 6 April 2028 will be £6.00 per share.

Required:

(a) Explain the extent to which the receipt of the £20,000 lump sum inducement payment, and the relocation package in relation to Demeter's move to London, will give rise to taxable employment income for him. **(5 marks)**

(b) Identify, and calculate, with brief explanations, the relief(s) available to Demeter to reduce the chargeable gain of £94,000 on the sale of his house in Manchester on 31 October 2022. **(6 marks)**

(c) Explain, with supporting calculations, the tax consequences for Demeter of participating in:

(i) Poseidon Ltd's occupational pension scheme in the tax year 2023/24.

(5 marks)

(ii) Poseidon Ltd's non-tax advantaged share option scheme, in respect of the grant of the options on 1 December 2022 and the exercise of the options and subsequent sale of the shares on 6 April 2028. **(4 marks)**

Note: Ignore national insurance contributions (NIC).

(Total: 20 marks)

6   YACON LTD AND DAIKON

You should assume that today's date is 1 December 2022.

Daikon, the managing director of Yacon Ltd, has requested advice on the tax implications of Yacon Ltd setting up a tax advantaged share incentive scheme for its employees. He also requires advice on the capital gains tax relief(s) available on the sale of his house, and the potential inheritance tax liability arising on the gift of an apartment.

Yacon Ltd:

– Is a UK resident trading company.

– Is considering setting up either a company share option plan (CSOP), or a share incentive plan (SIP), both of which would be offered to selected employees.

Yacon Ltd – criteria for its tax advantaged share incentive scheme:

- Employees will be selected to join the scheme dependent on their period of employment with the company.
- If the scheme is a CSOP, each employee will be offered options to purchase shares worth up to £3,000 each year.
- Employees will exercise the options five years after being granted them.
- If the scheme is a SIP, each employee will be given free shares worth up to £3,000 each year.
- Employees will remove the shares from the plan after five years.

Daikon:

- Was gifted an apartment by his aunt, Jicama, on 5 June 2020.
- Has never lived in this apartment.
- Will sell the house he currently lives in, and move in to this apartment on 31 December 2022.

Daikon – sale of his current house:

- Daikon purchased this house on 1 July 2014, when he was employed overseas.
- Daikon did not own any other property between 1 July 2014 and 4 June 2020.
- The sale of the house on 31 December 2022 will give rise to a chargeable gain of £145,000, before any reliefs.

Daikon – occupation of his current house:

- Daikon moved in to the house on 1 January 2015, on his return to the UK.
- Daikon has occupied the house since 1 January 2015, apart from the period from 1 July 2016 to 31 December 2017, when he was, once again, employed overseas.
- Daikon resumed exclusive occupation of the house on 1 January 2018.
- Since 1 April 2018, Daikon has let the basement of the house (which comprises 25% of the property) for residential use, retaining exclusive occupation of the remaining 75% for himself.

Gift of the apartment by Jicama:

- When Jicama gifted the apartment to Daikon on 5 June 2020, it was on condition of her continuing to live in the property for the foreseeable future.
- On 12 March 2022, Jicama began living with her sister, and she removed the condition she had previously imposed on the gift from that date.

Required:

(a) **Explain whether or not (1) a company share option scheme (CSOP) and (2) a share incentive plan (SIP) will satisfy Yacon Ltd's criteria for a tax advantaged share incentive scheme, and the income tax implications for the employees of acquiring the shares in each case.** **(8 marks)**

(b) **Calculate, with brief explanations, the private residence relief (PRR), and letting relief (if any), which are available to reduce the chargeable gain on Daikon's sale of his house.** **(7 marks)**

(c) **Explain the inheritance tax implications of Jicama's gift of the apartment to Daikon on 5 June 2020, if Jicama were to die in December 2025.** **(5 marks)**

(Total: 20 marks)

UNINCORPORATED BUSINESSES

7   GLORIA SEAFORD (ADAPTED)   *Online question assistance*

You should assume that today's date is 6 December 2022.

Gloria Seaford is UK resident but is not domiciled in the UK. She has owned and run a shop in the UK selling books, cards and small gifts as a sole trader since coming to the UK in June 2010.

Gloria was born on 4 January 1955 and on 1 November 2022 she started looking for a buyer for the business so that she could retire. She has received an offer of £335,000 for the shop premises from Ned Skillet who intends to convert the building into a restaurant.

The following information has been extracted from her client files and from a recent meeting with Gloria.

Gloria's business

– Purchased current premises, which were built in 2002, in July 2020 for £267,000.

– Registered for value added tax.

– Plans to sell the shop premises to Ned on 28 February 2023 and cease to trade on that day.

– Estimates that on 28 February 2023 she will be able to sell the shelving and other shop fittings to local businesses for £1,400 (no item will be sold for more than cost).

– Has agreed to sell all inventory on hand on 28 February 2023 to a competitor at cost plus 5%. This is expected to result in sales revenue of £8,300.

– Only other business asset is a van that is currently used 85% for business purposes. The van is expected to be worth £4,700 on 28 February 2023 and Gloria will keep it for her private use.

– Tax adjusted trading profit for the year ended 31 October 2022 was £39,245.

– Forecast tax adjusted trading profit for the period ending 28 February 2023, before taking account of the final sale of the business assets on that date and before deduction of capital allowances, is £11,500.

– Gloria has overlap profits brought forward of £15,720.

Capital allowances

– The tax written down value on the capital allowance main pool at 31 October 2022 was £4,050.

– Purchased equipment for £820 in November 2022.

– The tax written down value of the van at 31 October 2022 was £4,130.

Other income in 2022/23

– Pension income of £5,662.

– Bank interest of £16,875.

Capital assets and capital disposals

– On 1 November 2020 Gloria inherited the following assets from her aunt.

	Probate value
	£
Painting	15,200
17,500 shares in All Over plc	11,400

– Gloria sold the painting in May 2022 and realised a chargeable gain of £7,100.

– At the end of April 2021 Gloria received notification that All Over plc, a quoted trading company, was in receivership and that there would be a maximum payment of 3 pence per share.

– In August 2022 Gloria sold a UK residential property realising a gain of £80,000. Gloria had never lived in this property.

– A payment on account of £10,248 has been made in respect of the capital gains tax on the residential property.

– Gloria has unused capital losses as at 6 April 2022 of £31,100.

Investment opportunities

– Eric Sloane, a business associate of Gloria, has provided her with the details of a number of investment opportunities including Bubble Inc, an investment company incorporated in the country of Oceania where its share register is maintained.

– Gloria plans to buy a 2% share in Bubble Inc in May 2023, and expects to receive dividends of £12,000 per annum from the tax year 2023/24, which she will leave in an overseas bank account.

– There is no foreign tax withheld on these dividends.

– Gloria paid Eric £300 for his advice.

Required:

(a) State the value added tax implications of the sale by Gloria of her business assets and cessation of trade.

Calculations are not required for this part of the question. **(3 marks)**

(b) Compute Gloria's total income tax and national insurance liability for the tax year 2022/23. **(7 marks)**

(c) (i) Compute Gloria's capital gains tax payable for the tax year 2022/23 ignoring any claims or elections available in respect of All Over plc. **(5 marks)**

(ii) Explain, with reasons, the relief available in respect of the fall in value of the shares in All Over plc, identify the years in which it can be claimed and state the time limit for submitting the claim. **(3 marks)**

(d) (i) Explain the options available to Gloria in respect of the UK tax on the dividends paid by Bubble Inc.

You should calculate the tax payable under each alternative for the tax year 2023/24, assuming that Gloria's other income remains the same as in 2022/23, and advise which basis should be chosen. **(8 marks)**

(ii) Explain the capital gains tax and inheritance tax implications of a future disposal of the shares.

Clearly state, giving reasons, whether or not the payment made to Eric is allowable for capital gains tax purposes. **(8 marks)**

You should assume that the rates and allowances for the tax year 2021/22 apply throughout this question. **(Total: 34 marks)**

 Online question assistance

---

8   **PIQUET AND BURACO** *Walk in the footsteps of a top tutor*

You should assume that today's date is 1 June 2022.

Your firm has been asked to provide advice to two unrelated clients, Piquet and Buraco. Piquet, an unincorporated sole trader, requires advice on a proposed change to the date to which he prepares his accounts. Buraco requires advice on his residence status and the remittance basis.

(a) **Piquet:**

- Began trading as an unincorporated sole trader on 1 January 2015.
- Has always prepared accounts to 31 October.
- Has overlap profits of £15,000 for a five-month overlap period.
- Is planning to change his accounting date to 28 February 2023.

Actual and budgeted tax adjusted trading profit of Piquet's business:

	Profit per month	Profit for the period
	£	£
Year ended 31 October 2021	4,500	54,000
16 months ending 28 February 2023	5,875	94,000
Year ending 29 February 2024	7,333	88,000
Year ending 28 February 2025	9,000	108,000

Alternative choice of accounting date:

– Piquet is also considering a year end of 30 April.

– To achieve this, Piquet would prepare accounts for the 18 months ending 30 April 2023 and annually thereafter.

Required:

(i) On the assumption that Piquet changes his accounting date to 28 February, state the date by which he should notify HM Revenue and Customs of the change, and calculate the taxable trading profit for each of the tax years 2022/23 and 2023/24. **(3 marks)**

(ii) On the assumption that Piquet changes his accounting date to 30 April, state the basis periods for the tax years 2022/23 and 2023/24 and the effect of this change on Piquet's overlap profits. **(3 marks)**

(iii) Identify and explain TWO advantages for Piquet of using a year end of 30 April rather than 28 February. **(4 marks)**

(b) **Buraco's links with the country of Canasta:**

– Buraco is domiciled in Canasta.

– Buraco owns a home in the country of Canasta.

– Buraco's only income is in respect of investment properties in Canasta.

– Buraco frequently buys and sells properties in Canasta.

Buraco's links with the UK:

– Buraco's ex-wife and their 12 year-old daughter moved to the UK on 1 May 2021.

– Buraco first visited the UK in the tax year 2021/22 but was not UK resident in that year.

– Buraco did not own a house in the UK until he purchased one on 6 April 2022.

– Buraco expects to live in the UK house for between 100 and 150 days in the tax year 2022/23.

Required:

(i) Explain why Buraco will not satisfy any of the automatic overseas residence tests for the tax year 2022/23, and, on the assumption that he does not satisfy any of the automatic UK residence tests, explain how his residence status will be determined for that tax year. **(7 marks)**

(ii) On the assumption that Buraco is resident in the UK in the tax year 2022/23, state the tax implications for him of claiming the remittance basis for that year and explain whether or not there would be a remittance basis charge.

(3 marks)

(Total: 20 marks)

9   RAY AND SHANIRA (ADAPTED)   *Walk in the footsteps of a top tutor*

You should assume that today's date is 9 June 2022.

Your manager has received schedules of information from Ray and Shanira in connection with their personal tax affairs. These schedules and an extract from an email from your manager are set out below.

Schedule of information from Ray – dated 8 June 2022

I was born in 1964. I am resident and domiciled in the UK. Shanira and I are getting married on 17 September 2022.

Ray – unincorporated business

I was employed part-time until 31 March 2022. The annual salary in respect of my part-time job was £15,000. The whole of my income tax liability has always been settled via tax deducted at source.

I began trading on 1 June 2022. I purchased a computer on 3 June 2022, which is used both in the business and personally. I am not registered for the purposes of value added tax (VAT).

You have advised me that my taxable trading profits are calculated using the accruals basis, rather than the cash basis, and the budgeted taxable trading profits of the business are:

Eight months ending 31 January 2023   £35,000

Year ending 31 January 2024   £66,000

You have already informed me that my taxable trading profit based on these budgeted profits, and my income tax liability in respect of all of my income will be:

Tax year	Taxable trading profit	Income tax liability
2022/23	£46,000	£6,686
2023/24	£66,000	£13,832

What tax payments will I be required to make between 1 July 2022 and 31 March 2025?

Schedule of information from Shanira – dated 8 June 2022

I was born in 1966. I am resident and domiciled in the UK. Ray and I are getting married on 17 September 2022.

Gifts from Shanira to Ray

On 1 February 2022, I gave Ray a house situated in the country of Heliosa. We have only ever used this house for our holidays. The house was valued at £360,000 at the time of this gift. I purchased the house on 1 September 2005 for £280,000.

I will make the following further gifts to Ray between now and the end of the calendar year 2022:

–   Painting

       I purchased this painting at auction for £15,000 on 1 March 2018. It is a painting which we both love and would never sell. However, I obviously paid too much for it, as its current market value is only £7,000.

> – Shares in Solaris plc
>
> I will give Ray the whole of my holding of 7,400 ordinary shares in Solaris plc. The current market value is £9.20 per share.
>
> I acquired these shares on 1 October 2020 when Solaris plc purchased the whole of the ordinary share capital of Beem plc. This takeover was a genuine commercial transaction.
>
> At the time of the takeover:
>
> – I owned 3,700 ordinary shares in Beem plc, which I had purchased on 1 June 2014 for £12,960.
> – In addition to the shares in Solaris plc, I also received £14,800 in cash from Solaris plc.
> – An ordinary share in Solaris plc was worth £8.40 on 1 October 2020.

Extract from an email from your manager – dated 9 June 2022

> **Additional information in relation to Shanira**
>
> – Shanira is a higher rate taxpayer.
> – The gift of the house to Ray on 1 February 2022 was Shanira's first lifetime gift.
> – You should use the current market values of the painting and the shares in Solaris plc in order to calculate the chargeable gains arising on these gifts.
> – Neither gift holdover relief nor business asset disposal relief will be available in respect of the proposed gift of the shares in Solaris plc.
> – Shanira has not made any other chargeable disposals since 5 April 2021.
> – There is capital gains tax in the country of Heliosa but no inheritance tax.
> – There is no double tax treaty between Heliosa and the UK.
>
> **Please prepare a memorandum for the client files which addresses the following issues:**
>
> **(a) Ray – unincorporated business**
>
> – Calculations of the income tax and national insurance contribution payments to be made between 1 July 2022 and 31 March 2025 and the dates on which they will be payable.
> – Ray has told me that he does not intend to withdraw all of the profits of the business. Instead, he will either increase his inventory levels or acquire additional equipment, and he has asked how this will affect his taxable income.
> – Ray is incurring input tax and is considering registering voluntarily for VAT. Set out the information we need in order to advise him on whether or not voluntary registration is possible and/or financially beneficial and explain why the information is needed.
> – An explanation of whether or not Ray can recover the input tax in respect of the computer purchased on 3 June 2022 if he registers for VAT.

> **(b)** **Gifts from Shanira to Ray**
>
> – A calculation of the capital gains tax payable in respect of the gift of the house in Heliosa based on the currently available information, together with any further information required to finalise the liability, and the due date of payment.
>
> – An explanation, with supporting calculations, of when the further gifts should be made to Ray. The objective here is to maximise Ray's capital gains tax base cost without creating a capital gains tax liability for Shanira. In order to achieve this objective, you should consider dividing the proposed gift of the shares into two gifts to be given on different days.
>
> – The maximum possible inheritance tax liability which could arise in respect of the proposed gifts to Ray of the painting and the shares, if Shanira were to follow our advice in respect of their timing, together with the circumstances in which this liability would occur.
>
> **Tax manager**

Required:

Prepare the memorandum as requested in the email from your manager. The following marks are available:

(a) **Ray – unincorporated business.**

    (i) **Income tax and national insurance contribution payments, and the level of his taxable income.** **(11 marks)**

    (ii) **Value added tax (VAT).** **(5 marks)**

(b) **Gifts from Shanira to Ray.**

    (i) **Capital gains tax.** **(10 marks)**

    (ii) **Inheritance tax.** **(5 marks)**

Professional marks will be awarded for the approach taken to problem solving, the clarity of the explanations and calculations, the effectiveness with which the information is communicated and the overall presentation. **(4 marks)**

(Total: 35 marks)

10 AMY AND BEX *Walk in the footsteps of a top tutor*

You should assume that today's date is 10 March 2022.

Bex has recently left employment and entered into a business partnership with Amy. Bex requires advice in respect of a loan to the partnership, the calculation of her share of profits and the tax treatment of her redundancy payment.

Bex:

– Is resident and domiciled in the UK.

– Received an annual salary of £120,000 from her former employer, Cape Ltd.

– Was made redundant by Cape Ltd on 30 September 2021.

– Joined Amy, a sole trader, to form a partnership on 1 January 2022.

– Has no other source of income.

Amy and Bex partnership:

- Will prepare its first set of accounts for the 16-month period to 30 April 2023.
- Is expected to make a tax-adjusted profit of £255,000 (before deducting interest and capital allowances) for the period ending 30 April 2023.
- The tax written down value on its main pool at 1 January 2022 is £Nil.
- Except for the computer referred to below, no further assets will be purchased by either Amy or Bex for use in the partnership in the period ending 30 April 2023.

Profit sharing arrangements:

- The partnership's profit sharing agreement is as follows:

	Amy	Bex
Annual salary	£0	£30,000
Profit sharing ratio	3	1

Bex – loans:

- In addition to her capital contribution, Bex will make a £20,000 loan to the partnership on 1 August 2022. The partnership will use this money wholly for business purposes.
- This loan will be financed by a £25,000 personal loan from Bex's bank, taken out on the same date.
- The remaining £5,000 of the bank loan will be used to purchase a computer for use in the partnership. Bex will have 20% private use of this computer.
- Both the loan from Bex to the partnership and the personal bank loan to Bex will carry interest at the rate of 5% per annum.

Bex – redundancy package from Cape Ltd:

- The package comprised a £12,000 statutory redundancy payment and an additional ex-gratia payment of £58,000.
- Bex also received three months' salary in lieu of notice.

Required:

(a) (i) Explain, with the aid of calculations, the tax deductions which will be available in respect of the loan interest payable on both the loan from Bex to the partnership and the personal bank loan to Bex. **(7 marks)**

    (ii) In respect of the period ending 30 April 2023, show the allocation between the partners of the taxable trading profit of the partnership. **(4 marks)**

    (iii) Calculate Bex's taxable trading income in respect of her share of the partnership profits for all relevant tax years.

       Note: Your answer to (a)(iii) should clearly state the tax years and basis periods involved. **(3 marks)**

(b) Explain the income tax implications for Bex of the receipt of the redundancy package from Cape Ltd and calculate her total income tax liability for the tax year 2021/22. **(6 marks)**

(Total: 20 marks)

11   JUANITA *Walk in the footsteps of a top tutor*

You should assume today's date is 1 August 2022.

Juanita has contacted you following the death of her husband, Don. As the executor of his estate, she is seeking advice regarding the inheritance tax liability arising as a result of his death on shares which he owned. She also requires advice on the timing of her ceasing to trade.

Don:

—   Died on 1 July 2022.

—   Had always been UK resident and domiciled.

—   Was married to Juanita, and they have one daughter, Lexi.

Lifetime gifts:

—   Don made only two lifetime gifts.

—   On 9 May 2017, Don gifted his overseas villa to Lexi.

—   The villa was valued at £355,000 on 9 May 2017, and at £370,000 on 1 July 2022.

—   On 1 March 2019, on the advice of a financial adviser, Don gifted 3,500 of his shares in Estar Ltd to Lexi.

—   Prior to receiving this advice, Don had been planning to leave these shares to Lexi on his death.

—   Under the terms of Don's will, Don's cousin will inherit the remaining 3,500 shares in Estar Ltd owned by Don at his death.

Estar Ltd:

—   Is an investment company; no business property relief is available on the transfer of its shares.

—   Before the gift on 1 March 2019, Don owned 7,000 ordinary shares in Estar Ltd.

—   The remaining 3,000 ordinary shares issued by Estar Ltd are held by Juanita.

—   The shares were valued as follows:

Percentage shareholding	Value per share	
	1 March 2019	*1 July 2022*
0%–50%	£9.00	£10.80
51%–75%	£15.00	£18.00
76%–100%	£20.00	£24.00

Juanita:

—   Has carried on a business as a sole trader for many years, preparing accounts to 30 June annually.

—   Following Don's death, intends to cease trading and retire.

—   Would like to cease trading on 28 February 2023, in which case the business will be sold to an unconnected person.

—   Is willing to continue to trade until 30 April 2023, when Lexi will be able to take over the business.

—   Does not anticipate having any other source of taxable income in either of the tax years 2022/23 or 2023/24.

Juanita's business:

– Has taxable trading profits of £51,000 for the year ended 30 June 2022.

– Has budgeted tax-adjusted profits of £48,000 (before capital allowances) in the period ending 28 February 2023.

– Has budgeted further taxable profits of £4,000 per month if Juanita continues to trade after 28 February 2023.

– Has overlap profits from commencement of £17,000.

– The tax written down value on the main pool was £nil at 1 July 2022.

– The market value of the assets in the main pool will be £6,000 at the date of cessation.

Required:

(a) Advise Juanita of the reduction in the inheritance tax liability arising on Don's death in respect of the shares in Estar Ltd as a result of Lexi having received her shares as a lifetime gift, rather than on Don's death. **(8 marks)**

(b) Advise Juanita, by reference to the increase in her trading income after tax and national insurance contributions, whether it would be beneficial for her to continue to trade until 30 April 2023, rather than ceasing to trade on 28 February 2023. You should assume any elections which are beneficial to Juanita are made and should support your advice with a brief explanation of the available capital allowances in each case.

Note: You should assume that the rates and allowances for the tax year 2021/22 apply throughout the question. Where necessary, you should assume that there are four weeks in each month of the years 2022 and 2023. **(12 marks)**

(Total: 20 marks)

12   MEG AND LAURIE   *Walk in the footsteps of a top tutor*

You should assume that today's date is 1 April 2022.

Meg is an unincorporated sole trader. She requires advice regarding a planned change of accounting date, bringing her husband into the business, either as an employee or as a partner, and the value added tax (VAT) implications of purchasing services from an overseas supplier.

Meg:

– Is 60 years old and is married to Laurie.

– Owns an unincorporated sole trader business, MT Travel.

– Has rental income of £8,600 each year in addition to any profits from MT Travel.

MT Travel:

– Was set up by Meg on 1 January 2017.

– Has had accounts prepared to 31 December annually.

– Generated overlap profits of £7,400 on commencement.

– Meg will change its accounting date to 31 March by preparing accounts for the 15 months ending 31 March 2023.

– Currently has no employees.

MT Travel – recent and forecast tax-adjusted trading profits:

	£
Year ended 31 December 2021	17,000
15 months ending 31 March 2023	9,000

MT Travel – the future:

– From 1 April 2023, Meg's husband, Laurie, will start to participate in the business.

– Meg will either:

1. employ Laurie part-time, paying him an annual salary of £12,000, the commercial rate for the work he will perform, or

2. admit Laurie into the business as a partner, sharing profits and losses in the ratio 75% to Meg, and 25% to Laurie.

– The business is expected to generate a tax-adjusted trading loss in the tax year 2023/24 of £20,000, before making any payment to Laurie.

– The business is expected to become profitable again in the tax year 2024/25 and thereafter, but profits are not expected to exceed £30,000 per year for the foreseeable future.

Laurie:

– Is 63 years old.

– Was employed for many years by Hagg Ltd, earning gross annual remuneration of £60,000, until 31 March 2022.

– Has received annual dividends of £18,000 for many years. This is currently his only source of taxable income.

MT Travel – VAT:

– MT Travel is registered for the purposes of VAT.

– MT Travel currently buys standard-rated marketing services from a UK supplier, who is VAT registered.

– MT Travel can buy the same services from a supplier located in an overseas country where the rate of VAT is 12%.

Required:

(a) (i) Calculate the taxable trading profit of MT Travel for each of the tax years 2021/22 and 2022/23 before considering relief for the anticipated trading loss of the tax year 2023/24. **(3 marks)**

(ii) Identify and explain ONE practical tax disadvantage of MT Travel having a 31 March year end, rather than a 31 December year end. **(2 marks)**

(b) (i) Calculate the allowable trading loss available to each of Meg and Laurie for the tax year 2023/24 if Laurie becomes an employee or, alternatively, a partner in MT Travel on 1 April 2023. **(3 marks)**

(ii) Advise Meg and Laurie of the alternative ways in which their respective trading losses as calculated in (b)(i) could be used depending on whether Laurie is taken on as an employee or as a partner, and state the rate at which income tax would be saved in each case. **(8 marks)**

(c) Explain the value added tax (VAT) effect of MT Travel purchasing the services from the overseas supplier, rather than the UK supplier. **(4 marks)**

(Total: 20 marks)

13 ROD

You should assume that today's date is 1 June 2022.

Rod has requested advice in relation to the capital gains tax implications of selling shares he obtained through his employer's enterprise management incentive (EMI) scheme, and the potential income tax relief available in respect of his share of a trading loss of a partnership which he has recently joined.

Rod:

– Is resident and domiciled in the UK.

– Was employed for many years by Lumba plc, before taking early retirement on 30 June 2021.

– Joined the Thora Partnership on 1 December 2021.

– Made no disposals for capital gains tax in the tax year 2021/22, other than the sale of his shares in Lumba plc (as detailed below).

Sale of Lumba plc shares:

– In May 2017, Lumba plc granted Rod options to purchase 20,000 shares under its EMI scheme.

– The market value of a share at the date of the grant was £2.60 and the option price was £2.30 per share.

– Rod exercised all of the options on 1 June 2021, when the market value was £3.90 per share.

– Rod sold all the shares on 1 December 2021, when the market value was £4.00 per share.

– The gain is eligible for business asset disposal relief.

The Thora Partnership:

– Has been carried on for many years by two partners, Abe and Bob.

– Prepares accounts to 30 November annually.

– Admitted Rod into the partnership on 1 December 2021.

– Is expected to make a tax-adjusted trading loss of £47,000 in the year ending 30 November 2022.

The Thora Partnership – profit/loss sharing arrangements:

– The partnership's profit/loss sharing arrangements from 1 December 2021 are as follows:

	Abe	Bob	Rod
Annual salary	£20,000	£20,000	£0
Profit/loss sharing ratio	1	1	1

Rod's income in the tax years 2018/19 to 2021/22:

Tax year	Employment income	Dividends
	£	£
2018/19	82,000	0
2019/20	90,000	16,000
2020/21	86,000	12,000
2021/22	26,000	8,000

Required:

(a)   Calculate Rod's after-tax proceeds from the sale of his shares in Lumba plc and explain your calculation of the base cost for the shares.   **(6 marks)**

(b)   (i)   Calculate Rod's share of the tax-adjusted trading loss in the Thora Partnership for the tax years 2021/22 and 2022/23.

Note: Your answer to this part (b)(i) should clearly show the relevant basis periods.   **(6 marks)**

(ii)   State how Rod is able to relieve the trading loss(es) calculated in (b)(i) above as early as possible, and explain, with supporting calculations, the total amount of income tax saved if Rod follows this strategy.

Note: You should assume the tax rates and allowances for the tax year 2021/22 apply to all tax years.   **(8 marks)**

(Total: 20 marks)

14   TOMAS AND INES

You should assume that today's date is 1 June 2022.

Tomas requires advice on the tax implications of commencing to trade, the choice of accounting date for his business, and whether or not to register voluntarily for value added tax (VAT) purposes. Ines, his wife, requires advice on the tax implications of selling shares in respect of which relief has been obtained under the enterprise investment scheme (EIS).

Tomas:

–   Is UK resident and domiciled.

–   Uses his capital gains tax (CGT) annual exempt amount every year.

–   Receives dividends of £2,000 every year.

Tomas – sale of sporting memorabilia:

–   Tomas started selling items of sporting memorabilia from his collection during the tax year 2021/22.

–   HM Revenue and Customs (HMRC) agreed that these sales should be subject to CGT in the tax year 2021/22.

–   In April 2022, Tomas started purchasing and selling more items of sporting memorabilia, such that HMRC have said that he will be regarded as trading with effect from 6 April 2022.

–   Tomas will not be required to register for value added tax (VAT) for the foreseeable future.

–   Tomas will, however, consider registering voluntarily for VAT if it is financially beneficial for him to do so.

Tomas – expected trading results from the sale of sporting memorabilia:

- Tomas is considering either a 31 March or 30 April year end for his business.
- Tomas estimates that his total income less expenditure for the 12 months ending 31 March 2023 will be £11,500.
- Each item of memorabilia is purchased and sold for no more than £1,000.
- All of the costs he incurs are deductible for tax purposes.
- Tomas expects his profits to increase steadily after 1 April 2023.

Ines:

- Is UK resident and domiciled.
- Is a higher rate taxpayer.
- Has made/will make no disposals for CGT purposes, other than as described below.

Ines – sale of painting:

- Ines sold a painting on 4 July 2020 for proceeds of £196,000.
- The sale gave rise to a gain of £86,000.

Ines – acquisition of shares in Tavira Ltd:

- Ines subscribed £72,000 for 20,000 shares in Tavira Ltd on 8 October 2020.
- These shares are qualifying enterprise investment scheme (EIS) shares.
- Ines elected to defer the maximum possible amount of the gain on the sale of the painting against the acquisition of these shares.
- Ines obtained EIS relief of £18,600 against her income tax liability for the tax year 2020/21.
- Ines intends to sell all of the shares in Tavira Ltd for £95,000 on 1 June 2023.
- If undertaken, this sale would qualify for business asset disposal relief.

Required:

(a) On the assumption that Tomas prepares his first set of accounts to 31 March 2023, explain, with supporting calculations, the difference in the total amount of tax payable by him for the tax year 2022/23 as a result of the profit on the sales of sporting memorabilia being treated as trading income, rather than chargeable gains.

(5 marks)

(b) Identify Tomas' basis period for the tax year 2023/24 if he adopts a year-end date of (1) 31 March, or (2) 30 April, and state TWO tax advantages for Tomas of adopting 30 April as his year-end date. (5 marks)

(c) Explain TWO matters which Tomas should consider in deciding whether or not it will be financially beneficial to voluntarily register for value added tax (VAT). (3 marks)

(d) Explain the tax implications for Ines of her intended sale of the Tavira Ltd shares on 1 June 2023, and calculate her after-tax proceeds from this sale. (7 marks)

You may assume that the rates and allowances for the tax year 2021/22 will continue to apply for the foreseeable future.

(Total: 20 marks)

15 AMELIA

You should assume that today's date is 8 September 2022.

Amelia is a sole trader. She is seeking advice in respect of a loss incurred by her business, the tax implications of replacing a warehouse, and deregistration for value added tax (VAT) purposes.

Amelia:

– Has owned her unincorporated business, AS Trading, for many years.

– Has savings income of £6,000 each year.

– Had rental income of £11,600 from a UK residential property in the tax year 2021/22.

– Has no rental income in the tax year 2022/23 as the letting ceased on 31 March 2022.

– Sold this property on 30 April 2022.

AS Trading – tax adjusted trading profit/(loss):

	£
Year ended 31 December 2021	30,000
Year ending 31 December 2022 (forecast)	(14,000)

Amelia – recent capital disposals:

– Amelia's capital disposals are as follows:

Asset	Date of disposal	(loss)/gain
Painting	1 June 2021	(11,000)
UK rental property	30 April 2022	45,000
Shares in Swartz Ltd	16 August 2022	28,000

– All of these disposals were made to unconnected persons.

– Amelia had never lived in the UK rental property.

– Swartz Ltd is an unquoted trading company.

– Amelia sold the whole of her 3% shareholding in Swartz Ltd.

Proposed sale of Warehouse 1:

– Amelia acquired Warehouse 1 on 1 May 2016 for £86,000.

– Amelia will sell Warehouse 1 on 1 May 2023 for its expected market value at that date of £118,000.

– AS Trading occupies three out of the four floors of Warehouse 1.

– The remaining floor has been rented to tenants throughout Amelia's ownership of the building.

Proposed purchase of Warehouse 2:

– Amelia will purchase this warehouse, and a forklift truck for use in the warehouse, on 1 March 2023.

– Amelia will pay £83,000 for Warehouse 2, and will pay £23,000 for the forklift truck.

– Amelia will start to use the whole of Warehouse 2 in her business from 1 May 2023.

AS Trading – taxable turnover for value added tax (VAT) purposes:

	£
Year ended 31 December 2021	92,000
Year ending 31 December 2022 (forecast)	65,000
Year ending 31 December 2023 (forecast)	79,000

– Amelia expects that the taxable turnover of the business will continue to increase gradually in the next few years.

– AS Trading makes wholly standard-rated supplies.

– Amelia wishes to apply for voluntary deregistration for VAT purposes on 31 December 2022.

Required:

(a) (i) State the reliefs available to Amelia in respect of her trading loss of the year ending 31 December 2022, on the assumption that Amelia does not wish to carry forward any of the loss. **(3 marks)**

     (ii) Explain, with supporting calculations, how much tax would be saved for each of the reliefs identified in requirement. **(8 marks)**

(b) Explain, with supporting calculations, the capital gains tax and income tax implications for Amelia of the proposed sale of Warehouse 1, and the acquisition of Warehouse 2 and the forklift truck. **(6 marks)**

(c) Explain why Amelia can apply to voluntarily deregister for value added tax (VAT) purposes on 31 December 2022, from what date her VAT registration would be cancelled, and the immediate consequences for her of deregistering. **(3 marks)**

(Total: 20 marks)

CHANGING BUSINESS SCENARIOS

16   STANLEY BEECH (ADAPTED)

You should assume that today's date is 6 April 2022.

Stanley Beech, a self-employed landscape gardener, intends to transfer his business to Landscape Ltd, a company formed for this purpose.

The following information has been extracted from client files and from meetings with Stanley.

Stanley:

–   Commenced trading on 1 July 2012.

–   Constructed a storage building for £46,000 (including land of £10,000) on 1 July 2021 and began using it in the trade on 1 September 2021.

–   Has no other sources of income.

–   Has capital losses brought forward from the tax year 2020/21 of £9,700.

The whole of the business is to be transferred to Landscape Ltd on 1 September 2022:

–   The market value of the assets to be transferred is £118,000.

–   The assets include the storage building and goodwill, valued at £87,000 (including land of £12,000) and £24,000 respectively, and various small pieces of equipment and consumable stores.

–   Landscape Ltd will issue 5,000 £1 ordinary shares as consideration for the transfer.

Advice given to Stanley in respect of the sale of the business:

–   "No capital gains tax will arise on the transfer of your business to the company."

–   "You should take approximately 65% of the payment from Landscape Ltd in shares with the balance left on a loan account payable to you by the company, such that you can receive a cash payment in the future."

Advice given to Stanley in respect of his annual remuneration from Landscape Ltd:

–   "The payment of a dividend of £21,000 is more tax efficient than paying a salary bonus of £21,000 as you will pay income tax at only 32.5% on the dividend received, whereas you would pay income tax at 40% on a salary bonus. The dividend also avoids the need to pay national insurance contributions."

–   "There is no tax in respect of an interest free loan from an employer of less than £10,000."

–   "The provision of a company car is tax neutral as the cost of providing it is deductible in the corporation tax computation."

Stanley's proposed remuneration package from Landscape Ltd:

–   An annual salary of £55,000 and an annual dividend of approximately £21,000.

–   On 1 December 2022 an interest free loan of £3,600, which he intends to repay in two years' time.

–   A hybrid-electric company car with CO_2 emissions of 48g/km and an electric range of 39 miles. The only costs incurred by the company in respect of this car will be lease rentals of £400 per month.

–   The list price of the car is £34,200.

Landscape Ltd:

–   Will prepare accounts to 31 March each year.

Required:

(a) (i) Explain why there would be no capital gains tax liability on the transfer of Stanley's business to Landscape Ltd in exchange for shares.

Calculate the maximum loan account balance that Stanley could receive without giving rise to a capital gains tax liability and state the resulting capital gains tax base cost of the shares. **(9 marks)**

(ii) Explain the benefit to Stanley of taking part of the payment for the sale of his business in the form of a loan account, which is to be paid out in cash at some time in the future. **(1 mark)**

(iii) Explain how much structures and buildings allowance Landscape Ltd can claim in the year ended 31 March 2023. **(2 marks)**

(b) Comment on the accuracy and completeness of the advice received by Stanley in respect of his remuneration package.

Supporting calculations are only required in respect of the company car. **(10 marks)**

Ignore value added tax (VAT) in answering this question.

You may assume that the rates and allowances for the financial year to 31 March 2022 and the tax year 2021/22 will continue to apply for the foreseeable future.

(Total: 22 marks)

17   DESIREE (ADAPTED) *Walk in the footsteps of a top tutor*

You should assume that today's date is 6 June 2022.

Desiree requires advice on whether she should run her new business as an unincorporated sole trader or via a company together with the financial implications of registering voluntarily for value added tax (VAT).

The following information has been obtained from a meeting with Desiree.

Desiree:

– Resigned from her job with Chip plc on 31 May 2022.
– Had been employed by Chip plc on an annual salary of £60,000 since January 2019.
– Has no other income apart from bank interest of £1,000 per year.
– Intends to start a new business, to be called Duchess, on 1 September 2022.

The Duchess business:

– The business will sell kitchen equipment and utensils.
– Market research consultants have estimated that 80% of its sales will be to commercial customers.
– The market research consultants were paid fees by Desiree in November 2021 and March 2022.

Budgeted results of the Duchess business:

– The budgeted tax-adjusted trading profit/(loss) for the first three trading periods is:

	£
Ten months ending 30 June 2023	(46,000)
Year ending 30 June 2024	22,000
Year ending 30 June 2025	64,000

– The fees paid to the market research consultants have been deducted in arriving at the loss of the first period.

Desiree's financial position:

– Desiree has not yet decided whether to run the business as an unincorporated sole trader or via a company.

– Her primary objective when deciding whether or not to operate the business via a company is the most beneficial use of the trading loss.

Registration for VAT:

– The turnover of the business is expected to exceed the VAT registration limit in January 2023.

– Desiree would consider registering for VAT earlier if it were financially advantageous to do so.

– Desiree will import some of her products from overseas, but is unsure of the VAT treatment.

Required:

(a) (i) Calculate the taxable trading profit or allowable trading loss of the business for each of the first three taxable periods for the following alternative structures:

- the business is unincorporated

- the business is operated via a company. **(4 marks)**

(ii) Provide Desiree with a thorough and detailed explanation of the manner in which the budgeted trading loss could be used depending on whether she runs the business as an unincorporated sole trader or via a company and state which business structure would best satisfy her primary objective.

You are not required to prepare detailed calculations for part (ii) of this part of this question or to consider non-taxation issues. **(9 marks)**

(b) Explain in detail the financial advantages and disadvantages of Desiree registering voluntarily for VAT on 1 September 2022 and the VAT consequences of the imports, assuming she is VAT registered. **(7 marks)**

(Total: 20 marks)

18   ZITI   *Walk in the footsteps of a top tutor*

You should assume that today's date is 6 June 2022.

Your manager has received a letter from Ziti. Ziti owns and runs an unincorporated business which was given to him by his father, Ravi. Extracts from the letter and from an email from your manager are set out below.

Extract from the letter from Ziti

I have decided that, due to my father's serious illness, I want to be able to look after him on a full-time basis. Accordingly, I am going to sell my business and use the proceeds to buy a house nearer to where he lives.

My father started the business in 2007 when he purchased the building referred to in the business assets below. He gave the business (consisting of the goodwill, the building and the equipment) to me on 1 July 2018 and we submitted a joint claim for gift holdover relief, such that no capital gains tax was payable. I have no sources of income other than this business.

I have identified two possible methods of disposal.

(i)   My preferred approach would be to close the business down. I would do this by selling the building and the equipment on 31 January 2023 at which point I would cease trading.

(ii)   My father would like to see the business carry on after I sell it. For this to occur, I would have to continue trading until 30 April 2023 and then sell the business to my cousin who would continue to operate it.

In each case I would prepare accounts for the year ending 30 April 2022 and then to the date of cessation or disposal.

I attach an appendix setting out the information you requested in relation to the business.

Sadly, I have been told that my father is unlikely to live for more than three years. Please let me know whether his death could result in an inheritance tax liability for me in respect of the gift of the business.

My father's only lifetime gift, apart from the business given to me, was of quoted shares to a discretionary (relevant property) trust on 1 May 2014. The shares had a market value of £190,000 at the date of the gift and did not qualify for business property relief.

Appendix

Business assets (all figures exclude value added tax (VAT))

	Goodwill	Building	Equipment
	£	£	£
Original cost of the business assets	0	60,000	18,000
Market value at the time of my father's gift on 1 July 2018	40,000	300,000	9,000
Expected market value as at 31 January 2023 and 30 April 2023	40,000	330,000	10,000

Financial position of the business

The tax adjusted trading profits for the year ended 30 April 2021 were £55,000.

From 1 May 2021, it can be assumed that the business generates trading profits of £5,000 per month. The only tax adjustment required to this figure is in respect of capital allowances.

The tax written down value of the main pool as at 30 April 2021 was nil. I purchased business equipment for £6,000 on 1 August 2021. There have been no disposals of equipment since 30 April 2021.

Extract from an email from your manager

Additional background information

–   Ziti and Ravi are both resident and domiciled in the UK.

–   Ziti has overlap profits from when he took over the business of £9,000.

–   All of the equipment is movable and no item has a cost or market value of more than £6,000.

–   The business is registered for VAT.

–   No election has been made in respect of the building in relation to VAT.

Please prepare notes, which we can use in a meeting with Ziti, which address the following issues:

(a)   Sale of the business

(i)   Calculations to enable Ziti to compare the financial implications of the two possible methods of disposal. You will need to calculate:

–   Ziti's taxable trading profits from 1 May 2021 onwards and the income tax thereon; and

–   any capital gains tax (CGT) payable.

You should include:

–   explanations of the availability of any CGT reliefs

–   a summary of the post-tax cash position; and

–   any necessary assumptions.

(ii)   Explanations of whether or not VAT would need to be charged on either or both of the alternative disposals.

(b)   Inheritance tax

Calculations of the amount of inheritance tax which would be payable by Ziti for all possible dates of his father's death between 7 June 2022 and 30 June 2025. You should include an explanation of the availability of any inheritance tax reliefs.

When calculating these potential inheritance tax liabilities, you should assume that Ziti will sell the business on 30 April 2023.

The best way for you to approach this is to identify the particular dates on which the inheritance tax liability will change.

Tax manager

Required:

Prepare the meeting notes requested in the email from your manager.

The following marks are available.

(a)   Sale of the business.

    (i)   Comparison of the financial implications of the alternative methods for disposing of the business.

        Ignore national insurance contributions.   **(17 marks)**

    (ii)   Value added tax (VAT).   **(5 marks)**

(b)   Inheritance tax.   **(9 marks)**

Professional marks will be awarded for adopting a logical approach to problem solving, the clarity of the calculations, the effectiveness with which the information is communicated, and the overall presentation of the notes.   **(4 marks)**

(Total: 35 marks)

19   JONNY (ADAPTED) *Walk in the footsteps of a top tutor*

You should assume that today's date is 10 September 2022.

Your manager has had a meeting with Jonny who is establishing a new business. An extract from an email from your manager, a schedule and a computation are set out below.

Extract from the email from your manager

Jonny's new business will begin trading on 1 November 2022. Jonny will use an inheritance he received following the death of his mother to finance this new venture.

We have been asked to advise Jonny on his business and his inheritance. Some of the work has already been done; I want you to complete it.

Please prepare a memorandum for Jonny's client file addressing the following issues:

(a)   **Unincorporated business**

I attach a schedule which sets out Jonny's recent employment income and his plans for the new business. I think you will find it useful to read the schedule before you go through the rest of this email.

You should assume that Jonny does not have any other sources of income or any taxable gains in any of the relevant tax years.

    (i)   **Jonny's post-tax income**

        Jonny has asked for an approximation of his post-tax income position for the first two trading periods. I want you to prepare calculations in order to complete the following table, assuming that any available trading loss reliefs will be claimed in the most beneficial manner.

        You should include explanations of the options available to relieve the loss, clearly identifying the method which will maximise the tax saved (you do not need to consider carrying the loss forward).

Table to be completed

	Strong demand	Weak demand
	£	£
Aggregate budgeted net profit of the first two trading periods	39,200	2,800
Aggregate income tax (payable)/refundable in respect of the profit/loss for the first two tax years	?	?
Budgeted post-tax income	?	?

Include a brief explanation as to why these calculations are only an approximation of Jonny's budgeted post-tax income.

(ii) Salesmen

Jonny intends to hire two salesmen to get the business started. Their proposed contractual arrangements are as set out in the attached schedule.

Explain which of the proposed contractual arrangements with the salesmen indicate that they would be self-employed and state any changes which should be made to the other arrangements in order to maximise the likelihood of the salesmen being treated as self-employed.

(iii) New contracts for the business

Jonny is hoping to obtain contracts with local educational establishments and has asked us to help. One of our clients is a college and an ex-client of ours provided services to a number of schools and colleges. Accordingly, we have knowledge and experience in this area.

Explain the extent to which it is acceptable for us to use the knowledge we have gained in respect of our existing client and ex-client to assist Jonny.

(b) Jonny's inheritance from his mother

Jonny's mother died on 31 July 2022. She left the whole of her estate, with the exception of a gift to charity, to Jonny. I attach a computation of the inheritance tax due; this was prepared by a junior member of staff and has not yet been reviewed. I can confirm, however, that all of the arithmetic, dates and valuations are correct. In addition, there were no other lifetime gifts, and none of the assets qualified for business property relief.

I want you to review the computation and identify any errors. You should explain each of the errors you find and calculate the value of the inheritance which Jonny will receive after inheritance tax has been paid.

Tax manager

Schedule – Employment income and plans for the new business

Jonny's income

Jonny worked full-time for many years until 30 June 2020 earning a salary of £6,000 per calendar month. From 1 July 2020, he worked part-time earning a salary of £2,000 per calendar month until he ceased employment on 31 March 2022.

Two budgets have been prepared for Jonny's business based on customer demand being either strong or weak. You should assume that no tax adjustments are required to Jonny's budgeted profit/loss figures for the first two trading periods.

For strong demand, the taxable trading profit for the first two tax years has been computed; these figures are correct and you do not need to check them. You will, however, need to calculate the equivalent figures for weak demand.

	Strong demand £	Weak demand £
Budgeted net profit/(loss):		
Eight months ending 30 June 2023	9,200	(15,200)
Year ending 30 June 2024	30,000	18,000
Aggregate budgeted net profit of the first two trading periods	39,200	2,800
Taxable trading profit/(loss):		
2022/23	5,750	?
2023/24	19,200	?

Salesmen

Jonny is proposing to enter into the following contractual arrangements with two part-time salesmen:

– They will work on Tuesday and Wednesday mornings each week for a two-month period.

– They will be paid a fee of £300 for each new sales contract obtained. No other payments will be made.

– They will use their own cars.

– Jonny will lend each of them a laptop computer.

Computation – Inheritance tax payable on the death of Jonny's mother

Mother's lifetime gift	£
1 June 2018 – Gift of cash to Jonny	30,000

Mother's chargeable estate at death on 31 July 2022		
	£	£
Freehold property – Mother's main residence		530,000
UK quoted shares		400,000
Chattels – furniture, paintings and jewellery	40,000	
Less: Items individually worth less than £6,000	(25,000)	
	————	
		15,000
Cash		20,000
		————
		965,000
Less: Gift to charity		(70,000)
Annual exemption		(3,000)
		————
Chargeable estate		892,000
Less: Nil rate band	325,000	
Gift in the seven years prior to death (£30,000 – £6,000)	(24,000)	
	————	
		(301,000)
		————
		591,000
		————
Inheritance tax (£591,000 × 40%)		236,400
		————

Required:

Prepare the memorandum as requested in the email from your manager. The following marks are available:

(a)   **Unincorporated business:**

(i)   **Jonny's post-tax income.**   **(15 marks)**

(ii)   **Salesmen.**   **(4 marks)**

(iii)   **New contracts for the business.**   **(5 marks)**

(b)   **Jonny's inheritance from his mother.**   **(7 marks)**

Professional marks will be awarded for following the manager's instructions, the clarity of the explanations and calculations, problem solving, and the overall presentation of the memorandum.   **(4 marks)**

Notes

1   Assume that the tax rates and allowances for the tax year 2021/22 apply to all tax years.

2   Ignore national insurance contributions throughout this question.

(Total: 35 marks)

20 SNOWDON *Walk in the footsteps of a top tutor*

You should assume that today's date is 7 June 2022.

Your manager has had a meeting with Snowdon, a potential new client. Extracts from the memorandum prepared by your manager following the meeting, an inheritance tax computation prepared by Snowdon, and an email from your manager detailing the work you are required to do are set out below.

Extracts from the memorandum prepared by your manager – dated 6 June 2022

Snowdon is resident and domiciled in the UK. He requires advice in respect of a cottage he purchased from his sister, Coleen, and his unincorporated business, 'Siabod', which he started on 1 July 2013.

Purchase of the cottage from Coleen

Snowdon's sister, Coleen, died on 1 June 2022.

Coleen had sold a holiday cottage to Snowdon on 1 May 2018 for £225,000. At that time, the cottage was worth £260,000. Coleen had purchased the cottage for £165,000. The cottage qualified for capital gains tax gift holdover relief and Snowdon and Coleen submitted a valid joint claim.

Coleen made a gift to a trust on 1 March 2014. This resulted in a gross chargeable transfer after all exemptions of £318,000.

Snowdon provided me with a computation he had prepared of the inheritance tax due as a result of Coleen's death in respect of the cottage. Snowdon is aware that he is not an expert when it comes to inheritance tax, such that this computation is unlikely to be totally accurate.

Siabod business

Budgeted figures relating to the unexpanded Siabod business for the year ending 30 June 2023 are:

	£
Turnover	255,000
Tax adjusted trading profit	85,000
Income tax on £85,000 using current rates	21,432
Class 4 national insurance contributions on £85,000 using current rates	4,358

The Siabod business is partially exempt for the purposes of value added tax (VAT). Snowdon's budgeted input tax for the unexpanded business for the year ending 30 June 2023 was £18,000. He would have been able to recover the whole of this amount because the business would have been below the de minimis limits.

Extracts from the memorandum prepared by your manager – dated 6 June 2022 (continued)

Since the above figures were prepared, Snowdon has decided to expand the Siabod business and increase its budgeted turnover for the year ending 30 June 2023 from £255,000 to £435,000. In order to carry out this expansion, Snowdon will adopt either strategy A or strategy B. Whichever strategy is adopted, the partial exemption percentage of the business will continue to be 76% (recoverable).

Strategy A

Under this strategy Snowdon will recruit an additional employee with an annual salary of £48,000.

Strategy B

Under this strategy Snowdon will appoint a sub-contractor, Tor Ltd, which will carry out the work required for the expansion. Tor Ltd will charge fees of £90,000 plus VAT each year.

Budgeted costs of expanding the business

	Strategy A	Strategy B
	£	£
Salary of additional employee	48,000	N/A
Other expenditure relating to the expansion, net of VAT at 20%:		
Overheads	38,000	N/A
Advertising	2,000	2,000
Fees payable to Tor Ltd, net of VAT at 20%	N/A	90,000

Additional information

–   Prior to the expansion of the Siabod business, Snowdon's liability to employer's class 1 national insurance contributions for the year exceeded £4,000.

–   Apart from the profits of the Siabod business, Snowdon's only income is £740 of bank interest each year.

Inheritance tax computation prepared by Snowdon – dated 6 June 2022

Inheritance tax due in respect of the cottage

	£
Value of the cottage as at 1 May 2018 (no annual exemption on death)	260,000
Less: Taper relief (£260,000 × 40%) (between four and five years)	(104,000)
	156,000
Nil rate band	325,000
Less: Gifts in the seven years prior to death	nil
Available nil rate band	325,000
Inheritance tax (the gift is fully covered by the available nil rate band)	nil

Email from your manager – dated 7 June 2022

Please prepare a memorandum for Snowdon's client file covering the following:

(i) **Purchase of the cottage from Coleen**

– Identification and explanation of the errors in the inheritance tax (IHT) computation prepared by Snowdon, and a calculation of the correct amount of IHT due.

I have already established that the cottage did not qualify for business property relief.

– The capital gains tax gift holdover relief claimed by Coleen in respect of the cottage and Snowdon's base cost for the purposes of a future disposal by him.

(ii) **Expansion of the Siabod business**

– Calculations to show which of the two strategies is the most financially advantageous, i.e. the one which is expected to generate the most additional tax adjusted trading profit for the year ending 30 June 2023.

– A calculation of the additional budgeted post-tax income for the tax year 2023/24 which is expected to be generated by the most financially advantageous strategy.

(iii) **Procedures we should follow before we agree to become Snowdon's tax advisers**

A summary of the procedures we should follow before we agree to become Snowdon's tax advisers.

Tax manager

Required:

Prepare the memorandum as requested in the email from your manager. The following marks are available:

(i) Purchase of the cottage from Coleen. **(9 marks)**

(ii) Expansion of the Siabod business. **(17 marks)**

(iii) Procedures we should follow before we agree to become Snowdon's tax advisers. **(5 marks)**

Professional marks will be awarded for the approach taken to problem solving, the clarity of the explanations and calculations, the effectiveness with which the information is communicated, and the overall presentation and style of the memorandum. (4 marks)

(Total: 35 marks)

21 NELSON *Walk in the footsteps of a top tutor*

 Question debrief

You should assume that today's date is 3 December 2022.

Your manager has received a letter from Nelson, a potential new client, in relation to his unincorporated business. Extracts from the letter, and from an email from your manager detailing the work he requires you to do, are set out below.

Extracts from the letter from Nelson – dated 2 December 2022

Background

I was employed from 1 May 2017 until I was made redundant on 28 February 2021. My gross annual salary was £80,000.

Just over a year later, on 1 June 2022, I began trading as an unincorporated business preparing accounts to 30 April each year. My tax adviser advised me to trade as an unincorporated business because it was expected that I would make a tax adjusted trading loss for my first trading period ending on 30 April 2023. However, due to the speed with which the business has grown, the forecast for this period now shows a budgeted tax adjusted trading profit of £77,550.

Transfer of my business to NQA Ltd

In the future, I expect sales to be generated mainly from overseas customers, possibly via companies incorporated and trading outside the UK. In view of this, it has become clear to me that I need to be operating the business through a limited company.

Accordingly, I intend to incorporate my business by transferring its trade and assets to a new unquoted company, NQA Ltd, in exchange for ordinary shares. I will own the whole of the ordinary share capital of NQA Ltd and, for the time being, I will be its only director and employee. This incorporation will take place on 1 May 2023.

I will realise chargeable gains of £45,000 in respect of the goodwill of the business and £30,000 in respect of the Arch building (which I use as my business premises). I understand from our discussions that these gains will not be subject to capital gains tax due to the relief available when a business is transferred to a company in exchange for shares.

Other information

– Since 1 March 2021, I have had no source of income other than my unincorporated business.

– In the tax year 2023/24, I will not make any disposals for the purposes of capital gains tax other than the sale of my business to NQA Ltd.

Advice required

1   I am trying to determine whether or not I should have been advised to begin trading through a limited company from 1 June 2022 rather than as an unincorporated business.

I would like to know if I will pay more tax as a result of the advice I was given. I would also like to understand the relevance of the expected trading loss in the first trading period together with any other reasons my existing tax adviser might have had for advising me to begin trading as an unincorporated business rather than through a limited company.

2   Ideally, I would prefer to retain personal ownership of the Arch building when I incorporate my business, rather than transfer it to NQA Ltd. However, this will depend on how it affects my capital gains tax position.

3   Once NQA Ltd has begun trading, I would like to be able to borrow any excess funds in the company for my personal use. I would then repay the loan as and when I can afford to. I appreciate there may be an employment income benefit in respect of this.

4   One of my customers has gone into liquidation, and I do not expect to be able to recover any part of the outstanding debt.

   –   Does this mean that the value added tax (VAT) which I have already paid to HM Revenue and Customs (HMRC) in respect of this sale is lost?

   –   Am I correct in thinking that, if I had used the cash accounting scheme for VAT, I would not have had this particular problem, and that my cash flow generally would have benefited?

Extract from the email from your manager – dated 3 December 2022

Please prepare a memorandum for the client file consisting of the work set out below.

(a)   Becoming tax advisers to Nelson

Explain the information we require, the matters we should consider and the actions we should take before we agree to become Nelson's tax advisers.

(b)   Trading through a limited company rather than as an unincorporated business

Total taxes payable

The total taxes payable by Nelson for the tax year 2022/23 in respect of his budgeted tax adjusted trading profit will be £19,833. Prepare calculations to determine whether or not a lower amount would have been payable if Nelson had commenced trading through a limited company rather than as an unincorporated business.

You should assume:

–   the company's accounting period ends on 31 March 2023

–   the company's MONTHLY trading profit for this accounting period is £7,050. This figure is before deducting the cost of Nelson's monthly salary

–   the company pays Nelson a gross salary of £1,300 per month and a dividend equal to its post-tax profits.

Reasons for advice given by existing tax adviser

Explain why the expectation that Nelson's business would make a tax adjusted trading loss would have been an important consideration when deciding on whether he should begin trading as an unincorporated business or through a limited company. You should refer to Nelson's first two tax years of trading.

State any other reasons why Nelson's existing tax adviser may have advised him to commence trading as an unincorporated business rather than through a limited company.

(c) **Other matters**

–   Explain the capital gains tax (CGT) implications for Nelson of retaining personal ownership of the Arch building when he incorporates his business. You ARE NOT REQUIRED to consider CGT gift holdover relief.

–   Explain the tax implications for NQA Ltd of Nelson borrowing excess funds from the company and the subsequent repayment of those funds. You ARE NOT REQUIRED to explain any matters relating to employment income benefits in respect of this arrangement.

–   Provide explanations in response to the two questions raised by Nelson in respect of value added tax (VAT).

Tax manager

Required:

Prepare the memorandum as requested in the email from your manager. The following marks are available:

(a)   Becoming tax advisers to Nelson.   **(5 marks)**

(b)   Trading through a limited company rather than as an unincorporated business.

For guidance, there are 7·5 marks for the calculations and 6·5 marks for the reasons for the advice given.   **(14 marks)**

(c)   Other matters.   **(12 marks)**

Professional marks will be awarded for the approach taken to problem solving, the clarity of the explanations and calculations, the effectiveness with which the information is communicated, and the overall presentation and style of the memorandum.   **(4 marks)**

(Total: 35 marks)

22   ROSA

You should assume that today's date is 3 December 2022.

Your client, Rosa, has requested advice in relation to the consequences of her daughter, Siena, becoming either an employee or a partner in her unincorporated business, the options available to her to relieve a trading loss incurred by the business, and the value added tax (VAT) implications of selling a retail unit.

Rosa:

– 	Is 62 years old and is widowed.

– 	Has one daughter, Siena.

– 	Owns an unincorporated business, RS Trading, which she has run for many years.

– 	Currently has no employees in her business.

– 	Will bring her daughter, Siena, into the business either as an employee or a partner, on 1 April 2023.

– 	Has a budgeted income tax liability of £22,232, and a budgeted capital gains tax liability of £22,316 for the tax year 2022/23.

Siena:

– 	Will have no source of taxable income in the tax year 2023/24, other than from RS Trading.

RS Trading:

– 	Has an accounting date of 31 March each year.

– 	Has a budgeted tax adjusted trading profit of £27,000 for the year ending 31 March 2023.

– 	Has a budgeted trading loss of £62,000, before any payment to Siena, for the year ending 31 March 2024.

– 	Is registered for VAT and makes only standard-rated supplies.

RS Trading – future plans:

– 	Siena will become either an employee or a partner in RS Trading on 1 April 2023.

– 	If Siena becomes an employee, she will receive an annual salary of £22,000 which is a commercial rate for the duties she will perform.

– 	Alternatively, if Siena becomes a partner, the profit sharing arrangements from 1 April 2023 will be:

	Rosa	Siena
Annual salary	£0	£12,000
Profit sharing ratio	80%	20%

Rosa – investment properties:

– 	Rosa will receive net rental income of £60,000 from a portfolio of residential properties and a retail unit in the tax year 2022/23.

– 	Rosa sold all the residential properties on 30 November 2022, realising total chargeable gains of £92,000.

Disposal of the retail unit:

- Rosa will sell the retail unit, which is currently being rented to tenants up to 5 April 2023, for its market value of £280,000 on 6 April 2023.
- Rosa had bought the retail unit when it was newly constructed, on 1 May 2016, for £290,000 plus VAT at 20%.
- Rosa used the retail unit in her business until 30 April 2020, since when she has let it to unconnected tenants.
- The retail unit is subject to the capital goods scheme for VAT.
- Rosa has not opted to tax the retail unit for VAT purposes.

Required:

(a) Advise Rosa of the difference in the total amount of income tax and national insurance contributions (NICs) payable by her and Siena for the tax year 2023/24, if Siena is taken on as (i) a partner, or (ii) an employee by RS Trading on 1 April 2023.

(9 marks)

(b) Assuming Siena is employed by RS Trading from 1 April 2023, identify and explain the relief(s) available to Rosa to relieve her trading loss of the year ending 31 March 2024, and calculate the maximum tax saving available to her as a result of claiming such relief(s) in the tax year 2022/23.

Note: You should NOT consider the possibility of Rosa carrying all, or any part, of the loss forward for relief for part (b). (7 marks)

(c) Explain the value added tax (VAT) implications of the disposal of the retail unit on 6 April 2023, and calculate the final VAT adjustment under the capital goods scheme.

(4 marks)

(Total: 20 marks)

23   FREYA *Walk in the footsteps of a top tutor*

You should assume that today's date is 8 September 2022.

Your manager has had a meeting with Freya, a client of your firm. She has sent you the memorandum she prepared following the meeting and an email detailing the work you are required to do.

Memorandum extract from your manager: dated 7 September 2022

> **Background**
>
> Freya has been domiciled and resident in the UK more than 30 years and has not spent any significant periods of time overseas. She started trading as an unincorporated business in 2013 and has always prepared accounts to 31 May each year. Freya's business is her only source of income.

Sale of Freya's business

Freya has received an offer of £2,300,000 from an unconnected party for all of the assets of her business. If the offer is accepted, her only chargeable assets for capital gains tax purposes will be goodwill and her business premises. The aggregate chargeable gains arising in respect of these assets will be £850,000. However, once she is no longer working full time, Freya intends to live in the country of Benida and has asked us to consider whether she would save UK tax if she were to delay the sale of her business until after she has left the UK.

I agreed to advise Freya on the following strategy:

31 October 2022	Freya will sell all of the assets of her business to FIM Ltd, a UK resident limited company, in exchange for ordinary shares worth £2,300,000. Freya will own the whole of the ordinary share capital of FIM Ltd.
5 April 2023	Freya and her family will move to Benida.
30 April 2023	Freya will sell the whole of the ordinary share capital of FIM Ltd for cash proceeds.

Freya's ideal scenario

Freya would like to live in Benida for no more than three years. She would buy a home there and would also retain her home in the UK. Freya would stay in her UK home for 55 days in each tax year, of which 25 would be working days. She would spend the rest of her time in Benida. Freya does not intend to carry out any work in Benida. Freya's husband and children would remain in Benida throughout the three-year period and would not be resident in the UK.

Unincorporated business – financial information

– A single set of accounts will be prepared for the 17-month period ending 31 October 2022. The budgeted tax adjusted profit for this period, before deduction of capital allowances, is £94,000.

– The tax written down values as at 31 May 2021 were: main pool – zero, car with private use – £8,700.

– On 1 September 2021, Freya purchased plant and machinery for use in her business costing £4,200.

– On 31 October 2022, the plant and machinery used in her business (excluding the motor car) will have a market value on that date of £6,300. Every item will be sold for less than its cost.

– Freya will withdraw a motor car from the business on 30 September 2022. The car has always been used 65% for business purposes and will have a market value of £11,100, which is less than the car's original cost.

– Freya and FIM Ltd will submit a succession election to HM Revenue and Customs (HMRC).

– There are unrelieved overlap profits from the commencement of the business of £31,400.

Land in Benida

Freya's father, Alvaro, moved to the UK (and became UK resident) on 6 April 2008. He is domiciled in Benida and has owned a plot of land there for many years. He is considering giving this land to Freya within the next 12 months. I agreed to advise Freya on whether or not such a gift could result in an inheritance tax (IHT) liability for her.

Alvaro is not well and is unlikely to live for a further seven years: we should therefore assume all future potentially exempt transfers will become chargeable to IHT.

Because Alvaro makes regular, substantial lifetime gifts of assets situated in the UK, we should also assume there will be no nil rate band or annual exemptions available in respect of a gift of this land.

Email extract from your manager: dated 8 September 2022

Additional information in respect of the country of Benida

– There is no capital gains tax (CGT) in Benida

– There is no double tax treaty between the UK and Benida.

Please carry out the following work:

(a) **Sale of business**

– Calculate the CGT which would be payable by Freya on the sale of her business if she does not incorporate her business but simply sells all of her business assets for £2,300,000 on 31 October 2022 to an unconnected purchaser. Explain the rate of CGT which would be charged.

The annual exempt amount WILL NOT be available to Freya, and she will be a higher rate taxpayer in the tax year of sale.

– Explain the CGT implications of the proposed sale of Freya's business to FIM Ltd in exchange for shares worth £2,300,000. I can confirm that all of the conditions necessary for incorporation relief to apply to this transaction will be satisfied and that no election will be made to disapply this relief.

– On the assumption Freya lives in Benida for three years from 5 April 2023 in accordance with her ideal scenario, explain her UK residence status for those three tax years.

I have done some preliminary work on Freya's residence status and can confirm that Freya will be neither automatically non-UK resident nor automatically UK resident whilst she is living in Benida.

– On the assumption that Freya is non-UK resident for the tax year 2023/24, explain any changes which would need to be made to Freya's ideal scenario in respect of her time in Benida in order for there to be no UK CGT on the sale of her shares in FIM Ltd.

(b) **Liability to income tax and class 4 national insurance contributions (NIC)**

On the assumption Freya sells her business to FIM Ltd on 31 October 2022, calculate her liability to income tax and class 4 NIC for her final tax year of trading.

I can confirm that Freya will not receive any taxable income from FIM Ltd.

(c) **Land in Benida**

Explain whether or not a gift of the land by Alvaro to Freya at some time in the next 12 months could result in a UK inheritance tax (IHT) liability.

Tax manager

Required:

Carry out the work required as requested in the email from your manager. The following marks are available:

(a) **Sale of business.** **(13 marks)**

(b) **Liability to income tax and class 4 national insurance contributions (NIC).** **(8 marks)**

(c) **Land in Benida.** **(4 marks)**

(Total: 25 marks)

24 **JOE** *Walk in the footsteps of a top tutor*

You should assume that today's date is 1 June 2022.

Your manager has received two schedules from Joe, the finance director of VNL Ltd. The two schedules and extracts from an email from your manager detailing the work she requires you to do are included in the exhibits.

Schedule 1:

Liquidation of VNL Ltd

Background

As we have discussed, the company's shareholders have decided to liquidate the company. A liquidator will be appointed on 1 August 2022.

I set out below the information you asked for in relation to the sale of the company's intangible fixed assets together with a request for further advice in relation to the payments to be made by the company to its shareholders.

Sale of intangible fixed assets

On 1 September 2019, VNL Ltd purchased the trade and assets of a business from an unrelated company. The assets included goodwill and a brand name, as detailed below. These assets will be sold on 31 July 2022.

	Goodwill	*Brand name*
	£	£
Sale proceeds	75,000	47,000
Cost	95,000	36,000
Amortisation since acquisition	19,000	5,760

Further advice – payments to the shareholders

An interim payment will be made to the shareholders followed by a final payment at the conclusion of the liquidation which will take place in February 2023. I have been asked to consider the possibility of making the interim payment prior to the appointment of the liquidator.

Schedule 2:

New unincorporated business

Background

I can now confirm that I will commence trading as an unincorporated trader on 1 November 2022.

Tax adjusted trading profits (TATP)

When we last met you calculated that, with an accounting date of 31 March (and making my first accounts up to 31 March 2023), my taxable trading profits based on the monthly budgeted TATP of the business would be:

Tax year: 2022/23   £24,500
            2023/24   £97,000

I set out below a reminder of the monthly profit figures on which you based your calculations.

Period	Number of months	TATP per month £
1 November 2022 to 31 December 2022	2	4,000
1 January 2023 to 31 March 2023	3	5,500
1 April 2023 to 31 August 2023	5	7,500
From 1 September 2023	N/A	8,500

I have now realised that making my first accounts up to 31 July 2023 and continuing with an accounting date of 31 July would also be suitable commercially, and I would like some guidance from you as to which date I should choose.

Costs already incurred

Since 1 October 2021, I have been purchasing consultancy services every month in respect of the design and manufacture of the product the new business will be selling.

On 1 May 2022 I purchased computer equipment for use in the new business.

Business premises

I have identified a building for use as my business premises. It is a commercial property unit, which was constructed in 2005. I have agreed a price with the vendor of £190,000 plus value added tax (VAT). I intend to lease a third of the building to an unrelated business until my trading activities have grown sufficiently to require the use of the whole building.

Email extract from your manager:

> **Please prepare notes for a meeting with Joe in accordance with the following:**
>
> **(a)** **Liquidation of VNL Ltd**
>
> **Additional information:**
>
> – VNL Ltd is a trading company. It has always made significant trading profits and will be profitable in its final accounting period. It prepares accounts to 31 March each year.
>
> – The amortisation of the goodwill was not a tax deductible expense for VNL Ltd.
>
> – No election was made to write off the cost of the brand name at the 4% rate.
>
> – The company's shareholders are all individuals, some of whom are employed by VNL Ltd, and include both basic rate and higher rate taxpayers.
>
> – The shares in VNL Ltd were subscribed for prior to 17 March 2016, such that investors' relief will not be available in respect of any disposal.
>
> **(i)** **Sale of intangible fixed assets**
>
> Calculate the post-tax proceeds for VNL Ltd as a result of the sale of the intangible fixed assets.
>
> **(ii)** **Timing of payments to shareholders**
>
> Explain the tax rates which the shareholders will pay on the amounts received from VNL Ltd depending on when the payment is made.
>
> **(b)** **Unincorporated business**
>
> Additional information:
>
> – The taxable trading profit figures for the first two tax years in respect of a 31 March accounting date (as set out in Schedule 2) are correct; there is no need for you to check them.
>
> – There will be no further significant capital expenditure on buildings or plant and machinery.
>
> – The trading activity will be standard-rated for value added tax (VAT) purposes.
>
> **(i)** **Accounting date**
>
> In order to assist Joe in choosing between the two alternative accounting dates of 31 March and 31 July:
>
> – Calculate Joe's taxable trading profits for his first two tax years of trading if he were to adopt an accounting date of 31 July.
>
>   You should base your calculations for the 31 July accounting date on the monthly tax adjusted trading profit (TATP) figures in Schedule 2 from Joe, and you should ignore the expenditure incurred prior to 1 November 2022.
>
> – Without preparing any further calculations, comment on the possible effect on Joe's income tax liabilities for the first two tax years of trading of adopting a 31 July accounting date rather than one of 31 March.
>
> – State two advantages, other than in relation to Joe's income tax liabilities, of Joe adopting an accounting date of 31 July rather than 31 March.

> **(ii) Costs already incurred and the business premises**
>
> In respect of the costs already incurred, and the planned purchase of the business premises, explain whether or not:
>
> – Joe will be able to obtain a tax deduction when calculating his taxable trading profit
>
> – Joe will be able to recover the related input tax for VAT purposes.

Required

Prepare the notes for the meeting as requested in the email from your manager. The following marks are available:

(a) Liquidation of VNL Ltd.

    (i)   Sale of intangible fixed assets. **(4 marks)**

    (ii)   Timing of payments to shareholders. **(7 marks)**

(b) Unincorporated business.

    (i)   Accounting date. **(8 marks)**

    (ii)   Costs already incurred and the business premises. **(12 marks)**

Professional marks will be awarded for the approach taken to problem solving, the clarity of the explanations and calculations, the effectiveness with which the information is communicated, and the overall presentation and style of the meeting notes. **(4 marks)**

(Total: 35 marks)

CAPITAL TAXES

25 JOAN ARK

You should assume that today's date is 6 April 2022.

Joan Ark, aged 76, has asked for your advice regarding the following gifts that she has made during the tax year 2021/22.

(a) On 13 July 2021, Joan made a gift of 250,000 ordinary shares in Orleans plc, a quoted company into a discretionary trust for the benefit of her granddaughters.

On that day, the shares were quoted at 146p – 150p, with recorded bargains of 140p, 144p, 149p and 155p.

Joan originally purchased 200,000 shares in Orleans plc during 2006 at a cost of £149,000. Joan also bought 75,000 shares on 15 August 2019 for £69,375 and has subsequently bought 10,000 shares on 21 July 2020 for £14,800.

Orleans plc has an issued share capital of 10 million ordinary shares and Joan has never been a director or employee of the company.

(b) On 15 July 2021, Joan gave 20,000 of her 40,000 ordinary shares in Rouen Ltd, an unquoted trading company, to her son Michael. Rouen Ltd has an issued share capital of 100,000 ordinary shares. Joan's husband also owns 40,000 ordinary shares in the company.

On 15 July 2021, the relevant values of Rouen Ltd's shares were as follows:

Shareholding	Value per share
	£
100%	22.30
80%	17.10
60%	14.50
40%	9.20
20%	7.90

Joan purchased her 40,000 shares in Rouen Ltd during 2008 for £96,400. Her husband works for the company but Joan does not.

(c) On 4 November 2021, Joan gave her grandson an antique vase worth £18,500 as a wedding present. Joan purchased the vase during 2006 for £14,150.

(d) On 15 January 2022, Joan gave agricultural land with an agricultural value of £175,000 to her son Charles. Joan had purchased the land during 2010 for £92,000, and it has always been let out to tenant farmers.

The most recent tenancy agreement, which started in June 2012, will soon end, and Joan has obtained planning permission to build residential accommodation on the land. The value of the land with planning permission is £300,000.

Charles owns adjoining agricultural land, and the value of this land will increase from £210,000 to £250,000 as a result of the gift.

(e) On 31 March 2022, Joan made a gift of her main residence in Wales valued at £265,000 to her daughter Catherine. However, as a condition of the gift, Joan has continued to live in the house rent free.

The house was purchased on 1 July 2000 for £67,000, and Joan occupied it as her main residence until 31 December 2004. The house was unoccupied between 1 January 2005 and 31 December 2008, and it was rented out as furnished accommodation between 1 January 2009 and 30 June 2021.

Since 1 July 2021, Joan has again occupied the house as her main residence.

Joan has not previously made any lifetime transfers of assets. She is to pay any IHT liabilities arising from the above gifts.

Required:

(i) Advise Joan of the IHT and CGT implications arising from the gifts made during the tax year 2021/22.

Your answer should be supported by appropriate calculations, and should include an explanation of any reliefs that are available.

You should ignore the instalment option and the effect of the annual exemption for IHT purposes and the annual exempt amount for CGT purposes.

Marks for this part of the question will be allocated on the basis of:

5 marks to (a), 5 marks to (b), 3 marks to (c), 5 marks to (d), 6 marks to (e)

(24 marks)

(ii) Explain the main advantages of an individual making lifetime gifts for IHT purposes and the main factors to be considered in choosing which assets to gift. (6 marks)

Joan is a higher rate taxpayer for income tax purposes.

(Total: 30 marks)

26 ALEX (ADAPTED)

You should assume that today's date is 20 February 2022.

Alex, a widower, died on 5 February 2022. His will leaves £150,000 to charity and the remainder of his assets split in equal shares to his son, Brian and his daughter, Beatrice, who support his decision to benefit charitable causes.

The assets comprised in Alex's estate were as follows:

	Market value 5 February 2022 £
Main residence	575,000
Building society account	15,000
NS&I investment account	55,000
NS&I savings certificates	180,000
Various chattels	40,000
Shares in Touriga Ltd	Note 1
Shares in Nacional plc	Note 2
Other quoted investments	115,000

Notes

1   Touriga Ltd is an unquoted trading company. Alex bought his 2,450 ordinary shares (representing 35% of the issued shares) in September 2019 for £8.50 per share. The shares were worth £11.00 per share at the time of his death.

2   Nacional plc is a quoted company in which Alex held 20,000 shares (representing less than 1% of the issued shares) at the time of his death. On 5 February 2022, the shares were listed ex div at 624p – 632p with marked bargains at 625p, 629p and 630p. A dividend of 18 pence per share was declared on 5 December 2021, and was received on 11 February 2022 by the executors.

Alex had made two lifetime gifts. The first was a villa in Spain. This was given to Brian in July 2016. The value at that time was £338,000. In addition, Alex settled an equal amount on a relevant property trust in March 2017. Alex agreed to pay any tax due on the gifts.

Prior to his death, Alex had the following income in the tax year 2021/22:

	£
Pension (gross – PAYE deducted at source £2,120)	10,600
Building society interest	1,600
NS&I investment account interest	870
Dividends (other than from Nacional plc (Note 2 above))	9,000

Brian, Alex's son, is aged 58, is in poor health, and is not expected to live more than a few years. His wife died ten years ago, since when he has lived alone. He owns a house, currently worth £400,000 with an £80,000 mortgage outstanding and has other assets in the form of cash investments worth £80,000, and personal belongings worth £50,000.

Consequently, Brian has no need of his inheritance from Alex and so intends to gift his share of his father's estate to his two children, Colin and Charlotte, in equal shares.

Colin, who is 20, is in his second year at university, but Brian is worried that his son will spend all of the money at once. Charlotte, who is 17, is still at school but is likely to go to university in the near future.

Again, Brian worries about the money being spent unwisely, and therefore wishes to use some form of trust to control the capital sums gifted to both his children. Brian has made no lifetime gifts to date.

Required:

(a)   Calculate the income tax (IT) payable/repayable for Alex for the tax year 2021/22.
(5 marks)

(b)   Explain, with supporting calculations, the inheritance tax (IHT) implications (including any additional tax due on his lifetime gifts) arising on the death of Alex, and quantify the inheritance (after tax) due to Brian and Beatrice.

Assume that Alex's wife utilised all of her nil rate bands when she died.   (10 marks)

(c)   (i)   Explain how Brian could use a trust to maintain control of the capital he intends to gift to Colin and Charlotte following Alex's death and the inheritance tax (IHT) treatment of the trust.   (4 marks)

(ii)   State, giving reasons, what other inheritance tax (IHT) planning advice you would offer Brian with regard to setting up a trust for Colin and Charlotte with the assets he has inherited.   (3 marks)

(Total: 22 marks)

27   MABEL PORTER  *Online question assistance*

You should assume that today's date is 1 December 2022.

Mabel Porter is elderly and in poor health. Her husband, Luke, died on 1 June 2022 and she has no children.

Luke fully utilised his nil rate band for inheritance tax purposes during his lifetime.

In her will, Mabel has left the whole of her estate to Bruce and Padma, her brother's children. Bruce and Padma have always visited Mabel regularly although, since emigrating to South Africa in January 2019, Bruce now keeps in touch by telephone.

Mabel owns the following assets:

	Probate value	Market value	
	1 June 2022	Today	Estimated at 30 June 2027
	£	£	£
House and furniture		325,000	450,000
Rolls Royce motor car		71,000	55,000
Diamond necklace		70,000	84,000
Cash and investments in quoted shares		120,000	150,000
Assets inherited from her husband, Luke:			
40,000 ordinary shares in BOZ plc	44,500	77,000	95,000
Land in the country of Utopia	99,000	75,000	75,000

Mabel has decided to give a substantial present to both Bruce and Padma on each of their birthdays on 1 February 2023 and 5 March 2023 respectively. She does not want to gift any asset that will give rise to a tax liability prior to her death and hopes that the gifts will reduce her eventual inheritance tax liability.

Bruce and Padma have agreed to sign any elections necessary to avoid tax arising on the gifts. It can be assumed that the market values of the assets will not change between now and when these gifts are made.

Mabel will give Bruce either the shares in BOZ plc or the land in the country of Utopia. Utopia is not a member of the EEA.

Luke purchased the shares in BOZ plc on 1 March 2019. BOZ plc is a quoted manufacturing company with an issued share capital of 75,000 ordinary shares. It owns investment properties that represent 8% of the value of its total assets. The land in Utopia consists of a small farm that has always been rented out to tenant farmers. It was purchased by Luke on1 May 2018 and has an agricultural value at today's date of £58,000.

Mabel will give Padma either the Rolls Royce or the necklace.

Mabel purchased the Rolls Royce, new, in June 2017, for £197,000. She inherited the necklace from her grandmother in April 1997; its probate value at that time was £21,500.

Mabel's only lifetime gift was a gift of £210,000 to a discretionary trust on 1 May 2016 and she does not intend to make any further substantial gifts between now and her death. Mabel has capital losses of £15,100 as at 5 April 2022.

Required:

(a)   Explain the immediate capital gains tax and inheritance tax implications of each of the four possible gifts.

Quantify the chargeable gain or loss and the potentially exempt transfer in each case and comment on the availability or otherwise of any reliefs.   (12 marks)

(b)   Mabel has two objectives when making the gifts to Bruce and Padma:

1   To pay no tax on any gift in her lifetime; and

2   To reduce the eventual liability to inheritance tax on her death.

Advise Mabel which item to gift to Bruce and to Padma in order to satisfy her objectives. Give reasons for your advice.

Your advice should include a computation of the inheritance tax saved as a result of the two gifts, on the assumption that Mabel dies on 30 June 2027.   (10 marks)

(c)   Without changing the advice you have given in (b), or varying the terms of Luke's will, explain how Mabel could further reduce her eventual inheritance tax liability and quantify the tax saving that could be made.   (3 marks)

You should assume that the rates and allowances for the tax year 2021/22 will continue to apply for the foreseeable future.

(Total: 25 marks)

 Online question assistance

28   KEPLER (ADAPTED)

You should assume that today's date is 1 June 2022.

Kepler gave his nephew, Galileo, 600 shares (a 30% holding) in Messier Ltd on 1 June 2018. On 1 May 2022, Kepler died and left the remaining 1,400 shares in Messier Ltd to Galileo. Galileo intends to move to the UK from the country of Astronomeria to participate in the management of Messier Ltd.

The following information has been obtained from client files and meetings with the parties involved.

Kepler:

–   Died on 1 May 2022.

–   Was UK resident and domiciled.

–   Has two nephews; Galileo and Herschel.

–   In his will he left 1,400 shares in Messier Ltd valued at £546,000 to Galileo and the residue of his estate valued at £480,000 to Herschel.

Kepler – Lifetime gifts:

–   1 February 2017   Gave a house to Herschel valued at £311,000.

–   1 July 2017   Gave a watch costing £900 to each of his two nephews.

–   1 June 2018   Gave 600 shares in Messier Ltd to Galileo.

Messier Ltd:

– Unquoted company that transports building materials.

– Incorporated in the UK on 1 February 2009 when Kepler subscribed for 2,000 shares, the whole of its share capital.

Messier Ltd – Value of an ordinary share:

– As at	1 June 2018	1 May 2022
	£	£
As part of a 100% holding	485	570
As part of a 70% holding	310	390
As part of a 30% holding	230	260

Messier Ltd – Asset values:

– As at 1 June 2018	£
Premises	900,000
Surplus land rented to third party	480,000
Vehicles	100,000
Current assets	50,000

Galileo:

– Resident and domiciled in the country of Astronomeria where he has lived since birth.

– Lives in rented accommodation in Astronomeria.

– Intends to sell two paintings in order to provide funds to go towards the cost of relocating to the UK and purchasing a house here.

– Has a full time employment contract with Messier Ltd commencing on 1 September 2022.

– Intends to stay in the UK for at least five years.

The two paintings:

– Are situated in Astronomeria and are worth approximately £20,000 each.

– Have been owned by Galileo since 1 May 2007; their cost is negligible and can be ignored.

Employment contract with Messier Ltd:

– Galileo will be paid an annual salary of £52,000.

– Messier Ltd will assist Galileo with the cost of relocating to the UK.

Required:

(a)   (i)   Calculate the inheritance tax payable (if any) by Galileo in respect of:

            1   the gift of shares in June 2018, and

            2   the inheritance of shares in May 2022.   **(8 marks)**

       (ii)   Explain why Galileo is able to pay the inheritance tax due in instalments, state when the instalments are due and identify any further issues relevant to Galileo relating to the payments.   **(3 marks)**

(b)   Prepare a reasoned explanation of how any capital gains tax arising in the UK on the sale of the paintings can be minimised.   **(2 marks)**

(c)   (i)   Explain how Messier Ltd can assist Galileo with the cost of relocating to the UK and/or provide him with interest-free loan finance for this purpose without increasing his UK income tax liability.   **(3 marks)**

       (ii)   State, with reasons, whether Messier Ltd can provide Galileo with accommodation in the UK without giving rise to a UK income tax liability.

                                            (3 marks)

                                                      (Total: 19 marks)

29   SURFE *Walk in the footsteps of a top tutor*

You should assume that today's date is 1 December 2022.

Surfe has requested advice on the tax implications of the creation of a discretionary trust and a calculation of the estimated inheritance tax liability on her death. The following information was obtained at a meeting with Surfe.

Surfe:

–   Is an elderly widow who has two adult nephews.

–   Intends to create a trust on 1 January 2023.

Death of Surfe's husband:

–   Surfe's husband, Flud, died on 1 February 2009. He had made no gifts during his lifetime.

–   In his will, Flud left £140,000 in cash to his sister and the remainder of his estate to Surfe.

–   The inheritance tax nil rate band for the tax year 2008/09 was £312,000.

The trust:

–   The trust will be a discretionary (relevant property) trust for the benefit of Surfe's nephews.

–   Surfe will give 200 of her ordinary shares in Leat Ltd and £100,000 in cash to the trustees of the trust on 1 January 2023.

–   The inheritance tax due on the gift will be paid by Surfe.

–   The trustees will invest the cash in quoted shares.

Leat Ltd:

- Leat Ltd has an issued share capital of 1,000 ordinary shares.

- Surfe owns 650 of the company's ordinary shares.

- The remaining 350 of its ordinary shares are owned by 'Kanal', a UK registered charity.

- Leat Ltd is a property investment company such that business property relief is not available.

Leat Ltd – Value of an ordinary share:

- As at

	1 January 2023	1 July 2025
	£	£
As part of a holding of 75% or more	2,000	2,400
As part of a holding of more than 50% but less than 75%	1,000	1,200
As part of a holding of 50% or less	800	1,000

Surfe – Lifetime gifts:

- 1 February 2011   Surfe gave 350 ordinary shares in Leat Ltd to 'Kanal', a UK registered charity.

- 1 October 2022   Surfe gave £85,000 in cash to each of her two nephews.

Surfe's death:

- It should be assumed that Surfe will die on 1 July 2025.

- Her death estate will consist of the house in which she lives, worth £1,400,000, quoted shares worth £600,000 and her remaining shares in Leat Ltd.

- Her will divides her entire estate between her two nephews and their children.

Required:

(a) Outline BRIEFLY:

    (i)   **The capital gains tax implications of:**

        1   **the proposed gift of shares to the trustees of the discretionary trust**

        2   **any future sale of the quoted shares by the trustees; and**

        3   **the future transfer of trust assets to Surfe's nephews.**   **(4 marks)**

    (ii)   **The inheritance tax charges that may be payable in the future by the trustees of the discretionary trust.**

        You are not required to prepare calculations for part (a) of this question.

        (2 marks)

(b) **Calculate the inheritance tax liabilities arising as a result of Surfe's death on 1 July 2025.**   **(11 marks)**

        (Total: 17 marks)

30   ASH *Walk in the footsteps of a top tutor*

You should assume that today's date is 1 December 2022.

Ash requires a calculation of his capital gains tax liability for the tax year 2021/22, together with advice in connection with business asset disposal relief, registration for the purposes of value added tax (VAT) and the payment of income tax.

Ash:

- Is resident in the UK.
- Had taxable income of £29,000 in the tax year 2021/22.
- Was the owner and managing director of Lava Ltd until 1 May 2021, when he resigned and sold the company.
- Is a partner in the Vulcan Partnership.

Ash – disposals of capital assets in the tax year 2021/22:

- The sale of the shares in Lava Ltd resulted in a capital gain of £235,000, which qualified for business asset disposal relief.
- Ash assigned a 37-year lease on a property for £110,000 on 1 May 2021.
- Ash sold two hectares of land on 1 October 2021 for £30,000.
- Ash sold quoted shares and made a capital loss of £16,500 on 1 November 2021.

The lease:

- The lease was previously assigned to Ash for £31,800 when it had 46 years remaining.
- The property has always been used by Lava Ltd for trading purposes.
- Lava Ltd paid Ash rent, equivalent to 40% of the market rate, in respect of the use of the property.

The sale of the two hectares of land:

- Ash purchased eight hectares of land for £27,400 on 1 June 2014.
- Ash sold six hectares of the land for £42,000 on 1 August 2017.
- The remaining two hectares of land were worth £18,000 on 1 August 2017.

Vulcan Partnership (Vulcan):

- Has a 31 March year end
- Has monthly turnover of:

Standard-rated supplies	£400
Exempt supplies	£100
Zero-rated supplies	£5,600

- Its turnover is expected to increase slightly in 2023.
- None of its customers are registered for the purposes of VAT.
- Ash expects to receive less profit from Vulcan for the tax year 2022/23 than he did in 2021/22.

Required:

(a) (i) State the conditions that must be satisfied for Ash's assignment of the lease to be an associated disposal for the purposes of business asset disposal relief.

(3 marks)

(ii) Calculate Ash's capital gains tax liability for the tax year 2021/22 on the assumption that the assignment of the lease does qualify as an associated disposal and that business asset disposal relief will be claimed where possible.

The following lease percentages should be used, where necessary.

37 years   93.497

46 years   98.490   (7 marks)

(b) Discuss in detail whether the Vulcan Partnership may be required to register for value added tax (VAT) and the advantages and disadvantages for the business of registration.   (7 marks)

(c) Set out the matters that Ash should consider when deciding whether or not to make a claim to reduce the payment on account of income tax due on 31 January 2023.

(3 marks)

(Total: 20 marks)

31   BRAD (ADAPTED)   *Walk in the footsteps of a top tutor*

You should assume that today's date is 1 June 2022.

Your manager has had a meeting with Brad, a client of your firm. Extracts from your manager's meeting notes together with an email from your manager are set out below.

Extracts from meeting notes

Personal details

Brad is 70 years old. He is married to Laura and they have a daughter, Dani, who is 38 years old.

Brad had lived in the UK for the whole of his life until he moved with his wife to the country of Keirinia on 1 January 2019. He returned to live permanently in the UK on 30 April 2022. Whilst living in Keirinia, Brad was non-UK resident and he is now resident in the UK. He has always been domiciled in the UK.

Brad has significant investment income and has been a higher rate taxpayer for many years.

Capital gains

Whilst living in the country of Keirinia, Brad sold various assets as set out below. He has not made any other disposals since 5 April 2018.

Asset	Date of sale	Proceeds	Date of purchase	Cost
		£		£
Quoted shares	1 December 2018	18,900	1 October 2017	14,000
Painting	1 June 2021	36,000	1 March 2017	15,000
Antique bed	1 March 2022	9,400	1 May 2019	7,300
Motor car	1 April 2022	11,000	1 February 2019	8,500

I explained that, although Brad was non-UK resident whilst living in Keirinia, these disposals may still be subject to UK capital gains tax because he will be regarded as only temporarily non-UK resident.

There is no capital gains tax in the country of Keirinia.

Inheritance tax planning

Brad's estate is worth approximately £5 million. He has not made any lifetime gifts and, in his will, he intends to leave half of his estate to his daughter, Dani, and the other half to his wife, Laura. I pointed out that it may be advantageous to make a lifetime gift to Dani. Brad agreed to consider giving Dani 1,500 of his shares in Omnium Ltd and has asked for a general summary of the inheritance tax advantages of making lifetime gifts to individuals.

Omnium Ltd is an unquoted manufacturing company which also owns a number of investment properties. Brad was given his shares in the company by his wife on 1 January 2018. The ownership of the share capital of Omnium Ltd is set out below.

	Shares
Laura (Brad's wife)	4,500
Brad	3,000
Vic (Laura's brother)	1,500
Christine (friend of Laura)	1,000
	10,000

The current estimated value of a share in Omnium Ltd is set out below.

Shareholding	Value per share
	£
Up to 25%	190
26% to 50%	205
51% to 60%	240
61% to 74%	255
75% to 80%	290
More than 80%	300

Email from your manager

In preparation for my next meeting with Brad, please prepare the following:

(a) Capital gains tax

An explanation, with supporting calculations, of the UK capital gains tax liability in respect of the disposals made by Brad whilst living in the country of Keirinia.

Your explanation should include the precise reasons for Brad being regarded as only temporarily non-UK resident and a statement of when the tax was/will be payable.

(b) Inheritance tax

(i) An explanation of the inheritance tax advantages of making lifetime gifts to individuals, in general.

> (ii) In respect of the possible gift of 1,500 shares in Omnium Ltd to Dani:
>
> – a calculation of the fall in value of Brad's estate which will result from the gift
>
> – a detailed explanation of whether or not business property relief would be available in respect of the gift and, on the assumption that it would be available, the manner in which it would be calculated
>
> – a brief statement of any other tax issues arising from the gift, which will need to be considered at a later date.
>
> **Tax manager**

Required:

Carry out the work required as requested in the email from your manager.

The following marks are available.

(a) **Capital gains tax.** **(8 marks)**

(b) **Inheritance tax.**

(i) **Explanation of the inheritance tax advantages of making lifetime gifts to individuals.** **(7 marks)**

(ii) **In respect of the possible gift of 1,500 shares in Omnium Ltd to Dani.**

(10 marks)

(Total: 25 marks)

32 PESCARA (ADAPTED) *Walk in the footsteps of a top tutor*

 Question debrief

You should assume that today's date is 1 December 2022.

Pescara requires advice on the inheritance tax payable on death and on the gift of a property, and on the capital gains tax due on a disposal of shares, together with the relief available in respect of the purchase of seed enterprise investment scheme shares.

Pescara and her parents:

– Pescara is a higher rate taxpayer who is resident and domiciled in the UK.

– Pescara's father, Galvez, died on 1 June 2008.

– Pescara's mother, Marina, died on 1 October 2022.

– Both Galvez and Marina were resident and domiciled in the UK.

Galvez – lifetime gifts and gifts on death:

– Galvez had not made any lifetime gifts.

– In his will, Galvez left cash of £80,000 to Pescara and a further £80,000 to Pescara's brother.

– Galvez left the remainder of his estate to his wife, Marina.

Marina – lifetime gifts and gifts on death:

– On 1 February 2017, Marina gave Pescara 375,000 shares in Sepang plc.

– Marina had made no other lifetime gifts.

Marina – gift of 375,000 shares in Sepang plc to Pescara:

–   1 January 2014   Marina purchased 375,000 shares for £420,000.

–   1 February 2017   Marina gave all of the shares to Pescara.

                            The shares were quoted at £1.84 – £1.96

                            The highest and lowest marked bargains were £1.80 and £1.92.

–   The shares did not qualify for business property relief or capital gains tax gift holdover relief.

–   The inheritance tax nil rate band for the tax year 2008/09 was £312,000.

Acquisition of Sepang plc by Zolder plc and subsequent bonus issue:

–   1 January 2019   Zolder plc acquired the whole of the ordinary share capital of Sepang plc.

                            Pescara received 30 pence and two ordinary shares in Zolder plc, worth £1 each, for each share in Sepang plc.

                            The takeover was for genuine commercial reasons and not for the avoidance of tax.

–   1 July 2020   Zolder plc declared a 2 for 1 bonus issue.

Pescara's actual and intended capital transactions in the tax year 2022/23:

			£
15 November 2022	Sale	1,000,000 shares in Zolder plc	445,000
1 April 2023	Purchase	Qualifying seed enterprise investment scheme (SEIS) shares	90,000

Pescara – gift of a UK property:

–   Pescara intends to give a UK property to her son on 1 October 2023.

–   Pescara intends to continue to use this property, rent-free, such that this gift will be a gift with reservation.

Required:

(a)   Calculate the inheritance tax payable in respect of Marina's gift of the shares in Sepang plc, as a result of her death.   **(7 marks)**

(b)   (i)   Calculate Pescara's capital gains tax liability for the tax year 2022/23 on the assumption that seed enterprise investment scheme (SEIS) relief is claimed in respect of the shares to be purchased on 1 April 2023 and that business asset disposal relief is not available.   **(6 marks)**

       (ii)   State the capital gains tax implications of Pescara selling the SEIS shares at some point in the future.   **(3 marks)**

(c)   Explain how the proposed gift of the UK property will be treated for the purposes of calculating the inheritance tax due on Pescara's death.   **(4 marks)**

                                                   (Total: 20 marks)

 Calculate your allowed time, allocate the time to the separate parts.

33   CADA (ADAPTED)   *Walk in the footsteps of a top tutor*

You should assume that today's date is 1 December 2022.

Your firm has been asked to provide advice in connection with inheritance tax and capital gains tax following the death of Cada. The advice relates to the implications of making lifetime gifts, making gifts to charity, varying the terms of a will and other aspects of capital gains tax planning.

Cada and her family:

– Cada, who was UK domiciled, died on 20 November 2022.

– Cada is survived by two daughters: Raymer and Yang.

– Raymer has an adult son.

– Yang has no children.

Cada – Lifetime gifts and available nil rate band:

– Cada had not made any lifetime gifts since 30 November 2018.

– Cada's nil rate band available at the date of her death was £220,000.

Cada's death estate and the details of her will:

– Cada owned assets valued at £1,000,000 at the time of her death.

– Cada left her house, valued at £500,000, to Raymer.

– Cada left cash of £60,000 to a UK national charity.

– Cada left her remaining assets (including a portfolio of shares) valued at £440,000, to Yang.

– None of the remaining assets qualified for any inheritance tax reliefs.

Raymer:

– Is not an accountant, but has some knowledge of the UK tax system.

– Has made four observations regarding her mother's estate and her inheritance.

Raymer's four observations:

– 'My mother should have made additional gifts in her lifetime.'

– 'The tax rate on the chargeable estate should be less than 40% due to the gift to charity.'

– 'I do not intend to live in the house but will give it to my son on 1 July 2023.'

– 'My mother paid capital gains tax every year. However, when she died, some of her shareholdings had a value of less than cost.'

Cada's shareholdings at the time of her death:

– Quoted shares in JW plc valued at more than cost.

– Quoted shares in FR plc valued at less than cost.

– Unquoted shares in KZ Ltd valued at £nil.

Required:

(a) Explain the inheritance tax advantages, other than lifetime exemptions, which could have been obtained if Cada had made additional lifetime gifts of quoted shares between 1 December 2018 and her death. **(4 marks)**

(b) Calculate the increase in the legacy to the charity which would be necessary in order for the reduced rate of inheritance tax to apply and quantify the reduction in the inheritance tax liability which would result. **(5 marks)**

(c) Explain the capital gains tax and inheritance tax advantages which could be obtained by varying the terms of Cada's will and set out the procedures required in order to achieve a tax effective variation. **(6 marks)**

(d) In relation to capital gains tax, explain what beneficial actions Cada could have carried out in the tax year of her death in respect of her shareholdings. **(5 marks)**

(Total: 20 marks)

34 ERIC (ADAPTED) *Walk in the footsteps of a top tutor*

You should assume that today's date is 10 March 2023.

Your client, Eric, requires advice on the capital gains tax implications arising from the receipt of insurance proceeds and the disposal of some shares, and the inheritance tax reliefs available in respect of assets in his estate at death. His son Zak requires advice regarding the application of the personal service company (IR35) legislation.

Eric:

–   Is UK resident and domiciled.

–   Is a higher rate taxpayer.

–   Is in ill health and is expected to die within the next few months.

Capital transactions in the tax year 2021/22:

–   Eric made no disposals for capital gains tax purposes in the tax year 2021/22 other than those detailed below.

–   Eric received insurance proceeds of £10,000 following damage to a valuable painting.

–   Eric sold half of his shareholding in Malaga plc for £11.50 per share.

Damaged painting:

–   Eric purchased the painting for £46,000 in July 2019.

–   The painting was damaged in October 2021 such that immediately afterwards its value fell to £38,000.

     The insurance proceeds of £10,000 were received by Eric on 1 December 2021.

–   Eric has not had the painting repaired.

Malaga plc shares:

–   Malaga plc is a quoted trading company with 200,000 issued shares.

–   80% of Malaga plc's chargeable assets have always been chargeable business assets.

–   Eric was given 12,000 shares in Malaga plc by his sister on 5 August 2018, when they were valued at £126,000.

–   Eric's sister had purchased the shares for £96,000 on 1 March 2016.

- Gift holdover relief was claimed in respect of the gift of the shares to Eric on 5 August 2018.
- Eric paid the inheritance tax arising in respect of this gift following his sister's death on 1 September 2018.
- Eric has never worked for Malaga plc.
- Eric sold 6,000 shares in Malaga plc on 1 March 2022.

Assets owned by Eric and a previous lifetime gift:

- Eric owns farmland in the UK, which has been leased to a tenant farmer for the last ten years.
- The farmland has a market value of £420,000 and an agricultural value of £340,000.
- Eric's other assets, excluding the remaining Malaga plc shares, are valued at £408,000.
- Eric has made only one previous lifetime gift, of £60,000 cash to his son Zak on 1 July 2016.

Zak:

- Is the sole shareholder, director and employee of Yoyo Ltd, a company which provides consultancy services.
- In the year ended 31 March 2023, Yoyo Ltd's gross fee income from relevant engagements performed by Zak will be £110,000.
- All of the consultancy clients are small organisations for the purposes of the personal service company legislation.
- In the tax year 2022/23, Zak will draw a salary of £24,000 and dividends of £50,000 from Yoyo Ltd.
- Neither Yoyo Ltd nor Zak has any other source of income.

Required:

(a) Calculate Eric's total after-tax proceeds in respect of the two capital gains tax disposals in the tax year 2021/22. **(6 marks)**

(b) (i) On the assumption that Eric dies on 31 March 2023, advise on the availability and effect (if any), of agricultural property relief, business property relief and quick succession relief in respect of the farmland and the retained shares in Malaga plc.

Note: You are not required to prepare calculations for this part of the question. **(6 marks)**

(ii) Explain, with the aid of calculations, the impact on the inheritance tax liability arising on Eric's death if Eric does not die until 1 August 2023. **(3 marks)**

(c) Calculate Zak's taxable income for the tax year 2022/23 if the personal service company (IR35) legislation were to apply to the fee income received by Yoyo Ltd. **(5 marks)**

(Total: 20 marks)

35   SABRINA AND ADAM *Walk in the footsteps of a top tutor*

You should assume that today's date is 10 September 2022.

Adam would like advice on the capital gains tax and inheritance tax implications of being given Eastwick Farm by his mother, Sabrina, and on recent changes in tax law which affect his investment planning.

Sabrina:

–   Is UK resident and domiciled.

–   Has made one previous lifetime gift of £350,000 into a discretionary trust for her grandchildren on 1 September 2022.

–   Inherited Eastwick Farm from her husband, Sam, on his death on 1 July 2021.

–   Has managed the farm since this date.

Sam:

–   Owned and farmed Eastwick Farm for many years prior to his death on 1 July 2021.

–   Had made lifetime gifts which used the whole of his nil rate band for inheritance tax purposes.

Sabrina – proposal to gift Eastwick Farm to Adam:

–   Sabrina plans to retire from running the farm on 31 December 2022.

–   She has been informed by a financial adviser that she could gift the farm to Adam when she retires without paying any capital gains tax or inheritance tax.

–   She has decided to gift the farm to Adam on 1 January 2023.

Eastwick Farm – valuation of land and buildings:

	1 July 2021	1 January 2023 (estimated)
	£	£
Agricultural value	385,000	396,000
Market value	502,000	544,000

Adam:

–   Is UK resident and domiciled.

–   Is 42 years old.

–   Is an additional rate taxpayer, with adjusted income (for the purpose of calculating Adam's annual allowance for pension contributions) of £290,000 per year, which he expects to continue for the foreseeable future.

–   Uses his annual exempt amount for capital gains tax purposes each year.

–   Is in full-time employment and will lease Eastwick Farm to a tenant farmer.

Adam – investments:

–   Adam has regularly contributed the maximum allowed into a personal pension scheme using his available annual allowance each year.

–   Adam has invested the maximum amount each year in an individual savings account (ISA).

Adam – thoughts on investments:

– 'I have been advised that my annual allowance for pension contributions was £15,000 for the tax year 2021/22. Please can you explain how this figure is calculated?'

– 'Is there now any point in investing in either a cash or a stocks and shares ISA as savings income and dividends are now exempt from tax anyway up to £2,000 per year?'

Required:

(a) (i) Explain the capital gains tax and inheritance tax implications for Sabrina of the planned gift of Eastwick Farm to Adam on 1 January 2023, and the reasons why the financial adviser has determined that neither tax may be payable by her as a consequence of this gift.

Note: Detailed calculations are NOT required for this part. **(3 marks)**

(ii) Explain, with supporting calculations, Adam's potential capital gains tax liability on a future sale of Eastwick Farm and the inheritance tax implications for him of being gifted the farm by Sabrina on 1 January 2023 if, as he intends, he leases the farm to a tenant farmer, and Sabrina dies before 1 January 2030. **(11 marks)**

(b) Comment on the thoughts expressed by Adam in relation to his personal pension contributions and investment in individual savings accounts (ISAs). **(6 marks)**

(Total: 20 marks)

36 LIBER

You should assume that today's date is 10 September 2022.

Liber has requested advice on the timing of the sale of the shares which he acquired in a recent company takeover. His sister, Vesta, requires advice on the tax consequences of making a lifetime gift, rather than leaving an asset in her estate upon her death.

Liber:

– Is UK resident and domiciled.

– Has taxable income of £30,000 each year.

Liber – acquisition of ordinary shares in Mercury plc:

– Liber purchased 800 ordinary shares (a 40% holding) in Vulcan Ltd for £14,000 on 1 July 2012.

– Mercury plc acquired 100% of the ordinary share capital of Vulcan Ltd on 1 June 2022.

– In exchange for each ordinary share in Vulcan Ltd Liber received the following:

– Four ordinary shares in Mercury plc valued at £20 per share immediately after the takeover; and

– £15 cash.

– Mercury plc has 200,000 issued ordinary shares.

– Liber has never been a director or employee of either Vulcan Ltd or Mercury plc.

– The takeover was for *bona fide* commercial reasons and not for the avoidance of tax.

Liber – proposed transaction in Mercury plc shares:

– Liber now wishes to sell all of his shares in Mercury plc.

– He has received an offer from an unconnected person to purchase these shares on 1 January 2023 at a price of £28 per share.

– Liber would prefer to sell the shares to his nephew, Janus. However, this would delay the sale as his nephew will not have the necessary funds to purchase the shares until 1 May 2023.

– Janus has said he will also pay £28 per share.

Vesta:

– Is 66 years old and has never married or had a civil partner.

– Is in ill-health and is expected to die at some time within the tax year 2023/24.

– Has made no disposals for capital gains tax purposes in the tax year 2022/23 to date and will not make any in the tax year 2023/24.

– Has made one previous lifetime gift, of £350,000 cash, to her son, Janus, on 1 June 2022.

Vesta – investment property:

– Vesta owns an investment property, which has never been used as her private residence.

– The current market value of the property is less than the price Vesta paid for it, and its value is expected to fall further throughout the tax year 2023/24.

– Vesta is considering gifting the investment property to Janus in her lifetime, rather than leaving it to him in her estate on death.

– Janus is the sole beneficiary of Vesta's estate.

Required:

(a) (i) Explain, with supporting calculations, the capital gains tax implications for Liber of the takeover of Vulcan Ltd by Mercury plc on 1 June 2022, and a subsequent sale of his Mercury plc shares on 1 January 2023. **(8 marks)**

(ii) Explain, with supporting calculations, why it would be beneficial for Liber to sell his Mercury plc shares on 1 May 2023, instead of on 1 January 2023.

(4 marks)

(b) Advise Vesta whether or not there are any capital gains tax or inheritance tax advantages, for herself, or for Janus, if she were to gift the investment property to Janus on 31 December 2022, rather than leaving it to him in her estate on death.

(8 marks)

(Total: 20 marks)

37 MAIA *Walk in the footsteps of a top tutor*

You should assume that today's date is 4 June 2022.

Your manager has had a meeting with Maia, a client of your firm. Extracts from the memorandum prepared by your manager following the meeting and an email from her detailing the work she requires you to do are set out below.

Extracts from the memorandum prepared by your manager – dated 3 June 2022

Maia

Maia is 63 years old and has significant personal wealth. She has taxable income of approximately £120,000 each year, much of which she is able to save. She uses her capital gains tax annual exempt amount and her inheritance tax annual exemption every year. She is resident and domiciled in the UK.

Maia has agreed to provide financial assistance to her nephew, Josh.

Josh – financial position

Josh recently left university and, on 6 April 2022, he started working for NL Ltd, an unquoted company. He earns an annual gross salary of £25,200. Since 6 April 2022, NL Ltd has provided Josh with the use of a mobile telephone (market value of £650) and a home cinema system (market value of £1,700).

On 1 June 2022, NL Ltd issued 200 £1 ordinary shares to Josh. This share issue was not made as part of a tax advantaged share scheme. Josh paid £300 for these shares, which had a market value of £2,100 at that time. The shares are not readily convertible assets and Josh does not intend to sell them until 1 April 2026.

Josh currently receives dividend income of £420 each year. He is resident and domiciled in the UK.

Josh estimates that from 6 April 2022 he needs £2,500 per month to pay his rent and living expenses. Maia has asked us to calculate how much cash Josh will need for the tax years 2022/23 and 2023/24, over and above his post-tax income from all sources.

Providing financial assistance to Josh – alternative strategies

Maia is considering three alternative strategies to provide financial assistance to Josh.

(i) Gift of investment property on 1 July 2022

This investment property is currently worth £370,000.

Maia purchased the property for £130,000 on 1 July 2011. Since its acquisition, this property has been rented out for taxable net rental income of £1,100 per month. It is a residential building, but I do not know whether or not it has been rented out as furnished holiday accommodation.

Under this strategy, Josh would continue to rent out the property on the same basis from 1 July 2022 onwards.

(ii)	**Gift of shares in Far Ltd on 1 July 2022**

These shares are worth £420,000. They represent the whole of Maia's shareholding in the company and constitute 14% of the company's issued ordinary share capital.

Maia's father gave the shares to Maia on 1 November 2021 when they were worth £375,000. That gift resulted in a chargeable gain of £225,000 of which £140,000 was held over via a gift holdover relief claim.

Far Ltd is an unquoted trading company. It owns chargeable non-business assets which represent 16% of its total chargeable assets.

(iii)	**Monthly cash gifts commencing on 1 July 2022**

Maia would simply make a cash gift to Josh of £1,000 each month commencing on 1 July 2022.

Extract from the email from your manager – dated 4 June 2022

Please prepare a memorandum for the client files consisting of the work set out below.

(a) **Josh – additional cash requirement**

Calculate the total additional cash required by Josh, over and above his income from all sources, for the tax years 2022/23 and 2023/24, after deducting tax and national insurance contributions (NIC).

In order to prepare the calculations efficiently, you should think about how Josh's taxable income in 2023/24 will differ from that in 2022/23. There is no need to provide any narrative explanation of your calculations.

(b) **Providing financial assistance to Josh – alternative strategies**

In respect of each of the three alternative strategies set out in my memorandum, explain:

– The increase in Josh's post-tax income for the 21-month period ending 5 April 2024.

You should ONLY consider the post-tax income to be received by Josh in relation to strategies (i) and (iii) and NOT strategy (ii).

There is no need to consider the capital values of any of the strategies as, in the short term, Josh will not realise any of this value.

– The capital gains tax liabilities FOR MAIA ONLY on the assumption that those reliefs which are available will be claimed.

– The inheritance tax implications for Maia and Josh including consideration of the availability of business property relief.

As I noted in my memorandum, I do not know whether the investment property qualifies as furnished holiday accommodation or not. You should explain the liabilities for both possibilities regarding this property. You SHOULD NOT provide a definition of furnished holiday accommodation.

Tax manager

Required:

Prepare the memorandum as requested in the email from your manager. The following marks are available:

(a)	Josh – additional cash requirement.	**(9 marks)**
(b)	Providing financial assistance to Josh – alternative strategies.	
	(i) Gift of investment property.	**(12 marks)**
	(ii) Gift of shares in Far Ltd.	**(7 marks)**
	(iii) Monthly cash gifts.	**(3 marks)**

Professional marks will be awarded for the approach taken to problem solving, the clarity of the explanations and calculations, the effectiveness with which the information is communicated, and the overall presentation and style of the memorandum. **(4 marks)**

(Total: 35 marks)

MULTI TAX PERSONAL INCLUDING OVERSEAS

38 NUCLEUS RESOURCES (ADAPTED)

  Online question assistance and Walk in the footsteps of a top tutor

You should assume that today's date is 1 December 2022.

You have received the following memorandum from your manager.

To	Tax senior
From	Tax manager
Date	28 November 2022
Subject	Maria Copenhagen and Nucleus Resources

I spoke to Maria Copenhagen this morning. We arranged to meet on Thursday 4 December to discuss the following matters.

Nucleus Resources

Maria is planning a major expansion of her business, Nucleus Resources. I attach a schedule, prepared by Maria, showing the budgeted income and expenditure of the business for a full year. Maria wants to know how much additional after-tax income the expansion of the business will create depending on whether she employs the two additional employees or uses a sub-contractor, Quantum Ltd.

Quoted shares

In October 2020 Niels, Maria's husband, received a gift of shares with a value of £170,000 from his uncle. The shares are quoted on the Heisenbergia Stock Exchange. The uncle died in November 2022 and Maria wants to know whether there will be any UK inheritance tax in respect of the gift. The uncle had been living in the country of Heisenbergia since moving there from the UK in 2001 and had made substantial gifts to other close relatives in 2019 and 2020. Inheritance tax of £30,600 has been charged in Heisenbergia in respect of the gift to Niels.

According to Maria, Niels is considering transferring the shares to a trust for the benefit of their two sons.

Please prepare the following:

(a)   In respect of Nucleus Resources:

Calculations of the additional annual after-tax income that would be generated by the expansion of the business under the two alternatives i.e. the recruitment of the additional employees and the use of the sub-contractor. You should check to see if Maria is currently an additional rate taxpayer. If she is, you can simply deduct tax and national insurance at the marginal rates from the additional profits.

Don't worry about the precise timing of the capital allowances in respect of the car, just spread the total allowances available for the car equally over the period of ownership. Also, watch out for the VAT implications of the expansion; there is bound to be an effect on the recoverability of input tax due to the business being partially exempt.

(b)   In respect of the quoted shares:

(i)   A list of the issues to be considered in order to determine whether or not the gift from the uncle is within the scope of UK inheritance tax and the treatment of any inheritance tax suffered in the country of Heisenbergia.

(ii)   A brief outline of the tax implications of transferring the shares to the trust and the taxation of the trust income paid to the beneficiaries. The shares are currently worth £210,000.

(iii)   Notes on the extent to which it is professionally acceptable for me to discuss issues relating to the shares with Maria.

I want to be able to use the calculations and notes in my meeting with Maria (or in a subsequent meeting with Niels) and I may not have much time to study them beforehand so please make sure that they are clear, concise and that I can find my way around them easily.

Thank you

Tax manager

The schedule prepared by Maria is set out below.

Nucleus Resources – Estimated income and expenditure for a full year

Notes

1   The figures in the 'expansion' column relate to the expansion only and will be in addition to the existing business.

2   Nucleus Resources is registered for VAT.

3   All amounts are stated exclusive of VAT.

4   Materials and overheads are subject to VAT at 20%. The expenditure cannot be attributed to particular supplies.

		Existing business £	Expansion £
Turnover:	Standard-rated	40,000	190,000
	Exempt	90,000	–
Expenditure:			
Materials and overheads		37,000	See
Wages		35,000	below

Costs relating to the expansion

I already employ two part-time workers to cope with current business demands. In order to expand the business, I will either recruit two additional employees or sub-contract the work to Quantum Ltd, an unconnected company. Details of the expenditure relating to these two possibilities are set out below.

Employees

Employee 1 would be paid a salary of £55,000. He/she would also be provided with a newly purchased petrol driven motor car with a list price of £12,800 (including VAT) and a CO_2 emission rate of 99 grams per kilometre. It can be assumed that the car will be sold in five years' time for £2,000. Employee 2 would be paid a salary of £40,000 and would not be provided with a car.

There would also be additional materials and overheads, net of VAT at 20%, of £20,000.

Quantum Ltd

Quantum Ltd would charge an annual fee of £140,000 plus VAT.

There would be no additional materials or overheads.

Niels and Maria Copenhagen are both clients of your firm. The following information has been obtained from their files.

Niels Copenhagen

–   Resident and domiciled in the UK.

–   Niels has not made any previous transfers for the purposes of inheritance tax.

–   Married to Maria. They have two children; Hans (11 years old) and Erik (8 years old).

Maria Copenhagen

–   Resident and domiciled in the UK.

–   Trades as 'Nucleus Resources', an unincorporated business.

–   Receives annual gross rental income from an interest in possession trust of £110,000.

Required:

Prepare the meeting notes requested by your manager. The following marks are available.

(a) Calculations of the annual additional after-tax income generated by the expansion of Maria's business under each of the two alternatives. **(14 marks)**

(b) (i) The issues to be considered in order to determine whether or not the gift from the uncle is within the scope of UK inheritance tax and the treatment of any inheritance tax suffered in the country of Heisenbergia. **(6 marks)**

(ii) The tax implications of transferring the shares to the trust and the taxation of any trust income paid to the beneficiaries, Hans and Erik. **(7 marks)**

(iii) The extent to which it is professionally acceptable to discuss issues relating to the shares with Maria. **(4 marks)**

Appropriateness of the format and presentation of the notes and the effectiveness with which the information is communicated. **(4 marks)**

You should assume that the rates and allowances for the tax year 2021/22 apply throughout the question.

(Total: 35 marks)

 Online question assistance

---

39 POBLANO (ADAPTED) *Walk in the footsteps of a top tutor*

You should assume that today's date is 7 June 2022.

Your manager has had a meeting with Poblano. Poblano is the Finance Director of Capsicum Ltd, a subsidiary of Scoville plc. He is a higher rate taxpayer earning £60,000 per year and currently has no other income. Scoville plc together with its subsidiaries and its directors have been clients of your firm for many years.

The memorandum recording the matters discussed at the meeting and an extract from an email from your manager detailing the tasks for you to perform are set out below.

Memorandum recording matters discussed at meeting with Poblano

To	The files
From	Tax manager
Date	4 June 2022
Subject	Poblano

I had a meeting with Poblano on 3 June 2022.

(i) Working in Manchester

Poblano currently lives and works in Birmingham. However, Capsicum Ltd has recently acquired the Manchester operations of the group from a fellow subsidiary of Scoville plc. As a result of this, Poblano is going to be based in Manchester from 1 August 2022 for a period of at least five years. He will be paid an additional £15,000 per year during this period.

Poblano does not want to relocate his family to Manchester for personal reasons. He has been offered the use of a furnished flat in Manchester belonging to Capsicum Ltd to live in during the week. He will drive home each weekend.

Details of the company's flat are set out below.

	£
Current market value	560,000
Purchase price (1 June 2018)	517,000
Annual value	9,605
Monthly contribution required from Poblano	200

Alternatively, if he does not live in the flat, Capsicum Ltd will pay him a mileage allowance of 50 pence per mile to cover the cost of travelling to Manchester every Monday and returning home every Friday. During the week, whilst he is in Manchester, Poblano will stay with his aunt, paying her rent of £325 per month.

Poblano estimates that he will drive 9,200 miles per year travelling to Manchester each week and that he will spend £1,400 per year on petrol. There would also be additional depreciation in respect of his car of approximately £1,500 per year. Capsicum Ltd has a policy of not providing its employees with company cars.

Poblano expects to be better off due to the increase in his salary. He wants to know how much better off he will be depending on whether he lives in the company flat or receives the mileage allowance and stays with his aunt.

(ii) Poblano's cottage in Cornwall

Poblano owns a cottage in Cornwall which he uses for family holidays. He is now thinking about renting out the cottage to long term tenants, but does not understand the tax implications of doing this.

The cottage can be rented out for £1,500 a month, received in advance on the first day of the month. Poblano would incur annual letting agent's fees of £1,800 as well as annual insurance costs of £580.

Poblano has a mortgage on the cottage with interest of £2,000 payable each year.

(iii) Uncle's property in the country of Chilaca

Paprikash (Poblano's uncle) owns a property in the country of Chilaca that he uses for holidays. It has always been intended that the property would be left to Poblano in his uncle's will. However, Paprikash has recently agreed to give the property to Poblano now, if to do so would make sense from a tax point of view. Paprikash may still wish to use the property occasionally in the future.

The property is currently worth £600,000. However, due to the economic situation in the country of Chilaca, it is possible that this figure could either rise or fall over the next few years.

Paprikash is domiciled in the UK. He is in poor health and is not expected to live for more than a further five years. His total assets, including the property in the country of Chilaca, are worth £2 million.

Paprikash makes gifts on 1 May each year in order to use his inheritance tax annual exemption. His only other gift in the last seven years was to a trust on 1 June 2021. The gift consisted of a number of minority holdings of quoted shares valued at £290,000 in total. The trust is for the benefit of Poblano's daughter, Piri. It can be assumed that Paprikash will not make any further lifetime gifts.

There is no capital gains tax or inheritance tax in the country of Chilaca.

(iv) Trust created for the benefit of Poblano's daughter

The trust was created on 1 June 2021 as noted above. Poblano's daughter, Piri, received income from the trust for the first time in March 2022. Poblano did not have any further information on the trust and agreed to bring the relevant documentation to our next meeting. Piri's only other income is an annual salary of approximately £35,000.

Tax manager

E-mail from your manager

I want you to prepare notes for a meeting that we will both attend with Poblano. You will be leading the meeting.

Set out the information so that it is easy for you to find what you need as we go through the various issues. Include the briefest possible notes where the numbers are not self-explanatory.

The meeting notes need to include:

(i) Working in Manchester

–   Calculations showing how much better (or worse) off Poblano will be under each of the alternatives as compared to his current position. If he is worse off under either of the alternatives, include a calculation of the amount of salary he would have to be paid, in addition to the £15,000, so that he is not out of pocket.

–   An explanation of the tax treatment for the recipients of the mileage allowance to be paid to Poblano and the rent to be paid to his aunt.

–   Any further information required and the effect it could have on the calculations you have prepared.

(ii) **Poblano's cottage in Cornwall**

– An explanation of the income tax treatment for Poblano of the rental income received and expenses incurred in relation to the cottage.

This explanation should not include any calculations.

(iii) **Uncle's property in the country of Chilaca**

– Calculations of the inheritance tax liability that will become due in respect of the property in the country of Chilaca depending on whether the property is gifted to Poblano on 1 August 2022 or via his uncle's will.

You should assume the following:

– His uncle, Paprikash, will die on either 31 December 2024 or 31 December 2026.

– The property will be worth £600,000 on 1 August 2022.

– Three possible values of the property at the date of Paprikash's death: £450,000, £600,000 and £900,000.

You should calculate the inheritance tax for each of the 12 possible situations on the property only, assuming that Paprikash does not use the property after the date of the gift.

You should start by calculating the tax on a lifetime gift with Paprikash's death on 31 December 2024. If you then think about the relationships between the different situations you should find that the calculations do not take too long.

In order for the calculations to be comparable, when calculating the tax on the gift via Paprikash's will, you should assume that any available nil rate band is deductible from the property.

– Conclusions drawn from the calculations.

– Any other issues that we should draw to Poblano's attention.

(iv) **Trust created for the benefit of Poblano's daughter**

– A summary of the tax treatment of the income received by Poblano's daughter Piri, as beneficiary, depending on the nature of the trust.

I understand from Poblano that the only income of the trust is dividend income.

Required:

Prepare the meeting notes requested in the email from your manager.

The following marks are available.

(i)	Working in Manchester	**(10 marks)**
(ii)	Poblano's cottage in Cornwall	**(3 marks)**
(iii)	Uncle's property in the country of Chilaca	**(12 marks)**
(iv)	Trust created for the benefit of Poblano's daughter.	**(6 marks)**

Professional marks will be awarded for the appropriateness of the format and presentation of the notes and the effectiveness with which the information is communicated.

(4 marks)

(Total: 35 marks)

40   MIRTOON (ADAPTED)

  Online question assistance and Walk in the footsteps of a top tutor

You should assume that today's date is 9 December 2022.

Your manager has sent you an email, together with an attachment, in respect of a client called Mirtoon. The email and the attachment are set out below.

Email from your manager

Mirtoon intends to leave the UK in January 2023 in order to live in the country of Koro. He has entered into a full time contract of employment for a fixed term of four years but he may stay in Koro for as long as ten years. He will buy a house in Koro and will not make any return trips to the UK whilst he is living in Koro.

Mirtoon plans to sell his house in the UK and his UK business premises and cease his business prior to his departure. Details of these proposals, together with information regarding agricultural land owned by Mirtoon, are set out in the attached extract from his email.

Background information

Mirtoon is 52 years old and divorced. He has always been resident and domiciled in the UK. He will continue to be UK domiciled whilst living in the country of Koro.

He does not own any buildings other than his home and his business premises. He receives bank interest in respect of UK bank deposits of £28,950 per year. He will continue to hold these bank deposits whilst living in the country of Koro.

Mirtoon has not made any disposals for the purposes of capital gains tax in the tax year 2022/23. He has capital losses brought forward as at 5 April 2022 of £2,200.

Mirtoon is self-employed. He has overlap profits brought forward in respect of his business of £7,600. He is registered for value added tax (VAT) and makes standard-rated supplies only. He has never made any claims in respect of business asset disposal relief.

I want you to prepare the following:

(a)   Mirtoon's financial position

Mirtoon wants to know how his plans to dispose of assets and his departure from the UK will affect his financial position. The details of his plans are in the following attachment. He has asked us to prepare a calculation of **the total** of the following amounts:

–   The after-tax proceeds from the sale of his home and business assets.

–   The tax saving in respect of the offset of his trading losses.

The trading losses should be offset against the total income of the tax year 2021/22; there is no need to consider any other loss reliefs.

In order to accurately determine the tax effect of the relief available, you should prepare calculations of Mirtoon's income tax liability for 2021/22 both before and after the offset of the losses.

–   Any other tax liabilities arising as a result of Mirtoon's plans to leave the UK.

You should include explanatory notes where this is necessary to assist Mirtoon's understanding of the calculations. This may be particularly useful in relation to the availability of any reliefs and allowances and the tax relief available in respect of the offset of the trading losses.

(b)   A letter to be sent from me to Mirtoon that addresses the following matters

(i)   VAT: The VAT implications of the cessation of the business and the sale of the business assets.

(ii)   Income tax and capital gains tax: Whether or not Mirtoon will be liable to UK income tax and capital gains tax whilst he is living in the country of Koro by reference to his residence and domicile status.

You should include specific reference to the capital gains tax implications of the proposed sale of the agricultural land in June 2024. Also comment on the implications of Mirtoon selling his UK home whilst he is in Koro rather than prior to his departure.

There is no double tax treaty between the UK and the country of Koro.

(iii)   Inheritance tax: Mirtoon has asked me to discuss some ideas he has had in relation to reducing the potential inheritance tax liability on his death. To help me with this, please include a summary of the rules relating to gifts with reservation.

Tax manager

Attachment – Extract from an email from Mirtoon

Sale of house

I plan to sell my house on 31 December 2022 for £730,000. I purchased the house for £540,000 on 1 July 2018 and I have lived there ever since that date.

Sale of business assets

My business made a tax adjusted profit in the year ended 30 June 2021 of £97,000. However, in the year ended 30 June 2022 it made a tax adjusted loss of £20,000. I have not been able to find a buyer for the business and will therefore cease trading on 31 December 2022. I will sell my business premises, a small office unit, for £120,000 on 31 December 2022. I purchased this office unit for £58,000 on 1 May 2014. I will then sell any remaining business assets.

I expect to be able to sell the remaining business assets, consisting of machinery and inventory, for £14,000, with no asset being sold for more than cost. The business will make a tax adjusted loss of £17,000 in the six months ending 31 December 2022 after taking account of the sale of the business assets.

Agricultural land

In May 2018 my father gave me 230 hectares of agricultural land situated in the UK. A capital gain of £72,000 arose in respect of this gift and my father and I submitted a joint claim for gift holdover relief. I expect the value of the land to increase considerably in 2023 and I intend to sell it in 2024.

Required:

(a) The calculations showing how Mirtoon's disposal of assets and subsequent departure from the UK will affect his financial position as requested in the email from your manager, assuming that the house is sold on 31 December 2022.

 Ignore national insurance contributions. **(16 marks)**

(b) Prepare the letter to Mirtoon requested in the email from your manager. The following marks are available.

 (i) Value added tax (VAT) **(3 marks)**

 (ii) Income tax and capital gains tax **(8 marks)**

 (iii) Inheritance tax. **(4 marks)**

Professional marks will be awarded for the extent to which the calculations are approached in a logical manner in part (a) and the effectiveness with which the information is communicated in part (b). **(4 marks)**

(Total: 35 marks)

 Online question assistance

41 SHUTTELLE (ADAPTED) *Walk in the footsteps of a top tutor*

You should assume that today's date is 9 April 2022.

Your firm has been asked to provide advice to Shuttelle in connection with personal pension contributions and to three non-UK domiciled individuals in connection with the remittance basis of taxation for overseas income and gains.

(a) **Personal pension contributions:**

– Shuttelle has been the production director of Din Ltd since 1 February 2009.

– Shuttelle joined a personal pension scheme on 6 April 2019.

Shuttelle's tax position for the tax year 2021/22:

– Shuttelle's only source of income is her remuneration from Din Ltd.

– Shuttelle's annual salary is £204,000. This is a substantial increase on the previous year.

– Shuttelle lived in a house owned by Din Ltd for a period of time during the tax year 2021/22.

The house provided by Din Ltd for Shuttelle's use:

– Was purchased by Din Ltd on 1 January 2009 for £500,000 and has an annual value of £7,000.

– Shuttelle lived in the house from 1 February 2009 until 30 June 2021.

– The house had a market value of £870,000 on 6 April 2021.

Contributions to Shuttelle's personal pension scheme:

– Shuttelle has made the following gross contributions:
6 April 2019 – £9,000
6 April 2020 – £38,000
6 April 2021 – £120,000

– Din Ltd contributes £4,000 to the scheme in each tax year.

Required:

(i) Calculate Shuttelle's income tax liability for the tax year 2021/22. **(8 marks)**

(ii) Calculate the amount of tax relief obtained by Shuttelle as a consequence of the gross personal pension contributions of £120,000 she made on 6 April 2021.

You can assume that no reduction to the pensions annual allowance was necessary for tax years prior to 2021/22. **(3 marks)**

(b) **The remittance basis of taxation:**

– Advice is to be provided to three non-UK domiciled individuals.

– Each of the three individuals is more than 18 years old.

Details of the three individuals:

Name	Lin	Nan	Yu
Tax year in which the individual became UK resident	2011/12	2006/07	2011/12
Tax year in which the individual ceased to be UK resident	Still resident	2019/20	Still resident
Overseas income and gains for the tax year 2021/22	£39,200	£68,300	£130,700
Overseas income and gains remitted to the UK for the tax year 2021/22	£38,500	0	£1,400

Required:

(i) **In respect of each of the three individuals for the tax year 2021/22:**

1 **explain whether or not the remittance basis is available**

2 **on the assumption that the remittance basis is available to ALL three individuals, state, with reasons, the remittance basis charge (if any) that they would have to pay in order for their overseas income and gains to be taxed on the remittance basis.**

The following mark allocation is provided as guidance for this requirement:

1 **3 marks**

2 **4 marks** **(7 marks)**

(ii) **Set out briefly the circumstances under which a non-UK domiciled individual born overseas would be deemed to be UK resident for the purposes of income tax and capital gains tax.** **(2 marks)**

(Total: 20 marks)

42 CATE AND RAVI *Walk in the footsteps of a top tutor*

You should assume that today's date is 9 April 2022.

Cate requires advice on the after-tax cost of taking on a part-time employee and the tax implications of starting to sell items via the internet. Cate's husband, Ravi, requires advice in relation to capital gains tax on the disposal of an overseas asset.

Cate:

– Is resident and domiciled in the UK. She is aged 48.

– Is married to Ravi.

– Runs a successful unincorporated business, D-Designs.

– Receives dividends of £30,000 each year.

– Wants to sell some second-hand books online.

D-Designs business:

- Was set up by Cate in 2014.
- Is now making a taxable profit of £90,000 per annum.
- Operates a number of dress shops and already employs six full-time staff.
- Requires an additional part-time employee.

Part time employee – proposed remuneration package:

- Salary of £12,000 per annum.
- Medical insurance costing £1,300 per annum, which would have cost the employee £1,450 per annum to purchase.
- Mileage allowance of 50 pence per mile for the 62 mile round trip required each week to redistribute stock between the shops. This will be for 48 weeks in the year.
- This employment will be the employee's only source of taxable income.

Sale of second-hand books:

- Cate inherited a collection of books from her mother in December 2020.
- Cate intends to sell these books via the internet.
- Some of the books are in a damaged state and Cate will get them rebound before selling them.

Ravi:

- Is domiciled in the country of Goland.
- Has been resident in the UK since his marriage to Cate in February 2014.
- Has UK taxable income of £126,000 in the tax year 2021/22.
- Realises chargeable gains each year from disposals of UK buy-to-let residential properties equal to the capital gains tax annual exempt amount.
- Sold an investment property (residential) in Goland in February 2022 for £130,000, realising a chargeable gain of £70,000. None of the proceeds from the sale of this property have been remitted to the UK.

Required:

(a) Calculate the annual cost for Cate, after income tax and national insurance contributions, of D-Designs employing the part-time employee. **(9 marks)**

(b) Discuss whether the profit from Cate's proposed sale of books via the internet will be liable to either income tax or capital gains tax. **(5 marks)**

(c) Advise Ravi on the options available to him for calculating his UK capital gains tax liability for the tax year 2021/22. Provide supporting calculations of the tax payable by him in each case. **(6 marks)**

(Total: 20 marks)

43 WAVERLEY (ADAPTED) *Walk in the footsteps of a top tutor*

You should assume that today's date is 8 September 2022.

Your manager has been advising a client, Waverley, on his plans to sell his business. An email from your manager setting out the current situation and some notes on the tax system in the country of Surferia are set out below:

Email from your manager – dated 8 September 2022

Waverley

Waverley was born in the UK to UK domiciled parents in 1982. He divorced his wife in 2020. His three children, all of whom are under 18, live with his ex-wife in the UK.

Waverley began trading as a sole trader on 1 March 2014. We are advising him on the sale of his unincorporated business with the objective of minimising his capital gains tax liability. It has been concluded that it will be very difficult to sell the business as an unincorporated entity, so Waverley is going to sell the business to a newly-formed company which he owns, Roller Ltd. Waverley will then sell his shares in Roller Ltd.

Waverley has decided to emigrate to the country of Surferia. He wants to make a fresh start and has heard from friends that moving abroad could be advantageous from the point of view of UK tax. He will move to Surferia on 5 April 2023.

Waverley wants to see his children regularly and is also an enthusiastic member of an amateur football team in the UK. As a result, he intends to spend as many days as possible in the UK in the tax year 2023/24. He will continue to work for Roller Ltd until the company is sold and it is also possible that the purchaser of Roller Ltd will ask Waverley to do further work for the company whilst he is in the UK.

Waverley will sell his home in the UK in March 2023. The house is Waverley's private residence, such that there will be no capital gains tax in respect of its disposal. Once the house has been sold, whenever Waverley is in the UK he will stay in a hotel, as he does not have any other UK property available for his use. When he is not in the UK, he will live in a new house which he plans to buy in Surferia.

Unincorporated business

Waverley will cease trading as a sole trader on 15 January 2023 when he sells his unincorporated business to Roller Ltd. Roller Ltd will be wholly-owned by Waverley.

The tax adjusted trading profits of the business (actual and budgeted) up to the date of cessation are:

Year ended 30 June 2022   £125,400
Period ended 15 January 2023   £72,150

The assets of the unincorporated business are expected to be worth £540,000 on 15 January 2023. They will be sold at market value to Roller Ltd in exchange for 270,000 £1 ordinary shares in the company. This will result in chargeable gains, before incorporation relief, of £140,000 on the business premises and £50,000 in respect of goodwill.

The shares in Roller Ltd will be sold for £600,000 at some point during the six months following Waverley's emigration to Surferia on 5 April 2023.

Residence status

Waverley has always been resident and domiciled in the UK, but it is likely to be beneficial for him to be non-UK resident for the tax year 2023/24.

Investment property

Waverley owns a number of offices located in the UK which he rents out. One of these offices is tenanted under a lease which expires on 31 October 2027.

Waverley plans to sell this office as soon as possible following the end of the lease. He will then give the proceeds from the sale to his sister.

Please carry out the following work:

(a)   Unincorporated business

–   State the basis period for 2022/23, the final tax year of trading, and calculate the taxable trading profits for that year, noting any further information required in order to finalise this figure.

–   State the conditions which must be satisfied in order for incorporation relief to be available on the sale of the unincorporated business to Roller Ltd.

–   Explain whether Waverley will qualify for business asset disposal relief on the disposal of the shares in Roller Ltd.

–   Prepare calculations of Waverley's total capital gains tax liability, in the UK and in the country of Surferia, in respect of both the sale of the unincorporated business to Roller Ltd in the tax year 2022/23 (if any) and the sale of the Roller Ltd shares in the tax year 2023/24. In respect of the sale of the Roller Ltd shares, you should consider two possible situations: first where Waverley is resident only in the UK at the time of the sale; and second where he is resident only in Surferia at the time of the sale. You should not consider the rules concerning individuals who are temporarily non-UK resident.

You should assume that Waverley will be a higher rate taxpayer in the tax years 2022/23 and 2023/24 (if UK resident) and that he realises sufficient additional chargeable gains every year to use his annual exempt amount.

(b)   Residence status

Explain the maximum number of days which Waverley will be able to spend in the UK in the tax year 2023/24 without being UK resident. I have already concluded that for the tax year 2023/24, Waverley will be neither automatically resident overseas nor automatically resident in the UK.

(c)   Investment property

–   Explain the capital gains tax implications in the tax year 2027/28 of the sale of the investment property, assuming that it gives rise to a chargeable gain and that Waverley is resident only in the country of Surferia in that tax year.

–   Discuss, by reference to Waverley's domicile status, whether or not Waverley's gift to his sister of the proceeds from the sale of the investment property will be within the scope of UK inheritance tax.

Tax manager

Notes on the tax system in the country of Surferia

- Individuals who are resident in Surferia are subject to capital gains tax on disposals of worldwide assets at the rate of 12%. There is no annual exempt amount.
- For the purposes of capital gains tax in Surferia, Waverley's chargeable gains will be the same as they would be in the UK.
- The payment date for capital gains tax in Surferia is the same as the payment date for capital gains tax in the UK.
- There is no inheritance tax in Surferia.
- There is a double tax treaty between the UK and Surferia.

Required:

Carry out the work requested in the email from your manager. The following marks are available:

(a)	**Unincorporated business.**	**(12 marks)**
(b)	**Residence status.**	**(6 marks)**
(c)	**Investment property.**	**(7 marks)**

(Total: 25 marks)

44 NOAH AND DAN (ADAPTED) *Walk in the footsteps of a top tutor*

You should assume that today's date is 9 June 2022.

Your client, Dan, requires advice on the inheritance tax implications arising as a result of the recent death of his father, Noah, Dan's own UK residence status, and the potential chargeable gain arising on his proposed disposal of his UK house.

Noah:

- Was resident in the UK from 1 April 2003 until his death on 31 May 2022, following a short illness.
- Had a domicile of origin in the country of Skarta and did not acquire a domicile of choice in the UK.
- Has one child, Dan.

Noah – information for inheritance tax:

- Noah had not made any lifetime gifts.
- Noah left all the assets in his estate upon his death to Dan.

Noah – valuation of assets owned at death on 31 May 2022:

	£
House located in the country of Skarta (used as main residence)	367,000
Chattels and cash in the UK	360,000

Inheritance tax and liabilities in the country of Skarta:

- Under the tax system in Skarta, the inheritance tax payable will be £56,080.
- Legal and administration fees of £18,500 will be payable in Skarta in respect of Noah's house.
- There is no double tax treaty between the UK and Skarta.

Dan:

- Is domiciled in the country of Skarta.
- Is unmarried, and has no children.
- First became resident in the UK on 1 July 2017.
- Left the UK on 1 January 2021 to go travelling.
- Returned to the UK for the first time on 15 May 2022, when his father was taken ill.
- Intends to work part time in the UK throughout the month of July 2022 only.
- Will remain in the UK until 5 August 2022, when he intends to move permanently to Skarta.

Dan – disposal of his UK house:

- Dan purchased a house in the UK on 6 April 2018 for £293,000, where he lived until 1 January 2021.
- Dan stayed in the house when he returned to the UK on 15 May 2022 up until the date of sale.
- He allowed his father, Noah, to live in the house, rent-free, until his father's death.
- He has agreed to sell the UK house on 1 August 2022 for £318,000.

Required:

(a) (i) **State, giving reasons, whether or not the house in Skarta will be included in Noah's chargeable estate on death for the purposes of UK inheritance tax.**

(3 marks)

(ii) **Assuming that the house in Skarta is subject to inheritance tax in the UK, calculate the value of Dan's inheritance from Noah after all taxes and liabilities have been paid.** (6 marks)

(b) (i) **On the assumption that Dan does not satisfy either of the automatic tests for determining his UK residence status, explain why Dan will NOT be resident in the UK for tax purposes in the tax year 2022/23.** (5 marks)

(ii) **Calculate the chargeable gain arising on the disposal of Dan's UK house on 1 August 2022 under the residential property rules applicable to non-UK residents.** (4 marks)

(Total: 18 marks)

45 MAX (ADAPTED) *Walk in the footsteps of a top tutor*

You should assume that today's date is 9 April 2022.

Max ceased trading two years ago, and is now about to move overseas. He would like advice on the capital gains tax (CGT) implications of the disposal of two assets previously used in his unincorporated business, and the inheritance tax (IHT) implications of gifting one of them.

Max:

- Has always been UK resident and domiciled – Is widowed and has one daughter, Fara.
- Is a higher-rate taxpayer.
- Makes disposals each year to use his annual exempt amount for capital gains tax.
- Has made one previous lifetime gift to Fara on 6 May 2019, which resulted in a gross chargeable transfer of £194,000.

Max – unincorporated business:

– Max operated as a sole trader for many years, but ceased trading on 31 May 2020.

– Max still owns office premises and a machine which had been used exclusively in his business until 31 May 2020.

– Max now wishes to dispose of these assets prior to moving overseas.

Proposed gift of the office premises:

– Max is proposing to gift the office premises to Fara on 30 June 2022.

– Max acquired the premises on 1 April 2014.

– Since 1 June 2020, the premises have been let to an unconnected company.

– The market value of the premises in June 2022 is £168,000, which exceeds the original cost.

Max – move overseas:

– Max has decided to move overseas for a period of around two and a half years commencing on 1 November 2022. – Max does not intend to return to the UK at all during this period.

– Max will return to live permanently in the UK on 30 June 2025.

– Max is not entitled to use the split year treatment for determination of his residence status in any tax year.

Proposed sale of the machine:

– The machine was acquired on 1 August 2018 for a cost of £72,000.

– Max has received an offer of £84,000 for the immediate sale of the machine in June 2022.

– An alternative buyer has offered £90,000 for the machine, but will not be able to complete the purchase until June 2023.

Required:

(a)   In respect of the proposed gift of the office premises to Fara on 30 June 2022:

   (i)   Advise Max whether or not capital gains tax (CGT) gift holdover relief will be available, and if so, to what extent. **(3 marks)**

   (ii)   Advise Max of the maximum potential inheritance tax (IHT) liability, and the circumstances in which this would arise. **(5 marks)**

(b)   Explain the effect of Max's period of living overseas on his UK residence status for all relevant tax years, and advise him of the CGT consequences of the sale of the machine (1) in June 2022, or alternatively (2) in June 2023.

   Note: No calculations are required for this part. **(6 marks)**

(c)   Explain whether or not business asset disposal relief will be available on the sale of the machine, and calculate the increase in Max's after-tax proceeds if he sells the machine in June 2023 rather than in June 2022. **(6 marks)**

(Total: 20 marks)

46   EMMA   *Walk in the footsteps of a top tutor*

You should assume that today's date is 3 December 2022.

Your manager has forwarded an email to you from Emma, a client of your firm, which details the work you are required to do. Extracts from that email, and from an email from your manager which provides further information, are set out below.

Extracts from the email from Emma – dated 2 December 2022

As I approach my 75th birthday, I have decided to make some significant changes to my personal and financial affairs.

(a)   Rental income in the country of Falgar

I have not been happy since I moved to Falgar. Consequently, I have decided to return to the UK on 1 May 2023. However, I will keep my house in Falgar, so that I can return to it at some future time. In the meantime, from 1 May 2023 I will rent it out.

My understanding of the UK tax position in relation to this rental income is as follows:

–   provided I do not bring the rental income into the UK, it will not be subject to UK income tax

–   if I do bring the income into the UK, I will then have to pay UK income tax upon it.

Please explain whether or not my understanding is correct.

(b)   Gift of shares in Vyc Ltd

Our family company, Vyc Ltd, has had another excellent year and its value continues to increase. On 1 July 2023, I will give my son, Edward, 10,000 ordinary shares in the company. Edward has spent most of the last few years travelling in Asia and I am hoping that this gift of shares will persuade him to return to the UK.

I appreciate there may be a UK inheritance tax (IHT) liability if I die within seven years of this gift.

–   Please explain the circumstances which would result in the maximum IHT liability on this gift and provide me with a calculation of the amount which would then be due.

–   Also, please explain whether I am right to assume that capital gains tax gift holdover relief will be available in respect of this gift.

(c)   Sale of shares in Barb plc

I am going to sell my 2% holding in Barb plc, which I have owned as an investment since 1 December 2018. I could sell them now, in which case I would realise a chargeable gain of £330,000. Alternatively, if I wait until I am back in the UK, I would be able to increase the selling price by £60,000.

–   I plan to sell the shares now, for the lower price, as I believe this will mean that no UK capital gains tax will be due. Please explain whether or not this is the best thing to do from a tax perspective.

Extracts from the email from your manager – dated 3 December 2022

Emma

Emma is 74 years old and married to Bill. The couple have two adult children: a son, Edward, and a daughter, Lily. Emma has always been domiciled in the country of Falgar. She was resident in the UK from 6 April 1999 until she and Bill moved to Falgar on 1 February 2020. On her return to the UK on 1 May 2023, Emma will resume UK residency.

When carrying out this work, you should assume that Emma is a higher rate taxpayer.

Taxation in Falgar

– Income tax is charged at 26% on all income arising in Falgar.

– There is no capital gains tax or inheritance tax.

– There is no double tax treaty between the UK and Falgar.

Vyc Ltd

Vyc Ltd is an unquoted manufacturing company, which is registered in the UK. It does not own any assets other than those which are used in its trade.

The shareholders in Vyc Ltd are set out below. The shareholdings have not changed for many years.

	Number of shares
Emma	35,000
Bill (Emma's husband)	19,000
Lily (Emma's daughter)	10,000
Charlotte (Emma's sister)	20,000
Louis (Charlotte's husband)	16,000
	————
	100,000
	————

You should use the following values for an ordinary share in Vyc Ltd when carrying out this work.

Shareholding	Value per share
	£
Up to 25%	10
26% to 50%	13
51% to 74%	19
More than 75%	22

On 1 October 2018, Emma made a cash gift to her daughter, Lily. This resulted in a transfer of value after deduction of exemptions of £280,000. This is the only gift Emma has made. When explaining the maximum inheritance tax (IHT) liability, you should focus on the date on which Emma's future death may occur and the availability of business property relief.

Please provide the explanations requested by Emma in respect of:

(a) Rental income in the country of Falgar.

(b) Gift of shares in Vyc Ltd.

(c) Sale of shares in Barb plc.

Tax manager

Required:

Carry out the work required as requested in the email from your manager. The following marks are available:

(a)	Rental income in the country of Falgar.	**(4 marks)**
(b)	Gift of shares in Vyc Ltd.	**(13 marks)**
(c)	Sale of shares in Barb plc.	**(8 marks)**

(Total: 25 marks)

47 FIONA *Walk in the footsteps of a top tutor*

You should assume that today's date is 1 June 2022.

Your manager has had a meeting with Fiona, a potential new client of your firm. Extracts from the memorandum prepared by your manager following the meeting, and from an email which details the work you are required to do, are included in the exhibits.

Memorandum extract from your manager:

Background

Fiona is 74 years old and in poor health. She has lived in the country of Parella since 1991. She has a son, Hugo, and a daughter, Elena, both of whom live in the UK. Fiona will move to the UK on 1 August 2022 and acquire a home there.

Fiona's domicile and residence status

I have already established that, as a result of moving to the UK:

– Fiona will become UK resident on 1 August 2022 under the split year basis.

– Fiona will also be UK resident in the tax year 2023/24.

– Fiona is domiciled in Parella. However, once she becomes UK resident, Fiona will be deemed domiciled in the UK for the purposes of income tax and capital gains tax (CGT) because she was born in the UK with a UK domicile of origin.

Gifts made by Fiona

On 1 May 2021, Fiona gave Elena £430,000 in cash. The money was transferred from one of Fiona's UK bank accounts.

Fiona's previous gifts are set out below. These were all gifts of assets located in the UK, such that they were subject to UK inheritance tax (IHT) despite Fiona being domiciled in Parella. The amounts shown are after the deduction of any available annual exemptions.

1 August 2013	a potentially exempt transfer of £94,000
1 July 2016	a chargeable lifetime transfer of £74,000
1 September 2020	a potentially exempt transfer of £204,000

When Fiona's husband died in 2013, the whole of his nil rate band was used when calculating the IHT liability in respect of his estate.

Gift to be made to Hugo

Fiona owns a number of houses, which she rents out to long-term residential tenants. These houses are located in either Parella or the UK. Fiona intends to give one of these houses (either Aber House or Bleb House) to Hugo within the next three months. Both of the houses were acquired in May 2017. CGT gift holdover relief will not be available in respect of a gift of either property.

The expected (loss)/gain on the disposal of each of the two houses is set out below:

Location	Aber House Parella £	Bleb House UK £
(Loss)/gain on disposal	(50,000)	85,000

Property and interest income

Fiona's anticipated income for the tax year 2023/24, the year after she moves to the UK, is set out below.

	£
Property income	
Properties situated in the UK	26,270
Properties situation in Parella	31,000
Interest income	
UK bank interest	1,700
Parellian bank interest	1,200

The income arising in Parella is stated gross of Parellian tax. Fiona will remit all of the rental income in respect of the properties situated in Parella to the UK. The interest arising on the Parellian bank accounts will be retained in Parella.

Tax system in Parella

– The rate of income tax is 18%.

– There is no CGT or IHT.

– There is no double tax treaty between the UK and Parella.

Email extract from your manager:

Please carry out the following work:

(a) Becoming Fiona's tax advisers

Explain the actions which we should carry out before we become Fiona's tax advisers. I have already obtained her address and proof of her identity.

(b) Gifts to Elena and Hugo

You should assume that Fiona's death will occur on 30 April 2024.

(i) Inheritance tax (IHT) payable in respect of Fiona's gift on 1 May 2021

Calculate the IHT payable as a result of Fiona's death in respect of the gift made by Fiona to Elena on 1 May 2021.

> **(ii) Proposed gift to Hugo**
>
> In respect of Fiona's proposed gift to Hugo, explain, for each of the two houses:
>
> – whether or not a chargeable gain or an allowable capital loss will arise in the UK
>
> – whether or not the gift will be within the charge to UK IHT.
>
> On the basis of your explanations, advise Fiona which of the two houses she should give to Hugo and whether the gift should be made before or after Fiona has moved to the UK.
>
> You SHOULD NOT prepare any calculations for this part of the question.
>
> **(c) Taxation of overseas income**
>
> – Explain why the remittance basis will be available to Fiona in the tax year 2023/24 and whether or not she will be subject to the remittance basis charge.
>
> – Calculate Fiona's income tax liability for the tax year 2023/24 based on her anticipated income figures.

Required:

Carry out the work required as requested in the email from your manager. The following marks are available:

(a) Becoming Fiona's tax advisers. **(5 marks)**

(b) Gifts to Elena and Hugo.

(i) Inheritance tax (IHT) payable in respect of Fiona's gift on 1 May 2021.

(3 marks)

(ii) Proposed gift to Hugo. **(7 marks)**

(c) Taxation of overseas income. **(10 marks)**

(Total: 25 marks)

PERSONAL FINANCE, BUSINESS FINANCE AND INVESTMENTS

48   MONISHA AND HORNER (ADAPTED) *Walk in the footsteps of a top tutor*

 Question debrief

You should assume that today's date is 3 June 2022.

Your firm has been asked to advise two unrelated clients, Monisha and Horner. The advice relates to furnished holiday accommodation, tax planning for a married couple, and the personal service company (IR35) rules.

(a)   Monisha:

– Is married to Asmat.

– Earns a salary of £80,000 per year and realises chargeable gains on residential properties of £6,300 per year.

– Owns a UK investment property, which is let to short-term tenants.

Asmat:

– Looks after the couple's children and has no income or chargeable gains.

– Expects to return to work on 6 April 2028 on an annual salary of £18,000.

The UK investment property owned by Monisha:

– The property cost £270,000 and is currently worth £300,000.

– The letting does not qualify as a commercial letting of furnished holiday accommodation.

– Annual income and expenditure

	£
Rental income	20,000
Repairs and maintenance	3,480
Council tax	1,200
Agent's fees	2,000

– The property will be sold on 5 April 2029 and is expected to create a chargeable gain of £100,000.

Proposals to reduce the couple's total tax liability:

– Monisha will give a 20% interest in the investment property to Asmat on 1 April 2023.

– The couple will ensure that, from 6 April 2023, the letting of the investment property will qualify as a commercial letting of furnished holiday accommodation.

Required:

(i) State the conditions which must be satisfied in order for the letting of a UK furnished property to qualify as a commercial letting of furnished holiday accommodation. **(3 marks)**

(ii) Calculate the total tax saving in the six tax years 2023/24 to 2028/29 if ALL of the proposals to reduce the couple's tax liabilities are carried out.

In respect of the second proposal, you should assume that the letting will qualify as a commercial letting of furnished holiday accommodation for the whole of the period of joint ownership and that all beneficial reliefs are claimed.

You should ignore inheritance tax. **(10 marks)**

(b) **Horner:**

– Horner owns all of the shares of Otmar Ltd.

– Horner works for Otmar Ltd providing IT repair services to Florentine Ltd. This provision of services is subject to the personal service company (IR35) legislation.

– Florentine Ltd is classified as a medium or large sized organisation for the purposes of the IR35 legislation.

– Figures for Otmar Ltd for the year ending 5 April 2022 are set out below.

Where applicable, these amounts are stated exclusive of value added tax (VAT).

	£
Income in respect of relevant engagements carried out by Horner	85,000
Costs of materials used in repairs	3,900
Horner's annual salary	50,000
Contributions paid into an occupational pension scheme in respect of Horner	2,000

Required:

(i) Outline the circumstances in which the personal service company (IR35) rules apply. **(3 marks)**

(ii) Explain, with supporting calculations, the tax implications for Florentine Ltd of engaging Otmar Ltd. **(4 marks)**

(Total: 20 marks)

 Calculate your allowed time, allocate the time to the separate parts...................

49   STELLA AND MARIS (ADAPTED) *Walk in the footsteps of a top tutor*

You should assume that today's date is 3 June 2022.

Your firm has been asked to provide advice to two unrelated clients, Stella and Maris. Stella requires advice on the tax implications of making an increased contribution to her personal pension scheme. Maris requires advice regarding the lump sum payment she has received from her pension scheme and the inheritance tax exemptions available on her proposed lifetime gifts.

(a)   Stella:

–   Is resident and domiciled in the UK.

–   Received a gross salary of £203,000 in the tax year 2022/23. This was a substantial increase on the previous year.

–   Does not have an occupational pension.

–   Has property income from a portfolio of unfurnished properties, totalling £92,000 in the tax year 2022/23.

–   Has no other source of taxable income.

–   Wishes to make an increased contribution to her personal pension scheme in the tax year 2022/23.

Personal pension scheme contributions:

–   Stella has contributed £40,000 (gross) to her personal pension scheme in each of the tax years 2021/22 and 2020/21 and £30,000 (gross) in each of the tax years 2019/20 and 2018/19.

–   The full annual allowance (without restriction) was available for the tax years 2018/19 to 2021/22.

–   Stella wishes to make an increased contribution of £90,000 (gross) in the tax year 2022/23.

Required:

Calculate Stella's income after tax and pension contributions for the tax year 2022/23 if she does pay £90,000 (gross) into her personal pension scheme.

(10 marks)

(b)   Maris:

–   Is resident and domiciled in the UK and is widowed.

–   Has three married children and five grandchildren under the age of 12.

–   Attained the age of 68 on 30 January 2022 and decided to vest some of her pension benefits on that date.

–   Wishes to make regular gifts to her family in order to reduce inheritance tax on her death.

Personal pension fund:

–   Maris had a money purchase pension scheme which was valued at £1,550,000 on 30 January 2022.

–   Maris would like some advice on the tax implications of drawing a lump sum from this pension.

Assets and income:

–   In addition to pension income and savings income totalling around £60,000, Maris receives dividends from shareholdings in quoted companies of around £45,000 each year.

–   The shareholdings in quoted companies are currently valued at £980,000.

–   Maris wishes to gift some of the shares or the dividend income to her children and grandchildren on their birthdays each year.

–   Maris already makes gifts each year to use her annual exemption for inheritance tax purposes.

Required:

(i)   **Explain how an amount withdrawn by Maris as a lump sum from her pension may be taxed.** **(4 marks)**

(ii)   **Advise Maris of TWO relevant exemptions from inheritance tax which she will be able to use when making the birthday gifts, together with any conditions she will need to comply with in order to obtain them.** **(6 marks)**

(Total: 20 marks)

50   PIPPIN *Walk in the footsteps of a top tutor*

You should assume that today's date is 8 June 2022.

Your manager has sent you the notes she prepared following a meeting with Pippin, an established client of your firm who is resident and domiciled in the UK. The notes together with an email from your manager are set out below.

Meeting notes from your manager – dated 8 June 2022

Commencement of 'Pinova' business

Pippin intends to start a new unincorporated business, 'Pinova', on 1 August 2022. He has identified two alternative strategies: strategy A and strategy B.

The budgeted tax-adjusted profit/(loss) of the two strategies are set out below. These figures are before the adjustments necessary in respect of the equipment purchases and employment costs (see below).

	Strategy A		Strategy B	
	Period ending 31 March 2023	Year ending 31 March 2024 and future years	Period ending 31 March 2023	Year ending 31 March 2024 and future years
	£	£	£	£
Profit/(loss)	13,000	60,000	(10,000)	130,000

Equipment purchases and employment costs

The above profit/loss figures need to be adjusted in respect of the following:

– Both strategies will require Pippin to purchase equipment in August 2022 for £8,000.

– Strategy B will require two employees from 1 April 2023. Pippin will pay each of them a gross salary of £2,000 per month. He will also pay them £0.50 per business mile for driving their own cars. He expects each of them to drive 250 business miles per month.

– Strategy A will not require any employees.

Pippin will claim the maximum capital allowances available to him. He will also claim opening years' loss relief in respect of the trading loss arising under strategy B.

Cessation of previous business

Pippin's previous unincorporated business ceased trading on 31 December 2021. The taxable profits of the business for its final three tax years were:

	£
2019/20	82,000
2020/21	78,000
2021/22	14,000

Pippin had no other taxable income during these three years.

Receipt of £75,000

Pippin's aunt, Esme, died on 31 January 2022.

On 1 September 2016, Esme's father (Pippin's grandfather) died leaving the whole of his estate to Esme. However, on 1 January 2017 Pippin received £75,000 but cannot remember whether the money came from Esme or from his grandfather's estate.

On 1 November 2016, Esme had transferred cash of £375,000 to a trust for the benefit of her children.

Shares in Akero Ltd

Pippin owns 16,000 shares in Akero Ltd which have a current market value of £4.50 per share. Pippin subscribed £16,000 for these shares on 4 January 2020. Pippin obtained income tax relief of £4,800 (£16,000 × 30%) under the enterprise investment scheme (EIS) in the tax year 2019/20. He also claimed EIS deferral relief in that year of £16,000 in relation to a chargeable gain on the sale of a painting.

Pippin is considering selling 5,000 of his Akero Ltd shares in order to fund his personal expenditure during the start-up phase of the Pinova business.

Extract from an email from your manager – dated 8 June 2022

Please prepare a memorandum for the client files which addresses the following issues:

(i) **Additional funds required for the 20-month period from 1 August 2022 to 31 March 2024**

Pippin's taxable income will consist of the profits of the Pinova business and, for the tax year 2023/24 onwards, he expects to receive dividend income of £1,500 per year. His personal expenditure is £4,000 per month.

I want you to complete the table below to calculate the additional funds which Pippin would require during the first 20 months of the business under each of the two strategies (A and B) after putting aside sufficient funds to settle his tax liabilities for the tax years 2022/23 and 2023/24. You should then evaluate the two strategies by reference to the results of your calculations.

Pippin and I calculated his total **pre-tax** cash receipts; you do not need to check them. The only adjustment required to these pre-tax cash receipts is the cost of employing the two employees.

	Strategy A £	Strategy B £
Total pre-tax cash receipts for the 20-month period	61,000	109,500
Cost of employing the two employees	Nil	( )
Pippin's total income tax and national insurance contribution liabilities for the tax years 2022/23 and 2023/24	( )	( )
Personal expenditure (£4,000 × 20)	(80,000)	(80,000)
Additional funds required		

(ii) **Receipt of £75,000**

Explain, with supporting calculations, the inheritance tax implications for Pippin of the receipt of the £75,000.

(iii) **Sale of shares in Akero Ltd**

Explain the tax liabilities which would result if Pippin were to sell 5,000 of his Akero Ltd shares in the tax year 2022/23.

Tax manager

Required:

Prepare the memorandum as requested in the email from your manager. The following marks are available:

(i) Additional funds required for the 20-month period from 1 August 2022 to 31 March 2024. **(20 marks)**

(ii) Receipt of £75,000. **(5 marks)**

(iii) Sale of shares in Akero Ltd. **(6 marks)**

Professional marks will be awarded for the approach taken to problem solving, the clarity of the explanations and calculations, the effectiveness with which the information is communicated, and the overall presentation and style of the memorandum. (4 marks)

(Total: 35 marks)

51 FLORINA, KANZI AND WINSTON (ADAPTED) *Walk in the footsteps of a top tutor*

You should assume that today's date is 7 September 2022.

Your manager has had a meeting with Florina and Kanzi who are clients of your firm. Florina's father, Winston, also attended the meeting. The notes prepared following the meeting and an email from your manager setting out the work he requires you to do are set out below.

Meeting with Florina, Kanzi and Winston on 6 September 2022

The meeting was attended by Florina and Kanzi (who have been living together since 2003 but are not married) and Winston (Florina's father).

All three individuals are resident and domiciled in the UK. They have no sources of income or chargeable gains other than those referred to below.

Florina

Florina is a director of and shareholder in Flight Hip Ltd. She earns an annual salary of £50,000 and receives a dividend of £20,000 from the company every year. She received total taxable benefits of £25,000 from the company in the tax year 2021/22. Flight Hip Ltd is not a close company.

Florina's benefits include a company car together with free petrol for both business and private use. The car's benefit percentage by reference to its CO_2 emissions is 26%. Florina drives 19,000 miles per year of which 2,000 miles are in the performance of her employment duties. The total cost of all of the petrol used by Florina in the tax year 2021/22 was £3,000.

Florina's only other income consists of dividends of £1,500 received in June every year from Landing Properties Ltd. Landing Properties Ltd is an unquoted UK resident company, unrelated to Flight Hip Ltd.

Florina purchased 4,000 shares (a holding of less than 1%) in Landing Properties Ltd for £8,000 on 1 August 2006. She is considering selling these shares to Padarn, an unconnected individual, for their market value of £40,000. This would result in a capital gains tax liability of £3,940. I suggested that it may be possible to reduce the tax due by making a gift of some of the shares to Kanzi, who would then sell them to Padarn, and I agreed to provide Florina with further details.

Kanzi

Kanzi is an artist. His annual taxable trading income is approximately £14,000.

Although Kanzi is not employed by Flight Hip Ltd, the company provides him with a car and free petrol. The car's benefit percentage by reference to its CO_2 emissions is 23%. Kanzi drives 5,000 miles per year; the total cost of the petrol used by Kanzi in the tax year 2021/22 was £800.

Winston

Winston is in very poor health and is not expected to live for more than 12 months. It is estimated that Winston's total chargeable estate is currently worth £1,500,000. This figure includes his main residence, which is worth £500,000. The values of his assets are not expected to change between now and his death.

Winston intends to make a donation of £150,000 to a registered UK charity. This donation will be either a lifetime gift or a legacy from his estate on death.

Winston's current will leaves the whole of his estate to Florina and his two other children.

Winston's only previous lifetime gift was a chargeable transfer, after the deduction of exemptions, of £225,000 to a trust on 1 June 2020.

Winston wants to carry out some sophisticated tax-planning in order to reduce the inheritance tax which will be payable in respect of his death estate.

Email from your manager – dated 7 September 2022

Please carry out the following work.

(a)   Florina and Kanzi

Florina's remuneration from Flight Hip Ltd

Calculate the total tax saving which could be achieved by Florina and Flight Hip Ltd if, in the tax year 2022/23, the company were to make a single lump sum payment of £20,000 into a personal pension fund for Florina instead of paying her a dividend of £20,000. These calculations should take account of the tax which Florina will pay when she eventually withdraws the £20,000 from the pension fund.

You should assume that:

1   there will be no further contributions into the fund in future years; and

2   Florina will be a basic rate taxpayer when she makes a withdrawal from the fund.

Provision of free petrol

By comparing the income tax due in respect of the petrol with the value of the petrol received, determine whether Florina and Kanzi would be better off if:

–   Florina were to reimburse Flight Hip Ltd for the cost of the petrol used by her for private purposes; and/or

–   Flight Hip Ltd were to stop providing Kanzi with free petrol.

Sale of shares in Landing Properties Ltd

Explain whether or not gift holdover relief would be available in respect of a gift of shares in Landing Properties Ltd from Florina to Kanzi.

On the assumption that gift holdover relief would be available, calculate, with supporting explanations, the number of shares which Florina should give to Kanzi, prior to the eventual sale of the shares to Padarn, and the maximum reduction in the total capital gains tax payable which could be achieved.

(b) Winston's charitable donation

Prepare calculations, with supporting explanations, to show, by reference to inheritance tax only, whether it is more tax-efficient for Winston to make the charitable donation now or via his will. You should ignore the possibility of any further inheritance tax planning taking place.

(c) Becoming Winston's tax adviser

Winston wants to appoint us to replace his existing tax advisers.

Explain any difficulties which we may have complying with the fundamental principles of professional ethics in relation to acting for Winston and suggest appropriate safeguards.

Tax manager

Required:

Carry out the work requested in the email from your manager. The following marks are available:

(a) Florina and Kanzi.

> **Note: The following mark allocation is provided as guidance for this requirement:**

Florina's remuneration from Flight Hip Ltd	4.5 marks
Provision of free petrol	4 marks
Sale of shares in Landing Properties Ltd	5.5 marks

(14 marks)

(b) Winston's charitable donation.   **(6 marks)**

(c) Becoming Winston's tax adviser.   **(5 marks)**

(Total: 25 marks)

52   JESSICA *Walk in the footsteps of a top tutor*

You should assume that today's date is 8 June 2022.

Your client, Jessica, has requested advice in relation to the tax liability arising on a redundancy payment, the options available to relieve her share of a partnership trading loss, and the maximum contribution she can make to a personal pension scheme.

Jessica:

–   Is resident and domiciled in the UK.

–   Was employed by Berens Ltd up to 31 March 2022, when she was made redundant.

–   Will become a partner in the Langley Partnership on 1 July 2022.

–   Has never made any disposals for capital gains tax (CGT) purposes.

Jessica – income from Berens Ltd:

–   Jessica received an annual salary from Berens Ltd of £145,000 each year from the tax year 2019/20.

–   From 6 April 2021, Jessica was provided with a new company laptop computer, which cost Berens Ltd £850. Jessica had significant private use of this laptop computer.

Jessica – other income:

–   Prior to the tax year 2021/22 Jessica had no other source of income.

–   Starting from the tax year 2021/22, Jessica receives rental income of £6,000 each tax year.

Jessica – redundancy package from Berens Ltd:

–   The package, received on 31 March 2022, included a statutory redundancy payment of £13,000 and an ex-gratia payment of £37,000.

–   As part of the package, Berens Ltd also allowed Jessica to keep the laptop computer, which had a market value of £540 on 31 March 2022.

The Langley Partnership:

–   Prior to 1 July 2022, there were two partners in the partnership – Issa and Finn.

–   From 1 July 2022, the profit sharing ratio will be: Issa 20%, Finn 40%, and Jessica 40%.

–   The budgeted tax-adjusted trading (loss)/profit of the partnership is:

    –   Year ending 31 March 2023 – (£160,000)

    –   Year ending 31 March 2024 – £205,000.

Jessica – personal pension plan contributions:

–   Jessica joined a personal pension scheme on 1 May 2022.

–   She has not previously been in any pension scheme.

–   She wishes to make the maximum possible contributions which will qualify for tax relief in each of the tax years 2022/23 and 2023/24.

Required:

(a) Explain, with supporting calculations, the taxable amount of the redundancy package received from Berens Ltd on 31 March 2022, and calculate the income tax payable on it by Jessica.   (5 marks)

(b) (i) Advise Jessica of the options available to her to relieve her share of the Langley Partnership loss for the year ending 31 March 2023, on the assumption that she does not wish to carry any of her share of the loss forward.   (3 marks)

  (ii) Determine, by reference to the amount of income tax saved in each case, which of the available loss relief options (as identified in (i) above) will result in the highest overall income tax saving for Jessica.   (7 marks)

(c) Explain, with supporting calculations, the maximum amount of the contributions Jessica can pay into her pension scheme in each of the tax years 2022/23 and 2023/24 without incurring an annual allowance charge.   (5 marks)

(Total: 20 marks)

53 DEE 👣 *Walk in the footsteps of a top tutor*

You should assume that today's date is 4 September 2022.

Your manager has forwarded a schedule to you from Dee, a new client of your firm. The schedule and an email from your manager detailing the work he requires you to do are set out below.

Schedule from Dee – dated 4 September 2022

> I am resident and domiciled in the UK. My husband, Cam, moved to the UK in January 2017 and we married in June 2018. Cam is resident in the UK but domiciled in the country of Riviera. I have a 16-year-old son, Oder, who is resident and domiciled in the UK.
>
> **My father's London house**
>
> My father died on 1 June 2022 and I inherited his London house. The house had a value for probate purposes of £390,000, but is now worth £450,000. My father purchased the house for £130,000 in 1988. I intend to sell the house as soon as possible.
>
> **Investment plan in respect of the proceeds from the sale of the London house**
>
> I plan to invest the £450,000 proceeds as follows:
>
> – £300,000, purchase of UK shares; and
> – £150,000, cash deposit in the UK.
>
> **Alternative investment plan**
>
> It has been suggested to me by a friend (who is a tax adviser) that I should consider an alternative investment plan, which would result in a lower income tax liability for me and my family.
>
> Under my friend's suggestion I would give £150,000 of the sales proceeds from the London house to Cam, leaving me with £300,000. We would then each invest two-thirds of our respective funds in shares with the remaining third left on cash deposit.
>
> I would like to know what the income tax saving would be if I followed my friend's advice rather than my original plan.

Gift to Oder

I am also considering making a cash gift to Oder of £20,000 out of my existing funds (i.e. not from the proceeds from the sale of the London house). Oder would place this amount on cash deposit.

Our annual income

I set out below our current annual income.

The bank interest and dividends are in respect of cash deposits and shares all of which are held within ISAs. We invest the maximum possible amount into ISAs on 1 May each year.

Oder has no income. None of us have made any previous chargeable gains.

	Dee £	Cam £
Annual income		
Employment income	170,000	18,000
Bank interest (within ISA)	1,500	1,200
Dividends (within ISA)	2,500	1,800

Tax-efficient investments

I have considered investing in enterprise investment scheme (EIS) shares but have not done so due to the high level of risk involved. However, I understand that venture capital trusts (VCTs) have a lower level of risk.

Please let me have a comparison of the income tax implications of these two forms of investment on the assumption that I will invest £50,000 in the tax year 2022/23. I do not know for how long I will want to hold these shares.

Thank you

Dee

Email from your manager – dated 4 September 2022

Please prepare notes for me to use in a meeting with Dee. The notes should cover the following:

(a)   Minimising income tax on investment income

When carrying out this work you should assume:

1   The shares purchased will yield a 4% return per annum and the cash deposits will yield a 1% return per annum.

2   The whole of the £450,000 will be available to invest, i.e. Dee will pay any capital gains tax due in respect of the sale of the London house out of her existing funds.

3   None of the investments will consist of either enterprise investment scheme (EIS) shares or venture capital trust (VCT) shares.

–   Calculations of the income tax saving which would be achieved in a complete tax year if Dee were to follow her friend's advice and give £150,000 of the proceeds from the sale of the London house to Cam in accordance with the alternative investment plan.

To do this efficiently, you should just calculate the additional tax payable by Dee and Cam on the income generated by the inherited funds, rather than preparing complete income tax computations.

To save you some time, I have already calculated that if Dee invested the whole of the £450,000 herself, she would incur an additional income tax liability in respect of the bank interest and dividend income for a complete tax year of £4,485.

– It seems to me that the total income tax liability of Dee and Cam could be reduced further whilst still retaining the fundamentals of Dee's alternative investment plan. Dee would still give Cam £150,000 but, rather than each of them investing 2/3 of their funds in shares and leaving the remainder on cash deposit, the total investment of £300,000 in shares and £150,000 in cash deposits would be split between them in a different way.

Set out the factors which are relevant to obtaining a more income tax-efficient split of the total investment. You should only consider the income tax positions of Dee and Cam and the nature of the proposed investments. I do not require you to produce calculations of any potential tax savings.

– The matters to be considered in relation to income tax in respect of the proposed gift of £20,000 to Oder.

(b)   Gift to Cam

– By reference to Cam's domicile status, explain why Dee's proposed gift of £150,000 to Cam could result in an inheritance tax liability and how this potential liability might be avoided.

You should note that Dee gave Cam a half interest in her home on 1 August 2018. The value of this gift was £600,000.

– Calculations in order to show the capital gains tax saving which would be achieved if Dee were to give Cam a one-third interest in the London house prior to its sale (as opposed to cash of £150,000 following its sale).

(c)   Tax-efficient investments

– A comparison of the income tax implications for Dee of investing £50,000 in either EIS shares or VCT shares as requested.

Thank you

Tax manager

Required:

Prepare the notes as requested in the email from your manager. The following marks are available:

(a)	**Minimising income tax on investment income.**	**(11 marks)**
(b)	**Gift to Cam.**	**(9 marks)**
(c)	**Tax-efficient investments.**	**(5 marks)**
		(Total: 25 marks)

54 PEDRO

You should assume that today's date is 4 September 2022.

Pedro requires advice on the reason he has had to pay inheritance tax in respect of a holiday cottage following the death of his aunt, Marina, an explanation of why his letting of this cottage qualifies as a furnished holiday letting, and the income tax implications of a significant contribution into his personal pension scheme.

Pedro:

– Was given a holiday cottage in the UK by his aunt, Marina, on 4 March 2012.

– Paid inheritance tax in respect of this gift of the holiday cottage, following Marina's death on 8 June 2022.

– Inherited a portfolio of UK unfurnished residential properties, valued at £670,000 on Marina's death.

Gift of the holiday cottage in the UK by Marina:

– Marina and Pedro agreed that she could stay in the house for two months each year, rent-free, which she did every year until her death.

– For the remainder of each year, Marina lived in her main home.

Pedro – property income:

– The cottage (which is fully furnished) has been available for rental on a commercial basis since 1 July 2022, and will have a 70% occupancy rate for the first year of letting.

– No tenant will have stayed in the cottage for more than 14 consecutive days during the first year of letting.

– The net rental income from the cottage in the tax year 2022/23 will be £14,500.

– In the tax year 2022/23, Pedro will also receive net rental income of £32,000 from the unfurnished residential properties which he inherited from Marina.

Employment income:

– Pedro has been employed by Loule Ltd since 6 April 2021.

– Pedro receives an annual gross salary of £75,000 from Loule Ltd.

– Loule Ltd has contributed £8,000 in each of the tax years 2021/22 and 2022/23 to its occupational pension scheme on behalf of Pedro.

Personal pension scheme:

– Pedro had never been a member of a pension scheme prior to taking up employment with Loule Ltd.

– Pedro wishes to start contributing to a personal pension scheme in the tax year 2022/23.

– Pedro intends to make his first contribution into the new personal pension scheme, of £85,000 (gross), on 31 March 2023.

– The annual allowance available to Pedro was not restricted in any previous tax year.

– Pedro's income tax liability for the tax year 2022/23, before taking into account the planned contribution into his personal pension scheme, is £40,332.

Required:

(a) Explain the inheritance tax implications of the gift of the cottage to Pedro at the time the gift was made, and as a result of Marina's death. **(5 marks)**

(b) Explain, by reference to the relevant conditions, why the holiday cottage will qualify as a furnished holiday letting for the first 12-month period of letting. **(5 marks)**

(c) Calculate the reduction in Pedro's income tax liability for the tax year 2022/23 as a result of making the planned contribution of £85,000 (gross) into his personal pension scheme on 31 March 2023. Your answer should include an explanation of the amount of the personal allowance available to Pedro in this case. **(10 marks)**

You may assume that the rates and allowances for the tax year 2021/22 will continue to apply for the foreseeable future.

(Total: 20 marks)

TAXATION OF CORPORATE BUSINESSES

FAMILY COMPANY ISSUES

55 TRIFLES LTD (ADAPTED) *Walk in the footsteps of a top tutor*

You should assume that today's date is 4 September 2022.

Trifles Ltd intends to carry out a purchase of its own shares. The shareholders from whom the shares are to be purchased require advice on their tax position. Trifles Ltd also intends to loan a motorcycle to one of the shareholders.

The following information has been obtained from the shareholders in Trifles Ltd.

Trifles Ltd:

– Is an unquoted company specialising in the delivery of small, high value items.

– Was incorporated and began trading on 1 February 2015.

– Has an issued share capital of 10,000 ordinary shares subscribed for at £2 per share.

– Has four unrelated shareholders: Torte, Baklava, Victoria and Melba.

– Intends to purchase some of its own shares from Victoria and Melba.

– Victoria and Melba have been directors of the company since they acquired their shares but will resign immediately after the purchase of their shares.

The purchase by Trifles Ltd of its own shares:

– Will take place on 28 February 2023 for Victoria's shares, and on 31 March 2023 for Melba's shares at an agreed price of £30 per share.

– Will consist of the purchase of all of Victoria's shares and 450 shares from Melba.

Victoria:

–   Is resident in the UK.

–   Is a higher rate taxpayer with taxable income (all non-savings) of £55,000.

–   Will make no other capital disposals in the tax year 2022/23.

–   Has a capital loss carried forward as at 5 April 2022 of £3,500.

–   Will have no link with Trifles Ltd following the purchase of her shares.

–   Inherited her holding of 1,500 ordinary shares on the death of her husband, Brownie, on 1 February 2021.

–   Brownie paid £16,500 for the shares on 1 February 2019.

–   The probate value of the 1,500 ordinary shares was £16,000 on 1 February 2021.

Melba:

–   Is resident in the UK.

–   Is a higher rate taxpayer with annual non-savings income of £60,000 and dividends of £15,000 per annum.

–   Acquired her holding of 1,700 ordinary shares when Trifles Ltd was incorporated.

–   Following the purchase of her shares Melba's only link with Trifles Ltd will be her remaining ordinary shareholding and the use of a motorcycle belonging to the company.

The motorcycle:

–   Will be purchased by Trifles Ltd for £9,000 on 1 April 2023.

–   Will be made available on loan to Melba for the whole of the tax year 2023/24.

–   Melba will pay Trifles Ltd £30 per month for the use of the motorcycle.

Required:

(a)   **Explain whether or not Victoria and/or Melba satisfy the conditions relating to period of ownership and reduction in level of shareholding such that the amount received from Trifles Ltd on the purchase of own shares may be treated as a capital event.** **(7 marks)**

(b)   **Calculate Victoria's after-tax proceeds from the purchase of her shares:**

–   **if the amount received is treated as capital; and**

–   **if the amount received is treated as income.** **(7 marks)**

(c)   **Explain, with supporting calculations where necessary, the tax implications of the purchase and loan of the motorcycle for both Melba and Trifles Ltd.** **(6 marks)**

Ignore value added tax (VAT).

(Total: 20 marks)

56 NOCTURNE LTD (ADAPTED) *Walk in the footsteps of a top tutor*

You should assume that today's date is 4 September 2022.

Nocturne Ltd, a partially exempt company for the purposes of value added tax (VAT), requires advice on the corporation tax implications of providing an asset to one of its shareholders; the income tax implications for another shareholder of making a loan to the company; and simplifying the way in which it accounts for VAT.

Nocturne Ltd:

– Is a UK resident trading company.

– Prepares accounts to 31 March annually.

– Has four shareholders, each of whom owns 25% of the company's ordinary share capital.

– Owns a laptop computer, which it purchased in October 2018 for £1,200, and which has a current market value of £150.

– Has purchased no other plant and machinery for several years and the tax written down value of its main pool at 31 March 2022 was £Nil.

Provision of a laptop computer to one of Nocturne Ltd's shareholders:

– Nocturne Ltd is considering two alternative ways of providing a laptop computer in the year ending 31 March 2023 for the personal use of one of its shareholders, Jed.

– Jed is neither a director nor an employee of Nocturne Ltd.

– Option 1: Nocturne Ltd will buy a new laptop computer for £1,800 and give it immediately to Jed.

– Option 2: Nocturne Ltd will gift its existing laptop to Jed and will purchase a brand new replacement for use in the company for £1,800.

Loan from Siglio:

– Siglio will loan £60,000 to Nocturne Ltd on 1 October 2022 to facilitate the purchase of new equipment.

– Siglio is both a shareholder of Nocturne Ltd and the company's managing director.

– Nocturne Ltd will pay interest at a commercial rate on the loan from Siglio.

– Siglio will borrow the full amount of the loan from his bank on normal commercial terms.

VAT – partial exemption:

– Nocturne Ltd is partially exempt for the purposes of VAT.

– Nocturne Ltd's turnover for the year ended 31 March 2022 was £240,000 (VAT-exclusive).

– Nocturne Ltd's turnover for the year as a whole for VAT purposes comprised 86% taxable supplies and 14% exempt supplies.

– The input VAT suffered by Nocturne Ltd on expenditure during the year ended 31 March 2022 was:

	£
Wholly attributable to taxable supplies	7,920
Wholly attributable to exempt supplies	1,062
Unattributable	4,150

- Nocturne Ltd expects its turnover and expenditure figures to increase by approximately 25% next year.

- Siglio has heard about an annual test for computing the amount of recoverable input VAT during an accounting period and would like more information about this.

Required:

(a) **Explain, with the aid of supporting calculations, which of the two proposed methods of providing the laptop computer to Jed would result in the lower after-tax cost for Nocturne Ltd.**

You should ignore value added tax (VAT) for part (a) of this question. **(7 marks)**

(b) **Explain the income tax implications for Siglio of providing the loan to Nocturne Ltd.** **(4 marks)**

(c) (i) **Determine, by reference to the de minimis tests 1 and 2, Nocturne Ltd's recoverable input VAT for the year ended 31 March 2022.** **(4 marks)**

(ii) **Advise Siglio of Nocturne Ltd's eligibility for the annual test for computing the amount of recoverable input VAT for the year ending 31 March 2023 and the potential benefits to be gained from its use.** **(5 marks)**

(Total: 20 marks)

57 GAIL (ADAPTED) *Walk in the footsteps of a top tutor*

You should assume that today's date is 9 June 2022.

Your manager has had a meeting with Gail. Gail owns the whole of the ordinary share capital of Aero Ltd. An email from your manager setting out the matters discussed in the meeting and a schedule prepared by Mill, a junior member of your firm's tax department, are set out below.

Email from your manager – dated 9 June 2022

Gail

Gail was born in 1975 and is resident and domiciled in the UK. She owns the whole of the ordinary share capital of Aero Ltd (A Ltd) and works full-time as a director of the company. A Ltd owns the whole of the ordinary share capital of Zephyr Ltd (Z Ltd). A Ltd and Z Ltd are both UK resident trading companies.

Historical transactions in respect of A Ltd and Z Ltd – all transactions took place at market value

1 January 2014	A Ltd acquired the whole of the ordinary share capital of Z Ltd for £180,000.
1 October 2018	A Ltd sold a building (the Simpson Building) to Z Ltd for £110,000. A Ltd had purchased this building for £75,000 on 1 December 2010.
1 March 2020	A Ltd sold a brand to Z Ltd for £170,000, its market value at the time was £230,000. A Ltd had purchased this brand for £115,000 on 1 June 2016.

Proposed transactions – all transactions will take place at market value

Gail intends to raise a substantial sum of money by carrying out the following transactions:

1	24 June 2022	Z Ltd will sell the Simpson Building to an unrelated purchaser for £140,000. Rollover relief will not be claimed in respect of this disposal.
		Z Ltd will pay a dividend to A Ltd equal to the post-tax proceeds of this sale.
2	1 July 2022	A Ltd will sell the whole of the ordinary share capital of Z Ltd for £250,000.
3	15 July 2022	All of the cash realised by A Ltd as a result of transactions 1 and 2 will be paid to Gail in the form of either a dividend or a bonus.

Please carry out the following work:

(a)   Schedule prepared by Mill

I can confirm that there are no computational errors in the schedule but I suspect that Mill will have made a few technical errors.

Please identify and explain any errors in the schedule, explain whether or not the notes to the schedule are or are not correct, and calculate the correct amount of total cash available to pay to Gail.

(b)   Payment to Gail

Calculate the additional tax and national insurance contributions due, as reduced by any corporation tax savings, if all of the cash realised by A Ltd as a result of the proposed transactions 1 and 2 is paid to Gail in the form of:

(i)   a bonus

(ii)   a dividend.

Gail's annual income tax liability in respect of her annual salary of £85,000 from A Ltd is £21,432. This will be her only source of income in the tax year 2022/23 other than any payments received from A Ltd as outlined above.

(c)   Non-disclosure of income

Gail has realised that she has not declared some of her income in respect of the tax year 2017/18. As a result of this, her income tax liability for that tax year was understated. I have already explained the interest and penalties which may be charged in respect of this error.

State the other matters which need to be considered, by us and by Gail, in relation to the disclosure of this error to HM Revenue and Customs (HMRC).

Tax manager

Schedule prepared by Mill

Cash which will be available to pay to Gail as a result of the proposed transactions 1 and 2	
	£
Sale of the Simpson Building by Zephyr Ltd	
Sale proceeds	140,000
Less: Cost	(110,000)
Indexation allowance (October 2018 to June 2022)	
£110,000 × 0.105	(11,550)
	————
Chargeable gain	18,450
Less: Corporation tax payable by Zephyr Ltd at 19 %	(3,506)
	————
Dividend of post-tax proceeds paid to Aero Ltd	14,944
Less: Corporation tax payable by Aero Ltd at 19%	(2,839)
	————
Cash available in respect of the sale of the Simpson Building	12,105
Sale proceeds in respect of Zephyr Ltd	250,000
	————
Total cash available for Gail	262,105
	————

Notes

1   I do not think there will be a chargeable gain on the sale of Zephyr Ltd due to the substantial shareholding exemption.

2   I think there will be a degrouping charge in respect of the brand but I do not know how to compute it.

Mill

Required:

Carry out the work requested in the email from your manager. The following marks are available:

(a)   **Schedule prepared by Mill.**   (11 marks)

Note: The following movements in the Retail Prices Index should be used, where necessary.

December 2010 to December 2017	**0.218**
January 2014 to December 2017	**0.101**
June 2016 to December 2017	**0.057**

(b)   **Payment to Gail.**   (9 marks)

(c)   **Non-disclosure of income.**   (5 marks)

                                                                                                      (Total: 25 marks)

58 MARIA AND GRANADA LTD (ADAPTED) *Walk in the footsteps of a top tutor*

You should assume that today's date is 10 March 2022.

Your firm has been asked to provide advice to Granada Ltd, and one of its shareholders, Maria. Maria wants advice on the tax consequences of selling some of her shares back to Granada Ltd. Granada Ltd wants advice on the corporation tax and value added tax (VAT) implications of the recent acquisition of an unincorporated business.

Maria:

– Is resident and domiciled in the UK.

– Is a higher rate taxpayer with annual dividend income in excess of £10,000, and will remain so in the future.

– Has already realised chargeable gains of £15,000 in the tax year 2021/22.

Shares in Granada Ltd:

– Maria subscribed for 10,000 £1 ordinary shares in Granada Ltd at par in June 2012.

– Maria is one of four equal shareholders and directors of Granada Ltd.

– Maria intends to sell either 2,700 or 3,200 shares back to the company on 31 March 2022 at their current market value of £12.80 per share.

– All of the conditions for the capital treatment are satisfied, except for, potentially, the condition relating to the reduction in the level of shareholding.

Granada Ltd:

– Is a UK resident trading company which manufactures knitwear.

– Prepares accounts to 31 December each year.

– Is registered for VAT.

– Acquired the trade and assets of an unincorporated business, Starling Partners, on 1 January 2022.

Starling Partners:

– Had been trading as a partnership for many years as a wholesaler of handbags within the UK.

– Starling Partners' main assets comprise a freehold commercial building and its 'Starling' brand, which were valued on acquisition by Granada Ltd at £105,000 and £40,000 respectively.

– Is registered for VAT.

– The transfer of its trade and assets to Granada Ltd qualified as a transfer of a going concern (TOGC) for VAT purposes.

– The business is forecast to make a trading loss of £130,000 in the year ended 31 December 2022.

Granada Ltd – results and proposed expansion:

- The knitwear business is expected to continue making a taxable trading profit of around £100,000 each year.

- Granada Ltd has no non-trading income but realised a chargeable gain of £10,000 on 1 March 2022.

- Granada Ltd is considering expanding the wholesale handbag trade acquired from Starling Partners into the export market from 1 January 2023.

- Granada Ltd anticipates that this expansion will result in the wholesale handbag trade returning a profit of £15,000 in the year ended 31 December 2023.

Required:

(a) (i) Explain, with the aid of calculations, why the capital treatment WILL NOT apply if Maria sells 2,700 of her shares back to Granada Ltd, but WILL apply if, alternatively, she sells back 3,200 shares. **(4 marks)**

    (ii) Calculate Maria's after-tax proceeds per share if she sells:

        1   2,700 shares back to Granada Ltd; and alternatively

        2   3,200 shares back to Granada Ltd. **(4 marks)**

(b) (i) Describe the corporation tax treatment of the acquisition of the 'Starling' brand by Granada Ltd, if no charge for amortisation was required in its statement of profit or loss. **(3 marks)**

    (ii) Discuss how Granada Ltd could obtain relief for the trading loss expected to be incurred by the trade acquired from Starling Partners, if it does not wish to carry any of the loss back. **(5 marks)**

(c) Explain the value added tax (VAT) implications for Granada Ltd in respect of the acquisition of the business of Starling Partners, and the additional information needed in relation to the building to fully clarify the VAT position. **(4 marks)**

(Total: 20 marks)

---

59   ACRYL LTD AND CRESCO LTD (ADAPTED) *Walk in the footsteps of a top tutor*

You should assume that today's date is 10 December 2022.

Acryl Ltd and Cresco Ltd are two unrelated companies. Acryl Ltd requires advice on the implications of being placed into liquidation, particularly the timing of distributions to its shareholders. Cresco Ltd requires advice on the relief for losses on the cessation of trade, and its obligations in relation to value added tax (VAT).

(a) **Acryl Ltd:**

- Is a UK resident trading company.

- Has always prepared accounts to 30 June annually.

- Has substantial distributable profits.

- 70% of the company's share capital is owned by Mambo Ltd.

- The remaining 30% of the share capital is owned by Mambo Ltd's managing director, Alan. Mambo Ltd and Alan both subscribed for their shares at par value on 1 March 2016.

Mambo Ltd:

- Is a UK resident trading company.

Alan:

- Will be an additional rate taxpayer in the tax year 2022/23.
- Will receive a salary from Acryl Ltd. This will be his only income in the tax year 2022/23 other than the distribution from Acryl Ltd in December 2022/March 2023.
- Will be eligible for business asset disposal relief on the disposal of his shares in Acryl Ltd.

Liquidation of Acryl Ltd:

- Winding up will commence on 1 January 2023 with the appointment of a liquidator.
- It is anticipated that the winding up will be completed on 31 March 2023, when the company will cease trading.

Alternative timing of distributions being considered by Acryl Ltd:

- Acryl Ltd is prepared to distribute the available profits to its shareholders on 31 December 2022.
- Alternatively, Acryl Ltd will delay the distribution until the completion of the winding up of the company on 31 March 2023.

Required:

(i) **State the corporation tax consequences arising from the commencement of Acryl Ltd's winding up on 1 January 2023.** **(2 marks)**

(ii) **Explain the tax implications for both Mambo Ltd and Alan if the distribution to be made by Acryl Ltd occurs either on 31 December 2022, or alternatively on 31 March 2023, and conclude as to which date would be preferable.**

(7 marks)

(b) **Cresco Ltd:**

- Is a UK resident trading company.
- Commenced trading on 1 June 2018.
- Is registered for the purposes of value added tax (VAT).
- Has made significant trading losses in recent months such that the company will need to cease trading on 31 December 2022.

Cresco Ltd – trading losses:

- Recent and anticipated results are as follows:

	Year ended 31 May 2019	Year ended 31 May 2020	Year ended 31 May 2021	Year ended 31 May 2022	Period ending 31 December 2022
	£	£	£	£	£
Trading (loss)/profit	(5,000)	17,000	8,000	(24,000)	(40,000)
Bank interest receivable	5,000	3,000	3,000	0	0

- Cresco Ltd always claims relief for trading losses as early as possible.

Required:

(i) Set out, together with supporting explanations, how Cresco Ltd will claim relief for the trading losses incurred and identify the amount of trading losses which will remain unrelieved after all available loss reliefs have been claimed.

(8 marks)

(ii) Advise Cresco Ltd of the value added tax (VAT) implications of the cessation of its trade.

(3 marks)

(Total: 20 marks)

60 TRAISTE LTD (ADAPTED) *Walk in the footsteps of a top tutor*

You should assume that today's date is 10 June 2022.

Jordi is a director and shareholder of Traiste Ltd. He has asked for your advice in connection with the forthcoming redundancy of an employee, the sale of shares in Traiste Ltd by his sister, Kat, and the payment implications for Traiste Ltd of alternative ways for Jordi to extract profits from the company.

Traiste Ltd:

– Is a UK resident unquoted trading company.

– Has two shareholders, Jordi and Kat, who each own 50% of the 1,000 £1 shares in issue.

Traiste Ltd – proposed redundancy package for an employee:

– An employee, Esta, will be made redundant on 30 June 2022.

– Esta will receive statutory redundancy pay of £12,000 and an *ex-gratia* payment of £36,000 from Traiste Ltd.

– Traiste Ltd will continue to lease a motor car for Esta's personal use until 31 December 2022, although she has no contractual entitlement to this.

– The monthly lease payments are £420.

– The motor car has CO_2 emissions of 143 grams per kilometre and is petrol powered.

– The motor car is currently worth £10,300. Its list price when new was £18,400.

Kat:

– Is resident and domiciled in the UK.

– Is 58 years old.

– Is a director and shareholder of Traiste Ltd.

– Will receive employment income of £40,350 from Traiste Ltd and dividends from other UK companies of £1,000 in the tax year 2022/23.

– Has already used her annual exempt amount for capital gains tax purposes for the tax year 2022/23.

Kat – proposed sale of shares:

– Kat subscribed for her 500 shares in Traiste Ltd at par on the incorporation of the company on 1 March 2018.

– She wishes to sell all of her shares before the end of 2022, and retire from the company.

– Kat's brother, Jordi, has offered to buy these shares for £47 each. He is not prepared to sign any tax election in relation to this offer.

– Alternatively, Traiste Ltd will buy these shares for their market value of £52 each.

Jordi:

- Is resident and domiciled in the UK.
- Is 53 years old.
- Is a director and shareholder of Traiste Ltd.
- Is paid a gross annual salary of £55,000 by Traiste Ltd.
- Wishes to extract an additional cash sum of £20,000, net of all taxes, from Traiste Ltd, to be paid on 31 March 2023.
- The additional sum will be extracted as either a bonus or a dividend.
- Will not receive any other taxable income in the tax year 2022/23.

Required:

(a) (i) **Explain briefly the income tax implications for Esta in respect of each of the three components of the proposed redundancy package.**

   Note: Calculations are NOT required for this part.   **(3 marks)**

   (ii) **Calculate the corporation tax deductions available to Traiste Ltd in respect of the redundancy package provided to Esta.**   **(4 marks)**

(b) **Explain, with reference to the after-tax proceeds in each case, why Kat should accept Jordi's offer to buy her shares in Traiste Ltd, rather than sell her shares back to Traiste Ltd.**   **(8 marks)**

(c) **Explain, with supporting calculations, the amount of any payments to be made by Traiste Ltd to HM Revenue and Customs (HMRC) in respect of each of the two ways for Jordi to extract the additional £20,000 cash from the company, and state the due date of any such tax payments.**   **(5 marks)**

   (Total: 20 marks)

61 DENT LTD (ADAPTED)

You should assume that today's date is 10 June 2022.

Dent Ltd requires advice on registering for value added tax (VAT), the corporation tax treatment of its expenditure on research and development (R&D) activities, and the after-tax cost of remuneration to be provided to a key employee.

Dent Ltd:

- Will be incorporated and start trading on 1 July 2022.
- Will undertake a research project to develop an innovative new process related to its trade.
- Will be a small enterprise for the purposes of R&D expenditure.
- Will prepare its first set of accounts to 30 June 2023.
- Will make wholly taxable supplies for VAT purposes.

Dent Ltd – budgeted income for the year ending 30 June 2023:

- The value of trading receipts in the first few months will be low; such that Dent Ltd will not be required to be compulsorily registered for VAT until 1 April 2023.
- Dent Ltd expects, however, to receive substantial fees in April to June 2023, such that it anticipates generating an overall taxable trading profit for the year ending 30 June 2023.
- All of Dent Ltd's customers will be registered for VAT.

Dent Ltd – budgeted R&D expenditure for the year ending 30 June 2023:

	£
Specialist equipment (second-hand)	110,000
Property costs	46,000
Consumables	12,000
Staff costs	185,000
	353,000

- The above figures are all exclusive of VAT, where applicable.
- The property costs entirely comprise heat, light and water expenses.
- The staff costs include a fee of £25,000 to an agency (which is VAT registered) for the provision of an unconnected external contractor's services for the year.
- The remainder of the staff costs wholly relate to amounts payable to, or on behalf of, Dent Ltd's employees, including pension contributions totalling £14,000.
- The property costs, consumables and agency fees are incurred evenly throughout the year.

Alina – design engineer:

- Alina will commence employment with Dent Ltd on 1 July 2022 to lead the R&D project.
- Alina's annual salary of £80,000 is included in the budgeted staff costs figure above.
- On 1 July 2022, Dent Ltd will additionally provide Alina with the following, none of which are included in the budgeted staff costs figure above:
    - a lump sum payment of £10,000 in recognition of her forthcoming employment
    - a second-hand computer costing £1,000, of which Alina will have use, including significant private use, for the first nine months of her employment; and
    - temporary living accommodation for the first six months of her employment (as detailed below).

Alina – provision of temporary living accommodation:

- Dent Ltd will rent a flat for Alina's use from 1 July 2022 to 31 December 2022.
- Dent Ltd will pay the rental cost of £660 per month.
- The market value of the flat is currently £225,000, and its annual value is £2,800.

Required:

(a) Advise Dent Ltd on the implications for the recovery of input value added tax (VAT) of registering for VAT with effect from 1 April 2023, when it will be compulsory to do so, and explain why it is beneficial for the company instead to register voluntarily with effect from 1 July 2022.

Note: Calculations are NOT required for this part (a). **(6 marks)**

(b) Explain the corporation tax treatment of the research and development (R&D) expenditure of £353,000 to be incurred by Dent Ltd in the year ending 30 June 2023, and, on the assumption that Dent Ltd registers voluntarily for VAT with effect from 1 July 2022, calculate the amount of the deduction which will be available in respect of this R&D expenditure for corporation tax purposes. **(6 marks)**

(c) State the income tax implications of the receipt of the lump sum payment for Alina, and calculate the after-tax cost for Dent Ltd in respect of the lump sum payment and provision of the computer and the temporary living accommodation to Alina in its year ending 30 June 2023.

Note: You should ignore VAT in this part (c). **(8 marks)**

(Total: 20 marks)

62 DORIAN

You should assume that today's date is 8 September 2022.

You have been asked to provide advice to Dorian, the managing director of Taupe Ltd, in relation to Taupe Ltd's status as a close company, the company's provision of employment benefits to Dorian, and the late filing of the company's corporation tax return.

Dorian and Taupe Ltd

Taupe Ltd:

– Is a UK resident trading company, and is also a close company.

– Has six directors, Dorian and five other, unrelated, individuals.

– Prepares accounts to 30 April each year.

– Always pays all amounts due to HM Revenue and Customs (HMRC) by the due date.

– Is not a large company for the purpose of being required to pay its corporation tax liability in instalments.

Taupe Ltd – shareholders:

– The shares in Taupe Ltd are held as follows:

	Percentage of issued ordinary shares
Dorian	5%
The other five directors (each holding 5%)	25%
Basil (Dorian's father)	23%
Other, unrelated, shareholders (each holding less than 2%)	47%
	100%

Dorian:

– Has an annual salary of £78,000 from Taupe Ltd.

– Was provided with an interest-free loan of £7,500 from Taupe Ltd on 6 April 2021. Notional tax was payable on this loan by Taupe Ltd.

– Is due to repay this loan on 30 June 2024, but may repay it earlier, on 30 April 2024.

– Has no other income.

– Works full time at Taupe Ltd's office in London.

Taupe Ltd – assistance with Dorian's home to work travel costs:

– Taupe Ltd is considering two alternatives to assist Dorian with the costs of his daily travel from home to work for the tax year 2023/24.

Alternative 1:

– On 6 April 2023, Taupe Ltd will make an interest-free loan to Dorian of £4,800, equal to the cost of his annual travel season ticket.

– Taupe Ltd will write off this loan on 5 April 2024.

– Dorian will incur no additional travel costs under this alternative.

Alternative 2:

– Taupe Ltd will pay Dorian a mileage allowance for driving his own car to work, amounting to £3,600 for the year ending 5 April 2024.

– Taupe Ltd will pay an unconnected company an annual fee of £1,200 for a car parking space for Dorian near the company's London office.

– Dorian has estimated that his current annual cost of driving from home to work is £5,220, including £1,320 for parking.

Taupe Ltd – late filing of corporation tax returns:

– Taupe Ltd filed its corporation tax return for the year ended 30 April 2021 on 29 August 2022.

– HMRC issued a notice requiring the filing of this return on 8 June 2021.

– Taupe Ltd had filed its corporation tax return for the year ended 30 April 2020 on 6 July 2021.

– All previous corporation tax returns had been filed on time.

Required:

(a) Explain why Taupe Ltd is classed as a close company. **(4 marks)**

(b) Explain, with supporting calculations, the tax implications for both Dorian and Taupe Ltd, if Dorian repays the £7,500 loan on 30 April 2024 rather than on 30 June 2024. **(5 marks)**

(c) Explain, with supporting calculations, which of the two alternatives for providing assistance with travel costs, will produce the lower overall cost for Dorian. **(8 marks)**

(d) State, with reasons, the due date for filing Taupe Ltd's corporation tax return for the year ended 30 April 2021, and the implications for Taupe Ltd in respect of filing it late. **(3 marks)**

(Total: 20 marks)

63 SAMPHIRE LTD AND KELP LTD

You should assume that today's date is 1 March 2023.

Samphire Ltd requires advice on the cost of gifting a computer, or, alternatively, making a loan to one of its shareholders. Kelp Ltd has requested advice on the tax implications of replacing a factory and acquiring a new warehouse.

Nori:

– Owns 75% of the ordinary shares in Samphire Ltd.

– Has been a director of Samphire Ltd for many years.

– Owns the whole of the ordinary share capital of Kelp Ltd.

Samphire Ltd:

– Is a UK resident close trading company, which prepares accounts to 31 March annually.

– Will either gift a computer to Nori on 6 April 2023, or make a loan to Nori on the same date, to allow him to purchase a computer.

Alternative 1 – Samphire Ltd gifts the computer to Nori:

– The computer was purchased by Samphire Ltd in March 2021 for £2,600 and has a current market value of £1,500.

– Samphire Ltd has purchased no other plant and machinery for several years, and the written down value of its main pool at 6 April 2023 will be £nil.

– The sale proceeds for the purpose of capital allowances will be £nil.

– Nori's private use of the computer has been insignificant throughout Samphire Ltd's period of ownership.

Alternative 2 – Samphire Ltd makes a loan to Nori:

– On 6 April 2023 Samphire Ltd will make an interest-free loan of £1,500 to Nori.

– Samphire Ltd will write off the loan on 6 April 2025.

Kelp Ltd – disposal of lease on Factory 1:

– Kelp Ltd is a UK resident trading company.

– Kelp Ltd was assigned a 48-year lease on a factory building ('Factory 1') on 1 November 2016, for which it paid a premium of £165,000.

– Kelp Ltd used Factory 1 in its trade until 30 April 2022, since when it has been rented to tenants who are not connected with the company.

– On 1 November 2022 Kelp Ltd sold the lease with 42 years remaining for £206,000.

Kelp Ltd – acquisition of Factory 2:

– Kelp Ltd acquired a factory building ('Factory 2') from Samphire Ltd on 1 May 2022, and immediately started to use it in its trade.

– Samphire Ltd had acquired Factory 2 for £96,000 on 5 August 2012.

– Kelp Ltd paid £138,000 for Factory 2, which was its market value on 1 May 2022.

Kelp Ltd – acquisition of warehouse:

– Kelp Ltd will acquire a warehouse from an unconnected company for £78,000 on 1 April 2023.

– Kelp Ltd will occupy 70% of this warehouse for its own trade, and will rent out the remaining 30%.

Required:

(a) Explain, with supporting calculations, the total additional taxes payable by Samphire Ltd:

    (i)   If Samphire Ltd gifts the computer to Nori (Alternative 1)   **(4 marks)**

    (ii)   If Samphire Ltd makes a loan of £1,500 to Nori, and then writes off the loan on 6 April 2025 (Alternative 2).   **(6 marks)**

    Note: ignore value added tax (VAT).

(b) (i)   Calculate the chargeable gain for Kelp Ltd on the sale of the lease on Factory 1.   **(3 marks)**

    (ii)   Explain, with supporting calculations, the amount of the chargeable gain calculated in (b)(i) which will remain liable to corporation tax (if any), if Kelp Ltd claims the maximum amount of rollover relief available.   **(7 marks)**

Notes:

(1) The following lease percentages should be used, where necessary:

    42 years   96.593

    48 years   99.289

(2) The following indexation factors should be used, where necessary:

    August 2012 to December 2017   0.144

    November 2016 to December 2017   0.047

(Total: 20 marks)

GROUPS, CONSORTIA AND OVERSEAS COMPANY ASPECTS

64   DAUBE GROUP (ADAPTED) *Walk in the footsteps of a top tutor*

You should assume that today's date is 6 December 2022.

Your manager has had a meeting with Mr Daube, a potential new client. The memorandum recording the matters discussed at the meeting and an extract from an e-mail from your manager detailing the tasks for you to perform are set out below.

Memorandum recording matters discussed at meeting with Mr Daube

To:	The files
From:	Tax manager
Date:	3 December 2022
Subject:	Mr Daube – Corporate matters

I had a meeting with Mr Daube on 2 December 2022. He wants us to advise him on the sale of Shank Ltd, one of his companies, and on the sale of a number of buildings.

Mr Daube owns the Hock Ltd group of companies and Knuckle Ltd as set out below. The dates in brackets are the dates on which the companies were purchased. Neither Mr Daube nor his companies have any interests in any other companies.

All five companies are UK resident trading companies with a 31 March year end. All of the companies, with the exception of Shank Ltd, are profitable.

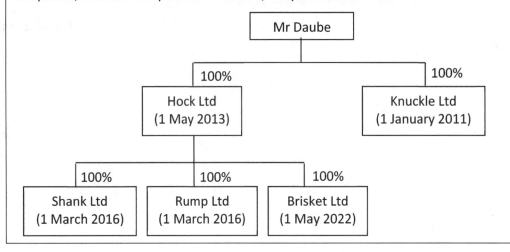

(i) **Sale of Shank Ltd**

Shank Ltd has made trading losses for a number of years and, despite surrendering the maximum possible losses to group companies, it has trading losses to carry forward as at 31 March 2022 of £35,000. Shank Ltd is expected to make a further trading loss of £19,000 in the year ending 31 March 2023 and has no other sources of income.

Mr Daube is of the opinion that the company will only become profitable following significant financial investment, which the group cannot afford, together with fundamental changes to its commercial operations.

Accordingly, Hock Ltd entered into a contract on 1 November 2022 to sell the whole of the ordinary share capital of Shank Ltd to Raymond Ltd (an independent third party) on 1 February 2023 for £270,000; an amount that is considerably less than the group paid for it.

(ii) **Sales of buildings**

The following buildings are to be sold during the year ending 31 March 2023, with the exception of the Monk building which was sold on 1 March 2022. Rollover relief will not be claimed in respect of any of the gains arising.

	Gar building	Cray building	Monk building	Sword building
Owned by:	Shank Ltd	Rump Ltd	Brisket Ltd	Knuckle Ltd
Cost:	£210,000	£24 million	£380,000	See below
Indexation allowance factors:	0.350	0.250	N/A	0.168
Date of sale:	1 January 2023	1 February 2023	1 March 2022	1 February 2023
Purchaser:	Hock Ltd	Quail plc	Hare plc	Pheasant plc
Estimated proceeds:	£370,000	£42 million	£290,000	£460,000

On 30 June 2012 Knuckle Ltd sold its original premises, the Pilot building, for £270,000 resulting in a chargeable gain of £60,000. On 1 January 2013 it purchased the Sword building for £255,000 and claimed rollover relief in respect of the gain on the Pilot building.

Rump Ltd has capital losses brought forward as at 1 April 2022 of £10 million.

Tax manager

Email from your manager

I have just had a further conversation with Mr Daube. He informed me that:

- Brisket Ltd acquired the Monk building on 1 January 2018.
- Quail plc, Hare plc and Pheasant plc are all unrelated to Mr Daube and his companies.
- None of the companies will make any other chargeable gains or allowable losses in the year ending 31 March 2023.
- Knuckle Ltd has identified a number of potential overseas customers and expects to begin selling its products to them in 2023. At the moment, all of Knuckle Ltd's supplies are standard-rated for the purposes of value added tax (VAT).

I want you to draft a report for Mr Daube dealing with the matters set out below.

(i)   Sale of Shank Ltd

- The alternative ways in which the company's trading losses can be relieved. I want some precise detail here so please try to consider all of the possibilities and any anti-avoidance legislation that may restrict the use of the losses.
- The tax treatment of the loss arising on the sale of Shank Ltd.
- An explanation of the threshold applicable for all of the companies for the payment of corporation tax by instalment for the year ending 31 March 2023.

(ii)   Sales of buildings

On the assumption that the three future building sales go ahead as planned:

- Calculations of the chargeable gain/allowable loss arising on the sale of each of the four buildings.
- The alternative ways in which any capital losses arising can be relieved, including the capital loss brought forward in Rump Ltd. I need a detailed explanation of the options available together with any restrictions that will apply. Watch out for the Monk building because the loss was incurred prior to the purchase of Brisket Ltd.
- The need to charge VAT on the sales of the buildings.
- The stamp duty land tax implications of the sales of the buildings.

(iii) Potential sales by Knuckle Ltd to overseas customers

- The VAT implications.

Tax manager

Required:

(a)   **Prepare the report as set out in the e-mail from your manager.**

   The following marks are available.

   (i)   **Sale of Shank Ltd**   **(12 marks)**

   (ii)   **Sales of buildings**   **(12 marks)**

   (iii)   **Potential sales by Knuckle Ltd to overseas customers.**   **(2 marks)**

   Professional marks will be awarded in part (a) for the appropriateness of the format of the report and the effectiveness with which the information is communicated.

                                                                          (4 marks)

(b)   **Prepare a summary of the information required and any action that should be taken before the firm agrees to become tax advisers to Mr Daube and his companies.**

                                                                          (5 marks)

                                                                    (Total: 35 marks)

65   DRENCH, HAIL LTD AND RAIN LTD (ADAPTED)

     Online question assistance and Walk in the footsteps of a top tutor

You should assume that today's date is 9 December 2022.

Your manager has sent you a schedule of information received from a client, named Drench, who is the managing director of Hail Ltd. Hail Ltd is a UK resident trading company with a year end of 30 June and Drench owns the whole of the company's ordinary share capital. The schedule is set out below together with an email from your manager.

Schedule of information from Drench

Acquisition of Rain Ltd

I intend to buy 100% of the ordinary share capital of Rain Ltd, a UK resident trading company, on 1 January 2023. I will either purchase the shares personally or Hail Ltd will acquire Rain Ltd as a 100% subsidiary.

Rain Ltd is one of two companies currently wholly-owned by Flake Ltd. All three of the companies in the Flake Ltd group are trading companies. Following its acquisition Rain Ltd will change its year end from 30 September to 30 June such that it will prepare accounts for the nine months ending 30 June 2023.

Budgeted results of Rain Ltd

The budgeted financial results of Rain Ltd for the nine months ending 30 June 2023 are set out below. The results depend on whether or not the company acquires new contracts in 2023. All of the company's sales are standard-rated for the purposes of value added tax (VAT). The chargeable gain is in respect of the disposal of a 0.3% shareholding in a quoted company.

	Nine months ending 30 June 2023	
	Without the new contracts	With the new contracts
	£	£
Sales revenue (exclusive of VAT)	380,000	1,425,000
Tax adjusted (loss)/profit	(110,000)	285,000
Chargeable gain	50,750	50,750

Other relevant information

In the year ended 30 September 2022 Rain Ltd realised a tax adjusted trading loss of £27,000 and had no other income or chargeable gains. The trading loss was surrendered as group relief to companies within the Flake Ltd group.

Rain Ltd's main asset is a building which is currently worth £340,000. The building was purchased from Mist Ltd, the other 100% subsidiary of Flake Ltd, on 1 July 2019 for its book value of £248,000. The market value of the building at that time was £260,000. Mist Ltd had purchased the building on 1 January 2010 for £170,000.

Hail Ltd is budgeted to realise taxable total profits in the year ending 30 June 2023 of £100,000.

Email from your manager

I want you to prepare the following:

(a) **A memorandum for the client file that explains the following matters, providing supporting calculations where relevant:**

    (i) **Acquisition of Rain Ltd**

        A comparison of the tax implications of:

        –   Drench acquiring Rain Ltd personally; and

        –   Hail Ltd acquiring Rain Ltd.

        Drench is aware of the general implications of forming a group. Accordingly, your comparison should focus on the following specific issues.

        On the assumption that Rain Ltd DOES NOT obtain the new contracts:

        –   The manner in which the loss for the nine months ending 30 June 2023 should be relieved in order to maximise the tax relief obtained; the tax relief should be quantified where possible.

        Drench wants the loss to be used as soon as possible and only to be carried forward as a last resort.

        –   The tax implications of Hail Ltd making a payment to Rain Ltd in respect of any group relief losses surrendered.

        On the assumption that Rain Ltd DOES obtain the new contracts

        –   The corporation tax liability of Rain Ltd for the nine months ending 30 June 2023.

        –   The date by when Rain Ltd will need to pay its corporation tax liability for the period in order to avoid interest charges.

        The tax treatment of Rain Ltd's building, including:

        –   any potential tax liabilities that may arise on the acquisition of Rain Ltd, and

        –   the base cost of the building for the purposes of calculating the chargeable gain or loss arising on the future disposal by Rain Ltd.

    (ii) **Loan from Hail Ltd to Drench and VAT cash accounting scheme**

        –   The tax implications for Hail Ltd of Drench borrowing £18,000 from the company on 1 February 2023. The loan will be interest-free and will be repaid by Drench on 1 February 2029.

        –   The advantages of the VAT cash accounting scheme and whether it will be possible for Rain Ltd to operate the scheme.

(b) **A briefing note to me**

Our firm will be assisting Rain Ltd to obtain the new contracts. We have experience in this area as we used to have a client that successfully applied for government building contracts. The client moved to a rival firm at the end of 2020.

To what extent is it acceptable for us to use the knowledge we gained in respect of our ex-client to assist Rain Ltd?

Tax manager

Required:

(a)   Prepare the memorandum including supporting calculations requested in the email from your manager. The following marks are available.

   (i)   Acquisition of Rain Ltd   **(15 marks)**

   (ii)   Loan from Hail Ltd to Drench and VAT cash accounting scheme.   **(8 marks)**

   Professional marks will be awarded in part (a) for the extent to which the calculations are approached in a logical manner and the effectiveness with which the information is communicated.   **(2 marks)**

   The following indexation factor should be used where necessary.

   January 2010 to December 2017   0.276

(b)   Prepare the briefing note requested in the email from your manager.   **(5 marks)**

                                                                    (Total: 30 marks)

 Online question assistance

66   JANUS PLC GROUP (ADAPTED) *Walk in the footsteps of a top tutor*

You should assume that today's date is 15 June 2022.

Your manager has had a meeting with Mrs Pairz, the Group Finance Director of the Janus plc group of companies. The memorandum recording the matters discussed at the meeting is set out below.

Memorandum recording matters discussed at the meeting with Mrs Pairz

To	The files
From	Tax manager
Date	15 June 2022
Subject	Janus plc group

Mrs Pairz has recently been appointed the Group Finance Director of the Janus plc group. She has asked for advice on the use of the trading loss of Janus plc for the year ended 31 March 2022 and on a number of other matters.

The Janus plc group of companies

The group structure indicating the trading loss of Janus plc and the taxable total profits of each of the other group companies for the year ended 31 March 2022 is set out below. All of the companies are UK resident trading companies.

Janus plc purchased Seb Ltd, together with its subsidiary, Viola Ltd, on 1 December 2021 from Mr Twinn. Mr Twinn has never owned any other companies. There have not been any other changes to the group structure in recent years.

The minority holdings in Castor Ltd and Pollux Ltd are owned by UK resident individuals. The minority holding in Duet Ltd is owned by Bi plc, a UK resident company, such that Duet Ltd is a consortium company.

The group policy is for an amount equal to the corporation tax saved to be paid for any losses transferred between group companies.

Each of the companies is separately registered for the purposes of value added tax (VAT).

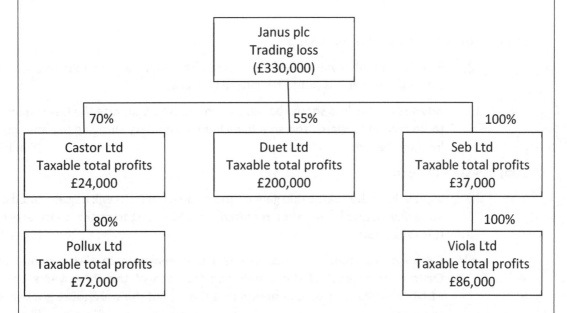

Additional information in respect of Janus plc

- Janus plc made a chargeable gain of £44,500 in the year ended 31 March 2022.

- Janus plc had taxable total profits in the year ended 31 March 2021 of £95,000 and did not make any charitable donations in the year.

Assets to be sold

(i) Pollux Ltd is to sell its administrative premises, 'P HQ', to Janus plc on 1 July 2022 for their market value of £285,000. Pollux Ltd acquired these premises from Castor Ltd on 1 March 2019 for their market value of £240,000.

(ii) Viola Ltd is to sell a warehouse to an unrelated company on 1 August 2022 for £350,000 plus VAT of £70,000. Viola Ltd acquired this warehouse on 1 February 2021 for £320,000 plus VAT of £64,000.

Mrs Pairz understands that the input tax relating to the warehouse should be recovered in accordance with the capital goods scheme because Viola Ltd is a partially exempt company, but suspects that the calculations may not have been done correctly.

The relevant VAT recovery percentages for Viola Ltd are:

Year ended 31 March 2021	70%
Year ended 31 March 2022	55%
Period from 1 April 2022 to 1 August 2022	50%

(iii) Castor Ltd is to sell patent rights to an unrelated company on 1 September 2022 for £41,000. Castor Ltd acquired these patent rights for use in its trade on 1 September 2018 for £45,000. The patent rights are being written off in Castor Ltd's accounts on a straight-line basis over a ten-year period.

Investment in Kupple Inc

Janus plc intends to purchase 15% of the ordinary share capital of Kupple Inc on 1 October 2022. Kupple Inc is a profitable trading company, resident in the country of Halven. Kupple Inc will provide consultancy services to Janus plc. This is intended to be a short-term commercial investment; Janus plc will sell the shares at some point in the next two years.

Required:

(a) Use of the trading loss of Janus plc:

(i) Explain the alternative ways in which the loss can be relieved, on the assumption that it is not to be carried forward.

(ii) Advise how the loss should be relieved in order to minimise the loss remaining to be carried forward. You should include a summary showing the amount of loss unrelieved. **(8 marks)**

(b) Assets to be sold:

(i) Explain how the chargeable gain on the disposal of P HQ will be calculated and state any further information required from Mrs Pairz to enable us to carry out this calculation. **(5 marks)**

(ii) Calculate the input tax recoverable from/repayable to HM Revenue and Customs in respect of the warehouse for each of the three years ending 31 March 2023, on the assumption that the sale of the warehouse goes ahead as planned. **(4 marks)**

(iii) Explain, with supporting calculations, the corporation tax implications of the sale of the patent rights. **(3 marks)**

(c) Investment in Kupple Inc:

(i) Explain the VAT implications for Janus plc of purchasing consultancy services from Kupple Inc. **(2 marks)**

(ii) Explain the corporation tax treatment of any profit or loss arising on the eventual sale of the shares in Kupple Inc. **(4 marks)**

(Total: 26 marks)

67 LIZA 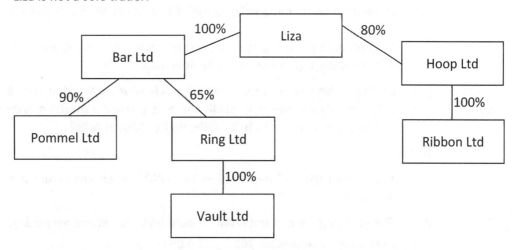 *Walk in the footsteps of a top tutor*

You should assume that today's date is 15 June 2022.

Liza requires detailed advice on rollover relief, capital allowances and group registration for the purposes of value added tax (VAT).

Liza's business interests:

– Liza's business interests, which have not changed for many years, are set out below. Liza is not a sole trader.

– All six companies are UK resident trading companies with a 31 March year end.
– All of the minority holdings are owned by individuals, none of whom is connected with Liza or with each other.

A building ('Building I') sold by Bar Ltd:

– Bar Ltd sold Building I on 31 May 2022 for £860,000.
– Bar Ltd had purchased the building on 1 June 2016 for £315,000 plus legal fees of £9,000.
– On 5 June 2016, Bar Ltd had carried out work on the building's roof at a cost of £38,000 in order to make the building fit for use.
– On 1 July 2021, Bar Ltd spent £14,000 repainting the building.
– Bar Ltd used Building I for trading purposes apart from the period from 1 January 2018 to 30 June 2019.
– It is intended that the chargeable gain on the sale will be rolled over to the extent that this is possible.

A replacement building ('Building II') purchased by Bar Ltd:

– Bar Ltd purchased Building II, newly constructed on 20 January 2022 and unused, for £720,000 on 1 May 2022.
– The purchase price includes £200,000 in respect of land and £150,000 in respect of electrical, water and heating systems.
– Bar Ltd brought the building into use immediately and uses two thirds of this building for trading purposes; the remaining one-third is rented out.

The trading activities of the Bar Ltd and Hoop Ltd groups of companies:

–   The number of transactions between the Bar Ltd group and the Hoop Ltd group is increasing.

–   Vault Ltd makes zero-rated supplies; all of the other five companies make standard-rated supplies.

Required:

(a)   (i)   Calculate the chargeable gain on the sale of Building I, ignoring any potential claim for rollover relief.   **(3 marks)**

(ii)   In relation to claiming rollover relief in respect of the disposal of Building I, explain which of the companies in the Bar Ltd and Hoop Ltd groups are, and are not, able to purchase qualifying replacement assets, and state the period within which such assets must be acquired.   **(4 marks)**

(iii)   Explain, with the aid of supporting calculations, the additional amount that would need to be spent on qualifying assets in order for the maximum amount of the gain on Building I to be relieved by rollover relief.   **(4 marks)**

Notes:

1   You should ignore Value Added Tax (VAT) when answering part (a) of this question.

2   The following indexation factor should be used, where necessary.

    June 2016 to December 2017   0.057

(b)   Explain the capital allowances that are available in respect of the acquisition of Building II.   **(4 marks)**

(c)   Explain which of the companies in the Bar Ltd and Hoop Ltd groups would be able to register as a single group for the purposes of value added tax (VAT), discuss the potential advantages of registering them as a single VAT group and the whether all companies would benefit from joining the VAT group.   **(5 marks)**

(Total: 20 marks)

68   SPETZ LTD GROUP (ADAPTED) *Walk in the footsteps of a top tutor*

 Question debrief

You should assume that today's date is 15 December 2022.

The management of the Spetz Ltd group requires advice on the value added tax (VAT) annual adjustment for a partially exempt company, the tax position of a company incorporated and trading overseas.

The Spetz Ltd group of companies:

–   Spetz Ltd has a large number of subsidiaries.

–   Novak Ltd and Kraus Co are two of the 100% subsidiaries of Spetz Ltd.

–   Novak Ltd has a VAT year end of 30 September.

–   Spetz Ltd acquired Kraus Co on 1 October 2021.

Novak Ltd – Figures for the year ended 30 September 2022:

	£
Taxable supplies (excluding VAT)	1,190,000
Exempt supplies	430,000
Input tax:	
– attributed to taxable supplies	12,200
– attributed to exempt supplies	4,900
– unattributed	16,100
– recovered on the four quarterly returns prior to the annual adjustment	23,200

Kraus Co:

- Is incorporated in, and trades through, a permanent establishment in the country of Mersano.
- Has no taxable income or chargeable gains apart from trading profits.
- Has taxable trading profits for the year ended 30 September 2022 of £520,000, all of which arose in Mersano.
- Is not a controlled foreign company.
- Has not made an election to exempt its overseas trading profits from UK tax.

The tax system in the country of Mersano:

- It can be assumed that the tax system in the country of Mersano is the same as that in the UK.
- However, the rate of corporation tax is 17%.
- There is no double tax treaty between the UK and Mersano.

Required:

(a) Calculate the value added tax (VAT) partial exemption annual adjustment for Novak Ltd for the year ended 30 September 2022 and state when it must be reported to HM Revenue and Customs. You should state, with reasons, whether or not each of the three de minimis tests is satisfied. **(7 marks)**

(b) (i) Explain how to determine whether or not Kraus Co is resident in the UK.
(3 marks)

(ii) Explain, with supporting calculations, the UK corporation tax liability of Kraus Co for the year ended 30 September 2022 on the assumption that it is resident in the UK, and discuss the advantages and disadvantages of making an election to exempt its overseas profits from UK tax. **(5 marks)**

(Total: 15 marks)

 Calculate your allowed time, allocate the time to the separate parts...................

69 KLUBB PLC *Walk in the footsteps of a top tutor*

You should assume that today's date is 1 June 2022.

Klubb plc, a client of your firm, requires advice on the penalty in respect of the late filing of a corporation tax return, the establishment of a tax advantaged share scheme, and its shareholding in an overseas resident company.

Klubb plc:

– Is a UK resident trading company.

– Has been charged a penalty in respect of the late filing of corporation tax returns.

– Intends to establish a tax advantaged share plan.

– Purchased 30% of the ordinary share capital of Hartz Co from Mr Deck on 1 April 2022.

Late filing of corporation tax returns:

– Klubb plc prepared accounts for the 16-month period ended 31 March 2021.

– The corporation tax returns for this period were filed on 31 May 2022.

Tax advantaged share plan:

– The plan will be either a tax advantaged share incentive plan (SIP) or a tax advantaged company share option plan (CSOP).

– If a SIP, the shares would be held within the plan for five years.

– If a SIP, members will not be permitted to reinvest dividends in order to purchase further shares.

– If a CSOP, the options would be exercised within five years of being granted.

– In both cases it can be assumed that the plan members would sell the shares immediately after acquiring them.

Klubb plc wants the share plan to be flexible in terms of:

– The employees who can be included in the plan.

– The number or value of shares which can be acquired by each plan member.

Hartz Co:

– Is resident in the country of Suta.

– Mr Deck continues to own 25% of the company's ordinary share capital.

– Kort Co, a company resident in the country of Suta, owns the remaining 45%.

Budgeted results of Hartz Co for the year ending 31 March 2023:

– Trading profits of £330,000.

– Chargeable gains of £70,000.

– All of Hartz Co's profits have been artificially diverted from the UK.

– Hartz Co will pay corporation tax at the rate of 11% in the country of Suta.

– Hartz Co will not pay a dividend for the year ending 31 March 2023.

Required:

(a) State the corporation tax returns required from Klubb plc in respect of the 16-month period ended 31 March 2021 and the due dates for filing them.

Explain the penalties which may be charged in respect of the late filing of these returns. **(4 marks)**

(b) Compare and contrast a tax advantaged share incentive plan with a tax advantaged company share option plan in relation to:

– the flexibility desired by Klubb plc regarding the employees included in the plan and the number or value of shares which can be acquired by each plan member; and

– the income tax and capital gains tax implications of acquiring and selling the shares under each plan. **(9 marks)**

(c) (i) Explain whether or not Hartz Co will be regarded as a controlled foreign company (CFC) for the year ending 31 March 2023 and the availability or otherwise of the low profits exemption. **(4 marks)**

(ii) On the assumption that Hartz Co is a CFC, and that no CFC exemptions are available, calculate the budgeted CFC charge for Klubb plc based on the budgeted results of Hartz Co for the year ending 31 March 2023. **(3 marks)**

(Total: 20 marks)

70 SPRINT LTD AND IRON LTD (ADAPTED) *Walk in the footsteps of a top tutor*

You should assume that today's date is 1 September 2022.

Your manager has received a letter from Christina. Christina is the managing director of Sprint Ltd and owns the whole of that company's ordinary share capital. Sprint Ltd is a client of your firm. Extracts from the letter from Christina and an email from your manager are set out below.

Extract from the letter from Christina

I intend to purchase the whole of the ordinary share capital of Iron Ltd on 1 November 2022. My company, Sprint Ltd, purchases components from Iron Ltd, so the two companies will fit together well. I hope to increase the value of Iron Ltd over the next three to five years and then to sell it at a profit.

I need your advice on the following matters.

Corporation tax payable

Iron Ltd has not been managed particularly well. It has had significant bad debts and, as a result, is in need of more cash. To help determine its financial requirements, I need to know how much corporation tax Iron Ltd will have to pay in respect of its results for the 16-month period ending 30 June 2023. Iron Ltd's tax adjusted trading income for this period is budgeted to be only £30,000. In fact, if we discover further problems, it is quite possible that Iron Ltd will make a trading loss for this period; but please base your calculations on the budgeted profit figure of £30,000.

Iron Ltd has no income other than trading income. Following the acquisition, Iron Ltd will sell a small industrial building for £160,000 and an item of fixed machinery for £13,700 on 1 December 2022. The industrial building and the item of fixed machinery were both purchased on 1 June 2017 for £100,000 and £13,500 respectively. At that time, rollover relief of £31,800 was claimed against the acquisition of the industrial building and £3,200 against the acquisition of the item of fixed machinery.

Ownership of Iron Ltd

I need to decide whether I should purchase the shares in Iron Ltd personally or whether the shares should be purchased by Sprint Ltd. I will be the managing director of Iron Ltd regardless of who purchases the shares.

My preference would be to own Iron Ltd personally. However, I would be interested to learn of any advantages to the company being owned by Sprint Ltd. When Iron Ltd is eventually sold, I intend to use the proceeds to purchase a holiday home in Italy.

Value added tax (VAT)

Iron Ltd is not registered for the purposes of VAT. The current management of the company has told me that the level of bad debts is keeping the company's cash receipts in a 12-month period below the registration limit of £85,000. However, I suspect that when I have the opportunity to look at the figures in more detail, it will become apparent that the company should be registered.

Extract from the email from your manager

Additional information

1   Sprint Ltd owns the whole of the ordinary share capital of Olympic Ltd. Both these companies are profitable and prepare accounts to 30 June each year. Both companies are registered for the purposes of VAT.

2   Sprint Ltd, Olympic Ltd and Iron Ltd are all UK resident trading companies.

3   Sprint Ltd will sell a warehouse on 1 February 2023. This will result in a capital loss of £38,000.

4   Iron Ltd currently makes up its accounts to 28 February each year. Following its acquisition, however, its next set of accounts will be for the 16 months ending 30 June 2023.

5   Iron Ltd currently has no 51% group companies.

Please carry out the work set out below.

There will be quite a few points to draw to Christina's attention, so keep each one fairly brief.

(a) **Iron Ltd – Corporation tax payable**

Assuming the entire ordinary share capital of Iron Ltd is purchased by Christina personally on 1 November 2022, calculate the corporation tax payable by Iron Ltd in respect of the 16-month period ending 30 June 2023, and state when this tax will be due for payment.

(b) **Ownership of Iron Ltd**

Explain the tax matters which Christina needs to be aware of in order to decide whether the ordinary share capital of Iron Ltd should be purchased by herself, personally, or by Sprint Ltd. You should assume that Iron Ltd will be required to register for VAT. You should consider the tax implications of both:

– the ownership of Iron Ltd, and

– the eventual sale of Iron Ltd (by either Christina or Sprint Ltd).

You should recognise that, regardless of who purchases and subsequently sells Iron Ltd, Christina intends to use the proceeds for personal purposes and that she is a higher rate taxpayer with a substantial amount of investment income.

(c) **VAT registration**

Set out the matters which Christina should be aware of in relation to the need for Iron Ltd to register for VAT and the implications for that company of registering late.

Tax manager

Required:

Carry out the work required as requested in the email from your manager. The following marks are available:

(a) **Iron Ltd – Corporation tax payable.**

Note: The following figures from the Retail Prices Index should be used, where necessary.

June 2017 to December 2017   0.021

(9 marks)

(b) **Ownership of Iron Ltd.** **(13 marks)**

(c) **Value added tax (VAT) registration.** **(3 marks)**

(Total: 25 marks)

71   HAHN LTD GROUP (ADAPTED)   *Walk in the footsteps of a top tutor*

You should assume that today's date is 8 September 2022.

Your manager has had a meeting with the finance director of Hahn Ltd, which is a client of your firm. Extracts from the memorandum she prepared following the meeting, and an email from her in connection with the Hahn Ltd group are set out below:

Extracts from the memorandum – dated 8 September 2022

Hahn Ltd group

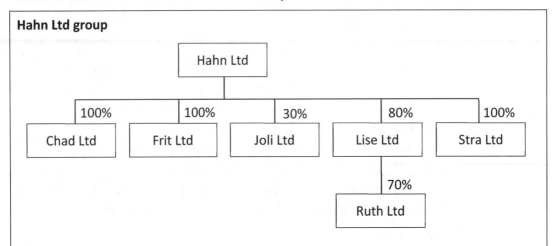

Notes

1   All of the companies are UK resident trading companies with a year end of 31 March.

2   All of the companies are registered for the purposes of value added tax (VAT).

3   With the exception of Chad Ltd, all of the companies have been members of the Hahn Ltd group for many years.

4   Hahn Ltd purchased Chad Ltd from Zeno Ltd on 1 September 2022. Prior to its disposal to Hahn Ltd, Zeno Ltd had owned Chad Ltd, and six other wholly-owned subsidiaries, for many years.

5   Joli Ltd is not a consortium company.

Budgeted results for the year ending 31 March 2023

	Hahn Ltd	Chad Ltd	Frit Ltd	Joli Ltd	Lise Ltd	Ruth Ltd	Stra Ltd
	£000	£000	£000	£000	£000	£000	£000
Tax adjusted trading profit/(loss)	180	675	(540)	410	375	320	38
Chargeable gains	–	–	65	–	–	–	–
Trading loss brought forward	–	–	–	–	–	–	(28)
Capital loss brought forward	–	–	(31)	–	–	–	–
Assets purchased which qualify for rollover relief	–	–	14	–	–	6	10

Notes

1   The budgeted results include £94,000 of sales made by Hahn Ltd to Stra Ltd. The arm's length price of these sales would be £104,000. Both of these figures are exclusive of VAT. No tax adjustments have been made in respect of these sales. The Hahn Ltd group is a large group for the purposes of the transfer pricing rules.

2   Frit Ltd's chargeable gain will be in respect of the sale of a building to an unconnected third party for £125,000. The building is a qualifying business asset for the purposes of rollover relief.

3   None of the companies will receive any dividends other than from 51% related group companies in the year ending 31 March 2023.

4   Frit Ltd will not be able to carry its loss back to the year ended 31 March 2022.

5   All of the companies, with the exception of Frit Ltd and Stra Ltd, were required to pay their corporation tax liabilities for the year ended 31 March 2022 by instalments.

VAT

–   The Hahn Ltd group is considering registering as a VAT group. Frit Ltd makes some exempt supplies, such that it is a partially exempt company. The other six companies all make standard-rated supplies only. Stra Ltd uses both the annual accounting scheme and the cash accounting scheme.

–   On 1 September 2022, Chad Ltd received a refund of VAT from HM Revenue and Customs (HMRC). The company has not been able to identify any reason for this refund.

Email from your manager – dated 8 September 2022

Please prepare a memorandum for the client files which addresses the following issues:

(a) **(i)** **Chargeable gain of Frit Ltd**

Calculate the additional amount which would need to be spent on assets qualifying for rollover relief, such that the unrelieved gain would be fully covered by Frit Ltd's brought forward capital loss.

(ii) **Relieving the trading loss of Frit Ltd**

– Prepare explanations, together with supporting calculations, to show how the trading loss of Frit Ltd should be allocated between the companies in the group. The group's priority is its cash flow position and the need to minimise the corporation tax payable by instalments.

When preparing these calculations, you should assume that the whole of the chargeable gain of Frit Ltd will be relieved by rollover relief.

– Prepare a schedule setting out the amounts of corporation tax payable by Hahn Ltd, and the companies it controls (i.e. not Joli Ltd) in respect of the year ending 31 March 2023, together with the related payment dates.

(b) **Group registration for the purposes of value added tax (VAT)**

By reference to the specific information in my memorandum only, set out the matters which will need to be considered when deciding which of the companies should be included in a group registration.

(c) **Chad Ltd – refund of VAT**

Prepare a summary of the actions which we should take, and any matters of which Chad Ltd should be aware, in respect of the refund of VAT.

Tax manager

Required:

Prepare the memorandum as requested in the email from your manager. The following marks are available:

(a)	**(i)**	Chargeable gain of Frit Ltd.	**(3 marks)**
	(ii)	Relieving the trading loss of Frit Ltd.	**(18 marks)**
(b)		Group registration for the purposes of value added tax (VAT).	**(5 marks)**
(c)		Chad Ltd – refund of VAT.	**(5 marks)**

Professional marks will be awarded for the approach taken to problem solving, the clarity of the explanations and calculations, the effectiveness with which the information is communicated, and the overall presentation. **(4 marks)**

(Total: 35 marks)

72 HEYER LTD GROUP *Walk in the footsteps of a top tutor*

You should assume that today's date is 8 June 2022.

Your manager has asked you to take charge of some work in connection with the Heyer Ltd group of companies. A schedule of information from the client files and an email from your manager detailing the work he requires you to do are set out below.

Heyer Ltd group – schedule of information from the client files

Group structure

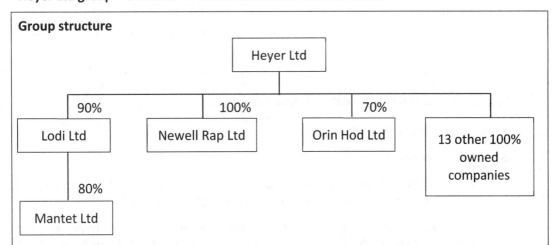

General information

– All of the companies are resident in the UK and prepare accounts to 31 December each year.

– The figures given below of taxable total profits (TTP) take account of all possible rollover relief claims.

– None of the companies has received any dividend income from non-group companies.

Specific information

Mantet Ltd

– Mantet Ltd has TTP of between £40,000 and £50,000 every year.

Newell Rap Ltd

– Heyer Ltd acquired Newell Rap Ltd on 1 May 2021.

– Newell Rap Ltd has a capital loss brought forward as at 1 January 2022 of £94,000. This loss arose on a sale of land on 1 February 2019.

Orin Hod Ltd

– The TTP of Orin Hod Ltd exceeds £200,000 every year.

– In the year ending 31 December 2022 Orin Hod Ltd will make chargeable gains of £86,000.

Other 100% owned companies

– Each of these companies has TTP of more than £130,000 every year.

– Four of them will have substantial chargeable gains in the year ending 31 December 2022.

– Five of them will have capital losses in the year ending 31 December 2022.

Group restructuring

- It is intended that the trade and assets of five group companies (Newell Rap Ltd and four of the other 100% owned companies) will be sold to Lodi Ltd at some point in January 2023.
- The assets of the five companies, including the business premises, machinery and equipment will be sold to Lodi Ltd for their market value.
- The tax written down value of the main pool of each of the five companies immediately prior to the sale will be zero.

Pink Time Ltd

Heyer Ltd intends to incorporate a new subsidiary, Pink Time Ltd, on 1 September 2022. Pink Time Ltd will have a monthly turnover of £35,000. All of its sales will be to members of the public and will be zero-rated for the purposes of value added tax (VAT).

Email from your manager – dated 8 June 2022

Please carry out the following work:

(a) Group planning

The group's objective is to minimise the corporation tax payable in instalments by group companies in respect of the year ended 31 December 2022.

I have asked Cox, our tax assistant, to carry out this work and I have provided him with the details of the companies' budgeted results for 2022. There is no group relief available within the group.

Cox has not done this type of work before and he has had very little experience of capital gains groups, so I want you to prepare some guidance for him. The guidance should consist of explanations of:

- the circumstances in which a member of the Heyer Ltd group would be required to pay corporation tax in instalments, assuming that the profits threshold should be divided by 18
- which companies are members of a capital gains group
- how Cox should determine the amount of chargeable gains and capital losses to transfer between the group companies in order to achieve the group's objective; and
- the relevance to the group's objective of the **specific information** provided in the schedule of information.

(b) Group restructuring

Identify, with reasons, the implications of the proposed group restructuring in relation to chargeable gains, stamp duty land tax and capital allowances, and what will happen to any capital losses belonging to the five companies whose trade and assets are transferred.

(c) Pink Time Ltd

Explain whether it will be compulsory for Pink Time Ltd to register for value added tax (VAT) and why the company would benefit from registering.

(d) **Disclosure of transfer pricing**

It has been realised by the management of Heyer Ltd that transfer pricing adjustments should have been made in respect of the year ended 31 December 2018 for three of the companies in the group. The corporation tax liability of the group was understated as a result of this non-disclosure.

I have already explained the interest and penalties which may be charged in respect of this. I want you to list the other matters which need to be considered, by us, as tax advisers to the group, and by the management of the group, in relation to the disclosure or non-disclosure of this information to HM Revenue and Customs (HMRC).

Tax manager

Required:

Carry out the work requested in the email from your manager. The following marks are available:

(a)	Group planning.	(11 marks)
(b)	Group restructuring.	(4 marks)
(c)	Pink Time Ltd.	(5 marks)
(d)	Disclosure of transfer pricing.	(5 marks)
		(Total: 25 marks)

73 **ACHIOTE LTD** *Walk in the footsteps of a top tutor*

You should assume that today's date is 8 June 2022.

The finance director of Achiote Ltd would like your advice on the tax implications of the acquisition of two intangible fixed assets, various transactions involving an overseas subsidiary, and opting to tax a commercial building.

Achiote Ltd:

–   Owns 100% of the ordinary shares in Borage Ltd and 80% of the ordinary shares in Caraway Inc.

–   Achiote Ltd and Borage Ltd are resident in the UK. Caraway Inc is resident in the country of Nuxabar.

–   All three companies are trading companies and prepare accounts to 31 March annually.

Borage Ltd – purchase of intangible fixed assets:

- Borage Ltd purchased the goodwill of an unincorporated business for £62,000 on 1 September 2021.

- Borage Ltd will amortise this goodwill in its accounts on a straight-line basis over a five-year period.

- Borage Ltd also purchased a patent from Achiote Ltd for £45,000 on 1 January 2022.

- Achiote Ltd had purchased the patent for £38,000 on 1 January 2019.

- The patent was being amortised in Achiote Ltd's accounts on a straight-line basis over a ten-year period.

- Borage Ltd will continue to amortise the patent over the remainder of its ten-year life.

Achiote Ltd – loan to Caraway Inc:

- Achiote Ltd made a loan of £100,000 to Caraway Inc on 1 April 2021.

- The rate of interest on the loan is 6% per annum, which is 2% below the rate applicable to an equivalent loan from an unrelated party.

- There is no double tax treaty between the UK and Nuxabar.

Achiote Ltd – sale of equipment to, and proposed sale of shares in, Caraway Inc:

- Achiote Ltd acquired its 80% shareholding in Caraway Inc on 1 January 2022 for £258,000.

- Achiote Ltd is now proposing to sell an 8% shareholding in Caraway Inc to an unconnected company on 1 October 2022 for £66,000.

- An item of equipment owned by Achiote Ltd and used in its trade was sold to Caraway Inc on 1 March 2022 for its market value of £21,000.

- The item of equipment had cost Achiote Ltd £32,000 in May 2021.

Achiote Ltd – purchase and rental of a commercial building:

- Achiote Ltd has recently purchased a two-year-old commercial building from an unconnected vendor.

- The building will be rented to an unconnected company, Rye Ltd.

- Rye Ltd is a small local company, which supplies goods to Achiote Ltd but does not charge value added tax (VAT) on these sales.

Required:

(a) **Explain, with supporting calculations where appropriate, the corporation tax treatment in the year ended 31 March 2022, of the goodwill and the patent acquired by Borage Ltd.** (4 marks)

(b) **Explain the implications of the rate of interest charged by Achiote Ltd on the loan to Caraway Inc by reference to the transfer pricing legislation, and any action which should be taken by Achiote Ltd.** (5 marks)

(c) **Advise Achiote Ltd of the chargeable gains implications arising from (1) the sale of the item of equipment to Caraway Inc; and (2) its proposed sale of the shares in Caraway Inc.** (5 marks)

(d) (i) **On the assumption that Rye Ltd makes only taxable supplies, state TWO legitimate reasons why it might not charge value added tax (VAT) on its sales to Achiote Ltd.** (2 marks)

(ii) **Explain whether or not it would be financially beneficial for Achiote Ltd to opt to tax the commercial building, and the implications for Rye Ltd if it chooses to do so.** (4 marks)

(Total: 20 marks)

74 HARROW TAN LTD *Walk in the footsteps of a top tutor*

 Question debrief

You should assume that today's date is 7 September 2022.

Your manager has sent you a memorandum in relation to the Harrow Tan Ltd group. An extract from the memorandum and a schedule of group information prepared by Corella, the group finance director, are set out below.

Memorandum from your manager – dated 7 September 2022

Background

– We are advising Corella, the group finance director, on a number of matters. I've attached a schedule from Corella, which sets out much of the relevant information.

– Corella was only recently appointed the Harrow Tan Ltd group finance director. She has had very little experience of practical tax since qualifying as an accountant in 1998. I have carried out a brief review of Corella's schedule and concluded that it is mathematically correct but that we cannot rely on its tax technical content.

– All five group companies are UK resident trading companies which prepare accounts to 31 December each year.

Memorandum from your manager – dated 7 September 2022 (continued)

Sale of shares in Rocha Ltd

Harrow Tan Ltd acquired the whole of the ordinary share capital of Rocha Ltd (100,000 shares) on 1 December 2021 for £8,900,000.

On 1 January 2022, Seckel Ltd (owned 80% by Harrow Tan Ltd) sold a commercial building to Rocha Ltd for £800,000, its market value on that date. The group claimed exemption from stamp duty land tax in respect of this transaction. Seckel Ltd had purchased the building on 1 May 2003 at a cost of £330,000. However, the results of Rocha Ltd for the year ending 31 December 2022 are now expected to be significantly worse than originally budgeted and an agreement was signed on 31 July 2022 for Harrow Tan Ltd to sell 60,000 Rocha Ltd ordinary shares for £10,300,000. It is planned that the sale of these shares will take place on 1 October 2022, although the sale could be delayed by up to three months if necessary.

Tosca Ltd – promotion of new product

Tosca Ltd manufactures high quality glass bowls. It accounts for value added tax (VAT) using the annual accounting scheme.

Tosca Ltd has developed a new product, which is expected to increase the company's annual turnover from £1,200,000 to £2,000,000. The new product is to be marketed to the company's customers, all of whom are UK based retailers, via promotional evenings in various parts of the UK.

At the promotional evenings the retailers will be provided with a meal. They will also be given a sample of the new product costing approximately £90, and a pen costing £40.

Please prepare notes for us to use in a meeting with Corella, which EXPLAIN the following matters:

(i)   **Sale of shares in Rocha Ltd**

–   The error(s) and omission(s) in part A of Corella's schedule together with any tax saving opportunities or other matters, including stamp duty land tax, which are not addressed in part A of her schedule. Please include a corrected calculation of the taxable gain on the sale on the assumption that it occurs on 1 October 2022.

–   Take some time to think about this. From my brief review I think there may be three or four issues which need to be brought to Corella's attention.

(ii)   **Group relief – year ending 31 December 2022**

–   By reference to the information in part B of Corella's schedule, the maximum amount of Seckel Ltd's trading loss which can be surrendered to each of the other companies in the Harrow Tan Ltd group.

(iii)   **Rollover relief**

–   The rollover relief potentially available to the group and the accuracy of part C of Corella's schedule.

(iv)   **Tosca Ltd – promotion of new product**

–   The VAT implications of:

–   the expected increase in the turnover of Tosca Ltd, and

–   the entertainment and gifts at the promotional evenings.

Schedule of group information – from Corella, the group finance director

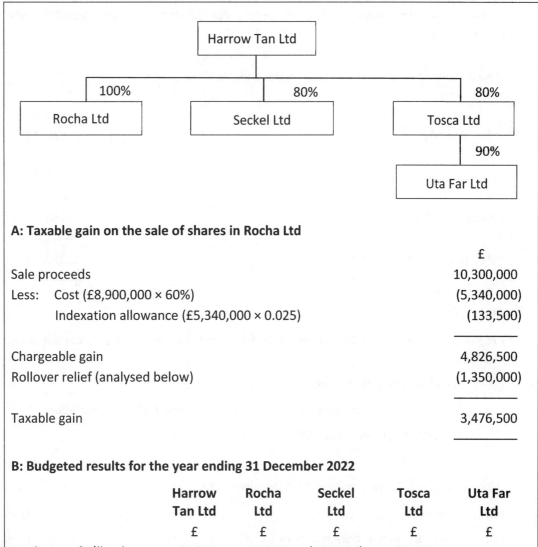

A: Taxable gain on the sale of shares in Rocha Ltd

	£
Sale proceeds	10,300,000
Less: Cost (£8,900,000 × 60%)	(5,340,000)
Indexation allowance (£5,340,000 × 0.025)	(133,500)
Chargeable gain	4,826,500
Rollover relief (analysed below)	(1,350,000)
Taxable gain	3,476,500

B: Budgeted results for the year ending 31 December 2022

	Harrow Tan Ltd	Rocha Ltd	Seckel Ltd	Tosca Ltd	Uta Far Ltd
	£	£	£	£	£
Trading profit/(loss)	40,000	60,000	(180,000)	70,000	600,000
Chargeable gains	Note 1	–			Note 2

Notes:

1 Disposal of shares in Rocha Ltd.

2 Uta Far Ltd sold a building used in its business on 1 May 2022 for £1,800,000. This resulted in a chargeable gain of £85,000.

Schedule of group information – from Corella, the group finance director (continued)

C: Harrow Tan Ltd – Acquisitions in the year ending 31 December 2022 qualifying for rollover relief	£
New factory, to be used in carrying on the company's business, consisting of:	
Land	410,000
Building	370,000
Total cost of factory	780,000
Machinery	430,000
Patents and Trademarks	140,000
Total qualifying additions	1,350,000

Required:

Prepare the meeting notes as requested by your manager. The following marks are available:

(i)   Sale of shares in Rocha Ltd.

      Note: The following indexation factor should be used where applicable:

      May 2003 to December 2017   0.532

                                            (12 marks)

(ii)   Group relief – year ending 31 December 2022.   **(6 marks)**

(iii)   Rollover relief.   **(7 marks)**

(iv)   Tosca Ltd – promotion of new product.   **(6 marks)**

Professional marks will be awarded for the ability to follow instructions, the clarity of the explanations and calculations, the effectiveness with which the information is communicated, and the overall presentation.   **(4 marks)**

(Total: 35 marks)

 Calculate your allowed time, allocate the time to the separate parts...................

75   SET LTD GROUP (ADAPTED) *Walk in the footsteps of a top tutor*

You should assume that today's date is 7 June 2022.

Your manager has forwarded an email to you from Ms Driver, the acting finance director of Set Ltd. Background information from your manager and the email from Ms Driver are set out below.

Background information from your manager – dated 7 June 2022

The finance director of the Set Ltd group of companies has become seriously ill and Ms Driver is standing in for him. I attach an email from Ms Driver requesting explanations of a number of matters.

Set Ltd has three wholly owned subsidiaries, Ghost Ltd, Steam Ltd and Wagon Ltd, and also owns shares in a number of other companies. Set Ltd and all of its wholly owned subsidiaries are resident in the UK.

You should assume that all of the UK resident companies in the Set Ltd group, including Ghost Ltd, pay corporation tax in instalments every year and will continue to do so, regardless of any loss relief planning entered into.

Please provide the explanations requested by Ms Driver in her email.

Thank you

Tax manager

Email from Ms Driver – dated 7 June 2022

(a)   **Ghost Ltd – corporation tax payments**

I'm working on the corporation tax instalment payments which Ghost Ltd will be required to pay in the period from now until 31 December 2022.

Set Ltd acquired the whole of the ordinary share capital of Ghost Ltd on 1 June 2022. Ghost Ltd had always prepared accounts to 30 April but following its acquisition has changed its year end to 31 December in line with all of the other companies in the Set Ltd group.

The finalised corporation tax liability of Ghost Ltd for the year ended 30 April 2022 was £597,500. I am now estimating the company's liability for the eight-month period ending 31 December 2022 so that I can determine the instalment payments required. As part of this work, I need to know if the company's corporation tax liability can be reduced in respect of the following:

–   Steam Ltd will sell a building on 1 August 2022, which is expected to result in a loss.

–   Wagon Ltd has a trading loss brought forward as at 1 January 2022 of £31,500. It is expected to make a further trading loss in the year ending 31 December 2022.

Please explain:

–   how Ghost Ltd could make use of the losses of Steam Ltd and Wagon Ltd in the period ending 31 December 2022.

–   the payments of corporation tax which will need to be made by Ghost Ltd in the period starting today, 7 June 2022, and ending on 31 December 2022. For the purpose of this explanation, please assume that Ghost Ltd's corporation tax liability for the eight-month period ending 31 December 2022 is £460,000.

Email from Ms Driver – dated 7 June 2022 (continued)

(b)   Wagon Ltd – value added tax (VAT)

Wagon Ltd intends to purchase manufacturing components from Line Co. Line Co is a company resident in the country of Terminusa. There is no VAT in Terminusa.

Wagon Ltd is also planning to sell goods to Signal Co. Signal Co is resident in France. Signal Co is a small company which is not required to be registered for VAT in France.

Neither Line Co nor Signal Co has any links with the Set Ltd group.

Please explain the VAT implications of these transactions.

(c)   Dee Co and En Co – controlled foreign company (CFC) charge

Set Ltd owns shares in two CFCs: Dee Co and En Co. Both of these companies have chargeable profits for the purposes of the CFC legislation. Estimates of the relevant financial information in respect of the year ending 31 December 2022 are as follows:

	Dee Co	En Co
Percentage of ordinary share capital owned by Set Ltd	21%	37%
	£	£
Non-trading income	nil	65,000
Operating expenditure	8,100,000	3,200,000
Accounting profit	1,100,000	280,000
Taxable total profit	1,300,000	350,000

I can see from my files that the only exemptions from a CFC charge requiring consideration are the low profits exemption and the low profit margin exemption.

Please explain whether Set Ltd will be subject to a CFC charge in respect of either Dee Co or En Co.

(d)   Steam Ltd – Project Whistle

Steam Ltd will commence Project Whistle in 2023. As part of the project, Steam Ltd will engage in scientific research, some of which will qualify for the additional 130% tax deduction available in respect of qualifying research and development expenditure. Due to the significant costs involved, Steam Ltd is expected to make a trading loss in the year ending 31 December 2023.

Please explain:

–   how any trading loss made by Steam Ltd in the year ending 31 December 2023 can be relieved.

–   the factors to consider when choosing between the available reliefs.

Regards

Ms Driver

Required:

Provide the explanations requested in the email from Ms Driver. The following marks are available:

(a)	Ghost Ltd – corporation tax payments.	**(9 marks)**
(b)	Wagon Ltd – value added tax (VAT).	**(4 marks)**
(c)	Dee Co and En Co – controlled foreign company (CFC) charge.	**(4 marks)**
(d)	Steam Ltd – Project Whistle.	**(8 marks)**

(Total: 25 marks)

76   GRAND LTD GROUP *Walk in the footsteps of a top tutor*

You should assume that today's date is 4 September 2022.

Your manager has had a meeting with Bryce, the managing director of Grand Ltd. Extracts from the email prepared by your manager following the meeting, together with a schedule of information from Bryce, are set out below.

Extract from the email from your manager – dated 3 September 2022

> **(a)   Grand Ltd group of companies**
>
> Grand Ltd has two wholly owned subsidiaries, Colca Ltd and Sautso Ltd, and also owns shares in a number of other companies. All of the group companies are UK resident trading companies, which prepare accounts to 31 March each year. All supplies made by the group are subject to value added tax (VAT) at the standard rate. Sautso Ltd has been a member of the Grand Ltd group for many years.
>
> **Sale of Colca Ltd**
>
> Grand Ltd purchased the whole of the ordinary share capital of Colca Ltd for £800,000 on 1 November 2015. The value of Colca Ltd has fallen and the company is to be sold on 1 December 2022. Two separate offers have been received: offer A and offer B.
>
> **Offer A – in respect of a sale of the company's shares**
>
> –   The purchaser will pay £730,000 for the whole of the ordinary share capital of Colca Ltd. This amount will be reduced by any tax liabilities payable by Colca Ltd arising as a result of the company being sold.

Extract from the email from your manager – dated 3 September 2022 (continued)

Offer B – in respect of a sale of the company's trade and assets

– The purchaser will pay £695,000 for the trade and assets of Colca Ltd.

Colca Ltd – expected asset values on 1 December 2022

	£
Oribi building	410,000
Atuel building	230,000
Items of machinery	25,000
Net current assets (at cost)	30,000
	695,000

There is further information in respect of these assets in the attached schedule from Bryce.

The value of Colca Ltd's goodwill is negligible and should be ignored for the purposes of this work.

Please prepare a memorandum for the client file.

Note: When calculating the post-tax proceeds in respect of the two offers, you should assume that tax relief at the rate of 19% will be obtained in respect of any allowable capital losses.

The memorandum should cover the following:

(i) **Offer A – in respect of a sale of the company's shares**

– An explanation of whether or not tax relief will be available in respect of the capital loss arising on the sale of the shares.

– An explanation of the tax implications of Colca Ltd leaving the Grand Ltd group whilst still owning the Atuel building. This explanation should not include any calculations.

– A calculation of the expected post-tax proceeds.

(ii) **Offer B – in respect of a sale of the company's trade and assets**

– A calculation of the expected post-tax proceeds. For this purpose, you should ignore any chargeable gains or allowable losses arising on the sale of the items of machinery.

– In relation to the sale of the items of machinery, an explanation as to whether or not they will result in chargeable gains or allowable capital losses and of the availability of rollover relief.

– An explanation of the companies to which Colca Ltd can transfer any capital losses arising on the assets sold.

(iii) **Offer B – value added tax (VAT)**

– In respect of offer B: an explanation as to whether or not Colca Ltd should charge VAT on the sale of its buildings and/or its machinery.

Extract from the email from your manager – dated 3 September 2022 (continued)

(b) **Tax evasion and tax avoidance**

Bryce and his daughter (who is a tax expert in the field of capital allowances) have drawn up a plan which they claim will enable a company to claim a tax deduction of 180% of the cost of new machinery. The plan is complicated in that it involves the creation of a new, wholly-owned subsidiary and a series of contracts involving the leasing and sub-leasing of the machinery between the two companies.

I have not looked at the plan in detail because, even if it would appear to have the intended tax effect, I am sure that it would fall within the general anti-abuse rule (GAAR).

Please prepare notes which:

– Distinguish between tax evasion and tax avoidance and state the purpose of the GAAR.

– Explain why the GAAR is likely to apply to this particular plan.

Tax manager

Schedule of information from Bryce – dated 3 September 2022

Colca Ltd – details of assets

Colca Ltd uses both the Oribi and Atuel buildings in its trade.

	Oribi building	*Atuel building*	*Machinery*
Date of purchase	1 February 2016	1 April 2020	N/A
Purchase cost	£320,000 (note 1)	£255,000 (note 2)	(note 3)
Value added tax option to tax made?	No	No	N/A

Notes

1 On 1 December 2015, Colca Ltd sold a machine for £74,000 resulting in a chargeable gain of £17,000. This gain was rolled over against the purchase of the Oribi building.

2 Colca Ltd purchased the Atuel building from Sautso Ltd for £255,000, its market value at that time. As Colca Ltd and Sautso Ltd are both 100% subsidiaries of Grand Ltd, the transfer of the building took place at no gain, no loss.

Sautso Ltd had purchased the Atuel building, new and unused, for £340,000 on 1 January 2020. Structures and buildings allowances have not been claimed by Sautso Ltd or Colca Ltd.

3 All of the items of machinery are movable. The sale of the machinery will give rise to a balancing charge of £12,100.

Most of the items of machinery are worth less than their original cost. However, a small number of items are particularly specialised, such that their current market value exceeds their original cost.

Required:

(a) Prepare the memorandum as requested in the email from your manager. The following marks are available:

   (i) Offer A – in respect of a sale of the company's shares. **(8 marks)**

   (ii) Offer B – in respect of a sale of the company's trade and assets. **(11 marks)**

   (iii) Offer B – value added tax (VAT). **(7 marks)**

(b) Tax evasion and tax avoidance. **(5 marks)**

Professional marks will be awarded for the approach taken to problem solving, the clarity of the explanations and calculations, the effectiveness with which the information is communicated, and the overall presentation and style of the memorandum and notes.

(4 marks)

Note: The following indexation factors should be used, where necessary.

November 2015 to December 2017	0.070
February 2016 to December 2017	0.070

(Total: 35 marks)

---

77 PLAD LTD AND QUIL LTD (ADAPTED) *Walk in the footsteps of a top tutor*

You should assume that today's date is 4 March 2022.

Your manager has sent you a schedule prepared by Claire Falkner concerning her company, Plad Ltd, and a new company, Quil Ltd, which she intends to incorporate on 1 April 2022. The covering email from your manager details the work he requires you to do. The two documents are set out below.

Attachment: Schedule from Claire Falkner – dated 3 March 2022

> **Plad Ltd**
>
> I have owned the whole of the ordinary share capital of Plad Ltd since 2007. Plad Ltd trades mainly in the UK and is a UK resident company. It purchases components from third parties to be assembled into finished products. It also has a permanent establishment in the country of Chekka. The profits realised in Chekka are subject to 14% Chekkan business tax. There is no double tax treaty between the UK and the country of Chekka.
>
> The budgeted taxable profits of Plad Ltd for the year ending 31 March 2023 are set out below. Plad Ltd's profitability is very stable, so please assume that the figures for the following year will be the same.
>
> | | £ |
> |---|---|
> | Trading profit in the UK | 58,000 |
> | Trading profit in the country of Chekka (before deduction of 14% Chekkan tax) | 7,000 |
> | | ——— |
> | Taxable total profits | 65,000 |
> | | ——— |

Attachment: Schedule from Claire Falkner – dated 3 March 2022 (continued)

Quil Ltd

Quil Ltd will be incorporated, registered for value added tax (VAT) and commence trading on 1 April 2022. It will trade in the UK and be a UK resident company.

From a commercial standpoint, my intention was to own Quil Ltd personally. However, if there is a sufficient tax advantage, I will consider establishing the company as a wholly-owned subsidiary of Plad Ltd.

The first two years of budgeted results of Quil Ltd are set out below. The trading profit/(loss) figures are before the deduction of capital allowances, but have otherwise been adjusted for the purposes of corporation tax. The chargeable gain will not qualify for rollover relief.

Year ending 31 March 2023 – trading loss   £(5,000)
Year ending 31 March 2024 – trading profit   £162,000   Chargeable gain   £16,000

On 1 April 2022, Quil Ltd will purchase the following capital assets:

New machinery and equipment   £40,000 (excluding VAT)
Newly constructed building used for   £600,000 (excluding VAT)
manufacturing and storage

Construction of the building will begin on 1 April 2022. Quil Ltd will start using the building in its trade from 1 January 2023.

The cost of the building includes £230,000 in respect of thermal insulation and air cooling equipment in order to create the appropriate conditions for manufacturing. The cost also includes £150,000 in respect of land.

Value added tax (VAT)

I would like the two companies to register as a group for VAT purposes (to avoid the need to charge VAT on intra group supplies and to generally reduce administration) and for the group to continue to use the annual accounting scheme currently used by Plad Ltd. I appreciate this would mean that the two companies would be jointly and severally liable for the group's VAT liability.

Plad Ltd – unreported chargeable gain

I have just discovered that a chargeable gain of £21,600 realised by Plad Ltd in the year ended 31 March 2018 was omitted from its corporation tax return. However, because the gain arose in respect of the sale of land, it was reported for the purposes of stamp duty land tax. Accordingly, I assume we do not need to do anything and that HM Revenue and Customs (HMRC) will contact us about this at some point.

Extract from the email from your manager – dated 4 March 2022

Please carry out the following work:

(a) Group relief

In order to help Claire make her decision on the ownership of Quil Ltd, advise her of the tax advantage of Quil Ltd being a wholly-owned subsidiary of Plad Ltd, such that the two companies form a group relief group. You should carry out this work in three stages:

(i) Explain, with supporting calculations, the maximum amount of group relief which Plad Ltd would need to receive for the year ending 31 March 2023 such that none of its double tax relief in respect of the Chekkan tax would be wasted and its UK corporation tax payable would be £nil. You should assume the rate of corporation tax is 19% for all accounting periods.

(ii) Prepare calculations of the corporation tax liabilities of the two companies for the two years ending 31 March 2024. Your calculations should be on the basis that the trading loss of Quil Ltd will be used as soon as possible whilst restricting the amount of group relief in an accounting period to the maximum figure you calculated in part (i).

You SHOULD NOT provide any explanations of these calculations.

(iii) Conclude by explaining the tax advantage of Quil Ltd becoming a wholly-owned subsidiary of Plad Ltd, as opposed to being owned personally by Claire.

When carrying out this work, you should be aware of the following:

- in the year ending 31 March 2023, £200,000 of the annual investment allowance will be available to Quil Ltd, and Quil Ltd will claim the maximum capital allowances available

- neither of the two companies will be required to pay corporation tax in quarterly instalments. This will be true regardless of who owns Quil Ltd.

(b) Group registration for value added tax (VAT) purposes

Explain any additional matters of which Claire should be aware in relation to group registration for VAT purposes. Note that Claire is not a sole trader.

(c) Plad Ltd – unreported chargeable gain

Explain the implications for Plad Ltd, and our firm, of the failure to report the chargeable gain to HM Revenue and Customs (HMRC). You SHOULD NOT address money laundering or the possibility of penalties, as I have already spoken to Claire about these matters.

Tax manager

Required:

Prepare the notes as requested in the email from your manager. The following marks are available:

(a) Group relief. **(17 marks)**

(b) Group registration for value added tax (VAT) purposes. **(3 marks)**

(c) Plad Ltd – unreported chargeable gain. **(5 marks)**

(Total: 25 marks)

78   KITZ LTD

You should assume that today's date is 4 September 2022.

The finance director of Kitz Ltd has requested advice on the tax implications of selling shares in a subsidiary company, making a loan to another subsidiary company, and selling an intangible fixed asset.

Kitz Ltd:

–   Kitz Ltd owns 100% of the ordinary shares in Feld Ltd.

–   Kitz Ltd and Feld Ltd are UK resident trading companies.

–   Both companies prepare accounts to 31 March annually.

–   Neither company is a small or medium-sized enterprise (SME) for the purpose of transfer pricing.

Kitz Ltd – sale of 7,500 ordinary shares (a 75% holding) in Mayr Ltd on 1 July 2022:

–   Mayr Ltd is a UK resident trading company.

–   The shares, which represent the whole of Kitz Ltd's shareholding, were sold to an unconnected purchaser for £790,000.

–   Kitz Ltd had acquired these shares on 1 March 2015 for £455,000.

–   Kitz Ltd had sold a warehouse to Mayr Ltd on 8 April 2017 for its market value on that date of £165,000.

–   Kitz Ltd had purchased the warehouse on 12 May 2015 for £129,000.

–   Mayr Ltd still owned the warehouse on 1 July 2022.

Kitz Ltd – loan to Feld Ltd:

–   Kitz Ltd will make a loan of £450,000 to Feld Ltd on 1 April 2023.

–   Feld Ltd will use the loan to purchase goodwill and office premises for use in its business, and 70% of the ordinary share capital of Durn Ltd.

–   The cost of these acquisitions is as follows:

	£
Goodwill	68,000
Office premises	137,000
70% shareholding in Durn Ltd	245,000

–   Kitz Ltd will charge interest at the rate of 7% per year on this loan.

–   Feld Ltd has been offered a loan of £450,000 from a bank at an interest rate of 10% per annum.

–   In the year ending 31 March 2024, Feld Ltd will have a trading profit of £587,000 and interest receivable of £48,100.

Kitz Ltd – proposed sale of a patent:

–   Kitz Ltd will sell a patent to Durn Ltd on 3 May 2023 for £72,000.

–   Kitz Ltd purchased the patent for £60,000 on 3 May 2018.

–   The tax written down value of the patent on 3 May 2023 will be £30,000.

–   Kitz Ltd has always used the patent in its business.

Required:

(a) **Explain the chargeable gains implications for Kitz Ltd arising from the sale of its shares in Mayr Ltd on 1 July 2022.**

Note: No calculations are required for part (a). **(6 marks)**

(b) **Explain, with brief supporting calculations, the corporation tax implications for both Kitz Ltd and Feld Ltd in respect of the interest charged on the loan by Kitz Ltd to Feld Ltd for the year ending 31 March 2024.** **(7 marks)**

(c) (i) **Explain the corporation tax implications for Kitz Ltd of the sale of the patent to Durn Ltd on 3 May 2023, assuming Kitz Ltd does not make a claim for intangible fixed asset rollover relief.** **(3 marks)**

(ii) **Explain why rollover relief for intangible fixed assets will be available in respect of the sale of the patent to Durn Ltd, and, on the assumption the maximum rollover relief is claimed, calculate the impact of the claim on Kitz Ltd's corporation tax liability for the year ending 31 March 2024.** **(4 marks)**

(Total: 20 marks)

79 MITA *Walk in the footsteps of a top tutor*

You should assume that today's date is 3 March 2023.

Your manager has received a letter from Mita, the owner and managing director of Porth Ltd, a client of your firm. Extracts from that letter, together with extracts from an email from your manager detailing the work you are required to do, are set out below.

Extracts from the letter from Mita – dated 2 March 2023

Sale of 4,000 ordinary shares in Porth Ltd

On 1 May 2023, I am going to sell 4,000 shares in Porth Ltd to my brother, Ned. I note from the work you have already done that the current market value of these shares is £260,000. However, because I am keen to get Ned involved, I have agreed a price of £200,000. Ned, who is UK resident, will sign the claim for capital gains tax gift holdover relief in respect of this sale.

Joint venture – Quod Ltd

On 1 April 2023, I shall incorporate a new company, Quod Ltd. On that day, Quod Ltd will register for value added tax (VAT) and begin to trade. It will develop a range of products over the next few years.

The planned ownership of the ordinary share capital of Quod Ltd is as follows:

Porth Ltd	60%
Either Mr Berm or Mr Berm's company, BJB Ltd	30%
CX Ltd	10%

Porth Ltd, BJB Ltd and CX Ltd are UK resident companies. Mr Berm is resident in the UK.

Quod Ltd – financial information

I have calculated Quod Ltd's budgeted tax adjusted trading loss for the year ending 31 March 2024 to be £44,000.

When calculating the loss, I deducted the whole of the costs attributable to scientific research amounting to £102,000 (note 1). I also deducted £1,000 in respect of the Cloque brand (note 2), as it will be amortised over a period of 35 years.

Note 1: Scientific research costs

	£
Equipment and computer hardware	27,500
Materials	21,000
Rent	17,400
Electricity and water	6,600
Staff costs	29,500
	───────
	102,000
	───────

– The rent is an appropriate allocation of the rent payable for Quod Ltd's premises for the year.

– All of the staff costs relate to employees of Quod Ltd with the exception of £7,000 paid to an external contractor provided by an unconnected company.

Note 2: Purchase of the Cloque brand

On 1 April 2023, Quod Ltd will purchase the Cloque brand for £35,000. Advice will then be required on how to develop this brand through the use of social media. It is intended that Quod Ltd will purchase this advice from a company based outside the UK (in a country where the rate of VAT is 9%) rather than as a standard-rated supply from a VAT registered supplier based in the UK.

Acquisition of Ryb Ltd

On 1 May 2023, Porth Ltd will purchase the whole of the ordinary share capital of Ryb Ltd. For the purposes of UK tax, Ryb Ltd is resident in the UK. Ryb Ltd trades through a permanent establishment (PE) in the country of Tirona.

Ryb Ltd's budgeted taxable trading profit for the year ending 31 March 2024, all of which relates to its activities in Tirona, is £75,000. Ryb Ltd has no other source of taxable income and is not expected to make any chargeable gains during the year.

Once we are confident of the profitability of the PE in Tirona, it is intended that Ryb Ltd will establish PEs in two other countries.

Extracts from the email from your manager – dated 3 March 2023

Additional information in respect of Porth Ltd, Quod Ltd and Ryb Ltd

Porth Ltd

– Mita owns the whole of the ordinary share capital of Porth Ltd, which is an unquoted trading company.

– Mita began trading as an unincorporated business on 1 June 2015. On 1 April 2018, when the assets of her business were worth £120,000, she incorporated her business by selling all of the assets to Porth Ltd in exchange for 10,000 ordinary shares. This sale resulted in total chargeable gains of £37,400, all of which were relieved by incorporation relief.

– Porth Ltd prepares accounts to 31 March each year. It does not own any assets other than those which are used in its trade.

Quod Ltd

– Quod Ltd will be a small enterprise for the purposes of the additional tax relief available for expenditure on research and development.

– I have already established that the research to be carried out by Quod Ltd will qualify for this relief.

– Quod Ltd WILL NOT surrender any part of the loss in return for a cash refund from HM Revenue and Customs (HMRC).

Ryb Ltd

– Ryb Ltd has not made an election to exempt the profits of its overseas permanent establishment (PE) from UK tax.

– The rate of corporation tax in the country of Tirona is 14%. Other than that, the tax system in Tirona is the same as that in the UK. There is no double tax treaty between the UK and Tirona.

Please carry out the following work:

(a) **Sale of 4,000 shares in Porth Ltd on 1 May 2023**

– Calculate Mita's capital gains tax (CGT) liability in respect of this proposed sale to Ned assuming all available reliefs will be claimed.

Mita is resident in the UK. You should assume she will be a higher rate taxpayer in the tax year 2023/24 and that the CGT annual exempt amount WILL NOT be available to her.

(b) **Quod Ltd**

- Explain the tax deduction which will be available to Quod Ltd in respect of the scientific research costs of £102,000 to be incurred in the year ending 31 March 2024.

- Explain the tax treatment of the proposed purchase of the Cloque brand (an intangible fixed asset) for £35,000.

- Calculate the amended budgeted tax adjusted trading loss for Quod Ltd for the year ending 31 March 2024 taking into account the explanations requested above.

- Explain how much of Quod Ltd's amended budgeted trading loss will be available for use by Porth Ltd.

- Explain the value added tax (VAT) implications of Quod Ltd purchasing advice from the overseas supplier, rather than the one based in the UK.

(c) **Ryb Ltd**

- Explain why the profits of Ryb Ltd are subject to UK corporation tax.

- Calculate Ryb Ltd's expected UK corporation tax liability for the year ending 31 March 2024 based on the information available.

- Discuss the advantages and disadvantages of Ryb Ltd making an election to exempt the profits of its PE in Tirona from UK tax.

Tax manager

Required:

Carry out the work required as requested in the email from your manager. The following marks are available:

(a)	Sale of 4,000 shares in Porth Ltd on 1 May 2023.	(4 marks)
(b)	Quod Ltd.	(15 marks)
(c)	Ryb Ltd.	(6 marks)

You may assume that the rates and allowances for the tax year 2021/22 will continue to apply for the foreseeable future.

(Total: 25 marks)

80   REP LTD *Walk in the footsteps of a top tutor*

You should assume that today's date is 8 September 2022.

Your manager has received an email from Lamar. Lamar is the managing director and majority shareholder in REP Ltd. Lamar and REP Ltd are clients of your firm. Your manager has forwarded the email to you together with an email detailing the work you are required to do.

Email extract from Lamar: dated 7 September 2022

Potential investment in JAY Ltd

We are in discussion with the management of CRO Ltd regarding the establishment of a new company, JAY Ltd. If it proceeds, JAY Ltd will commence trading on 1 April 2023 and carry on its business activities in the country of Garia, where it will manufacture computer components.

CRO Ltd is proposing that REP Ltd would own 30% of the ordinary share capital of JAY Ltd with CRO Ltd owning the remaining 70%. However, we regard this potential investment as somewhat risky, such that if we decide to proceed, we may prefer to own just 20% of JAY Ltd rather than 30%.

JAY Ltd is expected to be profitable in the year ending 31 March 2024. However, there is the possibility that it will be loss making in either that year or in future years.

JAY Ltd's tax adjusted trading profit for the year ending 31 March 2024 is budgeted to be £135,000, all of which will relate to its activities in Garia. JAY Ltd will have no other source of taxable income and will not make any chargeable gains during this year.

We have not been involved in a joint venture like this before and we have no experience of carrying on a business outside the UK. We would appreciate your advice on the following three extracts from the documentation provided to us by CRO Ltd:

(i)   'It has not yet been determined whether JAY Ltd will be resident in the UK or in Garia. If JAY Ltd is resident in the UK, it will be considered to be carrying on its business through a permanent establishment in Garia.'

(ii)   'If JAY Ltd is resident in the UK, we will consider making an election to exempt its overseas trading profits from UK tax.'

(iii)   'We have been advised that if JAY Ltd is resident in Garia, this will not result in a charge under the controlled foreign company (CFC) rules.'

Purchase of investment property

We are considering the purchase by REP Ltd of a new, unused commercial building for £200,000 plus 20% value added tax (VAT). REP Ltd would then grant a 20-year lease of this building to a retailer. Will REP Ltd be able to recover the VAT charged by the vendor on the sale of this building?

Proposed gift of shares to trust

I established a discretionary trust for the benefit of my nieces and nephews on 1 August 2012.

On 1 November 2022, I am planning to give 20,000 of my shares in REP Ltd to this trust. After I have made the gift, I will still own 60,000 shares (60% of the company). You have already advised me that these shares are not relevant business property for the purposes of business property relief, due to the investment activities of REP Ltd. Accordingly, I am aware that the gift on 1 November 2022 may result in an inheritance tax (IHT) liability. If I decide to make the gift, I will pay any IHT due.

I have made the following gifts in the past:

- 1 August 2012 Cash to trustees on the creation of the trust 120,000
- 1 February 2018 Cash to brother 35,000
- 1 May 2018 Additional cash to trustees 170,000
- 1 July 2022 Cash to sister 45,000

None of these gifts have resulted in an IHT liability.

Email extract from your manager: dated 8 September 2022

Please prepare notes for use at a meeting with Lamar.

I want you to lead the meeting. You should therefore set out the notes in a manner which will make it easy for you to refer to them during the meeting.

The notes should cover the following matters:

(a)   Knowledge obtained from advising other clients

We have a number of existing clients which trade from permanent establishments situated overseas, and a few years ago we had a client with a presence in the country of Garia.

Set out the points you will make in order to explain the extent to which REP Ltd can benefit from the knowledge we have gained from advising these other clients.

(b) **Investment in JAY Ltd**

Additional information

– REP Ltd and CRO Ltd are UK resident companies which prepare accounts to 31 March each year.

– Business profits generated in Garia are subject to 13% business tax in that country.

– There is no double tax treaty between the UK and Garia.

(i) **Residency of JAY Ltd**

Explanations of the relevance of the country of residency of JAY Ltd in relation to:

– the amount of corporation tax payable in the UK and Garia in respect of its profits; and

– the relief available to REP Ltd if JAY Ltd's business in Garia were to make a trading loss.

Before you start, take some time to identify the different possibilities which need to be addressed, recognising that we do not yet know what percentage of JAY Ltd will be owned by REP Ltd.

(ii) **Election to exempt the profits of JAY Ltd's overseas permanent establishment from UK tax**

List the implications of JAY Ltd making this election.

(iii) **Controlled foreign company (CFC) rules**

I can confirm that a CFC charge will not arise if JAY Ltd is resident in Garia. However, I want to provide Lamar with an explanation of the purpose of the CFC rules and the charge which can be levied under them.

(c) **Purchase of investment property**

Explain the matters which Lamar should be aware of in relation to REP Ltd recovering the value added tax (VAT) which would be incurred on the purchase of the investment property.

There is no need to consider partial exemption or the capital goods scheme.

(d) **Proposed gift of shares to trust on 1 November 2022**

A calculation of the inheritance tax (IHT) which would be payable by Lamar if he were to give 20,000 shares in REP Ltd to the trust on 1 November 2022 as planned. Your calculation should indicate the availability or otherwise of all relevant annual exemptions.

Where relevant, you should use the following values for a single ordinary share in REP Ltd:

Shareholding	Up to 25%	26% to 50%	51% to 74%	75% or more
Value per share	£8	£11	£17	£24

Lamar currently owns 80% of the ordinary share capital of REP Ltd. The remaining shares in the company are owned by individuals who have no connection with Lamar.

Tax manager

Required:

Prepare the meeting notes as requested in the email from your manager. The following marks are available:

(a)   Knowledge obtained from advising other clients.   (5 marks)

(b)   Investment in JAY Ltd.

    (i)   Residency of JAY Ltd.   (9 marks)

    (ii)   Election to exempt the profits of JAY Ltd's overseas permanent establishment from UK tax.   (3 marks)

    (iii)   Controlled foreign company (CFC) rules.   (3 marks)

(c)   Purchase of investment property.   (5 marks)

(d)   Proposed gift of shares to trust on 1 November 2022.   (6 marks)

Professional marks will be awarded for the approach taken to planning the content, the clarity of the explanations and calculations, the effectiveness with which the information is communicated, and the overall presentation and style of the notes.   (4 marks)

(Total: 35 marks)

Section 2

ANSWERS TO PRACTICE QUESTIONS

TAXATION OF INDIVIDUALS

EMPLOYMENT

1   MORICE AND BABEEN PLC *Walk in the footsteps of a top tutor*

Key answer tips

This question covers provision of benefits to employees and CGT with investors' relief. It is not likely to have been a popular question in the exam, as there are ten marks purely on the SAYE scheme – an area that had not been tested before in the ATX exam. However, part (b) covers some much more mainstream benefits.

Part (a) requires in-depth knowledge of the SAYE scheme conditions, which may have put off many students. However, there are six and a half marks available for applying the tax treatment of a tax advantaged share scheme to figures given in the question, so a solid pass could still have been obtained without precise knowledge of the SAYE conditions.

Part (b) on the income tax and national insurance implications of private medical insurance, beneficial loans and the use of an employee's own car for business journeys should have been straight forward. These are all TX areas.

Part (c) offers some easy marks, as long as you recognised that investors' relief would be available.

This question contains a mix of numerical and discursive requirements. It is advisable to use the spreadsheet functionality for calculations and the word processor functionality for any discursive requirements when in the exam. Ensure you label your answer clearly so it is clear which requirement you are answering.

The highlighted words in the written sections are key phrases that markers are looking for.

(a)   **SAYE scheme**

Tutor's top tips

This part of the question is slightly unusual for a section B question as the requirement at the end of the question does not actually tell you what you need to do.

If you look back at the information in the question you will see that there are really two requirements here:

1   *Explain whether or not each of the proposed rules will be acceptable for a SAYE scheme.*

2   *Explain, with calculations, the tax and national insurance liabilities for the employee in the illustrative example.*

Whether or not the proposed rules will be acceptable for a SAYE scheme

Tutor's top tips

You need to have a good knowledge of the SAYE scheme conditions to be able to answer this part of the question, and then you need to apply these conditions to the scenario to ensure that you score a good mark.

The investment period of five years is acceptable. SAYE schemes can run for three or five years.

The minimum monthly investment of £5 is acceptable, but the maximum of £750 is not acceptable. The maximum monthly investment for a tax advantaged scheme is £500.

The scheme must be open to all employees:

- It is not acceptable to have a minimum age limit of 21.
- It is also not acceptable to exclude part time employees.
- However, it is acceptable to exclude employees who have worked for the company for less than three years.

Tutorial note

It is acceptable to exclude employees who have worked for the company for less than a qualifying period, as long as the period chosen does not exceed five years.

The share options can be granted at a discount, as long as the exercise price is no less than 80% of the market value at the date of grant. The price of £2.48 will, therefore, be acceptable, as long as the market value at 1 January 2023 is not more than £3.10 (£2.48/80%) per share.

Tutor's top tips

You are asked to explain, with calculations, the tax and national insurance liabilities for the employee in respect of:

- *grant of the share options*
- *exercise of the share options, and*
- *sale of the shares.*

Even if you did not know the conditions for the SAYE scheme, you should still be able to answer most of this part of the requirement if you knew the general tax treatment for tax advantaged share option schemes.

Note that there are three different aspects to deal with here, so make sure that you cover all of these and clearly label your answer.

Grant of share options

There is no tax liability on the grant of the share options.

Exercise of share options

There is no tax liability on the exercise of the share options.

Sale of shares

There will be a chargeable gain on the sale of the shares, which will be subject to capital gains tax.

The cost of the shares will be:

	£
Amount saved (£250 × 12 months × 5 years)	15,000

The number of shares purchased at exercise will therefore be £15,000/£2.48 per share	6,048

The gain on disposal of 6,048 shares will be as follows:

	£
Proceeds (6,048 × £4.00)	24,192
Less: Cost	(15,000)
Chargeable gain	9,192

Tutor's top tips

Don't stop here. You need to explain how the gain will be taxed, but there is no information about the tax position of the illustrative employee.

Have they used their annual exempt amount?

Are they a basic rate or a higher rate taxpayer?

You need to consider all possibilities.

This gain may be covered by the annual exempt amount of £12,300, if the employee has no other chargeable disposals in 2027/28 (the tax year of sale), in which case no tax will be payable.

If the annual exempt amount is not available, the rate of capital gains tax will depend on the level of the employee's taxable income:

- If the employee has taxable income of more than £37,700, then the gain will be taxed at 20%.
- If the employee has taxable income of less than £37,700, gains falling into the basic rate band will be taxed at 10% with the excess being taxed at 20%.

Business asset disposal relief (formerly entrepreneurs' relief) will not be available as the employee will not own 5% of the company's ordinary share capital.

National insurance

There are no national insurance implications in respect of a SAYE scheme.

(b)   Income tax and national insurance implications for the employees of Babeen plc

Tutor's top tips

*The benefits set out here were tested at TX. TX level knowledge is often tested at ATX, and **explaining** the tax treatment of benefits, rather than just calculating them, is a popular requirement.*

Note that you are only asked to talk about the tax implications for the employees in this question, not the employer.

(i)   Medical care scheme

Private health insurance

Private health insurance is a taxable benefit.

The benefit will be the cost to the employer of £470.

Interest-free loans

As long as the amount borrowed does not exceed £10,000 at any point in the tax year, there will be no taxable benefit.

If the employee borrows more than £10,000 there will be a taxable benefit.

The benefit is calculated by multiplying the official rate of interest of 2% by the amount outstanding during the tax year, giving a maximum annual benefit of:

$$(£12,500 × 2\%) = £250$$

If the amount borrowed changes during the year, there are two alternative methods of calculating the benefit:

- The average method, based on the average amount outstanding
  = (balance b/f + balance c/f) ÷ 2
- The strict method, based on the actual amounts outstanding during the year.

Either the taxpayer or HMRC can elect for the strict method.

These taxable benefits will be subject to income tax at 20% if they fall within the basic rate band or 40% if the employee is a higher rate taxpayer.

Employees do not pay national insurance contributions on private health insurance or beneficial loans.

(ii)   Payments for driving their own cars

Tutor's top tips

Don't forget to refer to the tax tables given in the exam. The approved mileage allowances are provided.

However, you do need to learn the approved allowance for passengers, as this is not given.

Mileage allowance

Employees are allowed to receive a tax free mileage allowance of 45p per mile for the first 10,000 business miles per tax year, and 25p per mile thereafter.

- If they receive less than these approved amounts, the shortfall can be deducted from taxable employment income. This means that employees of Babeen plc will be able to deduct a shortfall of 9p per mile (45p – 36p) for the first 10,000 business miles.
- If they receive more than the approved amounts, the excess will be subject to income tax.

Passenger allowance

There is a tax free allowance of 5p per mile for carrying a passenger, so the 3p per mile paid will be tax free. However, the shortfall of 2p per mile (5p – 3p) is not tax deductible.

National insurance

As the mileage allowance is no more than 45p per mile, there will be no national insurance contributions payable. There will also be no national insurance contributions payable on the additional 3p per mile.

Tutorial note

Even if the employee drove more than 10,000 miles and had a taxable benefit in respect of the mileage allowance, there would still be no national insurance contributions payable.

However, if the employer paid more than 45p per mile, the excess would be subject to class 1 national insurance.

(c)   Sale of shares in Wind Ltd

	£
Proceeds	150,000
Less: Cost (3,500 × £1)	(3,500)
Chargeable gain	146,500
Less: Annual exempt amount	(12,300)
Taxable gain	134,200
CGT (£134,200 × 10%)	13,420

The gain qualifies for investors' relief because the shares have been subscribed for in an unlisted trading company, have been owned for at least three years and Morice does not work for the company. The gain can therefore be taxed at 10%.

Tutorial note

The availability of investors' relief would be subject to the availability of the £10 million lifetime limit. As this relief is relatively new, it is assumed that Morice would have a sufficient amount of this lifetime limit available.

Examiner's report

In order to score well in part (a) it was important for candidates to address each of the detailed rules in the question as opposed to writing generally about share option schemes. Many candidates who attempted this question were knowledgeable about Save As You Earn schemes but only a minority took a sufficiently disciplined approach to score well.

The explanation of the tax liabilities in respect of the shares acquired under the scheme was not done particularly well. Many candidates lacked precise knowledge of this area such that they did not know that no tax would be charged until the shares were sold. In addition, it needed to be recognised that the position of each employee would vary depending on whether or not they had made any other capital gains and on the level of their taxable income; very few candidates considered these matters.

The medical care scheme in part (b) was not handled particularly well in that many candidates incorrectly stated that the provision of health insurance would be an exempt benefit for the employees. However, this was not too important as it was only a minor part of the answer. The provision of an interest free loan was also not dealt with as well as might have been expected. The question stated that the loan would be 'up to £12,500' so it was necessary to point out that loans of no more than £10,000 would be exempt.

The explanation of the implications of the payments to employees for driving their own cars was handled well. The only common error was the failure to recognise that there would be no national insurance implications.

The question asked for the tax implications 'for the employees' as opposed to the tax implications generally. Accordingly, it was necessary to consider the national insurance issues for the employees (but not the employer) and there was no need to address the ability of the employer to obtain tax relief for the costs incurred.

The final section of the question was not part of the question when it was originally set.

ACCA marking scheme		Marks
(a) Scheme rules		
Investment period and investment limits		1.5
Eligible employees		1.5
Share price		1.5
Illustrative example		
Grant and exercise of option		1.0
Gain		1.5
Capital gains tax		3.0
National insurance contributions		1.0
		11.0
	Maximum	10.0
(b) (i) Health insurance		0.5
Interest-free loan		2.5
National insurance contributions		0.5
(ii) Driving on company business		
Income tax		2.0
National insurance contributions		1.0
Carrying passengers		1.5
		8.0
	Maximum	7.0
(c) Capital gain		0.5
Annual exempt amount		0.5
CGT liability		0.5
Investors' relief conditions		2.0
		3.5
	Maximum	3.0
Total		**20.0**

2   HYSSOP LTD *Walk in the footsteps of a top tutor*

Key answer tips

This question is really three separate questions covering employment benefits, payment of a lease premium by a company and the VAT capital goods scheme. As usual, there are a few twists, such as partial business use for rollover relief and the fact that the lease is a depreciating asset, but there are still enough basic marks here for you to score a pass if you missed these trickier points.

The highlighted words in the written sections are key phrases that markers are looking for.

(a)   Assistance with home to work travel costs for Corin

Tutor's top tips

This part requires explanation and calculation of the cost of two alternative benefits from the point of view of the employee and the company. This type of requirement regularly appears in the ATX exam.

The key is to think about cash flows and to remember to include tax payable and tax savings.

Don't forget to consider national insurance contributions; these are payable by the employer on all benefits, but the employee only pays them on cash earnings.

You are specifically asked which is the most cost efficient for both Corin and Hyssop Ltd, so there will be marks for following through your figures and stating this.

    (i)   Cost to Corin

    Alternative 1 – Provision of a motorcycle

    Corin is a higher rate taxpayer, so will pay income tax at 40% on the annual taxable benefit.

    Corin will have no national insurance liability in respect of this benefit.

    The total cost of this option will be:

    Income tax on benefit (£3,160 × 40%) = total cost   £1,264
                                                     —————

    Alternative 2 – Payment towards the cost of driving and provision of parking place

    Provision of a parking place at or near an employee's normal place of work is an exempt benefit for income tax.

    Corin will pay income tax at 40% on the cash received as reimbursement of his driving costs, together with class 1 national insurance contributions at 2%.

The total cost of this option will be:

	£
Cost of driving	2,820
Less: Amount reimbursed	(2,240)
Additional cost of driving	580
Income tax and NICs on cash received (£2,240 × 42%)	941
Total cost	1,521

The most cost efficient option for Corin is therefore provision of the motorcycle.

Tutorial note

The approved mileage allowances are not relevant in this case as the driving costs are not related to journeys made in the course of Corin carrying out his duties of employment.

(ii)   **Cost to Hyssop Ltd**

Alternative 1 – Provision of a motorcycle

Hyssop Ltd will have to pay class 1A national insurance contributions of 13.8% in respect of the provision of the motorcycle.

The total cost to Hyssop Ltd is therefore:

	£
Lease cost	3,160
Employer's class 1A NICs (£3,160 × 13.8%)	436
Total cost	3,596

Alternative 2 – Payment towards the cost of driving and provision of parking place

As the provision of the parking place is an exempt benefit for income tax, there will be no class 1A liability for Hyssop Ltd.

Hyssop Ltd will have a class 1 national insurance liability at 13.8% in respect of the reimbursement of driving costs.

The total cost to Hyssop Ltd is therefore:

	£
Cost of driving reimbursed	2,240
Parking cost	920
Employer's class 1 NICs (£2,240 × 13.8%)	309
Total cost	3,469

The most cost efficient option for Hyssop Ltd is therefore the payment towards the cost of driving and provision of the parking place.

Hyssop Ltd will be able to deduct all the costs for corporation tax purposes under both options.

Tutorial note

As the amounts are deductible for corporation tax purposes under both options, there is no need to calculate the after-tax cost to Hyssop Ltd.

(b)   Corporation tax implications of the acquisition of the 40-year lease

Tutor's top tips

This part tests TX knowledge of the allowable deduction for a premium paid on a short lease. You may have forgotten the formula, but could still gain marks for knowing that there is a deduction from trading profits over the life of the lease and that it should be time apportioned in the year of payment.

There are also marks here for discussing rollover relief – a very popular topic in the ATX exam, so make sure that you are able to explain and apply the rules.

Allowable deduction

As Hyssop Ltd has paid a premium on the grant of a short lease on a property which is going to be used in its trade, a deduction is available for each year of the lease in calculating Hyssop Ltd's taxable trading income.

The annual deduction is calculated as:

$$\frac{\text{Amount of premium taxed as income on the landlord}}{\text{Number of years of the lease}}$$

The amount of the premium which is taxed as income on the landlord is £57,200 ((£260,000 × (51 – 40)/50)).

The annual deduction available to Hyssop Ltd is £1,430 (£57,200/40).

As the lease was only acquired on 1 February 2022, the deduction available in the year ended 31 December 2022 is restricted to £1,311 (£1,430 × 11/12).

Tutorial note

Alternatively, the amount of premium taxed as income on the landlord could be calculated as (£260,000 – (£260,000 × (40 – 1) × 2%)) = £57,200.

Rollover relief: gain on warehouse

The factory is used in Hyssop Ltd's trade, so the lease is a qualifying business asset, and it was acquired within the 12 months before the disposal of the warehouse. Therefore the full business use element of the gain arising may be deferred to the extent that the proceeds relating to the business use of the warehouse have been reinvested in the lease.

The warehouse will have been owned by Hyssop Ltd for four years (1 January 2019 to 31 December 2022).

The warehouse has been used by Hyssop Ltd in its trade for three years (1 January 2019 to 31 December 2021).

The proceeds relating to the business use element of the gain are £236,250 (75% × £315,000). This is less than the £260,000 premium reinvested in the acquisition of the lease, therefore the full 75% of the chargeable gain relating to the business use of the warehouse can be deferred against the acquisition of the lease. Accordingly, £12,390 (£16,520 × 75%) may be deferred.

The lease is for less than 60 years and so is a depreciating asset for capital gains purposes. Accordingly, the gain will be deferred until the earliest of:

–   The date of disposal of the lease

–   The date the leased factory ceases to be used in Hyssop Ltd's business

–   1 February 2032 (ten years after the acquisition of the lease).

The remaining gain of £4,130 (£16,520 × 25%), relating to the non-business use, will be included in Hyssop Ltd's corporation tax computation for the year ending 31 December 2022.

(c)   Value added tax (VAT) implications of the disposal of the warehouse

Tutor's top tips

VAT for land and buildings and the capital goods scheme are popular topics in the ATX exam, so you should be prepared to answer a question on this area.

At the date of sale, the warehouse is more than three years old. Accordingly, because Hyssop Ltd has not opted to tax it, the disposal will be exempt from VAT.

As the warehouse was newly constructed when it was purchased, VAT of £54,000 (£270,000 × 20%) would have been charged and, as the warehouse was used in its standard-rated business, this would have been wholly reclaimed by Hyssop Ltd in the year ended 31 December 2019.

As the disposal is exempt from VAT, VAT will have to be repaid to HM Revenue and Customs (HMRC) because the warehouse is deemed to have 0% taxable use for the remainder of the ten-year adjustment period under the capital goods scheme. The amount of £32,400 (£54,000 × 6/10 × (100% − 0%)) will be repayable to HMRC as a result of the disposal.

Tutorial note

A further £5,400 (£54,000 × 1/10 × (100% – 0%)) will also be repayable to HMRC in respect of the year ending 31 December 2022 as the warehouse has been rented out throughout this year, with no option to tax.

Examiner's report

The first part required candidates to consider two possible ways in which an employer could provide financial assistance to an employee in respect of home to work travel and to advise on the most cost efficient method.

Although this was, arguably, very straightforward, it was not easy to get right. As always, those candidates who thought before writing did considerably better than those who simply wrote. In particular, they recognised the importance of national insurance contributions.

Most candidates identified the income tax and corporation tax implications of the two alternatives. The one point that many missed out on was the fact that the provision of a parking space is an exempt benefit.

The problems related to the national insurance position. Some candidates missed this out completely. Others were simply not orderly enough, such that they did not earn as many marks as they could have done.

Candidates needed to recognise that the provision of a motorcycle to an employee would result in a liability to class 1A national insurance contributions for the employer but no liability to national insurance contributions for the employee. Whereas, making a payment towards an employee's driving costs would result in a liability to class 1 national insurance contributions for both the employer and the employee.

Many candidates wrote about the statutory mileage rates, but these are only relevant where payments are in respect of journeys made when carrying out employment duties, which was not the case here.

The second part of the question concerned a premium paid in respect of a lease and the availability of rollover relief. This part was not done particularly well.

There were two distinct aspects to this part of the question.

The first concerned the tax deduction available in respect of the premium paid. Most candidates were able to make a start on this but very few made it to the end. The first task was to determine the amount of the premium that would be taxed on the landlord as income. This amount was then divided by the number of years of the lease in order to determine the annual deduction. The deduction in the current period was then 11/12 of the annual deduction because the lease was entered into when there were eleven months of the accounting period remaining.

The second part of the question concerned the availability of rollover relief. Most candidates knew the basics of rollover relief. However, they did not score as well as they could have done for two reasons:

- The asset sold had not been used for the purposes of the trade for the whole of the period of ownership. As a result, although rollover relief was available, only the business-use proportion of the gain could be relieved and only that proportion of the proceeds needed to be reinvested in qualifying business assets.

- They failed to realise that the lease was a depreciating asset for the purposes of rollover relief, such that the gain would be deferred until the earliest of the date of disposal of the lease, the date the leased building ceased to be used in the business and ten years after the acquisition of the lease.

The final part of the question concerned the capital goods scheme for VAT and was not done particularly well. The capital goods scheme is not easy to explain and many candidates were unable to organise their thoughts and provide a coherent explanation of the implications of the disposal of a building.

Candidates would help themselves if they told the story from the beginning.

- The first point to make was that the input tax on the purchase of the building would have been recovered in full.

- It was then necessary to recognise that the sale of the building would be an exempt supply.

- As a result of the exempt supply, there will be deemed to be 0% taxable use of the building for the remainder of the ten-year adjustment period resulting in a repayment of VAT to HMRC.

		ACCA marking scheme		Marks
(a)	(i)	Cost of motorcycle option		1.5
		Cost of driving costs reimbursement option		3.0
		Conclusion		0.5
				5.0
	(ii)	Cost of provision of motorcycle		1.5
		Cost of driving costs reimbursement		1.0
		All costs deductible for corporation tax		0.5
		Conclusion		0.5
				3.5
			Maximum	3.0
(b)		Deduction:		
		Available against taxable trading income		1.0
		Amount		3.0
		Deferral relief available		3.0
		Date gain crystallises		2.0
				9.0
			Maximum	8.0

(c)	Disposal exempt		1.5
	Initial reclaim		1.0
	Repayment of VAT reclaimed previously y/e 31 December 2022		2.0
			–––
			4.5
		Maximum	4.0
			–––
Total			**20.0**
			–––

3 METHLEY LTD (ADAPTED) *Walk in the footsteps of a top tutor*

Key answer tips

This income tax focused section B question is really three separate questions about three independent taxpayers.

Requirement (a) tests the advanced level topic of share schemes, specifically the tax advantaged company share option plan.

Requirement (b) tests the income tax cost for an employee of taking a company car compared with a loan from the employer to buy the car themselves.

Requirement (c) tests the remittance basis.

All of these areas are regularly tested and should not cause problems for well-prepared students. As the three requirements are independent they could have been attempted in any order. Whichever order you attempt them in, make sure you allocate enough time to each requirement.

The highlighted words in the written sections are key phrases that markers are looking for in your answer.

(a) Simon – company share option scheme (CSOP) versus an award of shares

Tutor's top tips

Share schemes are a new topic at the strategic professional level and are regularly tested, so make sure you have learnt the detail. It is important to tailor your answer to the scenario and not just write everything you know about a particular scheme.

Acquisition of the shares

Under a CSOP, there will be no charge to income tax in respect of the grant or exercise of the option given that Simon intends to exercise the option between three and ten years after the date of the grant.

There will be a charge to income tax if Simon receives free shares. Simon would have an income tax liability of £10,000 (£25,000 × 40%) in the tax year 2023/24.

Disposal of the shares

On disposal of the CSOP shares by Simon in the tax year 2029/30, any gain will be subject to capital gains tax (CGT). The gain (or loss) will be calculated by reference to the amount paid for them.

If Simon is awarded free shares worth £25,000, the disposal in the tax year 2029/30 will again be subject to CGT. However, the cost will be the market value at the date of award, i.e. £25,000. Any gains will be subject to CGT and any losses will be allowable.

Tutorial note

As Simon is a director of Methley Ltd, and will have held the shares for more than two years, any gain on disposal under both options may qualify for business asset disposal relief (formerly entrepreneurs' relief). This gives a 10% rate of CGT provided Methley Ltd remains a trading company and Simon has at least a 5% shareholding.

(b)   Chris – provision of benefits

Tutor's top tips

Comparisons are a regular feature of the advanced taxation exam, so make sure you are ready to answer questions on the common scenarios. These include:

- *Employees: employment benefits vs. extra salary/loan*
- *Sole traders: lease an asset vs. buy an asset or take on an employee vs. take on a partner, and*
- *Small companies: take extra salary vs. take a dividend/pension contribution.*

Provision of the company motor car

List price of the motor car: £10,400 (£9,600 + £800)

Percentage to be used: 19% [15% + 1/5(75 – 55)]

Annual benefit: £1,976 (£10,400 × 19%)

The total amount taxable as employment income is therefore £10,128 (£3,828 ((£1,976 – £700) × 3) + £6,300) and the income tax cost to Chris is £4,051 (£10,128 × 40%).

Tutorial note

Remember that there is no 4% surcharge where a diesel car meets the RDE2 standard.

Provision of the loan

As the amount of the interest-free loan never exceeds £10,000, there is no taxable benefit in respect of it.

When the loan is written off, this will be treated as a distribution as Chris is a shareholder in Methley Ltd, which is a close company. Accordingly, an income tax charge of £3,120 (£9,600 × 32.5%) will arise in the year the loan is written off.

Provision of the loan will therefore result in a lower overall income tax liability for Chris.

(c) Yara – UK income tax on overseas income in the tax year 2021/22

Tutor's top tips

The remittance basis is tested frequently in the exam for a varying number of marks. It is important to tailor your answer to the scenario here and to not write everything you know about the remittance basis.

It would have been possible to answer this question by presenting full income tax computations including Yara's salary as well. However, Yara's salary is subject to UK income tax whether Yara claims the remittance basis or not, so it is quicker to 'work in the margin' and just think about the impact on Yara's overseas income given that her UK income will make her a higher rate taxpayer.

As Yara has been resident in the UK for seven tax years prior to 2021/22, she will be liable to pay a remittance basis charge of £30,000 if she continues to elect for the remittance basis.

In previous years Yara paid UK income tax of £4,000 (£10,000 × 40%) on her foreign rental income remitted to the UK. She would not have been liable to pay the remittance basis charge.

Claiming the remittance basis in 2021/22 would increase her income tax liability by £30,000 to £34,000 (£4,000 + £30,000).

However, if Yara does not claim the remittance basis in 2021/22, she will be taxed on the arising basis instead. In this case, she will pay tax on the full amount of the foreign rental income arising in the tax year of £24,000. This will result in UK income tax payable of £9,600 (£24,000 × 40%).

Yara will also be entitled to the personal allowance, which she lost in previous years when the remittance basis was claimed. As her net income will be £106,000 (£82,000 + £24,000), the personal allowance available will be restricted to £9,570 ((£12,570 − 0.5 × (£106,000 – £100,000))). This will result in an income tax saving of £3,828 (£9,570 × 40%).

Therefore Yara's income tax on her foreign rental income on the arising basis, net of the tax saving as a result of the personal allowance, will be £5,772 (£9,600 – £3,828).

Claiming the remittance basis would not be beneficial for Yara in 2021/22. Accordingly, her income tax liability for 2021/22 in respect of her foreign rental income will increase by £1,772 (£5,772 – £4,000) compared to that payable in previous years.

Examiner's report

Part (a) of this question required candidates to compare and contrast the tax implications of an employee acquiring and disposing of shares in their company if these are acquired either through a tax advantaged company share option scheme (CSOP), or alternatively as free shares.

Most candidates demonstrated good knowledge of the tax implications of acquiring the shares through a CSOP, which has been tested many times before. Some candidates omitted to answer this part of the requirement; a significant number of those who did confused the scheme with a Share Incentive Plan (SIP), whose rules are totally different. Share incentive schemes are tested on a regular basis at ATX, so candidates should be confident with the tax implications of each, and ensure that they don't confuse the implications of the different schemes.

Note that this part of the question has been amended since it was originally set.

Part (b) of this question tested the income tax implications of two very commonly provided taxable benefits – a company motor car, and a beneficial loan. This is essentially brought forward knowledge from TX, but there were quite a lot of details to assimilate, and the majority of candidates did not take all of these into account. In order to provide a meaningful comparison of the income tax cost of each benefit, a candidate must ensure that all aspects of each scenario are considered. In particular, the car was to be provided for a three year period, before being transferred to the employee, and the loan was to be made for the same three year period, before being written off. The majority of candidates focused on the annual benefit calculation, but failed to consider that this situation would apply for three years, and then recognise the impact of the transfer/writing off. This is what essentially distinguished this as an ATX question – the ability to 'see the full picture' and advise on a holistic basis, taking into account all relevant details within a scenario. Candidates should be prepared for more questions of this style in future exams.

Part (c) dealt with the consequences of a UK resident, but non-domiciled individual claiming the remittance basis of taxation in respect of overseas income. This was clearly a question which candidates were prepared for and most scored well on this question part, recognising the need to compare the individual's income tax liability for the tax year on both an arising and a remittance basis, to determine which was lower. Almost all identified and dealt correctly with the remittance basis charge, which would be charged for the first time in the current tax year due to the individual's period of residence in the UK. However, very few actually answered the precise question set, which was to calculate the increase in the taxpayer's income tax liability in this tax year, compared with previous years, rather than just the difference between the arising and the remittance basis for the current year only. While this didn't lose the candidate many marks, it does highlight the need to read the question carefully, and ensure that the actual requirement is being addressed, rather than a requirement which the candidate is perhaps more used to seeing.

ACCA marking scheme		Marks
(a)	Acquisition of the shares	
	Company share option scheme	2.0
	Award of shares	2.0
	Disposal of shares	
	Company share option scheme	1.5
	Shares awarded	1.5
		7.0
(b)	Company car	3.0
	Beneficial loan	2.5
	Conclusion	0.5
		6.0
(c)	2021/22 remittance basis	3.0
	2021/22 arising basis	3.5
	Remittance basis claim not beneficial	0.5
	Increase in liability	0.5
		7.5
	Maximum	7.0
Total		20.0

4 DAMIANA PLC *Walk in the footsteps of a top tutor*

Key answer tips

This question covers R&D relief for a large company, corporation tax administration and share incentives for an employee.

The first part should be reasonably straightforward if you have learnt the R&D relief rules.

Part (b) tests TX level knowledge of corporation tax administration, and again should provide easy marks – provided you have retained this knowledge.

The final part of this question requires comparison of two alternative share incentives for an employee: sale of shares by the employer to the employee at less than market value versus share options issued under the enterprise management incentive (EMI) scheme. This is the trickiest part of the question, and requires some careful thought about the income tax and capital gains tax implications.

The highlighted words in the written sections are key phrases that markers are looking for in your answer.

(a)   **Relief for research and development (R&D) expenditure**

Tutor's top tips

Remember that additional relief is available for companies incurring qualifying expenditure on R&D. The method of relief depends on the size of the company: the company in this question is a large company. You must learn the rates of relief available as these are not provided in the tax tables in the exam.

*Note the requirement to **explain** with supporting calculations. If you just prepare calculations with no explanations, you will not score full marks.*

As Damiana plc is a large company for R&D purposes, it can claim an 'above the line' (ATL) tax credit for its qualifying R&D expenditure of £169,000. The amount of the credit is calculated as 13% of the qualifying R&D expenditure in the accounting period. This is treated as a taxable receipt of £21,970 (13% × £169,000), and a tax credit to be offset against its corporation tax liability equal to the same amount.

Accordingly, the total corporation tax saving attributable to the R&D expenditure is:

	£
Qualifying R&D expenditure	169,000
ATL credit (taxable receipt)	(21,970)
Net amount deductible for corporation tax	147,030
Corporation tax saving (19% × £147,030)	27,936
Add: ATL tax credit deducted from liability	21,970
Total corporation tax saving	49,906

Tutor's top tips

You may find it easier to do the calculation for this requirement in the spreadsheet functionality in the exam. Make sure you reference through to your calculations in the word processor if you choose to answer in this way. Alternatively, you could insert a table in the word processor function, but remember there is no ability to use formulae in the word processor.

Tutorial note

Alternatively, you could have calculated the corporation tax saving as follows:

	No R&D £	With R&D £
Taxable total profit (before R&D)	1,675,000	1,675,000
Less: R&D expenditure		(169,000)
Add: ATL credit		21,970
TTP	1,675,000	1,527,970
Corporation tax at 19%	318,250	290,314
Less: ATL tax credit		(21,970)
Corporation tax liability	318,250	268,344

Corporation tax saving attributable to R&D (£318,250 – £268,344) = £49,906.

(b) **Late filing of corporation tax returns**

Tutor's top tips

Filing dates for companies and late filing penalties are key areas of corporation tax administration that you must learn.

There are two accounting periods within the 18-month period ended 31 March 2021 for which corporation tax returns should have been filed. The first is the 12 months ended 30 September 2020 and the second is the six months ended 31 March 2021.

Both returns should have been filed by 31 March 2022 (12 months after the end of the 18-month period of account).

As the returns have been filed more than three months late, each return will attract a fixed late filing penalty of £200, as previous returns have been filed on time.

Tutorial note

It has been assumed that HMRC issued notices requiring the returns to be made before 1 January 2022, so that the later three-month filing rule does not apply.

(c)   Alternative 1 – transfer of shares to Luiza on 1 November 2022

Tutor's top tips

*The requirement asks you to **explain** the tax implications, so you need to provide a written answer as well as calculations.*

Note that you are asked to calculate Luiza's net increase in wealth under each alternative, which means that you should calculate the net cash that she will receive after deducting any tax due. This should provide easy marks, and you will be given credit for your method, even if the tax that you have calculated is incorrect.

As Luiza is an employee of Damiana plc, she will be treated as receiving a taxable benefit equal to the amount underpaid in respect of her shares. She is an additional rate taxpayer, so she will incur an income tax liability of £52,875 ((£24.50 – £1) × 5,000 = £117,500 × 45%) in the tax year 2022/23.

The shares are in a quoted company, so fall within the definition of 'readily convertible assets', therefore Luiza will also have a liability to class 1 national insurance contributions (NICs) of £2,350 (£117,500 × 2%).

On the sale of the shares on 10 November 2025, there will be a chargeable gain of £41,000 ((£32.70 – £24.50) × 5,000) arising in the 2025/26 tax year. As Luiza will have already used her annual exempt amount, capital gains tax will be payable on £41,000 at the rate of 20%. Business asset disposal relief will not be available as Luiza will not hold 5% of the shares in Damiana plc. The capital gains tax payable will therefore be £8,200 (£41,000 × 20%).

Tutorial note

Business asset disposal relief was formerly known as entrepreneurs' relief.

Luiza's net increase in wealth will be:

	£
Proceeds from sale of shares (£32.70 × 5,000)	163,500
Less: Cost of shares (£1 × 5,000)	(5,000)
Income tax	(52,875)
NICs	(2,350)
Capital gains tax	(8,200)
Net increase in wealth	95,075

Alternative 2 – Enterprise management incentive (EMI) scheme

The value of shares in the scheme on 1 November 2022 will be £122,500 (£24.50 × 5,000), which is within the £250,000 limit.

No income tax or NICs will be payable by Luiza on the granting of the options in 2022/23.

On exercise of the options on 2 November 2025, income tax and NICs will be payable on the difference between the market value at the date of grant and the exercise price of the options, i.e. £7,500 ((£24.50 – £23) × 5,000). This is the amount chargeable as it is less than the difference between the market value at the date of exercise and the exercise price. The income tax and NICs payable are therefore £3,525 (£7,500 × 47%).

As before, a chargeable gain will arise on disposal of £41,000. The gain will be charged at 10% as business asset disposal relief will be available. This is because for an EMI scheme there is no requirement for the shareholder to have a minimum 5% shareholding in the company, as long as the option was granted at least two years before the date of disposal, and the individual has worked for the company for at least two years prior to the date of disposal. The capital gains tax payable will therefore be £4,100 (£41,000 × 10%).

Luiza's net increase in wealth will be:

	£
Proceeds from sale of shares (£32.70 × 5,000)	163,500
Less: Cost of options (£23 × 5,000)	(115,000)
Income tax and NICs	(3,525)
Capital gains tax	(4,100)
Net increase in wealth	40,875

Examiner's report

The first part related to the tax relief for research and development expenditure in a 'large' company. Most candidates were comfortable with the calculation of this, scoring full, or almost full, marks. However, many ignored the requirement to 'explain' the relief, and so were not able to pick up the marks for this. Candidates should ensure that they fully address all aspects of the requirements.

The second part of the question required explanation of the corporation tax return filing dates in relation to a long period of account.

Surprisingly, this was not done at all well. Most candidates recognised that the long period would be split into two accounting periods for tax purposes, but fewer were able to state the correct split of the long period. Fewer still correctly identified the filing dates, with the most common error being to state the payment dates instead.

The implications for a company in respect of late filing of returns elicited a number of answers stating that 'penalties will arise', or 'interest will be charged', but candidates must be precise as to the nature and amounts of such penalties/interest in order to gain marks in this type of question.

The final part of the question concerned the acquisition of shares by an employee, either by means of a transfer, or by exercising options in an enterprise management incentive (EMI). Although few candidates scored high marks on this question part, a good number achieved a respectable score. It appeared that many candidates ignored the last part of the requirement to calculate the taxpayer's increase in wealth under each of the alternatives, which was a shame as this should have represented relatively easy marks. It is similar to the, perhaps more familiar, requirement to calculate 'after-tax proceeds' from a transaction. In these cases, follow through marks are available as long as the candidate picks up the correct figures from their earlier calculations. The message, again, is to read the requirements of a question very carefully to ensure that what should be relatively easier marks, marks like these, are not overlooked.

ACCA marking scheme		
		Marks
(a)	Above the line tax credit	2.5
	Calculation of tax saving	2.5
		5.0
(b)	Returns required	2.0
	Implications of late filing	2.0
		4.0
	Maximum	3.0
(c)	Alternative 1	7.0
	Alternative 2	7.0
		14.0
	Maximum	12.0
Total		**20.0**

5 DEMETER

Key answer tips

Part (a) of this question looks at the treatment of a lump sum and relocation package. It is important to explain why certain amounts are taxable rather than just stating that they will be taxed.

Part (b) is testing PRR and letting relief but you may find the numbers tricky due to the fact that the property has been let out for some of the time. Remember that any time the property is occupied it will qualify for PRR but the let part won't. You also need to think about the periods of deemed occupation which you can use. Once you have reduced your gain by PRR think about the available letting relief.

Part (c) is looking at pensions. You need to explain the initial treatment of the employer contributions but you also need to consider the impact of the other contributions Demeter has already made. Think about the level of annual allowance he has and whether this could cause an issue.

> Finally part (d) is looking at share options. In this case it is a non-tax advantaged share option plan. In order to score well you need to explain the tax implications at all three stages of the option lifespan (grant, exercise and sale). Try not to get confused with the rules for tax advantaged option plans.
>
> The highlighted words in the written sections are key phrases that markers are looking for.

(a) **Receipt of the one-off lump sum inducement payment and relocation package**

The one-off lump sum inducement payment of £20,000 paid on commencement of Demeter's employment is fully taxable as it wholly relates to future services to be performed by Demeter.

The total amount received by Demeter in relation to his relocation is £11,000 (£5,000 + (£1,500 × 4)). Demeter did not previously live within a reasonable daily travelling distance of his new employment, so is eligible for a maximum tax allowable amount of £8,000, provided he has spent at least this amount on qualifying expenditure.

Demeter's qualifying expenditure comprises all the costs relating to his move, including the estate agent fees on the sale of his house of £2,800, and the rent on his accommodation in London of £1,700 per month from 1 December 2022 until he purchases a new house on 1 April 2023. His total qualifying expenditure is therefore £12,800 (£6,000 + (£1,700 × 4)). This clearly exceeds £8,000, so the taxable amount of Demeter's relocation package is £3,000 (£11,000 – £8,000).

(b) **Reliefs available to Demeter to reduce the chargeable gain on the sale of his house in Manchester**

As the house was Demeter's only residence, private residence relief (PRR) will be available to exempt the proportion of the gain which relates to his actual or deemed occupation of the property. The relief is calculated as follows:

Demeter owned the house for 13.5 years (162 months) (1 May 2009 to 31 October 2022).

Availability of PRR:

		Exempt months
1 May 2009 to 30 April 2011	100% occupation	24
1 May 2011 to 31 Jan 2022	70% occupation (129m × 70%)	90
1 Feb 2022 to 31 Oct 2022	Last nine months treated as 100% occupation	9
Total exempt months		123

The PRR will exempt £71,370 (£94,000 × 123/162) of the gain. The remainder of the gain, i.e. £22,630 (£94,000 × 39/162), is attributable to the let part of the property.

Letting relief provides an extension to PRR in relation to the gain arising on the part of Demeter's house which was let. The additional exemption is restricted to the lowest of:

1   The amount of the gain which is exempt under PRR (£71,370).

2   The gain attributable to the letting (£22,630).

3   £40,000.

Therefore, the letting relief available is £22,630.

(c)   **(i)**   **Tax consequences for Demeter of participating in Poseidon Ltd's HM Revenue and Customs registered occupational pension scheme in 2023/24**

Poseidon Ltd's contribution into its occupational pension scheme on Demeter's behalf of £13,000 (10% × £130,000) will be an exempt benefit for Demeter, so no tax liability will arise on this.

However, the contributions will count towards Demeter's annual allowance. This will remain at £40,000 as Demeter's threshold income of £90,000 (net income (£130,000) less Demeter's personal pension contributions (£40,000)) does not exceed the £200,000 threshold.

Demeter has no unused annual allowance to bring forward from earlier tax years as he has made contributions up to the maximum amount each year. As the total contributions in 2023/24 of £53,000 (£13,000 + £40,000) will exceed the annual allowance, an annual allowance charge will be payable. Accordingly, as a higher rate taxpayer Demeter will pay an annual allowance charge of £5,200 (40% × £13,000 (£53,000 − £40,000)).

Tutorial note

There is no need to calculate Demeter's adjusted income as the amount of annual allowance will not be reduced regardless because his threshold income is below £200,000.

(ii)   **Tax consequences for Demeter of participating in Poseidon Ltd's non-tax advantaged share option scheme**

No income tax will be payable by Demeter on the grant of the options on 1 December 2022.

When Demeter exercises the options on 6 April 2028, income tax will be payable on the excess of the market value of the shares at the date of exercise over the price paid by Demeter, i.e. £6,030 ((£6.00 − (£4.20 × 95%) × 3,000). The income tax payable is therefore £2,412 (£6,030 × 40%).

The exercise of the shares has no impact on Demeter's personal allowance because his adjusted net income is below £100,000. There will also be no impact on Demeter's annual allowance charge because his threshold income remains below £200,000.

As Demeter will sell the shares immediately following the exercise of the options, the shares will not have increased in value and so no chargeable gain will arise.

Examiner's report

This question concerned various matters in relation to an individual relocating to take up employment. There were four parts to the question broadly covering a relocation package, sale of a residence, pension scheme contributions and a non-tax advantaged share option scheme.

Part (a) asked candidates to consider the extent to which an inducement package and relocation expenses would be taxable. Most candidates knew that the inducement package would be taxable but were not able to explain the reason why. Similarly most candidates knew that there was a relocation allowance of £8,000 but did not know the rules for qualifying relocation expenditure.

Part (b) required candidates to calculate and briefly explain the relief(s) available upon sale of a residence, which had been partially let to tenants. Many candidates were aware of the availability of private residence relief (PRR) in the scenario but made some mistakes in their calculations of the relief. Candidates should have known that periods of occupation are completely exempt and that the last nine months are treated as 100% occupation and therefore exempt.

Any remaining gain after private residence relief was eligible for letting relief although this proved to be a less well-known relief. Letting relief is restricted to the lowest of the following three values.

- The amount of the gain which is exempt under PRR
- The gain attributable to letting
- £40,000.

This is not a particularly tricky subject area and candidates should have been able to identify these points from the question.

Part (c)(i) considered the implications of an employer's contribution to an occupational pension scheme, when the employee is already making annual contributions to a personal pension scheme equal to the annual allowance. There was a general awareness of the rules in this area such as the £40,000 allowance but a lack of precision in relation to the detailed calculations required.

The final part of the question, part (c)(ii), concerned the tax implications of a non-tax advantaged share option scheme, from option grant through to exercise and disposal. Candidates should have been able to identify the following tax points from the facts of the question.

- No income tax payable on grant of the options
- Income tax payable on exercise of the options
- No gain on sale of the shares because it immediately follows the exercise of the options and the shares will not have increased in value.

This part was not done particularly well since candidates did not have a sufficiently precise knowledge of the rules concerning a non-tax advantaged share option plan.

					Marks
ACCA marking scheme					
(a)		One-off lump sum payment			2.0
		Financial assistance with relocation			3.5
					5.5
				Maximum	5.0
(b)		Private residence relief			4.0
		Letting relief			3.0
					7.0
				Maximum	6.0
(c)	(i)	Poseidon Ltd's contributions			1.5
		Annual allowance charge			4.5
					6.0
				Maximum	5.0
	(ii)	Grant of options			1.0
		Exercise of options			2.0
		Sale of shares			1.0
		Consideration of impact on personal allowance/annual allowance charge			1.0
					5.0
				Maximum	4.0
Total					**20.0**

6 YACON LTD AND DAIKON

Key answer tips

This question covers provision of two alternative share schemes: CSOP and SIP, the disposal of a private residence and finally IHT on a lifetime gift.

Part (a) requires in-depth knowledge of CSOP and SIP conditions, which may have put off many students. However, there are eight marks available for applying the conditions of the two schemes and no calculations are required. Share schemes are examined fairly regularly and you need to be confident with being able to discuss and apply the conditions.

Part (b) covers the disposal of a private residence with private residence relief and letting relief. If you follow a logical, step by step approach when dealing with the reliefs available and the dates of occupation and non-occupation you should do well in this type of question. These are all TX areas.

Part (c) covers IHT in respect of a gift with reservation, with the twist that the reservation is lifted before the donor's death. In order to spot this, you need to make sure you read the information in detail to see what has happened to the apartment that was given, who it was occupied by and for how long.

(a) Company share option plan (CSOP)

Ability to select employees

In a CSOP, Yacon Ltd would be free to select employees as it wishes to participate in the scheme.

Value of options granted

Yacon Ltd can choose to award options to purchase a different number of shares to each member of a CSOP. There is no annual maximum amount, but an employee can only be granted options over shares up to a total value of £30,000, as at the date of the grant.

Holding period required and tax implications for employees

There are no tax implications for employees on the grant of the options, or on their exercise after five years as the exercise will be between three and ten years of being granted.

Share incentive plan (SIP)

Ability to select employees

Under the rules for a SIP, all employees must be offered the opportunity to participate in the plan. Yacon Ltd can specify a minimum period of employment in order to qualify, but this cannot exceed 18 months.

Value of free shares given

Yacon Ltd can give each employee free shares up to the value of £3,600 each tax year, such that the proposal to offer shares with a value of up to £3,000 to each employee each year will be acceptable. The free shares must be offered on similar terms to all employees, such that different amounts of shares can be offered to different employees, depending on their meeting certain objective criteria, such as length of service or performance targets.

Holding period required and tax implications for employees

There are no tax implications for employees when the free shares are put into the plan.

As the free shares will be held in the plan for five years, there will be no income tax liability when they are withdrawn from the plan.

Tutorial note

The requirement only asked for the income tax implications on acquisition. It is vital to double check the precise scope of the requirement so you do not waste time on something that will not get you any marks.

(b) **Daikon – reliefs available on the sale of his house**

Private residence relief (PRR):

	Exempt years	Chargeable years
1 July 2014 to 31 December 2014		
Absent – no prior occupation		0.5
1 January 2015 to 30 June 2016		
Occupied	1.5	
1 July 2016 to 31 December 2017		
Absent but deemed occupation as employed overseas	1.5	
1 January 2018 to 31 March 2018		
Occupied	0.25	
1 April 2018 to 31 March 2022		1
Occupied (4 years × 75%)	3	
1 April 2022 to 31 December 2022		
Last 9 months treated as 100% occupation	0.75	
	7	1.5

PRR is £119,412 (£145,000 × 7/8.5).

Letting relief

The additional amount of the gain which will be exempt under letting relief is the lowest of:

(1)   The amount of the gain which is exempt under the PRR exemption (£119,412).

(2)   The gain attributable to the letting £17,059 (£145,000 × 1/8.5).

(3)   £40,000.

Letting relief is therefore £17,059.

(c) **Inheritance tax implications of Jicama's gift of the apartment**

The gift of the apartment on 5 June 2020 was a potentially exempt transfer (PET), valued at the market value of the apartment on that date. The gift was also a gift with reservation of benefit, due to the condition imposed by Jicama that she would continue to live there.

However, the reservation of benefit was lifted on 12 March 2022, when Jicama went to live with her sister. This created a further PET, which would be valued at the market value of the apartment on that date.

If Jicama dies in December 2025, this is within seven years of the date of the original gift, so both the original PET and the later deemed PET become chargeable. Taper relief would be available to reduce the liability to inheritance tax in both cases. To avoid a double tax charge, only the PET which results in a higher tax charge overall will actually be chargeable

Examiner's report

Requirement (a) – 8 marks

This requirement asked for an explanation of whether two different share schemes, a company share option plan (CSOP) and a share incentive plan (SIP), would satisfy Yacon Ltd's criteria for a tax advantaged share scheme. In addition, the income tax implications for the employees of acquiring the shares in each case needed to be explained.

Those candidates who knew the rules for share option schemes were able to apply them to the facts of the question with relative ease. Those with only a superficial understanding of the rules struggled to score well on this part. A detailed knowledge of the underlying rules is required for ATX-UK and those who don't possess this will struggle to do well on questions where this needs to be demonstrated.

A number of candidates went on to discuss the capital gains tax consequences of disposing of the shares, despite the fact that the requirement only asked for the income tax implications on acquisition. It is vital to double check the precise scope of the requirement such that time is not wasted in terms of doing something that has not been requested.

Requirement (b) – 7 marks

This requirement was to calculate, with brief explanations, the private residence relief (PRR) and potential letting relief, available to reduce the gain on the sale of a house.

It was encouraging to see that many candidates had a strong understanding of the PRR rules and were able to apply their knowledge to the facts of the question. However, common areas of confusion involved the first six month period when the owner was working overseas; this was a chargeable period because there had been no prior period of occupation. Also it should be noted that the last nine months of ownership is always exempt, even if some of the property is rented out during that period (as long as it has been occupied as the private residence at some point in the past).

Some candidates only provided calculations, and others only explanations. The requirement did however stipulate 'a calculation, with brief explanations', so to score well a combination of the two was required.

Not all candidates were as familiar with letting relief, which is given after consideration of PRR. Those who did understand the rules were able to score the marks for knowing that it is the lower of three comparative amounts; namely £40,000, the gain already exempt under PRR and the gain attributable to the let period.

Requirement (c) – 5 marks

This part of the question related to the inheritance tax implications of a gift of an apartment, on the assumption that the donor were to die within seven years.

The facts contained within the question are that when the apartment was first gifted, the donor retained the right to continue to live in it. Many candidates correctly identified this scenario as a 'gift with reservation of benefit' and a potentially exempt transfer (PET) at the time. The question then goes on to explain that, some time later, the donor removed the condition of her right to live in the property. Not all candidates realised that the removal of this 'reservation of benefit' created a further deemed PET at the date the condition was lifted.

Since the donor then went on to die within seven years of the first PET, both PETs in theory become chargeable but tax will only be due on the one giving rise to the higher liability.

ACCA marking scheme			
			Marks
(a)	Company share option plan		4.0
	Share incentive plan		5.0
			9.0
		Maximum	8.0
(b)	Private residence relief		5.5
	Letting relief		2.5
			8.0
		Maximum	7.0
(c)	Original gift 5 June 2020		2.0
	Reservation lifted		2.0
	Death in December 2025		3.0
			7.0
		Maximum	5.0
Total			**20.0**

UNINCORPORATED BUSINESSES

7   GLORIA SEAFORD (ADAPTED) *Online question assistance*

Key answer tips

Parts (a) to (c) of this question are reasonably straightforward sections dealing with the income tax, VAT and capital gain implications of a trader who is selling their business.

Whenever a question refers to an individual's residence and domicile status, you should be on the lookout for income and assets whose tax treatment may be affected. In this question it was part (d) where this information was relevant.

(a)   Value added tax (VAT) implications of the sale by Gloria of the business assets

- The sale of the premises is an exempt supply for VAT purposes because they are more than three years old. Accordingly, Gloria cannot recover any VAT incurred on any costs relating to the sale.

- Gloria must charge VAT on the shelving, shop fittings and the inventory of cards and small gifts.

- The sale of the inventory of books will be zero-rated.

- Gloria is making a taxable supply to herself of the van. However, there is no need to account for VAT as the amount due of £940 (£4,700 × 20%) is less than £1,000.

- Gloria must inform HMRC by 30 March 2023 that she has ceased to trade. Her VAT registration will be cancelled with effect from 28 February 2023.

Tutorial note

This is not a transfer of a going concern: the assets are being sold to different purchasers and the building is to be used for a different purpose.

(b)   Income tax and national insurance liability – 2022/23

Tutorial note

An individual's tax status is only important for income tax in determining their liability to UK tax on overseas income and the availability of the personal allowance.

The question says that Gloria is resident in the UK, but not UK domiciled.

As she is UK resident in the tax year 2022/23, Gloria is liable for tax on all of her UK income and is entitled to a personal allowance.

Her domicile is not important in this part as she has no source of overseas income.

This requirement is best answered in the spreadsheet in the exam. Make sure to show workings for any calculations done on a calculator rather than with a formula.

Income tax liability

	£
Trading income (W1)	32,435
Retirement pension	5,662
Bank interest	16,875
Total income	54,972
Less: Personal allowance	(12,570)
Taxable income	42,402

Analysis of income:
Savings income £16,875, Non-savings income £25,527

£	£
25,527 × 20% (non-savings income)	5,105
500 × 0% (savings income)(Note)	0
11,673 × 20% (savings income)	2,335
37,700	
4,702 × 40% (savings income)	1,881
42,402	
Income tax liability	9,321

Tutorial note

As Gloria is a higher rate taxpayer, she has a savings income nil rate band of £500.

National insurance liability

Gloria has no class 2 or class 4 national insurance contributions liability as she was over the state pensionable age on 6 April 2022.

Workings

(W1) Trading income

Closing year rules apply:

Year of cessation	2022/23
Penultimate year	2021/22

Accounts assessed in penultimate year (CYB) = y/e 31 October 2021

The year of cessation will assess all profits not yet assessed less overlap relief.

	£	£
Year ended 31 October 2022		39,245
Period ending 28 February 2023	11,500	
Profit on closing inventory (£8,300 × 5/105)	395	
Capital allowances (W2)	(2,985)	
	———	8,910
		———
		48,155
Less: Overlap profits		(15,720)
		———
Trading income		32,435
		———

(W2) Capital allowances – p/e 28 February 2023

	Main Pool	Van	B.U.	Allowances
	£	£	%	£
TWDV b/f	4,050	4,130		
Addition	820	–		
Less: Proceeds	(1,400)	(4,700)		
	———	———		
	3,470	570		
Balancing allowance	(3,470)	–		3,470
Balancing charge	–	(570)	× 85%	(485)
	———	———		———
	0	0		
	———	———		
Total allowances				2,985
				———

(c) **(i)** **Capital gains tax liability – 2022/23**

Tutorial note

The question says that Gloria is resident in the UK, but not UK domiciled.

Her non-UK domicile status is however not important in this part as she has not disposed of any overseas assets.

Accordingly, in 2022/23, Gloria is liable to capital gains tax on the net taxable gains arising on all of her UK asset disposals after deducting the annual exempt amount.

Calculation ignoring the negligible value claim

	Qualifying for business asset disposal relief (BADR)	Other gains	Residential property gains
	£	£	£
Gain on painting		7,100	
Gain on UK residential property			80,000
Gain on shop (£335,000 – £267,000)	68,000		
Less: Annual exempt amount (Note)			(12,300)
Less: Capital losses b/f (Note)			(31,100)
	———	———	———
	68,000	7,100	36,600
	———	———	———
Capital gains tax:			
Qualifying gains (£68,000 × 10%) (Note)			6,800
Other gains (£7,100 × 20%)			1,420
Residential property gains (£36,600 × 28%)			10,248
			———
Capital gains tax liability			18,468
Less: Payment on account			(10,248)
			———
Capital gains tax payable			8,220
			———

Tutorial note

Business asset disposal relief is available on the disposal of the shop as although Gloria is not disposing of the whole or part of the business as a going concern, the relief is available on the disposal of assets of an individual's trading business that has now ceased.

Furthermore, the business has been run for at least two years prior to the disposal and the disposal of assets is to take place within three years of the cessation of trade.

AEA and capital losses are set against non-qualifying residential property gains first, as these would otherwise be taxed at 28% (as Gloria is a higher rate taxpayer).

The rate of CGT on a gain qualifying for business asset disposal relief is 10%.

(ii)   Relief in respect of the fall in value of the shares in All Over plc

The shares in All Over plc are worth three pence each and are of negligible value. Gloria can make a negligible value claim in order to realise the loss on the shares without selling them.

	£
Value (17,500 × 3p)	525
Cost (probate value)	(11,400)
Capital loss on making the claim	(10,875)

Gloria can claim the loss in any year in which the shares are of negligible value provided she notifies HMRC within two years of the end of that year.

Accordingly, she can claim to realise the loss in the tax year 2021/22 or even in 2020/21 if she can show that the shares were of negligible value in that year.

Alternatively, she can claim the loss in the tax year 2022/23 or a later year if that would give rise to a greater tax saving.

(d)   (i)   Options for UK tax in respect of dividends paid by Bubble Inc

If Gloria invests in Bubble Inc shares, she will own an overseas asset and will be in receipt of overseas income. Her tax status is therefore important in determining how she will be assessed to UK taxes.

The important factors in determining Gloria's liability to UK tax are as follows:

- She is resident in the UK, but not UK domiciled
- Her unremitted dividends from Bubble Inc will be > £2,000.

Accordingly, she will be taxed as follows:

Income tax

- She will be assessed on the dividends on an arising basis with her personal allowance available **unless** a claim for the remittance basis is made
- If a claim for the remittance basis is made:
  - The dividends arising in that year will only be assessed in the UK if they are remitted into the UK

- As Gloria plans to leave the dividends in her overseas bank account, they will not be taxed in the UK
- Note that they will be taxed even if remitted in a later year when the remittance basis is not claimed
- No personal allowance available in the year the remittance basis is claimed
- In addition, Gloria will be liable to a £60,000 remittance basis tax charge as she has been UK resident for more than 12 out of the previous 14 tax years.

Income tax liability

	Arising basis £	Remittance basis £
Pension income	5,662	5,662
Bank interest	16,875	16,875
Dividends from Bubble Inc	12,000	0
Total income	34,537	22,537
Less: Personal allowance	(12,570)	(0)
Taxable income	21,967	22,537

Analysis of income:

Arising basis: Dividend income £12,000, Savings income £9,967

Remittance basis: Savings income £16,875, Non-savings income £5,662

Income tax

£	£	£	£
5,000 × 0% (savings)	5,662 × 20% (NSI)	0	1,132
1,000 × 0% (SNRB)	1,000 × 0% (SNRB)	0	0
3,967 × 20% (savings)	15,875 × 20% (savings)	793	3,175
9,967	22,537		
2,000 × 0% (dividends)		0	
10,000 × 7.5% (dividends)		750	
21,967	22,537		
		1,543	4,307
Plus: Remittance basis charge		0	60,000
Income tax liability = payable		1,543	64,307

Tutorial notes

1   *Under the arising basis, the non-savings income is covered by the personal allowance so that the first £5,000 of savings income falls into the 0% starting rate band.*

2   *As Gloria is a basic rate taxpayer, the savings income nil rate band is £1,000.*

3   *If the dividends had foreign tax withheld, they would be grossed up for the foreign tax. Double tax relief would then be available for the foreign tax in the normal way.*

- Gloria should clearly not claim the remittance basis in the tax year 2023/24.
- Note that the remittance basis claim is made on a year by year basis.

Tutorial note

Note that even if Gloria had not been UK resident for at least 7 out of the last 9 years, it would not be beneficial for her to claim the remittance basis.

If Gloria remains resident for three more tax years, she will have been UK resident for more than 15 of the previous 20 tax years and will be deemed to be UK domiciled. The remittance basis will then no longer be available for her to claim, and she will be taxed on the arising basis.

(ii)   **Implications of future disposal of shares**

Capital gains tax

- Individuals are subject to capital gains tax on worldwide assets if they are resident in the UK.

- However, because Gloria is non-UK domiciled and the shares are situated abroad, the treatment of gains and losses on the disposal of overseas assets depends on whether Gloria's unremitted overseas income and gains in the tax year that the shares are sold exceed £2,000 as follows:

    If unremitted overseas income and gains < £2,000

    – Only assessed on gains if proceeds are remitted to the UK

    – Overseas losses will be allowable

    – The annual exempt amount is available

    If unremitted overseas income and gains ≥ £2,000

    – Assessed on gains on all overseas disposals on an arising basis **unless** an election is made for the remittance basis to apply

    – If the election is not made (i.e. arising basis applies)

        – all gains assessed

        – annual exempt amount available

        – overseas losses are allowable

- If the election is made (i.e. remittance basis applies)
  - only assessed on gains if proceeds are remitted into the UK
  - annual exempt amount is not available
  - overseas losses are not allowable unless a further election is made
  - the election will apply to both income and gains
  - Gloria cannot elect for it to apply to just one or the other.

Tutorial note

The remittance basis election applies to both income and gains.

*As Gloria has been resident in the UK for 12 out of the last 14 tax years she will have to pay the remittance basis charge of £60,000 in any tax year where her unremitted income and gains exceed £2,000 **and** she claims the remittance basis.*

Again, if Gloria is UK resident for more than 15 of the previous 20 tax years she will be deemed to be UK domiciled for CGT purposes and the remittance basis will then no longer be available for her to claim. However, if her unremitted income and gains are < £2,000 she will still be able to use the remittance basis.

- Any tax suffered in Oceania in respect of the gain is available for offset against the UK capital gains tax liability arising on the shares.

Investment advice costs

In computing a capital gain or allowable loss, a deduction is available for the incidental costs of acquisition. However, to be allowable, such costs must be incurred wholly and exclusively for the purposes of acquiring the asset.

The fee paid to Eric related to general investment advice and not specifically to the acquisition of the shares and therefore, would not be deductible in computing the gain.

Inheritance tax

For IHT, Gloria's domicile status is important in deciding how she will be taxed.

Assets situated abroad owned by non-UK domiciled individuals are excluded property for the purposes of inheritance tax.

However, Gloria will be deemed to be UK domiciled for the purposes of inheritance tax only if she has been resident in the UK for 15 out of the 20 tax years immediately preceding the tax year in which the disposal occurs.

Gloria has been living in the UK since June 2010 and would therefore appear to have been resident for 13 tax years (2010/11 to 2022/23 inclusive). She will be deemed to be UK domiciled for IHT purposes from 2025/26.

If Gloria is deemed to be UK domiciled such that the shares in Bubble Inc are not excluded property, business property relief will not be available because Bubble Inc is an investment company.

8   PIQUET AND BURACO *Walk in the footsteps of a top tutor*

Key answer tips

This section B question covers two areas of the syllabus: change of accounting date and residence, including the remittance basis. These are both new topics at ATX level and if you had not studied these two areas in detail you would struggle to gain a pass here.

Part (a) requires calculations of assessable profits following a change of accounting date, with explanations of the implications of choosing alternative dates. These assessments are tricky, and require very good knowledge of the rules. There are easier marks for stating the date for notifying HMRC, and also the advantages of having a 30 April year end.

Part (b)(i) requires application of the statutory residence tests. Although this is a technically challenging area, lots of help could be gained by looking at the tax rates and allowances at the front of the exam and applying to the scenario.

Part (b)(ii) offers three marks for the remittance basis rules, which have been tested several times before. The main pitfall here would be spending too long explaining all the rules, rather than just answering the specific question set.

The highlighted words in the written sections are key phrases that markers are looking for.

Tutor's top tips

This is really two separate, standalone questions. You could attempt parts (a) and (b) in whichever order you like, as long as you clearly label your answer.

(a)   (i)   Accounting date changed to 28 February

Tutor's top tips

The basis of assessment rules for sole traders are very important and are often tested in the ATX exam. You need to be confident in dealing with:
- *Opening years*
- *Change of accounting date*
- *Closing years.*

Piquet must notify HM Revenue and Customs of the change by 31 January 2024 (31 January following the tax year in which the change is made).

Taxable trading profit

	£
2022/23	
16 months ending 28 February 2023	94,000
Less: Relief for overlap profits (£15,000 × 4/5)	(12,000)
	82,000
2023/24	
Year ended 29 February 2024	88,000

(ii) **30 April year end – Basis periods and overlap profits**

The basis period for the tax year 2022/23 will be the 12 months ended on the new accounting date in the tax year (i.e. the 12 months ended 30 April 2022).

This will create additional overlap profits, as the profits for the six months ended 31 October 2021 have already been subject to tax in the tax year 2021/22. The additional overlap profits will be £27,000 (6/12 × £54,000).

The basis period for the tax year 2023/24 will be the 12 months ending 30 April 2023.

Tutorial note

The level of overlap profit depends on the sole trader's accounting year end date, and will change if the accounting year end is changed.

The number of months' worth of overlap profit can be found by counting the number of months from the accounting year end to the end of the tax year (5 April).

Applying this to the dates in the question:

Year end:	No. of months of overlap
31 October	*5*
28 February	*1*
30 April	*11*

This means that if the year end is changed from 31 October to 28 February, the overlap profit must fall from five months' worth to one month worth (i.e. four months' worth will be used).

If the year end is changed from 31 October to 30 April, the overlap profit must increase from five months' worth to 11 months' worth (i.e. six months' worth of extra overlap will be created).

(iii)   The advantages of a 30 April year end

Tutor's top tips

You are asked to identify and explain TWO advantages of using a 30 April year end, so try to make sure you do this.

Choice of year end for a sole trader is a popular planning area that you should be prepared to discuss.

Financial benefit

It would be financially advantageous for Piquet to have an accounting date earlier in the tax year (30 April) rather than later in the tax year (28 February) because the profits of his business are increasing.

The earlier year end date will result in an earlier period of profits, and therefore a lower amount of profits, being subject to tax.

For example, in the tax year 2023/24, the profit for the 12 months ending 30 April 2023 will be less than the profit for the 12 months ending 29 February 2024.

Time for tax planning

The nearer an accounting date is to the start of the tax year, the sooner the taxable profit for that tax year will be known. This means that there will be more time for plans to be made and carried out in relation to, for example, payments on account and pension contributions.

Cash flow benefit

The interval between earning profits and paying the tax on those profits is greater where the year end is earlier rather than later in the tax year.

For example, the payments of tax for the year ended 30 April 2024 are due on 31 January 2025 and 31 July 2025, whereas the payments for the year ended 29 February 2024 would be due a year earlier.

Tutorial note

Note that only two advantages were required.

Credit was also available to candidates who explained the effect of a trader's year end on the basis period in the tax year of cessation.

(b)   (i)   Residence status – 2022/23

Tutor's top tips

The requirement for this part of the question is very specific, and you will not be given credit for providing information that is not requested.

There are only two aspects of residency to discuss:

1   The automatic overseas residence tests (i.e. automatic non-UK residence tests)

2   The sufficient ties tests.

No credit was given for considering the automatic UK residence tests in detail as the question clearly states that these are not satisfied.

You must apply your knowledge to the scenario, and you will not score marks for writing about residency in general terms.

When considering the sufficient ties tests, you should discuss all possibilities. Buraco could either fall into the '91 – 120 days in the UK' bracket, or the '121 – 182 days in the UK' bracket.

Automatic overseas residence tests

Buraco will not satisfy any of the automatic overseas residence tests for the tax year 2022/23 because he will have been in the UK for 46 days or more in that tax year.

Tutorial note

The 90-day test does not apply to Buraco because he does not work full time overseas.

Residence status – 2022/23

Buraco was not UK resident for any of the three previous tax years, accordingly:

–   if he is in the UK for between 100 and 120 days, he will be resident if he has three or more of the four relevant UK ties; or

–   if he is in the UK for between 121 and 150 days, he will be resident if he has two or more UK ties.

Buraco does not satisfy the tie relating to work, as he does not work in the UK.

Buraco satisfies the close family tie and the accommodation tie, as he has a minor child in the UK and a house which he has stayed in during the year.

Accordingly, as he satisfies two of the ties, he will be UK resident if he is in the UK for more than 120 days.

If he is in the UK for less than 120 days, he will only be resident if he satisfies the final tie relating to time spent in the UK during either of the two previous tax years. This tie will be satisfied if Buraco spent more than 90 days in the UK during the tax year 2021/22.

(ii)   **Tax implications of claiming the remittance basis**

Tutor's top tips

Make sure that you apply your knowledge to the scenario and set out the implications for Buraco. He has only been in the UK since 2021, so there will be no remittance basis charge.

There are just three marks available, so you should try to have three separate points in your answer.

If Buraco claims the remittance basis in 2022/23, he will only be subject to UK tax on his overseas income and overseas chargeable gains remitted to the UK.

However, Buraco would not be entitled to the income tax personal allowance or the capital gains tax annual exempt amount.

There would not be a remittance basis charge because Buraco was not resident in the UK for seven of the nine tax years prior to 2022/23.

Examiner's report

The calculations in parts (a)(i) and (ii) would have been straight forward for those candidates who knew the rules and had practised applying them. Unfortunately, most candidates who attempted this question did not know the rules, such that very few scored well on these parts of the question.

In part (a)(iii) many candidates were able to identify one advantage but few were able to come up with two. This was disappointing as the choice of year end is a basic aspect of tax planning for the unincorporated trader and one that candidates should be confident of.

Candidates should recognise that change of accounting date is not part of the TX (UK) syllabus and must therefore be regarded as an area that will be examined regularly in future ATX (UK) exams.

In part (b)(i) candidates appeared to be well-prepared for a question on this area of the syllabus with good levels of knowledge.

However, it was important for candidates to realise that this was a question that required their knowledge to be applied to the specific facts and that it was not enough to simply set down everything they knew on the topic. For example, candidates should have realised that, depending on the number of days spent in the UK (which was left imprecise in the question) the relevant number of ties was either two or three. Then, it was not sufficient to list the ties, it was necessary to state whether or not they were met by the individual concerned. It was then good exam technique to draw the various aspects of the explanation together into a form of summary or conclusion.

The other common mistake made by candidates when answering this question was to include irrelevant information in their answers. A significant number of candidates explained the automatic UK residency tests despite the wording of the requirement. Such explanations would not have scored any marks as they were irrelevant to the requirement and thus such candidates put themselves under unnecessary time pressure as a result.

Part (b)(ii), the final part of the question, concerned the remittance basis. This was answered well by many candidates. There were only two matters to note here. Firstly, some candidates' knowledge of the rules governing the remittance basis charge was somewhat imprecise. Secondly, a minority of candidates set out the rules but did not apply them to the individual concerned.

		ACCA marking scheme		Marks
(a)	(i)	Date		1.0
		Calculations		2.0
				3.0
	(ii)	Basis periods		1.5
		Overlap profits		1.5
				3.0
	(iii)	Identification of issue – one mark each		2.0
		Explanation of issue – one mark each		2.0
				4.0
(b)	(i)	Automatic overseas residence tests		1.0
		Days and ties		2.5
		Work, family and accommodation ties		3.0
		90 days tie		1.5
		Conclusion		1.0
				9.0
			Maximum	7.0
	(ii)	UK tax on overseas income and gains		1.0
		Personal allowance and annual exempt amount		1.0
		No remittance basis charge		2.0
				4.0
			Maximum	3.0
Total				**20.0**

9   RAY AND SHANIRA (ADAPTED) *Walk in the footsteps of a top tutor*

Key answer tips

This section A multi-tax question covers income tax and NIC payment dates for a new sole trader, the effect of various expenditure options on levels of taxable income, VAT registration and the CGT and IHT implications of gifts between a couple before and after marriage. Most of the technical knowledge in the question is included in the TX syllabus and so illustrates the importance of maintaining TX knowledge.

The first section of part (a)(i) requires some basic income tax and class 2 and 4 NIC calculations (you have already been given the relevant taxable trading income and income tax liability figures) followed by an understanding of when relevant payments need to be made. As this is a new sole trader now receiving income that has not been taxed at source, you will need to consider the rules for payments on account.

The second section of part (a)(i) requires you to consider the effect that reinvesting profits in equipment or stock will have on the level of taxable profits. This is not something that would have necessarily been seen in question practice before the exam and so required some logical thinking.

Part (a)(ii) focuses on the very common exam topic of voluntary VAT registration. However, the question requires you to think a bit more specifically about when it is possible and *financially* beneficial to voluntarily register, rather than just generically noting a standard list of the pros and cons of voluntary registration.

Part (b) focuses on the IHT and CGT implications of gifts between couples who are either married or unmarried, in particular the timing of gifts before/after marriage so as to optimise the position re CGT annual exempt amounts, losses and base costs going forward. There is also a company takeover for a mixture of shares and cash to contend with. CGT and IHT are very frequently tested together and so it is important to understand the differences and interaction between the rules.

The highlighted words in the written sections are key phrases that markers are looking for in your memorandum.

Tutor's top tips

The requirements at the end of the question serve only to highlight the number of marks available for each section. The real requirements are in the email from your manager.

Highlight the requirements as you come across them, and don't forget to keep looking back at them to make sure your answer is focused.

With the written elements in the exam you should try and get your points down as succinctly as possible which will help you make as many relevant points as possible and keep your answers focused and structured.

Memorandum

Client	Ray and Shanira
Subject	Various personal tax matters
Prepared by	Tax senior
Date	9 June 2022

(a) Ray – unincorporated business

(i) Payments of tax and national insurance contributions

Income tax and class 4 national insurance contributions

Tutor's top tips

You are only asked to set out the payments due between 1 July 2022 and 31 March 2025, so there is no need to consider any further payments after that period.

31 January 2024	Amount payable in respect of 2022/23 (W)	£9,965
	First payment on account for 2023/24 (£9,965 × 0.5)	£4,983
31 July 2024	Second payment on account for 2023/24	£4,982
31 January 2025	Balancing payment in respect of 2023/24	
	(£17,810 – £9,965) (W)	£7,845
	First payment on account for 2024/25 (£17,810 × 0.5)	£8,905

Class 2 national insurance contributions

2022/23 £132 (£3.05 × 52 × 10/12)

Payable 31 January 2024

2023/24 £159 (£3.05 × 52)

Payable 31 January 2025

Tutorial notes

1   *Ray will not be required to make payments on account of his tax liability for the tax year 2022/23 because the whole of his tax liability for the previous year was settled via tax deducted at source.*

2   *The payment required in respect of the class 2 national insurance contributions for 2022/23 will be calculated by reference to the number of weeks in the tax year that Ray is carrying on his trade. This has been simplified to the nearest month in this answer.*

Working: Income tax and class 4 national insurance contributions payable

2022/23

	£	£
Income tax liability (per schedule)		6,686
Class 4 national insurance contributions		
(£46,000 – £9,568) × 9%		3,279
		————
		9,965
		————

2023/24

	£	£
Income tax liability (per schedule)		13,832
Class 4 national insurance contributions		
(£50,270 – £9,568) × 9%	3,663	
(£66,000 – £50,270) × 2%	315	
	————	
		3,978
		————
		17,810
		————

Effect on taxable income of increasing inventory or acquiring additional equipment

Tutor's top tips

Remember that drawings for a sole trader are not tax deductible. This means that, regardless of the level of drawings taken, a sole trader is taxed on all of their taxable trading profits.

You may find it easier to do the calculations in the spreadsheet part of the exam software. Here you can use formulas to do the calculations for you. Don't forget to reference through your workings to any explanations in the word processor. Ensure you use clear headings to distinguish the different parts of your answer.

Ray will be subject to income tax on his tax adjusted trading profit regardless of whether or not he withdraws the profits from the business.

However, the cost of any additional equipment will be deducted from his tax adjusted trading profit due to the availability of the 100% annual investment allowance, such that using the profits in this way will reduce Ray's taxable trading profit and thus his taxable income for the period in which the expenditure is incurred.

Conversely, because Ray's profits are calculated on the accruals basis, an increase in inventory levels will not have an immediate effect on his tax adjusted trading profit; the increase in purchases will be cancelled out by the corresponding increase in the closing level of inventory. Accordingly, using the profits in this way will not reduce Ray's taxable income for the period in which the expenditure is incurred.

An immediate tax deduction would be available for the cost of the inventory purchased if the cash basis were used instead of the accruals basis when calculating profits.

Tutorial note

Under the accruals basis, the sales in the statement of profit or loss are matched with the cost of goods actually sold, not the total purchases in the period.

However, under the cash basis, purchases can be deducted as soon as the cost is incurred.

(ii)   Value added tax (VAT)

Information required in order to advise on voluntary registration

Tutor's top tips

*Note that the requirement is to set out the **information needed** to advise on whether or not voluntary VAT registration is **possible** and/or **financially beneficial** and explain **why** the information is needed.*

There are no marks for discussing any other aspects of voluntary VAT registration.

–   The nature of the goods or services supplied by Ray's business.

Ray cannot register for VAT if he is only making exempt supplies; he must be making some taxable supplies.

–   The extent to which Ray's customers are registered for VAT.

Once he is registered for VAT, Ray will have to charge VAT on his standard-rated supplies. Those customers who are not registered for VAT will be unable to recover this VAT, such that the addition of VAT would represent a price increase for them. If these customers will not bear such an increase, then Ray may well be worse off because his recovery of input tax will not be sufficient to compensate him for the output tax which he has been unable to pass on to his customers.

Input tax in respect of the computer

It is possible to recover input tax incurred in the four years prior to registering for VAT in respect of goods (whether inventory for resale or non-current assets) provided the goods are still owned at the date of registration. However, the recovery of input tax in respect of the computer will be restricted to the proportion of the time for which it is used for the purposes of the business.

(b) Gifts from Shanira to Ray

(i) Capital gains tax

Tutor's top tips

Watch out for the dates in this part of the question. The gift of the house has already happened in 2021/22.

As today's date is 9 June 2022, it is too late to make any further gifts in the tax year 2021/22. Any future gifts will arise in the tax year 2022/23 (or possibly later).

House in the country of Heliosa

The chargeable gain on the gift of the house was £80,000 (£360,000 – £280,000). This will result in a UK capital gains tax (CGT) liability of £18,956 ((£80,000 – £12,300) × 28%).

The UK CGT will be reduced by double tax relief in respect of any CGT payable in Heliosa. Therefore, in order to finalise Shanira's CGT liability, we will need to confirm the amount of CGT payable in Heliosa on the sale of the house.

The UK CGT is due to be paid on 31 January 2023.

Proposed gifts

Tutor's top tips

Try not to get bogged down with all of the different options here.

The key points to identify are:

– *Gifts after the wedding will be at no gain, no loss and the base cost for the donee will be the original cost.*

– *Gifts before the wedding will be at market value, so a gain or loss will arise and the base cost for the donee will be the market value.*

– *The painting is standing at a loss, so this should be given before the wedding, and enough gains should be crystallised to use this loss.*

Before the wedding, a gift from Shanira to Ray will be treated as a disposal at market value, giving rise to either a chargeable gain or an allowable loss. After the wedding, no chargeable gain or allowable loss will arise on any assets sold or gifted by Shanira to Ray, or vice versa. Instead, the asset will be treated as having been disposed of for an amount equal to the disposer's CGT base cost.

Painting

The painting is currently worth less than its cost. Accordingly, it should be given to Ray before the wedding in order to realise the capital loss of £8,000 (£7,000 – £15,000).

Tutorial note

Although a gift of the painting prior to the wedding will result in a lower CGT base cost for Ray (£7,000 as opposed to £15,000), given that the couple wish to retain the painting rather than sell it in the future, this is not an issue.

Shares in Solaris plc

Shares given to Ray prior to the wedding will have a CGT base cost for Ray equal to their market value at the time of the gift, i.e. £9.20 per share. Shares given after the wedding will have a CGT base cost for Ray equal to Shanira's base cost, which is substantially lower. Accordingly, prior to the wedding, Shanira should give Ray the maximum number of shares which she can without giving rise to a CGT liability.

Shanira will have a capital loss in respect of the gift of the painting of £8,000. She will also have her annual exempt amount for the tax year 2022/23 of £12,300. Accordingly, she can make a chargeable gain of £20,300 without giving rise to a CGT liability.

The chargeable gain on a gift of all 7,400 shares would be:

	£
Proceeds at market value (7,400 × £9.20)	68,080
Less: Cost (W)	(10,468)
Chargeable gain	57,612
Chargeable gain per share sold (£57,612/7,400)	7.79

In order to realise a chargeable gain of £20,300, Shanira should give Ray 2,605 (£20,300/£7.79) of the shares prior to the wedding. The remaining 4,795 shares should not be gifted until after they are married.

Working

Sale proceeds in respect of the shares in Beem plc

	£
Shares in Solaris plc (7,400 × £8.40)	62,160
Cash	14,800
Total proceeds	76,960

Base cost in respect of Solaris plc shares (paper-for-paper):

£12,960 × (£62,160/£76,960) = £10,468

(ii)   Inheritance tax

Tutor's top tips

Marks will be given for consistency here. As long as your answer reflects the advice you gave in part (b)(i) regarding which assets should be transferred, you should be awarded credit.

The maximum inheritance tax (IHT) liability in respect of the gift of the painting and the first tranche of shares made before the wedding will arise if Shanira were to die within three years of the gifts, such that no taper relief would be available. There would be no IHT payable in respect of the gift of shares made after the wedding, as this will be an exempt inter-spouse transfer.

There would also be IHT to pay in respect of the gift of the house in Heliosa, but this will arise regardless of whether the CGT planning is carried out or not.

	£	£	£
Painting			7,000
Shares in Solaris plc (2,605 × £9.20)			23,966
			———
Transfer of value			30,966
Less: Annual exemption for 2022/23			(3,000)
			———
			27,966
Nil rate band at time of death		325,000	
Less:			
Chargeable transfers in the previous seven years	360,000		
Less: Annual exemptions for 2021/22 and 2020/21	(6,000)		
	———		
		(354,000)	
		———	
Available nil rate band			(0)
			———
			27,966
			———
IHT at 40%			11,186
			———

Tutorial note

A marriage exemption of £2,500 would be available if one of the gifts was made in consideration of marriage. However, the exemption would be conditional on the marriage taking place.

Examiner's report

Part (a) concerned an individual who had begun trading as a sole trader. It covered his income tax and NIC position as well as aspects of VAT and was in two parts. Candidates often overcomplicated this part of the question because they did not answer the question set and they produced a lot of additional calculations and narrative.

The first part of (a) had two aspects to it. The main issue was the individual's cash flow position and when payments of tax and NIC needed to be made. The taxable profits for the tax years were provided in the question so there was no need to apply the opening year rules. Also, the tax liabilities were provided, so there was no need to calculate them. Instead, the question was testing candidates' abilities to identify when the taxes needed to be paid via self-assessment.

This aspect of the question was not done well. Some candidates provided answers that were not consistent with the requirement. Other candidates did not correctly apply the basic self-assessment payment dates to the facts of the question. Many candidates wasted time by providing additional answers that were not required, for example recalculating the opening year rules and the tax liabilities. The timing of tax payments, particularly where an individual has commenced trading, is of considerable importance in the real world and is examined and will continue to be examined regularly.

The second aspect of this first part of (a) concerned the purchase of inventory or additional equipment as an alternative to taking drawings. Again, candidates found this to be a challenging area.

Candidates were expected to be aware that the level of drawings was irrelevant when determining the taxable profits of an unincorporated trader.

Many candidates provided incorrect responses about the tax implications of purchasing inventory. The most common was to write that this would reduce taxable profits, which of course is not the case. The purchase of additional equipment was handled reasonably well.

The second part of part (a) concerned VAT, in particular, voluntary registration. The majority of candidates were able to score reasonably well. However, a number of candidates did not pay attention to the requirements and instead wrote everything they knew about the subject as opposed to simply addressing the specific issues of the question. Finally, in respect of part (a), the recovery of pre-registration input tax was not handled particularly well because most candidates did not state that it was pre-registration input tax.

Part (b) of the question concerned capital gains tax and inheritance tax where there were to be gifts made either before or after the donor and donee got married.

Part (i), relating to capital gains tax, was challenging for many candidates. This was despite the fact that the rules being tested were fairly basic and that guidance as to how to approach the question was provided in the question.

From a capital gains tax point of view, most candidates knew that gifts prior to marriage would take place at market value, whilst those after the marriage would be at no gain, no loss. But candidates did not demonstrate that they can apply this knowledge to the question in order to come up with some advice.

They were also unclear as to the knock-on effect of these rules on the donee's base cost.

There were two things that candidates should have recognised when answering this part of the question.

The first was to recognise that the painting should be given before the wedding in order to realise the loss that was available. The second was to recognise that, in order to create a higher base cost for the shares, it was better to give them before the wedding, but only to the extent that the gains arising would be covered by the loss on the painting and the annual exempt amount. It was then simply a question of working out how many shares needed to be given in order to realise that amount of gain.

This question could not be answered well by just taking the numbers in the question and calculating some gains. Candidates needed to read the guidance from the manager in the question and then think about how to solve the problem.

The second part of (b) concerned the inheritance tax implications of the same gifts. The performance in this part was better than the rest of the question. Candidates needed to take care as regards the annual exemptions and the available nil rate band due to the earlier chargeable lifetime transfer. There was also the need to apply the spouse exemption to any gifts made after the marriage.

		ACCA marking scheme		Marks
(a)	(i)	Class 4 national insurance contributions payable		2.0
		Class 2 national insurance contributions payable		1.5
		Payments and dates		5.0
		Non-withdrawal of profits		4.0
				12.5
			Maximum	11.0
	(ii)	Information required		4.0
		Input tax in respect of the computer		2.0
				6.0
			Maximum	5.0
(b)	(i)	House in Heliosa		
		Capital gains tax liability		1.5
		Information required – double tax relief		1.0
		Information required – other		1.0
		Due date		0.5
		Rationale re timing of proposed gifts		1.0
		Painting		2.0
		Shares in Solaris plc		
		Explanations		2.0
		Calculations		3.5
				12.5
			Maximum	10.0

			Marks
(ii)	Explanation		2.5
	Calculation		3.5
			——
			6.0
		Maximum	5.0
			——
	Problem solving		1.0
	Clarity of explanations and calculations		1.0
	Effectiveness of communication		1.0
	Overall presentation and style		1.0
			——
			4.0
			——
Total			**35.0**
			——

10   AMY AND BEX   *Walk in the footsteps of a top tutor*

Key answer tips

This section B question is mostly made up of areas which are within the TX syllabus, specifically the allocation of partnership profits and opening year rules and also a loan made by a partner to a partnership, emphasising the importance of retaining TX knowledge. The question also includes the very commonly-tested exam topic of redundancy payments.

Part (a)(i) requires an explanation of the tax relief available for interest payable on a loan taken out by a partner which is then lent to a partnership. Both the partner and the partnership are paying interest and so the question requires an analysis of how relief is claimed from both perspectives.

Part (a)(i) and (ii) involve the allocation of partnership profits for a new business and then the application of the opening year rules to these profits to ascertain the taxable profits for each relevant year.

Part (b) requires an understanding of the different rules that apply to the various elements of a typical redundancy package.

The highlighted words in the written sections are key phrases that markers are looking for.

(a) (i) **Tax treatment of the interest payable**

Tutor's top tips

When a partnership pays interest on a loan taken out for business purposes the interest is simply deducted from trading profits. However, when a partner takes out a loan to provide money to his or her partnership, the interest paid is deducted from the partner's total income rather than his or her trading income from the partnership.

The interest payable by the partnership on the loan from Bex will be deductible in calculating the taxable trading profit of the business.

As the loan will be made on 1 August 2022, the interest payable in the period ending 30 April 2023 will be £750 (£20,000 × 5% × 9/12).

The interest payable on the loan taken out by Bex to provide the loan to the partnership will qualify for income tax relief as it is a loan for a qualifying purpose. The annual deduction from Bex's total income will be £1,000 (£20,000 × 5%), and the deduction in the tax year 2022/23 will be £667 (£1,000 × 8/12).

The purchase of a computer for use in a partnership is also a qualifying purpose for income tax relief, but the interest payable is only allowable for three years from the end of the tax year in which the loan was taken out, i.e. up to 2025/26. The allowable amount is also restricted where there is private use of the asset by the partner.

Bex will get a deduction against her total income of £133 (£5,000 × 5% × 80% × 8/12) in the tax year 2022/23 and an annual deduction of £200 (£5,000 × 5% × 80%) in each of the tax years 2023/24, 2024/25 and 2025/26.

(ii) **Allocation of taxable trading profit**

	£
Adjusted profit before loan interest and capital allowances	255,000
Less: Loan interest payable (from (a)(i))	(750)
Less: AIA on the computer (£5,000 × 80%)	(4,000)
Taxable trading profit	250,250

Allocation:

	Total	Amy	Bex
	£	£	£
16 months ending 30 April 2023			
Salary (£30,000 × 16/12)	40,000	0	40,000
Balance in profit sharing ratio (3:1)	210,250	157,688	52,562
Total share of profit	250,250	157,688	92,562

Tutorial note

As no other assets will be purchased by the partners in the period ending 30 April 2023, the computer equipment purchased by Bex will qualify for the annual investment allowance (AIA). This will be restricted to reflect her private use of the computer. Remember that the 130% super deduction is not available here, as that is only available to companies.

(iii) Bex – taxable trading income

Bex is treated as commencing a new business on 1 January 2022, the date she joined the partnership. She will be assessed on her £92,562 share of profits for the period ending 30 April 2023 as follows:

2021/22 (1 January 2022 to 5 April 2022)
£92,562 × 3/16 = £17,355

2022/23 (6 April 2022 to 5 April 2023)
£92,562 × 12/16 = £69,422

2023/24 (1 May 2022 to 30 April 2023)
£92,562 × 12/16 = £69,422

(b) Bex – redundancy package from Cape Ltd

Tutor's top tips

Remember that although statutory redundancy payments are always exempt from income tax, they do reduce the £30,000 tax free exemption that applies to certain qualifying discretionary (ex-gratia) lump sum payments.

When it comes to calculating the income tax payable for the tax year 2021/22 don't forget to include the partnership share that you have calculated for 2021/22 in part (a)(iii)!

The statutory redundancy pay is fully exempt from income tax. However, it reduces the £30,000 exemption available for the ex-gratia payment.

The taxable amount of the ex-gratia payment is therefore £40,000 (£58,000 – (£30,000 – £12,000)).

Three months' pay in lieu of notice (PILON) is £30,000 (£120,000/4). This is fully taxable as earnings.

Tutorial note

This question just asked for the income tax treatment of the redundancy package. Remember that for NIC purposes any ex-gratia payment would be exempt from employee's class 1 NICs, but the excess over £30,000 would be subject to class 1A NICs for the employer. The pay in lieu of notice would be subject to class 1 NICs in the same way as any other cash earnings.

Bex – income tax liability 2021/22

	£
Employment income – salary (£120,000 × 6/12)	60,000
– PILON	30,000
Partnership profit	17,355
Taxable portion of ex-gratia payment	40,000
	———
	147,355
Less: Personal allowance	0
	———
Taxable income	147,355
	———

Income tax liability:

£		£
37,700 × 20%		7,540
109,655 × 40 %		43,862
———		
147,355		
———		
Income tax liability		51,402
		———

Tutorial note

The contractual payment in lieu of notice is taxable as normal employment income, but the taxable portion of the ex-gratia payment is assessed to tax as the top slice of Bex's income.

As Bex's income exceeds £125,140 her personal allowance would be reduced to nil.

Examiner's report

Part (a)(i) required an explanation of the tax deductions available in respect of interest on two loans; The new partner took out a personal loan, which qualified for income tax relief in her personal tax computation, and she used this to make a loan to the partnership, which qualified for tax relief in the computation of the partnership's taxable trading profit. A good number of candidates produced rather muddled answers to this part, not making it clear which of the loans they were referring to in their explanations or supporting calculations, and therefore potentially not attracting as many marks as they could have done. The adoption of a logical approach in this sort of question requiring a discussion of two very similar issues can save considerable confusion and avoid wasting time. Candidates should pause and think before they start writing. Dealing fully with the implications of one of the loans first, and then the other, tended to provide a much clearer answer than those who adopted something of a random approach, apparently writing points as they occurred to them, without making it clear which loan they were dealing with, and leading to confusion for the reader.

In part (a)(ii) candidates were required to calculate the taxable trading profit for the first accounting period for the partnership and show the allocation between the partners. The majority of candidates correctly identified the deductions available for loan interest and capital allowances, and allocated the profit between the two partners in the profit sharing ratio. The most common error was a failure to deal correctly with the salary paid to one of the partners, treating this as an allowable deduction from the partnership profit, rather than as part of the profit allocation.

Part (a)(iii) required candidates to go on and calculate one partner's taxable trading income for all relevant tax years. It was good to see that most candidates were able to correctly identify the relevant tax years, but only a small minority correctly identified the actual basis periods for all three relevant years. Unincorporated businesses are tested in every exam, and questions frequently demand identification of basis periods – particularly in the opening years (as here) or closing years of a business. This is fundamental knowledge from TX which candidates must bring forward and be able to apply to given scenarios at ATX.

Part (b) required explanation of the tax treatment of various items within a redundancy package, and calculation of the taxpayer's income tax liability for the year in which this was received. In the main, this was done well, with the majority of candidates appearing to be very comfortable with this topic.

		ACCA marking scheme		
				Marks
(a)	(i)	Interest payable by the partnership		2.0
		Interest payable by Bex		5.5
				———
				7.5
			Maximum	7.0
				———
	(ii)	Adjustment to profit		2.5
		Allocation of profit		2.0
				———
				4.5
			Maximum	4.0
				———
	(iii)	Correct tax years		1.0
		Correct basis periods		1.0
		Correct calculations		3.0
				———
				5.0
			Maximum	3.0
				———
(b)		Taxable redundancy payment		3.0
		Calculation of tax		4.0
				———
				7.0
			Maximum	6.0
				———
Total				**20.0**
				———

11   JUANITA *Walk in the footsteps of a top tutor*

Key answer tips

This section B question tests two unrelated areas – inheritance tax with related property considerations, and the income tax and NIC impact of ceasing to trade on two alternative dates.

This demonstrates that often section B questions will test you on two totally different areas of the syllabus! This one could really be approached as two separate questions, one on inheritance tax for eight marks and one on income tax and NIC for twelve marks.

Make sure you allocate your time in accordance with the marks available – don't spend too long on part (a) and scrimp on the time available for part (b).

The highlighted words in the written sections are key phrases that markers are looking for in your answer.

(a)   Inheritance tax (IHT) liability on the Estar Ltd shares

Tutor's top tips

Related property is a commonly tested area of the syllabus which is new at the strategic professional level. It is tested in a tricky way here as you need to consider the impact of related property being gifted in lifetime on the IHT due on an individual's estate. However, if you have revised the topic and think carefully about how best to set out your answer before beginning to write, you should be able to score well here.

Regardless of whether the shares in Estar Ltd were gifted to Lexi in Don's lifetime or on his death, IHT will be payable at the rate of 40% because the gift of the villa in 2017 has used the full nil rate band.

However, whether the shares were gifted or not will impact on their value in Don's death estate under the related property valuation rules.

The IHT due in respect of the Estar Ltd shares on Don's death as a result of his making the lifetime gift to Lexi is £52,240 (£27,040 + £25,200) (W).

If all the shares had been retained by Don until his death, the IHT payable in respect of the shares would have been £67,200 (7,000 × £24 × 40%).

Therefore, there is a reduction in the IHT liability on the Estar Ltd shares of £14,960 (£67,200 – £52,240).

Working: Value of the lifetime gift of 3,500 shares

Related property rules apply as the shares in Estar Ltd were held by both Don and Juanita at the date of the gift.

	£
Value before the gift: 7,000 shares at £20 (70% + 30%)	140,000
Value after the gift: 3,500 shares at £15 (35% + 30%)	(52,500)
	———
Diminution in value	87,500
Business property relief not available (as per question)	
Less: AE 2018/19	(3,000)
AE 2017/18 (used on gift of villa)	0
	———
Gross chargeable transfer	84,500
	———
IHT at 40%	33,800
Less: Taper relief at 20% (3-4 years)	(6,760)
	———
IHT payable by Lexi	27,040
	———

The remaining 3,500 shares held by Don at the date of his death will give rise to an IHT liability on his death of £25,200 (40% × 3,500 × £18 (35% + 30%)).

(b)   Cessation of trade on 28 February 2023

Tutor's top tips

Although basis periods are a basic level topic, they are commonly tested at the advanced level too. The examining team often set questions based around unincorporated businesses and therefore basis periods are easy to include in most advanced taxation exams! Make sure you refresh your knowledge on this area. Choice of business cessation date is a classic scenario that you should be prepared for.

This requirement requires both explanations and calculations. Using a mixture of both the spreadsheet and word processor in the exam would be the best approach to answering the question. Make sure it is clear which requirements are answered where by use of headings, and reference through to any workings in the spreadsheet.

The profits of the year ended 30 June 2022 of £51,000 will be taxed in the tax year 2022/23.

If Juanita ceases to trade on 28 February 2023, the profits of her final accounting period will also be taxed in this tax year.

The tax liability in respect of the profits of the final accounting period will therefore be as follows:

	£
Tax-adjusted profit for the eight months ending 28 February 2023	48,000
Add: Balancing charge (£0 – £6,000)	6,000
Less: Overlap profits	(17,000)
Taxable trading profit	37,000

	£
Income tax (£37,000 × 40%)	14,800
Class 4 NIC (£37,000 × 2%)	740
Class 2 NIC (£3.05 × 8 × 4)	98
Total deductions	15,638

Income after tax and national insurance contributions is £32,362 (£48,000 – £15,638).

Tutor's top tips

Don't forget that you were asked to calculate after-tax income. Even if your figures are incorrect you will still score a follow through mark provided you remember to do this.

The £51,000 is provided so that you know Juanita is already a higher rate taxpayer in 2022/23 and has exceeded the upper profits threshold for NIC. The £51,000 does not need to be included in any calculations (although you would not be penalised if you had included it).

Cessation of trade on 30 April 2023

If Juanita continues to trade until 30 April 2023, the profits of her final accounting period will be taxed in the tax year 2023/24.

The liability for this final period will therefore be:

	£
Tax-adjusted profit for the ten months ending 30 April 2023 (£48,000 + £4,000 + £4,000)	56,000
Add: Balancing charge	0
Less: Overlap profits	(17,000)
Taxable trading profit	39,000

	£
Income tax ((£39,000 − £12,570) × 20%)	5,286
Class 4 NIC ((£39,000 − £9,568) × 9%)	2,649
Class 2 NIC (£3.05 × 10 × 4)	122
	————
Total deductions	8,057
	————

Income after tax and national insurance contributions is £47,943 (£56,000 − £8,057).

The increase in income after tax and national insurance contributions of £15,581 (£47,943 − £32,362) exceeds the amount of the additional two months profits of £8,000 (2 × £4,000). It is therefore beneficial for Juanita to continue to trade until 30 April 2023.

Availability of capital allowances

No writing down allowance is available in the final accounting period of a business. A balancing adjustment will, however, arise on the disposal of the assets. The sale proceeds will exceed the written down value of the assets at the start of the final period, so a balancing charge will arise.

If the sale is delayed until 30 April 2023, and the business is transferred to Lexi, then as Juanita and Lexi are connected persons, a succession election can be made to transfer the plant and machinery to Lexi at its written down value at 30 April 2023, thereby avoiding the balancing charge.

Examiner's report

Part (a) examined two key principles in valuing unquoted shares which are gifted in lifetime, namely related property and diminution in value (comparing the value of the shareholding before and after the gift). Both of these were relevant in respect of the gift in this case, and it was pleasing to see that a significant number of candidates identified these, but unfortunately in many cases were not then able to apply them correctly to the figures given. An earlier lifetime gift was included, so that candidates had to recognise that there would be no annual exemption to bring forward, and no nil rate band available. This is a common examination technique which candidates should be familiar with if they have practised similar past examination questions. However, a common issue here was for candidates to provide a full calculation of the inheritance tax payable in respect of this earlier gift, despite this being totally irrelevant in order to address the requirement, which was to focus on the tax payable only in respect of the shares. In some cases, this wasted a considerable amount of time for no marks. This highlights the need to read the wording of the requirement very carefully to ensure that the right approach is taken and time is not wasted on unnecessary calculations.

Part (b) required advice on which of two proposed dates for ceasing to trade would be beneficial for the taxpayer. The focus of the decision was the additional income after tax and national insurance contributions in each case.

The requirement was deliberately worded, instructing candidates to do this by reference to the increase in net trading income, to encourage them to adopt a marginal approach to the question, considering only the additional income, tax, and national insurance contributions in each case, but the majority of candidates ignored this, and produced full computations, resulting in unnecessary and repetitive computations, including figures which were common to both scenarios. It was still possible to score full marks on this basis, but would have been much more time-consuming, and care had to be taken to ensure that comparable calculations were prepared in each case in order to come to a meaningful conclusion.

In ATX questions involving opening or closing years for an unincorporated business, it is extremely important always to identify the relevant tax years for which the assessments are being calculated. This is something which several candidates omitted to do, and as a consequence missed the significance of the fact that the second proposed cessation date fell into a later tax year such that a new personal allowance, and class 4 national insurance contributions threshold would be available.

The majority of candidates did not address the final part of the requirements relating to an explanation of the capital allowances available. There were two aspects to this; the first is the need to calculate a balancing adjustment in the final period, and explain why, in this case it is a balancing charge. The second relates to the 'beneficial election' which was referred to in this context in the requirements. This concerns the succession election to transfer assets at written down value when the business is transferred to her daughter. This is an important election, and one which ATX candidates should always consider when a business is being transferred to a connected person.

ACCA marking scheme			
			Marks
(a)		Value of shares gifted	3.0
		IHT on gifted shares	3.0
		IHT on remaining shares in the death estate	1.5
		IHT if all the shares are in the death estate	1.0
		IHT saving	0.5
			————
			9.0
		Maximum	8.0
			————
(b)		Cessation on 28 February 2023	
		Taxable trading profit 2022/23	2.0
		Income tax	1.0
		Class 4 NIC	0.5
		Class 2 NIC	1.0
		Income after tax and NIC	0.5
		Cessation on 30 April 2023	
		Taxable trading profit 2023/24	2.0
		Income tax	1.0
		Class 4 NIC	1.0
		Class 2 NIC	0.5
		Income after tax and NIC	0.5
		Comments re capital allowances	3.5
		Conclusion	0.5
			————
			14.0
		Maximum	12.0
			————
Total			**20.0**
			————

12   MEG AND LAURIE *Walk in the footsteps of a top tutor*

Key answer tips

This question covers change of accounting date for an unincorporated business, the tax implications of taking on an employee or a partner, and overseas aspects of VAT.

The first part asks for calculations of taxable trading profits for a business that is changing its accounting date. This should offer relatively easy marks if you have learnt the change of accounting date rules.

Part (b) covers the common scenario of taking on a spouse either as an employee or as a partner, but for a loss-making business. Most of the marks in this part are for discussing the trading loss reliefs available and for providing advice on the possible tax savings.

The final part of the question requires knowledge of the VAT implications of purchasing overseas services. Overseas aspects of VAT are tested fairly regularly in the exam.

The highlighted words in the written sections are key phrases that markers are looking for in your answer.

(a)   (i)   Taxable trading profit

Tutor's top tips

The requirement just asks for calculation of taxable trading profits, so there is no need to provide explanations here.

		£
2021/22		
Year ended 31 December 2021		17,000
2022/23		
15 months ended 31 March 2023		9,000
Less: Relief for overlap profits		(7,400)
		1,600

Tutorial note

As Meg has changed her accounting date to 31 March, all the overlap profits from commencement are relieved. This represents three months' profits from 1 January 2017 to 5 April 2017.

(ii) Disadvantage of 31 March year end

Tutor's top tips

Although there are two disadvantages described here, you only need to identify and explain ONE disadvantage to gain full marks.

A year end of 31 March means that the taxable profit for the current tax year is unlikely to be known with certainty until after the end of the tax year on 5 April. This means that payments to be made within the tax year – such as a payment on account or pension contributions – will have to be based on estimates.

A year end of 31 March gives the minimum interval between earning profits and paying the associated tax liability. The profits earned in January, February and March of any calendar year will be taxed one year earlier than they would have been if Meg had retained a 31 December year end.

(b) (i) Allowable trading losses if Laurie is an employee

	£
Tax adjusted trading loss in 2023/24 before any payment to Laurie	20,000
Add: Salary paid to Laurie	12,000
Employer's NICs (Note)	0
	———
Allowable trading loss for Meg in 2023/24	32,000
	———

Laurie will not have an allowable trading loss in this case.

Note: Laurie's salary of £12,000 each year is an allowable expense for Meg's business. No Class 1 employer's national insurance contributions (NICs) will be payable in respect of this as they will be covered by the £4,000 annual employment allowance.

Tutorial note

The NIC employment allowance is available here, even though Laurie is the only employee, as this is an unincorporated business. It is not available for a company where a director is the sole employee.

It is also not available to businesses whose employers NIC liability was £100,000 or more in the previous year. As MT Travel did not previously have any employees this rule will not be applicable here.

Allowable trading losses if Laurie is a partner

	Total £	Meg £	Laurie £
Tax-adjusted trading loss (allocated 75:25)	20,000	15,000	5,000

(ii)   Loss relief available to Meg

Tutor's top tips

Trading losses for unincorporated businesses are often tested in the exam, so you must learn the rules.

The key to scoring well is to be very specific when describing the reliefs available, avoid discussing reliefs that are not relevant and apply your knowledge to the specific scenario. For example, the additional relief for losses in opening years will be available to Laurie if he commences trade as a partner, but will not be available to Meg.

In the tax year 2023/24 Meg has an allowable loss of £32,000, if Laurie is taken on as an employee, and £15,000, if Laurie becomes a partner.

Loss relief is available against Meg's total income of the tax year 2023/24 and/or 2022/23. In the tax year 2023/24 Meg's only income will be £8,600 rental income. In 2022/23 her income will include a taxable trading profit of £1,600 (see part (a)(i)) in addition to the rental income of £8,600. In both these tax years her total income is covered by her personal allowance for the year, and therefore a loss relief claim will not result in any tax saving in either year.

Alternatively, the full amount of the loss can be carried forward for relief against the first available future profits from the same trade, which are expected to occur in 2024/25. The maximum rate of relief will be 20% on the amount of Meg's taxable income (all non-savings), which falls within the basic rate band.

Loss relief available to Laurie

If Laurie becomes a partner in the business, he will have an allowable trading loss of £5,000 in 2023/24. His total income in each of the tax years 2023/24 and 2022/23 is £18,000, which is wholly dividend income, so he could relieve the loss in either year resulting in tax being saved at the rate of 7.5% in respect of the dividends in excess of his personal allowance and dividend nil rate band.

As 2023/24 is the tax year of commencement of business for Laurie, he can carry back the loss against his total income of the three tax years prior to the loss making year on a FIFO basis. Accordingly, he can offset the loss against his total income of the tax year 2020/21, when he was employed. This will result in a tax saving at the rate of 40% as the loss will be relieved against his employment income, and Laurie was a higher rate taxpayer in 2020/21.

(c)   Implications of purchasing services from the overseas supplier

Tutor's top tips

You should make sure that you know the VAT rules for imports/exports of goods, and for supply/purchase of overseas services. Be prepared to explain these rules in the exam.

As MT Travel is registered for value added tax (VAT), this is a business to business (B2B) service, so will be treated as supplied in the UK, as this is where the customer (MT Travel) is established. MT Travel must therefore pay VAT at the UK standard-rate of 20% to HM Revenue and Customs under the 'reverse charge' principle. The rate of VAT overseas is irrelevant.

Input VAT can be reclaimed on this expense in the normal way.

MT Travel's VAT position is therefore the same as if the services had been purchased from the UK supplier.

Examiner's report

This question concerned an unincorporated business which was about to change its accounting date, and which was anticipating a trading loss in a future period.

The first part concerned the tax implications of a change of accounting date for an unincorporated business. Unfortunately, relatively few candidates appeared to be aware of the assessment rules on a change of accounting date, so this part was not done well. However, many candidates were able to identify and explain a disadvantage of choosing an accounting date which fell later in the tax year.

The second part of this question required a calculation of the loss available to the trader, and their spouse, on the basis that firstly, the spouse became an employee of the business, or, secondly, the spouse became a partner in the business. In general this was done well. Candidates were then required to go on and advise both taxpayers as to the reliefs available for their losses. The rules relating to trading losses are frequently examined, and while many candidates scored reasonably here, more precise answers would have scored higher marks. Candidates would do well to invest time at the revision stage of their studies to memorising the rules concerning relief for trading losses, and ensuring that they are able to recognise those rules which apply in a given scenario. In particular, they should be able to identify those which apply in certain situations only, such as the opening years of a business, which was applicable to just one of the partners here.

Those candidates who scored well on this particular part:

- adopted a structured approach to outlining the reliefs for the trading loss separately for each of the individuals, and clearly stating the rate of tax saved, as required.

- Didn't waste time considering irrelevant reliefs.

In order to gain a good mark in this type of question it is vital that candidates attempt past exam questions which are available in the question banks. Reading through model answers, while providing useful information, is often of limited help in these cases; candidates need to practise the structured approach necessary to produce a good, coherent answer.

		ACCA marking scheme			*Marks*
(a)	(i)	Taxable trading profits			3.0
					3.0
	(ii)	Tax planning disadvantage			2.0
					2.0
(b)	(i)	Laurie as employee	– loss available to Meg		2.0
			– no loss available to Laurie		0.5
		Laurie as a partner	– split of loss in PSR		1.0
					3.5
				Maximum	3.0
	(ii)	Loss relief available to Meg			5.0
		Loss relief available to Laurie			4.5
					9.5
				Maximum	8.0
(c)		Reverse charge principle			3.0
		Further implications			1.5
					4.5
				Maximum	4.0
Total					20.0

13   ROD

Key answer tips

This question tests a mixture of new areas (EMI share options) as well as brought forward knowledge from TX (partnerships and loss relief).

Part (a) asks for a calculation of after tax proceeds for the sale of some shares acquired via an EMI option. In order to do this you need to think about how much would be chargeable to CGT and tax this at the appropriate rate to take away from proceeds. You were also asked to explain how the base cost is calculated for CGT so make sure you do this and not just the calculations.

(a)   After-tax proceeds from the sale of the Lumba plc shares

The capital gain on the sale of the Lumba plc shares is calculated as follows:

	£	£
Sale proceeds (£4.00 × 20,000)		80,000
Less: Exercise price (£2.30 × 20,000)	46,000	
Amount charged to income tax on exercise (see below)	6,000	
Base cost		(52,000)
Chargeable gain		28,000
Less: Annual exempt amount		(12,300)
Taxable gain		15,700

The capital gains tax payable is £1,570 (£15,700 × 10%).

The after-tax proceeds are £78,430 (£80,000 – £1,570).

As the options were granted at a discount to the market value at the date of grant, a charge to income tax will have arisen on 1 June 2021, when Rod exercised the options, on an amount of £6,000 (£0.30 per share × 20,000 shares), being the difference between the market value of the shares at the date of grant and the exercise price of the options (£2.60 – £2.30). This is added to the price paid for the shares (£2.30 per share) in calculating the base cost of the shares.

(b) **(i)** **Rod's share of the tax-adjusted trading loss in the Thora Partnership for the tax years 2021/22 and 2022/23.**

	£
2021/22 (1 December 2021 to 5 April 2022)	
£29,000 (W) × 4/12	9,667
2022/23 (1 December 2021 to 30 November 2022)	
Loss 1 December 2021 to 30 November 2022 (W)	29,000
Less: Used in 2021/22	(9,667)
	———
	19,333
	———

Tutorial note

A new partner will be taxed under the opening year basis of assessment rules. Where a loss is made in the opening years it is not possible to create overlap losses. Any loss already used in a tax year cannot be used again in a later tax year, so must be deducted from the later assessment.

Working:

	£
Tax-adjusted trading loss year ending 30 November 2022	47,000
Add: Salaries for Abe and Bob (£20,000 + £20,000)	40,000
	———
Balance of loss to be allocated in the profit/loss sharing ratio	87,000
	———

Rod's share of the loss is £29,000 (£87,000/3).

(ii) **Tax saving available to Rod as a result of taking the earliest possible relief for his share of the trading losses of the Thora Partnership**

Rod has a trading loss of £9,667 in 2021/22 and a trading loss of £19,333 in 2022/23.

The losses can be carried back and offset against Rod's total income of the three years prior to the tax year of the loss in each case, on a FIFO basis. This is the earliest possible relief available to Rod.

The loss of the tax year 2021/22 will be carried back and offset against Rod's total income of the tax year 2018/19 of £82,000, which will result in a tax saving of £3,867 (£9,667 × 40%).

The loss of the tax year 2022/23 will be carried back and offset against Rod's total income of the tax year 2019/20 of £106,000 (£90,000 + £16,000). This will result in a tax saving of £7,733 (£19,333 × 40%), as the relief will be taken against the employment income in priority to the dividends. Additionally, as Rod's total income originally exceeded £100,000, his personal allowance was restricted to £9,570 (£12,570 – ((£106,000 –— £100,000)/2)). After taking loss relief, his full personal allowance will be available, generating a further tax saving of £1,200 ((£12,570 – £9,570) × 40%).

Therefore, Rod's total tax saving as a result of taking loss relief is £12,800 (£3,867 + £7,733 + £1,200).

Tutorial notes

1   Rod is eligible to claim opening years' loss relief as the trading loss arose within the first four years of him joining the partnership.

2   In calculating an individual's income tax liability, losses are usually offset against non-savings income first, before savings income (if any), and then dividends. This will maximise the amount of tax relief obtained.

Examiner's report

This question concerned various matters in relation to an individual who had been an employee of a company and had just become a partner in a partnership. There were three parts to the question, broadly covering the capital gain arising on the sale of shares awarded through an enterprise management incentive (EMI) scheme, partnership loss allocation and a partner's loss relief.

The first part of the question required a calculation of the after-tax proceeds from the sale of shares and also an explanation of the base cost of the shares. Many candidates were able to calculate the capital gains tax arising upon sale of the shares and then to calculate proceeds less tax, earning themselves many of the calculation marks. However unfortunately, many candidates appeared to lack knowledge of the detailed rules for the EMI scheme and so were unable to fully explain the base cost of the shares.

The second part of the question required candidates to allocate a trading loss between partners in a partnership and then to calculate, for a new partner who had just joined the partnership, the share of the loss available over two tax years. The question specifically asked candidates to show the relevant basis periods. It was very pleasing to see that many candidates were able to earn marks for the calculations however, fewer candidates were able to state the dates of the relevant basis periods.

The third and final part of the question required candidates to state how the new partner could relieve his trading loss as early as possible and then to explain, with supporting calculations, the total amount of income tax which could be saved with this strategy. Most candidates were able to discuss a possible loss relief strategy although not all chose the loss relief strategy which would relieve the loss as early as possible. Many candidates were able to explain the subsequent tax saving and to support this with calculations. A minority of candidates recognised that claiming the loss relief would affect the amount of personal allowance available and went on to identify the tax implications of this.

ACCA marking scheme			
			Marks
(a)	Calculation of chargeable gain		2.0
	Calculation of after-tax proceeds		2.0
	Explanations		3.0
			———
			7.0
		Maximum	6.0
			———
(b)	Calculation of Rod's share of the loss (working)		2.0
	2021/22 loss		2.0
	2022/23 loss		2.5
			———
			6.5
		Maximum	6.0
			———
	Identification of earliest relief		3.0
	Calculation of tax saving – 2018/19		1.5
	– 2019/20		4.0
	Total saving		1.0
			———
			9.5
		Maximum	8.0
			———
Total			**20.0**
			———

14 TOMAS AND INES

Key answer tips

This question covers some basic aspects of business tax, VAT and also the enterprise investment scheme (EIS). With the exception of part (c) all of this question could be answered with brought forward knowledge from TX. Please do not underestimate how important it is to ensure you revise this brought forward knowledge.

Part (a) offers some easy marks for calculating tax on trading income. Make sure you consider all taxes that would be relevant to this income.

The second part of the question tests basis periods and the advantage of a 30 April year end as opposed to a 31 March year end. Make sure you are happy with the basis period rules as these often get tested despite being brought forward knowledge from TX.

Next you are asked for two matters to consider when deciding whether to voluntarily register for VAT. Think about what the consequences of registration would be and what this would mean in relation to the stakeholders of the business.

The final part of the questions tests the enterprise investment scheme (EIS). Here some EIS shares are being sold on which IT relief and reinvestment relief has been claimed. The key here is to consider whether the shares have been sold within three years or not. This will determine the treatment of the gain on the shares and the IT relief. You should also consider what happens to the deferred gain now that the shares have been sold.

(a) **Tax treatment of the sale of sporting memorabilia**

As Tomas is carrying on a trade of selling sporting memorabilia, the following liabilities will arise:

	£
Income tax	
Tomas' trading income is covered by his personal allowance	0
No tax will arise on the dividends, as they are covered by the dividend nil rate band	0
National insurance contributions (NIC)	
Class 2: £3.05 × 52	159
Class 4: (£11,500 − £9,568) × 9%	174
Total tax payable	333

If the sales were treated as capital disposals, there would be no capital gains tax to pay as the memorabilia are chattels, with cost and proceeds both less than £6,000.

So the difference in the total tax which will be payable by Tomas for the tax year 2022/23 is an increase of £333.

(b) **Basis periods if Tomas adopts a 31 March, or a 30 April year end, and tax advantages of adopting a 30 April year end**

The tax year 2023/24 will be Tomas' second tax year from commencement of trading.

1   If Tomas adopts a 31 March year end, his basis period will be the 12 months ending 31 March 2024.

2   If Tomas adopts a 30 April year end, his basis period will be the 12 months ending 30 April 2023.

Advantages of adopting a 30 April year end are as follows:

–   The income tax liability for the tax year 2023/24 will be due for payment by 31 January 2025. Adopting a 30 April year end maximises the interval between earning profits and paying the tax on those profits.

–   A 30 April year end is financially beneficial for Tomas as the profits of his business are expected to rise each year. So a basis period of 30 April 2023, rather than 31 March 2024, will result in an earlier period of profit, and therefore a lower level of profits, being taxed.

–   30 April 2023 is near the start of the tax year 2023/24, whereas 31 March 2024 is at the end. So, with a 30 April year end, the taxable profit for 2023/24 will be known much earlier, which means there is more time for planning in respect of, for example, the amounts of payments on account, or pension contributions.

Tutorial note

Although three advantages have been explained here, candidates were only required to explain TWO to gain full marks.

(c) **Matters to be considered by Tomas in deciding whether it is financially beneficial to register voluntarily for value added tax (VAT)**

The VAT status of his suppliers. If Tomas' suppliers are VAT registered, Tomas will be charged VAT on his purchases, which he will only be able to reclaim if he is registered for VAT himself. However, if he purchases from non-VAT registered businesses, or members of the public, he will not suffer any input VAT, so there will be no financial benefit from registering.

The VAT status of his customers. If Tomas' customers are registered for VAT, they will be able to reclaim the VAT charged by Tomas on the memorabilia. However, if they are not registered, the VAT will represent an additional cost for them, which may make Tomas' prices uncompetitive, or Tomas will have to bear the burden of the VAT himself.

Tutorial note

Marks were also awarded where candidates made other sensible comments.

(d) **Sale of shares in Tavira Ltd**

If the shares in Tavira Ltd are sold on 1 June 2023, Ines will have owned them for less than three years. The following consequences will therefore arise:

– A chargeable gain of £23,000 (£95,000 – £72,000) will arise on the sale; and

– The enterprise investment scheme (EIS) income tax relief obtained when the shares were acquired will be withdrawn. As the shares will be sold at a profit, the full amount of the tax credit originally given of £18,600 will be reclaimed by HM Revenue and Customs (HMRC).

In addition, the sale of the Tavira Ltd shares will result in the gain on the sale of the painting, which was deferred on the acquisition of the shares, being brought back into charge. The gain on this disposal was £86,000, but the maximum amount of the gain deferred was restricted to the qualifying expenditure of £72,000.

Ines will have a capital gains tax (CGT) liability in the tax year 2023/24, calculated as follows:

	Gain eligible for business asset disposal relief	Gain not eligible for business asset disposal relief
	£	£
Gain on Tavira Ltd shares	23,000	
Deferred gain on painting		72,000
Less: Annual exempt amount (best use)	0	(12,300)
Taxable gains	23,000	59,700

Ines' CGT liability is £14,240 ((£23,000 × 10%) + (£59,700 × 20%)).

Ines' income tax liability is £18,600.

Accordingly, Ines' after-tax proceeds from the sale of the Tavira Ltd shares is £62,160 (£95,000 − £14,240 − £18,600).

Examiner's report

This question concerned the taxation of profits, determination of basis periods, and voluntary registration for VAT for a new unincorporated business, and the sale of shares in respect of which enterprise investment scheme (EIS) relief had been claimed.

The first part of the question required candidates to explain the difference in the total amount of tax payable by the taxpayer due to his profits now being taxed as trading income rather than as chargeable gains. When specific taxes are not mentioned in the question, candidates need to think broadly. Although the majority of candidates correctly identified the income tax implications, very few considered that there would also be national insurance (NIC) implications as well. In relation to the CGT implications, only a minority recognised that the items being sold constituted chattels under £6,000, and so were exempt. So, the majority of candidates were only able to score two out of a possible five marks. The question did ask for supporting calculations, but many candidates produced detailed, comprehensive income tax and CGT computations, in addition to explaining the implications. Calculations were only needed to support the explanation, and so needed to only be brief. In particular, many candidates doing the CBE explained the position in the word processing document, referring the relevant numbers, and also produced comprehensive calculations in the spreadsheet, which did not gain them any additional marks.

The second part of this question related to the basis period for the second tax year of the taxpayer's business if he adopted firstly a 31 March, and secondly a 30 April year end. Very few candidates were able to correctly identify both, which was surprising. A thorough knowledge of the opening and closing year basis period rules for unincorporated businesses is essentially brought forward knowledge from TX. Both of these are frequently tested in scenarios at ATX, and candidates should ensure that they have a sound knowledge of these rules. The requirement to explain the advantages of a 30 April year-end date was done better, with the majority of candidates being able to state one or two advantages in general terms, but relatively few went on the relate these to the specific circumstances of the taxpayer's business.

The third part of the question required candidates to explain two matters the taxpayer should consider in deciding whether it would be financially beneficial to register voluntarily for VAT. On the whole this was done well, although some candidates wasted time explaining more than two, and/or producing lengthy answers including what appeared to be all they knew about voluntary registration, without considering whether these would, in fact, have a financial impact. Candidates are encouraged to take time to read and understand the question fully before starting to write. A little more time spent reading the specific requirements here might have saved quite a bit of wasted effort in some cases.

The final part of the question tested the rules relating to the sale of shares, which qualified under the EIS scheme, being sold within three years of their acquisition. Many candidates were aware of the main principles relating to the taxation of the gain and the withdrawal of the EIS relief previously given but very few managed to get the calculation of the CGT right, particularly in relation to the treatment of the previously deferred gain, which was, admittedly quite a tricky aspect.

ACCA marking scheme

			Marks
(a)	Income tax implications		2.0
	National insurance implications		2.0
	Capital gains tax – chattels < £6,000		1.0
	Difference in tax payable		0.5
			5.5
		Maximum	5.0
(b)	Recognition of basis periods		2.0
	Advantages of 30 April year end		4.0
			6
		Maximum	5.0
(c)	VAT status of suppliers		2.0
	VAT status of customers		2.0
			4.0
		Maximum	3.0
(d)	Consequences of sale		5.0
	Tax liabilities		3.0
	After-tax proceeds		0.5
			8.5
		Maximum	7.0
Total			20.0

15   AMELIA

Key answer tips

This question looks at a sole trader whose business is currently loss making, is in the process of replacing a warehouse and is considering voluntarily deregistering for VAT.

Part (a)(i) requires a fairly generic answer just stating the different ways in which the loss could be offset. Make sure you provide precise answers detailing what the loss can be offset against and whether the use of the loss can be restricted.

Part (a)(ii) moves on from part (i) and asks you to explain and calculate the tax savings for each of the reliefs identified earlier. Your approach to the answer will require some thought and planning, and a logical approach dealing with each option in turn is advisable. Rather than preparing full tax computations, which are time consuming, try to work in the margins just considering the rate at which tax will be saved.

Part (b) is mostly about rollover relief. CGT reliefs are expected to be tested in the exam, so spend some time learning in detail the conditions for each relief as well as the detail of how they operate.

Part (c) requires an explanation of the immediate consequences of the individual deregistering for VAT. VAT will be tested at some point in the exam; registration and de-registration are frequently examined.

(a)   (i)   Reliefs available in respect of Amelia's trading loss of the year ending 31 December 2022

The loss of the year ending 31 December 2022 is a loss of the tax year 2022/23. Accordingly, Amelia can offset the loss against her total income of 2022/23 and/or 2021/22. If she chooses to offset the loss against her total income of 2022/23, she can then offset any remaining loss against her chargeable gains of that year.

Tutorial notes

Amelia has been trading for many years; this means she will be using the current year basis to identify the basis periods for her profits/(losses).

The trading loss of the year ended 31 December 2022 falls into the tax year 2022/23.

Amelia can make a current year claim and/or a prior year claim against total income for both years, either year and in any order. After a claim has been made against total income it is then possible for Amelia to make a claim against chargeable gains in that same year.

(ii) **Relief against income and chargeable gains in the tax year 2022/23**

In the tax year 2022/23, Amelia's only income will be savings income of £6,000. This will be covered by her personal allowance, such that she will have no liability to income tax for this year. Accordingly, if she chooses to take relief for the loss against this income, there will be no income tax saving. However, the remaining loss of £8,000 (£14,000 – £6,000) could then be offset against her chargeable gains for the year.

Tutorial note

If Amelia wishes to make a claim against her chargeable gains in the tax year 2022/23, it is mandatory that an all or nothing claim must first be made against her total income.

Amelia's chargeable gains comprise total gains less the capital loss brought forward i.e. £62,000 (£45,000 + £28,000 – £11,000). Accordingly, the full £8,000 of trading loss could be offset.

Ignoring offset of the trading loss, Amelia would have taxable gains of £49,700 after deducting the annual exempt amount of £12,300. As Amelia will have no taxable income in 2022/23, £37,700 of her taxable gains will fall within her basic rate band, and the remaining £12,000 will be taxed at the higher rate.

The trading loss should therefore be offset against the gain on the UK rental property, as this will be taxed at the higher, residential property rates of 18%/28% (working). The capital gains tax (CGT) saving will be £2,240 (£8,000 × 28%).

Working: Offset of remaining trading loss against chargeable gains

	Residential property gain	Other gain	Total gains
	£	£	£
Gain on UK rental property	45,000		45,000
Gain on Swartz Ltd shares		28,000	28,000
Less: Trading loss converted to capital loss			
	(8,000)		(8,000)
Less: Annual exempt amount	(12,300)		(12,300)
Less: Capital loss brought forward	(11,000)		(11,000)
	———	———	———
Gain remaining chargeable	13,700	28,000	41,700
	———	———	———

Tutorial notes

After taking relief for the trading loss, only £4,000 (£41,700 – £37,700) of Amelia's taxable gains will be taxed at the higher rate, instead of £12,000.

The trading loss would be treated as a current year capital loss in the CGT computation, (i.e. it would be deducted from Amelia's chargeable gains before deducting the annual exempt amount and the capital loss brought forward), as shown above. However, candidates were awarded full credit regardless of the order in which they deducted the trading loss.

Relief against income in the tax year 2021/22

In the tax year 2021/22 Amelia's total income is £47,600 (£30,000 + £11,600 + £6,000), so the full amount of the loss of £14,000 can be offset. Amelia's taxable income was £35,030 (£47,600 – £12,570), such that she was a basic rate taxpayer. The loss offset (which is against her non-savings income of this year) would generate a tax saving of £2,800 (£14,000 × 20%).

Relief against income in the tax years 2022/23 then 2021/22

Amelia could offset the loss against her income of £6,000 in 2022/23, with the remaining £8,000 offset against her income in 2021/22. This would save no tax in 2022/23, and only £1,600 (£8,000 × 20%) in 2021/22.

(b) **Capital gains tax and income tax implications of the sale of Warehouse 1 and the acquisition of Warehouse 2 and the forklift truck**

The sale of Warehouse 1 will give rise to a chargeable gain of £32,000 (£118,000 – £86,000).

Rollover relief will be available to defer part of this gain because Amelia acquired a qualifying replacement asset, Warehouse 2, during the year prior to the sale.

The acquisition of the forklift truck does not qualify for rollover relief as it is a movable asset.

Tutorial note

Rollover relief is available to defer the gain arising on the disposal of a qualifying asset, where a replacement qualifying asset is purchased within a qualifying time period.

Qualifying assets include: –   *Land and buildings (used in the trade)*

                              –   *Goodwill (individuals only – not companies)*

                              –   *Fixed (not movable) plant and machinery*

The gain which is eligible for rollover relief is restricted to £24,000 (£32,000 × 3/4) because Amelia only occupied three of the four floors of Warehouse 1 for business purposes.

The rollover relief available will be further restricted because not all of the proceeds relating to the business use of Warehouse 1 have been used to acquire Warehouse 2:

	£
Proceeds of business element (£118,000 × 3/4)	88,500
Cost of replacement	(83,000)
Gain remaining chargeable	5,500

The balance of the eligible gain of £18,500 (£24,000 – £5,500) will be available for rollover relief. Amelia's chargeable gain in respect of the sale of Warehouse 1 will therefore be £13,500 (£32,000 – £18,500).

The gain of £18,500 will be rolled over and deducted from the base cost of Warehouse 2. The base cost of Warehouse 2 will be £64,500 (£83,000 – £18,500).

Tutorial note

Rollover relief is restricted where there is non-trade use of the qualifying asset being sold or replaced.

Rollover relief is also restricted where the proceeds received on the sale of the original asset are not fully re-invested into a replacement qualifying asset.

The cost of the forklift truck of £23,000 will be eligible for the annual investment allowance in AS Trading's year ending 31 December 2023.

(c) **Deregistration for value added tax (VAT)**

Amelia is able to apply to voluntarily deregister for VAT on 31 December 2022 as the value of her taxable supplies in the following year are not expected to exceed the deregistration limit of £83,000. Her registration will be cancelled from 31 December 2022, or from a later date agreed with HM Revenue and Customs (HMRC).

On deregistration, output VAT will be payable on all non-current assets and inventory held by Amelia, on which input VAT was previously reclaimed. If the total VAT payable does not exceed £1,000, no payment is needed.

As a result of deregistration, Amelia will not be able to reclaim input VAT on the acquisition of Warehouse 2 and the forklift truck.

Tutor's top tips

Don't forget you can find the VAT de-registration threshold in your tax rates and allowances.

Examiner's report

This question concerned a sole trader whose business is currently loss-making, who is also going to replace a warehouse used in the business and is considering voluntarily deregistering for VAT.

Part (a)(i) asked candidates to state the reliefs available to the trader in respect of her trading loss, other than carrying it forward.

This is another area where precision is required. Candidates need to learn whether a loss can be relieved against total income, or trading income only. Candidates should also practise referring to the relevant tax years when dealing with an unincorporated business; just stating 'current year' or 'prior year' is not sufficient, without providing some context to this in terms of the tax years involved. If disposals of capital assets are included in the scenario, candidates are normally expected to consider extending the loss relief to any chargeable gains arising, which, surprisingly, many candidates omitted. Candidates are reminded that relief for trading losses, both for unincorporated businesses and companies, remains a frequently tested area, and would be advised to ensure that they learn the precise rules applicable in each situation.

Part (a)(ii) required candidates to explain and calculate the tax saving for each of the reliefs that they had identified in (a)(i).

This type of question requires a structured, organised approach, and candidates should spend a little time planning an efficient way to address the requirement. The standard of the explanations and calculations was very mixed. Candidates who were well-prepared chose to use a marginal approach to calculate the tax saving, which is an efficient approach to use when tax savings are required. This approach has been used in many past exam questions involving the tax implications of taking loss relief, which candidates would be well advised to practise. Additionally, these candidates had identified the available chargeable gains, and were able to score well on this part by including an explanation and calculation of the CGT saved, in addition to the income tax saving.

Weaker answers often comprised full tax computations, before and after taking loss relief, and, in some cases without actually calculating the tax saving at the end. Additionally, the CGT implications were overlooked by a number of candidates.

Part (b) required an explanation, together with relevant calculations, of the CGT and income tax implications of replacing a warehouse and acquiring movable equipment.

The CGT implications were the more obvious, and most candidates recognised that the disposal of the original warehouse qualified for rollover relief, and that the replacement had been acquired within the required time period. However, the details of the computation proved to be trickier. A good number restricted the eligible gain correctly, by reference to the proportion of the building which had been used in the trade, but relatively few also restricted the qualifying sale proceeds and then went on to calculate the correct chargeable gain. The most common error in this question part, was the failure to recognise that the movable equipment was not a qualifying asset for rollover relief purposes. Many candidates appeared to forget, or ignore, the income tax element, but those who did address this correctly recognised that the movable equipment would qualify for the AIA, to reduce the individual's income tax liability.

Part (c) required an explanation of the immediate consequences of the individual deregistering for VAT.

Many candidates were able to score at least half of the three marks available here, although there were a number of inaccuracies in the detail again here, relating to the level of 'profits' rather than sales, or turnover, and a lack of knowledge regarding the date from which the deregistration would be effective.

					Marks
ACCA marking scheme					
(a)	(i)	Reliefs available			3.5
				Maximum	3.0
	(ii)	Relief in 2022/23	– against income		1.5
			– against gains		5.0
		Relief in 2021/22			2.5
		Relief in 2022/23 and 2021/22			1.0
					10.0
				Maximum	8.0
(b)		Availability of rollover relief			2.5
		Calculation of rollover relief			3.5
		AIA on forklift truck			1.0
					7.0
				Maximum	6.0
(c)		Deregistration for VAT			4.0
				Maximum	3.0
Total					**20.0**

CHANGING BUSINESS SCENARIOS

16   STANLEY BEECH (ADAPTED)

Key answer tips

This question is taken from the old pilot paper, and is not in the current exam format. However, it still provides useful practice of some key areas.

The key to success in part (a) is understanding that Stanley can afford to have some chargeable gains after incorporation relief, because these can be covered by his capital losses and the annual exempt amount, and being able to work backwards to find this amount.

In part (b) it is important to answer the question set and not do unnecessary calculations. Also remember that an owner managed company like this will always be a close company and look out for any close company implications.

(a)   **Transfer of the business to Landscape Ltd**

   (i)   **Capital gains tax liability**

   Where all of the assets of Stanley's business are transferred to Landscape Ltd as a going concern wholly in exchange for shares, any capital gains arising are relieved via incorporation relief such that no capital gains tax liability arises.

   However, where part of the payment received from the company is in the form of a loan account, Stanley will have chargeable gains as set out below.

   For Stanley to have no liability to capital gains tax in the tax year 2022/23, assuming he has no other chargeable gains in the year, his chargeable gains must be covered by his capital losses brought forward (£9,700) and the annual exempt amount of £12,300.

	£
Gain on building ((£87,000 – £46,000)	41,000
Gain on goodwill	24,000
Total capital gains before reliefs	65,000

   Incorporation relief should therefore be:
   (£65,000 – £9,700 – £12,300)   43,000

   Therefore the MV of the shares to be accepted should be:

   $$£43,000 = £65,000 \times \frac{\text{MV of shares}}{£118,000}$$

   MV of shares = £78,062

   Therefore the loan account to accept as part of the consideration can be up to the value of £39,938 (£118,000 – £78,062) and there will be no capital gains tax arising on the transfer.

The shares will have a capital gains tax base cost of £35,062 computed as:

	£
MV of shares (see above)	78,062
Less: Incorporation relief	(43,000)
	———
Base cost of shares	35,062
	———

Tutorial note:

Proof that incorporation relief of £43,000 will avoid a CGT liability is as follows:

	£
Total capital gains	*65,000*
Less: Incorporation relief	
$£65,000 \times \dfrac{£78,062}{£118,000}$	*(43,000)*
	———
	22,000
Less: Annual exempt amount	*(12,300)*
	———
	9,700
Less: Capital losses brought forward	*(9,700)*
	———
Taxable gains	*Nil*
	———

No business asset disposal relief is used as there is no chargeable gain arising on incorporation.

A chargeable gain will arise on the disposal of shares and business asset disposal relief may then be available subject to the normal conditions based on the ownership of the shares.

This should not be an issue as the ownership of the sole trader business can be aggregated with that of the shares, and so Stanley has already owned the combined businesses for the two years required to qualify for business asset disposal relief.

Tutorial note:

When a building on which structures and buildings allowance has been claimed is transferred on incorporation, there is no adjustment required to the sale proceeds for capital gains tax purposes, provided incorporation relief has not been disapplied.

(ii)   **The benefit of using a loan account**

The loan account crystallises capital gains at the time of incorporation without giving rise to a tax liability due to the availability of capital losses, and the annual exempt amount.

This reduces the gains deferred against the base cost of the shares in Landscape Ltd from £65,000 to £43,000 such that any future gains on the disposal of the shares will be smaller.

Stanley can extract the loan account of £39,938 from Landscape Ltd in the future with no 'tax cost', by having the loan repaid.

Tutorial note:

The subsequent disposal of the shares will be eligible for business asset disposal relief provided the conditions are satisfied, as none of Stanley's lifetime allowance of £1,000,000 has been utilised.

(iii)   **Landscape Ltd structures and buildings allowance for the year ended 31 March 2023**

Landscape Ltd can claim structures and buildings allowance from the date that the building is transferred to it. The company will claim the allowance based on the original qualifying cost of £36,000 (excluding land) and will claim for the remainder of the 33 ⅓ year period.

The amount available for the year ended 31 March 2023 will be £630 (£36,000 × 3% × 7/12).

(b)   **Advice on Stanley's remuneration package**

(i)   **Dividend**

The advice in respect of the dividend is accurate but not complete.

The first £2,000 of dividend income will effectively be tax free, as it will fall into Stanley's dividend nil rate band.

Also, the advice ignores the cost to Landscape Ltd. Because Stanley owns Landscape Ltd, he must consider the effect on the company's position as well as his own.

Dividends are not tax deductible. The profits paid out as a dividend to Stanley will have been subject to corporation tax at 19%. On the other hand, Landscape Ltd will obtain a tax deduction at 19% for a salary bonus together with the related employer's national insurance contributions.

There will be an overall tax saving from paying a dividend as opposed to a salary bonus. However, the benefit will not be as great as suggested by the advice that Stanley has received due to the different treatment of the two payments in hands of the company.

(ii)   Interest free loan

The advice in respect of the loan is again accurate but not complete. The loan will not give rise to an employment income benefit as it is for not more than £10,000, but the advice again ignores the position of the company.

As the company is controlled by Stanley, Landscape Ltd will be a close company. Accordingly, the loan to Stanley is a loan to a participator in a close company, and as Stanley owns more than 5% of the company's share capital there is no de minimis in this case.

Thus, Landscape Ltd must pay an amount equal to 32.5% of the loan (£1,170) to HMRC. The payment will be due on 1 January 2024 (i.e. nine months and one day after the end of the accounting period in which the loan is made).

When the loan is repaid by Stanley, Landscape Ltd may reclaim the £1,170. The repayment by HMRC will be made nine months and one day after the end of the accounting period in which the loan is repaid.

(iii)   Company car

The advice in respect of the company car is not correct because of the difference in the tax rates applying to the company and to Stanley, and the liability to class 1A national insurance contributions.

Tax cost of providing car:	£
Class 1A national insurance contributions	
(£3,762 (W) × 13.8%)	519
Income tax on benefit (£3,762 (W) × 40%)	1,505
	———
	2,024
	———

	£
Tax saved:	
Cost of providing car (£400 × 12)	4,800
Class 1A national insurance contributions	519
	———
	5,319
	———
Corporation tax (£5,319 × 19%)	1,011
	———
Net tax cost (£2,024 – £1,011)	1,013
	———

Working: Car benefit

CO_2 emissions 48g/km, electric range = 30 to 39 miles

Appropriate percentage = 11%

Car benefit (£34,200 × 11%) = £3,762

		ACCA marking scheme	
			Marks
(a)	(i)	Split of consideration	
		Incorporation relief – 3 conditions	1.5
		Amount of future cash payment:	
		Rationale – gains to equal capital losses	
		and annual exempt amount	1.5
		Gains on transfer of business	1.0
		Gains after incorporation relief:	
		Incorporation relief	1.0
		Calculation of gains after incorporation relief	0.5
		Solving to find value of the loan account	1.0
		Business asset disposal relief	1.0
		CGT base cost of shares:	
		Value of assets transferred for shares	0.5
		Incorporation relief	1.0
	(ii)	Benefit of using a loan account	
		Capital gains	1.0
		Extract funds with no tax cost	0.5
	(iii)	Landscape Ltd SBA for year ended 31 March 2023:	
		Claim based on original cost for remainder of 33 ⅓ years	1.0
		Calculation of allowance	1.0
			────
			12.5
		Maximum	12.0
			────

			Marks
(b)		Advice on remuneration package	
		Dividend	
		Advice is correct but incomplete with reason	1.0
		CT position re dividend	0.5
		CT position re bonus	0.5
		Conclusion with reason	1.0
		Interest free loan	
		Advice is correct but incomplete with reason	1.0
		Close company	0.5
		Loan to a participator and reason	1.0
		Tax due/when	1.0
		Repayment position	0.5
		Company car	
		The advice is not correct with reason	1.0
		Calculation	
		Car benefit	1.0
		Tax cost	1.0
		Tax saving	1.0
			────
			11.0
		Maximum	10.0
			────
Total			**22.0**
			────

17   DESIREE (ADAPTED) *Walk in the footsteps of a top tutor*

Key answer tips

This section B question covers the often tested scenario of sole trader versus company, with some easy marks on voluntary VAT registration.

Part (a) requires calculation of taxable profits or losses for the first three periods, and was almost identical to a requirement set in one of the section A questions in a previous exam.

Part (a)(ii) requires discussion of the use of losses for a sole trader compared to a company. This is a typical textbook scenario with no tricks, and you should score well here as long as you have learnt the rules.

Part (b) requires discussion of voluntary VAT registration – a TX topic, but one which most students are likely to be happy with. There are also marks for discussing imports – a popular exam topic. The danger here is not applying the discussion to the specific scenario.

The highlighted words in the written sections are key phrases that markers are looking for.

(a)   (i)   Taxable profit/allowable loss for each of the first three taxable periods

Tutor's top tips

Think carefully before attempting this section.

If the business is unincorporated, the losses must be matched to tax years before reliefs can be claimed.

However, if the business is set up as a company, the loss reliefs will be for accounting periods, so no further adjustments will be needed.

Make sure that your answer is clearly labelled!

Business is unincorporated

	Loss	Assessable profit
	£	£
2022/23 – Actual basis (1 September 2022 to 5 April 2023) (£46,000 × 7/10)	(32,200)	0
2023/24 – First 12 months (1 September 2022 to 31 August 2023) 1 September 2022 to 30 June 2023 – Loss	(46,000)	
Loss allocated to 2022/23	32,200	
1 July 2023 to 31 August 2023 – Profit (£22,000 × 2/12)	3,667	
	(10,133)	0
2024/25 – Current year basis (Year ending 30 June 2024)		22,000

Tutorial note

Remember that when you apply the opening year rules to losses there is no overlap!

Losses can only be relieved once, and if they are matched with two tax years in the assessments, they must be removed from the later year.

Business is operated via a company

	Loss	Assessable profit
	£	£
Ten months ending 30 June 2023	(46,000)	0
Year ending 30 June 2024		22,000
Year ending 30 June 2025		64,000

(ii)   **Advice on whether or not the business should be incorporated**

Tutor's top tips

You must learn the loss reliefs available to individuals and companies, as these often feature in exam questions.

Don't write about all the loss reliefs available; just pick the ones that are relevant. For example, in this question there is no point in talking about reliefs on cessation of trade.

When writing about loss reliefs, make sure that you use very specific language. For example, don't just say 'losses can be carried forward'; say that 'losses can be carried forward against the first available future trading profits from the same trade'.

You must also apply the reliefs to the scenario.

The two key considerations for both the unincorporated business and the company are:

- *Amount of tax saved, and*
- *Timing of the relief.*

There is no point in preparing full computations of the tax saved, as the question states that detailed calculations are not required.

Business is operated via a company

If the business is operated via a company, the loss of the ten month period ending 30 June 2023 will be carried forward for offset against future total profits of the company.

The earliest that any of the company's losses will be relieved is the year ending 30 June 2024 thus reducing the corporation tax payable on 1 April 2025.

However, the tax savings will only arise if the budgeted profits are achieved as the company doesn't appear to have any other income or gains. If the business does not achieve profitability the losses will be wasted.

Business is unincorporated

If the business is unincorporated, the loss in each of the two tax years can be offset against:

- The total income of the year of loss and/or the previous year
- The total income of the three years prior to the year of loss starting with the earliest of the three years.

This enables Desiree to obtain immediate relief for the losses.

Desiree has employment income in the tax year 2022/23 of only £10,000 (£60,000 × 2/12) together with bank interest of £1,000. All of this income will be covered by her personal allowance.

Her total income in earlier years is her salary of £60,000 and the bank interest. Accordingly, she should offset the losses against the income of the tax year 2021/22 and earlier years rather than the income of the tax year 2022/23.

The loss of the tax year 2022/23 could be offset against the total income of the tax year 2021/22 (the previous year) or 2019/20 (the first of the three years prior to 2022/23).

The loss of the tax year 2023/24 could be offset against the total income of 2020/21 (the first of the three years prior to 2023/24).

This will obtain full relief for the losses at a mixture of basic and higher rates of tax.

Conclusion

Desiree's primary objective is the most beneficial use of the loss.

She should therefore run the business as an unincorporated sole trader in order to obtain relief for the losses as soon as possible.

Tutor's top tips

Make sure that you state your conclusion. As long as it is consistent with your analysis, you will be given credit.

There is no loss relief cap for the relief as the trading loss is less than £50,000.

(b)   Financial advantages and disadvantages of Desiree registering voluntarily for VAT

Tutor's top tips

This section of the question is mainly based on TX knowledge and is very straightforward.

You could attempt this part of the question first, just in case you run out of time on part (a).

Advantages

- Registering for VAT will enable the business to recover input tax, where possible, on expenses and capital expenditure.
  This will reduce the costs incurred by the business thus reducing its losses and its capital allowances.

- The VAT incurred on the fees paid to the market research consultants in March 2022 can be recovered as pre-registration input tax.
  The payment in November 2021 is more than six months prior to registration and therefore the input tax in relation to it cannot be recovered.

Disadvantages

- The business will have to charge its customers VAT at 20%.
  This will represent an increase in the prices charged to those customers who are unable to recover VAT (i.e. domestic customers and non-registered business customers).
  Desiree may need to consider reducing prices in order to reduce the impact of the additional VAT on these customers.

Treatment of imports

- Desiree must account for output VAT on importation.
- This can be recovered as input VAT on the same VAT return.
- As the VAT can be recovered the treatment is tax neutral.

Examiner's report

Part (a)(i) required candidates to calculate the taxable trading profit or allowable trading loss depending on whether the business vehicle was a company or an unincorporated business. The majority of candidates scored high marks here although some had difficulty calculating the figure for the second tax year of an unincorporated business based on the first 12 months of trading. Those who did not do so well simply did not know the basic mechanical rules and either missed out this part of the question or tried to make it up. The opening and closing years rules for unincorporated traders are examined regularly and candidates preparing for future sittings are likely to benefit from being able to handle them.

Part (a)(ii) required candidates to provide a 'thorough and detailed explanation' of the manner in which the losses could be used depending on the choice of business vehicle. This part of the question was done well by almost all of the candidates who attempted it. In order to maximise marks here it was necessary to be precise in terms of language used. For example, it was not sufficient to state that losses can be carried forward against future profits. Instead, candidates needed to state that losses could be carried forward for offset against future profits of *the same trade*.

There was also a requirement to state which business structure would best satisfy the client's objectives. The mark available for this was missed by those candidates who had stopped thinking and were simply writing down everything they knew about loss relief.

The other difficulty which candidates had with this part of the question was a failure to recognise that not all possible loss reliefs were available due to the particular facts of the question. Candidates should ensure that they do not write at length about matters which are irrelevant.

The final part of the question concerned the 'financial' advantages and disadvantages of registering voluntarily for VAT. Many candidates let themselves down by not reading the question carefully such that they simply listed all the advantages and disadvantages they could think of without focusing on the word financial or the particular facts surrounding the client. This meant that they missed the possibility of recovering pre-registration VAT, which was often the difference between an OK mark and a good mark.

ACCA marking scheme				
				Marks
(a)	(i)	Business is unincorporated		
			Application of opening year rules	2.5
			Losses counted once only	1.0
		Business is operated via a company		1.0
				————
				4.5
			Maximum	4.0
				————
	(ii)	Business is operated via a company		2.5
		Business is unincorporated		
			Reliefs available	2.5
			Application to Desiree's position	3.0
		Conclusion		1.0
				————
				9.0
				————
(b)		Advantages		
			Recovery of input tax	1.5
			Pre-registration input tax	1.5
		Disadvantages		1.5
		VAT treatment of imports		3.0
				————
				7.5
			Maximum	7.0
				————
Total				**20.0**
				————

18 ZITI *Walk in the footsteps of a top tutor*

Key answer tips

This section A question has two distinct parts:

Part (a) relates to the disposal of an unincorporated business on two alternative disposal dates (31 January 2023 and 30 April 2023). The examining team expects you to compare the after-tax sale proceeds after payment of both income tax and capital gains tax.

This is the most demanding part of the question and a methodical approach is necessary together with a sound understanding of the closing year rules and capital allowances.

With regard to capital gains tax, Ravi (Ziti's father) gave the business to Ziti back in July 2018 and claimed full gift holdover relief, so you need to consider the impact of this on Ziti's disposal and also think about whether business asset disposal relief is available.

There are five easy marks on VAT, for a comparison of the disposal of assets following a cessation of trade and the disposal of a business as a going concern. This is commonly tested, so make sure you know the conditions.

Part (b) relates to the inheritance tax payable by Ziti if Ravi were to die any time between 7 June 2022 and 30 June 2025. This is challenging as you need to consider when the inheritance tax liability would change. As long as you realise that the two main factors affecting the IHT liability are business property relief and taper relief, you should be able to earn sufficient marks to pass this part of the question.

The highlighted words in the written sections are key phrases that markers are looking for.

Tutor's top tips

As is the norm for section A questions, the formal requirements that appear at the end of the question only tell you how many marks are available for each section of the answer. The detailed requirements can be found in the information provided.

As you read through the question, highlight any requirements and instructions that you find. The requirements in this particular question are all in the email from the manager.

The question has asked for meeting notes which address certain issues and you may find it useful to strike through the issues as you attempt them.

Make sure that you set out your answer in the required format. For meeting notes you need a suitable heading which will identify the subject. Use of sub-headings for each part which agree to the points in the manager's email will make your answer easier to mark.

Section A will always have four professional marks to cover presentation, relevant advice and quality of communication.

NOTES FOR MEETING

Prepared by   Tax senior

Date   6 June 2022

Subject   Ziti – sale of business and inheritance tax

(a)   Sale of the business

      (i)   Post-tax income and sales proceeds

            Income tax position

Tutor's top tips

As long as you methodically deal with each alternative disposal date, it should be easy to pass this part of the question, which is all based on TX knowledge.

Step 1:   Find Ziti's profits assessed under the closing year rules.

Step 2:   Find the income tax payable on Ziti's profits.

The key to success is recognising that the two alternative cessation dates fall into two different tax years.

If Ziti ceases to trade on 31 January 2023 then the final tax year is 2022/23, whereas if he ceases just three months later on 30 April 2023, the final tax year will be 2023/24.

This has an impact on the closing year assessments.

Cessation on 31 January 2023 would require two sets of accounts, for:

- *the year ended 30 April 2022*
- *the nine months ended 31 January 2023.*

However, both of these will be assessed in 2022/23.

Cessation on 30 April 2023 would also require two sets of accounts, for:

- *the year ended 30 April 2022*
- *the year ended 30 April 2023.*

The year ended 30 April 2022 will be assessed in the tax year 2022/23, and the year ended 30 April 2023 will be assessed in the tax year 2023/24, requiring two income tax computations.

In both cases the profits for the year ending 30 April 2021 would be assessed under the current year basis in the tax year 2021/22, but you were only required to consider the trading profits from 1 May 2021 onwards in this question.

It was also important to appreciate the effect that the capital allowances would have on the assessment of profits on cessation, based on the timing of capital additions and disposals.

Remember to get the easy mark for deducting overlap profits (profits taxed twice on commencement) from the final year's assessment!

Business cessation on 31 January 2023 in the tax year 2022/23

Adjusted profits for accounting periods	y/e 30.4.2022 £	9 m/e 31.1.2023 £
Trading income		
(12 × £5,000)/(9 × £5,000)	60,000	45,000
Less: Capital allowances (£6,000 × 100% AIA)	(6,000)	
Add: Balancing charge (TWDV £0 – £10,000 MV)		10,000
	———	———
Adjusted trading profit	54,000	55,000
	———	———

Assessment of profit	
2022/23	£
Year ended 30 April 2022	54,000
Period ended 31 January 2023	55,000
Less: Overlap profits	(9,000)
	———
Taxable trading profit	100,000
	———

Tutor's top tips

Strictly, the capital allowances should be calculated for each accounting period before matching the profits to the tax year using the closing year rules, as set out above.

The alternative presentation below shows you how the answer could be calculated more quickly by taking some shortcuts.

Either presentation would be acceptable in the exam.

Alternative presentation:

Assessment of profits

2022/23	£
Trading income (1 May 2021 to 31 January 2023)	
(21 × £5,000)	105,000
Add: Net balancing charge (£6,000 – £10,000) (Note)	4,000
Less: Overlap profits	(9,000)
	———
Taxable trading profit	100,000
	———

Tutorial note

There would be an AIA of £6,000 on the purchase of the equipment during the year ended 30 April 2022, leaving a tax written down value of zero, then a balancing charge of £10,000 in the final accounting period on the sale of all the equipment in the main pool.

With cessation on 31 January 2023, both the AIA and the balancing charge will be assessed in 2022/23, but with cessation on 30 April 2023 the allowance and charge will fall into two different tax years.

Tutor's top tips

The examining team wants you to quantify the after-tax proceeds so you have to find the income tax payable based on profits of £100,000 in the tax year 2022/23. Remember the personal allowance of £12,570 is only restricted once income exceeds £100,000, so the full PA is available.

Don't worry if you have the wrong figure for taxable trading profit. As long as you calculate the income tax correctly based on your figure, you would still score full marks here.

Income tax payable	**2022/23**
	£
Taxable trading profit (above)	100,000
Less: Personal allowance	(12,570)
Taxable income	87,430

£	
37,700 × 20%	7,540
49,730 × 40%	19,892
87,430	
Income tax payable	27,432

Business disposal on 30 April 2023 in the tax year 2023/24

Adjusted profits for accounting periods	y/e 30.4.2022	y/e 30.4.2023
	£	£
Trading income		
(12 × £5,000)/(12 × £5,000)	60,000	60,000
Less: Capital allowances (£6,000 × 100% AIA)	(6,000)	
Add: Balancing charge (TWDV £0 – £10,000 MV)		10,000
Adjusted trading profit	54,000	70,000

Assessment of profits	
2022/23	£
Year ended 30 April 2022	54,000
2023/24	
Year ended 30 April 2023	70,000
Less: Overlap profits	(9,000)
Taxable trading profit	61,000

Income tax payable

	2022/23	2023/24
	£	£
Taxable trading profit (above)	54,000	61,000
Less: Personal allowance	(12,570)	(12,570)
Taxable income	41,430	48,430

£ £		
37,700 / 37,700 × 20%	7,540	7,540
3,730 / 10,730 × 40%	1,492	4,292
41,430 / 48,430		
Income tax payable	9,032	11,832

Capital gains tax (CGT) position

Tutor's top tips

When computing the capital gain on the disposal of the business, it is necessary to deal with each asset separately. Gains will only arise on chargeable assets.

With cessation on 31 January 2023, Ziti is closing down the business so a disposal only arises on the building and the equipment, not the goodwill.

Alternatively, with the disposal on the 30 April 2023, the business is being sold as a going concern so it is necessary to consider the gain on the goodwill as well.

The question asks for explanations of the availability of any CGT reliefs as well as any necessary assumptions, so there will be marks available for these.

Sale of assets on 31 January 2023

	£
Capital gains:	
Building (£330,000 – £60,000 (W))	270,000
Equipment	0
	270,000
Less: Annual exempt amount	(12,300)
Taxable gains	257,700
CGT at 10%	25,770

No capital gains or losses will arise in respect of the equipment, as movable items (chattels) with a cost and market value of not more than £6,000 are exempt from CGT.

Working: Deemed cost of building

	£
Market value at date of gift	300,000
Less: Gain on gift held over (£300,000 – £60,000)	(240,000)
	———
Deemed cost for Ziti	60,000
	———

Tutorial note

The assets were originally given to Ziti by Ravi, and a gift holdover relief claim was made, which means that when Ziti now disposes of the business, his base cost will be the same as the original cost (Ravi's cost).

Sale of business on 30 April 2023

Tutor's top tips

There will now be a gain on the goodwill in addition to the gain on the building.

The CGT liability computed earlier on the building will simply increase by the tax on this goodwill gain which is £4,000 (£40,000 × 10%).

You do not have to do the entire computation again.

	£
CGT due in respect of the sale of the building on 31 January 2023 (as above)	25,770
CGT due in respect of the sale of goodwill (£40,000 × 10%)	4,000
	———
	29,770
	———

Availability of business asset disposal relief (BADR):

BADR is available where a business which has been owned for at least two years:

* is sold; or
* ceases to be carried on and its assets are sold within three years of cessation.

Accordingly, the relief will be available in both situations.

Tutorial note

BADR may be denied on chargeable gains relating to goodwill where the goodwill is acquired by a close company and the individual making the disposal becomes a shareholder in the company.

However, in this scenario the business is being sold to an individual so the potential restriction does not apply.

Summary of post-tax cash

Tutor's top tips

When computing the after-tax proceeds consider only the cash inflows and cash outflows. This type of requirement features very regularly in the exam.

Cash inflows will consist of the trading income and sale proceeds received from the sale of the assets.

Cash outflows will consist of the capital cost of the equipment and the income tax and capital gains tax liabilities payable.

	Sale on 31 January 2023	Sale on 30 April 2023
	£	£
Trading income (£5,000 × 21/24)	105,000	120,000
Equipment purchased 1 August 2021	(6,000)	(6,000)
Sale proceeds:		
Goodwill	–	40,000
Building	330,000	330,000
Equipment	10,000	10,000
Less: Income tax	(27,432)	
(£9,032 + £11,832)		(20,864)
CGT	(25,770)	(29,770)
Post-tax cash	385,798	443,366

Delaying the sale until 30 April 2023 would:

- be financially beneficial; and
- delay the payment of both the income tax for the profits taxed in the tax year 2023/24 and the CGT.

Assumption:

Ziti has not used his annual exempt amount.

(ii) Value added tax (VAT)

Tutor's top tips

The VAT implications arising on a cessation of trade is an area that is regularly examined and should be an easy five marks, provided that you have revised this topic.

In both cases, Ziti is ceasing to trade and would have to deregister for VAT.

The difference between the two options is that the disposal on 31 January 2023 is not a transfer of a going concern (so output VAT would be payable) whereas the transfer on 30 April 2023 is a TOGC (so no output VAT is payable as long as certain conditions are satisfied).

Watch out for the building; remember that there are special rules for buildings. The question has confirmed that no option to tax has been made and the building is more than three years old.

Sale on 31 January 2023

VAT will need to be charged at 20% on the sale of the equipment.

The sale of the building will be an exempt supply, as it is a commercial building, more than three years old and no election has been made for it to be a taxable building.

Sale on 30 April 2023

VAT will need to be charged at 20% on the equipment and the goodwill unless the sale qualifies as a transfer of a going concern.

For the sale of the business to be regarded as a transfer of a going concern, the following conditions must be satisfied:

- The business must be a going concern.
- The purchaser must use the assets to carry on the same kind of business as that carried on by Ziti.
- The purchaser must be VAT registered or be required to be VAT registered as a result of the purchase (based on the supplies made by the purchased business in the previous 12 months).
- There should be no significant break in trading before or after the purchase of the business.

(b) **Inheritance tax**

Tutor's top tips

The question asked you to compute the IHT liability payable by Ziti for all possible dates based on Ravi dying between 7 June 2022 and 30 June 2025. The question did also give a hint and indicated that the best way to approach this is to identify the dates on which the IHT liability would change.

The first aspect to consider is the availability of 100% business property relief. If Ravi died while Ziti still owned the business, then 100% BPR would be available. However, if Ravi died after Ziti had sold the business then no BPR would be available.

After computing the inheritance tax liability, you then need to consider how the liability would change if Ravi was fortunate enough to survive for a longer period. For every consecutive year thereafter, the IHT liability would be reduced by 20% as a greater amount of taper relief would be available.

As with previous section A questions, it is imperative to spend a few minutes planning your approach prior to starting the question.

You should have identified four different periods.

1   7.6.2022 – 30.4.2023

During this period Ziti still owns the business so 100% BPR is available and no IHT liability would arise.

2   1.5.2023 – 30.6.2023

During this period no BPR is available as Ziti will have sold the business.

The IHT liability would be reduced by 40% taper relief as the period between the gift to Ziti and the date of Ravi's death is between 4 – 5 years.

3   1.7.2023 – 30.6.2024

Taper relief of 60% is available as the period between the gift to Ziti and the date of Ravi's death is between 5 – 6 years.

4   1.7.2024 – 30.6.2025

Taper relief of 80% is available as the period between the gift to Ziti and the date of Ravi's death is between 6 – 7 years.

The easiest way to approach the question is to compute the IHT liability based on the second period above and then reduce this liability by the increased taper relief.

Summary

Date of death	Note	Liability
		£
7 June 2022 to 30 April 2023	1	0
1 May 2023 to 30 June 2023	2	48,480
1 July 2023 to 30 June 2024	3(i)	32,320
1 July 2024 to 30 June 2025	3(ii)	16,160

Notes

1   If Ravi were to die whilst Ziti still owns the business, there would be no inheritance tax liability due to the availability of 100% business property relief on the transfer of an unincorporated business which has been owned by the transferor (Ravi) for at least two years.

2   Business property relief will not be available if Ziti does not own the business when Ravi dies, because he does not intend to reinvest all of the proceeds into replacement business property.

Taper relief will only be available once Ravi has survived the gift by at least three years.

	£	£	£
Value transferred			
(£40,000 + £300,000 + £9,000)			349,000
Less: Annual exemptions			
(2018/19 and 2017/18 b/f)			(6,000)
			343,000
Nil rate band		325,000	
GCTs in 7 years before the gift			
(1.7.2011 – 1.7.2018):			
Chargeable transfer	190,000		
Less: Annual exemptions			
(2014/15 and 2013/14)	(6,000)		
		(184,000)	
NRB available			(141,000)
Taxable amount			202,000
			£
Inheritance tax at 40%			80,800
Less: Taper relief (4 – 5 years) (40% × £80,800)			(32,320)
Inheritance tax payable			48,480

3   IHT liability with additional taper relief

			£
(i)	Taper relief of 60% (5 – 6 years)		32,320
	(IHT liability £80,800 × 40%)		————
(ii)	Taper relief of 80% (6 – 7 years)		16,160
	(IHT liability £80,800 × 20%)		————

Examiner's report

The first part of part (a) concerned the tax implications of the disposal of the business and was split into two sub-requirements. It was quite substantial and was worth 17 marks. Stronger candidates structured their answers in such a way that it was very clear which of the possible methods of disposal they were addressing and then dealt with the two methods one at a time. Weaker candidates did not spend sufficient time thinking about the facts of the question and simply dealt with a disposal without making it clear which of the possibilities they were considering.

The income tax aspects of the disposal revolved around the closing year rules for the unincorporated trader. There were two possible dates for the disposal: 31 January 2023 (in the tax year 2022/23) and 30 April 2023 (in the tax year 2023/24). It was important to be able to identify the tax years of the proposed disposal and the basis of assessment for each of the relevant years.

Many candidates did not have a clear understanding of these basic rules, such that they were not able to identify the relevant tax years or to accurately calculate the taxable profits for each of the relevant tax years. The unincorporated trader is an important element of the syllabus and is examined at almost every sitting; candidates must ensure that they are competent at applying the opening years rules, closing year rules and relief for losses.

The trader had purchased equipment, which was then to be sold on the cessation of the business. This required knowledge of the fundamentals of capital allowances including the annual investment allowance (AIA) and the balancing charge on disposal. Most candidates identified the AIA but many then omitted to follow the story through to the disposal, such that the balancing charge was left out. In addition, weaker candidates prepared comprehensive (and time-consuming) calculations of capital allowances in order to arrive at an AIA of £6,000, when all that was required was a statement in the calculation of the trading profit that the AIA was £6,000.

The treatment of overlap profits, the personal allowance and the calculation of income tax was done well by the vast majority of candidates.

The capital gains tax implications of the sale of the business were straightforward and were handled reasonably well. However, one common error was to treat the sale of the business as if it were a sale of a single asset as opposed to a sale of the individual assets of the business. It is important to calculate a chargeable gain on the disposal of each individual asset and not to group assets together as a single disposal.

Many candidates concluded that the capital gains tax implications were the same regardless of which of the methods of disposal took place. However, this was not the case because there was a disposal of goodwill only where the business was sold as a going concern. This affected both the disposal proceeds of the assets and the capital gains tax arising.

Finally, candidates were required to prepare a summary.

From the point of view of the client there are many detailed issues and calculations to consider here so it is important to be able to bring matters together in a manner which is useful and informative.

The summary was worth a maximum of three marks and simply required figures from earlier calculations to be brought together in one place. In order to score the maximum marks available, candidates had to include the trading income and the proceeds from the sale of the assets together with both the income tax and the capital gains tax. It was also important to exclude any non-cash items. Very few candidates managed to score all three marks; and many candidates failed to produce any sort of summary.

The second part of part (a) was handled well by the majority of candidates with many candidates demonstrating a good knowledge of the various conditions necessary for a sale to be regarded as a transfer of a going concern.

The second part of the question concerned the basic mechanics of inheritance tax; it was done well by many candidates. The question concerned the gift of a business and the subsequent death of the donor.

Almost all candidates identified the gift of the business as a potentially exempt transfer that would become chargeable following the death of the donor within seven years. They were also competent at dealing with the annual exemptions, the nil rate band (with one exception – see below), the tax rate and taper relief.

The one area where a lot of candidates did not perform as well was when it came to business property relief (BPR). To begin with, many candidates omitted BPR altogether. BPR is a significant relief that all candidates should be aware of. It is important to slow down in the exam and make sure that you work through the tax implications of the particular situation in a logical way. So, with inheritance tax, assets need to be valued, then reliefs (including BPR) need to be considered, then exemptions, followed by the nil band, tax rate and taper relief.

Those candidates who did include BPR in their answers often failed to realise that if the business was sold by Ziti (the donee) before the death of his father (the donor), BPR would not be available because the rules require the donee to own the assets gifted at the date of the donor's death.

The point referred to above regarding the nil rate band relates to the relevance of the chargeable lifetime transfer (CLT) made by the donor of the business on 1 May 2014. It was thought by some candidates that this gift would have no effect on the nil rate band available as it was more than seven years prior to the death of the donor. However, because the CLT was made within seven years of the gift of the business on 1 July 2018, the nil rate band available when calculating the tax due in respect of the gift of the business has to be reduced by the amount of the CLT.

ACCA marking scheme			
			Marks
(a)	(i)	Income tax position	
		Basis periods	2.0
		Trading income	1.5
		Capital allowances	3.0
		Overlap profits	1.0
		Cessation on 31 January 2023	
		Income tax payable	1.0
		Cessation on 30 April 2023	
		Income tax payable	1.0
		Capital gains tax position	
		Capital gains	2.5
		Capital gains tax	1.5
		Availability of business asset disposal relief	2.0
		Summary	3.0
		Assumption	1.0
			———
			19.5
		Maximum	**17.0**
			———
	(ii)	Sale on 31 January 2023	1.5
		Sale on 30 April 2023	
		Charge VAT unless it is a transfer of a going concern	1.0
		Conditions (one mark each, maximum three marks)	3.0
			———
			5.5
		Maximum	**5.0**
			———
(b)		Death prior to disposal of business	2.0
		Death post disposal of business	
		Value of gift	1.5
		Annual exemptions	1.0
		Business property relief	1.5
		Taper relief	1.0
		Nil rate band	1.5
		Inheritance tax liabilities	2.0
			———
			10.5
		Maximum	**9.0**
			———
		Approach to problem solving	1.0
		Clarity of calculations	1.0
		Effectiveness of communication	1.0
		Overall presentation	1.0
			———
		Maximum	**4.0**
			———
Total			**35.0**
			———

19   JONNY (ADAPTED)   *Walk in the footsteps of a top tutor*

Key answer tips

This question is in four separate parts, which could be answered in any order.

All of the areas covered are mainstream areas, and much of the technical knowledge tested is brought forward knowledge from TX: unincorporated businesses and trading losses, employed vs. self-employed factors and basic inheritance tax.

It is very important to retain your TX knowledge, as it is often tested in the ATX exam.

Remember that there will always be five marks available in section A of the exam for discussing ethical issues. These are often some of the easiest marks to obtain, as there are a limited number of different scenarios that could be examined.

The detailed information in the question would be shown as three separate exhibits in the real exam, which you can find of the left hand side of the screen. Make sure that you access the information in each exhibit, as well as in the requirements button.

The highlighted words in the written sections are key phrases that markers are looking for in your letter.

Tutor's top tips

As is usual for section A questions, the formal requirements at the end of the question just tell you how many marks are available for each part of the question. The detailed requirements are in the email from the manager.

As you read through, you may find it useful to highlight any requirements and instructions that you find. Refer back to these and tick them off as you answer the question, to ensure that you do not leave anything out.

Note that the requirement asks for a memorandum, so there will be marks available for using the correct format.

Memorandum

To	The files
Prepared by	Tax senior
Date	10 September 2022
Subject	Jonny – new business, inheritance tax and other matters

(a)   Unincorporated business

(i)   Jonny's post-tax income

Tutor's top tips

Although unincorporated businesses and trading losses are TX topics, the ATX examining team has said that unincorporated businesses will be tested in every exam, so you must ensure that you can remember and apply the rules.

In order to answer this question, there are a number of steps to be undertaken:

1   Apply the opening year assessment rules and calculate the taxable trading profit/loss for the first two tax years based on the weak demand figures.

2   Explain the options available for relieving the loss and select the most tax efficient option.

3   Calculate the tax payable/saved for each of the first two tax years for both strong and weak demand.

4   Calculate the post-tax income.

Do not waste time in calculating the taxable trading profits for strong demand as these figures are provided in the question.

Weak demand – taxable trading profit/(loss) for the first two tax years

	£	£
2022/23 (1 November 2022 to 5 April 2023)		
Loss (£15,200 × 5/8)		(9,500)
2023/24 (1 November 2022 to 31 October 2023)		
1 November 2022 to 30 June 2023		
Loss	(15,200)	
Less: Recognised in the tax year 2022/23	9,500	
		(5,700)
1 July 2023 to 31 October 2023		
Profit (£18,000 × 4/12)		6,000
Profit		300

Options for loss relief with weak demand

The loss of £9,500 for the tax year 2022/23 can be offset against:

(i) Total income of the tax year 2022/23 and/or 2021/22.

In the tax year 2022/23, Jonny will have no taxable income.

In the tax year 2021/22, Jonny had employment income of £24,000 (12 × £2,000), such that he was a basic rate taxpayer.

Or

(ii) Total income of the tax years 2019/20, 2020/21 and 2021/22 in that order.

In the tax year 2019/20, Jonny had employment income of £72,000 (12 × £6,000), such that he had more than £9,500 of income taxable at the higher rate.

The loss should therefore be offset in the tax year 2019/20, resulting in a tax refund of £3,800 (£9,500 × 40%).

Income tax payable/refundable

	Strong demand		Weak demand	
	2022/23	2023/24	2022/23	2023/24
	£	£	£	£
Taxable trading profit	5,750	19,200	0	300
Less: Personal allowance	(5,750)	(12,570)	0	(300)
Taxable income	0	6,630	0	0
Income tax payable at 20%	0	1,326	0	0
Income tax refundable (above)			(3,800)	

Tutor's top tips

The question provides a table to be completed, so make sure that you do this. There are easy marks available for following through and calculating the post-tax income figures, regardless of whether your figures for the tax payable and tax savings are correct.

Post-tax income position

	Strong	Weak
	£	£
Aggregate budgeted net profit of the first two trading periods (per email)	39,200	2,800
Aggregate income tax (payable)/refundable for the first two tax years	(1,326)	3,800
Budgeted post-tax income	37,874	6,600

These post-tax income figures are an approximation because the total income arises in a period of 20 months (1 November 2022 to 30 June 2024), whereas the total income tax payable is in respect of only 17 months (five months in the tax year 2022/23 and the whole of the tax year 2023/24).

Tutorial note

You could also have stated that the figures are an approximation as they are based on estimates, which may change.

(ii) Salesmen

Tutor's top tips

This part requires straightforward application of employed vs. self-employed factors. The key to scoring well here is to apply the factors to the scenario, not just list them all out. The requirement asks specifically for indicators of self-employment, so there is no need to discuss anything else.

Proposed contractual arrangements indicating self-employed status

– The salesmen will be paid a fee by reference to the work they do. This will enable them to earn more by working more efficiently and effectively.

– The salesmen will not be paid sick pay or holiday pay; such payments would be indicative of employed status.

– The salesmen will be required to use their own cars.

Suggested changes in order to maximise the likelihood of the salesmen being treated as self-employed

– It would be helpful if the salesmen were able to work on the days they choose rather than being required to work on specific days.

– The salesmen should be required to provide their own laptop computer rather than borrowing one from Jonny.

Tutorial note

The period for which the salesmen will work is not a relevant factor in determining their status. However, the longer they are appointed for, the more likely it is that the factors indicating employment (for example, the degree of control over the worker) will be present.

(iii)   New contracts for the business

Tutor's top tips

There are five marks available here, so try to make sure that you make five separately identifiable points in your answer.

-   ACCA's Code of Ethics and Conduct includes confidentiality as one of the fundamental principles of ethics on which we should base our professional behaviour.
-   Where we have acquired confidential information as a result of our professional and business relationships, we are obliged to refrain from using it to our own advantage or to the advantage of third parties.
-   This principle of confidentiality applies to both ex-clients and continuing clients.
-   As a result of this, we should not use any confidential information relating to our existing clients or ex-clients to assist Jonny.
-   We are permitted to use the experience and expertise we have gained from advising our clients.

(b)   Jonny's inheritance from his mother

Tutor's top tips

This part of the question involves correcting errors in an inheritance tax computation, which requires good basic knowledge of inheritance tax.

Take note of the information in the email from the manager: you are told that the arithmetic, dates and valuations are correct, and also that there were no other lifetime gifts and no business property relief. It is important to not waste time recalculating figures you are told are correct.

The exclusion of chattels less than £6,000 and application of the annual exemption to the death estate are common errors, so should have been easy to spot.

Even if you did not spot all of the errors, you would still score marks for following through and calculating the value of the inheritance receivable by Jonny.

Errors identified

1   Chattels (for example, furniture, paintings and jewellery) with a value of less than £6,000 are not exempt for the purposes of inheritance tax (although they are exempt for the purposes of capital gains tax).

2   The annual exemption is not available in respect of transfers on death.

3   There is a residence nil rate band of £175,000 available, as Jonny's mother's main residence was passed to him (a direct descendant) on her death.

4   The reduced rate of inheritance tax of 36% will apply. This is because:

–   the chargeable estate, before deduction of the charitable donation and the residence nil rate band but after deduction of the nil rate band, is £689,000 (£619,000 (£591,000 + £25,000 + £3,000) + £70,000); and

–   the gift to the charity of £70,000 is more than 10% of this amount.

Value of inheritance receivable by Jonny

	£
Chargeable estate per draft computation	892,000
No exemption for chattels valued at less than £6,000	25,000
No annual exemption	3,000
	———
	920,000
Less: Residence nil rate band	(175,000)
Nil rate band	(301,000)
	———
	444,000
	———
Inheritance tax at 36%	159,840
	———
Assets inherited by Jonny	
(£530,000 + £400,000 + £40,000 + £20,000 – £70,000)	920,000
Less: Inheritance tax payable	(159,840)
	———
Inheritance receivable by Jonny	760,160
	———

Examiner's report

Part (a), which was in three parts, related to a sole trader business. Part (a)(i) required candidates to calculate an individual's post- tax income for the first two tax years of trading, after considering the optimum relief for a trading loss in the first accounting period. A small number of candidates achieved full, or nearly full marks for this part but a significant minority made no or very little attempt to address this part of this question, suggesting a lack of preparation for this type of question. Unincorporated business are tested in every exam, and questions frequently demand consideration of basis periods and/or relief for trading losses, so question practice on these areas should always form an important part of all candidates' preparation for this exam.

Relief for trading losses is a technically demanding area, which requires accurate knowledge of what reliefs are available in which situations, and the precise rules or conditions in each case. Many candidates confined themselves to discussing just one method of loss relief, whereas careful reading of the question indicated that there were different options available and a decision was to be made regarding the optimum method of relief, thereby suggesting that more than one method of relief was available.

It appeared that many candidates would have benefited from pausing and thinking more before they started to write. It is important in a question dealing with relief for losses that a well-considered and logical approach is taken. Weaker candidates prepared detailed income tax computations for several tax years in the apparent hope that this would eventually lead to being able to determine the rate of tax paid in each year, and an ability to calculate the tax refund suggested by the question. The problem with this approach was that it was very time consuming and tended to produce redundant information as tax years were included for which it was not possible to offset the loss. Candidates should be advised to consider first of all the tax years in which they believe loss relief is available, before launching into a series of detailed computations for which there are no marks available.

Part (a)(ii) concerned the employment status of two part-time salesmen and was done extremely well. The majority of candidates were able to identify which of the specific contractual arrangements given in the question concerning the work to be done by the salesmen indicated self-employment and any changes required to the other arrangements in order to maximise the likelihood of the salesmen being treated as self-employed. Many candidates gave the impression of being very confident with this topic, and happy to write at length about the different arrangements, giving the impression that they may well have exceeded the four marks worth of time which should have been allocated to this part. Candidates should always take note of the number of marks available for each question part and resist the temptation to elaborate unnecessarily on areas with which they are very comfortable.

Part (a)(iii) covered the ethical issue of confidentiality in relation to using knowledge and experience gained from dealing with both current and ex-clients to assist a new client. This part was done very well by the vast majority of candidates, with many scoring full marks. It was pleasing to see that most candidates related well to the specific client and the facts given in the scenario.

Part (b) of this question required candidates to identify errors in an inheritance tax computation on a death estate, and to calculate the amount to be received by the sole beneficiary of the estate, after the correct inheritance tax had been paid.

Performance on this part of the question was mixed, with a disappointing number of candidates believing that the capital gains tax exemption for chattels with a value below £6,000 also applies to inheritance tax, and that inheritance tax annual exemptions are available against assets in the death estate. These are fundamental errors which candidates at ATX should not be making. Candidates should ensure that they are able to identify and apply correctly the different exemptions available for capital gains tax and inheritance tax as these are tested on a very regular basis.

In order to calculate the correct amount of inheritance tax to be paid after correcting the errors found, the majority of candidates rewrote the entire death estate. This succeeded in gaining the relevant marks, but was probably fairly time-consuming, and candidates are encouraged to try and adopt a more efficient approach, focusing on the effect of correcting the error on the value of the chargeable estate as this would save time.

Questions at ATX frequently ask for a calculation of after-tax proceeds – here, the amount receivable by the sole beneficiary of the estate. Candidates need to think more carefully about the starting point for this type of calculation. Here, it wasn't the value of the chargeable estate, as this includes a deduction for the nil rate band.

Candidates needed to identify the actual value which would be received prior to making this deduction. Failure to identify the correct starting point is a common error.

ACCA marking scheme				
				Marks
(a)	(i)	Taxable trading profit/(loss) for weak demand		3.0
		Income tax payable or refundable		
		Strong demand		2.0
		Weak demand		2.0
		Advice on use of loss		
		Options available		3.0
		Recommendation		3.0
		Summary		1.0
		Calculation only an approximation		2.0
				——
				16.0
			Maximum	15.0
				——
	(ii)	One mark for each relevant point	Maximum	4.0
				——
	(iii)	One mark for each relevant point	Maximum	5.0
				——
(b)		Identification of errors		5.5
		Calculations		
		Inheritance tax liability		2.0
		Inheritance receivable by Jonny		1.5
				——
				9.0
			Maximum	7.0
				——
		Followed instructions		1.0
		Clarity of explanation and calculations		1.0
		Problem solving		1.0
		Overall presentation		1.0
				——
			Maximum	4.0
				——
Total				35.0
				——

20 SNOWDON *Walk in the footsteps of a top tutor*

Key answer tips

This question covers inheritance tax and capital gains tax implications of lifetime gifts, basic sole trader computations, VAT partial exemption and procedures around taking on a new client. There are many typical section A features to this question.

The first part of the question is relatively straightforward as long as you know your IHT basics from TX! Once you have redone the calculations as they should have been done, it should be easy to spot what is wrong with the calculations in the question.

The second part is a little bit trickier as it requires you to consider various costs involved with expanding a business including national insurance contributions and irrecoverable VAT. If you take an organised approach and consider each extra cost in turn you can score well on this part.

The final part of the question allows for some easy marks to be earned by listing out the various procedures that should be followed when appointing a new client. Ensure that you leave sufficient time to do this part well, or even consider doing this first.

The highlighted words in the written sections are key phrases that markers are looking for in your answer.

Tutor's top tips

You are asked to prepare a memorandum, so make sure that you do this to gain the marks for presentation.

Use the headings from the manager's email to help to give your answer structure. Note the verbs in the question: some ask for calculations whereas others ask for explanations, so ensure that you follow the instructions and keep all explanations brief and to the point.

You may find it easier to prepare calculations in the spreadsheet, with explanations being done in the word processor. Don't forget that you can use formulae in the spreadsheet functionality to help with any calculations. These can be viewed by markers so they can see what workings have been carried out.

Memorandum

Client	**Snowdon**
Subject	**Personal tax matters**
Prepared by	**Tax senior**
Date	**7 June 2022**

(i)   Purchase of the cottage from Coleen

Errors in Snowdon's computation

1   The value of the gift for the purpose of inheritance tax (IHT) is the fall in value of Coleen's estate, i.e. £35,000 (£260,000 – £225,000) being the value of the cottage less the amount paid by Snowdon.

2   The cottage was a lifetime gift and not a gift on death. Accordingly, the annual exemption for both the year of the gift and the previous year are available: a total of £6,000 (2 × £3,000).

3   The 40% rate of taper relief is correct. However, the relief should be 40% of the inheritance tax due as opposed to 40% of the gift.

4   The nil rate band of £325,000 should be reduced by chargeable transfers in the seven years prior to 1 May 2018. Accordingly, it will be reduced by the chargeable lifetime transfer made by Coleen on 1 March 2014.

Inheritance tax due in respect of the gift of the cottage

	£
Value of the gift	35,000
Less: Annual exemptions (£3,000 × 2)	(6,000)
	29,000
Nil rate band	325,000
Less: Chargeable transfer in the seven years prior to 1 May 2018	(318,000)
Available nil rate band	7,000
Inheritance tax ((£29,000 – £7,000) × 40%)	8,800
Less: Taper relief (£8,800 × 40%) (between four and five years)	(3,520)
	5,280

Base cost of the cottage for the purposes of a future disposal

	£	£
Value of the cottage as at 1 May 2018		260,000
Less: Gift holdover relief		
Proceeds (market value)	260,000	
Less: Cost	(165,000)	
	95,000	
Less: £225,000 – £165,000	(60,000)	
Gift holdover relief		(35,000)
Base cost of cottage		225,000

Tutorial note

The question states that gift holdover relief is available on the gift of the holiday cottage. It is assumed therefore that it qualifies as a furnished holiday letting. You should always apply the information as it is provided in the question.

(ii)   Expansion of the Siabod business

Tutor's top tips

You are asked to calculate which strategy will generate the most additional tax adjusted trading profit. The question mentions the amount of extra turnover that will be generated and the extra costs that will be incurred, but don't forget the extra costs that are not mentioned, such as employers national insurance and irrecoverable VAT!

Strategy A

	£
Additional turnover (£435,000 – £255,000)	180,000
	———
Salary	48,000
Employer's class 1 NIC ((£48,000 – £8,840) × 13.8%)	5,404
Overheads and advertising (£38,000 + £2,000)	40,000
Irrecoverable VAT (W1)	0
	———
	93,404
	———
Additional tax adjusted trading profit (£180,000 – £93,404)	86,596
	———

Strategy B

	£
Additional turnover (as for strategy A)	180,000
	———
Fee paid to Tor Ltd	90,000
Advertising	2,000
Irrecoverable VAT (W2)	8,736
	———
	100,736
	———
Additional tax adjusted trading profit (£180,000 – £100,736)	79,264
	———

The most financially advantageous strategy would be strategy A.

Additional post-tax income in respect of strategy A

	£
Tax adjusted trading profit prior to expansion	85,000
Tax adjusted trading profit in respect of expansion (above)	86,596
	171,596
Interest income	740
	172,336
Personal allowance	0
	172,336

	£
Income tax on trading income	
£37,700 × 20%	7,540
(£150,000 – £37,700) × 40%	44,920
(£171,596 – £150,000) × 45%	9,718
	62,178
Income tax on interest income	
£740 × 45%	333
Class 4 NIC	
(£50,270 – £9,568) × 9%	3,663
(£171,596 – £50,270) × 2%	2,427
Total income tax and NIC	68,601
Less: Income tax and class 4 NIC on profit of £85,000 (£21,432 + £4,358)	(25,790)
Less: Income tax on interest income prior to expansion of business ((£740 – £500) × 40%)	(96)
Additional income tax and class 4 NIC in respect of expansion	42,715
Additional post-tax income (£86,596 – £42,715)	43,881

Tutorial note

Prior to expanding the business, Snowdon was a higher rate taxpayer and was therefore entitled to a savings income nil rate band of £500. Following the expansion of the business, he will be an additional rate taxpayer and will not be entitled to this allowance.

Workings

(W1) Strategy A – recoverable input tax

Partial exemption percentage	76%

	£
Total input tax (£18,000 + ((£38,000 + £2,000) × 20%))	26,000
Attributable to taxable supplies (£26,000 × 76%)	(19,760)
Attributable to exempt supplies	6,240

The VAT attributable to exempt supplies can be recovered in full as it is below the annual de minimis limit of £7,500 (£625 × 12) and is less than half of the total input tax.

(W2) Strategy B – recoverable input tax

Partial exemption percentage	76%

	£
Total input tax (£18,000 + ((£90,000 + £2,000) × 20%))	36,400
Attributable to taxable supplies (£36,400 × 76%)	(27,664)
Attributable to exempt supplies	8,736

The VAT attributable to exempt supplies cannot be recovered as it exceeds the annual de minimis limit of £7,500 (£625 × 12).

(iii)   **Procedures we should follow before we agree to become Snowdon's tax advisers**

– We must obtain evidence of Snowdon's identity (for example, his passport) and his address.

– We must have regard to the fundamental principles of professional ethics. This requires us to consider whether becoming tax advisers to Snowdon would create any threats to compliance with these principles.

– Integrity: we must consider the appropriateness of Snowdon's attitude to complying with the law and the disclosure of information to HM Revenue and Customs (HMRC).

– Professional competence: we must ensure that we have the skills and competence necessary to be able to deal with the matters which may arise in connection with Snowdon's affairs.

   If any such threats are identified, we should not accept the appointment unless the threats can be reduced to an acceptable level via the implementation of safeguards.

– We should contact Snowdon's existing tax adviser(s) in order to ensure that there has been no action by Snowdon which would preclude the acceptance of the appointment on ethical grounds.

– We must carry out a review in order to satisfy ourselves that Snowdon is not carrying on any activities which may be regarded as money laundering.

Examiner's report

This question required appropriate advice on a variety of personal tax matters, including inheritance tax, capital gains tax, income tax and value added tax (VAT) issues, together with consideration of the procedures to be considered before taking on a new client. It was quite a challenging question, requiring a structured logical approach in order to produce a good answer. A good number of candidates did achieve this, but a significant number appeared to struggle with the detailed calculations required. The use of subheadings, taken from the issues in the manager's email, provides a useful structure in this type of question, which future candidates should consider adopting.

The first part of the question, which was worth nine marks, required candidates to identify, explain, and correct errors made by the potential new client in their calculation of an inheritance tax liability on a lifetime gift, and calculate the implications for the recipient of having made a valid gift holdover relief claim in relation to this asset. This type of 'correction of errors' question has been used several times in the past in Section A questions, and it was pleasing to see many candidates try to both explain the errors, and provide a revised calculation, as required. Consequently, these candidates scored well. Weaker candidates tended to rely too much on just producing the revised calculations, without adequate explanations of the reasons for the revisions, which were required in order to score a high mark on this question part. This is a challenging question type, but one which candidates should expect to appear regularly on the ATX paper. Many candidates' knowledge of capital gains tax gift holdover relief was rather vague and very few dealt correctly with the fact that this was actually a sale at undervalue i.e. some proceeds had been received and therefore the deferred gain would be restricted. Candidates need to be familiar with the precise consequences of claiming capital gains tax reliefs such as this.

The second part of the question concerned the appraisal of two alternative strategies being considered by the potential client in relation to expanding their unincorporated business. This part was worth 17 marks and was wholly computational involving mainly income tax, and a few marks of VAT. It contained a considerable amount of detail relating to each of the strategies, and of the VAT implications, including possible partial exemption. Questions involving a series of detailed computations, such as this one, require careful reading, thinking and planning before starting to write, in order to produce a logical, easy to follow set of calculations. Lengthy computations such as this are challenging questions, with a number of different 'issues' embedded within them, such as the consideration of the impact of VAT, and in particular partial exemption, as there was here. Time spent in planning at the start ensures that candidates don't waste time with unnecessary calculations, which, in some cases were quite lengthy, but were irrelevant, so gained no marks. Also, candidates are able to recognise the point in the computation when specific aspects – such as partial exemption for VAT – need to be considered. It was clear where candidates had done such preparation; their computations were logically presented, and easy to mark. It cannot be stressed enough how vital it is to spend a few minutes reading, thinking and planning before starting to write an answer to these longer question parts.

The final part of the question required a summary of the procedures to be followed before agreeing to become tax advisers for the potential new client. This appeared to be a question for which most candidates were well prepared, and most scored well. Those that didn't tended to be too general in their comments, such as talking about the need to ensure adherence to ACCA's fundamental ethical principles, without identifying which of these principles is/are particularly relevant in this scenario. It is always important in an ethics requirement to relate your answer specifically to the (potential) client, and the scenario in the question.

Overall, candidates who prepared satisfactory answers to this question:

– clearly addressed each of the three issues set out in the manager's email

– read the requirements carefully

– did not waste time including irrelevant material

– produced clearly laid out and labelled computations.

ACCA marking scheme		Marks
(i) Identification of errors		
Value of the gift		1.5
Annual exemptions		1.5
Taper relief		2.0
Nil rate band		1.0
Calculation of inheritance tax		2.5
Base cost for the purpose of capital gains tax		2.0
		────
		10.5
	Maximum	9.0
		────
(ii) Additional tax adjusted trading profit – strategy A		
Additional turnover		0.5
Salary, class 1 NIC and overheads		2.0
Recoverable input tax		3.0
Additional tax adjusted trading profit – strategy B		
Additional turnover and fee paid to Tor Ltd		1.0
Recoverable input tax		3.0
Additional post-tax income		
Taxable income		3.0
Income tax and class 4 NIC on trading income		2.5
Income tax on interest income		1.0
Remainder of calculation		3.0
		────
		19.0
	Maximum	17.0
		────
(iii) Identity		1.0
Fundamental principles		3.0
Contact existing tax advisers		1.0
Money laundering		1.0
		────
		6.0
	Maximum	5.0
		────

Problem solving	1.0
Clarity of explanations and calculations	1.0
Effectiveness of communication	1.0
Overall presentation and style	1.0
	———
	4.0
Total	**35.0**
	———

21 NELSON *Walk in the footsteps of a top tutor*

Key answer tips

This question covers ethics, sole trader v company, loss relief, incorporation, close companies and irrecoverable debts for VAT. There is a lot to cover so it is important that you allocate your time carefully between the different requirements so that you don't run out of time.

The first part on ethics offers some easy marks as new client procedures get tested relatively often. You should ask yourself why you have been told about potential trade overseas- has our firm dealt with this before?

There are a lot of calculations to do in part (b) but as long as you keep moving through them you should score well. Note that the question has told you what the tax would be as a sole trader so don't waste time calculating this again!

You're also asked for explanations in part (b) about why Nelson was advised to set up as a sole trader due to making a loss. You are given information about how many marks are for the calculations and how many for explanations so use this to guide you in terms of how much time to spend on each area.

Part (c) looks at three independent areas. You may find some of these easier than others so start with whichever you find the easiest, but make sure you leave enough time to have a go at all three.

The highlighted words in the written sections are key phrases that markers are looking for in your answer.

Memorandum

For The files

Subject Nelson – Incorporation of business and other matters

Prepared by Tax senior

Date 3 December 2022

(a) Becoming tax advisers to Nelson

Information required:

– Proof of Nelson's identity and his address.

Matters to consider:

– We must give consideration to the fundamental principles of professional ethics, for example, integrity and professional competence and due care. This requires us to consider whether becoming tax advisers to Nelson would create any threats to compliance with these principles.

If any such threats are identified, we should not accept the appointment unless the threats can be reduced to an acceptable level via the implementation of safeguards.

Nelson is planning to sell mainly to overseas customers in the future, possibly via companies' resident overseas. We should consider the likelihood of these plans being realised and whether or not we would have the necessary technical expertise to provide Nelson with the best advice.

– We must assure ourselves that Nelson is not involved in any form of money laundering.

Actions to take:

– We need permission from Nelson to contact his existing tax advisers in order to ensure that there is nothing in the past which would preclude us from accepting the appointment on ethical grounds.

If Nelson refuses to give permission, we should seriously consider refusing to act for him.

(b) **Trading through a limited company rather than as an unincorporated business**

Total taxes payable if Nelson had commenced trading through a limited company

Taxes payable by the company for the accounting period ending 31 March 2023

	£	£
Trading profit (£7,050 × 10)	70,500	
Salary for Nelson (£1,300 × 10)	(13,000)	
Employer's class 1 national insurance contributions (NIC)		
£5,633 (£13,000 – (£8,840 × 10/12)) × 13.8%	(777)	777
Taxable total profits	56,723	
Corporation tax (£56,723 × 19%)	(10,777)	10,777
Available for dividend	45,946	
Total taxes payable		11,554

Taxes payable by Nelson for the tax year 2022/23

	£
Salary	13,000
Dividend income	45,946
	———
	58,946
Less: Personal allowance	(12,570)
	———
	46,376
	———

Income tax for the tax year 2022/23	£	£
Employment income		
£430 (£13,000 − £12,570) × 20%	86	
Dividend income		
£2,000 × 0%	0	
£35,270 (£37,700 − £430 − £2,000) × 7.5%	2,645	
£8,676 (£45,946 − £2,000 − £35,270) × 32.5%	2,820	
	———	
		5,551
Employee's class 1 NIC		
£5,027 (£13,000 − (£9,568 × 10/12)) × 12%		603
		———
Total taxes payable		6,154
		———
Total taxes payable (£11,554 + £6,154)		17,708
		———

The total tax payable for the tax year 2022/23 would have been £2,125 (£19,833 − £17,708) less if Nelson had commenced trading through a limited company rather than as an unincorporated business.

Tutorial note

The employment allowance which provides relief of up to £4,000 from employer's class 1 NIC would not be available to the company because Nelson would be the company's only employee.

Reasons for advice given by existing tax adviser

Tutor's top tips

Make sure your answer is specific to the scenario, don't just list out every possible loss relief you know! It is clear that this is a new business therefore opening years loss relief is relevant.

Trading loss

If Nelson's business had made a tax adjusted trading loss for the period ending 30 April 2023, Nelson would have had a trading loss for the tax year 2022/23 equal to 10/11 of the loss for the trading period.

Where a self-employed individual makes a trading loss in any of the first four tax years of trading, the loss can be offset against the individual's total income of the three tax years prior to the year of loss starting with the earliest year. Accordingly, Nelson could have offset the loss against his employment income for the tax years 2019/20 and 2020/21. This would have resulted in a repayment of income tax at 40% and 20%.

Nelson's tax adjusted trading profit/loss for the tax year 2023/24, the second tax year, is based on the results of the first 12 months of trading. However, the loss for the first 10 months would not have been counted again, such that the profit/loss would have been 1/11 of the loss for the first trading period less 1/12 of the profit of the second trading period. This is likely to be either a small loss or a profit.

If Nelson had begun trading through a limited company, there would have been no immediate relief for a trading loss. It would have been carried forward for relief against the future total profits of the company.

Other possible reasons

–   Trading via a company would have increased the complexity of Nelson's financial affairs.

–   Trading via a company would have meant that Nelson's ability to access the profits of the business would not have been as straight forward as it has been.

Tutorial note

Nelson would not have been able to relieve a trading loss against total income of the year of loss or the preceding year because he had no income in the tax year 2021/22 and, if his business had made a loss, he would have had no income in the tax year 2022/23.

(c)   Other matters

Nelson retaining personal ownership of the Arch building

If Nelson retains personal ownership of the business premises, incorporation relief (the relief which is available where a business is transferred to a company in exchange for shares) will no longer be available. This is because he will not be transferring all of the assets of the business (excluding cash) to NQA Ltd.

As a result, the chargeable gain arising in respect of the goodwill will be subject to capital gains tax (CGT). The annual exempt amount of £12,300 will be deducted from the gain and the balance of £32,700 will be taxed at 20% (on the assumption that Nelson will be a higher rate taxpayer in the tax year 2023/24). Accordingly, there will be a CGT liability of £6,540, which will be due on 31 January 2025.

Tutorial note

Business asset disposal relief is not available in respect of a chargeable gain on goodwill as a result of incorporating a company in this way. Even if it were, it would not be available to Nelson because he will not have owned the business for two years at the time of disposal.

Nelson borrowing money from NQA Ltd

Nelson will control NQA Ltd because he will own all of the company's issued share capital. As a result, because NQA Ltd will be controlled by five or fewer shareholders, it will be a close company.

Where a close company (NQA Ltd) makes a loan to a shareholder (Nelson), it is required to make a payment equal to 32.5% of the loan to HM Revenue and Customs (HMRC) within nine months and one day of the end of the accounting period.

There is no need to make this payment to HMRC if Nelson repays the loan prior to the date on which the tax is due to be paid. HMRC will repay the tax to NQA Ltd when the loan is repaid by Nelson.

Value added tax (VAT)

The VAT paid to HMRC in respect of the irrecoverable debt is not lost. It can be recovered, provided:

–   the debt has been written off by Nelson; and

–   six months have elapsed since the date on which the payment was due.

Use of the cash accounting scheme would have avoided this problem, as Nelson would not have had to account for output tax until he had received payment from the customer. This would also result in a cash flow advantage to Nelson where a customer does not pay promptly.

On the downside, Nelson would not be able to recover input tax until he has paid for the relevant goods or services.

Accordingly, whether or not the cash accounting scheme would benefit Nelson's cash flow position depends on the timing of payments to creditors and receipts from debtors.

Examiner's report

This question concerned a potential new client looking for financial assistance in relation to his unincorporated business, which he was considering incorporating. The question covered the areas of ethics, income tax, corporation tax, national insurance, capital gains tax, close companies and VAT.

The first part of the question required an explanation of matters to be considered and actions required before taking on a new client. It was pleasing to see many candidates scoring well on this question part. However a significant number of candidates failed to mention consideration of the fundamental principles of professional ethics. Ethics will be examined on every ATX-UK paper and candidates would be well advised to take the time to understand the ethical requirements of the ACCA.

The second part of the question was split into two further requirements. The first requirement was a comparison of tax payable if trading through a limited company compared to trading as an unincorporated trader. However the tax payable if trading as an unincorporated trader was given in the question and did not need to be recalculated. Despite this, a number of candidates recalculated this tax payable figure, wasting their valuable time and earning no marks. These candidates would have benefitted from spending time to ensure they were clear on the requirement and planning their answer, before they began to write. By doing this, they should save themselves time in the long run and earn more marks.

The question stated that after incorporation, the owner would take a mixture of dividend and salary from the company. Most candidates were able to calculate the corporation tax payable if the business were incorporated and recognised that employer's national insurance would be both payable and tax deductible for corporation tax purposes if the owner took a salary from the company. Many candidates then successfully went on to calculate the income tax payable by the owner of the company, given the mixture of dividends and salary withdrawn from the company. However most candidates failed to recognise that the owner would also have to pay employees' national insurance if he took a salary from the company.

The second requirement of this part of the question was an explanation of why the business owner may have been advised to trade as an unincorporated business rather than through a company when trading losses were anticipated in the first couple of years of the business. Many candidates wasted time and earned no marks by simply describing all the losses rules of companies and unincorporated businesses whereas what was needed was for the candidates to apply their knowledge to the specific facts of the question. This business anticipated losses in 'opening years' and the relevant loss relief to discuss was opening years loss relief for unincorporated businesses which is not available for companies. Those candidates who spoke generally about opening years loss relief would have earned extra marks if they had actually calculated the specific loss available in opening years but very few candidates did this.

The third part of the question concerned three other matters relevant to the business. The first matter was the capital gains tax implication of retaining ownership of a business asset when incorporating all other business assets. Many candidates correctly identified that this would mean that incorporation relief would not be available but some then went on to calculate capital gains tax on the asset which was being retained instead of the capital asset being transferred to the company.

The second matter concerned the tax implications of the owner borrowing funds from the company and subsequently repaying them. Many candidates recognised that this was a close company issue and would involve a payment from the company to HMRC, which would be repayable when the loan was repaid. However the requirement specifically asked candidates not to address employment income benefits in respect of the arrangement and yet many candidates went on to discuss these matters, again wasting their valuable time and earning no marks. Once again these candidates would have benefitted from spending time to ensure they were clear on the requirement and planning their answer, before they began to write. By doing this, they should save themselves time in the long run and earn more marks overall.

The third matter required an explanation of whether VAT on a bad debt could be recovered and whether this would not be a problem with the cash accounting scheme for VAT. Many candidates were very clear on the rules in this area and scored well. However once again, some candidates wasted time and earned no extra marks by explaining everything they knew about the cash accounting scheme instead of the specific aspect required by the question.

Many candidates were failing to produce answers that were sufficiently specific to the scenario, tending towards general statements of knowledge in the particular area. To score well at ATX-UK, candidates must 'apply' their knowledge. Writing out lots of rules in the hope that one of the rules might apply is not a good use of candidates' time.

Marks were awarded for professional skills in question one. These marks were awarded for clear and logical explanations and calculations, for a sensible approach to solving the problems set in the second part of the question, for answers that were scenario specific rather than general, and for a professionally acceptable style. Generally the candidates performed reasonably well in this area.

ACCA marking scheme		Marks
(a)	Information required	1.0
	Matters to consider	4.0
	Actions to take	1.0
		6.0
	Maximum	5.0
(b)	Trading as a limited company	
	Corporation tax	3.0
	Income tax	3.5
	Employee's class 1 national insurance contributions	1.0
	Reasons for advice to trade as an unincorporated business	
	Relief for expected trading loss	6.5
	Other reasons	2.0
		16.0
	Maximum	14.0

(c)	The Arch building		
	Incorporation relief not available		2.0
	Capital gains tax		2.0
	Loan to Nelson		
	Reason why NQA Ltd will be a close company		1.0
	Tax payment required		3.0
	Repayment of tax		1.0
	Value added tax		
	Recovery of output tax		3.0
	Cash accounting scheme and cash flow		2.0
			————
			14.0
		Maximum	12.0
			————
	Problem solving		1.0
	Clarity of explanations and calculations		1.0
	Effectiveness of communication		1.0
	Overall presentation and style		1.0
			————
			4.0
			————
Total			**35.0**
			————

22   ROSA

Key answer tips

This section B question focuses on the difference in tax between taking on an employee or a partner, loss relief for individuals and the capital goods scheme for VAT.

Part (a) is a higher skills requirement that looks at the difference in income tax and national insurance between taking on someone as a partner or an employee. There are lots of calculations to do here so it is important to plan what you need to do before you get started.

In part (b) you are asked to discuss the loss relief options available to an individual. Note that she has a relatively high level of income so you should always question whether the restriction on reliefs against total income is relevant. Make sure your answer is specific to the scenario and doesn't just list out every possible loss relief.

The capital goods scheme is the focus of the final part of this question. This is a topic which is often tested in the ATX exam so you should be prepared to tackle this, and to be able to perform calculations. Note that you are only asked for the final adjustment so don't waste time discussing the annual adjustments as this will score no marks.

(a) **Difference in the total amount of income tax and national insurance contributions (NICs) payable by Siena and Rosa for the tax year 2023/24 if Siena becomes (i) a partner, or (ii) an employee on 1 April 2023**

(i) **Siena becomes a partner**

If Siena becomes a partner in RS Trading on 1 April 2023, she will be allocated £2,800 of the partnership loss of the year ending 31 March 2024 (W), such that she will have no taxable income for the tax year 2023/24. Accordingly, she will have no liability to income tax or class 2 or class 4 NIC.

Rosa will be allocated a trading loss of £59,200 in the tax year 2023/24 (W). As she will have no other source of income in that year, Rosa will have no liability to income tax or class 2 or class 4 NIC.

(ii) **Siena becomes an employee**

If Siena becomes an employee, on an annual salary of £22,000, she will have an income tax liability of £1,886 ((£22,000 − £12,570) × 20%), and a class 1 employee's NIC liability of £1,492 ((£22,000 − £9,568) × 12%).

In this case, RS Trading will also have a liability to class 1 employer's NIC of £1,816 ((£22,000 − £8,840) × 13.8%). As this is covered by the £4,000 employment allowance, no class 1 contributions would be payable.

Rosa will, again, have no personal liability to income tax or NIC, as she will incur a trading loss of £84,000 (£62,000 + £22,000).

Therefore, the total income tax and NIC payable by Siena and Rosa for the tax year 2023/24 will be reduced by £3,378 (£1,886 + £1,492) if Siena becomes a partner.

However, although the total tax and NIC payable by Siena and Rosa is lower if Siena becomes a partner, the amount of trading loss available for relief is higher if Siena becomes an employee (£84,000, rather than £62,000).

Working:

Allocation of RS Trading loss for the year ending 31 March 2024:

	Total	Rosa	Siena
	£	£	£
Budgeted loss	(62,000)		
Salary to Siena	(12,000)		12,000
Balance (80:20)	(74,000)	(59,200)	(14,800)
Total share of loss	(62,000)	(59,200)	(2,800)

Tutorial note

Although Rosa will have no personal liability to NIC, she can voluntarily continue to pay Class 2 contributions in order to ensure entitlement to contributions based benefits.

(b) **Loss reliefs available to Rosa in respect of the budgeted trading loss of RS Trading**

Rosa will have a trading loss of £84,000 in the tax year 2023/24.

As Rosa has no other income in the tax year 2023/24, she can only carry back the loss to the tax year 2022/23 and offset the loss against her total income of that year, and then against the chargeable gains arising on the sale of the investment properties in the tax year 2022/23.

Rosa's total income in 2022/23 is £87,000 (£27,000 + £60,000). There is no restriction on the amount of loss which can be used against trading income from the same trade, but relief against the property income will be capped at the greater of £50,000 and 25% of Rosa's adjusted net income for the year, which is £21,750 (£87,000 × 25%).

Accordingly, a maximum of £50,000 can be offset against the property income. Therefore, a total of £77,000 (£27,000 + £50,000) can be offset against income leaving net income of £10,000 (£87,000 –- £77,000), which will be covered by Rosa's personal allowance.

The balance of the loss of £7,000 (£84,000 – £77,000) can be relieved against the chargeable gains of £92,000 on the sale of the investment properties.

Maximum tax saving 2022/23:

	£
Income tax (No liability to income tax remains, so the whole amount is repayable)	22,232
Capital gains tax (CGT) (Working)	5,730
	27,962

Working:

CGT payable after taking loss relief:

	£
Gains remaining chargeable (£92,000 –- £7,000)	85,000
Less: Annual exempt amount	(12,300)
Taxable gains	72,700
CGT: £37,700 × 18%	6,786
£35,000 × 28%	9,800
£72,700	16,586

CGT saving is £5,730 (£22,316 – £16,586)

Tutorial note

Before taking loss relief, Rosa's taxable gains would all be taxed at 28% as Rosa's taxable income exceeded £37,700. After taking loss relief against Rosa's total income for the tax year 2022/23, the full amount of the basic rate band will be available to use against taxable gains.

(c)   Value added tax (VAT) implications of the disposal of the retail unit

On 6 April 2023, when the retail unit is sold, it will be at least three years old. Accordingly, the sale will be exempt from VAT as Rosa has not opted to tax it.

On acquisition, the retail unit was newly constructed, so VAT of £58,000 (£290,000 × 20%) will have been charged. Rosa will have reclaimed the whole of this in the year ended 31 March 2017, as she used it in her business, making wholly standard-rated supplies.

However, as the sale of the retail unit will be an exempt disposal, for the purpose of the capital goods scheme it is deemed to have 0% taxable use for the remainder of the ten-year adjustment period. As the warehouse is sold during the eighth year of the adjustment period, there are two years of the adjustment period remaining, and therefore a final VAT adjustment of £11,600 (£58,000 × 2/10 × (100% − 0%)) will be repayable by Rosa to HM Revenue and Customs (HMRC) in respect of the sale.

Examiner's report

This question was in three main parts, concerning an unincorporated business looking to bring someone else into the business, trading losses of an unincorporated business and VAT on sale of a property.

The first part of the question required advice, based on calculations, on whether an unincorporated business owner should bring a new person into the business as an employee or as a partner. The calculations required were the total amount of income tax and national insurance contributions for each scenario. There were some excellent answers to this part of the question, dealing with each of the relevant tax liabilities in a clear and logical manner. Those candidates who did not do so well would have benefited from taking time to plan their answer before they began, thinking about which taxes affect which individual.

The second part of the question required an explanation of the loss relief available to the unincorporated trader and a calculation of the maximum tax saving available as a result of such relief. Some candidates wrote very generally about loss reliefs, without applying their knowledge to the facts of the question, which lost them marks. A significant number of candidates seemed unaware of the technical rules on restriction of income tax reliefs against total income and were unable to factor these into their calculations. A thorough understanding of the technical rules from all areas of the syllabus is a requirement to do well in this exam.

The third part of this question dealt with disposal of a retail unit which was subject to the capital goods scheme. Some candidates spent time writing everything they knew about the capital goods scheme when only the implications upon disposal were required. Only knowledge which addresses the question requirements will earn marks; candidates should not waste their time writing out tax rules if they are not asked for in the question. Even if a candidate writes lots of correct information about a particular tax topic, if it has not been asked for, it cannot earn any marks.

<table>
<tr><th colspan="3">ACCA marking scheme</th><th></th></tr>
<tr><td></td><td></td><td></td><td>Marks</td></tr>
<tr><td>(a)</td><td>Siena as partner</td><td></td><td>3.0</td></tr>
<tr><td></td><td>Siena as employee</td><td></td><td>4.0</td></tr>
<tr><td></td><td>Calculation of shares of loss</td><td></td><td>2.0</td></tr>
<tr><td></td><td>Conclusion</td><td></td><td>2.0</td></tr>
<tr><td></td><td></td><td></td><td>─────</td></tr>
<tr><td></td><td></td><td></td><td>11.0</td></tr>
<tr><td></td><td></td><td>**Maximum**</td><td>9.0</td></tr>
<tr><td></td><td></td><td></td><td>─────</td></tr>
<tr><td>(b)</td><td>Availability of loss relief</td><td></td><td>2.0</td></tr>
<tr><td></td><td>Relief against total income in 2022/23</td><td></td><td>3.5</td></tr>
<tr><td></td><td>Tax saving</td><td></td><td>3.5</td></tr>
<tr><td></td><td></td><td></td><td>─────</td></tr>
<tr><td></td><td></td><td></td><td>9.0</td></tr>
<tr><td></td><td></td><td>**Maximum**</td><td>7.0</td></tr>
<tr><td></td><td></td><td></td><td>─────</td></tr>
<tr><td>(c)</td><td>Disposal exempt</td><td></td><td>1.5</td></tr>
<tr><td></td><td>Initial reclaim</td><td></td><td>1.5</td></tr>
<tr><td></td><td>Implications of sale</td><td></td><td>2.0</td></tr>
<tr><td></td><td></td><td></td><td>─────</td></tr>
<tr><td></td><td></td><td></td><td>5.0</td></tr>
<tr><td></td><td></td><td>**Maximum**</td><td>4.0</td></tr>
<tr><td></td><td></td><td></td><td>─────</td></tr>
<tr><td>**Total**</td><td></td><td></td><td>**20.0**</td></tr>
<tr><td></td><td></td><td></td><td>─────</td></tr>
</table>

23   FREYA *Walk in the footsteps of a top tutor*

Key answer tips

This question primarily concerns an individual who is selling her business and moving overseas for a few years. The final requirement throws in a bit of IHT. As expected, there is quite a bit to cover, so allocate your timings to each part of the requirement and make sure you don't over run on any part of the question.

Part (a) is worth 13 marks. This is more than half of the marks available in the question, so make sure your answer covers all the key points and isn't too brief. Here, there are four clear requirements that need to be addressed; CGT on the sale of Freya's business, CGT implications on incorporating her business pre-sale, determination of her residency status and CGT implications on a planned sale of shares.

The question states that incorporation relief is available, and no election would be made to disapply it – so covering the conditions which must be satisfied is therefore a waste of time. Business asset disposal relief (BADR) is relevant to this part of the question. Detailed knowledge of CGT reliefs is required in this exam. As well as being able to apply the rules, you will also need to be able to explain them.

When determining Freya's residency status, you need to pay attention to the wording of the question; the question clearly states that neither the automatic non-UK residence test, nor the automatic UK residence test apply. Marks are therefore only available for a discussion of the sufficient ties tests. Always give a conclusion; is Freya, or is she not, UK resident? The conclusion will usually be worth at least one mark.

Finally, a consideration of CGT and the temporary non-UK residency rules is required. This is a common exam topic, so be prepared to define the rules and then apply the rules to the given scenario.

Part (b) requires a calculation of IT and NIC on the cessation of the individual's unincorporated business. This is really just knowledge from the TX exam put in to an ATX scenario. A good knowledge of the closing year rules for capital allowances and basis periods is essential for the exam (also the opening year rules).

Part (c) involves a brief consideration of IHT. The key issue here was the domicile status of the donor. The determination of the donor's domicile status is fundamental in establishing the extent to which they will suffer UK IHT; it is always worth a quick check before you start to write your answers.

The highlighted words in the written sections are key phrases that markers are looking for in your answer.

(a)   Sale of business

Capital gains tax (CGT) payable if Freya remains in the UK and sells business assets

If Freya remains in the UK, and sells her business assets rather than incorporating, her CGT liability would be £85,000 (£850,000 × 10%).

The rate of CGT would be 10% due to the availability of business asset disposal relief. This relief would be available because Freya would have disposed of the whole of her business which she will have owned for more than two years.

Tutor's top tips

CGT reliefs are a very regular feature in the exam. Make sure that as well as being able to identify which reliefs apply, you can also explain why they apply. Here you were expected to state that business asset disposal relief (BADR) was available because the entire business was being sold; had it not been an entire business BADR would not have been available.

Sale of business to FIM Ltd in exchange for shares

It has already been determined that the conditions for incorporation relief will be satisfied. Incorporation relief will defer all of the chargeable gains arising on the sale of the assets of the business, such that no CGT would arise. Instead, the gains will be deducted from Freya's base cost in the shares, giving a revised base cost of £1,450,000 (£2,300,000 − £850,000).

Tutorial notes

Incorporation relief defers the gain until the shares received on incorporation are sold.

The gain is deferred into the base cost of the shares, so that when the shares are sold in the future they will have a lower base cost and therefore a higher gain will arise.

Tutor's top tips

The question very clearly states that the conditions for incorporation relief will be satisfied and that there is no need to consider the election to disapply incorporation relief. Discussing these areas in your answer will just waste your time and no marks will be awarded.

Freya's residence status whilst living in Benida

Freya will not satisfy any of the automatic residency tests. Accordingly, it is necessary to consider the number of ties which she will have with the UK and the number of days she wishes to spend in the UK.

The ties to be considered in respect of a tax year are:

	Satisfied?
Spouse or children under 18 who are UK resident	No
Accommodation available in the UK for a continuous period of more than 90 days which was stayed in for at least one night during the tax year	Yes
Working in the UK for 40 days or more	No
In the UK for more than 90 days in either or both of the previous two tax years	
2023/24 and 2024/25	Yes
2025/26 onwards	No
Spend more time in the UK than in any other country	No

Freya will satisfy two ties in the tax years 2023/24 and 2024/25 and only one tie in subsequent years. Therefore, she can spend up to 90 days in the UK in each of the first two tax years and up to 120 days in each of the subsequent years without becoming UK resident.

In conclusion, if Freya were to live in Benida in accordance with her ideal scenario (returning to the UK for 25 working days and 30 additional days in each tax year) she will be non-UK resident in all years.

Tutor's top tips

The question tells you that none of the automatic UK residence or non-UK residency tests were met; this is to help you identify that it is only the sufficient ties test that needs to be considered.

The advice here is to consider each tie separately – does it or does it not apply? Always give a conclusion (usually worth at least one mark) as to whether the individual is UK resident or not.

Sale of shares in FIM Ltd without incurring a UK CGT liability

In order for there to be no UK CGT on the gain on the sale of the shares in FIM Ltd, Freya would need to be:

–   not resident in the UK in the tax year of sale; and

–   not a temporary non-UK resident.

It has already been determined that Freya will not be UK resident while she is living in Benida.

The temporary non-resident rules prevent individuals avoiding UK CGT by realising chargeable gains whilst they are outside the UK for relatively short periods.

The rules will apply:

–   to Freya because she will have been UK resident for at least four of the seven tax years immediately prior to the year of departure; and

–   to the shares in FIM Ltd because they will be owned by Freya on the day she leaves the UK.

In order not to be caught by these rules, Freya will need to remain non-UK resident for a minimum period of five complete years rather than the three years in her ideal scenario.

If she returned to the UK after no more than three years, the chargeable gain realised on the sale of the shares would be subject to CGT in the tax year in which she returned.

Tutor's top tips

The temporary non-UK residency rules are frequently tested, so make sure you know them, are ready to explain them in detail, and are able to apply them to the scenario.

(b) **Liability to income tax and class 4 national insurance contributions (NIC): tax year 2022/23**

Income tax

	£
Trading profit for the final 17-month period	94,000
Add: Balancing charge on sale of car (W)	1,560
Less: Overlap profits	(31,400)
Taxable trading profit	64,160
Less: Personal allowance	(12,570)
Taxable income	51,590

£		£
37,700 × 20%		7,540
13,890 × 40%		5,556
51,590		
Income tax liability		13,096

Class 4 NICs

	£
£40,702 (£50,270 – £9,568) × 9%	3,663
£13,890 (£64,160 – £50,270) × 2%	278
Class 4 NIC liability	3,941

Working: Capital allowances

	Main Pool	Private use car	B.U.	Allowances
	£	£	%	£
TWDV b/f	0	8,700		
Additions	4,200	–		
	4,200	8,700		
Disposals:				
Plant and machinery at TWDV (succession)	(4,200)	–		
Private use car at market value		(11,100)		
	0	(2,400)		
		–		
Balancing charge		2,400	× 65%	1,560

Tutorial note

Freya's unincorporated business is ceasing to trade. The closing year rules will therefore need to be applied and all profits will need to be taxed by the end of the final tax year of trade (2022/23) – there is no need to time apportion the profits!

In the capital allowances computation cessation rules also apply. There are no WDAs, FYAs or AIA available in the closing year. All pools will need to be bought down to nil with balancing adjustments (unless a succession election has been made).

Freya and FIM Ltd are connected; this allows a succession election to be made.

A succession election allows the assets that have been transferred, to transfer at their opening tax written down value (TWDV).

(c)   Land in Benida

The gift of the land could not result in a UK inheritance tax (IHT) liability if it were made whilst Alvaro is domiciled in Benida. This is because overseas assets owned by non-UK domiciled individuals are not subject to UK IHT.

However, Alvaro will become deemed domiciled in the UK on 6 April 2023 because he will then have been UK resident for the 15 tax years prior to the year of transfer.

Accordingly, in order to ensure that no UK IHT liability can arise, Alvaro should give the land to Freya prior to 6 April 2023.

Tutor's top tips

Before launching into a full explanation of IHT, take a moment to think – is Alvaro UK domiciled or not? If not UK domiciled at the moment, is there a possibility that soon he may become deemed UK domiciled? How will his domicile status affect his liability to UK IHT? This was where the marks were available in this question.

Examiner's report

This question primarily concerned an individual who is going to sell her business and move overseas for a few years.

Part (a), which was worth 13 marks, comprised four clearly distinguished requirements relating to the capital gains tax (CGT) consequences of selling her business, determination of her residence status, and the impact of this on a planned disposal of shares. A number of candidates' responses to this part were surprisingly, and disappointingly, brief.

Most candidates recognised that business asset disposal relief would be available on the sale of her business assets to an unconnected purchaser, but were not always able to correctly explain why, particularly in respect of the need for the whole of an unincorporated business to be transferred. Detailed knowledge of the different CGT reliefs available to individuals is a fundamental pre-requisite at ATX UK as these reliefs are tested on a very regular basis, and candidates must be precise in their discussion of the conditions to be satisfied, and the implications of the relief being applied/claimed.

Similarly, in relation to the requirement to explain the CGT implications if, alternatively, the business was sold to a company in return for shares in that company. Candidates were told that incorporation relief was available, and no election would be made to disapply it, but still some candidates wasted time discussing the conditions which must be satisfied in this case, which was not relevant here. Again, most candidates were able to state that the gain would be deferred, but some failed to describe correctly, if at all, the further implications that the gains would reduce the base cost of the shares on a subsequent disposal, thereby limiting the marks they could score here.

The third requirement of this part was to determine the individual's residence status for the three years for which she was planning to be away from the UK. Candidates were told that neither the automatic non-UK residence, nor the automatic UK residence tests were satisfied, so they had to focus on the number of ties which she would have with the UK. When considering the number of UK ties someone has, knowledge must be precise. A good approach is to consider each tie in turn, and state whether or not it applies. This will ensure candidates maximise their mark in this type of question. A conclusion is always required in this situation, which is usually worth one mark. Candidates should conclude sensibly from what they have written, but a minority of candidates did not do this.

Again, in the final part of this requirement some candidates did not score full marks due to lack of precision. Asked to explain the changes to be made to the individual's ideal scenario (to spend three years overseas) in order for there to be no CGT on her planned sale of shares, some candidates made vague comments which hinted at her being treated as a temporary non-resident for CGT purposes, but few stated why, or directly addressed the changes she would need to make.

Part (b) required a calculation of the individual's income tax and class 4 national insurance contributions (NIC) for the tax year of cessation of her business.

A thorough knowledge of the opening and closing year basis period rules for unincorporated businesses is essential brought forward knowledge from TX-UK. Both of these are frequently tested in scenarios at ATX-UK, and candidates should ensure that they have a sound knowledge of these rules, including the availability of capital allowances in these situations. The capital allowances computation proved to be a particular problem for candidates, with the main errors being calculating an annual investment allowance (AIA) and writing down allowance (WDA) for the final accounting period as well as, or instead of, a balancing adjustment, and not taking account of the fact that a succession election was to be made in respect of the assets in the main pool. The other main issue was that candidates time apportioned the trading profits of the final 17-month accounting period over the final two tax years, thereby wasting a considerable amount of time, and creating potential problems for the ensuing tax calculations.

On the whole, candidates who sat the computer based exam (CBE) and chose to use the spreadsheet response space for this question part presented clearer, easier to follow answers than those who did not. Where detailed calculations are required, the use of the spreadsheet response option can provide valuable time savings and help candidates to present their workings more clearly.

Part (c), which was worth 4 marks, asked for an explanation of whether or not a potential inheritance tax (IHT) lability could arise in respect of a proposed gift of land by the individual's father, who was expected to die within the next 12 months.

A surprising number of candidates took this requirement at face value and discussed the seven-year rule, availability of taper relief etc. These candidates did not appear to have gone back to the scenario to look at the other information which had been provided in relation to this part. The land was situated overseas; the father was overseas domiciled but would shortly become deemed domiciled in the UK due to having been resident for 15 years. These were the aspects that were required to be discussed for this part.

Overall, question 2 was not very well answered, with candidates failing to display the required level of technical knowledge, and a lack of precision and detailed explanations.

ACCA marking scheme			
			Marks
(a)	Sale of unincorporated business		2.0
	Sale of business to FIM Ltd		2.0
	Residency – consideration of ties		5.0
	– consideration of days and conclusion		2.5
	Sale of shares in FIM Ltd		4.0
			————
			15.5
		Maximum	13.0
			————
(b)	Capital allowances		3.5
	Other aspects of taxable income		2.5
	IT and class 4 NIC liability		2.0
			————
			8.0
			————
(c)	No IHT whilst non-UK domiciled		1.5
	Consideration of deemed domicile		2.5
			————
			4.0
			————
Total			**25.0**
			————

24 JOE *WALK IN THE FOOTSTEPS OF A TOP TUTOR*

Key answer tips

This question covers various aspects of the ATX syllabus including liquidations, intangible asset disposals, shareholder distributions, a new unincorporated business and pre-trade expenditure.

Part (a) requires calculation of the profit or loss on the disposal of an intangible asset recognition of how a loss would be treated within the corporation tax computation. You also need an in-depth knowledge of the tax implications of payments to shareholders pre and post appointment of a liquidator. Consideration of CGT reliefs is also required, to reduce or defer any CGT liability.

Part (b) on the income tax and national insurance implications of private medical insurance, beneficial loans and the use of an employee's own car for business journeys should have been straight forward. These are all TX areas.

Part (c) offers some easy marks, as long as you recognised that investors' relief would be available.

The highlighted words in the written sections are key phrases that markers are looking for.

Notes for meeting

For	**The files**
Client	**VNL Ltd – liquidation**
	Joe – establishment of new business
Prepared by	**Tax senior**
Date	**1 June 2022**

(a) Liquidation of VNL Ltd

    (i) Sale of intangible fixed assets

Tutor's top tips

This requirement is focused on the calculation of the profit or loss on the disposal of two intangible assets and the post-tax proceeds. Post-tax proceeds means the disposal proceeds (not the profit) less any tax due, or plus any tax saved. This is a common requirement in the exam so you need to make sure you are ready tackle a question like this.

Make sure you read all the information given to you in the scenario to pick up on the relevant information needed to calculate the profit or loss, especially the treatment of the amortisation for tax purposes. You are told that no election has been made to write off the cost of the brand at 4%, which means that you should follow the accounting treatment instead and assume that the amortisation is allowable.

	Goodwill	Brand	
	£	£	£
Sale proceeds on 31 July 2022	75,000	47,000	122,000
Cost	(95,000)		
Tax written down value			
(£36,000 – £5,760)		(30,240)	
(Loss)/profit	(20,000)	16,760	
Corporation tax at 19% on profit			(3,184)
Loss relieved against total profits at 19%			3,800
Post tax proceeds			122,616

Tutorial note

The loss on the sale of the goodwill is a non-trading debit. This loss can be offset against the total income and gains of the current accounting period.

(ii) Timing of payments to shareholders

Tutor's top tips

Liquidations are not tested regularly in the ATX exam. However, there can be some easy marks available if you are familiar with the tax treatment of distributions to shareholders both before and after the appointment of a liquidator.

Prior to the appointment of the liquidator

A payment made to the shareholders prior to the appointment of the liquidator will be subject to income tax as a dividend in the normal way.

The first £2,000 of an individual's dividend income in a tax year from all shareholdings is taxed at 0%. The excess over £2,000 will be taxed as a shareholder's top slice of income.

Any amount which falls into a shareholder's basic rate band will be subject to income tax at 7.5%. The balance of the dividend will be subject to income tax at 32.5%.

After the appointment of the liquidator

Once the liquidator has been appointed, amounts paid to shareholders will represent proceeds in respect of a part disposal of their shares for the purposes of capital gains tax (CGT).

Any amount of the chargeable gain which is not covered by the shareholder's annual exempt amount of £12,300 will be subject to CGT.

Where the disposal of the shares qualifies for business asset disposal relief, the whole of any chargeable gain (within the lifetime limit of £1,000,000) will be subject to CGT at 10% irrespective of whether the shareholders are basic rate or higher rate taxpayers.

As VNL Ltd is a trading company, business asset disposal relief will be available where:

– the shareholder had owned at least 5% of the company's ordinary share capital and been an officer or employee of the company for a period of at least two years prior to the cessation of VNL Ltd's trade, and

– the shares are disposed of within three years of the cessation of VNL Ltd's trade.

Where business asset disposal relief is not available, the chargeable gain will be taxed after calculating tax on income, by reference to the income tax bands.

Any amount of the chargeable gain which falls into a shareholder's basic rate band will be subject to CGT at 10%. The balance of the chargeable gain will be subject to CGT at 20%.

Tutor's top tips

Remember in this scenario the shareholders are all individuals and therefore your focus should just be on the tax implications for individuals and not companies.

The calculations in this requirement lend themselves well to the spreadsheet functionality in the exam. Don't forget to reference through to these in the word processor.

(b) Unincorporated business

(i) Accounting date

Tutor's top tips

This requirement covers the opening year rules for an unincorporated trader and is assumed knowledge from the TX paper. Make sure you revise this area as it is an area that has been examined frequently in the past.

You need to evaluate the tax implications of the two year ends proposed in the scenario. For the July year end you must work out the profits for each accounting period first, and then apply the opening year rules. If you miss out the first step you will not be awarded all of the marks available.

You may want to make some assumptions if there is a lack of information provided. Make sure you state those assumptions.

Taxable trading profits in the first two tax years

		March	July (W)
		£	£
Tax year:	2022/23	24,500	30,278
	2023/24	97,000	79,750
Total		121,500	110,028

– Joe's total taxable trading profits for the first two tax years would be lower if he were to adopt a 31 July accounting date.

– A 31 July accounting date results in a higher amount of taxable trading profits in the tax year 2022/23 and a lower amount in the tax year 2023/24.

  – As a result, Joe's income tax liability for the tax year 2022/23 would be higher than it would be with a 31 March accounting date.

  – However, depending on his other sources of income, Joe may be able to use more of his basic rate band in 2022/23 whilst having a lower amount subject to income tax at 40% in the following tax year.

Advantages of adopting a 31 July accounting date

– After the first tax year, there will be a greater time period between earning profits and paying the tax due in respect of them.

– There will be a greater time period between knowing the amount of taxable profits and the end of the tax year. This time period can be used to plan Joe's affairs, for example, in respect of pensions.

Working

	£
Trading profit for accounting periods	
Period ending 31 July 2023	
1 November 2022 to 31 December 2022 (£4,000 × 2)	8,000
1 January 2023 to 31 March 2023 (£5,500 × 3)	16,500
1 April 2023 to 31 July 2023 (£7,500 × 4)	30,000
	54,500
Year ending 31 July 2024	
1 August 2023 to 31 August 2023	7,500
1 September 2023 to 31 July 2024 (£8,500 × 11)	93,500
	101,000

Taxable trading profit

2022/23 – 1 November 2022 to 5 April 2023	
(£54,500 × 5/9)	30,278
2023/24 – 1 November 2022 to 31 October 2023	
(£54,500 + (£101,000 × 3/12))	79,750
	———
	110,028
	———

Tutorial note

Credit was also awarded for relevant comments regarding the impact of the change of accounting date on overlap profits.

(ii)   Costs already incurred and the business premises

Tutor's top tips

This part of the question requires you to explain the tax implications for pre-trade expenditure for both income tax and VAT.

This is an element of assumed knowledge from the TX paper. The key things to remember are the time periods for pre-trading expenses, services and capital expenditure and also the difference between capital and revenue expenses. The treatment varies between trade profits and VAT.

Make sure that you use clear headings, so that the marker can see which tax you are addressing in your answer.

Tax deduction when calculating taxable trading profit

–   **Consultancy services**

The cost of the consultancy services will be treated as an allowable expense incurred on 1 November 2022, i.e. the day Joe begins trading. This is because the expenditure will have been incurred in the seven years prior to the commencement of trade and would be allowable if it had been incurred after trading commenced.

–   **Computer equipment**

Capital allowances in the form of the 100% annual investment allowance will be available in respect of the cost of the computer equipment as it was purchased for the purposes of carrying on Joe's new trade.

This will result in a tax deduction equal to the whole of the cost when calculating the trading profit for Joe's first trading period.

   –   **Premises**

That part of the cost of the premises which relates to integral features or plant and machinery will qualify for plant and machinery capital allowances.

The balance of the cost of the premises will not qualify for any allowances. In particular, it will not qualify for structures and buildings allowance because the building was constructed prior to 29 October 2018.

Recovery of input tax for the purposes of value added tax (VAT)

   –   **Consultancy services**

Joe will be able to recover input VAT in respect of services provided to him for business purposes in the six months prior to registering for VAT.

Accordingly, because Joe first incurred these costs more than six months ago, he should consider registering for VAT as soon as possible in order to recover as much of the input tax relating to the consultancy services as he can.

   –   **Computer equipment**

Joe will be able to recover the input tax in respect of the computer equipment provided he registers for VAT by 30 April 2026 (i.e. within four years of purchasing the equipment). This is on the assumption that he still owns the equipment when he registers.

   –   **Premises**

The amount of input tax which Joe can recover will depend on whether or not he opts to tax the building for the purposes of VAT.

If he opts to tax the building, he will be able to recover all of the input tax.

Otherwise, he will only be able to recover two-thirds of it.

This is because the granting of the lease will be an exempt supply unless an option to tax is made in respect of the building.

The building will not be subject to the capital goods scheme because its VAT exclusive cost will be less than £250,000.

Examiner's report

Part (a) concerned the liquidation of a company which had always been profitable in the past.

Part (a)(i) – 4 marks

The company planned to sell two intangible assets just before the liquidator was appointed and part (a)(i) required a calculation of the post-tax proceeds of these disposals for the company.

It is important to always check the 'command' word being used in a question. In this part, it is to 'calculate'. Long explanations are therefore not required here and will not earn marks. Candidates should aim for clear labelling of figures and perhaps brief explanations of what is being done, but without wasting time on lots of narrative content.

It is also important to note that the question asks for 'post-tax proceeds'. To arrive at this figure there are distinct steps in the calculation which need to be followed. Given the facts in this scenario, it is first necessary to calculate any taxable profit or loss, then calculate any corporation tax paid or saved at 19%, and then finally calculate the proceeds less any tax paid, or plus any tax saved.

The tax treatment generally follows the accounting treatment for the sale of intangible assets which is why trading profits and losses as opposed to capital gains or losses are being calculated.

The first intangible asset sold was goodwill and candidates were told that the amortisation of this goodwill had not been a tax deductible expense for the company. As a result, the full unamortised cost of £95,000 should be used in calculating the loss on sale i.e. £75,000 − £95,000 = £20,000 loss.

The second intangible asset sold was the brand which had been amortised. As this is an intangible asset held by a company, it should be assumed that this amortisation is tax deductible, unless told otherwise. As such, the amortised cost should be used to work out the taxable profit on the sale of the brand i.e. £47,000 less (£36,000-£5,760) = £16,760. A number of candidates incorrectly calculated the amortisation of the brand at 4%, but the question specifically states that no election to write it off at this fixed rate had been made

Thus far only the taxable profits and losses on the disposal of these assets has been calculated. A number of candidates stopped at this point but it was important to appreciate that the requirement involved calculation of the 'post-tax proceeds' arising from these disposals.

The next stage is to therefore calculate the tax saved, or paid, at 19% on the relevant loss or profit.

Finally, this needs to be brought together to calculate the 'post tax proceeds' arising from these transactions. The starting point for this is to go back to the actual proceeds i.e. £75,000 + £47,000 = £122,000. Then to deduct any tax paid, or add any tax saved, to the total proceeds. A common mistake made in questions of this nature is to take the profit or loss on disposal and to adjust this for the tax figure. But it should be remembered that, when looking at post tax proceeds from the disposal of an asset, the cost itself is no longer relevant and although this does feature in the profit or loss on which the tax is based, it is the proceeds which are important, as adjusted for the tax paid or saved.

Part (a)(ii) – 7 marks

Part (a)(ii) of this question required an explanation of the tax rates which shareholders will pay on amounts received from the company, depending on the timing of the payment. Within the first exhibit, it was stated that there would be a final payment to shareholders at the conclusion of the liquidation but consideration was being given to making an interim payment, prior to the appointment of the liquidator.

The command word used here was 'explain'; it is important to identify this and to focus on what the requirement is actually requiring an explanation of i.e. 'tax rates'.

Many candidates were very good at dealing with the pre-liquidation payment, correctly identifying that it would be treated as a dividend and detailing the potential tax rates. The scenario had specifically stated that the shareholders would be a mix of basic and higher rate taxpayers. Some candidates merely referred to the dividend treatment but did not go on to discuss in sufficient detail the specific tax rates which would apply to these types of shareholders; therefore they did not score the marks available for this. In this context, it is important that candidates do ensure they are happy with the precise detail of a question requirement before beginning their answer. It's always worth going back to double check exactly what it is they have been asked to do, perhaps by highlighting key words in the question so that they stand out when working on the response.

Many candidates were able to identify that any final payment by a liquidator would be treated as a capital payment, but not all went on to discuss the rates of capital gains tax which the shareholders would then pay. Not only were the standard rates of capital gains tax of 10% and 20% relevant here, but also the single rate of 10% for both basic and higher rate taxpayers if business asset disposal relief were to apply.

Requirement (b) This part of the question was about Joe who was setting up in business as an unincorporated trader.

Requirement (b)(i) – 8 marks

There were three subparts within this requirement. The first asked for a calculation of Joe's taxable trading profits for his first two tax years of trading, assuming he were to adopt a 31 July accounting date.

This required knowledge of unincorporated traders' opening year rules from TX-UK. Firstly, it involved a calculation of the trading profits for the relevant accounting periods i.e. to 31 July 2023 and to 31 July 2024. And then the basis periods for the tax years 2022/23 and 2023/24 needed to be determined in order to establish how much of the accounting periods' profits would be assessed in each of the tax years concerned.

Some candidates missed out the first of these steps and therefore did not score the available marks for initially calculating the trading profits for the accounting periods based on the revised 31 July accounting date.

It is important to appreciate that TX-UK knowledge can be tested at this level; therefore, if candidates do feel less confident on certain brought forward knowledge areas, they should aim to identify these and work to improve their technical knowledge on these aspects.

The second part of this requirement asked for comment on the possible effect on Joe's income tax liabilities for the first two tax years of trading of adopting a 31 July accounting date (as previously calculated), rather than that of 31 March (given in the question). Many candidates were able to successfully compare the numbers under both scenarios and to provide appropriate comment on the impact on taxable amounts and resulting tax liabilities. Many also considered the impact of the alternative dates on overlap profits.

The third part asked for two advantages, other than in relation to income tax liabilities, of adopting a 31 July year end rather than that of 31 March. Many candidates were able to identify the increased time between earning the profits and paying the tax, and also the benefit of having a longer period for planning purposes in terms of increasing the gap between knowing the amount of taxable profits and the end of the relevant tax year.

Requirement (b)(ii) – 12 marks

This part of the question involved an explanation of whether or not Joe could obtain a tax deduction for certain expenses he had incurred before starting to trade. It also asked whether or not he could recover the associated input VAT on those costs.

The expenses incurred related to three things – consultancy services, computer equipment and business premises.

With respect to whether or not the expenses were tax deductible, many candidates were unaware that pre-trading expenses on services incurred in the seven years prior to trading were allowed. More candidates correctly identified that capital allowances would be available on the computer equipment but most didn't address the issue as to whether or not a tax deduction would be available for the cost of the premises. This involved an appreciation of the fact that the premises would not qualify for structures and building allowance since they were constructed before 29 October 2018.

As far as dealing with the VAT aspects of this question, a knowledge of the detailed rules and time limits for recovery of pre-registration VAT was required; namely six months prior to VAT registration for services, and four years prior to VAT registration for goods. A number of candidates demonstrated that they were aware that time limits existed, but were not sufficiently precise as to exactly what these were. A detailed, rather than purely superficial, knowledge of the tax rules is required in order to score well in this exam.

Many candidates were confused regarding the input VAT recovery on the business premises; this is a challenging area of the syllabus. Joe intended to use two thirds of the premises for his trade and to rent out the remaining one third. This meant that he could recover two thirds of the input VAT on the original cost, but given that leasing is an exempt supply for VAT purposes, would not be able to recover the remaining one third. In order to change this position, and to be able to recover the full amount including that relating to the part which was let out, Joe would need to opt to tax the building.

Professional skills – 4 marks

In this question the requirement was to prepare notes for use at a meeting with the client covering a number of different tax issues.

Candidates should try to remember two key points when addressing requirements of this nature. Firstly, any explanations provided should be concise but comprehensive enough to form the basis of discussions with the client. Secondly, the notes should be presented in a logical, structured way, such that they are easy to follow in a meeting.

Candidates who scored well addressed all parts of the question, structured their answers according to the matters to be addressed (which were clearly set out in the manager's email), wrote concisely in short, clear paragraphs, provided easy to follow calculations and demonstrated a logical thought process in addressing each of the relevant issues.

In summary, candidates who provided satisfactory answers to question 1 were able to do the following:

- directly address each of the tasks within the manager's email

- demonstrate a good knowledge of the tax rules for companies and unincorporated traders, including relevant areas of brought forward knowledge from TX-UK

- apply their knowledge appropriately to the scenario and provide concise explanations, where required.

				Marks
(a)	**(i)**	Loss on sale of goodwill		1.0
		Profit on sale of brand		1.0
		Post tax proceeds		2.0

				4.0

	(ii)	Prior to appointment		4.0
		After appointment		6.0

				10.0
			Maximum	7.0

(b)	**(i)**	Taxable profits		
		Trading profit		3.0
		Taxable trading profit		3.0
		Comments		2.0
		Advantages		2.0

				10.0
			Maximum	8.0

	(ii)	Income tax		
		Consultancy services		1.5
		Computer equipment and premises		4.0
		Value added tax		
		Consultancy services		2.0
		Computer equipment		2.5
		Premises		4.0

				14.0
			Maximum	12.0

		Problem solving		1.0
		Clarity of explanations and calculations		1.0
		Effectiveness of communication		1.0
		Overall presentation and style		1.0

				4.0

Total				**35.0**

ACCA marking scheme

CAPITAL TAXES

25   JOAN ARK

Key answer tips

This is a good practice question covering the IHT and CGT implications of lifetime gifts in part (a), with a written requirement on general IHT planning points in part (b).

The style of question is more like the section B questions, although it is much longer than the section B questions you will see under the current exam format.

When attempting part (a), the best approach is to run through each disposal twice: once to deal with the IHT implications, then again to deal with the CGT implications.

If you try to cover both taxes at once, it is very easy to get them confused! You must also make sure that your answer is clearly labelled so that the marker knows exactly which tax and which gift you are discussing.

In a question like this, any detailed calculations should be carried out in the spreadsheet in the exam. This will enable you to set pro formas out more easily and also make use of formulae to cut down on calculation time. Don't forget to reference through to any calculations you have performed in the discursive part of your answer in the word processor.

(i)   **IHT and CGT implications of gifts made in the tax year 2021/22**

(a)   **Ordinary shares in Orleans plc**

IHT implications

For IHT purposes, a discretionary trust is a 'relevant property trust' and lifetime gifts into trusts are chargeable lifetime transfers.

BPR is not available as the shares are quoted and Joan does not have a controlling interest.

Tutorial note

There would be two annual exemptions available against this gift; however, the question says to ignore the effect of the annual exemption.

The shares are valued at the lower of:

- Quarter up method = 147p (146p + 1/4 × (150p −146p)) per share, or
- Average of the marked bargains = 147.5p ((140p + 155p) ÷ 2).

As Joan is to pay any IHT, the gift is a net gift and will be taxed at 25%.

	£
Transfer of value (250,000 × 147p)	367,500
Less: BPR	(0)
Exemptions	(0)
Net chargeable transfer	367,500
Less: NRB	(325,000)
Taxable amount	42,500
IHT payable (£42,500 × 25%)	10,625

The tax payable by Joan is due by 30 April 2022.

Gross gift to c/f = (£367,500 + £10,625) = £378,125

If Joan dies within seven years, before 13 July 2028, a further IHT liability may arise.

CGT implications

For CGT purposes, the shares are deemed to have been sold for their market value.

This is calculated as the mid-price = 148p ((146p + 150p) ÷ 2)

There are no acquisitions on the same day or in the next 30 days; therefore, the disposal of shares is from the share pool as follows:

	Number	Cost
		£
2006 – Purchase	200,000	149,000
August 2019 – Purchase	75,000	69,375
July 2020 – Purchase	10,000	14,800
	285,000	233,175
July 2021 – Gift	(250,000)	(204,539)
	35,000	28,636

The chargeable gain is calculated as follows:

	£
Market value (250,000 × 148p)	370,000
Less: Cost	(204,539)
Chargeable gain	165,461

Joan does not have a 5% interest in the company and therefore the shares are not qualifying business assets for gift holdover relief purposes.

However, Joan can elect to defer all of the gain with a gift holdover relief claim as the disposal is immediately chargeable to IHT.

Therefore there is no capital gains tax payable.

Tutorial note

If gift holdover relief is claimed, the full gain is deferred, therefore business asset disposal (BADR) relief (formerly entrepreneurs' relief) is not a consideration.

However, even if gift holdover relief were not claimed, BADR would not be available as Joan is not an employee and does not own a 5% interest. The gain would therefore be taxed at 20% (as Joan is a higher rate taxpayer), not 10%.

(b)   Ordinary shares in Rouen Ltd

IHT implications

Joan's gift of shares in Rouen Ltd in July 2021 to her son will be a PET, calculated as follows:

	£
Value of shares held before the transfer (Note)	
40,000 × £17.10 (part of a 80% holding)	684,000
Value of shares held after the transfer	
20,000 × £14.50 (part of a 60% holding)	(290,000)
Value transferred	394,000
Less: BPR (100%) (Note)	(394,000)
Chargeable amount	0

As a PET there is no lifetime IHT payable.

If Michael still owns the shares at the date of Joan's death, 100% BPR is still available and there will be nil taxable amount.

An IHT liability will arise if Joan dies before 15 July 2028 and Michael has disposed of the shares before that date.

Tutorial note

When valuing the shares for IHT purposes, the related property provisions must be taken into account. Joan is therefore disposing of 20,000 shares out of a combined 80% holding of shares held by her husband.

Business property relief at the rate of 100% will be available as the shares are unquoted trading company shares held for at least two years.

CGT implications

A capital gain will arise as follows:

	£
MV of 20% holding (20,000 × £7.90)	158,000
Less: Cost £96,400 × (20,000/40,000)	(48,200)
Chargeable gain	109,800

Provided Joan and her son jointly elect, the gain can be held over as a gift of business assets, since Rouen Ltd is an unquoted trading company.

Therefore, there is no capital gains tax payable.

Tutorial note

If gift holdover relief is claimed, the full gain is deferred, therefore BADR is not a consideration.

However, even if gift holdover relief were not available, BADR would not be available as Joan does not work for Rouen Ltd. The gain would therefore be taxed at 20%.

Key answer tips

For IHT purposes, the diminution in the value of Joan's estate is the starting point.

For CGT purposes, the deemed proceeds is the market value of the asset gifted (i.e. a 20% holding).

Note that the diminution in value concept does not apply to CGT and the related property provisions do not apply to CGT.

(c) **Antique vase**

IHT implications

The gift of the vase is in consideration of marriage, and will therefore qualify for an exemption of £2,500 as it is a gift from a grandparent to grandchild.

The balance of the gift of £16,000 (£18,500 − £2,500) will be a PET made on 4 November 2021, with no tax unless Joan dies within seven years.

CGT implications

The gift of the vase is a disposal of a non-wasting chattel. The gain is calculated as £4,350 (£18,500 − £14,150).

Gift holdover relief is not available as a vase is not a qualifying business asset and there is no immediate charge to IHT.

The CGT liability due on 31 January 2023 is therefore £870 (£4,350 × 20%) (ignoring the annual exempt amount).

(d)   Agricultural land

IHT implications

The gift of the agricultural land will be a PET for £300,000 on 15 January 2022 and will not become chargeable unless Joan dies within seven years.

The increase in the value of her son Charles' property is irrelevant in valuing the PET. Only the diminution in the value of Joan's estate as a result of the gift is relevant.

If the PET becomes chargeable as a result of Joan dying before 15 January 2029, agricultural property relief at the rate of 100% based on the agricultural value of £175,000 will be available. This is because the land is let out for the purposes of agriculture and has been owned for at least seven years.

However, relief will only be available if, at the date of Joan's death, Charles still owns the land and it still qualifies as agricultural property.

CGT implications

The gift of agricultural land to Charles will be valued at its open market value on the date of the gift of £300,000.

Since the land qualifies for agricultural property relief it is also eligible for gift holdover relief for CGT purposes. Joan and Charles can therefore jointly elect that the gain of £208,000 (£300,000 – £92,000) is held over as a gift of business assets.

Therefore, there is no capital gains tax payable.

Tutorial note

BPR will not be available on the remainder of the market value as Joan has rented the farm out rather than use it as her farming business.

BADR is not a consideration as the full gain is deferred with a gift holdover relief claim.

However, even if gift holdover relief were not available, BADR would not be available for the disposal of a rented property, as this is classed as an investment asset. The gain would therefore be taxed at 20%.

(e)   Main residence

IHT implications

The gift of the main residence is a gift with reservation because although Joan has gifted the freehold interest, she retains an interest in the property as she has continued to live rent free in the property.

The gift will be treated as a PET for £265,000 as normal on 31 March 2022, but Joan will still be treated as beneficially entitled to the property.

If Joan continues to live in the property rent free until her death, it will be included in her estate when she dies at its market value at that date, although relief will be given should there be a double charge to IHT.

Joan could avoid these provisions by paying full consideration for the use of the property. The gift of the main residence will simply be a PET on 31 March 2022 with no gift with reservation implications.

CGT implications

The gift of the main residence is a chargeable disposal for CGT purposes and the time of the disposal is when the ownership of the asset passes to the donee.

The reservation of benefit is therefore not relevant for CGT, and a normal CGT computation is required on 31 March 2022.

	£
Deemed consideration	265,000
Less: Cost	(67,000)
	198,000
Less: PRR (W1)	(75,103)
Letting relief (W2)	(0)
Chargeable gain	122,897
Capital gains tax at 28%	34,411
Due date	30 April 2022

Tutorial note

When a UK residential property is disposed of a UK land return must be submitted and the relevant CGT paid within 30 days, rather than the usual deadline of 31st January following the end of the tax year.

Workings

(W1) Private residence relief

		Notes	Months	Exempt	Chargeable
1.07.2000 – 31.12.2004	Owner occupied		54	54	
1.01.2005 – 31.12.2008	Unoccupied	1	48	36	12
1.01.2009 – 30.06.2021	Rented out	2	150	0	150
1.07.2021 – 31.03.2022	Owner occupied		9	9	
			261	99	162

PRR = (99/261) × £198,000 = £75,103

Notes

1   Three years allowed for any reason provided the property is owner occupied at some time before and sometime after the period of absence.

2   The last nine months are always exempt. However, Joan occupies the property throughout this period anyway.

(W2) Letting relief

Letting relief is only available in respect of gains arising during periods of shared occupancy.

As Joan did not occupy any of the property while it was let out, no letting relief is available.

(ii)   Main advantages in lifetime giving for IHT purposes

Possible advantages of lifetime giving include:

*   Making use of lifetime IHT exemptions such as the annual exemption, small gifts exemption, marriage exemptions in reducing a taxpayer's chargeable estate at death.

*   Gifts between individuals will not become liable to IHT unless the donor dies within seven years of making the gift.

*   If the donor does die prematurely there may still be an IHT advantage in lifetime giving because usually:

    −   The value of the asset for calculating any additional IHT arising upon death is fixed at the time the gift is made, unless the asset falls in value, in which case fall in value relief may be available.

    −   The availability of taper relief (providing the donor survives at least three years) may help reduce the effective IHT rate.

Main factors to consider in choosing assets to gift

The main factors to consider include:

(i)   Whether or not a significant CGT liability will arise upon making the gift.

Lifetime gifting may give rise to CGT. This therefore needs to be balanced against the fact that no CGT liability will arise upon death (i.e. if the assets are left in the estate and gifted in a will). Death results in the 'tax free' uplift of the chargeable assets included in the deceased's estate to market value.

The availability of CGT reliefs (primarily gift holdover relief for business assets or if there is an immediate charge to IHT) and CGT exemptions (e.g. annual exempt amount) to ensure there is no CGT liability on the lifetime gift is therefore relevant in selecting assets.

Some assets are completely exempt from CGT, such as cash. Giving cash during lifetime would not give rise to a CGT liability.

(ii)   Whether an asset is appreciating in value.

Because any additional IHT arising as a result of death will be based on the (lower) value of the asset at the date of gift it may be advantageous to select assets that are likely to significantly appreciate in value.

Even if the value of the asset decreases, fall in value relief may be available so that lifetime giving does not result in more tax than leaving the asset in the death estate.

    (iii)   Whether the donor can afford to make the gift.

             Whilst lifetime gifting can result in significant IHT savings this should not be at the expense of the taxpayer's ability to live comfortably, particularly in old age.

    (iv)   The availability of significant IHT reliefs, particularly BPR.

             There may be little point in selecting an asset that already qualifies for 100% relief.

             Also, if residential property is gifted in lifetime, the residence nil rate band (RNRB) will not be available. However, if property the deceased lived in is passed to direct descendants on death, a RNRB of up to £175,000 may be available.

26   ALEX (ADAPTED)

Key answer tips

This section B question includes some straightforward marks for basic income tax and inheritance tax computations, with a written section on the use of trusts.

There are a few tricky points in part (b) – make sure that you calculate the lifetime tax before trying to calculate the death tax on lifetime transfers, as the PET uses the nil rate band on death but does not affect the nil band when calculating the lifetime tax on the CLT.

Where shares are quoted 'ex div' you must add the dividend to the estate too. Don't forget to include the income tax from part (a) – this will be a mark for consistency, even if your figure is wrong.

Trusts are only likely to feature as part of a question in the exam, as in part (c).

(a)   **Income tax payable/repayable – 2021/22**

	Total	Non-savings income	Savings income	Dividends
	£	£	£	£
Pension	10,600	10,600		
B.Soc interest	1,600		1,600	
NS&I interest	870		870	
Dividends – other	9,000	–		9,000
– Nacional plc (Note 1)	3,600			3,600
Total income	25,670	10,600	2,470	12,600
Less: PA (Note 2)	(12,570)	(10,600)		(1,970)
Taxable income	13,100	0	2,470	10,630

Income tax

£		£
2,470	× 0% (Savings income)	0
2,000	× 0% (Dividends)	0
8,630	× 7.5% (Dividends)	647
13,100		

Income tax liability	647
Less: Tax at source	
PAYE	(2,120)
Income tax repayable	(1,473)

Tutorial note

1   Alex will be taxed on his income due and payable up to the date of death. He will have a full (non-apportioned) personal allowance for 2021/22, the tax year of death.

Re-the Nacional plc dividends:

- The dividends are declared before Alex's death and are therefore included in Alex's last income tax computation even though they are received post death.

- Dividends to include = (20,000 × 18p) = £3,600

The ACCA have confirmed that this is the treatment they expect for dividends declared pre-death, received post death.

2   The PA is always set off in the most beneficial way, and should be set against non-savings income first.

The excess PA should not be set against Alex's savings income, as this all falls into the £5,000 starting rate band and will be taxed at 0%.

Instead, the excess PA should be set against the dividends to save tax at 7.5%, as the dividends are not fully covered by the £2,000 dividend nil rate band.

(b) Inheritance tax liability on Alex's death

Lifetime inheritance tax

July 2016 – PET

- The gift in July 2016 was a potentially exempt transfer (PET).
- No IHT is payable at the time of the gift.
- IHT only becomes payable when Alex dies within seven years.

March 2017 – CLT

- The transfer into the discretionary trust in March 2017 was a chargeable lifetime transfer (CLT).
- Lifetime IHT is due when the gift is made and additional tax is due as Alex dies within seven years of the gift.

- The value of the CLT was £338,000.

- No annual exemptions were available, as these are allocated in date order against the PET in July 2016.

- The lifetime tax on the CLT was as follows:
  (£338,000 – £325,000 nil rate band) × 25% = £3,250

- The gross chargeable transfer was therefore £341,250 (£338,000 + £3,250).

Tutorial note

1 *The question tells you that when Alex's wife died, she had utilised all of her nil rate band. As a result, only Alex's nil rate band is available.*

   Had his wife not utilised her nil rate band, the proportion of unused nil rate band could be transferred to Alex on his death.

2 *Where the donor suffers the lifetime tax due, the tax rate used to calculate lifetime tax is 25% (i.e. 20/80).*

3 *All of the nil rate band is available against this lifetime gift; the PET is ignored as it is not chargeable during Alex's lifetime, although it does use the annual exemptions.*

Additional inheritance tax due at death

IHT on PET in July 2016

The PET becomes chargeable on death, as Alex died within seven years of making the gift. As there are no lifetime transfers in the previous seven years, all of the nil rate band is available.

		£
Value transferred		338,000
Less: Annual exemptions: 2016/17		(3,000)
2015/16		(3,000)
		———
PET		332,000
		———
IHT due (£332,000 – £325,000) × 40%		2,800
Less: Taper relief (5 – 6 years) (60%)		(1,680)
		———
IHT due on death		1,120
		———

This additional tax is paid by Brian (see tutorial note).

IHT on CLT in March 2017

The PET has used up the nil rate band, so the CLT in March 2017 is fully taxable as follows:

	£
IHT due on gross gift (£341,250 × 40%)	136,500
Less: Taper relief (4 – 5 years) (40%)	(54,600)
	81,900
Less: IHT paid during lifetime	(3,250)
IHT due on death	78,650

This additional tax is paid by the trustees of the discretionary trust (see tutorial note).

Tutorial note

The additional tax on PETs and CLTs as a result of death is always paid by the donee.

Estate at death

	£	£
Main residence		575,000
Touriga shares (W1)	26,950	
Less: Business property relief	(26,950)	
		0
Nacional shares (W2)		128,800
Building society account		15,000
NS&I investment account		55,000
NS&I savings certificates		180,000
Chattels		40,000
Other quoted investments		115,000
Income tax repayment (part (a))		1,473
		1,110,273
Less: Exempt charitable legacy		(150,000)
Gross chargeable estate		960,273
Less: Residence nil rate band		(175,000)

The IHT nil rate band has already been used against gifts made in the seven years prior to death.

Taxable estate		785,273
IHT on estate (£785,273 × 36%) (W3)		282,698

The inheritance due to each of Brian and Beatrice is £352,263 (W4).

Workings

(W1) Touriga Ltd

The total value of Touriga Ltd shares at death = (£11.00 × 2,450) = £26,950.

As these shares are unquoted trading company shares and have been held for more than two years, 100% business property relief applies.

(W2) Nacional plc

The Nacional plc shares are valued at the lower of:

(i)   Quarter up method

= (624p + (632p – 624p) × 1/4) = 626p

(ii)   Average of highest and lowest marked bargains

= (625p + 630p) × ½ = 627.5p

Value of 20,000 shares = (626p × 20,000) = £125,200

As the shares are quoted ex-div at the date of death, the value of the shares in the death estate needs to include the value of the next dividend (18p × 20,000 = £3,600).

The total value of the shares is therefore £128,800 (£3,600 + £125,200).

(W3) Rate of tax

	£
Taxable estate	785,273
Add: Exempt legacy to charity	150,000
Residence nil rate band	175,000
Baseline amount	1,110,273
Apply 10% test	
£1,110,273 × 10%	111,027

As the exempt charitable legacy exceeds £111,027, the estate is taxed at 36% instead of 40%.

(W4) Share of inheritance

	£
Value of estate	960,273
Value of Touriga shares	26,950
	987,223
IHT payable from estate	(282,698)
Estate value to share	704,525

Half share to each of Brian and Beatrice (£704,525 ÷ 2) = £352,263.

(c)   (i)   Use of a trust

Relevant property trusts

Brian has the choice of setting up an interest in possession trust or a discretionary trust.

However, regardless of the type of trust set up, if the trust is set up by Brian during his lifetime it will be a 'relevant property trust' for IHT purposes.

A relevant property trust is taxed as follows:

- Gifts into a relevant property trust are chargeable lifetime transfers (CLTs). They attract IHT at half the death rate to the extent that the cumulative lifetime transfers in the last seven years of the settlor (Brian) exceed the nil rate band (£325,000).

- The tax can be paid by the trustees out of the settled assets (i.e. borne by the trust).

- Once the assets are settled in a relevant property trust, the trust will suffer a ten year charge (the 'principal charge').

- The charge is 6%.

- If capital assets are removed from the trust (i.e. distributed to the beneficiaries), an exit charge is also levied.

Type of trust

Given Brian's desire to retain control over the assets, it would appear that a discretionary trust would be advisable, rather than an interest in possession trust.

This is because:

- The trustees of a discretionary trust have the discretion (hence the name) over how the funds will be used.

- They can thus control the assets comprising the inheritance, while allowing Colin or Charlotte access to some or all of the income.

- It is likely that Brian himself would wish to be a trustee and he could therefore control how his children accessed the money, both the income and capital.

- In contrast, if an interest in possession trust is set up, the beneficiaries Colin and Charlotte would be legally entitled to the income generated by the trust each year and it must be paid to them.

- In the trust deed the capital must be directed to pass at a set future date or as a consequence of a future event.

(ii)   Inheritance tax planning

If Brian creates a discretionary trust by making a lifetime gift of the inherited assets, this will be a CLT and will give rise to a charge to IHT with a further liability arising if Brian dies within seven years.

Therefore, Brian should be advised to pass his inheritance directly to his children by using a deed of variation to alter the disposition of Alex's estate.

Provided the deed includes a statement that the deed is effective for inheritance tax purposes, the transfer into the trust will be treated as a legacy under the will.

There will be no alteration in the tax payable on Alex's estate but Brian will not have a CLT, there will be no lifetime tax on setting up the trust and Brian will have preserved his own nil rate band for use against future lifetime gifts or the value of his own estate on death.

Tutorial note

If Brian had chosen to set up an interest in possession trust, if set up on death (under a deed of variation of Alex's will), it will be an Immediate Post Death Interest trust (IPDI) and not a 'relevant property trust'. As a result, different rules apply to the taxation of trust. These rules are beyond the scope of the ATX syllabus.

27   MABEL PORTER *Online question assistance*

Key answer tips

This question covers the commonly-tested area of CGT versus IHT for lifetime gifts, with IHT calculations on death and further IHT planning.

You must make sure that your answer is well structured and well labelled in part (a) – you are looking at four gifts in total, and need to consider CGT and IHT for each. The best way to approach this is to deal with one tax at a time.   Think about all the CGT implications, remembering to state which reliefs are not available, as well as those that are; then deal with the IHT implications in the same way.

As long as your advice and calculation of the tax saving in (b) is consistent with your analysis in part (a), you could still score full marks here.

(a)   Tax implications of the four possible gifts

All four possible gifts would be potentially exempt transfers (PETs) such that no inheritance tax would be due at the time of the gift.

The chargeable gain or allowable loss arising on each gift will be computed by reference to the market value of the asset as at the date of the gift.

Gift to Bruce of shares in BOZ plc

Capital gains tax

The gift will result in a chargeable gain of £32,500 (£77,000 – £44,500).

BOZ plc is Mabel's personal trading company as she is able to exercise at least 5% of the voting rights. Accordingly, the shares qualify for gift holdover relief.

However, gift holdover relief would only be available if Bruce (the recipient of the gift) were UK resident. This is unlikely to be the case as he emigrated to South Africa in January 2019; therefore gift holdover relief is not available.

Business asset disposal relief is not available as although BOZ plc is Mabel's personal trading company and she has owned the shares for more than two years, she does not work for BOZ plc.

Key answer tips

Where an individual owns shares in a plc, you should generally assume that they hold less than a 5% interest and that they don't work for the company, unless clearly told otherwise.

Inheritance tax

The value transferred will be reduced by business property relief at the rate of 50% because Mabel owns a controlling shareholding in the company.

Luke's period of ownership can be taken into account in order to satisfy the two-year period of ownership requirement.

The relief is restricted because the company owns excepted assets.

	£
Value transferred	77,000
Less: BPR (£77,000 × 92% × 50%)	(35,420)
Annual exemptions – 2022/23 and 2021/22 (£3,000 × 2)	(6,000)
PET	35,580

Gift to Bruce of the land in Utopia

Capital gains tax

The gift will result in a capital loss of £24,000 (£99,000 – £75,000).

This loss is available for relief against chargeable gains made by Mabel in the tax year 2022/23 or later tax years.

Mabel and Bruce (aunt and nephew) are not connected persons for the purposes of capital gains tax and therefore, there is no restriction on Mabel's use of the losses.

Inheritance tax

Agricultural property relief is not available because the land is not situated in the UK or the EEA.

Business property relief is also not available because the farm is an investment asset, not a business asset.

The value of the PET will therefore be:

	£
Value transferred	75,000
Less: Annual exemptions – 2022/23 and 2021/22 (£3,000 × 2)	(6,000)
PET	69,000

Tutorial note

BPR is available on worldwide business property, whereas APR is only available on farmland and buildings situated in the UK or the EEA.

The minimum period of ownership rule also has to be satisfied. Even if the farm had been in the UK or EEA, APR would not be available as a tenanted farm must be owned by the donor and occupied and farmed by the tenant for at least seven years prior to the transfer.

Gift to Padma of the Rolls Royce motor car

Capital gains tax

No gain or loss will arise as cars are exempt assets for the purposes of capital gains tax.

Inheritance tax

The PET will equal the market value of the car of £71,000.

There are no annual exemptions available as they have already been used against the gift to Bruce.

Gift to Padma of the necklace

Capital gains tax

The gift will result in the following chargeable gain:

	£
Deemed proceeds (market value)	70,000
Less: Cost (probate value when inherited)	(21,500)
Chargeable gain	48,500

Gift holdover relief is not available as the necklace is not a business asset.

Inheritance tax

The value of the PET will equal the market value of the necklace of £70,000.

There are no annual exemptions available as they have already been used against the gift to Bruce.

Key answer tips

Watch out for the dates here – the gift to Padma will be made after the gift to Bruce.

(b)   Recommendation of gifts to make

Mabel's criteria in deciding which assets to give are:

- The gifts must not give rise to any tax liabilities prior to her death.

   The gifts will not give rise to inheritance tax prior to Mabel's death because they are potentially exempt transfers. Accordingly, in satisfying this criterion, it is only necessary to consider capital gains tax.

- If possible, the gifts should reduce the inheritance tax due on her death.

Bruce

A gift of the shares in BOZ plc would result in a chargeable gain of £32,500.

This exceeds Mabel's capital losses brought forward of £15,100 and the annual exempt amount of £12,300, such that a capital gains tax liability would arise.

Accordingly, she should give Bruce the land in Utopia. This will result in a capital loss of £24,000.

Padma

There would be no capital gains tax on either of the proposed gifts to Padma.

The car is an exempt asset and the chargeable gain arising on the necklace would be relieved by Mabel's capital losses and the annual exempt amount as follows:

		£
Chargeable gain		48,500
Less:	Capital loss on the gift to Bruce of the land	(24,000)
	Annual exempt amount	(12,300)
		────────
		12,200
Less:	Capital losses brought forward (restricted)	(12,200)
		────────
Taxable gain		0
		────────

Accordingly, the gift to be made to Padma should be chosen by reference to the amount of inheritance tax saved.

Mabel should give Padma the necklace as its value is expected to increase.

Key answer tips

Don't worry if you made some mistakes in part (a) – as long as you have provided clear, consistent advice with reasons, you should still score full marks here.

IHT payable if the lifetime gifts to Bruce and Padma are not made

IHT payable on Mabel's lifetime gift – during her lifetime

1 May 2016 – Gift into discretionary trust

		£
Transfer of value		210,000
Less: Annual exemptions – 2016/17		(3,000)
– 2015/16 b/f		(3,000)
Net chargeable amount		204,000

The gift is covered by the NRB and therefore no IHT was paid.

Gross chargeable amount	204,000

IHT payable on Mabel's lifetime gift – due to her death

If Mabel dies on 30 June 2027, this gift is more than seven years before death and therefore no IHT payable.

As there are no other lifetime gifts, the full NRB is available against the death estate.

Death estate

	£	£
House and furniture		450,000
Rolls Royce car		55,000
Diamond necklace		84,000
Cash and investments		150,000
Shares in BOZ plc	95,000	
Less: BPR (50% × £95,000 × 92%)	(43,700)	
		51,300
Land in Utopia		75,000
Chargeable estate		865,300
IHT payable (£865,300 – £325,000) × 40%		216,120

Tutorial note

Luke has fully utilised his nil rate band, so there is no unused proportion to transfer to Mabel.

The residence nil rate band is not available as the house is not being left to Mabel's direct descendants.

IHT payable if Mabel makes the lifetime gifts to Bruce and Padma

IHT payable on Mabel's lifetime gifts – during her lifetime

1 May 2016 – Gift into discretionary trust

As before, the IHT payable will be £0 as the gift of £204,000 is covered by the NRB.

1 February 2023 – Gift to Bruce – Land in Utopia

	£
Transfer of value	75,000
Less: Annual exemption – 2022/23	(3,000)
– 2021/22 b/f	(3,000)
PET – chargeable amount	69,000

No IHT payable during lifetime as the gift is a PET.

5 March 2023 – Gift to Padma – Diamond necklace

	£
Transfer of value	70,000
Less: Annual exemptions (already used)	(0)
PET – chargeable amount	70,000

No IHT payable during lifetime as the gift is a PET.

IHT payable on Mabel's lifetime gifts – due to her death

1 May 2016 – Gift into discretionary trust

As before, if Mabel dies on 30 June 2027, this gift is more than seven years before death and therefore no IHT payable.

1 February 2023 – Gift to Bruce – Land in Utopia

	£	£
Chargeable amount		69,000
NRB at death	325,000	
Less: Gross transfers in last 7 years (1.2.2016 – 1.2.2023)	(204,000)	(121,000)
Taxable amount		0

No IHT payable as the gift is covered by the NRB.

5 March 2023 – Gift to Padma – Diamond necklace

	£	£
Chargeable amount		70,000
NRB at death	325,000	
Less: Gross transfers in last 7 years (5.3.2016 – 5.3.2023)		
(£204,000 + £69,000)	(273,000)	
		(52,000)
Taxable amount		18,000
IHT payable (£18,000 × 40%)		7,200
Less: Taper relief (5.03.2023 to 30.06.2027) (4 – 5 years) (40%)		(2,880)
		4,320
Less: IHT paid in lifetime (PET)		(0)
IHT due on death		4,320

Death estate

	£	£
House and furniture		450,000
Rolls Royce car		55,000
Cash and investments		150,000
BOZ plc shares (as before)		51,300
Chargeable estate		706,300
NRB at death	325,000	
Less: Gross transfers in last 7 years (30.6.2020 – 30.6.2027)		
(£69,000 + £70,000)	(139,000)	
		(186,000)
Taxable estate		520,300
IHT payable (£520,300 × 40%)		208,120

Quantifying the IHT saving as a result of making the lifetime gifts

	£
Total IHT payable if the gifts are not made	216,120
Total IHT payable if the gifts are made (£4,320 + £208,120)	(212,440)
Total IHT saved	3,680

Key answer tips

Even if you recommended different gifts, you could still score full marks for calculating the tax saving by comparing the tax payable without the gifts and the tax payable with the gifts (remembering that the assets given would no longer be in the death estate!).

(c)   Further advice

Mabel should consider delaying one of the gifts until after 1 May 2023 such that it is made more than seven years after the gift to the discretionary trust.

Both PETs would then be covered by the nil rate band resulting in a saving of inheritance tax of £4,320 (from (b)).

Mabel should ensure that she uses her inheritance tax annual exemption of £3,000 every year by, say, making gifts of £1,500 each year to both Bruce and Padma. The effect of this will be to save inheritance tax of £1,200 (£3,000 × 40%) every year.

She could also make use of the normal expenditure out of income exemption.

28   KEPLER (ADAPTED)

Key answer tips

This is a reasonable capital taxes question but with some complications. The calculation of inheritance tax on the lifetime gift of shares is something a well prepared student should have no problems with. You might have been puzzled when asked to calculate Galileo's inheritance tax payable on the shares he inherited on Kepler's death when there is none. The examining team did give a clue by saying tax payable (if any).

Payment by instalments is important in practice and the rules should be learnt.

You must also make sure that you are happy with the overseas aspects of personal tax, as these are very often tested in the exam.

There are some easy marks in the last sections asking for advice about employment benefits, provided you have retained this TX knowledge.

In a question like this, any detailed calculations should be carried out in the spreadsheet in the exam. This will enable you to set pro formas out more easily and also make use of formulae to cut down on calculation time. Don't forget to reference through to any calculations you have performed in the discursive part of your answer in the word processor.

(a)   (i)   Galileo – Inheritance tax payable

Gift of shares in June 2018

The gift of shares to Galileo was a potentially exempt transfer. It has become chargeable due to Kepler's death within seven years of the gift.

Any tax arising on a PET which becomes chargeable on death is payable by the donee (i.e. Galileo).

	£	£
Value of Kepler's holding prior to the gift to Galileo (2,000 × £485)		970,000
Less: Value of Kepler's holding after the gift (1,400 × £310)		(434,000)
Transfer of value		536,000
Less: Business property relief (W1)		(367,843)
Less: Annual exemption – 2018/19		(3,000)
– 2017/18 b/f (W2)		(1,200)
Chargeable amount		163,957
Nil rate band at death	325,000	
Gross chargeable transfers in last 7 years (W2)	(305,000)	
Nil rate band available		(20,000)
Taxable amount		143,957
		£
Inheritance tax (£143,957 × 40%)		57,583
Less: Taper relief (3 – 4 years) (£57,583 × 20%)		(11,517)
Inheritance tax payable by Galileo		46,066

Inheritance of shares in May 2022

The inheritance tax payable in respect of the shares in the death estate will be paid by the executors and borne by Herschel, the residuary legatee.

None of the tax will be payable by Galileo.

Tutorial note

As Galileo is inheriting a specific gift, he will not suffer any tax. The tax will be taken from the balance of the estate.

Workings

(W1) Business property relief

BPR at 100% is available on unquoted trading company shares held for at least two years. However, BPR is restricted if the company has excepted assets.

Excepted assets and total assets

	Total assets	Excluding excepted assets
	£	£
Premises	900,000	900,000
Surplus land	480,000	–
Vehicles	100,000	100,000
Current assets	50,000	50,000
	1,530,000	1,050,000
BPR (£536,000 × 100% × (£1,050,000/£1,530,000))		367,843

Tutorial note

Excepted assets are those which have not been used wholly or mainly for business in the last two years and are not likely to be required for future use in the business.

(W2) Lifetime gifts in the seven years before 1 June 2018

	1 Feb 2017	1 July 2017
	£	£
Transfer of value	311,000	1,800
(2 × £900)		
Less Annual exemptions		
– 2016/17	(3,000)	
– 2015/16 b/f	(3,000)	
– 2017/18		(1,800)
	305,000	0

- No tax is due at the time of the gifts as they are PETs.
- Both gifts fall within seven years of Kepler's death and therefore become chargeable on death.
- Therefore, the GCTs in the seven years before the gift in June 2018 are £305,000.

(ii)   Payment by instalments

The inheritance tax can be paid by instalments because Messier Ltd is an unquoted company controlled by Kepler at the time of the gift and is still unquoted at the time of his death.

The tax is due in ten equal annual instalments starting on 30 November 2022.

All of the outstanding inheritance tax will become payable if Galileo sells the shares in Messier Ltd.

Tutorial note

Candidates were also given credit for stating that payment by instalments is available because the shares represent at least 10% of the company's share capital and are valued at £20,000 or more.

(b)   Minimising capital gains tax on the sale of the paintings

Galileo will only become resident from the date he arrives in the UK as he will be starting to work full time in the UK for a period of one year or more and he did not have sufficient ties in the UK in order to be UK resident prior to coming to the UK. Further, the split year basis applies to him as he was not UK resident in the previous year, is UK resident in the current year and arrived in the UK part way through the current year to begin work in the UK.

Prior to that date he will not be resident such that he will not be subject to UK capital gains tax.

Galileo should sell the paintings before he leaves Astronomeria; this will avoid UK capital gains tax completely.

Tutorial note

If Galileo sells the paintings after arriving in the UK and becoming UK resident, then as a non-domiciled individual, the taxation of his gains depends on how much of them he remits to the UK.

If his unremitted gains exceed £2,000 then Galileo must choose whether to be taxed on all his gains (arising basis) but keep his entitlement to the capital gains annual exempt amount, or to be taxed only on the gains remitted to the UK (remittance basis) and lose the annual exempt amount.

If he chooses the remittance basis then he will not have to pay the £30,000 annual charge as he has not been resident in the UK for at least seven out of the last nine tax years.

If his unremitted gains are less than £2,000, then the remittance basis of taxation applies automatically and he will be entitled to a capital gains annual exempt amount.

However, since he wants to use the proceeds of selling his paintings to help buy a house, it is likely he will bring in all the money raised from the sale and consequently will automatically be taxed on the whole of his gains. As he is not claiming the remittance basis the capital gains annual exempt amount will be available.

(c) **(i)** **Relocation costs**

Direct assistance

Messier Ltd can bear the cost of certain qualifying relocation costs of Galileo up to a maximum of £8,000 without increasing his UK income tax liability.

Qualifying costs include the legal, professional and other fees in relation to the purchase of a house, the costs of travelling to the UK and the cost of transporting his belongings. The costs must be incurred before the end of the tax year following the year of the relocation (i.e. by 5 April 2024).

Assistance in the form of a loan

Messier Ltd can provide Galileo with an interest-free loan of up to £10,000 without giving rise to any UK income tax.

(ii) **Tax-free accommodation**

It is not possible for Messier Ltd to provide Galileo with tax-free accommodation.

The provision of accommodation by an employer to an employee will give rise to a taxable benefit unless it is:

- necessary for the proper performance of the employee's duties (e.g. a caretaker); or

- for the better performance of the employee's duties and customary (e.g. a hotel manager); or

- part of arrangements arising out of threats to the employee's security (e.g. a government minister).

As a manager of Messier Ltd, Galileo is unable to satisfy any of the above conditions.

Examiner's report

This question concerned inheritance tax, capital gains tax and income tax together with certain implications of moving to the UK from overseas. There were five separate parts to this question, all of which had to be addressed in the time. A number of candidates failed to tailor their answers to the number of marks available and wasted time producing inappropriately long answers.

Part (a) required candidates to calculate the inheritance tax payable by the donee of a potentially exempt transfer following the death of the donor. This was done well by many candidates although a minority did not consider business property relief, which was an important element of the question. Those who did consider business property relief often failed to recognise the existence of excepted assets in the company.

Candidates were also asked to explain why the tax could be paid in instalments and to state when the instalments were due. This was not handled particularly well; many candidates did not know the circumstances in which payment by instalments is available and the payment dates given often lacked precision.

Part (b) concerned the liability to capital gains tax of an individual coming to the UK. It was only for two marks but it illustrated continued confusion on the part of many as to the treatment of someone who is not resident. Such a person is not subject to UK capital gains tax on personal investment assets and the remittance or otherwise of the proceeds is irrelevant. Candidates preparing for future exams should ensure that they fully understand the rules.

Part (c) involved the desire to assist an employee's relocation to the UK without giving rise to an income tax liability. This was done rather well with many candidates identifying the possibility of a tax free loan and relocation assistance.

ACCA marking scheme			
			Marks
(a)	(i)	Diminution in value	1.0
		Business property relief	1.5
		Annual exemptions	1.5
		Available nil band	1.5
		Inheritance tax at 40%	0.5
		Taper relief	1.0
		Tax due in respect of shares in death estate	1.0
			8.0
	(ii)	Valid reason for payment by instalments being available	1.0
		When due	1.0
		Implication of Galileo selling the shares	1.0
			3.0
(b)		Residence position	1.0
		Advice	1.0
			2.0
(c)	(i)	Relocation costs	
		Tax free with maximum	1.0
		Examples of qualifying costs (0.5 each, maximum 1)	1.0
		Deadline	0.5
		Interest-free loan	
		Maximum tax-free amount	1.0
			3.5
		Maximum	3.0
	(ii)	Provision of accommodation will be taxed	1.0
		Reasons why not exempt	2.0
			3.0
Total			**19.0**

29 **SURFE** *Walk in the footsteps of a top tutor*

Key answer tips

This is a section B question in two parts, covering CGT and IHT aspects of discretionary trusts, and textbook IHT computations for lifetime gifts and a simple death estate. This is likely to have been a popular question in the exam as IHT is always tested, and so should be very familiar to students.

Part (a) on trusts should offer some straightforward marks, as the level of knowledge tested is very basic. You may have been tempted to give chapter and verse on all aspects of trusts rather than just focusing on the specific areas requested and thus may have run out of time to complete the question.

Part (b) covers straightforward IHT computations. There are a couple of tricky points, such as the valuation of shares with related property and diminution in value, and also the calculation of the proportion of the husband's unused nil rate band. However, there should be enough marks available for basic computations for you to score a good mark.

The highlighted words in the written sections are key phrases that markers are looking for.

(a) **(i)** **Capital gains tax implications**

Tutor's top tips

*The examining team asks you to outline **briefly** the capital gains tax implications of:*

*1   transfer of shares **into** a trust*

*2   sale of shares by the trustees, **within** the trust*

*3   transfer of shares **out of** the trust.*

There are only four marks available here, and there is usually a half to one mark available per point, so that should give you an idea of how much you are expected to write.

Gift of shares to trustees of the discretionary trust

The gift of shares will be treated as a disposal at market value for capital gains tax purposes, and a chargeable gain will arise.

However, as the transfer will be a chargeable lifetime transfer for the purposes of inheritance tax, the gain may be deferred by making a gift holdover relief claim.

Surfe must elect to claim gift holdover relief by 5 April 2027 (i.e. within four years of the end of the tax year of the gift).

Tutorial note

Usually, a gift holdover relief claim requires a joint election to be signed by the donor and the donee.

However, where the claim relates to a transfer into a trust, only the donor has to sign the election.

Sale of quoted shares by the trustees

The gain on sale of shares will be taxable on the trustees, and the capital gains tax payable will be paid from the trust assets.

Tutorial note

You could also have stated that there will be an annual exempt amount available of £6,150 (half of the full annual exempt amount of £12,300), and that tax on any excess will be payable at 20%.

However, you are only expected to have a very basic knowledge of the capital gains tax treatment of trusts, so the examining team did not expect you to make these points.

Transfer of trust assets to Surfe's nephews

Transfer of assets from the trust will again be treated as a disposal at market value and a chargeable gain will arise.

As there will also be an inheritance tax charge, the gain may be deferred against the cost for the nephews by making a gift holdover relief claim.

Both the trustees and the nephew must sign the gift holdover relief election, which should be submitted within four years of the end of the tax year in which the transfer occurs.

(ii) **Inheritance tax**

The trustees will be subject to extra tax on the chargeable lifetime transfer from Surfe to the trust, if Surfe dies within seven years of the transfer.

There will be a principal charge of 6% of the value of trust assets payable by the trustees every ten years.

When assets are transferred out of the trust, there will be an exit charge of up to 6% of the value of the assets transferred.

These tax charges will be paid from the trust assets.

Tutorial note

The rules governing the inheritance tax treatment of discretionary trusts are complex. However, you are only expected to have a very basic knowledge of the tax charges that may arise within the trust.

(b)   Inheritance tax payable on Surfe's death on 1 July 2025

Tutor's top tips

There will be three different elements to the tax payable on Surfe's death:

1   Tax on potentially exempt transfers (PETs) within seven years prior to death.

2   Further tax on chargeable lifetime transfers (CLTs) within seven years prior to death.

3   Tax on the death estate.

Before you can calculate the death tax, you need to establish the tax that was paid during lifetime, as this will be deducted from the death tax.

It is very important that you clearly label your answer so that the marker can see whether you are calculating lifetime tax or death tax.

Lifetime tax

Tutor's top tips

Always work chronologically, starting with the earliest gift.

1 February 2011 – Gift to charity

Gifts to charity are exempt from IHT.

1 October 2022 – Gifts to nephews

These gifts are potentially exempt transfers.

	£
Transfer of value (£85,000 × 2)	170,000
Less: Annual exemption	
Current year (2022/23)	(3,000)
Previous year (2021/22)	(3,000)
	———
Gross transfer	164,000
	———

No lifetime tax is payable.

Tutorial note

Remember that PETs are not chargeable during lifetime, and do not affect the nil rate band, although they do still use up the annual exemptions.

1 January 2023 – transfer of shares and cash to trust

This transfer is a chargeable lifetime transfer.

	£	£
Value of shares (W1)		400,000
Cash		100,000
		———
Transfer of value		500,000
Less: Annual exemption		
Current year (2022/23)		(used)
Previous year (2021/22)		(used)
		———
Net chargeable amount		500,000
Nil rate band (NRB) at date of gift (2022/23)	325,000	
Less: Gross chargeable transfers in 7 years pre gift	(0)	
	———	
NRB available		(325,000)
		———
Taxable amount		175,000
		———
Inheritance tax at 25% (Surfe is paying the tax)		43,750
		———
Gross chargeable transfer c/f (£500,000 + £43,750)		543,750
		———

Tutorial note

The question states that Surfe (the donor) will pay the lifetime tax, so the rate of tax is 25% and you must add the tax to the gift to calculate the gross transfer for use in future calculations.

If the trustees (the donee) agreed to pay the tax, the tax would be at 20% and the gross amount would be £500,000.

Death tax: 1 July 2025

1 October 2022 – Gifts to nephews

This PET is within seven years prior to death and is now chargeable

	£
Gross chargeable amount	164,000
NRB at death (W2) (all available)	(504,167)
Taxable amount	0

There is no tax payable as this gift is covered by the NRB.

1 January 2023 – transfer of shares and cash to trust

		£
Gross chargeable transfer		543,750
NRB at death (W2)	504,167	
Less: Gross chargeable transfers in 7 years pre gift	(164,000)	
NRB available		(340,167)
Taxable amount		203,583
Inheritance tax at 40%		81,433
Less: Taper relief		
(1.1.2023 to 1.7.2025) less than 3 years		(0)
		81,433
Less: Lifetime tax paid		(43,750)
Inheritance tax payable on death		37,683

Tutor's top tips

You should only be penalised once for any mistake that you make.

If you have the wrong gross chargeable transfer brought forward, or the wrong NRB, you can still score marks for calculating the IHT at 40%, stating that taper relief is not available and deducting your figure for lifetime tax paid.

1 July 2025 – death estate

		£
House		1,400,000
Quoted shares		600,000
Shares in Leat Ltd (based on 80% holding) (W1)		
(450 × £2,400)		1,080,000
		3,080,000
NRB at death (W2)	504,167	
Less: Gross chargeable transfers in 7 years pre death		
(£164,000 + £543,750)	(707,750)	
NRB available		(0)
Taxable amount		3,080,000
Inheritance tax at 40%		1,232,000

Tutorial note

The value of the Leat Ltd shares included in the death estate is based on the value of the combined holding, including the related property held by the charity, at the date of death.

There is no residence nil rate band available as the house is not left to Surfe's direct descendants. Even if the house had been left to direct descendants, the residence nil rate band would have been reduced to £Nil in any case, as this gets tapered down by £1 for every £2 the value of the estate exceeds £2 million.

Workings

(W1) Gift of shares to the trust on 1 January 2023

	No. of shares before gift	No. of shares After gift
Surfe	650	450
Kanal (related property)	350	350
	1,000	800
Combined holding as a % of total shares	100%	80%
Value per share at date of gift	£2,000	£2,000

Transfer of value:	£
Value of Surfe's holding prior to the gift	
(650 × £2,000)	1,300,000
Less: Value of Surfe's holding after the gift	
(450 × £2,000)	(900,000)
Transfer of value	400,000

Tutorial note

The value of the Leat Ltd shares is based on the value of the combined holding, including the related property held by the charity, at the date of the gift.

The most common example of related property is property held jointly by spouses or civil partners, but property that has been transferred by the donor (or their spouse/civil partner) to a charity or political party is also deemed to be related property for as long as the charity still owns the property (and for five years after they dispose of it).

Remember also that the value for IHT is calculated as the diminution in value of the donor's estate, and is found by calculating the value of Surfe's shares before the gift and deducting the value after the gift.

(W2) Nil rate band on death

	£
Surfe's NRB as at the date of death	325,000
Unused nil rate band of Flud	
((£312,000 – £140,000)/£312,000) × £325,000)	179,167
	———
	504,167
	———

Tutorial note

As Surfe's husband did not use all of his NRB, the excess can be transferred to Surfe to be used on her death.

The amount transferred is based on the proportion that was unused when Surfe's husband died, but this proportion is then applied to the NRB in force at the date of Surfe's death.

Note that the fact that the date of the husband's death is more than seven years before Surfe's is irrelevant. The unused proportion of the deceased spouse's NRB can always be transferred regardless of the date of the first death.

Examiner's report

Part (a) required an outline of the capital gains tax implications of various transactions relating to the trust and the inheritance tax charges that may be payable in the future by the trustees. It was important for candidates to be methodical in their approach to this question. There were three transactions to be addressed in relation to capital gains tax whereas the inheritance aspects of the question were more open ended.

The majority of candidates knew some of the capital gains tax implications of the transactions but very few knew all of them. In particular, there was a lack of understanding that capital gains would arise when the trustees transfer trust assets to the beneficiaries of the trust. As always, when dealing with capital gains tax, it is vital to consider the availability of reliefs; gift holdover relief is available when assets are transferred to a discretionary trust and again when they are transferred to the beneficiaries.

The inheritance aspects of part (a) were not handled as well as the capital gains tax aspects. The majority of candidates failed to mention the ten-yearly charges and exit charges payable out of the trust's assets.

Part (b) required a calculation of the inheritance tax liability arising on the death of an individual who had made a number of lifetime gifts. This was a fairly straightforward question, albeit with a couple of tricky points within it, but it was not handled particularly well.

There was a lack of appropriate structure to candidates' answers that indicated that, perhaps, there had been insufficient practice of this area. Inheritance tax computations should all look the same, starting with the tax on any chargeable lifetime transfers, followed by the consideration of gifts within seven years of death and ending with the death estate. However, many candidates began with the death estate and worked their way backwards towards the lifetime gifts; a method that was never going to be successful.

There was confusion as to which gift benefited from the annual exemptions and in respect of the utilisation of the nil rate band. There was also a general lack of knowledge of the impact of related property on the valuation of a gift. Other technical errors, made by a minority of candidates, included the treatment of cash as an exempt asset and business property relief being given in respect of the shares owned by the taxpayer.

On the positive side, the majority of candidates identified the availability of the husband's nil rate band and the death estate was handled well.

ACCA marking scheme				
				Marks
(a)	(i)	Gift of shares		1.5
		Future sale of quoted shares		0.5
		Transfer of trust assets to beneficiaries		1.5
		Election details		1.0
	(ii)	Inheritance tax		2.5
				7.0
			Maximum	6.0
(b)		Inheritance tax in respect of lifetime gifts		
		Gift to charity		0.5
		Gifts to nephews		1.5
		Gift to trust		
		Shares – fall in value		2.0
		Cash and nil rate band		1.0
		Lifetime tax		1.0
		Gross chargeable transfer		0.5
		Nil rate band		2.5
		Inheritance tax payable on death		1.5
		Inheritance tax in respect of death estate		1.5
				12.0
			Maximum	11.0
Total				**17.0**

30 ASH *Walk in the footsteps of a top tutor*

Key answer tips

This is a question with three independent parts which could have been attempted in any order.

The first part deals with capital gains and is a mix of straightforward marks (land part disposal) and trickier marks (lease assignment).

The second part deals with VAT registration for a business dealing with both taxable and exempt supplies but does not require any calculations.

The third part covers a tax administration issue about whether to reduce a payment on account, which tests knowledge brought forward from TX.

The highlighted words in the written sections are key phrases that markers are looking for.

(a) (i) Availability of business asset disposal relief (BADR) – lease assignment

Tutor's top tips

You may have found this part on associated disposals tough, as it is a fringe element of the ATX syllabus which is not often tested.

There are three marks available and three conditions, so one mark for each. Even if you could not remember the details of associated disposals, a few basic points relating to BADR would likely have earned you one mark out of the three available.

The following conditions must be satisfied in order for the assignment of the lease to qualify as an associated disposal such that business asset disposal relief (BADR) will be available:

- Ash's disposal of the shares in Lava Ltd must qualify for BADR
- The lease must have been owned by Ash and used for the purposes of the trade of Lava Ltd for at least two years.
- Ash must have sold the shares in Lava Ltd and the lease as part of a process of withdrawing from participating in the business of Lava Ltd.

Tutorial note

BADR is not available on an associated disposal if full commercial rent is charged for the use of the asset.

In this question, rent is charged, but not the full market rate. Therefore, BADR is available on part of the gain, but not all of the gain.

(ii)   Capital gains tax liability – 2021/22

Tutor's top tips

You have already been told that the sale of shares in Lava Ltd qualified for BADR, and you can see that the land sale does not qualify as there is no mention of any business.

The best way to present the calculation of gains tax when there are gains both qualifying and non-qualifying for BADR is in two columns. The annual exempt amount and the capital loss on the sale of the quoted shares should be deducted from the non-qualifying gains first.

Even if you calculated the gain on the lease incorrectly you would still get the marks available for including it in your summary and taxing it.

It is best to perform detailed calculations like this in the spreadsheet in the exam. This will enable you to set them out more easily, and also use formulae. This can cut down on calculation time in the exam.

	BADR available	BADR not available
	£	£
Gain on sale of shares	235,000	
Gain on assignment of lease		
(£79,812 (W1) × 60%/40%) (Note 1)	47,887	31,925
Gain on sale of land (W2)		21,780
Loss on sale of quoted shares		(16,500)
	———	———
	282,887	37,205
Less: Annual exempt amount		(12,300)
	———	———
	282,887	24,905
	———	———

		£
Capital gains tax (Note 2)		
Gains qualifying for BADR		
(£282,887 × 10%)		28,289
Gains not qualifying for BADR		
(£24,905 × 20%)		4,981
		———
CGT liability		33,270
		———

Tutorial notes

1   BADR in respect of the lease will be restricted to 60% of the gain, due to the rent charged by Ash to Lava Ltd which is equivalent to 40% of the market rate.

2   Ash's taxable income is less than his basic rate band. However, the gains qualifying for BADR use up the remainder of the basic rate band first, such that all of the non-qualifying gains are taxed at 20%.

Workings

(W1) Gain on the assignment of the lease

	£
Proceeds (for a 37 year lease)	110,000
Less: Deemed cost (£31,800 × (93.497 ÷ 98.490))	(30,188)
Chargeable gain	79,812

Tutorial note

A lease is a wasting asset whose cost depreciates in accordance with a curved line table.

	£
Proceeds	*X*
Less: Cost × (% for life left at disposal ÷ % for life left at acquisition)	*(X)*
Capital gain	*X*

(W2) Gain on the sale of the remainder land

	£	£
Proceeds		30,000
Less: Deemed cost of the remainder		
Original cost	27,400	
Part disposal cost		
£27,400 × (£42,000 ÷ (£42,000 + £18,000))	(19,180)	
		(8,220)
Chargeable gain		21,780

(b)   **Vulcan Partnership (Vulcan) – Value added tax (VAT) registration**

Tutor's top tips

You are asked to discuss in detail whether the Vulcan Partnership may be required to register and the advantages and disadvantages of registration. This gives you three headings to structure your answer.

You must apply your knowledge to the facts of the question. You will not earn marks for listing everything you know about VAT registration.

You are not required to perform any calculations, although you may find it useful to establish the current level of annual taxable supplies.

Whether or not Vulcan may be required to register

Subject to the exceptions noted below, Vulcan will be required to register for VAT once its cumulative taxable supplies (those that are standard-rated and zero-rated) in a 12-month period exceed £85,000.

However, Vulcan will not be required to register if HM Revenue and Customs are satisfied that its total supplies for the following 12 months will be less than £83,000.

Vulcan could request to be exempt from registration because only a small proportion of its supplies are standard-rated. This exemption will be available provided it would be in a repayment position if registered.

Advantages of registration

Vulcan will be able to recover all of its input tax if the amount relating to exempt supplies is de minimis. Where Vulcan's exempt supplies is not de minimis, it will still be able to recover the majority of its input tax.

Registration will prevent third parties from knowing the size of Vulcan's business.

Disadvantages of registration

Registration will add to the amount of work required to administer the business. In addition, Vulcan may be subject to financial penalties if it fails to comply with the obligations imposed by the VAT regime.

The partnership's customers would be unable to recover any output tax charged by the partnership as they are not registered for VAT. Accordingly, the prices charged to the small proportion of customers purchasing standard-rated items would increase unless Vulcan decides to reduce its profit in respect of these sales.

(c)   Payment on account on 31 January 2023

Tutor's top tips

Payments on account are regularly tested at ATX, even though they are a TX topic.

The examining team usually asks for due dates of payments on account and/or amounts payable. Here they have tested the option to reduce payments on account and the potential impact of this, demonstrating the need to review this topic thoroughly prior to your exam.

The payment on account due on 31 January 2023 is the first payment in respect of Ash's income tax payable (income tax liability as reduced by tax deducted at source) for the tax year 2022/23. The payment due is half of the income tax payable for the tax year 2021/22 unless Ash makes a claim to reduce the payment.

Ash can make a claim to reduce the payment if he expects the amount payable for the tax year 2022/23 to be less than that for 2021/22. The income tax payable for the tax year 2022/23 is likely to be less than that for 2021/22 due, principally, to Ash receiving less profit from Vulcan.

Ash will need to estimate his income tax payable for the tax year 2022/23 in order to decide whether or not to reduce the payment on account. Ash will be charged interest if the payment on account is reduced to an amount that is less than half of the final agreed amount payable for 2022/23. In addition, a penalty may be charged if Ash is fraudulent or negligent when he makes the claim to reduce the payment.

Examiner's report

Part (a)(i) required a statement of the conditions necessary for the disposal of an asset to be an associated disposal for the purposes of business asset disposal relief and was not done well. This is not an area of the syllabus that one would expect to see examined regularly and many candidates will have known immediately on reading the requirement that they did not know the answer. However, the sensible approach would then have been to write a very brief answer with some sensible comments on business asset disposal relief. It was pretty likely that this would then score one of the three marks available.

In general part (a)(ii) was done well by many candidates. There was no problem in deciding what needed to be done, so those candidates who did poorly simply did not have sufficient knowledge of the rules.

The majority of part (b) was done very well including, in particular, the advantages and disadvantages of registering for VAT. However, some candidates' answers lacked precision when it came to the circumstances where compulsory registration is required in that taxable supplies were not clearly defined and/or the 12-month period was not clearly stated. Other candidates wasted time by writing far too much on the recovery of input tax. The one area where performance was not good was the exceptions to the need to register, which were only referred to by a very small number of candidates.

Part (c) concerned an area that candidates would have been familiar with but it approached it from a slightly unusual angle: it was not done well. Candidates needed to use their common sense as much as anything else here and to recognise that the claim would need to be made before the end of the tax year. This in turn meant that the tax liability would need to be estimated and that interest would be payable if the final liability turned out to be more than the estimated liability. Making these two points would have scored two of the three marks available for this part of the question.

ACCA marking scheme				
				Marks
(a)	(i)	Conditions – 1 mark each		3.0
				—
	(ii)	Taxable capital gains		
		Assignment of lease		2.5
		Sale of land		2.0
		Other matters		1.5
		Capital gains tax		1.5
				—
				7.5
			Maximum	7.0
				—
(b)		Requirement to register		1.5
		Exceptions		2.0
		Advantages		2.0
		Disadvantages		2.0
				—
				7.5
			Maximum	7.0
				—
(c)		Context		1.5
		Circumstance in which a claim can be made		1.0
		Interest and penalties		1.5
				—
				4.0
			Maximum	3.0
				—
Total				20.0
				—

31   BRAD (ADAPTED) *Walk in the footsteps of a top tutor*

Key answer tips

The question covers two unrelated issues.

Part (a) requires an explanation of why an individual is only temporarily non-UK resident and calculations of the UK capital gains tax.

The payment date is also required which is an easy mark to gain, but easily forgotten and lost if you are not careful.

Part (b) relates to IHT and is divided into two parts. The first part asks for a general explanation of the IHT advantages of making lifetime gifts. The second part concerns a particular gift of shares and requires knowledge of the valuation rules and business property relief in order to calculate a transfer of value and provide a detailed explanation of BPR. Finally, any other tax issues arising from the gift was another requirement.

The highlighted words in the written sections are key phrases that markers are looking for.

(a)   Capital gains tax

Tutor's top tips

The examining team frequently tests capital gains tax for an individual who leaves the UK, returns within five years, and disposes of assets whilst overseas. These are known as the temporary non-UK resident rules or temporary absence abroad rules. You are asked for an explanation of the rules as well as the calculations, so make sure you provide the explanations.

Note that the rules only apply to assets owned before the individual loses their UK resident status and as such the antique bed does not fall within the rules, as it is purchased whilst Brad is abroad. Also note that the disposal of the motor car is exempt, regardless of these rules.

Brad will be regarded as only temporarily non-UK resident whilst living in Keirinia because:

- he was absent from the UK for less than five years; and
- having always lived in the UK prior to moving to Keirinia, he was UK resident for at least four of the seven tax years immediately prior to the year of departure.

As a temporary non-UK resident, Brad will be subject to UK capital gains tax on the assets sold whilst he was temporarily overseas, which he owned at the date of his departure from the UK.

Accordingly, the antique bed is excluded from these rules as it was both bought and sold during the period of absence.

The profit on the sale of the motor car is ignored as motor cars are exempt assets for the purposes of capital gains tax.

The shares were sold in the tax year 2018/19, before Brad left the UK, so the gain on these shares was subject to tax in that year. However, there will have been no tax to pay as the capital gain of £4,900 (£18,900 – £14,000) was covered by the annual exempt amount for the tax year 2018/19.

The capital gains tax due on the sale of the painting is calculated as follows.

	£
Capital gain (£36,000 – £15,000)	21,000
Less: Annual exempt amount	(12,300)
Taxable gain	8,700
Capital gains tax at 20%	1,740

The gain on the sale of the painting is subject to tax in 2022/23, the tax year in which Brad returned to the UK, and not in the year of sale.

Accordingly, the tax is due on 31 January 2024.

(b) Inheritance tax

(i) The inheritance tax advantages of making lifetime gifts to individuals

Tutor's top tips

The question asks for the IHT advantages of lifetime gifts. Make sure you discuss all the issues as this part is worth seven marks.

Note that only the advantages are required, so there is no need to mention disadvantages.

A lifetime gift to an individual is a potentially exempt transfer. It will be exempt from inheritance tax if the donor survives the gift by seven years.

If the donor dies within seven years of making the gift, such that the gift is chargeable to inheritance tax, the value used will be the value at the time of the gift and not the value at the time of death. Any increase in the value of the asset will be ignored, although relief will be available if the asset falls in value following the gift.

Certain exemptions are only available in respect of lifetime gifts (i.e. they cannot be deducted from the death estate).

These exemptions are:

- the annual exemption of £3,000 each year
- gifts in consideration of marriage/civil partnership up to certain limits
- regular gifts out of income that do not affect the donor's standard of living
- the small gifts exemption of £250 per donee per tax year.

Any inheritance tax due on the donor's death will be reduced by taper relief if the donor survives the gift by more than three years.

The tax due will be reduced by 20% if the donor survives the gift by more than three but less than four years. The percentage reduction will increase by 20% for each additional year that the donor survives the gift.

(ii) **In respect of the possible gift of 1,500 shares in Omnium Ltd to Dani**

Tutor's top tips

There are three elements to this part of the question so make sure you attempt all parts.

*The first part is a calculation of the transfer of value. For IHT, this is based on the **fall in value** or **diminution in value** of Brad's estate.*

However, shares in Omnium Ltd are also owned by Brad's wife, so there is a related property calculation as part of the transfer of value.

*Remember that if we are dealing with related property and shares we apportion the value of the combined ownership based on the **number** of shares.*

The formula is:

A/(A+B) × combined ownership

where A is donor's number of shares and B is the related property's number of shares.

In this answer the examining team has used the short cut calculation possible for valuing shares. In the question you are given the value per share, so all you need to do is to value Brad's shares using the price per share based on the combined percentage ownership.

Fall in value of Brad's estate

Before the gift, Brad owned a 30% interest and his wife a 45% interest; therefore, the couple have a combined ownership interest of 75%.

After the gift, Brad's ownership would be 15% and therefore the combined ownership of the couple will drop to 60%.

The fall in value of Brad's estate on a gift of 1,500 shares in Omnium Ltd using the related property rules will be (see tutorial note):

	£
Value of shares held prior to the gift (3,000 × £290)	870,000
Value of shares held after the gift (1,500 × £240)	(360,000)
	510,000

Tutorial note

Using the A/(A + B) rules:

	£
Value of shares held prior to the gift: (7,500 × £290) × (3,000 ÷ (3,000 + 4,500))	870,000
Value of shares held after the gift: (6,000 × £240) × (1,500 ÷ (1,500 + 4,500))	(360,000)
	510,000

Ignoring the related property rules:

	£
Value of shares held prior to the gift (3,000 × £205)	615,000
Value of shares held after the gift (1,500 × £190)	(285,000)
	330,000

The higher fall in value of £510,000, produced by reference to related property, will be used.

Tutor's top tips

The model answer shows the transfer of value with and without using related property. Don't worry if you didn't get this point. Technically, both calculations are necessary and the higher transfer of value is the answer. However, this is almost always going to be the value used where related property is gifted.

Business property relief

Tutor's top tips

The requirement asks for a detailed explanation of whether or not BPR is available. The examining team has offered clues in the question as Omnium Ltd owns a number of investment properties. Business property relief will not be available if the business of Omnium Ltd consists wholly or mainly of dealing in securities, stocks or shares or land and buildings or the making or holding of investments.

If BPR is available then the investment properties are excepted assets such that BPR will only be available on:

The transfer of value × (Non-excepted assets ÷ Total assets)

Business property relief will not be available if the business of Omnium Ltd consists wholly or mainly of dealing in securities, stocks or shares or land and buildings or the making or holding of investments. Accordingly, it will be necessary to determine the significance of the investment properties to the activities of Omnium Ltd as a whole.

Brad must have owned the shares for at least two years at the time of the gift. This condition is satisfied.

Business property relief will not be available unless Dani still owns the shares at the time of Brad's death (or had died whilst owning the shares) and the shares continue to qualify for the relief.

If all of the conditions set out above are satisfied, business property relief will be available at the rate of 100%, because Omnium Ltd is an unquoted company.

However, where the company has excepted assets, business property relief will be restricted to:

100% × (Value of non-excepted assets ÷ Value of total assets) × the fall in value

Excepted assets are assets that have not been used for the purposes of the company's business in the two years prior to the transfer and are not required for such use in the future. Some or all of Omnium Ltd's investment properties may be classified as excepted assets.

Tutorial note

Business property relief will only be relevant if Brad were to die within seven years of making the gift, such that the potentially exempt transfer became a chargeable transfer.

Business property relief would also be available if Dani disposed of the shares prior to Brad's death and acquired qualifying replacement property within three years of the disposal.

Other tax issues

The gift of shares will be a disposal at market value for the purposes of capital gains tax. Gift holdover relief will be available but will be restricted because of the investment properties owned by Omnium Ltd.

Gifts of shares are not subject to stamp duty.

Tutorial note

The question asked for a brief statement only of the other tax issues.

The capital gains gift holdover relief restriction is calculated as:

Capital gain × (Chargeable business assets ÷ Chargeable assets).

Don't forget stamp duty – this is an easy mark!

Examiner's report

In part (a) the majority of candidates had some knowledge of the temporary non-UK resident rules and quite a reasonable knowledge of capital gains tax generally, such that they scored reasonably well. Most candidates knew the five-year rule although a much smaller number stated the four years out of seven rule.

A minority of candidates stated a rule correctly in general terms but failed to apply it to the facts of the question. For example, some candidates stated that assets bought and sold during the period of absence were not subject to UK capital gains tax but then went on to calculate a gain in respect of the antique bed.

Other candidates failed to apply the basics. For example, a minority of candidates omitted the annual exempt amount whilst others either provided an incorrect payment date or failed to provide one at all.

When providing a payment date it is important to make it clear which tax year is being addressed. There were several possible relevant tax years in this question so stating a date without a year could not score unless the candidate explained in general terms how the date is determined (i.e. 31 January after the end of the tax year).

In the first part of part (b) many candidates did very well but the performance of the majority was unsatisfactory.

The advantages of lifetime giving are scattered throughout the inheritance tax system with certain exemptions only being available in respect of lifetime gifts, potentially exempt transfers being exempt once the donor has lived for seven years, taper relief once the donor has lived for at least three years, and the value of a gift being frozen at the time of the gift together with the availability of relief for any fall in value of the assets gifted.

Most candidates would have known all of these rules but many did not include them all in their answers. Instead they wrote at length about some of them whilst omitting others. In particular, many candidates did not address the exemptions available in respect of lifetime giving. This is likely to be because candidates simply started writing and kept writing until they felt they had written enough. These candidates would have benefited from thinking their way through the inheritance tax system and noting each of the advantages of lifetime giving before they started writing.

The valuation, which involved fall in value together with related property, in the second part of (b) was done well with many candidates scoring full marks. A minority of candidates were not aware that it is only the spouse's property that is related whilst others failed to appreciate that it is only the donor's property that is valued (the related property is only relevant when determining the valuation).

The business property relief was done well with the majority of candidates identifying the two year rule and the relevance of the investments. Fewer candidates stated the need for the donee to continue owning the shares until the death of the donor.

Candidates did not do so well when it came to identifying other tax issues. Most candidates simply repeated the basics of the inheritance tax rules in relation to potentially exempt transfers when what was required here was consideration of capital gains tax and stamp duty.

		ACCA marking scheme		
				Marks
(a)		Conditions		2.0
		Antique bed and motor car		1.5
		Quoted shares		2.0
		Painting		3.5
				———
				9.0
			Maximum	8.0
				———
(b)	(i)	Seven year rule		1.0
		Valuation		2.0
		Exemptions		3.0
		Taper relief		2.0
				———
				8.0
			Maximum	7.0
				———
	(ii)	Fall in value		3.5
		Availability of business property relief		
		Business of Omnium Ltd		1.5
		Brad's ownership of the shares		1.0
		Circumstances on Brad's death		1.0
		Calculation of business property relief		
		Rate of relief		1.0
		Excepted assets		2.0
		Other tax matters		2.5
				———
				12.5
			Maximum	10.0
				———
Total				**25.0**
				———

32 PESCARA (ADAPTED) *Walk in the footsteps of a top tutor*

Key answer tips

Part (a) requires the calculation of death tax on a potentially exempt transfer. It is slightly complicated in that the donor is a widow and her husband did not utilise all of his nil rate band on death, but otherwise it is straightforward.

Part (b) requires the calculation of tax due on the sale of shares which were originally acquired via a gift and had subsequently been the subject of a takeover and a bonus issue. An explanation of the treatment on the subsequent disposal of an investment in SEIS shares is also required.

Part (c) requires a straightforward explanation of the IHT payable on death in respect of a gift with reservation. However, detailed knowledge needs to be displayed, including an explanation of double charges relief to score highly on this part.

The highlighted words in the written sections are key phrases that markers are looking for.

Tutor's top tips

The calculation of death tax due on a PET which becomes chargeable on death, with careful consideration of the nil rate band available, is a classic requirement. All of this part draws on basic level tax knowledge and should provide some relatively easy marks, provided you have refreshed your basic knowledge.

(a) **Marina**

Inheritance tax payable in respect of the gift of the shares in Sepang plc

	£	£
Transfer of value (375,000 × £1.86) (W1)		697,500
Less: Annual exemption – 2016/17		(3,000)
– 2015/16 b/f		(3,000)
Potentially exempt transfer now chargeable		691,500
Less: Marina's NRB at death	325,000	
NRB transferred from Galvez (W2)	158,333	
NRB available		(483,333)
Taxable amount		208,167
IHT at 40%		83,267
Less: Taper relief		
(1.2.2017 – 1.10.2022) (5 – 6 years) (60%)		(49,960)
		33,307
Less: IHT paid in lifetime		(0)
IHT payable		33,307

Workings

(W1) Value of shares in Sepang plc as at 1 February 2017

Lower of:

(i)	Quarter up = (£1.84 + ((£1.96 – £1.84) × 1/4))	£1.87
(ii)	Mid-market = ((£1.80 + £1.92) × 1/2)	£1.86
	Therefore, value of shares used	£1.86

(W2) Nil rate band transferred from Galvez

	£
Nil rate band available in 2008/09	312,000
Legacies to Pescara and her brother (2 × £80,000)	(160,000)
Unused NRB	152,000
Unused % of current year NRB available to transfer to Marina (£325,000 × (£152,000 ÷ £312,000))	158,333

Tutorial note

Galvez had no lifetime gifts and therefore the calculation of the unused NRB just considers legacies in his will.

If there had been any CLTs or PETs in the seven years pre death, they would have to be taken into consideration as they would also utilise some of Galvez's NRB available on death.

An alternative method of calculating Marina's NRB which is acceptable is:

- *Galvez had an unused NRB = (£152,000 ÷ £312,000) = 48.718%*
- *Marina can claim 148.718% of the current NRB = (£325,000 × 148.718%) = £483,333.*

Remember that an individual can never claim more than 200% of the current NRB.

(b) (i) Pescara

Capital gains tax liability – 2022/23

Tutor's top tips

The base cost of the original Sepang plc shares following the gift to Pescara must be established first. Then the takeover consideration received from Zolder plc, in return for the original shares in Sepang plc, must be quantified in order to allocate the base cost of the original shares to the two elements of the takeover consideration received.

The bonus issue must then be brought into the share pool of the new Zolder plc shares acquired before the gain is calculated on the disposal of some of the shares from the share pool.

	£
Proceeds: sale of 1,000,000 shares	445,000
Less: Cost (W1)	(275,362)
Chargeable gain	169,638
Less: SEIS reinvestment relief (50% × £90,000)	(45,000)
Annual exempt amount	(12,300)
Taxable gain	112,338
Capital gains tax at 20%	22,468

Tutorial note

SEIS reinvestment relief allows the exemption of gains on any asset.

The maximum amount of relief that can be claimed is the lowest of:

1 *50% of the chargeable gain = (50% × £169,638) = £84,819, or*

2 *50% of amount invested in qualifying SEIS shares (maximum 50% × £100,000)*
   = (50% × £90,000) = £45,000, or

3 *Any amount up to the lower of 1 or 2.*

Therefore, any amount up to £45,000 could be claimed.

Remember that this CGT reinvestment relief is in addition to the income tax relief available which allows the deduction of 50% of the cost of the investment in SEIS shares to be deducted from the income tax liability in the tax year of investment.

Workings

(W1) Base cost of 1,000,000 shares in Zolder plc

	Number	£
Original shares in Sepang plc		
Market value of gift (W2)	375,000	712,500
Exchanged for shares in Zolder plc		
Cost of new shares (W3)	750,000	619,565
Bonus issue (2:1)	1,500,000	0
	2,250,000	619,565
Cost of shares to be sold		
(1,000,000/2,250,000) × £619,565	(1,000,000)	(275,362)
Balance c/f	1,250,000	344,203

Tutorial note

1   The base cost of shares in Sepang plc to Pescara will be the market value at the time of the gift. Remember that for CGT purposes the value of quoted shares is calculated as the mid-price, which is the average of the highest and lowest quoted prices.

The question says that gift holdover relief is not available on these shares and therefore there will be no gain deferred against this base cost.

2   Bonus shares are free shares to existing shareholders. The number of shares received are therefore brought into the share pool at nil cost.

(W2) Value of shares in Sepang plc as at 1 February 2017

Mid-price = £1.90 ((£1.84 + £1.96) ÷ 2)

375,000 × £1.90 = £712,500

(W3) Takeover of Sepang plc

	MV of consideration received £	Allocation of original base cost £
Cash (375,000 × 30p)	112,500	
(£112,500/£862,500) × £712,500		92,935
Shares (375,000 × 2 × £1)	750,000	
(£750,000/£862,500) × £712,500		619,565
	———	———
	862,500	712,500
	———	———

(ii)   Pescara – Capital gains tax implications of selling the SEIS shares

Tutor's top tips

There are only three marks available here, so a short but succinct summary of the position is required.

This part could have been answered independently at the beginning to bank some easy marks first.

The treatment of the gain or loss arising on the SEIS shares depends on when they are sold.

- If they are sold within three years of their purchase, any gain arising will be chargeable and any loss will be allowable.

- If they are sold more than three years after their purchase, any gain arising will be exempt.

  If the sale results in a loss, the loss will be allowable but will be reduced by the SEIS income tax relief obtained in respect of the shares.

In addition, if the SEIS shares are sold within three years, all or part of the capital gains tax reinvestment relief will be withdrawn, depending on the amount of shares sold and whether or not the sale is at arm's length.

(c)   Pescara – Gift of a UK property

Tutor's top tips

This is a straightforward independent part on gifts with reservation which should produce some easy marks and could have been answered at the beginning if preferred.

The gift of a property will be a potentially exempt transfer (PET). The value of this PET will be the market value of the property at the time of the gift.

The amount which will be subject to inheritance tax in respect of this gift with reservation depends on whether or not the reservation of benefit is lifted (i.e. Pescara stops using the property rent-free, before she dies).

(i)   If the reservation of benefit is lifted prior to Pescara's death, there will be a further PET equal to the value of the property at that time. This will only be chargeable if Pescara dies within the subsequent seven years.

(ii)   If the reservation of benefit is still in place when Pescara dies, the value of the property at the time of her death will be included in her death estate.

In this case, the residence nil rate band will be available.

Where Pescara dies within seven years of the original PET, such that it is chargeable to inheritance tax, and either (i) or (ii) applies, the original PET or (i)/(ii) will be taxed, whichever results in the higher tax liability.

Tutorial note

1   Where Pescara dies within seven years of the original PET, double charges relief is available.

If the reservation has been lifted, the original PET and the deemed PET both become chargeable.

If the reservation is still in place, the original PET becomes chargeable but HMRC require the house to be included in the estate computation at death.

Double charges relief ensures that, in either case, the higher of these two liabilities will actually be chargeable.

2   *Pescara would be advised to stop using the property (or to start paying a market rent)
if she wishes the gift to be advantageous from the point of view of inheritance tax.*

3   *Note that if Pescara was just to make incidental use of the property (such as living in
the property while visiting her son) so that the benefit derived is minimal, then the GWR
rules would not apply.*

Examiner's report

The majority of candidates performed well in part (a) and scored high marks. Less well-prepared candidates were unable to value the shares in Sepang plc and/or the amount of the nil rate band to be transferred from the donor's deceased husband. This was because they either did not know the rules or were unable to apply them to the facts in the question. Some candidates failed to identify that the husband's nil rate band was available for transfer.

Part (b) concerned capital gains tax and was in two parts; neither part was done particularly well. In part (i) the calculation of the base cost of the shares required a certain amount of work.

It was first necessary to realise that, due to the fact that gift holdover relief was not claimed on the original gift (the question stated that gift holdover relief was not available), the base cost of the original shares was their market value at the time of the gift. Following the takeover, this original cost had to be split between the new shares and cash received by reference to the market value of the consideration. Finally, the bonus issue increased the number of shares but had no effect on the total base cost.

A significant number of candidates lost marks here because they side-stepped the first two stages of this calculation by attributing a cost to the new shares equal to their market value at the time of the takeover. The majority of candidates had no problem with the bonus issue.

When calculating the amount subject to capital gains tax it was necessary to deduct EIS deferral relief equal to the whole of the £50,000 invested in EIS shares. Many candidates confused this relief with the relief available in respect of income tax when EIS shares are acquired. *Note: This is the examiner's comment on the original question, which has since been adapted to test SEIS reinvestment relief instead of EIS relief.*

The first problem that some candidates had in part (b)(ii) was that they answered the question by reference to income tax rather than capital gains tax. Many of those who did address capital gains tax did not score as many marks as they might have done because they were not methodical in their approach. It was important to (briefly) consider four possible situations (i.e. sale of the shares at a profit or a loss both within and after the three-year period).

Part (c) was not done particularly well as those candidates who clearly had some knowledge did not pay sufficient attention to the requirement.

The question asked how the gift would be treated for the purposes of calculating the inheritance tax due on death. This required consideration of the value to be used, whether or not the reservation was lifted prior to death and the relief available in order to avoid double taxation.

Many candidates wrote more broadly about gifts with reservation, explaining the rationale behind the rules and the actions necessary in order for the reservation to be lifted. These generalisations did not score any marks.

	ACCA marking scheme		Marks
(a)	Value of shares		2.0
	Annual exemptions		1.0
	Nil rate band		2.5
	Inheritance tax liability		1.5
			7.0
(b)	(i)	Proceeds less cost	5.0
		SEIS reinvestment relief, annual exempt amount and liability	2.0
			7.0
		Maximum	6.0
	(ii)	Sale of SEIS shares	3.5
		Withdrawal of SEIS reinvestment relief	1.0
			4.5
		Maximum	3.0
(c)	The initial gift		1.0
	Reservation lifted within seven years		1.5
	Reservation in place at death		1.0
	Avoidance of double taxation		1.5
			5.0
		Maximum	4.0
Total			20.0

33   CADA (ADAPTED) *Walk in the footsteps of a top tutor*

Key answer tips

This section B question covers the very regularly tested area of CGT versus IHT, with planning points re: lifetime gifts, the reduced rate of IHT for substantial legacies to charity, deed of variation and CGT planning. It is likely to have been a very popular question, although parts of it are actually quite challenging.

Part (a) requires you to think about IHT advantages of lifetime gifts, but not the use of lifetime exemptions. The only other advantages were the freezing in value of appreciating assets, and taper relief.

Part (b) covers the reduced rate of IHT for substantial legacies to charity.

There are some easy marks in part (c) for stating the procedures for a deed of variation to be tax effective.

Part (d) is less obvious, and requires you to spot the issue that capital losses are not available at death, but can be crystallised during lifetime to save CGT, either by selling shares that have gone down in value or by making a negligible value claim for shares that are worthless.

The highlighted words in the written sections are key phrases that markers are looking for.

(a)   The inheritance tax advantages of additional lifetime gifts

Tutor's top tips

Think carefully before answering this part of the question. Cada would not have survived more than seven years after these lifetime gifts, so they would not become exempt. You are specifically told not to discuss lifetime exemptions, so there will be no marks if you do.

The question also states that 'none of the remaining assets qualified for any inheritance reliefs', so there is no point in discussing business property relief either.

Also, there are no marks here for discussing CGT, as the requirement only asks for IHT advantages.

It is therefore important to cover the points regarding appreciating assets and taper relief thoroughly in order to get the four marks available.

Any additional lifetime gifts of quoted shares would have become chargeable on Cada's death on 20 November 2022.

However, the value charged to tax would have been the value of the shares at the time of the gift and not their value at the time of death.

Any increase in the value of the shares would therefore have been ignored, although relief would have been available if the shares had fallen in value following the gift.

Taper relief would have been available in respect of any gifts made in the period 1 December 2018 to 20 November 2019 (i.e. those gifts made more than three years prior to death).

This would only be relevant in respect of that amount of the gifts made which exceeded the nil rate band available of £220,000. In these circumstances, because the gift would have been made between three and four years prior to death, taper relief would have reduced the tax charged on the gift by 20%.

(b)   Additional gift to charity

Tutor's top tips

It is a good idea to set out your computations before and after the additional gift to charity side by side, so that you only have to write out the headings once.

The breakdown of the estate is shown here for completeness, but you could obtain full credit by taking the total estate value of £1,000,000 straight from the question, as long as you remembered that the residence nil rate band would be available for Cada's house.

This section is only worth five marks, so is quite time pressured.

Make sure that you fully answer the question by identifying both the increase in the legacy required and the IHT saving. Even if your increased legacy is wrong, you will still score marks for calculating the tax saving based on your figures.

	Before additional gift to charity	After additional gift to charity
	£	£
House	500,000	500,000
Cash	60,000	60,000
Other assets including share portfolio	440,000	440,000
	1,000,000	1,000,000
Less: Gift to charity (W)	(60,000)	(78,000)
Gross chargeable estate	940,000	922,000
Less: Residence nil rate band	(175,000)	(175,000)
Nil rate band	(220,000)	(220,000)
Taxable estate	545,000	527,000
Inheritance tax at 40%/36%	218,000	189,720

Reduction in the inheritance tax liability (£218,000 – £189,720)	28,280
Additional gift to charity (£78,000 – £60,000)	18,000

Tutorial note

The reduced rate of 36% applies where the gift to charity is at least 10% of the individual's baseline amount.

The baseline amount consists of the assets owned at death reduced by liabilities, exemptions, reliefs, and the nil rate band but before the deduction of the charitable gift and the residence nil rate band.

An alternative method of calculating the baseline amount

= (Taxable estate plus charitable donation plus residence nil rate band)

Working: Additional charitable donation required

	£
Taxable estate	545,000
Add back: Charitable donation	60,000
Residence nil rate band	175,000
	———
Baseline amount	780,000
	———
Charitable donation required for 36% rate to apply:	
10% × baseline amount	78,000
	———

(c) Variation of Cada's will

Tutor's top tips

Although you may have learnt some of the tax advantages of a deed of variation, such as skipping a generation, you will not score marks in this section unless you apply your knowledge to the scenario.

Potential tax advantages

(i) Gift to charity

An additional £18,000 gift to charity could be carried out via a variation of Cada's will. This would result in the tax saving set out in (b) above.

(ii) The house

There are two reasons to vary the terms of Cada's will, such that the house is left directly to Raymer's son.

Capital gains tax

Without the variation, the proposed gift of the house by Raymer to her son will result in a chargeable gain equal to the excess of the value of the house on 1 July 2023 (the date of the proposed gift) over its probate value of £500,000.

Private residence relief would not be available, as Raymer does not intend to live in the house.

Gift holdover relief would not be available as a house is not a qualifying asset for this relief.

Inheritance tax

Without the variation, the gift of the house by Raymer to her son would be a potentially exempt transfer for the purposes of inheritance tax and would become a chargeable transfer if Raymer were to die within seven years of the gift.

Procedures

- The variation of the will must be made in writing within two years of death by the person(s) who would benefit under the will (i.e. Raymer and Yang).
- It must be stated that the variation is intended to replace the terms of the will for the purposes of inheritance tax and capital gains tax.

Tutorial note

The additional gift to charity would have to come out of the legacy to Yang, since Raymer only inherited the house.

It would be beneficial for Yang to sign the deed of variation, since it will cost £18,000 in additional charitable legacies, however, it will save tax of £28,280. All the inheritance tax due on the death estate will come out of Yang's inheritance, since she is the residuary legatee. By signing the deed of variation to give an additional £18,000 to charity, Yang will actually inherit an additional £10,280 (£28,280 – £18,000).

(d)   Capital gains tax – Beneficial actions in respect of shareholdings

Tutor's top tips

The key to success in this section was spotting that Cada owned shares that had fallen in value. As there is no capital gains tax on death, relief can only be obtained for these capital losses during lifetime.

There are no marks for discussing the annual exempt amount (AEA), as the question states that Cada pays capital gains tax every year, so must already be using her AEA.

Following her death, the capital gains tax base costs of Cada's shareholdings are equal to their market value as at the date of death. Accordingly, any losses which accrued up to the date of death are no longer available for relief.

Cada could have sold the shares in FR plc (valued at less than cost) prior to her death in order to realise the accrued capital losses. The capital losses could have been offset against any chargeable gains in the tax year 2022/23.

A negligible value claim could have been submitted in respect of the shares in KZ Ltd. The shares would have been treated as having been sold and reacquired at their market value, resulting in an allowable capital loss. This loss would have been available for relief against Cada's chargeable gains in the tax year 2022/23 (the year in which the claim would have been made) or in either of the two preceding tax years, provided the shares were of negligible value in those years.

Any capital losses in excess of chargeable gains in the tax year 2022/23 could have been carried back and offset against gains in the three tax years prior to death, relieving later years before earlier years.

Tutorial note

Candidates were not required to consider the possibility of a loss arising in respect of the unquoted shares being offset against the taxpayer's income.

Examiner's report

The first thing to note in part (a) was that this part of the question concerned inheritance tax and not capital gains tax. The question also stated that candidates should not consider lifetime exemptions, for example the annual exemption. Many candidates did not identify these important points and thus wrote about both of these areas rather than focussing on the question requirements.

In addition, many candidates wrote at length about business property relief. This was not relevant because business property relief is available in respect of both lifetime gifts and the death estate and thus additional lifetime gifts by the deceased would not have resulted in additional relief. Other candidates were of the opinion that lifetime gifts will reduce the value of the death estate (true) and therefore reduce the inheritance tax due on death (not necessarily true). These candidates had failed to recognise the inheritance tax due in respect of potentially exempt transfers in the seven years prior to death (which these transfers inevitably would be due to the facts of the question).

Most candidates would have benefited from reading the question more carefully (and, for example, ignoring the annual exemption) and thinking more (thus recognising that business property relief was not relevant) and then writing a shorter answer that may very well have scored more marks.

Having said that, the majority of candidates correctly identified taper relief as an advantage of lifetime gifts and many explained the concept of value freezing. However, very few candidates were able to explain fall in value relief correctly.

Part (b) required candidates to calculate the increase in the legacy to charity that would be necessary for the reduced rate of inheritance tax to apply. Candidates appeared to be well-prepared for a question on this area of the syllabus and this part was answered particularly well with the exception of a very small minority who were simply not aware of the rules regarding the 36% rate of tax.

In part (c) the tax advantages are not obscure, but they do require some thought and they are not particularly easy to explain. Candidates would have benefited from slowing down and thinking about how best to express what they wanted to say rather than writing in the hope that the necessary words would eventually appear on the page.

As always, candidates had to apply their knowledge to the facts in the question. As far as capital gains tax was concerned, many candidates knew that there was no capital gains tax on death but failed to think about the potentially undesirable implication of the proposed gift of the house and how that implication could be avoided. In respect of inheritance tax, many candidates saw that this was linked to generation skipping but mentioning the term 'generation skipping' was not in itself sufficient.

Candidates had to explain that the variation would avoid the need for Raymer to make a potentially exempt transfer and therefore removed the possibility of such a transfer being chargeable to inheritance tax in the event that Raymer died within seven years of making the gift.

The majority of candidates were able to explain the procedures necessary in order to achieve a valid variation of the terms of the will.

Many candidates were unsure of the answer to part (d) despite having sufficient knowledge to deal with it. Unfortunately, instead of calmly thinking about it, they wrote about various aspects of capital gains tax, and inheritance tax, until they ran out of time. In particular, many candidates wrote about using any unused annual exempt amount despite being told in the question that the individual paid capital gains tax every year.

The key issue here was that, because there is no capital gains tax on death, any unrealised losses in respect of shares worth less than cost are lost. Candidates simply had to point out, for example, that the quoted shares that were valued at less than cost at the time of death should have been sold prior to death in order to realise a loss that could then have been offset against chargeable gains.

ACCA marking scheme		Marks
(a) Value frozen		
Identify issue		1.0
Relief for fall in value		1.0
Taper relief for gifts more than three years prior to death		
Identify issue		1.0
Explain effect		1.5
		4.5
	Maximum	4.0
(b) Original liability		2.5
Additional gift to charity		2.5
Net saving		1.0
		6.0
	Maximum	5.0
(c) Potential tax advantages		
Additional gift to charity		1.0
House		3.5
Procedures		2.0
		6.5
	Maximum	6.0
(d) No relief for accrued losses		1.0
Quoted shares where cost exceeds market value		1.0
Unquoted shares		2.0
Use of losses		2.0
		6.0
	Maximum	5.0
Total		**20.0**

34 ERIC (ADAPTED) *Walk in the footsteps of a top tutor*

Key answer tips

This section B question includes aspects of CGT and IHT, which are very frequently tested together, and also tests the personal service company (IR35) rules.

Part (a) requires a calculation of the after-tax proceeds of two capital disposals, the first involving insurance proceeds received for a damaged asset and the second a sale of shares that had previously been gifted and were subject to a gift holdover relief claim.

Part (b)(i) requires written advice on the availability of some key IHT reliefs, namely agricultural property relief, business property relief and quick succession relief. Business property relief in particular is one of the most frequently tested reliefs in the exam and so detailed knowledge of the rules is essential.

Part (b)(ii) requires calculations of the IHT impact of the client living longer than expected, resulting in a PET falling more than seven years prior to death, thus leaving more nil rate band available.

Part (c) involves applying the personal service company (IR35) rules and calculations to consultancy income received. Ensure you apply the correct rules for the size of the client organisations!

The highlighted words in the written sections are key phrases that markers are looking for in your letter.

Tutor's top tips

The question includes two key, very frequently tested reliefs: CGT gift holdover relief and IHT business property relief. It is crucial to know the rules in detail to enable you to answer such questions.

Requirements (a) and (c) are best answered in the spreadsheet response option in the exam, due to the fact that they are purely computational. Requirement (b) is discursive, and so is better suited to the word processor. Make sure you clearly label your answers so it is clear to the marker which part of the question you are answering.

(a) Chargeable gains 2021/22

Tutor's top tips

Remember that the receipt of insurance proceeds for a damaged asset is treated like a normal part disposal using the A/A+B formula to calculate the proportion of the original cost to use in the gain calculation.

Effectively, it is treated as if the damaged part of the asset has been 'sold' for the insurance proceeds received (A), and the asset that is left has a remaining value (B).

Part disposal in respect of damaged painting

	£
Insurance proceeds received	10,000
Less: Cost £46,000 × £10,000/(£10,000 + £38,000)	(9,583)
Chargeable gain	417

Disposal of Malaga plc shares

	£
Sale proceeds (£11.50 × 6,000)	69,000
Less: Cost (W)	(51,000)
Chargeable gain	18,000

Total after-tax proceeds

	£
Total chargeable gains (£417 + £18,000)	18,417
Less: Annual exempt amount	(12,300)
Taxable gains	6,117
Capital gains tax payable (£6,117 × 20%)	£1,223

After-tax proceeds are £77,777 (£10,000 + £69,000 – £1,223).

Working:

5 August 2018: Gain on gift from sister (£126,000 – £96,000)	£30,000
Gain eligible for gift holdover relief (£30,000 × 80%)	£24,000
Base cost of shares for Eric (£126,000 – £24,000)	£102,000

Cost of the shares sold is £51,000 (£102,000 × 1/2).

Tutorial notes

1   The compensation received in respect of the damaged painting cannot be deducted from the cost of the painting rather than treated as a part disposal, because it exceeds 5% of the value of the painting.

2   Relief would be available in computing the gain on the disposal of the Malaga plc shares for the inheritance tax paid by Eric following his sister's death on 1 September 2018. However, no inheritance tax figures were given and candidates were not expected to consider this point.

3   As Eric's sister owned more than 5% of the issued ordinary shares in Malaga plc, it was her personal company for the purpose of gift holdover relief. Accordingly, the proportion of the gain which was eligible for gift holdover relief was restricted to the fraction chargeable business assets/total chargeable assets.

(b)   (i)   Inheritance tax reliefs available if Eric dies on 31 March 2023

Tutor's top tips

There are three reliefs to consider here, so make sure that you think about all of them for both the farmland and the Malaga plc shares.

There are marks for stating why a relief is available, and also for stating why a relief is not available; for example: BPR is not available for the farmland, as it has been held as an investment.

Farmland

Agricultural property relief will be available on the farmland, but only on its agricultural value of £340,000. It will be available at the rate of 100% as the land will have been owned by Eric for more than seven years prior to his death and occupied by a tenant farmer throughout this period.

Business property relief (BPR) will not be available on the excess of the market value over the agricultural value of the land as Eric does not farm the land himself.

Malaga plc shares

No BPR will be available in respect of these shares as they are quoted shares and Eric does not have control of the company.

Quick succession relief (QSR) will be available as a tax credit to reduce the inheritance tax payable in respect of these shares as part of Eric's death estate. This is because the shares will have been subject to inheritance tax twice within a five-year period, i.e. on the potentially exempt transfer becoming chargeable on the death of Eric's sister, and again within Eric's death estate.

QSR is calculated as:

Inheritance tax paid on his sister's death $\times \dfrac{\text{net transfer}}{\text{gross transfer}} \times$ relevant percentage

The relevant percentage is 20% as the period between the date of the gift from his sister (which gave rise to the first charge to inheritance tax), and Eric's death will be 4–5 years.

(ii) **Impact on inheritance tax liability if Eric does not die until 1 August 2023**

The lifetime gift to Zak of £60,000 on 1 July 2016 will now be more than seven years prior to the date of death so is no longer taken into account in calculating the inheritance tax on Eric's death estate. This will mean that there is an additional £54,000 (£60,000 – (2 × £3,000 annual exemptions)) of nil rate band available to use against the death estate than there would have been if Eric had died on 31 March 2023.

As Eric's chargeable estate is worth considerably in excess of £325,000, this will result in an inheritance tax saving of £21,600 (£54,000 × 40%).

There will be no impact on the amount of QSR available as the period between the date of the gift from his sister and Eric's death will still be 4–5 years.

(c) **Zak's 2022/23 taxable income**

Tutor's top tips

The rules for calculating income under the personal service company legislation is different depending on the size of the client organisation involved. Always look for the size of the client in order to see which rules apply.

You are asked to calculate taxable income, not income tax payable, so don't waste time calculating the income tax due as there will be no marks for this.

	£
Yoyo Ltd fee income	110,000
Less: 5% deduction	(5,500)
	104,500
Less: Salary	(24,000)
Employer's NIC on salary ((£24,000 – £8,840) × 13.8%)	(2,092)
	78,408
Less: Employer's NIC on deemed payment $\dfrac{13.8}{113.8} \times$ £78,408	(9,508)
Deemed employment income	68,900

Zak – taxable income 2022/23

	£
Total income from Yoyo Ltd (£24,000 + £68,900)	92,900
Less: Personal allowance	(12,570)
Taxable income	80,330

Tutorial notes

1 *As Zak is the sole employee of Yoyo Ltd, the employment allowance of £4,000 will not be available to deduct from the employer's NIC payable.*

2 *As all the profits of Yoyo Ltd are deemed to have been paid to Zak as employment income, no further tax will arise in respect of the dividends of £50,000 paid to Zak. This is treated as exempt income to avoid a double tax charge.*

Examiner's report

Part (a) required candidates to calculate the after-tax proceeds from two capital gains tax disposals.

Questions at ATX frequently ask for a calculation of after-tax proceeds – here, the amount of proceeds remaining after the payment of capital gains tax. Candidates need to think more carefully about the starting point for this type of calculation. Failure to identify the correct starting point is a common error, with many candidates in this case deducting the tax from the taxable gain, rather than the sale proceeds, which they have used at the start of the computation.

Very few candidates proved able to calculate the capital gain arising on receipt of insurance proceeds for a damaged asset where no repair was undertaken. Similarly, many missed the implications of the previous gift holdover relief claim when calculating the gain on disposal of quoted company shares. Candidates should expect to have to deal with some of the trickier aspects of the calculation of individual gains at this level, and should therefore ensure that they practise a sufficient number of these.

The requirements for part (b)(i) stated the inheritance tax reliefs to be considered in respect of the assets in the taxpayer's estate on death. Candidates demonstrated good knowledge of the availability and operation of agricultural property relief. Business property relief, despite being examined far more frequently, was handled less well, with many candidates omitting to consider it in relation to the farmland, and believing that it is available to a minority shareholder in a quoted company. Many candidates were able to identify the ability to take quick succession relief in the given scenario, but very few were able to provide the formula for calculating it. Precise knowledge of these reliefs, when they are available, and how they are calculated is essential at ATX.

Part (b)(ii) required an explanation, with supporting calculations, of the impact on the inheritance tax arising on the taxpayer's death estate if his death occurred four months later than originally assumed. An ability to recognise the relevance of the timing of events or transactions in respect of all taxes is an important skill at ATX. The key point here was that the lifetime gift would no longer be accumulated as it was made more than seven years prior to death, thereby leaving the full nil rate band for use against the death estate. It was pleasing to see that many candidates recognised this point, providing concise explanations to score the full three marks. However, a significant number provided comprehensive calculations of the death estate, often with no explanation at all, making it difficult to demonstrate understanding of the requirement and consequently to score marks. Once again this highlights the need to read the wording of the requirement very carefully to ensure that the correct approach is taken.

Part (c) was concerned with the application of the personal service company (IR35) legislation. It was generally not well attempted by many candidates, despite having been examined in a similar way on previous occasions. It remains an important topic within the ATX syllabus.

		ACCA marking scheme		Marks
(a)		Gain on damaged painting		2.0
		Gain on shares		2.5
		After-tax proceeds		2.0
				——
				6.5
			Maximum	6.0
				——
(b)	(i)	Farmland – Agricultural property relief		2.0
		– Business property relief		1.0
		Shares – Business property relief		1.0
		– Quick succession relief		2.5
				——
				6.5
			Maximum	6.0
				——
	(ii)	Lifetime gift no longer accumulated		1.0
		Calculation of effect		2.0
		No effect on quick succession relief		1.0
				——
				4.0
			Maximum	3.0
				——
(c)		Yoyo Ltd – fee income less 5% deduction		1.0
		Employer's NIC on salary deducted		1.5
		Employer's NIC on deemed payment		1.0
		Taxable income		2.5
				——
				6.0
			Maximum	5.0
				——
Total				20.0
				——

35   SABRINA AND ADAM *Walk in the footsteps of a top tutor*

Key answer tips

This question covers the tax implications of the gift of a farm, the annual allowance for pension contributions and advice regarding investment in ISAs.

Part (a) requires explanations of both capital gains tax and inheritance tax for a lifetime gift, including consideration of agricultural property relief and business property relief. Questions such as this are very common in the exam.

Part (b) tests the rules for reducing the annual allowance for pensions. However, there are easy marks here for discussing the tax treatment of ISAs, savings income and dividends.

The highlighted words in the written sections are key phrases that markers are looking for in your answer.

(a)   (i)   Implications for Sabrina of the gift of Eastwick Farm to Adam on 1 January 2023

Tutor's top tips

In this part, you are just considering the tax implications for Sabrina. Detailed calculations are not required so the marks are for your written explanations.

Make sure that you clearly label your answer so the marker can see which tax you are writing about.

Capital gains tax

On the gift of the farm to Adam, chargeable gains will arise on the chargeable assets gifted. These will be computed by reference to the market values of the assets at the date of the transfer, i.e. 1 January 2023. Their base costs will be their market values at the date of Sam's death, i.e. 1 July 2021.

However, gift holdover relief will be available as this is the gift of a business, and the financial adviser has assumed that this will be claimed. As no proceeds will have been received from Adam, the whole of the gain can be deferred, such that Sabrina will have no liability to capital gains tax.

Inheritance tax

The gift will be a potentially exempt transfer, so Sabrina will have no liability to inheritance tax.

(ii)   Implications for Adam of the gift of Eastwick Farm on 1 January 2023

Tutor's top tips

In this part, you are writing about the tax implications for Adam. Again, make sure that you clearly label your answer to this part of the question to show whether you are considering capital gains tax or inheritance tax.

Think carefully about the reliefs that may be available for the gift of a farm, and remember to apply them to the correct tax. Reliefs to consider here are:

CGT = gift holdover relief and business asset disposal relief

IHT = agricultural property relief and business property relief.

You must learn the conditions for these reliefs, and there will be marks for stating and applying these in your answer.

Capital gains tax

The claim for gift holdover relief is a joint claim by both the donor and donee, so Adam will have to agree to this.

If the claim is made, the chargeable gains on the gift of the farm of £42,000 (£544,000 – £502,000) will be deferred. Adam's base cost in each of the assets will be their market value less the chargeable gain on the gift. Accordingly, if a claim for gift holdover relief is made, Adam's chargeable gain on the future disposal of any or all of these assets will be greater.

If Adam leases the farm to a tenant farmer, business asset disposal relief will not be available on any subsequent disposal, as the farm will be an investment for Adam; he will not be carrying on a business. As Adam will be an additional rate taxpayer, this will generate an additional capital gains tax liability of £8,400 (£42,000 × 20%).

Inheritance tax

The gift of the farm by Sabrina on 1 January 2023 will qualify for agricultural property relief (APR) at the rate of 100% on the agricultural value on 1 January 2023 of £396,000. Sabrina has been managing the farm since her husband's death and although she has owned the farm herself for less than two years, as she inherited it from her husband on his death, his period of ownership can be added to hers, such that the two-year holding period is satisfied.

The excess of the market value over the agricultural value on 1 January 2023 of £148,000 (£544,000 – £396,000) is eligible for business property relief (BPR) at the rate of 100%, because Sabrina, as owner, has been farming the land herself, and, as above for APR, the two-year ownership requirement is satisfied.

In the case of Sabrina's death before 1 January 2030, i.e. within seven years of making the transfer, it is important that Adam still owns the farm at the date of her death. This is because, provided the farm still constitutes agricultural property, i.e. it is used for agricultural purposes by the tenant to whom it is let; APR will be available on the agricultural value.

However, as Adam is not intending to farm it himself, no BPR will be available on Sabrina's death. Accordingly, the £148,000 excess of the market value over the agricultural value of the farm will be liable to inheritance tax at the rate of 40%. Sabrina's annual exemptions for the tax years 2022/23 and 2021/22 and her nil rate band have been used on the earlier transfer into the discretionary trust.

Adam will therefore have a maximum potential inheritance tax liability of £59,200 (£148,000 × 40%).

Taper relief will be available to reduce this amount if Sabrina survives until at least 1 January 2026 (three years after making the gift).

Any inheritance tax payable by Adam will be deductible when computing the chargeable gain arising on a subsequent disposal of the farm (but cannot be used to create an allowable loss).

(b)   Personal pension scheme

Tutor's top tips

The reduction of the annual allowance for pension contributions is complex, but you are given the income limit in the tax tables in the exam, and the question actually states the amount of allowance available, which should have made this part of the answer easier.

Remember that you are also given the savings and dividends nil rate bands in the tax tables, as well as the rates of tax applicable to dividends. These would have been useful when considering the benefits of investing in ISAs.

As Adam's adjusted income exceeds £240,000, his annual allowance for obtaining tax relief on pension contributions has been reduced. There is a reduction of £1 for every £2 of income in excess of £240,000. As Adam's adjusted income is £290,000, this has reduced the annual allowance by £25,000 ((£290,000 – £240,000)/2), leaving an annual allowance of only £15,000 (£40,000 – £25,000).

Individual savings accounts (ISAs)

Adam's thoughts are only partially correct.

The first £2,000 of dividend income is exempt from income tax each year, but any dividends in excess of this will be taxed at Adam's highest marginal rate of tax, which, as an additional rate taxpayer, would be 38.1% on the excess dividends over the higher rate threshold.

If he is considering investing in stocks and shares, he needs to consider his current and potential future level of dividends. If these use his £2,000 nil rate band, a stocks and shares ISA, under which all dividends are exempt from income tax, is still worthwhile.

He should also remember that the disposal of investments within a stocks and shares ISA is exempt from capital gains tax. This will be particularly relevant to him if he continues to use his annual exempt amount each year.

Adam is incorrect in relation to savings income. As an additional rate taxpayer, Adam has no entitlement to the savings nil rate band, so all his savings income will be taxable. If Adam wishes to hold money in cash deposits, then a cash ISA will still be beneficial.

Examiner's report

The majority of this question was focused on the proposed gift of a farm, and required comprehensive consideration of the reliefs available for both capital gains tax – gift holdover relief and business asset disposal relief – and inheritance tax – agricultural property relief (APR) and business property relief (BPR). Many candidates scored around half marks, by demonstrating knowledge of the basic principles of capital gains tax and inheritance tax, including the use of exemptions and the recognition of the relevant tax rates to be applied. However, recognition of the reliefs available, and their application, was disappointing. An ability to identify and apply appropriate reliefs for both capital gains tax and inheritance tax is an important skill at ATX, and candidates are again encouraged to practise more past exam questions, particularly those involving both capital taxes, in order to improve on this.

Additionally, when a scenario involves a number of transactions, to be carried out at different times, by different people, it is important to provide this information – who is making the gift/sale, and when – to accompany calculations and provide appropriate context. Candidates who do this are able to score much higher marks, by demonstrating understanding of the tax implications in context, than those candidates who just provide calculations without any accompanying details.

The second part of the question concerned the rules for restriction of the annual allowance for pension contributions for taxpayers with high adjusted net income, and also discussion of the nil rate bands for both savings and dividend income. It was pleasing to see that the majority of candidates were aware of these, and consequently scored a pass on this question part.

		ACCA marking scheme		Marks
(a)	(i)	Capital gains tax		2.0
		Inheritance tax – potentially exempt transfer		1.0
				3.0
	(ii)	Gift holdover relief claim/CGT payable		3.5
		APR/BPR on original gift		4.5
		APR/BPR as a result of Sabrina's death within seven years		2.0
		Potential IHT payable		2.5
		IHT deductible on subsequent sale		1.0
				13.5
			Maximum	11.0
(b)		Personal pension scheme		2.0
		ISAs		5.5
				7.5
			Maximum	6.0
Total				20.0

36 LIBER

Key answer tips

The first part of this question tests takeovers along with tax planning. The calculations around takeovers can sometimes be a little tricky. You need to start by looking at the base cost of the original shares and what happens to this at takeover. Consider if there are any tax implications on the takeover itself. You can then move on to deal with the subsequent sale. Remember that there are easy marks available for calculating the tax, so don't miss out on these!

The second part of part (a) looks at tax planning and the benefits of delaying the sale. Notice that if the sale is delayed it will fall into a new tax year – think about why this might be beneficial.

Part (b) looks at comparing giving in lifetime to giving at death, which is something that is often tested in ATX. Remember that you have two taxes to consider so it is worth separating your answer into two parts so that the two taxes don't get confused.

The highlighted words in the written sections are key phrases that markers are looking for.

(a)   (i)   **Capital gains tax implications of the takeover of Vulcan Ltd on 1 June 2022 and a subsequent sale of the Mercury plc shares on 1 January 2023**

Gain on the cash received in the takeover

The share-for-share exchange rules will automatically apply on the takeover of Vulcan Ltd on 1 June 2022, as this was a *bona fide* commercial transaction, and Mercury plc has acquired more than 25% of the ordinary shares in Vulcan Ltd. The shares in Mercury plc will 'stand in the shoes' of the shares in Vulcan Ltd and no gain will be chargeable in respect of these shares until they are sold. The receipt of cash is treated as a part-disposal of the Vulcan Ltd shares and a chargeable gain will arise at the date of the takeover.

The chargeable gain in respect of the cash received is £9,789 (£12,000 − £2,211 (W)).

Business asset disposal relief will not be available in respect of the gain arising on the cash consideration, as Liber was not a director or employee of Vulcan Ltd.

Gain on the sale of the Mercury plc shares

	£
Proceeds (3,200 × £28)	89,600
Less: Cost (W)	(11,789)
Chargeable gain	77,811

Business asset disposal relief will not be available on the sale of the Mercury plc shares as Liber is not a director or employee of Mercury plc, and holds less than 5% of the ordinary shares in Mercury plc.

Tutorial note

Where there is a share-for-share exchange, the two year ownership requirement includes the holding period of the original shares.

	£
Gain on cash received on takeover	9,789
Gain on sale of shares in Mercury plc	77,811
Total chargeable gains	87,600
Less: Annual exempt amount	(12,300)
Taxable gains	75,300

Capital gains tax (CGT) payable is £14,290 (((£37,700 − £30,000) × 10%) + ((£75,300 − £7,700) × 20%)).

Working: Allocation of cost at time of takeover

	Market value £	Apportioned cost £
Consideration received:		
Ordinary shares in Mercury plc		
(800 × 4 × £20)	64,000	
(£64,000/£76,000) × £14,000		11,789
Cash (800 × £15)	12,000	
(£12,000/£76,000) × £14,000		2,211
	76,000	14,000

(ii) **Reasons why it is beneficial to sell the Mercury plc shares on 1 May 2023 instead of on 1 January 2023**

The calculation of the gain on the sale of the Mercury plc shares will be the same, but the sale will be in the following tax year, 2023/24, so the following tax implications will arise:

The gain on the cash received on the takeover in the tax year 2022/23 will be covered by the annual exempt amount for that year and so there will be no CGT liability in the tax year 2022/23.

The whole of the 2023/24 annual exempt amount will be available to be deducted from the gain on the sale of the Mercury plc shares. This will result in a CGT liability of £12,332 in the tax year 2023/24 (W). The overall tax saving if the Mercury plc shares are sold on 1 May 2023 is therefore £1,958 (£14,290 (as in (a)(i)) − £12,332).

Tutorial note

Alternatively, delaying the sale of the shares until 1 May 2023 results in the gain on the cash received in the takeover of £9,789 being fully covered by the annual exempt amount for the tax year 2022/23 and therefore a CGT saving of £1,958 (20% × £9,789).

The tax relating to the sale of the Mercury plc shares will be due a year later on 31 January 2025, rather than 31 January 2024.

Working: CGT liability if Mercury plc shares disposed of on 1 May 2023

	£
Gain on sale of shares in Mercury plc	77,811
Less: Annual exempt amount	(12,300)
Taxable gains	65,511

CGT payable is £12,332 (((£37,700 − £30,000) × 10%) + ((£65,511 − £7,700) × 20%)).

(b) Vesta

Capital gains tax and inheritance tax advantages of gifting the investment property on 31 December 2022

Capital gains tax (CGT)

If the property remains in Vesta's estate on her death, there will be no CGT implications, such that the fall in value of the property will not give rise to an allowable loss.

If the property is gifted to Janus on 31 December 2022, an allowable loss will arise as a result of the fall in value. However, as Vesta will make no disposals for CGT purposes in the tax year 2023/24, she will not be able to relieve this loss.

Therefore, for CGT purposes, Vesta will be indifferent as to whether to gift the property to Janus in her lifetime, or to leave it to him in her estate on death.

However, Janus's base cost of the property on a future disposal is its market value at the date it is transferred to him. Accordingly, as the property is expected to be worth less at the date of Vesta's death than it is currently, it will be advantageous from Janus's point of view if Vesta gifts the property to him on 31 December 2022 as he will then have a higher base cost for CGT purposes on a future sale.

Tutorial note

As Janus and Vesta are connected persons, the CGT loss on the gift of the property to Janus on 31 December 2022 could only have been relieved against a gain arising on a later disposal by Vesta to Janus.

Inheritance tax (IHT)

If the property remains in Vesta's estate at the date of her death, it will be included at its value on death, which is expected to be lower than its current market value.

If the property is gifted to Janus on 31 December 2022, it will be a potentially exempt transfer (PET), such that there will be no immediate charge to IHT. This PET will become chargeable as a result of Vesta's death within seven years.

As the value of the property is expected to have decreased between the date of the gift and the date of death, fall in value relief will be available (assuming that Janus still owns the property, or has sold it in an arm's length transaction), so the lifetime gift will not result in any more IHT being payable on the property than if it were left to Janus in the death estate.

No annual exemptions are available as they have been used on the cash gift to Janus on 1 June 2022. No taper relief will be available as Vesta will not have survived for three years after making the gift.

Therefore, for IHT purposes, both Vesta and Janus will be indifferent between a lifetime gift and leaving the property in her estate on death.

Examiner's report

This question was in two main parts. Part (a) concerned a takeover involving cash and shares being offered in exchange for shares. Part (b) concerned advice on the capital gains tax and inheritance tax advantages of a lifetime gift rather than a death estate bequest.

When looking at the first part of the question concerning the takeover, candidates should have been able to identify the following tax issues from the facts of the question.

- At the date of the takeover, share-for-share rules automatically apply but there will be a gain on the cash element of the takeover consideration. When the new shares are eventually sold, a gain will arise on the sale.

- If the new shares are sold in the same tax year as the takeover, the gain on the cash element at takeover and the gain on the new shares will be added together and the annual exempt amount set against the total gains.

- If instead, the new shares are sold in a subsequent tax year for the same price, the gain on the new shares may be the same as calculated above but it will be offset by a new annual exempt amount. This will result in a tax saving.

Clarity of thought was critical here. Candidates needed to identify the tax implications of what had already happened and then consider the implications of the alternative sale date scenarios. Candidates should not be writing their answers immediately; they should be planning what points they need to make in their answer. Candidates who start preparing calculations in the hope that they will eventually arrive at the correct answer do not score well.

For those candidates who took a moment to consider the facts and decide on a strategy for answering the question, the calculations were not very difficult and the two possible sale alternatives could be compared, scoring high marks.

A further issue in this part of the question was whether business asset disposal relief (BADR) would be available to the individual making the share disposals. Stronger candidates understood the BADR rules but more importantly, were able to apply them to the facts of the question and decide that BADR would not be available. Weaker candidates listed the BADR rules but were not able to apply them to the scenario. A significant minority of students considered the substantial shareholding exemption which is not relevant in the scenario of an individual disposing of shares.

The second part of the question required candidates to consider the capital gains tax and inheritance tax advantages of a lifetime gift rather than a death estate bequest. Candidates may have been familiar with this as a tax planning concept but once again, the key to answering this question was in applying knowledge to the facts given in this particular question.

Candidates should have found the following tax issues arising from the facts of the question.

- A lifetime gift would result in a capital loss, not a capital gain, since the value of the asset had fallen since purchase. However the facts of the question were that the donor would not be able to use a capital loss. Since there is no capital gains tax on a death estate bequest, from a capital gains tax point of view, the donor would be indifferent between lifetime and death gifting.

- For inheritance tax purposes, a lifetime gift would be a potentially exempt transfer. However the facts of the question were that the potentially exempt transfer would become chargeable within three years, with neither taper relief nor annual exemptions available. Furthermore, fall in value relief would be available, meaning that once again the donor would be indifferent between lifetime and death gifting.

Candidates need to consider the scenario given *before* they start writing their answer and not simply state general tax rules. Each client has their own particular set of circumstances which the tax rules must be applied to. Once again, candidates would benefit from taking some thinking time to consider the scenario before they put pen to paper.

		ACCA marking scheme		Marks
(a)	(i)	Gain on cash at date of takeover		4.5
		Gain on sale of Mercury plc shares on 1 January 2023		2.5
		Capital gains tax payable		2.0
				9.0
			Maximum	8.0
	(ii)	2023/24 annual exempt amount available		1.0
		Calculation of tax saving		3.0
		Tax payable later		1.0
				5.0
			Maximum	4.0
(b)		Capital gains tax implications		4.0
		Inheritance tax implications		5.5
				9.5
			Maximum	8.0
Total				**20.0**

37   MAIA *Walk in the footsteps of a top tutor*

Key answer tips

This question covers calculations of post-tax income, CGT and IHT implications of a variety of alternative options.

The first part of the question tests mostly TX knowledge, aside from the share scheme. Although this is mostly brought forward knowledge it is tested in a more advanced way as it gets you to think about post-tax income and how that has an effect on the amount of cash needed by an individual. It is important to think carefully and read the advice in the requirement before diving into the calculations.

The second part of the question may look quite overwhelming when you first read through. There is a lot to cover, but if you take an organised approach to ensure you cover each individual aspect you should be able to score well on this.

The highlighted words in the written sections are key phrases that markers are looking for.

Memorandum

Client   **Maia**

Subject   **Provision of financial assistance for Josh**

Prepared by Tax senior

Date   **4 June 2022**

Tutor's top tips

Note that the requirement at the bottom of the question does not give sufficient information for you to answer the question. You need to go and find the real requirement in the extract of the email from your manager.

(a)   Josh – additional cash requirement

Tutor's top tips

*Think carefully about what you are being asked to calculate in this part of the question. It is the **extra** cash over and above Josh's after tax income from two tax years.*

The cash required is given in the question as this is the rent that needs to be covered for two years. You then need to find the after tax income for the two tax years in question.

The requirement helps by telling you to think about how his income will differ in the tax year 2023/24 compared to 2022/23. The only difference is the share issue, so if you add back the tax on this to your result for the tax year 2022/23 you should get to the equivalent after tax figure for 2023/24.

2022/23	£	£
Salary	25,200	25,200
Shares in NL Ltd (£2,100 – £300)	1,800	
Home cinema (£1,700 × 20%)	340	
Mobile telephone (exempt)	0	
	———	
Employment income	27,340	
Dividend income	420	420
	———	
	27,760	
Less: Personal allowance	(12,570)	
	———	
	15,190	
	———	
		25,620
Income tax		
£14,770 (£27,340 – £12,570) × 20%	2,954	
£420 × 0% (nil rate band)	0	
	———	
		(2,954)
Class 1 national insurance contributions (NIC)		
(£25,200 – £9,568) × 12%	1,876	(1,876)
	———	———
Income after tax and NIC		20,790
		———

2023/24

As for 2022/23	20,790
Add: Tax in respect of shares in NL Ltd (£1,800 × 20%)	360
Income after tax and NIC	21,150
Cash required (24 × £2,500)	60,000
Anticipated income (£20,790 + £21,150)	(41,940)
Additional cash required	18,060

(b) Providing financial assistance to Josh – alternative strategies

Tutor's top tips

There is a lot to do in this part of the question and it is easy to get confused. Ensure you cover all aspects by using headings to structure your answer. For each alternative strategy you should consider:

1   The increase in post-tax income for Josh (not needed for strategy (ii))

2   The CGT liabilities for Maia

3   The IHT implication for Maia and Josh including consideration of BPR

For both 2 and 3 you also need to consider the position whether the property qualifies as furnished holding accommodation or not. You were told not to include the definition so make sure you don't include any unnecessary detail.

(i)   Gift of investment property

Increase in Josh's post-tax income

Josh would receive net rental income of £13,200 (£1,100 × 12) in a full tax year, such that he would continue to be a basic rate taxpayer. Accordingly, his additional post-tax income in the 21-month period from 1 July 2022 to 5 April 2024 would be £18,480 (£1,100 × 21 × 80%).

Capital gains tax (CGT) liabilities for Maia

Maia's gift of the building would be treated as a sale at market value for the purposes of calculating the chargeable gain. This gives rise to a gain of £240,000 (£370,000 – £130,000).

If the building IS NOT furnished holiday accommodation:

- The building would not be a business asset, such that neither gift holdover relief nor business asset disposal relief would be available.

- Maia is a higher rate taxpayer who uses her annual exempt amount every year. Accordingly, her CGT liability on the gift of the building will be £67,200 (£240,000 × 28%).

If the building IS furnished holiday accommodation:

- Gift holdover relief would be available because furnished holiday accommodation is included within the definition of business assets used in the trade. Accordingly, no CGT would be payable by Maia in respect of the gift.

Tutorial note

A claim for gift holdover relief would need to be signed by both Maia and Josh as it is a joint election. Those candidates who did not recognise the availability of gift holdover relief were given credit for explaining that business asset disposal relief would be available, such that the CGT rate applied to the gain would be 10%.

Inheritance tax (IHT) implications for Maia and Josh

If the building IS NOT furnished holiday accommodation:

- The gift would be a potentially exempt transfer, such that there would be no inheritance tax due unless Maia were to die within seven years of the gift.
- If Maia were to die within seven years of the gift, the excess of the market value of the property at the time of the gift (i.e. £370,000) over Maia's available nil rate band would be subject to IHT at 40%. This tax would be payable by Josh.
- Maia's available nil rate band would be the nil rate band for the year of death (assumed to be £325,000) less her chargeable transfers in the seven years prior to 1 July 2022.
- Taper relief would be available if Maia were to survive the gift by more than three years. This would reduce the IHT by 20% for each additional full year for which she survived the gift.

If the building IS furnished holiday accommodation:

- Since Maia will have owned the building for more than two years prior to the transfer, the gift could qualify for 100% business property relief (BPR). However, the building will only qualify as relevant business property if Maia is able to demonstrate to HM Revenue and Customs (HMRC) that it is operated as a business with substantial involvement by her (and subsequently by Josh) and additional services are provided. It should be anticipated that this treatment will be resisted by HMRC.
- Even if it does qualify for BPR, it will be necessary for Josh to still own the building (or replacement business property) and for it to still be qualifying business property at the time of Maia's death.

Tutorial note

If Josh no longer owned the property as at Maia's death, then if he had not replaced it with other qualifying business property BPR would be withdrawn and IHT would become chargeable at death. This would therefore give rise to the same consequences as if the building hadn't been furnished holiday accommodation.

(ii) Gift of shares in Far Ltd

CGT liabilities for Maia

Maia's gift of the shares would be treated as a sale at market value for the purpose of calculating the chargeable gain. Gift holdover relief would be available because Far Ltd is an unquoted trading company.

	£	£
Proceeds at market value		420,000
Less: Cost		
Market value on 1 November 2021	375,000	
Less: Gift holdover relief in respect of earlier gift	(140,000)	
		(235,000)
		185,000
Less: Gift holdover relief (£185,000 × 84% (100% – 16%))		(155,400)
Chargeable gain		29,600

Business asset disposal relief would not be available, regardless of whether or not Maia works for Far Ltd, because Maia will not have owned the shares for two years on 1 July 2022. Accordingly, as Maia is a higher rate taxpayer, her CGT liability would be £5,920 (£29,600 × 20%).

IHT implications for Maia and Josh

Business property relief would not be available because Maia will not have owned the shares for two years on 1 July 2022. Accordingly, the IHT implications would be the same as for the gift of the investment property, where it is not furnished holiday accommodation, as set out above.

(iii) Monthly cash gifts

Increase in Josh's post-tax income

There would be no income tax implications for Josh. He would therefore receive £21,000 over the 21-month period.

CGT liabilities for Maia

There would be no CGT implications for Maia because cash is an exempt asset.

IHT implications for Maia and Josh

These gifts are likely to be exempt from IHT as they would satisfy the following conditions:

- They would be part of Maia's expenditure out of her income.
- There would be a regular pattern of giving.
- They would not affect Maia's standard of living.

Examiner's report

This question concerned a wealthy aunt looking to provide financial assistance to her nephew. The aunt was considering three alternative strategies involving the gift of a property, gift of shares and a gift of cash.

The first part of the question required calculations to determine how much additional cash would be required by the nephew over a two-year period, by comparing his cash income to his cash outgoings. In order to calculate his outgoings, candidates needed to calculate his income tax and national insurance contributions. It was pleasing to see that many candidates answered this part well, with a significant number of candidates achieving almost full marks.

However, a number of candidates did not recognise that employees' national insurance contributions would not be payable on benefits-in-kind. Many candidates lost valuable time producing two full income tax computations for the two tax years instead of looking at the change that had occurred between the two years and simply calculating how this would affect income tax payable.

Despite the fact that this part of the question specifically asked candidates not to provide any narrative explanation of the calculations, many candidates spent time providing explanations for which although correct, there were no marks awarded.

The second part of the question was split into three sub-parts, asking candidates to consider three alternative strategies of gifting.

The first proposed strategy was for the aunt to gift an investment property to the nephew. The requirement asked for the capital gains tax consequence for the aunt and the inheritance tax consequences for both the aunt and the nephew of such a gift. The requirement stated that it was unclear if the property was furnished holiday accommodation or not but to explain the liabilities for both possibilities regarding the property. Many candidates failed to address both possibilities and often only addressed the possibility that the property was not a furnished holiday accommodation. Future candidates would be well advised to stop and think about the points they wish to address before they start writing.

Many candidates were able to identify that business property relief might be available when calculating inheritance tax but appeared to lack knowledge of the conditions required for this relief. A significant number of candidates gave a definition of furnished holiday accommodation when it was specifically stated in the requirement that they should not provide this definition. Again these candidates would have benefitted from spending time ensuring they fully understood the requirement and planning their answer, before beginning to write. By doing this, it is likely they would have saved themselves time in the long run and allowed themselves to earn as many of the available marks as possible.

The second proposed strategy was for the aunt to gift shares in an unquoted trading company. Many candidates were able to identify the possibility of gift holdover relief but did not restrict the gift holdover relief for chargeable non-business assets. As before, candidates were able to recognise that business reliefs such as business asset disposal relief and business property relief might be available but unfortunately did not apply the conditions for these reliefs to the facts of the question.

The third proposed strategy was for the aunt to make monthly cash gifts and it was very positive to see that many candidates scored full marks on the capital gains tax and inheritance tax implications of such cash gifts.

Marks were awarded for professional skills in this question. These marks were awarded for clear and logical explanations and calculations, for a sensible approach to solving the problems set in parts (a) and (b), for answers that were scenario specific rather than general, and for a professionally acceptable style. Generally the candidates performed reasonably well in this area.

ACCA marking scheme			Marks
(a)	Tax year 2022/23		
	Employment income		3.0
	PA and tax liability		2.0
	National insurance contributions		1.5
	Tax year 2023/24		1.5
	Monthly cash required		2.0
			10.0
		Maximum	9.0
(b)	(i)	Income tax	2.0
		Capital gains tax	
		Taxable gain	1.0
		If the building is not furnished holiday accommodation (FHA)	1.5
		If the building is FHA	2.0
		Inheritance tax	
		If the building is not FHA	4.0
		If the building is FHA	3.0
			13.5
		Maximum	12.0

			Marks
(ii)	Capital gains tax		
	Chargeable gain		1.5
	Gift holdover relief		2.5
	Tax payable		2.5
	Inheritance tax		2.0
			8.5
		Maximum	7.0
(iii)	Income tax		1.0
	Capital gains tax		1.0
	Inheritance tax		2.0
			4.0
		Maximum	3.0
Problem solving			1.0
Clarity of explanations and calculations			1.0
Effectiveness of communication			1.0
Overall presentation and style			1.0
			4.0
Total			**35.0**

MULTI TAX PERSONAL INCLUDING OVERSEAS

38   NUCLEUS RESOURCES (ADAPTED)

  Online question assistance and Walk in the footsteps of a top tutor

Key answer tips

This section A question is really two unconnected questions.

The first part is all about a sole trader expanding her business, either by taking on some employees or paying a company to do some work for her. You need to work out which option will leave her financially better off. Unincorporated businesses are very common in the ATX exam, even though much of the technical content is TX knowledge, so make sure that you revise this area.

The second part covers mainly IHT and CGT. There are a couple of issues here: you need to think about the impact of domicile on IHT, and the tax implications of a lifetime transfer into a trust. In addition, there is a small section on ethical issues.

The highlighted words in the written sections are key phrases that markers are looking for.

Tutor's top tips

Read the memorandum in the question carefully. The examining team gives you some helpful tips on how to approach this part of the question.

You need to check whether Maria is already an additional rate taxpayer, to avoid the need to prepare full income tax computations.

You also need to think about VAT as this is a partially exempt business. The examining team indicates that the recoverability of input VAT is bound to be affected.

If the amount of VAT recoverable changes as a result of the expansion, this will affect the amount of after-tax income for Maria.

Remember also that you are considering the options from Maria's point of view, so you do not need to consider the tax position of the employees or company doing the work for Maria, just the extra income after tax generated for Maria herself.

Make sure that you show your workings clearly, so that if you do make some mistakes you can still gain marks for consistency.

Notes for meeting with Maria Copenhagen

(a) **After-tax income generated by the expansion of Nucleus Resources**

Maria is an additional rate taxpayer, as the current net income from the business and IIP trust of £168,000 (£40,000 + £90,000 − £37,000 − £35,000 + £110,000) exceeds £150,000.

Maria's personal allowance would already be reduced to £0 as her net income exceeds £125,140.

Accordingly, the profit generated by the expansion will be subject to tax at a total of 47% (income tax at 45% and class 4 national insurance at 2%).

Tutorial note

In the real exam answer the examining team worked out the net after-tax income at £168,000 (i.e. ignoring the VAT impact).

However, the net after-tax income before considering the options is in fact £162,894 (£168,000 less irrecoverable VAT £5,106 (W1)).

Either way, with £168,000 or £162,894, the purpose of this first paragraph is just to establish that she is an additional rate taxpayer and therefore the impact of each option can be calculated at the marginal rates.

Employ additional employees :

	£
Additional turnover	190,000
Existing irrecoverable VAT will be recoverable (W1, W2)	5,106
	195,106
Salaries (£55,000 + £40,000)	95,000
Class 1 NIC ((£95,000 – (£8,840 × 2)) × 13.8%) (Note 1)	10,670
Cost in respect of car (W4)	2,566
Additional overheads	20,000
	128,236
Net additional income (£195,106 – £128,236)	66,870
Additional income after tax (£66,870 × 53% (Note 2))	35,441

Tutorial note

1   *The £4,000 employment allowance will already have been claimed against the class 1 secondary NICs relating to the existing employees. Accordingly, there is no £4,000 deduction against the additional class 1 secondary NICs in relation to the additional employees.*

2   *If the total tax rate at the margin is 47%, the after-tax income generated by the expansion will be 53% (100% – 47%).*

Use Quantum Ltd:

	£
Additional turnover	190,000
Additional irrecoverable VAT (£9,912 (W3) – £5,106 (W1))	4,806
Quantum Ltd annual fee	140,000
	144,806
Net additional income (£190,000 – £144,806)	45,194
Additional income after tax (£45,194 × 53%)	23,953

Tutor's top tips

Don't worry if you didn't get this completely right. If you have calculated after-tax income correctly based on your figures, you will still score marks here. There were some very easy marks for just putting in the extra income and expenses.

Workings

(W1) Existing business – Irrecoverable VAT due to partial exemption

Partial exemption percentage (£40,000 ÷ £130,000) (Note)	31%
	£
Total input tax (£37,000 × 20%)	7,400
Attributable to taxable supplies (£7,400 × 31%)	(2,294)
Attributable to exempt supplies	5,106

De minimis tests:

1   Total monthly input tax is £617 (£7,400 ÷ 12) on average, which is less than £625. However, as the value of exempt supplies is more than 50% of the total supplies, test 1 is not satisfied.

2   Total input tax less input tax directly attributable to taxable supplies is £7,400 (£7,400 – £0), which gives a monthly average of £617, as above, but again the value of exempt supplies is more than 50% of the total supplies, so test 2 is not satisfied.

3   Monthly input tax relating to exempt supplies is £425 (£5,106 ÷ 12) on average, which is less than £625. However, as the input VAT relating to exempt supplies is more than 50% of the total input VAT, test 3 is not satisfied either.

Therefore, the VAT attributable to exempt supplies cannot be recovered.

Tutorial note

Remember that when a business makes a mixture of both taxable and exempt supplies, input VAT can usually only be reclaimed on purchases attributable to taxable supplies.

Any mixed input VAT needs to be apportioned using the formula:

Taxable supplies ÷ total supplies = % recoverable.

This % is always rounded up to the next whole %.

However, if the input VAT relating to exempt supplies is very small (i.e. below the de minimis limits), then the whole amount can be reclaimed.

(W2) Expanded business with employees

Irrecoverable VAT due to partial exemption

Partial exemption percentage

((£40,000 + £190,000) ÷ (£130,000 + £190,000))	72%

	£
Total input tax ((£37,000 + £20,000) × 20%)	11,400
Attributable to taxable supplies (£11,400 × 72%)	(8,208)
Attributable to exempt supplies	3,192

This is below the annual de minimis limit of £7,500 (£625 × 12) and is less than half of the total input tax. Accordingly, all of the input tax can be recovered.

Tutorial note

As this de minimis test is satisfied, there is no need to consider the two further tests.

Therefore, as a result of expanding the business and taking on employees, £5,106 (W1) of irrecoverable VAT becomes recoverable.

Tutorial note

The approach in this answer is that used by the examining team in their model answer and was therefore the way in which they expected you to deal with the situation, given the hint that the recoverability of input VAT is 'bound to be affected'. However, you may have assumed that the comment in Note 4 that 'the expenditure cannot be attributed to particular supplies' only related to the existing business and that all of the input VAT on the additional overheads of £20,000 is fully recoverable as they directly relate to a wholly taxable supply (i.e. the new project).

If so, this is a very valid assumption. If you stated this assumption and prepared you answer on this basis, you should still have gained full marks.

(W3) Expanded business using Quantum Ltd

Irrecoverable VAT due to partial exemption

Partial exemption percentage (W2)	72%

	£
Total input tax ((£37,000 + £140,000) × 20%)	35,400
Attributable to taxable supplies (£35,400 × 72%)	(25,488)
Attributable to exempt supplies	9,912

De minimis tests:

1   Total monthly input tax is £2,950 (£35,400 ÷ 12) on average. As this exceeds £625, test 1 is not satisfied.

2   Total input tax less input tax directly attributable to taxable supplies is £35,400 (£35,400 – £0), which gives a monthly average of £2,950, as above. As this exceeds £625 test 2 is not satisfied.

3   Monthly input tax relating to exempt supplies is £826 (£9,912 ÷ 12) on average. As this exceeds £625, test 3 is not satisfied either.

Therefore, the VAT attributable to exempt supplies cannot be recovered.

Tutorial note

As in (W2), you may have assumed that the comment in Note 4 that 'the expenditure cannot be attributed to particular supplies' only related to the existing business and that all of the input VAT on the annual charge of £140,000 is fully recoverable as it directly relates to a wholly taxable supply (i.e. the new project).

If so, this is a very valid assumption. The examining team has said that if you stated this assumption and prepared you answer on this basis, you should still have gained full marks.

(W4) Cost in respect of car

	£
Annual cost ((£12,800 – £2,000) ÷ 5) (Note)	2,160
Class 1A NIC (£2,944 (W5) × 13.8%)	406
	2,566

Tutorial note

*The question specifically tells you to spread the effect of the capital allowances evenly. All you need to remember is that the **total** capital allowances available will be equal to the net cost of the car to the business (i.e. the proceeds less the original cost). This effect will actually be spread over a longer period than five years, as the car will be added to the special rate pool and no balancing allowance will be given on disposal, and instead WDAs will continue to be claimed on a reducing balance basis. However, you have been told in the question to spread the allowances over the period of ownership of the car.*

Don't forget that as an employer, Maria will have to pay class 1A NICs as she will be providing a benefit to an employee.

(W5) Car benefit

CO$_2$ emissions 99 g/km, available all tax year

Appropriate percentage = 15% + ((95g − 55g)/5g) = 23%

Car benefit (£12,800 × 23%) = £2,944

(b)   (i)   Inheritance tax on the quoted shares

Tutor's top tips

Make sure that you answer the specific question here. In the first part, the question asks you for the 'issues to be considered' in order to determine whether the gift will be subject to UK IHT.

What it is really asking you to consider is two things:

'is Neil's uncle UK domiciled', and

'are the shares UK or overseas assets'?

Consideration of the availability of double taxation relief is then required.

*There are six marks available, so try to make sure that you have at least six separately identifiable points in your answer, and show that you have **applied** your knowledge by using facts provided in the information in the question.*

The inheritance tax position depends on the domicile of the uncle and the location of the quoted shares.

- If the uncle was domiciled in the UK when he made the gift in October 2020, the value of the shares at the time of the gift will be subject to inheritance tax.

- If the uncle was domiciled in Heisenbergia, the gift will only be subject to UK inheritance tax if the shares are UK assets.

Uncle's domicile

- If the uncle was not UK domiciled in 2001 it seems very unlikely from what we know that he would have acquired a UK domicile whilst living in Heisenbergia.

- If the uncle was UK domiciled at the time he left the UK in 2001, he will continue to be UK domiciled unless he acquired a domicile of choice in Heisenbergia.

- In order to have acquired a domicile of choice in Heisenbergia, the uncle would have had to have severed his ties with the UK and exhibited a clear intention of making Heisenbergia his permanent home.

Location of the quoted shares

- The shares are UK assets if the company is incorporated in the UK or the shares are registered in the UK.

Tutorial note

The location of the shares may also be affected by any double tax treaty between the UK and Heisenbergia.

Inheritance tax suffered in Heisenbergia

- Any UK inheritance tax due in respect of the gift can be reduced by double tax relief in respect of the inheritance tax charged in Heisenbergia.

(ii)   Creation of the trust

Tutor's top tips

The first part of the requirement simply asks for the 'tax implications' of transferring the shares to the trust. So, you need to consider all of the capital tax implications of the gift here: IHT, CGT and also stamp duty.

The second part requires an outline of the taxation of trust income received by a beneficiary.

Inheritance tax

- The lifetime transfer of shares to the trust would be a chargeable lifetime transfer.

- The value transferred would be reduced by the annual exemptions for the year of the gift and the previous year.

- As the company is quoted, business property relief (at 50%) will only be available in respect of the shares if Niels controls the company, which is unlikely to be the case.

- As Niels has not made any previous chargeable transfers, the transfer would be covered by his £325,000 nil rate band; there would be no inheritance tax due.

Capital gains tax

- The transfer of the shares to the trust represents a chargeable disposal at market value.

- Gift holdover relief would be available (because the gift is immediately chargeable to inheritance tax) such that any gain arising could be deducted from the trustees' base cost of the shares rather than being charged.

Stamp duty

- There is no stamp duty on a gift.

Income tax

- Niels will be subject to income tax on any amounts received from the trust by his sons, subject to a *de minimis* limit of £100 per annum. This is because the boys are both minors and the trust was created with capital provided by their parent, Niels.

- A tax credit will be given in respect of the income tax paid by the trustees.

(iii)   Discussion of issues with Maria

Tutor's top tips

Ethical issues will always be included in the exam for five marks. These sections are usually very straightforward, as long as you have not run out of time!

- Maria and Niels are separate clients and must be treated as such from the point of view of confidentiality.

- We must not disclose information relating to Niels to anyone, including Maria, unless we have permission from Niels (or such disclosure as is required by law or professional duty). Accordingly, we should check to see if we have written permission from Niels to discuss his affairs with his wife.

- Unless we have permission from Niels, we should not discuss the situation relating to the proposed transfer of shares to the trust. This is because we cannot explain the situation to Maria without referring to Neils' tax position, i.e. the lack of previous chargeable transfers.

- Maria's question concerning inheritance tax on the gift from the uncle is different because it can be answered without making any reference to the tax affairs of Niels. It is, arguably, a general question on the workings of inheritance tax. There would be no breach of confidentiality if we discussed this matter with Maria.

- However, we know that it is not a general question and we should still consider the potential problems that could arise in discussing matters with Maria that relate to the personal affairs of Niels without first obtaining permission from Niels.

Examiner's report

Part (a) required calculations of the annual additional after-tax income generated by two alternative business expansion proposals. These calculations were made more complicated by the fact that the client's business was partially exempt for the purposes of VAT (value added tax).

This required an approach similar to that tested in question 2 of the Pilot paper but was only attempted by a minority of candidates. However, with the exception of the VAT aspects, the majority of candidates made a good attempt at this part of the question and produced clear, logical calculations which identified most of the relevant issues.

One surprising but common error was to treat the car benefit as a cost incurred by the business. In addition, a minority of candidates wasted time by providing lengthy explanations which were not asked for.

Part (b) tested three technical areas relating to the client. The general approach in this question was good, with well structured documents addressing the majority of the issues being prepared by many candidates.

Part (i) concerned the inheritance tax implications of a gift from an individual who may or may not have been domiciled in the UK. Somewhat surprisingly, many candidates struggled with this.

The most common error was to focus on the domicile status of the recipient of the gift rather than the donor. There was also some discussion of the remittance basis which had no relevance here.

Stronger candidates began by stating the general rule as regards domicile and location of assets in relation to inheritance tax and then applied the rules to the specific facts in the question.

The majority of candidates made sensible comments about the availability of double tax relief.

Part (ii) concerned the transfer of shares to a trust. The inheritance tax aspects were handled well and the stronger candidates also addressed the capital gains tax and income tax aspects. As always, it was important to identify all of the issues first and then ensure that they were all addressed in the time available. Otherwise, the only issue covered was inheritance tax and too few marks were earned.

Part (iii) concerned the extent to which it is acceptable to discuss a client's affairs with that client's spouse. The majority of candidates were quite clear on the inappropriateness of such behaviour and scored well. However, a significant minority did not attempt this part demonstrating either a lack of time management or poor knowledge of this area of the syllabus.

			Marks
		ACCA marking scheme	*Marks*
(a)		VAT position	
		Existing business	3.0
		Expand with employees	2.0
		Expand using Quantum Ltd	2.0
		Employ additional staff	
		Turnover	0.5
		Irrecoverable VAT	1.0
		Salaries and class 1 NIC	1.5
		Car	
		Cost	1.0
		Class 1A NIC	1.5
		Additional overheads	0.5
		Income after tax	1.0
		Use Quantum Ltd	
		Turnover	0.5
		Irrecoverable VAT	1.0
		Annual fee	0.5
		Income after tax	0.5
			――――
			16.5
		Maximum	14.0
			――――
(b)	(i)	Relevance of domicile	1.0
		Relevance of location of shares	1.0
		Uncle's domicile in 2001	2.0
		Acquisition of domicile of choice in Heisenbergia	1.0
		Location of shares	1.0
		Double tax relief	1.0
			――――
			7.0
		Maximum	6.0
			――――
	(ii)	Inheritance tax	
		Chargeable lifetime transfer	1.0
		Annual exemptions	0.5
		Business property relief	0.5
		Covered by nil rate band	1.0
		Capital gains tax	
		Gain by reference to market value	1.0
		Gift holdover relief available	1.0
		Income tax	
		Payable by Niels, with reasons	2.0
		Tax credit for tax paid by trustees	0.5
		Stamp duty	1.0
			――――
			8.5
		Maximum	7.0
			――――
	(iii)	Two separate clients	1.0
		Statement of general rule	1.0
		Transfer of shares to trust	1.5
		Inheritance tax on gift from uncle	2.0
			――――
			5.5
		Maximum	4.0
			――――
		Appropriate style and presentation	2.0
		Effectiveness of communication	1.0
		Logical structure	1.0
			――――
			4.0
			――――
Total			**35.0**
			――――

39 POBLANO (ADAPTED) *Walk in the footsteps of a top tutor*

Key answer tips

This is a lengthy section A question, and the biggest task is sorting out the information and the requirements whilst also leaving enough time to answer the question. There are really four separate questions here, which could be attempted in any order, as there is no follow through of information.

Part (i) covers a comparison of net income for two different employment packages. This type of question is very popular at ATX, and once you have seen one they are all very similar. The accommodation benefit is pure TX knowledge, and illustrates how important it is to retain this knowledge. However, even without this you should still be able to score a good pass here.

The second part of the question, part (ii), covers property income. The rules regarding finance costs for residential properties are covered here. Be careful, as the treatment of finance costs for individuals, such as Poblano, is very different from the treatment for companies.

Part (iii) covers the popular topic of inheritance tax, but in a rather unusual way. The '12 possible situations' may put you off attempting this section, but the examining team does provide guidance on how to approach it – so if you heed their words and do not panic you should be able to score some marks.

The final part of the question, part (iv), covers the income tax treatment of trusts. Trusts are generally not a popular area with students, although this section is actually very straightforward if you have learnt the rules.

The highlighted words in the written sections are key phrases that markers are looking for.

Tutor's top tips

Again, the formal requirements at the end of the question serve only to highlight the number of marks available for each section. The detailed requirements are mainly in the email from the manager and in the memorandum given at the start of the question.

Highlight the requirements as you come across them, and don't forget to keep looking back at them to make sure your answer is focused.

The first requirement asks for 'notes for a meeting', with the 'briefest possible notes' where the numbers are not self-explanatory. This means that you must keep narrative to a minimum and should write in very short sentences. Bullet points are ideal.

MEETING NOTES

Date   7 June 2022

Subject   Poblano

(i)   Working in Manchester – Poblano's financial position

Tutor's top tips

Poblano wants to know how much better or worse off he will be compared to his current position. This means that you need to think about the additional net cash (or deficit) after taking into account any tax charges and expenses.

The first paragraph of the question states that Poblano earns £60,000 per year, so it is clear that any extra taxable employment income will be subject to 40% income tax and 2% NICs.

Living in the company flat

The calculations set out below are based on the information currently available.

	£
Additional salary	15,000
Less: Income tax (£15,000 × 40%)	(6,000)
Class 1 primary NICs (£15,000 × 2%)	(300)
Petrol and depreciation (£1,400 + £1,500) (Note 1)	(2,900)
	————
Additional salary after income tax, NICs and motoring expenses	5,800
Less: Income tax on benefit in respect of the use of the flat	
(£16,045 (W) × 40%)	(6,418)
Contribution towards the flat to be made by Poblano (£200 × 12)	(2,400)
	————
Poblano would be worse off by	(3,018)
	————
Additional salary required for Poblano not to be out of pocket	
(£3,018 ÷ 58%)	5,203
	————

Tutor's top tips

Remember to state the additional salary needed, and remember that this will also be received net of 40% income tax and 2% NICs, so needs to be grossed up by 100/58 (or divided by 58%).

If Poblano's additional salary and benefits increased his adjusted net income to more than £100,000 he would start to lose his personal allowance but that is not the case here.

Not living in the company flat

		£
Additional salary after income tax, NICs and motor expenses (as above)		5,800
Plus:	Mileage allowance (9,200 × 50p)	4,600
Less:	Income tax and NICs on mileage allowance	
	(£4,600 × 42%) (Note 2)	(1,932)
	Rent (£325 × 12) (Note 3)	(3,900)
Poblano would be better off by		4,568

Notes

1 The depreciation is not an immediate cost but will increase the funds needed by Poblano to purchase his next car.

 Poblano will not be able to claim a tax deduction for these costs as they relate to travelling to and from work and not to the performance of his duties.

2 The mileage allowance would be subject to tax and national insurance contributions as Poblano would be travelling to and from work and not in the performance of his duties.

 Manchester will not be a temporary workplace for Poblano because he expects to work there for more than two years.

Tutorial note

The mileage allowance is not exempt and the approved mileage allowance of 45p per mile is irrelevant here, as the travel from home to work is private mileage, not a business trip.

If Poblano had been sent to Manchester for less than two years, then the travel would represent travel from home to a temporary workplace, and would qualify as a business trip.

In this case, only the excess allowance of 5p per mile (50p – 45p) would be taxable, rather than all of it.

3 Poblano's aunt will not be subject to income tax on the rent.

 This is because it will be in respect of a (presumably) furnished room in her house and the rent does not exceed £7,500 per year.

Tutor's top tips

The question specifically asks for an explanation of the tax treatment of the mileage allowance and the rent paid to Poblano's aunt, so make sure that you provide this.

Further information required

- The cost of the furniture provided in the flat – there will be an annual taxable benefit equal to 20% of the cost.

- Any running costs (utilities and maintenance etc.) in respect of the flat borne by Capsicum Ltd – there will be a taxable benefit equal to the costs incurred.

- Any capital improvements made to the property before the start of the tax year for which the benefit is being calculated.

Working: Taxable benefit in respect of the use of the flat

	£
Annual value	9,605
Additional benefit (£517,000 – £75,000) × 2% (Note)	8,840
	18,445
Contribution to be made by Poblano (£200 × 12)	(2,400)
Accommodation benefit	16,045

Note: The cost of £517,000 will be increased by any capital improvements made to the property before the start of the tax year for which the benefit is being calculated.

Tutorial note

The current value of the property (when Poblano moves in) is not relevant in this case, as the property has been owned by the employer for less than six years.

(ii)   Poblano's cottage in Cornwall

The rental income from the cottage will be subject to income tax on a cash basis. The rent will be assessed to income tax in the tax year in which it is received and the letting agent fees and insurance will be deductible from the rental income when they are paid.

The mortgage interest is not deductible against rental income, but will be given basic rate tax relief as a deduction against Poblano's income tax liability.

Tutor's top tips

Rental income is assessed on the cash basis if gross rental receipts do not exceed £150,000 for the tax year. It is possible that Poblano could elect to be taxed on the accruals basis, but you should assume the cash basis is used unless you are told otherwise.

(iii)   **Property in Chilaca**

Inheritance tax liabilities

Tutor's top tips

This section of the question may have appeared daunting, as there are 12 possible situations to deal with. However, there are actually very few calculations needed, as a number of the situations result in the same amount of tax.

The examining team does hint at this in the question, and often they do give advice concerning the approach they want you to take with parts of questions.

Make sure that you follow this advice!

Key answer tips

Watch out for the following:

- There is no annual exemption, as Paprikash already makes gifts each year that use this.
- There is no lifetime tax, as a gift to an individual is a PET. The issue therefore revolves around charges arising as a result of death.

  In all cases, the nil rate band will be reduced by the gift in 2021, as this is less than seven years before the date of the gift/death.
- The residence nil rate band is not available as the property is not being left to a direct descendant.
- Death tax on a lifetime gift is usually based on the value of the gift at the date of gift, not at the date of death (*unless* the property falls in value), so any increases in value since the date of the gift are irrelevant for calculating death tax on a lifetime gift.
- Taper relief will be available for lifetime gifts, but only if the donor survives for at least three years.

Lifetime on 1 August 2022 – PET

Assumed Value at death (Note 1)	Death on 31 December 2024: IHT arising: (Note 2)		Death on 31 December 2026: IHT arising (Note 3)	
£		£		£
450,000	(£450,000 – £35,000) × 40% =	166,000	(£166,000 × 60%) =	99,600
600,000	(£600,000 – £35,000) × 40% =	226,000	(£226,000 × 60%) =	135,600
900,000	(£600,000 – £35,000) × 40% =	226,000	(£226,000 × 60%) =	135,600

Gift via will on 31 December 2024 or 31 December 2026 (Note 4)

Assumed Value at death (Note 1)	Death on 31 December 2024 or 2026: IHT arising: (Note 2)	
£		£
450,000	(£450,000 – £35,000) × 40% =	166,000
600,000	(£600,000 – £35,000) × 40% =	226,000
900,000	(£900,000 – £35,000) × 40% =	346,000

Notes

1   When Paprikash makes the gift it will be a potentially exempt transfer, thus, if the value of the property at the time of death is less than it was at the time of the gift, the inheritance tax payable will reflect the fall in value.

If the value at the time of death is higher than at the time of the gift, the 'frozen' value at the time of the gift is charged to tax at the death rates.

2   The nil rate band remaining following the gift into trust on 1 June 2021 will be:

(£325,000 – £290,000 CLT in June 2021) = £35,000.

Tutorial note

The value of the CLT on 1 June 2021 is £290,000 as:

- *the gift is a gift of a minority shareholding in quoted shares, which does not qualify for business property relief (BPR), and*

- *the annual exemptions have already been utilised.*

3   31 December 2026 would be between four and five years after the gift such that 40% taper relief would be available. Accordingly, the liability will be 60% of the liability calculated in respect of death occurring on 31 December 2024.

4   The date of death will not affect the amount of inheritance tax due.

Tutorial note

Note 4 is true, but only because it is assumed in the answer that the nil rate band does not change in the future.

In practice, the nil rate band can change in each tax year and therefore the amount of tax payable could be affected by the date of death.

Inheritance tax liabilities – conclusions

If the property is gifted on 1 August 2022, the inheritance tax due on death will never be more than the amount due if the property is transferred via Paprikash's will, even if the value of the property falls prior to the date of death.

Making a lifetime gift would turn out to be particularly beneficial if:

- The value of the property increases, as the tax would be based on the value as at 1 August 2022 rather than the value at the time of death.

- Paprikash survives the gift by more than three years such that taper relief would be available.

Tutor's top tips

Even if your calculations are not correct, you will still be able to score marks for drawing sensible conclusions.

Other issues

Tutor's top tips

The question asks for any 'other issues' that should be drawn to Poblano's attention. The most obvious issue is the continuing use of the property by Paprikash, which is mentioned a couple of times in the information.

There is also the issue of capital gains tax potentially arising on lifetime gifts.

Gift with reservation

Once the property has been given to Poblano, the occasional use of it by Paprikash may result in the gift being treated as a gift with reservation.

In these circumstances, the gift would be ignored for inheritance tax purposes and the property would then be included in Paprikash's death estate at its value at the time of death.

In order to ensure that the gift is effective for inheritance tax purposes Paprikash should have only minimal use of the property unless he pays Poblano a market rent.

Tutorial note

HMRC guidance is that visits of up to two weeks a year without the nephew, and up to a month with the nephew, would be acceptable as 'minimal' use for these purposes. Knowledge of this guidance is not expected in the exam, but is of interest!

If the uncle pays a full commercial rent for the use of the property gifted, the gift with reservation rules will not apply. The gift will only be treated as a PET.

Capital gains tax

Lifetime gift

If Paprikash is resident in the UK in the year in which he gives the property to Poblano, it will be necessary to calculate a capital gain on the gift of the property.

The gain would be the market value of the property less its cost. The gain, less any available annual exempt amount, would be taxed at 18% or 28% (residential property rates) depending on Paprikash's taxable income.

Tutorial note

If Paprikash is not resident in the UK in the year in which he gives the property to Poblano, the gain will be exempt from capital gains tax (subject to the temporary residence overseas rule).

Gift on death in the will

There would be no capital gains tax if the property were given to Poblano on death, via Paprikash's will.

(iv)   Tax treatment of trust income received by Poblano's daughter

Tutor's top tips

*Be careful that you don't waste time here. You only need to talk about the tax treatment of the **income** received from the trust by Poblano's daughter.*

There are six marks available, so your answer needs to reflect this. Note that the question does not tell you what type of trust it is, so you need to discuss the different types of trust and the tax treatment of income received from each.

The question clearly states that the income is dividend income, so don't waste time discussing any other types of income.

The trust will be either an interest in possession trust or a discretionary trust:

*   It will be an interest in possession trust if Piri has an absolute right to the income generated by the trust assets.
*   It will be a discretionary trust if the trustees have the right to accumulate the income and pay it to Piri when they choose.

It is understood that the only income received by the trustees of the trust is dividend income.

Interest in possession trust

- The income to which Piri is entitled must be grossed up at 100/92.5.
- The first £2,000 of dividend income will be taxed at 0% (i.e. there will be no tax).
- Where dividend income exceeds £2,000 and falls into Piri's basic rate band (after calculating the tax on her salary) it will be taxed at 7.5%.
- The balance of the income will be taxed at 32.5%.
- There will be a 7.5% tax credit.

Discretionary trust

- The income received must be grossed up at 100/55.
- Where the income falls into Piri's basic rate band it will be taxed at 20%.
- The balance of the income will be taxed at 40%.
- There will be a 45% tax credit.

Tutorial note

There is no £2,000 nil rate band for dividends received from a discretionary trust as the income is assessed on the beneficiary as non-savings income.

The 7.5% tax credit in respect of the dividend from the interest in possession trust and the 45% tax credit relating to the income from the discretionary trust are refundable.

Examiner's report

Note that part of this examiner's report has been deleted as it relates to a part of the question that is no longer examinable.

This was a substantial question in three parts. Although some of the question parts could be seen as easier or harder than others, all of the parts had some easily accessible marks and candidates benefited from attempting all parts rather than only attempting those that appeared to be straightforward.

Part (i) concerned the implications of a change to an employee's location of work. On the whole this part of the question was done reasonably well. However, in order to score a high mark for this part it was necessary to focus on the client's financial position and calculate how much better or worse off he was going to be as a result of the change. This required candidates to think in terms of income and costs (with tax as a cost) and to recognise that costs that are not tax deductible are still costs and are therefore still relevant. This aspect of the question was not handled particularly well.

The calculation of the benefit in respect of the flat provided by the company was done well. However, the majority of candidates failed to recognise that the mileage allowance related to travel to and from work and was therefore taxable in full.

It was pleasing to note that fewer candidates than in the past provided lengthy explanations of what they were going to do before getting on and doing it. However, the question asked for an explanation of the tax treatment of two particular points; the receipt of the mileage allowance and the receipt of the rent. Many candidates failed to provide these explanations. As noted above, in respect of question 1, candidates must identify and carry out all of the tasks in the question in order to maximise their marks.

Note that part (ii) of this question has been added to the original question to test a new area.

Part (iii) of the question concerned inheritance tax and the advantages of lifetime giving. At first sight it was a daunting question requiring the consideration of three possible property values, two dates of death and a lifetime gift or gift via will; a total of 12 possible situations. However, there was guidance from the 'manager' as to where to start together with the reassurance that 'you should find that the calculations do not take too long'.

It was very pleasing to find that the majority of candidates had no problem with this part of the question and that their knowledge of the basic mechanics of inheritance tax was sound. Candidates benefited from thinking rather than writing such that they were then able to realise that, for example, with a lifetime gift, the only difference between the two possible dates of death was the availability of taper relief. The best answers were admirably short and to the point.

The one area where candidates could have done better was in identifying the possible gift with reservation. The failure by many candidates to do this indicates, yet again, that some candidates do not take enough care in identifying all that has been asked of them.

The final part of the question concerned the tax treatment of income received from a trust. This was a test of knowledge, as opposed to application of knowledge, and candidates should have scored well.

However, the marks for this part were not as high as expected because candidates were not sufficiently careful in their approach. As always, the advice here is to stop and think. The question made it clear that the nature of the trust was not known and therefore candidates were expected to consider the income tax position of receipts from both an interest in possession trust and a discretionary trust. There was also the need to be specific and precise, as regards grossing up fractions and tax rates, rather than superficial and general in order to maximise the marks obtained.

		Marks
ACCA marking scheme		

		Marks
(i)	Salary less tax, national insurance contributions and motoring expenses	2.0
	Living in the company flat	
	Tax on the benefit	2.0
	Contribution	0.5
	Additional salary required	1.0
	Further information required	2.0
	Staying with aunt in Manchester	
	Calculations	1.5
	Mileage allowance	1.5
	Rent paid to aunt	1.5
		————
		12.0
	Maximum	10.0
		————
(ii)	Cash basis	0.5
	Treatment of income and expenses	1.0
	Treatment of mortgage interest	1.5
		————
		3.0
		————
(iii)	Inheritance tax liabilities	
	Nil band	1.0
	Lifetime gift	
	Value at time of gift and tax rate	1.0
	Fall in value post gift	1.0
	Taper relief	1.0
	Gift via will	1.5
	Full set of outcomes	0.5
	Conclusions (1 mark each, maximum 2 marks)	2.0
	Explanatory notes (½ mark each)	2.0
	Gift with reservation	2.5
	Capital gains tax	1.5
		————
		14.0
	Maximum	12.0
		————
(iv)	Nature of the trust	2.0
	Tax treatment (2 × 2 marks)	4.0
		————
		6.0
		————
	Appropriate style and presentation	2.0
	Effectiveness of communication	2.0
		————
		4.0
		————
Total		**35.0**
		————

40   MIRTOON (ADAPTED)

  Online question assistance and Walk in the footsteps of a top tutor

Key answer tips

There are two separate parts to this section A question, which could be attempted in any order. There are a mix of numerical and discursive requirements in this question. It is best to set out any detailed calculations in the spreadsheet response option in the exam, with discursive elements better suited to the word processor. Ensure you make it clear which part of the question is being answered where by use of headings.

Part (a) requires calculation of how a disposal of assets, use of trading losses and departure from the UK will affect an individual's financial position. Although the calculations are generally straightforward, this part is challenging due to its size and the fact that there is no indication as to how the 16 marks available are split.

Part (b) asks for a letter that covers three totally separate issues, which could be dealt with in any order.

Part (b)(i) requires discussion of the VAT implications of cessation of a business, and is pure TX level knowledge.

Part (b)(ii) covers overseas aspects of income tax and capital gains tax for an individual who is leaving the UK. This area is tested regularly, so you must ensure that you learn the complex rules that apply.

Part (b)(iii) asks for explanation of the gifts with reservation rules relating to inheritance tax. These rules are tested regularly, so you should make sure you are familiar with them.

The highlighted words in the written sections are key phrases that markers are looking for.

Tutor's top tips

Again, the formal requirements at the end of the question just tell you how many marks are available for each section. The detailed requirements are all in the email from your manager.

There are four marks available for professional skills, such as preparing your answer in letter format in part (b). You should think about how you present your answer, and make sure you explain yourself clearly to score as many of these marks as possible.

(a)   Mirtoon's financial position

Tutor's top tips

*It is important that you answer the question here. You are asked to calculate **the total** of the after-tax proceeds from the sale of the house and business assets, the tax saving from the trading losses and 'any other tax liabilities'.*

A good approach to take would be to set out a pro forma working, fill in the easy figures such as the proceeds from the sale of the house and business, and then cross reference this to separate workings for the calculation of the other missing amounts.

Even if your individual workings are wrong, you will still gain a mark for satisfying the requirement and arriving at a total.

Total net proceeds

	£
Proceeds from sale of home	730,000
Proceeds from sale of business premises	120,000
Less: Capital gains tax in respect of business premises (W1)	(6,200)
Proceeds from sale of other business assets	14,000
After-tax proceeds from sale of home and business assets	857,800
Tax saving in respect of trading losses (W3)	22,868
Other tax liabilities	
Capital gains tax in respect of agricultural land (W1)	(11,500)
Total net proceeds	869,168

Workings

(W1) Capital gains tax

Tutor's top tips

*Think about **all** of the gains that will arise before you calculate the capital gains tax payable.*

There will be a held over gain that crystallises when Mirtoon leaves the country.

Remember that capital losses and the annual exempt amount can be set off against the gains in the most beneficial way, in order to minimise the tax payable.

	£	£
Gains qualifying for business asset disposal relief (BADR)		
Sale of business premises (W2)	62,000	
Not qualifying for BADR		
Sale of house (Note 1)		0
Gain crystallising on agricultural land (Note 2)		72,000
Less: Annual exempt amount (Note 3)		(12,300)
Less: Capital losses brought forward (Note 3)		(2,200)
	———	———
Taxable gains	62,000	57,500
	———	———
Capital gains tax:		
Qualifying gains (£62,000 × 10%) (Note 4)	6,200	
Non-qualifying gains (£57,500 × 20%) (Note 5)		11,500
	———	———

Explanatory notes

Tutor's top tips

Although the requirement is to 'calculate', you are asked to include explanatory notes, particularly in relation to the availability of reliefs and allowances and the offset of the trading losses. There will be marks available for providing these notes, so try to remember to do this.

1   Private residence relief is available to exempt the gain on the house, as it was used as Mirtoon's main residence.

2   As Mirtoon emigrates from the UK within six years of the end of the tax year in which the gift of the agricultural land was made, the held over gain from the time of the gift crystallises and is chargeable on the day before emigration (i.e. January 2023), and will be taxed in the tax year 2022/23.

Tutorial note

There is an exception to the rule regarding the emigration of the donee.

Where the donee goes overseas to take up full time employment abroad a chargeable gain will not crystallise on his departure from the UK provided:

1   he resumes his status as UK resident within three years, and

2   he has not disposed of the asset whilst abroad.

However, as Mirtoon is leaving the UK for at least four years, this exception does not apply here.

3   The capital losses and the annual exempt amount can be set off in the most tax-efficient manner. Accordingly, they will be deducted from gains that would otherwise be taxed at 20%.

4   The gain in respect of the business premises will qualify for BADR because this was an asset:

- used in a business that has now ceased, and
- was sold within three years of cessation, and
- was held for at least two years before the disposal

Accordingly, the gain will be taxed at 10%.

5   Mirtoon's basic rate band is fully used by his income and qualifying gains. Accordingly, the non-qualifying gains will all fall into the higher rate band and will be taxed at 20%.

Tutorial note

Even though Mirtoon does have some of his basic rate band remaining after deducting his taxable income, this must be set against the gains qualifying for BADR first. As these qualifying gains alone are greater than £37,700, there is clearly no basic rate band left. Had there been, any non-qualifying gains in the basic band would be taxed at 10% instead of 20%.

Tutor's top tips

Don't worry if you missed the gain crystallising on the agricultural land. In that case, you would have been given credit for setting off the capital losses and the annual exempt amount against the gain on the business premises, and you would still be given the mark for summarising the net cash position based on your figures.

(W2)   Chargeable gain on sale of business premises

	£
Sale proceeds	120,000
Less: Cost	(58,000)
Chargeable gain	62,000

(W3) Tax saving in respect of trading losses

Tutor's top tips

*The requirement specifically tells you to offset the loss against total income of the previous tax year (i.e. normal carry back relief) and **not** to consider any other loss reliefs.*

Accordingly, although terminal loss relief would be available here for the loss arising in the last 12 months of trading, there will be no marks for calculating the terminal loss or for discussing terminal loss relief.

Assessable trading loss for the tax year 2022/23

	£
Loss for year ended 30 June 2022	(20,000)
Loss for six months ending 31 December 2022	(17,000)
Less: Overlap profits	(7,600)
Loss for the tax year 2022/23 (Note 1)	(44,600)

Tutorial note

In the final tax year of trading the loss is matched to the tax year using the current year basis rules in exactly the same way as a profit, including the deduction of overlap profits from commencement, which will increase the loss available for relief.

There is no cap on the use of the trading loss against other income as the loss is less than £50,000.

Income tax liability for the tax year 2021/22

Tutor's top tips

Note that in this question, you are told to prepare calculations of the income tax liability both before and after the offset of losses. This is unusual, as the examining team normally likes you to work in the margin and not prepare full computations! However, you should always do as you are asked in order to maximise your marks.

Watch out for the personal allowance. Remember that this is reduced if adjusted net income is greater than £100,000, but will effectively be 'reinstated' after setting off the losses, as the adjusted net income then falls below the £100,000 limit.

	Before offset of losses	After offset of losses
	£	£
Trading income	97,000	97,000
Bank interest	28,950	28,950
Total income	125,950	125,950
Less: Loss relief	(0)	(44,600)
Net income	125,950	81,350
Less: PA (Note 2)	(0)	(12,570)
Taxable income	125,950	68,780

Analysis of income

Before: Savings £28,950, non-savings £97,000

After: Savings £28,950, non-savings £39,830

Income tax

£	£			
37,700	37,700	× 20% (Non-sav)	7,540	7,540
59,300	2,130	× 40% (Non-sav)	23,720	852
500	500	× 0% (Sav)(Note 3)	0	0
28,450	28,450	× 40% (Sav)	11,380	11,380
125,950	68,780			

	Before	After
Income tax liability	42,640	19,772

Tax saving (£42,640 – £19,772)   22,868

Explanatory notes

1 As the tax year 2022/23 is Mirtoon's final tax year, the assessment will include any losses not yet assessed (i.e. both of the accounting periods ending in the tax year 2022/23, less the overlap profits from commencement).

2 The personal allowance is reduced by £1 for every £2 by which adjusted net income exceeds £100,000, and is reduced to £0 where the adjusted net income is greater than £125,140.

3 As Mirtoon is a higher rate taxpayer he will have a savings income nil rate band of £500.

Tutorial note

As the non-savings income is greater than £5,000, the interest income does not fall within the starting rate band.

It is possible to calculate the tax saving at the margin as follows:

	£
Benefit of loss (£44,600 × 40%)	*17,840*
Benefit of PA now available (£12,570 × 40%)	*5,028*
	22,868

However, the email from the manager specifically asked you to prepare calculations of Mirtoon's income tax liability before and after the offset of the losses, so that is the approach you should have adopted.

(b) **LETTER**

Firm's address

Mirtoon's address

9 December 2022

Dear Mirtoon

Tutor's top tips

There are marks available for using the correct format for your letter. Try to make sure that your answer looks like a letter. Remember to address Mirtoon as 'you' as you are writing the letter to him, and remember to sign off your letter with 'yours sincerely'.

Departure from the UK

Please find below the information you require regarding the various tax matters to be considered on the cessation of your business and departure from the UK.

(i) **VAT implications of the cessation of your business**

You must deregister for VAT when you cease to make taxable supplies and notify HM Revenue and Customs within 30 days of cessation (i.e. by 30 January 2023). Failure to do so could result in a penalty.

As you are not selling your business as a going concern, you will need to charge output VAT on any assets sold prior to deregistration.

If you still hold inventory and non-current assets (on which you have recovered input VAT) at the date of deregistration, you must account for output VAT on the replacement value of these assets. However, this charge will be waived if the output VAT is less than £1,000.

Tutorial note

If Mirtoon was to sell his business as a going concern, to a VAT registered person, the transfer would not be a taxable supply. This is not the case here, as the question specifically tells you that Mirtoon has not been able to find a buyer for his business and is, therefore, going to cease trading and then sell any remaining business assets.

(ii)   Liability to UK income tax and capital gains tax whilst living in Koro

Tutor's top tips

Overseas aspects of income tax and capital gains tax are often tested in the exam. In order to gain a good mark in this type of question, you must ensure that you apply your knowledge to the scenario and don't just talk generally about the tax implications of residence and domicile.

You should deal with income tax and capital gains tax separately, as the rules are not the same for the two taxes.

As you are going abroad to work full time, and are not planning to make any return trips, you will automatically be non-UK resident for the tax years that you are away.

The tax year that you leave will be split, as you will be leaving to work full time overseas and will not spend any time in the UK after departure, having been UK resident in the previous tax year, UK resident in the current year and not UK resident in the following year.

Therefore, you will lose your residency from the date that you start working overseas, and will regain it on the date you return.

Income tax

As you will not be UK resident, you will not be taxed in the UK on your overseas income.

Your UK income is still taxable, so you will be taxed on your UK bank interest.

Capital gains tax

Generally, you will not be subject to UK capital gains tax if you are not resident in the UK unless you dispose of UK property.

However, as you have been resident in the UK for at least four of the seven years before leaving the UK, the temporary non-residence rules will apply.

According to these rules, you must remain outside the UK for five years to avoid capital gains tax on assets owned before your departure. If you sell such an asset while you are abroad, you will be taxed on the gain in the tax year of return to the UK.

Sale of agricultural land

If you sell the agricultural land in June 2024, while you are in Koro, then the disposal will be subject to non-UK resident capital gains tax. A gain will be chargeable equal to the proceeds less the market value as at 5 April 2019.

If you return to the UK within five years (i.e. before January 2028), a further gain will be taxed in the tax year of return. A gain will be calculated equal to proceeds less cost and then any gain already assessed to non-UK resident capital gains tax in 2024 will be deducted. However, if you return after January 2028 there will not be a further gain taxed in the UK.

Sale of UK residential home

Tutor's top tips

The examining team have stated that only residential properties acquired after 5 April 2015 will be examined so you do not need to be aware of how to calculate a gain or loss on a property acquired before this date.

If you were to sell your UK home whilst you are in Koro, the gain will not be exempt. However, only gains accruing after 5 April 2015 are chargeable and even then, only to the extent that they are not covered by private residence relief (PRR) or the annual exempt amount.

As your home was purchased after 5 April 2015, the whole gain would be chargeable to capital gains tax.

PRR will exempt any part of the gain that relates to periods of occupation.

For periods of non-occupation (once you have moved to Koro) the gain may be chargeable, although the last nine months of ownership will be covered by PRR.

If there are any further periods of non-occupation, the whole tax year (not just the actual period of occupation) will be treated as a period of non-occupation, and thus not exempt, unless you have stayed in your house for a total of at least 90 nights in the tax year.

Any gain remaining after PRR and the annual exempt amount will be taxed at 18% or 28%, depending on the level of your UK taxable income and consequential remaining basic rate band in the normal way.

You should note that HMRC must be notified of the disposal of any UK property by a non-UK resident individual within 30 days of the conveyance of the property, even if there is no CGT liability.

(iii) **Inheritance tax planning**

Gifts with reservation

Tutor's top tips

Gifts with reservation appear regularly in the ATX exam, so you should be familiar with the rules that apply here.

A 'gift with reservation of benefit' (GWR) is a lifetime gift where:

• the legal ownership of an asset is transferred, but

• the donor retains some benefit in the asset gifted.

For example, the gift of a house, but the donor continues to live in it.

Special anti-avoidance rules apply to a GWR to ensure that these gifts do not escape from an inheritance tax charge.

The gift is effectively ignored, and the asset is still included in the estate of the donor when they die.

Any tax arising is payable by the legal owner of the asset (i.e. the donee).

However, HMRC have the right to use an alternative treatment if this gives a higher overall liability on the death of the donor. This recognises the GWR as though it was a true gift at the time of the gift, and the asset is not then included in the donor's estate.

Usually including the asset in the estate gives the higher inheritance tax charge. This is because capital assets normally appreciate in value and no annual exemptions are available in the death estate.

There are some exceptions. A gift will not be treated as a gift with reservation if:

• the donor pays full consideration for the benefit retained. For example, if they pay full market rate rent for the use of a property; or

• the circumstances of the donor have changed in a way that could not be foreseen at the time of the gift. For example, if the donor moves out of the property but then later becomes ill and moves back in to be cared for by their family.

Please do not hesitate to contact me if you require any further information.

Yours sincerely

Tax manager

Examiner's report

In part (a), the sale of the house was handled well with almost all candidates identifying the availability of private residence relief. The crystallisation of the heldover gain in respect of the agricultural land (due to Mirtoon becoming non-resident), on the other hand, was spotted by only a small minority of candidates. However, this was an easy point to miss and it was possible to obtain a perfectly good mark without any reference to it.

The treatment of the losses arising on the cessation of the business was not handled well due to a lack of knowledge of the closing year rules. This meant that many candidates struggled to determine the assessment for the final years of trading. There was also a considerable number of candidates who erroneously treated the overlap profits brought forward as taxable profits in the final tax year as opposed to being part of the allowable loss. The unincorporated trader is examined with great regularity and candidates are likely to benefit from knowing, in particular, the opening and closing years rules.

A minority of candidates demonstrated a lack of precision when considering the tax due in respect of the sale of the house and business and the tax saving in respect of the offset of the trading losses. This lack of precision included a failure to take account of the capital losses brought forward and/or the annual exempt amount and the omission of the personal allowance from the income tax computations. It was important to consider the personal allowance as Mirtoon's income exceeded £100,000 such that the personal allowance was restricted.

Note that this part of the question has been amended since it was originally set.

Part (b) was in three parts and produced a wide variety of answers.

Part (i) concerned the VAT implications of Mirtoon ceasing to trade. This part was done reasonably well, although, perhaps not as well as expected. Some candidates made it hard for themselves by writing generally rather than addressing the facts of the question. In particular, many candidates wrote at length about the sale of a business as a going concern. However, the question made it clear that the business was to cease with the assets then being sold. The vast majority of candidates identified the need to deregister. However, a considerably smaller number pointed out the possible need to account for output tax on business assets owned as at cessation.

Part (ii) concerned Mirtoon's liability to income tax and capital gains tax whilst living overseas. There were some good answers to this part but also two particular areas of confusion.

The first area of confusion related to the taxation of income where an individual is not resident in the UK. It needs to be recognised that where an individual is not resident in the UK, any foreign income will not be subject to UK income tax. Where many candidates went wrong was to imagine that the remittance basis was relevant here (perhaps because Mirtoon was not resident but continued to be domiciled in the UK). This led candidates to write at length about the remittance basis thus wasting time.

The second area of confusion concerned the temporary non-resident rules. These rules relate to capital gains tax and cause gains that would otherwise not be taxable in the UK to be so taxable if the individual returns to the UK within five years of leaving. However, a minority of candidates incorrectly treated these rules as an extension of the residency rules as they relate to income tax.

The section concerning the sale of Mirtoon's UK home whilst non-UK resident is a new section added following the change in rules in FA2015.

Part (iii) concerned inheritance tax and gifts with reservation. The good news was that the vast majority of candidates knew all about gifts with reservation and answered this part of the question well.

The bad news, however, was that many candidates did not restrict their answers to the above area but wrote at length about inheritance tax generally. Candidates must take care in identifying what has been asked and try to avoid addressing other areas.

The original question also contained a section on the associated operations rules which have since been removed from the ATX syllabus.

		ACCA marking scheme		Marks
(a)		Sale of home and business premises		
		Chargeable gains		1.0
		Private residence relief		1.0
		Capital gains tax		1.0
		Agricultural land		2.5
		Trading losses		
		Loss available for relief		2.0
		Tax relief		4.0
		Total proceeds net of tax adjustments		2.0
		Explanatory notes (one mark each – maximum four marks)		4.0
				——
				17.5
			Maximum	16.0
				——
(b)	(i)	Requirement to deregister		1.5
		Output tax		2.0
				——
				3.5
			Maximum	3.0
				——
	(ii)	Status		2.5
		Income tax		1.5
		Capital gains tax		7.0
				——
				11.0
			Maximum	8.0
				——
	(iii)	Gifts with reservation		5.0
			Maximum	4.0
				——
		Approach to problem solving		1.0
		Appropriate style and presentation		1.0
		Effectiveness of communication		2.0
				——
				4.0
				——
Total				35.0
				——

41   SHUTTELLE (ADAPTED) *Walk in the footsteps of a top tutor*

Key answer tips

This section B question is divided into two distinct parts which are unrelated so could be attempted in either order.

Part (a) is a question on personal pension contributions and you are required to calculate the income tax liability of an individual who has contributed to a personal pension scheme in excess of the annual allowance. Based on your calculation, you are then required to calculate the tax relief obtained as a result of the personal pension contribution. In order to do this, you needed to determine if the annual allowance should be restricted. Note that this potential restriction has been introduced since this question was set in the ATX exam and therefore did not feature in the original question.

Part (b) is a question regarding the remittance basis for three individuals. In addition, you are required to state whether or not the remittance basis charge is applicable to the individuals and if so quantify it.

The highlighted words in the written sections are key phrases that markers are looking for.

(a)   Shuttelle

Tutor's top tips

You should score some easy marks for a basic income tax computation which includes salary and an accommodation benefit.

The key was recognising that there would also be an excess pension contribution. You may not have realised that the contributions by the employer must be included in the excess pension contribution calculation. However, you would still score some marks for recognising that the excess pension contributions needed to be included as part of the tax calculation.

In order to calculate the annual allowance available, you had to consider if there was any unused relief brought forward from the previous three years and whether the annual allowance for the tax year 2021/22 needed to be restricted. Remember the annual allowance is £40,000 for the tax year 2021/22 but can be increased by any unused AA in the previous three years, starting with the earliest year first.

The personal pension contributions also extend the basic and higher rate bands.

Note that the annual allowance charge is calculated using the taxpayer's marginal rate of tax.

A numerical requirement such as this is best suited to being prepared in the spreadsheet response option in the exam. You can make use of formulae to help bring figures from workings into the main computation, and also to calculate the tax for you. Make sure your figures are clearly labelled so it is clear to the marker what you are trying to calculate.

(i) **Income tax liability – 2021/22**

	£
Salary	204,000
Accommodation (W1)	3,875
	————
Net income	207,875
Less: Personal allowance (W2)	(12,570)
	————
Taxable income (all non-savings)	195,305
	————

£		£
157,700 × 20% (W3)		31,540
37,605 × 40%		15,042
————		
195,305		
59,000 × 40% (Annual allowance charge) (W4)		23,600
		————
Income tax liability		70,182
		————

Tutorial note

The basic rate and higher rate limits are extended due to the pension contributions. Accordingly, the excess pension contributions will be taxed at 40%.

Workings

(W1) Benefit in respect of accommodation

	£
Annual value	7,000
Expensive accommodation benefit	
((£500,000 – £75,000) × 2%)	8,500
	————
	15,500
	————
Benefit in 2021/22 (£15,500 × 3/12)	3,875
	————

(W2) Personal allowance

	£
Net income	207,875
Less: Gross PPCs	(120,000)
	————
Adjusted net income (ANI)	87,875
	————

As ANI is < £100,000; the full personal allowance is available.

(W3) Extended basic and higher rate bands

	£	£
Current bands	37,700	150,000
Add: Gross PPCs	120,000	120,000
Revised bands	157,700	270,000

(W4) Annual allowance charge

	£
Gross contributions by Shuttelle	120,000
Gross contributions by Din Ltd	4,000
Less: Annual allowance available in 2021/22 (W5)	(65,000)
Annual allowance charge	59,000

(W5) Annual allowance available – 2021/22

	£
Brought forward from 2019/20 (£40,000 – £9,000 – £4,000)	27,000
Used in 2020/21 (£40,000 – £38,000 – £4,000)	(2,000)
Current year available in 2021/22 (W6)	40,000
	65,000

(W6) Threshold income – 2021/22

	£
Net income	207,875
Less: Gross PPCs	(120,000)
Threshold income	87,875

As Shuttelle's threshold income does not exceed £200,000 it is not necessary to calculate her adjusted income to determine if a restriction to the 2021/22 annual allowance is needed.

(ii) **Total tax relief in respect of the gross personal pension contributions**

Tutor's top tips

This is a comparison of the income tax liability without the pension contribution with your answer from part (i).

Don't forget

* *the tax relief at source as personal pension contributions are paid net of 20% tax, and*
* *without the PPC relief, there would be no personal allowance available.*

	£		£
	37,700	× 20%	7,540
	112,300	× 40%	44,920
	———		
	150,000		
	57,875	× 45%	26,044
	———		
	207,875		
	———		———
Income tax liability – ignoring the gross PPCs			78,504
Income tax liability – reflecting the gross PPCs (part (i))			(70,182)
Pension contributions – tax relief at source			
(£120,000 × 20%)			24,000
			———
Total tax relief in respect of pension contributions			32,322
			———

Tutorial note

1 When calculating the liability ignoring the pension contributions, there would be no personal allowance due to the level of the net income.

2 By charging tax on the excess pension contributions, relief is effectively only given for £61,000 (£120,000 – £59,000), the balance of the contributions, as set out below:

	£		£
57,875 × 45% (additional rate)			*26,044*
3,125 × 40% (higher rate)			*1,250*
	———		
61,000			
	———		
Tax saved in respect of personal allowance becoming available:			
(£12,570 × 40%)			*5,028*
			———
Total tax relief in respect of pension contributions			*32,322*
			———

(b)   The three non-UK domiciled individuals

Tutor's top tips

Overseas aspects for individuals is a commonly tested syllabus area as it is a new topic in the ATX syllabus and the rules have changed significantly in recent years, so make sure you have learnt the rules.

(i)   The availability of the remittance basis and the remittance basis charge

The availability of the remittance basis

The remittance basis is available to UK resident individuals who are not domiciled in the UK.

Accordingly:

*   the remittance basis is available to Lin and Yu.

*   the remittance basis is not available to Nan as he is not UK resident.

The remittance basis charge

Tutor's top tips

Don't forget that if an individual is not domiciled in the UK then the level of unremitted overseas income and gains is significant.

If unremitted overseas income and gains is < £2,000 then the remittance basis is automatic, otherwise it must be claimed.

The remittance basis charge is assessed on individuals who have claimed the remittance basis (not where the remittance basis is automatically applied) and differs depending upon the length of time they have been resident in the UK.

*   *Resident for 7 out of the last 9 tax years the charge is £30,000*

*   *Resident for 12 out of the last 14 tax years the charge is £60,000.*

Lin has unremitted overseas income and gains of less than £2,000. Accordingly, the remittance basis will apply automatically, such that there will not be a remittance basis charge.

Nan has unremitted overseas income and gains of more than £2,000. If Nan were able to claim the remittance basis, the remittance basis charge would be £60,000 because he has been resident in the UK for 12 of the 14 tax years prior to the tax year 2021/22.

Yu has unremitted overseas income and gains of more than £2,000. The remittance basis charge would be £30,000 because Yu has been resident in the UK for 7 of the 9 tax years prior to the tax year 2021/22.

(ii)   **Deemed UK domicile**

A non-UK domiciled individual born overseas would be deemed to be UK domiciled for the purposes of income tax and capital gains tax if:

- they were resident for 15 of the 20 tax years preceding the relevant tax year, unless
- there is no tax year beginning after 5 April 2017 in which they were UK resident.

Examiner's report

Part (a) was a tricky question to get absolutely correct, and very few candidates did so, but there were plenty of marks available to candidates who knew how to put an income tax computation together and were aware of the rules relating to the determination of the annual allowance for a particular year. On the whole candidates scored reasonably well.

In particular, most candidates handled the accommodation benefit well and knew that the tax bands needed to be extended. Many candidates were also aware that there was a three-year rule in respect of the annual allowance, although many were not absolutely clear as to how the rule worked. Many candidates missed the fact that the personal allowance would be available in full possibly because they did not pause and think at that stage of the calculation. Tax calculations should be done as a series of small steps with thought at each step in order to ensure that important matters are not missed.

The second part of the question concerned the remittance basis and was not done particularly well. The problem here was that candidates did not have a clear set of rules. Instead, they had an awareness of a series of technical terms and time periods that were all confused. This made it very difficult to score well.

The first thing candidates had to do was to explain whether or not the remittance basis was available to each of three individuals. This required a statement of the availability of the remittance basis together with a reason. For those who did not know the rules there was a 50:50 chance as regards the availability of the remittance basis. However, the reason for its availability or non-availability caused a lot more problems.

Candidates must learn the rules and be able to apply them and state them clearly. In addition, the marks available for giving a reason are only awarded where the whole of the reason given is correct. For example, the remittance basis was available to Lin because he was UK resident but not UK domiciled. Candidates who stated this together with various time periods of residency could not score the mark for the reason as it was not clear from their answer whether it was his residence and domicile status that was relevant or the time periods.

The second thing candidates had to do was to state, with reasons, the remittance basis charge applicable to each of the individuals on the assumption that the remittance basis was available to all of them. Again, this was not done particularly well due to many candidates having a very confused knowledge of the rules. One particular area of confusion related to the automatic applicability of the remittance basis where unremitted income and gains are less than £2,000; many candidates thought the rule related to the level of remitted income and gains.

		ACCA marking scheme		
				Marks
(a)	(i)	Benefit in respect of accommodation		2.0
		Personal allowance		1.0
		Tax bands		1.5
		Relevance of employer's pension contributions		1.0
		Annual allowance		3.0
		Tax on excess pension contributions		1.5
				———
				10.0
			Maximum	8.0
				———
	(ii)	Comparison with original liability		2.5
		Tax relief at source on pension contributions		1.0
				———
				3.5
			Maximum	3.0
				———
(b)	(i)	Availability of remittance basis		
		General rule		1.5
		Application of the rule to the individuals		1.5
		The remittance basis charge		
		Lin		1.0
		Nan		1.5
		Yu		1.5
				———
				7.0
				———
	(ii)	Deemed UK domicile		2.0
				———
Total				**20.0**
				———

42 CATE AND RAVI *Walk in the footsteps of a top tutor*

Key answer tips

This section B question is about a husband, Ravi, who is UK resident but not domiciled and his wife, Cate who is a sole trader.

Part (a) requires calculation of the cost of Cate taking on an employee, and is similar to requirements seen in previous exam questions.

In part (b) Cate is planning to sell some items she inherited and you need to consider the badges of trade in relation to this new venture.

Part (c) covers the commonly tested topic of arising versus remittance basis for a non-UK domiciled individual, but for CGT rather than income tax.

The highlighted words in parts (b) and (c) are key phrases that markers are looking for.

(a)   Cate – After-tax cost of taking on the part time employee

Tutor's top tips

The first three headings from the scenario relate to this part of the question. Make sure you use all of the information given; in particular, consider why you have been provided with Cate's dividend income.

The requirement is to 'calculate', so you do not need to provide written explanations, although you should show all of your workings.

You are calculating the after-tax cost for Cate, so you do not need to consider the tax payable by the employee.

	£
Salary	12,000
Medical insurance – cost to employer	1,300
Class 1A NICs (1,300 × 13.8%)	179
Mileage allowance (£0.50 × 62 × 48 weeks)	1,488
Class 1 NICs (W1)	457
Total additional expenditure	15,424
Less: Income tax and class 4 NIC saving (£15,424 × 42%) (Note)	(6,478)
Income tax saving on personal allowance (£7,712 × 40%) (W2)	(3,085)
After-tax cost	5,861

Tutorial note

The additional expenditure is deductible from Cate's taxable trading profit and will save income tax and class 4 NICs.

The income tax saving is at 40% as Cate is a higher rate taxpayer. Class 4 NICs are saved at 2% as Cate's taxable trading profits are above the upper limit for class 4.

Workings

(W1) Class 1 NICs: employer's contributions

	£
Salary: (£12,000 − £8,840) × 13.8%	436
Mileage allowance: ((£0.50 − 0.45) × 62 × 48 weeks) × 13.8%	21
	457

Tutorial note

1   *Only the excess mileage allowance over 45p per mile is liable to NICs.*

2   *Medical insurance is subject to Class 1A.*

3   *The £4,000 employment allowance would already have been fully offset against the class 1 NICs payable in respect of D-Designs' existing employees.*

(W2) Personal allowance

	Before taking on employee		After taking on employee	
	£	£	£	£
Basic PA		12,570		12,570
Less: Abatement				
ANI (W3)	120,000		104,576	
Less: Limit	(100,000)		(100,000)	
	————		————	
	20,000		4,576	
	————		————	
50% deduction		(10,000)		(2,288)
		————		————
Revised PA		2,570		10,282
		————		————
Increase in PA (£10,282 – £2,570)			7,712	
			————	

Tutorial note

Before taking on the additional part time employee Cate's adjusted net income was £120,000, so her personal allowance would have been reduced to £2,570.

After taking on the employee, Cate's adjusted net income will be reduced by the total additional expenditure of £15,424. She will therefore be entitled to a reduced personal allowance for the year of £10,282.

(W3) Adjusted net income

	Before taking on employee	After taking on employee
	£	£
Trading profit	90,000	90,000
Dividends	30,000	30,000
	————	————
	120,000	120,000
Less: Additional allowable expenditure	–	(15,424)
	————	————
Total income = Net income = ANI	120,000	104,576
	————	————

(b)   Cate – Sale of second-hand books

Tutor's top tips

To score the marks here you must apply the badges of trade to the scenario.

Make sure you structure your answer with headings, and give a conclusion for an easy mark.

Badges of trade

The tax treatment of the income from the sale of the second-hand books will depend on whether or not Cate is deemed to be carrying on a trade of selling books.

If she is, the income will be treated as trading income, and subject to income tax in the same way as her taxable profits from D-Designs.

If not, then the sales will be dealt with under the capital gains tax rules.

In determining how Cate should be taxed, HMRC will make reference to the 'badges of trade', a series of factors to be considered in order to determine whether or not an individual is trading.

Factors indicating that the sale of books does not constitute a trade

– Cate has inherited the books; she did not buy them for resale.

– Selling second-hand books is not related in any way to Cate's existing business, the running of a chain of dress shops.

– The frequency of transactions; this would appear to be a one-off batch of sales.

Factors indicating that the sale of books does constitute a trade

– Having some of the books rebound may be viewed as 'supplementary work' in order to generate increased profit.

– Taking steps to find purchasers by advertising the books on the internet could indicate a trading motive.

Conclusion

Based on the above factors, it is more likely that the capital gains tax treatment will apply.

For capital gains tax purposes books are chattels so, as no individual book is likely to have a value in excess of £6,000, if the capital gains tax treatment does apply, any gains made by Cate will be exempt from tax.

Tutorial note

Marks were available for discussion of any relevant factors and for reaching a sensible conclusion.

(c) **Ravi – Capital gains tax on overseas property gain**

Tutor's top tips

It is more efficient to perform your workings for the two options alongside one another. This can be done easily in the spreadsheet response option in the exam.

Remember to give a conclusion as you have been asked to advise. This is best presented in the word processor, but remember to reference through to any workings in the spreadsheet.

Arising basis

Ravi is resident in the UK, so would normally be liable to pay UK capital gains tax on disposals of both his UK and overseas assets on an arising basis.

On this basis, the gain on the disposal of the overseas property is fully liable to UK capital gains tax, as his annual exempt amount for the tax year 2021/22 has already been used.

As Ravi is a higher rate taxpayer, capital gains tax will be charged at the residential property rate of 28% and the capital gains tax payable will therefore be £19,600 (W).

Double tax relief will be available against this UK capital gains tax liability for any tax suffered on the same gain in Goland.

Remittance basis

However, as Ravi is not domiciled in the UK, he should consider making a claim for the remittance basis for the taxation of his overseas gain.

As he has not remitted any of the proceeds from the sale, if he makes such a claim, there will be no gain chargeable in the UK.

However, he will lose his entitlement to the annual exempt amount, which will generate an additional capital gains tax liability of £3,444 (W) on his UK asset gains.

Additionally, as Ravi has been resident in the UK since February 2014 (at least seven out of the last nine tax years), he will be liable to pay a remittance basis charge of £30,000.

The total amount payable as a result of claiming the remittance basis would therefore be £33,444 (W).

Conclusion

A remittance basis claim will not be worthwhile for the tax year 2021/22.

Working: Capital gains tax

	Arising basis £	Remittance basis £
Overseas gain	70,000	N/A
UK gains	12,300	12,300
Less: AEA	(12,300)	N/A
Taxable gains	70,000	12,300
Capital gains tax at 28%	19,600	3,444
Plus: Remittance basis charge	N/A	30,000
Total capital gains tax	19,600	33,444

Examiner's report

Part (a) concerned an individual, Cate, running a successful unincorporated business that required an additional part-time employee. The requirement was to calculate the annual cost of employing the part-time employee.

The first thing candidates had to do was determine all of the costs that were going to be incurred. On the whole this was done reasonably well, although some candidates confused cost with tax deductibility, and some simply prepared tax computations for Cate, which was not what they had been asked to do. In addition, many candidates failed to consider the employer national insurance contributions aspects which were a key part of the question.

Once the costs had been determined, it was simply a case of recognising that Cate was a higher rate tax payer, such that she would save income tax at 40% and class 4 national insurance contributions at 2% as a result of the increased costs. This was not tackled well by the majority of candidates who tried to do before and after calculations rather than working at the margin. In addition, many failed to consider the class 4 national insurance contribution implications altogether.

There was a more subtle point in the question in relation to the income tax personal allowance. The reduction in Cate's taxable trading income due to the costs relating to the part-time employee meant that part of her personal allowance would be reinstated, thus reducing the after-tax cost to her of taking on the new employee.

Part (b) required a discussion of the tax treatment of the profit derived from the sale of books on the internet. This required candidates to consider the badges of trade in relation to the specific transactions taking place. This part of the question was done well by many candidates. However, some candidates did not give themselves sufficient thinking time, such that they failed to realise what the question was testing.

It was important that candidates tried to reach a conclusion based on the information provided and that they thought about the capital gains tax implications as well as the income tax implications. There was no right answer as such, just a need to think about the relevant issues and to express the implications in a clear manner.

The final part of the question was arguably more challenging. It concerned the capital gains tax position of an individual, Ravi, who was resident in the UK but domiciled overseas and focussed principally on the remittance basis.

Although some candidates did reasonably well here, almost all candidates could have scored more marks if they had organised their thoughts before they began writing. There was a mark for making the point that Ravi was liable to UK capital gains tax because he was UK resident and a further mark for recognising that the remittance basis was available because he was domiciled overseas. In order to score these two marks, candidates had to make it clear that the liability to capital gains tax was due to his residence status and the remittance basis was due to his domicile status. Many candidates did not make these two points clearly, such that they only scored one of the two available marks.

Candidates were then expected to address the remittance basis charge and the loss of the annual exempt amount. This was done well by the majority of candidates.

	ACCA marking scheme		Marks
(a)	Total additional expenditure		5.0
	Income tax and class 4 NIC saving		2.0
	Saving due to personal allowance		2.5
			9.5
		Maximum	9.0
(b)	Trading income v capital gain issue		1.0
	Relevant badges of trade factors		3.0
	Any reasonable conclusion		1.0
	Chattels, so exempt CGT		1.0
			6.0
		Maximum	5.0
(c)	CGT on an arising basis as UK resident		2.0
	Optional remittance basis as not UK domiciled		1.0
	CGT effect if remittance basis used		2.0
	Remittance basis charge		1.5
	Conclusion		0.5
			7.0
		Maximum	6.0
Total			**20.0**

43   WAVERLEY (ADAPTED) *Walk in the footsteps of a top tutor*

Key answer tips

This 25 mark section A question tests a wide range of topics, demonstrating the need to study the whole breadth of the syllabus.

Requirement (a) tests basis periods on cessation of trade, capital gains tax, incorporation relief and the taxation of non-UK residents. Basis periods are a basic level topic but remain very important for the advanced taxation exam so make sure you have revised this area.

Requirement (b) tests the frequently examined topic of personal tax residence. You must make sure you tailor your answer to the scenario given here to score well.

Requirement (c) tests UK property gains for non-UK residents and the impact of domicile on the UK inheritance tax applicable to lifetime gifts. Provided you have revised this topic there were straightforward marks to be had here, with no need for computations.

The three requirements were independent and could have been attempted in any order. Requirement (a) was likely to be the most time consuming so it may have been a good idea to leave this one until last to avoid running out of time on the other parts.

In section A questions the information needed to answer the question will usually be split over at least 2 exhibits. Ensure you open all exhibits and the requirements button so that you have all of the relevant information.

The highlighted words in the written sections are key phrases that markers are looking for in your answer.

(a)   Unincorporated business

Final tax year of trading

The basis period for 2022/23, the final tax year of trading, is from 1 July 2021 to 15 January 2023. Accordingly, the taxable trading profit will be £197,550 (£125,400 + £72,150).

Any overlap profits from when Waverley began trading are deductible from this figure; this information is required in order to finalise the taxable trading profit.

Incorporation relief – conditions

–   Waverley's unincorporated business must be transferred to Roller Ltd as a going concern.

–   All of the assets of the unincorporated business, other than cash, must be transferred.

–   The whole or part of the consideration for the transfer must be the issue of shares by Roller Ltd to Waverley.

Tutor's top tips

Business asset disposal relief is tested regularly as it is an important relief for business owners.

This requirement asks you to explain whether the share disposal will qualify for the relief. You need to think about what type of company it is, the level of shareholding, Waverley's employment status and the period of ownership.

Remember that where there is an incorporation which qualifies for incorporation relief the ownership period of the unincorporated business can be combined with that of the shares when identifying if the period of ownership requirement has been met.

Business asset disposal relief (BADR)

The disposal of shares in Roller Ltd will qualify for BADR because:

- Roller Ltd is a trading company,
- Waverley owns at least 5% of the shares (he actually owns 100%),
- Waverley will be an employee of the company,
- Waverley qualifies for incorporation relief and has owned both the unincorporated business and shares for at least two years in total.

Sale of the unincorporated business to Roller Ltd and subsequent sale of Roller Ltd

Tutor's top tips

You may have found it difficult to know how to approach this part of requirement (a), given you needed to consider two residency options. The best approach to many questions testing alternative scenarios is to set your answer out in columns. This will save you considerable time compared with setting out separate computations, and make it easier for you to compare the scenarios.

Sale of the unincorporated business to Roller Ltd (2022/23)

Country of residence of Waverley:		UK
	£	£
Chargeable gains arising (£140,000 + £50,000)	190,000	
Less: Incorporation relief	(190,000)	
	0	0

Sale of shares in Roller Ltd (2023/24)

Country of residence of Waverley:	UK		Surferia
	£	£	£
Proceeds	600,000		
Less: Cost (£540,000 − £190,000)	(350,000)		
	————		
Chargeable gain	250,000		
	————		
CGT in the UK at 10%		25,000	
		————	
CGT in Surferia at 12%			30,000
			————
Total CGT		25,000	30,000
		————	————

Conclusion

The tax cost on the disposal of the shares will be lower if he is resident in the UK at the time the shares are sold.

(b)   Residence status

Tutor's top tips

Residence and domicile for personal tax has been a frequently tested topic in the exam in recent sittings. Each time it has been tested, it has been important for students to limit their answer to the information given in the scenario, rather that write down everything they have learnt about this topic, to keep their answer on point and to avoid running out of time.

In this question you were told that Waverley would not be automatically resident in the UK or overseas. Therefore, you should have limited your answer to discussion of the significant ties tests.

The number of days which Waverley can spend in the UK in the tax year 2023/24 without being UK resident will depend on the number of ties he has with the UK.

Waverley will definitely satisfy two ties:

–   He was in the UK for more than 90 days in 2022/23, the previous tax year.
–   In 2023/24 Waverley will have children under the age of 18 who are resident in the UK.

Waverley will also satisfy a third tie if he works in the UK for 40 days or more in the tax year 2023/24.

Waverley will not satisfy the following two ties in respect of the tax year 2023/24:

– He will not have accommodation in the UK available for his use.

– He will not be in the UK for more days than in any other country.

Accordingly, Waverley will satisfy either two or three ties.

Waverley was UK resident in the previous three tax years. Accordingly, if he works in the UK for 40 days or more, such that he satisfies three ties, he will only be able to spend up to 45 days in the UK without becoming UK resident.

If Waverley does not work in the UK for 40 days or more, he will only satisfy two ties, and will therefore be able to spend up to 90 days in the UK without becoming UK resident.

Tutorial note

The question states that Waverley will not be automatically UK resident in the tax year 2023/24. Accordingly, he must be in the UK for less than 183 days. The question also states that he will live in Surferia when he is not in the UK. Accordingly, he will spend more days in Surferia than he will in the UK.

(c)   Investment property CGT

Tutor's top tips

The taxation of non-residential property gains for non-UK residents is a relatively new area of the syllabus. The topic is tested here at a high level with no explanation of the different methods of calculating the chargeable amount.

The lack of computational information given in the question on the disposal of the investment property and the relatively low mark allocation should have given you a clue that the examining team were not expecting much detail here.

The gain on the sale of the property will be subject to Surferian CGT because Waverley will be resident in Surferia when he sells the property.

That part of the gain which has accrued since 5 April 2019 will also be subject to CGT in the UK because non-residential property situated in the UK is subject to UK CGT regardless of the residence status of the person making the disposal.

It will therefore be necessary to consider the terms of the double tax treaty between the UK and Surferia. For example, the treaty might provide that the part of the gain on the property which would otherwise be taxed twice is only taxed in one of the two countries (double tax relief by exemption).

Alternatively, it might allow the tax chargeable in one country to be deducted from the tax charged in the other (double tax relief by credit).

Tutor's top tips

The examining team gave an additional discretionary mark here for discussion of the administrative implications of Waverley's gain being subject to capital gains tax.

Remember, capital gains tax is always due by 31 January following the end of the tax year (unless the disposal is that of a UK residential property) and stating this is often given credit in the exam.

Inheritance tax (IHT)

Tutor's top tips

The impact of a taxpayer's domicile on inheritance tax is often tested for written marks in the exam, so you need to be able to explain it clearly and concisely. Perhaps practise by trying to explain it to a family member or friend?

You should explain both the impact of Waverley's domicile and consider the impact of him being either UK domiciled or non-UK domiciled for IHT purposes to score well here. It is also important to include an explanation of the deemed domicile rules and how an individual can lose their UK domiciled status, as these points are often missed.

Whether or not Waverley's gift to his sister will be within the scope of UK IHT will depend on Waverley's domicile status and the country in which the money is situated.

If the money is in a UK bank account it will be a UK asset, such that the gift will be within the scope of UK IHT regardless of Waverley's domicile status. If the money is in an overseas bank account it will be an overseas asset, such that it will only be subject to UK IHT if Waverley is domiciled or deemed domiciled in the UK.

In order to acquire a domicile of choice outside the UK, Waverley will need to leave the UK permanently and sever all of his links with the UK. Accordingly, whilst he has young children in the UK, and wishes to continue with his UK-based social activities, he will remain domiciled in the UK even though he will be living overseas.

In addition, even if Waverley were able to acquire a domicile of choice overseas, such that he loses his UK domicile status, for the purposes of IHT he will be deemed domiciled in the UK for a further three years. Also, as he was born in the UK and has his domicile of origin in the UK, he will be deemed domiciled in the UK for any tax year where he is UK resident and was UK resident for at least one of the previous two tax years.

In conclusion, the gift of the proceeds from the sale of the investment property will be within the scope of UK IHT unless Waverley has acquired a domicile of choice overseas and is not deemed domiciled in the UK for the purposes of IHT.

Examiner's report

This report has been adapted to remove elements which are no longer examinable due to changes in legislation.

Part (a) of this question required candidates to deal with various aspects of incorporating a business, including the income tax implications of the cessation of trade for the sole trader, and the capital gains tax implications of a disposal of shares in the new company.

An ability to identify the basis periods for taxation of a business in its opening and closing years, is a fundamental skill which candidates are expected to apply at ATX. Relatively few candidates were able to do this correctly in the case of the final tax year for this business. This is regarded as essential brought forward knowledge, and is tested on a regular basis.

The assets of the business were transferred to the company on incorporation in return for consideration comprising wholly of shares, such that the total gains on the chargeable assets were eligible for incorporation relief.

The most common errors in this part of the question was failure to realise that the nominal value of the shares issued as consideration does not necessarily equal the market value of the shares. The nominal value of the shares issued is irrelevant; their market value must equal the total market value of the assets transferred where they represent the total consideration. This is a commonly tested examination point in this area, but was only picked up by a few candidates.

A logical approach was required for the final aspect of this part of the question, to calculate the capital gains tax liability arising on the subsequent disposal of shares on the alternative assumptions that the taxpayer was UK resident or overseas resident. Candidates needed to take a step back and ensure that they understood the full picture, before embarking on the calculations. This advice is also applicable more generally to Section A questions, where candidates need to stop and think about the scenario as a whole before starting to undertake the detailed work required.

Part (b) required candidates to identify the relevant 'ties' to determine the residence status, which applied to the taxpayer who has left the UK. The question clearly stated that the automatic tests for determining both UK and overseas residence were not satisfied, but a minority of candidates still discussed these rules, gaining no marks, and wasting time. However, overall this part of the question was done well, with candidates being aware of the relevant ties, and applying them to the taxpayer's situation.

Part (c) concerned the capital gains tax implications, both in the UK and overseas, of an overseas resident taxpayer disposing of a UK investment property acquired when previously resident in the UK. Most candidates realised that this was chargeable overseas, but very few appeared to be aware of recent legislation (FA2019), which now includes disposals of UK non-residential property by a non-resident individual as being within the scope of UK capital gains tax.

Note that this part of the question has been adapted since the question was originally set.

The taxpayer's domicile, rather than residence status was relevant to the second part of this requirement, which related to the gift of the proceeds from the sale of the investment property. This was not particularly well done, with many candidates not recognising the relevance of the concept of 'deemed domicile, and of the location of the asset being gifted. The definition and relevance of an individual's residence and domicile for the purposes of both capital taxes is a frequently tested area at ATX, and candidates should ensure that they are confident with applying these in context.

ACCA marking scheme			
			Marks
(a)	Taxable trading profits		2.5
	Sale of business to Roller Ltd		
	Incorporation relief conditions		2.0
	Business asset disposal relief		2.0
	Sale of Roller Ltd		
	Chargeable gain on disposal		2.5
	Capital gains tax		2.0
	Conclusion		2.0
			————
			13.0
		Maximum	12.0
			————
(b)	Consideration of each tie		5.0
	Conclusions		2.0
			————
			7.0
		Maximum	6.0
			————
(c)	Capital gains tax		
	Gain on UK property		2.0
	Relief under the treaty		2.0
	An additional discretionary mark may be given for the		
	administrative requirements of capital gains tax		
	Inheritance tax		
	Liability to UK inheritance tax		1.0
	Cessation of UK domicile		2.0
	Deemed domicile		1.0
	Conclusion		1.0
			————
			9.0
		Maximum	7.0
			————
Total			25.0
			————

44 NOAH AND DAN (ADAPTED)   *Walk in the footsteps of a top tutor*

Key answer tips

This section B question tests inheritance tax with some overseas aspects, the UK residence tests, and capital gains tax on the disposal of a UK residential property by a non-UK resident individual.

Parts (a) and (b) are unrelated, and could be attempted in any order as long as each part is clearly labelled.

The highlighted words in the written sections are key phrases that markers are looking for in your answer.

(a) **(i)** **Inheritance tax treatment of the house located in Skarta**

Tutor's top tips

The concept of domicile and deemed domicile is often tested in the exam, so you should be prepared to write about this.

An individual who is not domiciled or deemed domiciled in the UK is liable to UK inheritance tax only in respect of assets located in the UK.

An individual is deemed domiciled in the UK if they have been resident in the UK for 15 out of the 20 tax years immediately preceding the tax year in which the transfer is made, and accordingly are liable to UK inheritance tax on their worldwide assets.

Noah became resident in the UK on 1 April 2003, so by the time of his death on 31 May 2022, Noah had been resident in the UK for 19 tax years, so would be deemed domiciled in the UK for inheritance tax purposes. Therefore, the house located in Skarta will be included in his chargeable death estate.

(ii) **Value of Dan's inheritance**

Tutor's top tips

*Make sure that you answer the full requirement here. You are asked for the value of Dan's inheritance **after all taxes and liabilities**, not just the inheritance tax payable.*

Noah – death estate

	£
UK assets	360,000
House in Skarta (W)	348,650
	————
Chargeable estate	708,650
Residence nil rate band	(175,000)
Nil rate band available on death	(325,000)
	————
Taxable estate	208,650
	————
IHT (£208,650 × 40%)	83,460
Less: Double tax relief – the lower of:	
Overseas tax suffered £56,080	
UK IHT on the house (£348,650 × £83,460/£708,650)	(41,062)
	————
IHT payable	42,398
	————

Value of Dan's inheritance after all taxes and liabilities

	£
Value of assets in the estate (£360,000 + £367,000)	727,000
Less: Legal and administration fees in Skarta	(18,500)
IHT suffered (£56,080 + £42,398)	(98,478)
Value of inheritance	610,022

Working: House in Skarta

	£
Value of the house at 31 May 2022	367,000
Less: Legal and administration fees – the lower of:	
The fees incurred £18,500	
Maximum £18,350 (5% × £367,000)	(18,350)
Value to include in the estate	348,650

(b)   (i)   Reasons why Dan will be classed as non-UK resident in the tax year 2022/23.

Tutor's top tips

There is no point in discussing the automatic residence tests, as the question clearly states that Dan does not satisfy these.

The marks in this part of the question are for applying the sufficient ties tests to Dan. To score well, you should show that you have considered all of the ties.

As Dan does not satisfy the criteria under either of the automatic tests for determining his UK residence status, the 'sufficient ties' tests must be considered. These take into account the number of days spent in the UK and the number of 'ties' Dan has to the UK.

As Dan has previously been resident in the UK in at least one of the previous three tax years, and will spend between 46 and 90 days in the UK during 2022/23 (15 May to 5 August 2022), he would be considered to be UK resident in this tax year if he has at least three UK ties.

Dan will satisfy only two ties:

–   He will have owned his house in the UK up to the date of its sale on 1 August 2022 (i.e. for more than 91 days in 2022/23), and has spent several nights there.

–   He spent more than 90 days in the UK in the tax year 2020/21, as he did not leave the UK until 1 January 2021.

Dan will not satisfy the remaining three ties:

- He does not have any close family residing in the UK.
- He will not be present in the UK for the same number or more days in 2022/23 than in any other country.
- He will not have substantive work in the UK in 2022/23.

Accordingly, Dan will be classed as non-UK resident in 2022/23.

Tutorial note

1   *A parent (Noah) does not fall within the definition of close family for this purpose.*

2   *As Dan is planning to move permanently to Skarta on 5 August 2022, he will not be present in the UK for more days in 2022/23 than in any other country.*

3   *Dan will be working for 31 days in July 2022, which is insufficient to be regarded as 'substantive' (40 days or more).*

(ii)   Dan – capital gains tax liability on disposal of his UK house

Tutor's top tips

This part of the question tests the rules relating to the disposal of a UK residential property by a non-UK resident.

	£
Proceeds	318,000
Less: Cost	(293,000)
Gain	25,000

	£
Gain before private residence relief (PRR)	25,000
Less: PRR (W) £25,000 × 42/52	(20,192)
Chargeable gain	4,808

Working: PRR

	Total months	Exempt months	Chargeable months
Tax year			
2018/19			
– UK resident			
– actual occupation 6 April 2018 to 5 April 2019	12	12	–
2019/20			
– UK resident			
– actual occupation 6 April 2019 to 5 April 2020	12	12	–
2020/21			
– UK resident			
– actual occupation 6 April to 31 December 2020	9	9	–
– unoccupied 1 January to 5 April 2021	3	–	3
2021/22			
– non-UK resident			
– unoccupied 6 April to 31 October 2021	7		7
– last 9 months 1 November 2021 to 5 April 2022	5	5	–
2022/23			
– non-UK resident last 9 months 6 April to 1 August 2022	4	4	–
	52	42	10

Tutorial note

Usually, when considering PRR, the total ownership period is considered and it is not necessary to split the period into tax years.

However, for a non-UK resident, if the individual does not stay at the property for at least 90 nights during any tax year, the whole tax year will be treated as a period of non-occupation for PRR purposes.

There is no need to consider whether or not Dan qualifies for the 90-day rule in 2021/22 or 2022/23 because the period of ownership of the property in these two tax years is within the final nine months of ownership, which are exempt as long as the property qualified as the individual's main private residence at some point during the period of ownership.

Examiner's report

The first part concerned inheritance tax on assets situated overseas. Candidates performed quite well and displayed a strong knowledge of the rules. However, a minority did not score as many marks as they could have done because they did not follow the instructions in the question sufficiently carefully. In particular, they failed to finish off their answers by calculating the value of the inheritance after deduction of all taxes and liabilities.

The second part of the question required an explanation of an individual's resident status and a calculation of a chargeable gain on the sale of a property including the relief available in respect of a private residence.

The majority of candidates had a sound knowledge of the rules in connection with the determination of UK residence. There were just two minor problems; some candidates failed to note that there were only five marks available and simply wrote too much, whilst others did not do enough to apply the rules to the facts of the question.

Note that part of this examiner's report has been deleted, as it relates to part of the question that has now been removed.

Candidates who did well in this question:

- applied their knowledge of the detailed rules to the facts of the question

- managed their time carefully

- read the requirements carefully and ensured that they answered the question set.

		ACCA marking scheme		
				Marks
(a)	(i)	Inclusion of house in Skarta in death estate		3.0
	(ii)	Chargeable estate		2.0
		IHT liability		3.0
		Value of Dan's inheritance		2.0
				7.0
			Maximum	6.0
(b)	(i)	Need three ties		1.0
		Application of ties		4.5
				5.5
			Maximum	5.0
	(ii)	Gain before PRR		0.5
		PRR exemption		4.0
				4.5
			Maximum	4.0
Total				18.0

45   MAX (ADAPTED)   *Walk in the footsteps of a top tutor*

Key answer tips

The first two parts of this question look at the capital gains tax and inheritance tax aspects of a lifetime gift. It is important to pay attention to the dates in these parts of the question.

Part (b) covers the statutory residence tests and the temporary non residence rules for capital gains tax. It is important that both parts of the requirement are covered and not just one!

The final part of the question asks for an explanation of the availability of business asset disposal relief together with a calculation of the increase in post-tax proceeds if a different disposal date is used. This type of higher skills requirement is commonly set in ATX and should be expected.

The highlighted words in the written sections are key phrases that markers are looking for in your answer.

(a)   (i)   Availability of gift holdover relief in respect of the gift of the office premises

The office premises are eligible for gift holdover relief as they were used for the purpose of Max's trade. However, as they ceased to be used in the business on 31 May 2020, the proportion of the gain to be held over is restricted to the gain on disposal × period of business use/total period of ownership. Therefore, the proportion of the gain eligible for gift holdover relief is 74/99 ((1 April 2014 – 31 May 2020)/(1 April 2014 to 30 June 2022)).

Tutorial note

Max is disposing of the building used in his sole trader business. He hasn't used it in the trade for the whole period of ownership as his trade ceased several months before the gift to Fara. Therefore, gift holdover relief must be restricted so that only the proportion of the gain relating to business use qualifies.

(ii)   Maximum potential inheritance tax (IHT) liability in respect of the gift of the office premises

No IHT is payable at the time the gift is made, but a liability may arise if Max dies within seven years of making the gift.

Business property relief is not available as this is a gift of an individual asset which has been used in an unincorporated sole trader business, rather than the gift of the business itself. However, annual exemptions are available for the tax years 2022/23 and 2021/22, such that the gross chargeable value of the gift will be £162,000 (£168,000 – £3,000 – £3,000).

Max has made one prior gift, on 6 May 2019, which will use part of his nil rate band if he dies before 6 May 2026. Taper relief will be available if Max dies after 30 June 2025 (three years after the date of the gift on 30 June 2022), so the maximum potential IHT liability will arise if Max dies before this date.

The maximum potential inheritance tax liability is therefore £12,400 (£162,000 – (£325,000 – £194,000) × 40%) and will arise if Max dies on or before 30 June 2025.

(b) **Effect of Max's two-and-a-half-year period overseas on his UK residence status and the capital gains tax (CGT) consequences on the sale of the warehouse**

Tutor's top tips

It is important to consider the statutory residence tests before going into any implications for capital gains tax. Ensure that you run through the tests in order and address the ones that are not met and those that are met, and state why.

Max will leave the UK on 1 November 2022. As Max was resident in the UK for one or more of the previous three tax years, and he will spend more than 91 days in the UK in the tax year 2022/23, then he will NOT satisfy any of the automatic overseas tests.

Max WILL satisfy the first automatic UK residence test in the tax year 2022/23 as he will spend 183 days or more in the UK in that tax year.

In the tax years 2023/24 and 2024/25 Max will satisfy the first automatic overseas residence test as he will spend less than 16 days in the UK.

In the tax year 2025/26 Max's return to live permanently in the UK from 30 June 2025 means that he will not satisfy any of the automatic overseas residence tests, but will satisfy the UK residence test as he will spend 183 days or more in the UK in that tax year.

1   Sale in June 2022

As Max is resident in the UK in June 2022, the disposal will give rise to a chargeable gain in 2022/23.

2   Sale in June 2023

Disposals of assets made by non-UK resident individuals are not chargeable to CGT in the UK. However, Max will be regarded as a temporary non-resident, as his period of non-residence will be less than five years, and he has been UK resident for at least four of the seven tax years prior to the tax year of departure. Accordingly, any gains made in the period of non-residence in respect of assets held prior to Max's departure, and disposed of while he is overseas, will become chargeable in 2025/26 (the tax year of his return).

Tutorial note

Although a machine is a wasting chattel and would therefore normally be an exempt asset for capital gains purposes, the exemption does not apply if capital allowances would have been claimed on it, which is the case here. Accordingly, since cost and proceeds exceed £6,000, a gain has to be calculated.

(c) **Availability of business asset disposal relief (BADR) on the sale of the machine**

The sale of the machine will satisfy two of the conditions for BADR in that it was in use within Max's business at the date of cessation, and the business had been owned by Max for at least two years prior to cessation. However, the third condition that the disposal must be within three years of the date of cessation, will only be satisfied if the disposal takes place before 1 June 2023. Accordingly, if the sale takes place in June 2022, BADR will be available, but if it does not take place until June 2023, it will not.

Sale in June 2022

If the sale of the machine takes place in June 2022, this will give rise to a chargeable gain of £12,000 (£84,000 – £72,000).

As Max will be able to claim BADR in respect of this chargeable gain, the after-tax proceeds will be £82,800 (£84,000 – (£12,000 × 10%)).

Sale in June 2023

If the sale of the machine is delayed until June 2023, this will give rise to a chargeable gain of £18,000 (£90,000 – £72,000) in 2025/26.

As Max will not be able to claim BADR in respect of this chargeable gain, the after-tax proceeds will be £86,400 (£90,000 – (£18,000 × 20%)).

The increase in after-tax proceeds is therefore £3,600 (£86,400 – £82,800).

Tutorial note

Although the disposal occurs in June 2023 the gain does not become chargeable until 2025/26 under the temporary non-residence rules as this is the tax year that Max returns and becomes UK resident again.

Tutor's top tips

The final requirement asked for both explanations and calculations. It is important not to neglect the explanations.

Examiner's report

This question concerned the capital gains tax and inheritance tax implications of a lifetime gift, and also the implications of a taxpayer moving abroad on his UK residence status, and his proposed sale of a UK asset.

The first part related to the availability of gift holdover relief in respect of a commercial building which has previously been used in a business, but which is now being rented out. Most candidates who attempted this question part were able to identify the issues and score two out of the three possible marks. Very few candidates went on to quantify the proportion of the gain which would be eligible for relief. Candidates should remember that where dates or figures are given in a question, they are usually required to use these in their answer.

The second part of the question required advice on the maximum potential inheritance tax liability which could arise in respect of the gift of the commercial building. The majority of candidates produced a good computation, but only a minority provided the necessary supporting explanations to fully satisfy the requirement – in this case, the fact that taper relief is available to reduce an inheritance tax liability if the donor of the lifetime gift survives for at least three years. Where an explanation or justification is needed for including or omitting figures, candidates must provide this.

The third part of the question required explanation of the implications of an individual moving overseas for a few years on his UK residence status for each of those years, and the consequences for the timing of a proposed disposal for capital gains tax purposes. The majority of candidates appeared not to have read the question properly, and dived straight in to explaining the rules for temporary non-residence for capital gains tax purposes, with which they were clearly very familiar, but ignoring the need to first of all consider the individual's actual residence status by reference to the automatic rules for determining this. This meant that they restricted the number of marks which they were able to obtain. Candidates should ensure that they fully address all aspects of a requirement, not just what they perceive to be the key point, in order to score a high mark on a question.

The final part of the question concerned an explanation of the availability of business asset disposal relief, and the calculation of the increase in after-tax proceeds if the individual delayed selling a further business asset to a date when he would not be UK resident. Almost all candidates had identified that the temporary non-residence rules would apply, and implemented them correctly, and, it was pleasing to see, followed through the calculation to the end, quantifying the increase in after-tax proceeds, as required, and thereby scoring a high mark on this part. The main area of difficulty for this question was imprecise knowledge of the conditions for business asset disposal relief, and future candidates are reminded once again of the need to be very familiar with the precise rules in respect of all the capital gains tax reliefs.

ACCA marking scheme				Marks
(a)	(i)	Gift holdover relief		3.0
				———
	(ii)	Gross chargeable value of the gift		2.5
		Circumstances in which maximum liability arises		2.5
		Calculation of maximum liability		1.0
				———
				6.0
			Maximum	5.0
				———
(b)		Max's residence status		3.5
		Sale in June 2022		1.0
		Sale in June 2023		3.0
				———
				7.5
			Maximum	6.0
				———
(c)		Business asset disposal relief		2.5
		After-tax proceeds from sale in June 2022		1.5
		After-tax proceeds from sale in June 2023		1.5
		Increase in after-tax proceeds		0.5
				———
				6.0
				———
Total				**20.0**
				———

46 EMMA *Walk in the footsteps of a top tutor*

Key answer tips

This questions focuses primarily on the two capital taxes: inheritance tax and capital gains tax. Though there are a few marks on the overseas aspects of income tax.

Part (a) tests the deemed domicile rules in conjunction with the remittance basis. The question clearly signposts remittance basis but you need to ask yourself if it would actually be available to Emma based on her tax status.

Part (b) looks at inheritance tax – in particular the situation that would give rise to the maximum inheritance tax liability. You will have to make some assumptions here so ensure you state your assumptions. Don't forget the extra part about gift holdover relief for capital gains tax!

Finally, part (c) tests the popular temporary non-residence rules. It is important to explain why the rules are applicable as well as the impact that they will have. You're asked to advise when the best time to sell the shares is, so make sure you give a reasoned recommendation to score well.

The highlighted words in the written sections are key phrases that markers are looking for in your answer.

(a) **Rental income in the country of Falgar**

Tutor's top tips

The question mentioned the date Emma first became UK resident. You should think about why you are told this; this allows you to see how many tax years she has been UK resident for and therefore if the long term resident deemed domicile rules apply!

The rental income arising in Falgar will be subject to income tax in the UK because Emma will be UK resident. This will be true regardless of whether or not Emma brings the money into the UK because the remittance basis will not be available to Emma.

The remittance basis will not be available because, although Emma is domiciled in Falgar, she is deemed to be domiciled in the UK for the purposes of income tax. This is because she will have been UK resident for 15 of the 20 tax years prior to the tax year in which the income arises.

However, the UK income tax due in respect of the rental income will be reduced by double tax relief. Double tax relief will be the lower of the UK tax and the Falgarian tax on the rental income, such that the effective UK rate will be 14% (40% – 26%).

(b) **Gift of shares in Vyc Ltd**

Circumstances resulting in the maximum inheritance tax (IHT) liability

The maximum IHT liability will occur where both condition (i) and condition (ii), set out below, are satisfied.

(i)   Emma dies by 30 September 2025, i.e. within seven years of 1 October 2018, the date on which she made the cash gift to her daughter.

Once seven years have elapsed, the gift on 1 October 2018 will no longer be accumulated in determining the nil rate band available in respect of the gift of the shares in Vyc Ltd.

Tutorial note

If Emma dies within seven years of 1 October 2018, i.e. by 30 September 2025, she will have died within three years of the gift of the shares to Edward. Accordingly, taper relief will not be available.

(ii)   At the time of Emma's death, business property relief (BPR) IS NOT available.

The gift of the shares in Vyc Ltd will qualify for 100% BPR at the time of the gift because:

–   Vyc Ltd is an unquoted trading company, such that the shares are relevant business property; and

–   Emma has owned the shares for at least two years.

However, BPR will not be available on Emma's death if:

–   the shares are no longer qualifying business property; or

–   Edward has disposed of the shares prior to Emma's death, unless:

    –   Edward has replaced the shares with qualifying business property; or

    –   Edward has died before Emma, whilst still owning the shares (or qualifying replacement business property).

Tutorial note

The shares in Vyc Ltd are UK assets because Vyc Ltd is a UK registered company. Accordingly, a gift of the shares will be subject to UK inheritance tax regardless of Emma's domicile status.

Maximum possible IHT liability

	£	£
Transfer of value (W)		340,000
Annual exemptions:		
2023/24		(3,000)
2022/23		(3,000)
		_____
		334,000
Nil rate band	325,000	
Less: Chargeable transfer in the previous seven years	(280,000)	
	_____	
		(45,000)
		_____
Taxable amount		289,000
		_____
IHT payable (£289,000 × 40%)		115,600
		_____

Working

Transfer of value by reference to related property

	£
Value of shares held prior to the gift: (35,000 × £19 (54% (35% + 19%)))	665,000
Value of shares held after the gift: (25,000 × £13 (44% (25% + 19%)))	(325,000)
	_____
	340,000
	_____

Assumption: The transfer of value has been calculated by reference to related property on the assumption that the fall in value would be a lower figure if related property were ignored.

Tutorial note

1   The value of Emma's shares is determined by reference to the shares held by her and her husband under the related property rules.

2   Candidates who prepared calculations both with and without reference to related property to determine which resulted in the higher figure (rather than stating an assumption) received equal credit.

Capital gains tax (CGT)

Vyc Ltd is an unquoted trading company, such that shares in the company qualify for CGT gift holdover relief. However, for the relief to be available, it is necessary for Edward, the recipient of the gift, to be resident in the UK in the tax year in which the gift is made.

(c)   Sale of shares in Barb plc

Tutor's top tips

When advising on the timing of the sale of shares it is important that you don't just consider the tax cost, but think about the impact on post-tax proceeds. The aim should be to maximise post-tax proceeds, even if this means paying a bit more tax.

For the purposes of UK CGT, Emma is a temporary non-UK resident whilst she is living in Falgar. This is because:

–   she was UK resident for at least four of the seven tax years immediately prior to the tax year 2019/20 (the tax year of departure); and

–   on her return to the UK, she will have been absent for less than five years.

Accordingly, if Emma sells the shares now, the chargeable gain of £330,000 will still be subject to UK CGT, albeit in the tax year 2023/24 (the tax year in which she returns to the UK) as opposed to 2022/23, the tax year of sale. This rule applies because Emma owned the shares on 1 February 2020 (the date she left the UK) and will have disposed of them whilst living in Falgar.

If Emma waits until she has returned to the UK, the chargeable gain will increase by £60,000 to £390,000. It will be subject to CGT in the tax year 2023/24, the tax year of disposal.

Accordingly, the chargeable gain will be subject to CGT in the tax year 2023/24 regardless of the date of sale and therefore UK CGT, at the rate of 20%, will be due on 31 January 2025.

In order to maximise her post-tax proceeds, Emma should sell the shares after she has returned to the UK. By doing so, she will realise additional post-tax proceeds of £48,000 (£60,000 × 80% (100% – 20%)).

Tutorial note

Business asset disposal relief will not be available on the sale of the shares as Emma owns less than 5% of the shares.

Examiner's report

This question was split into three parts looking at international aspects of personal tax, inheritance tax and capital gains tax.

The first part of the question asked candidates to explain how the client's overseas rental income would be taxed in the UK based on their domicile and residence. Many candidates decided that the client was not UK domiciled but did not realise that the client would be 'deemed UK domicile'. It is vital that candidates have an in-depth understanding of the detail of the ATX-UK tax rules; a superficial understanding of the rules is not enough to score well in this exam.

The second part of the question concerned a proposed gift of shares from the client to her son and the requirement was for an explanation of the circumstances resulting in the maximum amount of inheritance tax payable and a calculation of this amount. The two key circumstances affecting the possible inheritance tax payable were a prior gift in the last seven years and the availability of business property relief. Not all candidates were able to see the link between a prior gift in the last seven years using up nil rate band for this potential gift and missed this point completely. Most candidates recognised the relevance of business property relief but failed to recognise that this relief could be unavailable if the donee did not own the shares at the date of the donor's death.

Candidates were generally able to score marks for their calculation of inheritance tax, although they were not all clear on the rules for related property share valuations.

An extra requirement in this part of the question concerned the availability of gift holdover relief for capital gains tax purposes on the gift of the shares. Although at first it may have appeared that gift holdover relief would be available and many candidates discussed this, most candidates missed the point that the donee would need to be resident in the UK in the tax year in which the gift is made. Again this required knowledge of a detailed tax rule, applied to the circumstances of the question. Candidates with only a limited knowledge of the tax rules are left exposed by the detailed question scenarios.

The third part of the question tested a knowledge and application of temporary non-UK residence rules. The client was unsure whether to sell a UK asset now whilst temporary non-UK resident or wait until they returned to the UK and sell it for substantially more proceeds. Many candidates correctly recognised that selling the asset at either time would result in a taxable gain, chargeable in the tax year of return to the UK. However, many candidates then incorrectly advised that since higher proceeds would result in a higher tax bill, the client should sell for a lower proceeds to reduce their tax bill. This is very unsound, uncommercial advice. The commercial point is that the advice should be based on maximising 'post tax proceeds' for the client. Candidates are expected to apply the detailed tax rules but also apply sound commercial judgement to their client advice.

	ACCA marking scheme		
			Marks
(a)	Basis of taxation		3.0
	Tax rate		2.0
			―――
			5.0
		Maximum	4.0
			―――
(b)	Emma's death		2.0
	Ownership of shares		5.0
	Calculation		
	Fall in value		3.5
	Inheritance tax liability		2.5
	Capital gains tax		2.0
			―――
			15.0
		Maximum	13.0
			―――
(c)	Temporary non-UK resident		3.0
	Capital gains tax liability		
	Sale before returning to the UK		2.0
	Sale after returning to the UK		1.5
	Payment date		1.0
	Advice		2.5
			―――
			10.0
		Maximum	8.0
			―――
Total			**25.0**
			―――

47 FIONA *Walk in the footsteps of a top tutor*

Key answer tips

This question covers an ethical issue, IHT on a lifetime gift as a result of death, CGT and IHT on a proposed gift with overseas aspects and taxation of overseas income.

Part (a) requires knowledge of the ethical issues for a firm accepting a new client. There will be five marks on ethical issues in section A of every ATX exam, and these can be easy marks to obtain.

Part (b) is split into two sub requirements. Part (b)(i) covers the impact of someone dying after making various lifetime transfers and is purely computational. This is only worth three marks so there is nothing too technical to deal with, and it is assumed knowledge from TX.

Part (b)(ii) is a written section on the CGT and IHT implications of lifetime gifts, one of which involves an overseas asset. You are told not to do any calculations for this part so do not waste time in performing any.

Part (c) requires you to discuss why the remittance basis is available to Fiona, which requires good knowledge of the conditions and potential charges, as well as calculating her income tax liability. Make sure you split the marks and your timing between these two requirements.

The highlighted words in the written sections are key phrases that markers are looking for.

(a) Becoming Fiona's tax advisers

Tutor's top tips

This is a standard ethical question and you need to make sure you apply the fundamental principles and address any threats to these.

There are five marks available, so try to make at least five separate points in your answer.

The actions we should carry out before we become Fiona's tax advisers:

- We must give consideration to the fundamental principles of professional ethics, for example, integrity and professional competence and due care. This requires us to consider whether becoming tax advisers to Fiona would create any threats to compliance with these principles.

  If any such threats are identified, we should not accept the appointment unless the threats can be reduced to an acceptable level via the implementation of safeguards.

  Fiona's move to the UK will significantly affect her tax affairs, and we must be sure that we are able to deal with the technical aspects of these matters.

- We must assure ourselves that Fiona is not involved in any form of money laundering.

- We should obtain permission from Fiona to contact her existing tax advisers in order to ensure that there is nothing in the past which would preclude us from accepting the appointment on ethical grounds.

- We should issue a letter of engagement setting out the terms of our agreement with Fiona and our agreed responsibilities.

(b) Gifts to Elena and Hugo

Tutor's top tips

This part of the question requires you to calculate the IHT on a lifetime gift as a result of death. This is stage two of calculating IHT. Watch out for the following information to guide you through this type of requirement:

- *Are there any annual exemptions available to deduct from the gift?*

- *Are there any other previous lifetime gifts that will impact the availability of the NRB?*

- *Are there any other reliefs available or lifetime tax paid that can deducted?*

This is an element of assumed knowledge from the TX exam.

(i) **Inheritance tax (IHT) payable in respect of Fiona's gift on 1 May 2021**

	£	£
Gift to Elena on 1 May 2021		430,000
Less: Annual exemption 2021/22		(3,000)
		———
		427,000
		———
Nil rate band	325,000	
Less: Chargeable transfers in the previous seven years		
1 July 2016 chargeable lifetime transfer (CLT)	(74,000)	
1 September 2020 potentially exempt transfer (PET)	(204,000)	
	———	
		(47,000)
		———
Amount chargeable to IHT		380,000
		———
IHT (£380,000 × 40%)		152,000
		———

Tutorial note

The gift was of a UK asset, such that it was subject to UK IHT even though Fiona was domiciled in Parella at the time it was made. This calculation assumes a date of death of 30 April 2024, as required in the email from the manager. This would be within three years of the gift on 1 May 2021, such that no taper relief would be available.

(ii) **Proposed gift to Hugo**

Tutor's top tips

*For a question like this you need to split the marks up according to the requirement. You need to discuss the CGT and IHT for **two** potential gifts. So this means there are **four** areas to address in your answer.*

Based on your explanation of the two alternative gifts you can then score some easy marks for advising which asset should be given and whether it should be given before or after Fiona becomes UK resident.

You need to ensure you do not spend too long on each of the areas. Using headings is important to ensure you cover all the areas and to show the marker which particular area you are discussing. A scattered approach to your answer will make it difficult to read and mark.

Capital gains tax (CGT)

Aber House

– Aber House is situated in Parella. Accordingly, tax relief will not be available in the UK in respect of the capital loss resulting from a gift of this house unless it is made after Fiona becomes UK resident.

However, because Fiona and Hugo are connected persons, the loss would only be available for relief against gains on future disposals to Hugo.

Bleb House

– On a gift of Bleb House, a gain of £85,000 would be subject to UK CGT regardless of whether or not Fiona is resident in the UK at the time of the gift.

– This is because, since 6 April 2015, residential properties situated in the UK have been subject to CGT regardless of the resident status of the person making the disposal.

IHT

Aber House

– Aber House is situated in Parella. Accordingly, a gift of this house will not be subject to IHT unless Fiona is domiciled or deemed domiciled in the UK for IHT purposes.

– It has already been determined that once Fiona is UK resident, she will be deemed domiciled in the UK for the purposes of income tax and CGT. However, she will not be deemed domiciled for the purposes of IHT because she was not resident for either of the two tax years prior to 2022/23.

– Accordingly, Aber House would be excluded property for the purposes of IHT regardless of when in the next three months the gift is made.

Bleb House

– Bleb House is situated in the UK. Accordingly, a gift of this house will be within the charge to UK IHT regardless of Fiona's domicile status.

Conclusion

– Fiona should give Aber House to Hugo after she has moved to the UK. This would create the possibility of obtaining relief for the capital loss and would not have any IHT implications.

(c)   Taxation of overseas income

Tutor's top tips

This question is based on the taxation of overseas income. To tackle a tricky area such as this you need to ensure you read the scenario carefully and pick up on any hints as to whether Fiona would be entitled to the automatic remittance basis. The main conditions to look out for are:

- *Is the individual UK resident but not UK domiciled?*

- *Does she have unremitted income and gains of less than £2,000?*

You were also asked to discuss if the remittance base charge would apply; a good understanding of when this charge applies would help you to answer this part of the question.

Availability of the remittance basis

– The remittance basis is available where an individual is UK resident but not UK domiciled.

– Where an individual is UK resident and deemed domiciled in the UK, the remittance basis is only available if unremitted overseas income and gains in a tax year is less than £2,000.

In these circumstances, the remittance basis applies automatically.

– Accordingly, for the tax year 2023/24, the amount of Fiona's taxable overseas income will be automatically calculated on the remittance basis. This is because her only unremitted overseas income will be her Parellian bank interest of £1,200.

– Fiona will not be subject to the remittance basis charge because she will qualify for the remittance basis automatically.

Fiona – income tax liability for the tax year 2023/24

Tutor's top tips

There are some easy marks here for preparing a basic income tax computation.

*The only tricky part is calculating the double tax relief. In order to do this, you need to calculate the UK tax on the overseas income. This is the difference between the UK tax **with** the overseas income, and the UK tax **without** the overseas income. Watch out for the impact on the savings income nil rate band!*

The calculation is best performed in the spreadsheet response option in the exam. This will enable you to use formulae to speed up workings. Remember to reference through to any workings performed in your narrative answer in the word processor.

	£	Working £
Property income:		
Properties in the UK	26,270	26,270
Properties in Parella	31,000	N/A
Interest income:		
UK bank interest	1,700	1,700
Parellian bank interest (unremitted)	–	–
Total income	58,970	27,970
Less: Personal allowance	(12,570)	(12,570)
Taxable income	46,400	15,400
Property income		
£37,700/£13,700 × 20%	7,540	2,740
£7,000 × 40%	2,800	
Interest income		
£500/£1,000 × 0%	0	0
£1,200 × 40%/£700 × 20%	480	140
	10,820	2,880
Double tax relief, the lower of:		
UK tax on overseas income		
£10,820 – £2,880 (W) = £7,940		
Parellian tax suffered		
£31,000 × 18% = £5,580	(5,580)	
Income tax liability	5,240	

Tutorial note

The personal allowance will be given because the remittance basis is available automatically.

Examiner's report

Requirement (a) – 5 marks

This part of the question tested knowledge of the actions to be taken before becoming Fiona's tax advisers.

This was a standard ethics requirement and many candidates were able to score well on this part of the question. However, when answering any ethics question dealing with aspects such as these, the need to address any threats to compliance with the fundamental principles such as integrity, professional competence and due care, should be borne in mind. If any such threats are identified, the point should be made that they can they be reduced to an acceptable level with the implementation of appropriate safeguards.

A small but significant number of candidates suggested that Fiona's address and proof of identity should be obtained, despite being specifically told in the question that this had already happened.

Before starting on an answer, it is always worth rechecking the requirement and information contained within the scenario in order to avoid wasting time on points that cannot earn marks.

Requirement (b)

Part (b) involved consideration of the inheritance tax and capital gains tax consequences of certain gifts being made by Fiona to her children.

Requirement (b)(i) – 3 marks

This part required a calculation of the inheritance tax payable on a gift made during Fiona's lifetime and arising as a consequence of her death. Once again, it is important to remember that if the command word in the requirement is to 'calculate', candidates should not be writing huge amounts in their answer. Brought forward TX-UK knowledge on how to calculate an inheritance tax liability was needed here. Some candidates appeared to be unfamiliar with how to work out the amount of nil rate band available for offset against a lifetime gift and the concept of reducing this by chargeable lifetime gifts in the seven years before the one for which the liability was being calculated.

Requirement (b)(ii) – 7 marks

This part of the question involved comparing two potential gifts which Fiona was planning to make to her son. Both were houses, one of which was located overseas and the other in the UK. The requirement involved consideration of both the capital gains tax (CGT) and inheritance tax (IHT) consequences of each of these gifts and also a consideration of the timing i.e. before, or after, becoming UK resident.

Many candidates addressed some parts of the requirement but failed to cover all aspects; for example, by only dealing with one of the properties and/or one of the taxes and/or not considering the timing of the gift.

When approaching this type of requirement, in the absence of any other specific instructions as to how the answer should be presented, it may be helpful to think about using a tabular format. This would ensure that all parts of the requirement are adequately dealt with.

The question also requested advice on which of the two houses Fiona should gift her son and the optimum timing of the gift. This therefore meant a conclusion needed to be drawn based on the previously provided analysis. If candidates are asked to give advice, there are specific marks allocated to this so it is essential to ensure that a relevant conclusion/recommendation is made in order to earn the available credit.

Requirement (c) – 10 marks

There were two subparts to this requirement.

The first asked for an explanation of why Fiona would be eligible for the remittance basis and whether or not she would be subject to the remittance basis charge.

The remittance basis is available where an individual is UK resident but not UK domiciled. Fiona's status for the tax year 2023/24 was that of resident and deemed domicile. In this case, the remittance basis is only available if unremitted overseas income and gains in any tax year is less than £2,000; in this situation it applies automatically and there is no remittance basis charge.

Some candidates appeared to know the rules but were unclear on the amount of 'unremitted' overseas income when applied to Fiona's specific circumstances. The question specifically stated that her overseas bank interest income of £1,200 would not be remitted to the UK whereas that from her overseas rental properties would be. As such, with an amount of overseas unremitted income of less than £2,000, the remittance basis automatically applies to Fiona for the relevant tax year.

The second subpart of this requirement asked for a calculation of Fiona's income tax liability for the tax year 2023/24. It's worth emphasising here once again that, if asked for a calculation, there is no need to spend time providing detailed explanations of all of the relevant numbers. As long as they are all clearly labelled, and brief explanations of any workings are given if necessary, the focus should be on doing the calculations themselves in order to earn the marks.

Many candidates were able to produce an income tax computation in response to this part of the question and showed an awareness of the fundamentals of double tax relief. Strictly, in order to calculate the UK tax suffered on the overseas income for double tax relief purposes, a calculation of the income tax liability with the overseas income included should be performed and this should then be compared with a calculation of the liability with the foreign income excluded. The difference in these two tax liabilities represents the UK tax on the overseas income, which is then compared with the foreign tax suffered. This method is demonstrated in the model answer.

ACCA marking scheme			
			Marks
(a)		Fundamental principles	3.0
		Other matters	3.0
			———
			6.0
		Maximum	5.0
			———
(b)	(i)	Calculation of inheritance tax	3.0
			———
			3.0
			———

(b)	(ii)	Capital gains tax		
		Aber House		2.0
		Bleb House		1.5
		Inheritance tax		
		Aber House		3.0
		Bleb House		1.0
		Conclusion		2.0
				——
				9.5
			Maximum	7.0
				——
(c)		Remittance basis		4.0
		Calculation of income tax liability		
		Liability before double tax relief		3.5
		Double tax relief		3.5
				——
				11.0
			Maximum	10.0
				——
Total				**25.0**
				——

PERSONAL FINANCE, BUSINESS FINANCE AND INVESTMENTS

48   MONISHA AND HORNER (ADAPTED) *Walk in the footsteps of a top tutor*

Key answer tips

This section B question tests your knowledge of furnished holiday lettings, tax planning for married couples (and civil partners) and the IR35 rules.

The first part of (a) concerns various aspects of income tax and capital gains tax in relation to tax planning for a married couple and in particular deals with furnished holiday accommodation. This is purely TX knowledge so should be an opportunity to score well if you have refreshed your TX knowledge!

The second part of (a) was the more difficult part of the question. It required a calculation of the total tax saving on the transfer of a 20% interest in a rental property from one spouse (Monisha) to the other (Asmat) together with the property being let as furnished holiday accommodation in the future. It is necessary to think very clearly about the taxes that would be saved and the impact on the computations of both husband and wife.

Part (b) covers the personal service company (IR35) rules and required an outline of the circumstances in which the rules apply, and clear explanations were needed to score highly. Then an explanation of the tax implications for the client was required, with supporting calculations. Here you should ensure that your main focus is the explanation, and not spend too long on the numbers.

The highlighted words in the written sections are key phrases that markers are looking for.

Tutor's top tips

The definition of furnished holiday accommodation should supply easy marks provided the conditions had been learnt.

(a)   Monisha

(i)   Furnished holiday accommodation in the UK – conditions

- The property must be available for commercial letting to the public as holiday accommodation for at least 210 days in the tax year.

- The property must be commercially let as holiday accommodation for at least 105 days in the tax year, excluding any periods of longer term occupation.

- There must be no more than 155 days of longer term occupation in the tax year.

Longer term occupation occurs where there is a continuous period of occupation by the same person for more than 31 days.

(ii)   The total tax saving for the six years ending 5 April 2029

Tutor's top tips

With the time allocation for this part, it is important to pause, think about which taxes are involved (i.e. income tax and capital gains tax) and then perform the calculations at the margin.

There is insufficient time to do full blown income tax computations before and after, and there is no need to do computations for multiple years as the levels of income and gains are the same for the first five years.

Once the situation is defined, the calculations are very straightforward. However, time needs to be spent making sure the requirement is fully understood before any calculations are performed to avoid time wasted doing unnecessary calculations.

Furnished holiday accommodation has several tax benefits. For income tax, the full cost of furniture is deductible (or capital allowances are available, if using the accruals basis) instead of claiming for replacement furniture relief and the income is relevant earnings for pension relief purposes. From a CGT point of view, the gain is eligible for business asset disposal relief, rollover relief and gift holdover relief.

Income tax

	£
Income tax saved in the first five tax years (£6,660 (W) × 40% × 5 years) (Note)	13,320
Income tax saved in the final tax year (£6,660 (W) × (40% − 20%))	1,332
Total income tax saved	14,652

Tutorial note

In the first five years, Monisha is a higher rate taxpayer but as Asmat has no other income his share of property income will be covered by his personal allowance (PA) and he will pay no tax on that income. The income tax saving will therefore be 40%.

Note that with or without the proposals, Asmat would not be able to transfer £1,260 of his unused PA to Monisha as she is a higher rate taxpayer. Therefore, his entire PA remains with him. Without the proposal to transfer income to him, his PA would be wasted.

In the final year (2028/29), Asmat will be earning £18,000 p.a. and therefore he will utilise his entire PA, even without the proposal, and he will be a basic rate taxpayer. The income tax saving from moving income from Monisha into his computation is therefore 20% (40% − 20%).

Working: Taxable property income

	£
Rental income	20,000
Less: Allowable expenses (£3,480 + £1,200 + £2,000)	(6,680)
Total property income	13,320
Amount subject to income tax in the hands of Asmat (£13,320 × 50%) (tutorial note)	6,660

For the first five tax years, Asmat will not have any other income, such that his share of the property income will be covered by his personal allowance.

Tutorial note

Despite the fact that Monisha gifts only a 20% interest in the investment property to Asmat, the income of a jointly held asset is automatically split equally between a married couple, regardless of their actual interests in the property.

Monisha and Asmat could elect to split the income between them in the ratio 80:20, but to do so would not be beneficial in their particular circumstances.

Accordingly, property income of £6,660 (W) will be subject to income tax in the hands of Asmat, rather than being taxed at 40% in the hands of Monisha, in each of the six tax years.

Capital gains tax

Tutor's top tips

Once the scenario is understood, this part follows on easily. However, remember that part of Monisha's annual exempt amount is still available.

Asmat will have a full annual exempt amount available and business asset disposal relief will be available if the property is treated as furnished holiday accommodation.

Inter spouse transfer

The gift of the 20% interest in the property will take place at no gain, no loss because Monisha and Asmat are married.

Capital gains tax saving on the disposal of the property

If the proposals are not carried out:

Monisha

	£
Total gain	100,000
Less: Annual exempt amount available	
(£12,300 – £6,300 other chargeable gains)	(6,000)
Taxable gain	94,000
CGT at 28%	26,320

If the proposals are carried out:

Monisha

	£	£
Share of gain (£100,000 × 80%)		80,000
Less: Annual exempt amount available		
(£12,300 – £6,300 other chargeable gains)		(6,000)
Taxable gain		74,000
Asmat		
Share of gain (£100,000 × 20%)	20,000	
Less: Annual exempt amount available	(12,300)	
Taxable gain		7,700
Total taxable gains		81,700
CGT at 10% (Business asset disposal relief)		8,170
Capital gains tax saved (£26,320 – £8,170)		18,150
Total tax saved (£14,652 + £18,150)		32,802

Tutorial note

1   The gain on the sale of the property will be allocated between Monisha and Asmat in the ratio 80:20.

2   A gain on the sale of furnished holiday accommodation qualifies for business asset disposal relief.

3   To be advantageous for capital gains tax purposes, it was not necessary for Monisha to transfer 50% of the interest in the property to Asmat. It was only necessary to utilise Asmat's annual exempt amount. The excess gain above the annual exempt amount is taxed at 10% regardless of who it accrues to.

(b)   Horner

Tutor's top tips

Clear explanations of when the rules apply are needed to score highly on this part.

As there are only three marks available, there is no need to go into great detail about the factors used to determine an employed or self-employed type relationship.

(i)   **The circumstances in which the personal service company (IR35) rules apply**

1   A company enters into a contract to provide services to a client.

2   The services are carried out by an individual.

3   If the services were provided under a contract between the individual and the client, the individual would be regarded as an employee of the client.

4   The individual has an interest of at least 5% in the company or an entitlement to receive payments from the company, other than salary, in respect of the services provided to the client.

In respect of condition three, when determining whether or not the individual would be regarded as an employee of the client, the rules used to distinguish between employees and the self-employed are used.

Tutorial note

It is possible for a partnership, rather than a company, to enter into the contract with the client.

(ii)   **Tax implications for Florentine Ltd of engaging Otmar Ltd.**

Tutor's top tips

When dealing with the personal service company legislation, it is important to identify the size of the client organisation involved. This determines whether it is the responsibility of the personal service company or the client to determine whether the rules apply.

As Florentine Ltd is a medium or large sized client organisation, they must determine whether Otmar Ltd falls within the personal service company legislation.

If they determine that Otmar Ltd does fall within the legislation, then they must provide a Status Determination Statement to Horner.

Florentine Ltd will be required to deduct income tax and NIC from the deemed direct payment at the relevant rates. This payment is calculated as follows:

	£
Otmar Ltd – income from relevant engagements	85,000
Less: Materials used to provide services	(3,900)
	———
Deemed direct payment	81,100
	———

Tutorial note

1   *When calculating the deemed direct payment, the cost of any materials used to carry out the services can be deducted, as well as any expenses which would normally be deductible against employment income (if any).*

2   *Horner's salary and the pension contributions are not deductible when calculating the deemed direct payment. These would only be relevant when calculating the deemed employment income where the client involved is a small organisation.*

Examiner's report

Part (a)(i) was answered very well by the majority of candidates. The only difficulty related to confusion over the meaning of 'longer term accommodation' and the maximum number of days of such occupation permitted in a tax year.

Part (a)(ii) was done poorly by many candidates who either did not have a thorough attempt at it or worked very hard but did not pause to think about how to approach the problem.

The key was to first calculate the taxable property income in order to identify the amount of taxable income that would be taxed in the hands of Asmat rather than Monisha.

It was then necessary to recognise that for the first five years under consideration, Monisha would be a higher rate taxpayer whereas Asmat's income would be covered by his personal allowance, such that no tax would be payable. Accordingly, by working at the margin, it was easy to see that for the first five years the saving would be 40% of the income transferred. In the sixth year, Asmat was expected to be employed, such that the income transferred would be taxed at 20% and the saving would therefore be 20% (40% − 20%) of the income transferred.

The problem was that very few candidates chose to work at the margin. Instead, many chose to prepare income tax computations for the two individuals before and after the transfer of the interest in the property in order to quantify the difference in the total liability. This was very time consuming. Some candidates even prepared calculations for each of the five years despite the fact that the figures were the same in each year.

Calculating tax liabilities can be very time consuming. Candidates should always stop and think about the most efficient way of approaching a set of calculations before they start writing.

The capital gains tax element of this part of the question was not handled particularly well. This was perhaps due to a shortage of time. It required candidates to recognise that an additional annual exempt amount would be available and that tax would be charged at 10%, due to the availability of business asset disposal relief, rather than at 28%. Only a minority of candidates were able to quantify the effect of these points.

The majority of candidates struggled to satisfy the requirement in part (b)(i) despite a reasonable knowledge of the rules. It was generally recognised that the rules were in place in order to prevent the avoidance of tax but there was some confusion as to exactly where tax was being avoided. Very few candidates were able to state the commercial relationship between the taxpayer, the personal service company and the client in a clear manner.

The final part of the examiner's report has been removed as it relates to part of the question which has been changed since the question was set.

		ACCA marking scheme		Marks
(a)	(i)	The conditions – one mark each		3.0
		Meaning of longer term occupation		1.0
				4.0
			Maximum	3.0
	(ii)	Income tax		
		Taxable property income		1.0
		Allocated equally		1.0
		First five tax years		1.5
		Final tax year		1.0
		Capital gains tax		
		Gift of 20% interest is at no gain, no loss		1.0
		Capital gains tax if the proposals are not carried out		1.5
		Capital gains tax if the proposals are carried out		2.5
		Total saving		0.5
				10.0
(b)	(i)	The conditions – one mark each		3.0
		Reference to rules used to determine employer, employee relationship		1.0
				4.0
			Maximum	3.0
	(ii)	Responsibility is with Florentine Ltd		1.0
		Status Determination Statement		0.5
		Deduct income tax and NIC		1.0
		Deemed direct payment		1.0
		No deduction for salary and pension contributions		0.5
				4.0
Total				**20.0**

49   STELLA AND MARIS (ADAPTED) *Walk in the footsteps of a top tutor*

Key answer tips

This section B question is really two separate questions which could be attempted in either order. The first covers income tax and relief for pension contributions; the second covers pension benefits and inheritance tax exemptions.

Given the heavy emphasis on pensions, this may not have been the most popular question in the exam.

Part (a) is similar to questions seen in other ATX exams and tests the pensions annual allowance charge. Note that the restriction of the annual allowance has been introduced since this question was set in the exam, so this aspect would not have needed consideration in the original question.

Part (b)(i) tests the application of the lifetime allowance for pensions, which is only tested rarely in the ATX exam.

Part (b)(ii) is a much more straightforward section covering the small gifts exemption and normal expenditure from income.

The highlighted words in the written sections are key phrases that markers are looking for.

(a)   Stella – Income after-tax and pension contributions 2022/23

Tutor's top tips

There are easy marks here for basic income tax computations and for calculating income after tax.

The key to scoring well was recognising that there would also be an excess pension contribution. In order to calculate the annual allowance available, you had to consider if there was any unused relief brought forward from the previous three years and also if the current year annual allowance needed to be restricted.

Remember the unrestricted annual allowance is £40,000 for 2022/23 but can be increased by any unused AA in the previous three years, starting with the earliest year first.

The personal pension contributions also extend the basic and higher rate bands.

Note that the annual allowance tax charge is calculated using the taxpayer's marginal rate of tax.

Detailed calculations such as those needed in requirement (a) are best completed in the spreadsheet response option in the exam. Formulae can be used to cut down on calculation time, but remember it is still important to label all workings.

Income tax liability

	£
Employment income	203,000
Property income	92,000
Net income	295,000
Less: Personal allowance (W1)	(0)
Taxable income (all non-savings income)	295,000

£		£
127,700	× 20% (W2)	25,540
112,300	× 40%	44,920
240,000	(W2)	
55,000	× 45%	24,750
295,000		
67,500	× 45% (annual allowance charge) (W3)	30,375
Income tax liability		125,585

Income after-tax and pension contributions

	£
Income received	295,000
Less: Income tax liability	(125,585)
Less: Pension contributions paid (W5)	(72,000)
Income after-tax and pension contributions	97,415

Tutorial note

The ATX examining team has stated that credit was also awarded to candidates who calculated the class 1 national insurance contributions on Stella's employment income.

Workings

(W1) Personal allowance

	£
Net income	295,000
Less: Gross PPCs	(90,000)
Adjusted net income (ANI)	205,000

As ANI is > £125,140; the personal allowance is reduced to £nil.

(W2) Extended basic and higher rate bands

	£	£
Current bands	37,700	150,000
Add: Gross PPCs qualifying for tax relief	90,000	90,000
Revised bands	127,700	240,000

(W3) Annual allowance charge

	£
Annual allowance for 2022/23 (W4)	12,500
Unused annual allowance for three previous tax years:	
2019/20 (£40,000 − £30,000)	10,000
2020/21 (£40,000 − £40,000)	0
2021/22 (£40,000 − £40,000)	0
Maximum gross pension contribution in 2022/23	22,500

Annual allowance charge is £67,500 (£90,000 − £22,500).

(W4) Threshold income 2022/23

	£
Net income	295,000
Less: Gross personal pension contributions	(90,000)
Threshold income	205,000

As threshold income is > £200,000 it is necessary to calculate adjusted income to determine if a restriction to the 2022/23 annual allowance is required.

Adjusted income 2022/23

	£
Net income	295,000
Plus: Employer/employee occupational pension contributions	0
Adjusted income	295,000

As adjusted income is > £240,000 (and threshold income is > £200,000) the annual allowance must be restricted.

	£
Annual allowance 2022/23	40,000
Less: (£295,000 – £240,000) × 50%	(27,500)
Revised annual allowance	12,500

Tutorial note

The minimum annual allowance for a tax year is £4,000, but this is not relevant to Stella as her annual allowance for the tax year 2022/23 exceeds this amount

(W5) Pension contributions paid

The amount actually paid in respect of the pension contribution by Stella is £72,000 (£90,000 × 80%).

(b) (i) Maris – Maximum receivable as a lump sum

Tutor's top tips

You should be aware of the basic rule that 25% of the pension fund can be taken tax free, and you are given the lifetime allowance in the tax rates and allowances. There are easy marks for discussing and applying these.

As this requirement is discursive it lends itself better to being completed in the word processor response option in the exam. Be sure to label up each requirement clearly so that it is clear to the marker what is being answered where.

The value of Maris's pension fund exceeds the lifetime allowance of £1,073,100.

Accordingly, the maximum lump sum which she can take tax-free is restricted to £268,275 (25% × £1,073,100).

The excess of the fund over the lifetime allowance may be taken as a lump sum, subject to an income tax charge at 55% on the value of this excess.

Any withdrawals from the balance of the lifetime allowance will be treated as taxable non savings income. As Maris is a higher rate taxpayer, these would be taxed at 40%, or possibly 45% if her total income increases above the higher rate limit of £150,000.

(ii) Inheritance tax – Lifetime exemptions available

Tutor's top tips

This section should offer easy marks as long as you write down the conditions for the exemptions to apply and refer to the information given in the question wherever possible.

There are six marks available, so try to make six separately identifiable points in your answer.

Small gift exemption

Maris can make exempt gifts valued at up to £250 each tax year to any number of recipients. If the total value of the gifts to any one recipient exceeds £250, the full value of the gifts will be taxable. The gifts can comprise either cash or shares.

Exemption for normal expenditure out of income

The following conditions must be satisfied for the gifts to be exempt:

– The gift is made as part of Maris's normal expenditure. As she is intending to make regular gifts to her family on their birthdays, she should be able to establish a regular pattern of giving.

– The gift is made out of income, not capital. Maris must therefore give cash, not part of her shareholdings.

– Maris is left with sufficient income to maintain her usual standard of living. As she appears to have fairly significant pension and savings income this condition should be satisfied.

There is no monetary limit on the amount of this exemption.

				Marks
		ACCA marking scheme		
(a)		Qualifying pension contributions		1.0
		Taxable income		2.0
		Restriction of annual allowance 2022/23		1.0
		Excess pension contribution		3.0
		Income tax liability		2.5
		Net income after-tax and pension contributions		2.0
				11.5
			Maximum	10.0
(b)	(i)	Tax free amount		1.5
		Taxed amount		2.5
				4.0
	(ii)	Small gift exemption		3.0
		Exemption for normal expenditure out of income		4.0
				7.0
			Maximum	6.0
Total				**20.0**

50   PIPPIN *Walk in the footsteps of a top tutor*

Key answer tips

This is a three-part Section A scenario question covering an individual setting up an unincorporated business, inheritance tax, and EIS shares.

The three requirements can be answered independently, so careful thought should be given to the order in which you attempt the question. Identify the parts that you think you can answer quickly and attempt these first, leaving parts of the question that you think you will be tempted to spend too long on until last.

Make sure that you set out the question as a memorandum with an appropriate heading, set out your answer neatly and express yourself clearly in order to score the presentation marks available. You should also try to answer the question succinctly; this will save you time and help with the professional marks!

The first part of the question requires some basic level income tax and national insurance computations, but is likely to be very time pressured.

Requirement (ii) tests the IHT implications of a gift that could either be a lifetime gift or a transfer from an estate.

Requirement (iii) covers the sale of shares that qualified for EIS relief.

The highlighted words in the written sections are key phrases that markers are looking for in your memorandum.

(i)   Memorandum

      Client: Pippin

      Subject: Pinova business

      Prepared by: Tax senior

      Date: 8 June 2022

Tutor's top tips

In the first part of this question, you are given a table to complete, so there will be marks available for doing this, even if your figures are incorrect.

You must adopt a methodical approach and label your answer. There are two strategies to consider, and two tax years for each strategy, so make sure that you address all of these.

Once you have decided how to set out your answer, the actual calculations are relatively straightforward, basic level calculations. Don't forget the NICs, as there are easy marks available for calculating these, and all of the rates and thresholds are given in the tax tables.

Additional funds required for the 20-month period from 1 August 2022 to 31 March 2024

	Strategy A	Strategy B
	£	£
Total pre-tax cash receipts for the 20-month period	61,000	109,500
Cost of employing the two employees:		
(£48,000 + £3,000 + £226)	0	(51,226)
Total income tax and national insurance contribution liabilities for the tax years 2022/23 and 2023/24		
(£0 + £15,449)	(15,449)	
(£23,334 – £7,560)		(15,774)
	45,551	42,500
Personal expenditure (£4,000 × 20)	(80,000)	(80,000)
Additional funds required	34,449	37,500

Strategy A

2022/23

	£
Budgeted profit	13,000
Less: Capital allowances 100% AIA	(8,000)
Tax adjusted trading profit	5,000
Less: Personal allowance	(5,000)
Taxable income	0

Tutor's top tips

Although this is a new unincorporated business, Pippin has chosen to have a 31 March year end, so the trading profits are assessed on the actual basis and there are no overlap profits.

Income tax:

	£
Covered by the personal allowance	0
Class 4 national insurance contributions (NICs):	
Below the lower profits limit	0
Class 2 NICs:	
Below the small profits threshold	0
	———
Total tax and NICs	0
	———

Tutorial note

Non-payment of class 2 NICs can affect the availability of state benefits, including the state pension.

Accordingly, it may be advisable for Pippin to pay the class 2 NICs even if his profit is below the small profits threshold.

2023/24

	£	£
Tax adjusted trading profit		60,000
Dividend income		1,500
Less: Personal allowance		(12,570)
		———
Taxable income		48,930
		———

Analysed as: Dividend income £1,500, non-savings income £47,430.

Income tax:

£	£	£
37,700 × 20% (non-savings)	7,540	
9,730 × 40% (non-savings)	3,892	
────		
47,430		
1,500 × 0% (dividend nil rate band)	0	
────		
48,930		
────		
	────	
		11,432
Class 4 NICs:		
(£50,270 − £9,568) × 9%	3,663	
(£60,000 − £50,270) × 2%	195	
	────	
		3,858
Class 2 NICs:		
(£3.05 × 52)		159
		────
Total tax and NICs		15,449
		────

Strategy B

2022/23

	£
Budgeted loss	(10,000)
Less: Capital allowances 100% AIA	(8,000)
	────
Tax adjusted trading loss	(18,000)
	────

Claiming opening years loss relief will result in a repayment of income tax and class 4 NICs of £7,560 (£18,000 × 42%) in respect of the tax year 2019/20.

2023/24

	£	£
Budgeted profit		130,000
Less: Cost of employees		
Salaries (£2,000 × 12 × 2)		(48,000)
Mileage allowance (£0.50 × 250 × 12 ×2)		(3,000)
Class 1 NICs:		
Salary (£2,000 × 12)	24,000	
Mileage payments ((£0.50 – £0.45) × 250 × 12)	150	
	24,150	
(£24,150 – £8,840) × 13.8% × 2)	4,226	
Less: Employment allowance	(4,000)	
		(226)
Tax adjusted trading profit		78,774
Income tax and NICs on profit of £60,000 (per strategy A)		15,449
Income tax and class 4 NICs on excess over £60,000		
(£78,774 – £60,000) × 42%		7,885
Total tax and NICs		23,334

Tutorial note

This answer calculates the income tax and NICs using the tax from strategy A as a base, and working in the margin to calculate the extra tax due. As Pippin is already a higher rate tax payer and his trading profit exceeds the upper threshold for national insurance, any additional income is subject to income tax at 40% and NICs at 2%.

Alternatively, you could have calculated the income tax and NICs on the tax adjusted trading profit of £78,774 from scratch. This gives the same answer and would gain the same marks in the exam, but takes considerably more time.

Evaluation of the two strategies

Tutor's top tips

You are asked to evaluate the two strategies by reference to the results of your calculations, so make sure you do this.

Even if your answer is not correct, you could still gain marks here for making some sensible comments about which strategy requires the least additional funding.

Strategy A requires less additional funding than strategy B over the 20-month period.

However, the annual profit under strategy A will only be £60,000. This will not be sufficient to generate the £48,000 (£4,000 × 12) of post-tax cash receipts required by Pippin.

The post-tax profit under Strategy B will be £55,440 (£130,000 − £51,226 − £23,334), such that there may be sufficient post-tax cash receipts for Pippin's needs.

(ii)   Receipt of £75,000

Tutor's top tips

This part of the question covers inheritance tax from the point of view of an individual who has received a gift of cash, and there are two alternatives to consider.

If Esme gave the cash to Pippin, the gift would be a potentially exempt transfer, so any tax liability would be borne by Pippin (the donee). You need to explain how much tax would be due.

However, if Pippin received the cash directly from Esme's father's death estate, the tax would be borne by the estate.

The question states that Esme's father left the whole of his estate to Esme, so the only way that Pippin could receive the cash from the estate would be if Esme changed her father's will using a deed of variation.

The tax implications for Pippin depend on whether the £75,000 was a direct gift from Esme or the result of Esme having made a tax-effective deed of variation of her father's will.

Gift from Esme

The gift would have been a potentially exempt transfer. Esme's death within seven years of the gift would result in an inheritance tax liability for Pippin as follows:

	£
Transfer	75,000
	————
Inheritance tax at 40% (Note)	30,000
Taper relief (5 to 6 years) (£30,000 × 60%)	(18,000)
	————
	12,000
	————

Note: Esme's annual exemptions and her nil rate band were used by the gift on 1 November 2016.

Deed of variation

A deed of variation whereby £75,000 of Esme's inheritance was transferred to Pippin would not be treated as a gift from Esme to Pippin. Instead, the money would be regarded as having passed to Pippin via his grandfather's will. Accordingly, in these circumstances, there would be no inheritance tax implications for Pippin as a result of the death of Esme.

(iii)   Sale of shares in Akero Ltd

Tutor's top tips

The treatment of EIS shares is a new topic at the strategic professional level, and often features in the exam. There are lots of rules to learn, and you should make sure that you learn the key rules at least.

This question deals with the sale of shares and possible withdrawal of relief if the sale occurs within less than three years of purchase.

As you are not given the date of sale, you need to consider the possibility that the sale could happen within less than three years of purchase or after more than three years.

There are three different aspects to write about:

1   The possible gain on the sale of the shares.

2   The deferred gain becoming chargeable.

3   The withdrawal of EIS income tax relief.

To score well, you should write about all of these.

Capital gains tax

Chargeable gain on the sale of the shares

Pippin will realise a chargeable gain of £17,500 ((£4.50 − £1) × 5,000) if the shares are sold prior to 4 January 2023 (i.e. within three years of purchase) at their current market value.

However, if the shares are sold on or after 4 January 2023, the chargeable gain arising on the sale will be exempt.

Chargeable gain deferred in respect of the painting

Regardless of when the shares are sold, the chargeable gain which was deferred on their acquisition will become chargeable.

The chargeable gain deferred was £16,000, or £1 per share, such that, on the sale of 5,000 shares, a gain of £5,000 will become chargeable.

Capital gains tax liability

Any chargeable gains realised by Pippin in the tax year 2022/23 will be reduced by his annual exempt amount of £12,300.

Any gains not covered by the annual exempt amount will be taxed at 10%, as Pippin has no taxable income.

Income tax

If the shares are sold prior to 4 January 2023 at their current market value, there will be a withdrawal of £1,500 (5,000 × £1 × 30%) of the income tax relief originally obtained by Pippin. This is because the shares will have been sold for more than their cost.

Tutor's top tips

Even if you were not sure how to calculate the withdrawal of the income tax relief, you would still be given credit for stating that there would be a withdrawal of relief.

Examiner's report

The first part concerned a plan to start a new unincorporated business. Candidates were asked to prepare a table of figures in order to determine the individual's cash position for two alternative business strategies after two years of trading. One of the strategies required the individual to take on two employees.

The technical content of this part of the question was reasonably straightforward and required candidates to:

- recognise the availability of the annual investment allowance
- determine the relief available in respect of a trading loss in the first tax year of trading
- deal with the tax implications for the employer of paying a mileage allowance to the employees
- calculate the employer's class 1 contributions in respect of the employees
- calculate the income tax, class 4 and class 2 liabilities of the individual.

Accordingly, in order to do well, candidates needed to concentrate on the detail, be brisk in their approach and avoid any unnecessary narrative. Many candidates were able to do this and there were some very high quality answers to this part of the question.

Weaker candidates were less willing to commit themselves to the numbers and instead wrote about the tax implications in more general terms. Some candidates also let themselves down by failing to consider the individual's national insurance contributions position, such that they did not attempt quite a few of the marks on offer.

There were few technical problems with this part of the question. The one common error was the implications of the mileage allowance, with most candidates knowing there was a rule regarding the excess over 45p per mile but many thinking it related to the tax deductibility of the payments made as opposed to the class 1 contributions due.

The second part of the question concerned inheritance tax and was done reasonably well. Candidates were very comfortable with the basic mechanics of the tax including death within seven years of a potentially exempt transfer (PET), the nil rate band and the availability of taper relief. Weaker candidates did not always relate the facts of the question to the requirement, such that they ignored the chargeable lifetime transfer which was made prior to, but in the same tax year as, the PET. This meant that they wrote in general terms about the availability of the annual exemption and the nil rate band rather than applying the rules to the specific facts of the question.

The final part of the question required candidates to explain the tax liabilities on the sale of shares in respect of which income tax relief under the enterprise investment scheme and EIS deferral relief had been claimed.

As is so often the case, in order to score well, candidates needed to stop and think. In particular, they needed to identify the three separate implications of the sale of the shares. It was important to do this first because candidates then knew how much needed to be explained in the relatively short amount of time available.

The three implications which needed to be explained were:

- the gain which was deferred when the shares would become chargeable
- an element of the income tax relief obtained when the shares were acquired would be withdrawn
- there would be a chargeable gain on the sale of the shares themselves.

Weaker candidates identified one of these points and wrote about it at length rather than identifying all of the points which needed to be made.

ACCA marking scheme		
		Marks
(i)	Completion of table	1.5
	Strategy A	
	2022/23	3.5
	2023/24	5.0
	Strategy B	
	Cost of employees	5.5
	2022/23	3.5
	2023/24	2.5
	Evaluation	2.0
		———
		23.5
	Maximum	20.0
		———
(ii)	PET and death within seven years	3.5
	Deed of variation	2.0
		———
		5.5
	Maximum	5.0
		———
(iii)	Gain on shares sold	2.0
	Deferred gain	2.0
	Capital gains tax liability	1.5
	Income tax	1.5
		———
		7.0
	Maximum	6.0
		———
	Problem solving	1.0
	Clarity of explanations and calculations	1.0
	Effectiveness of communication	1.0
	Overall presentation and style	1.0
		———
		4.0
		———
Total		**35.0**
		———

51   FLORINA, KANZI AND WINSTON (ADAPTED)   *Walk in the footsteps of a top tutor*

Key answer tips

This question covers various income tax and capital gains tax issues for an individual, inheritance tax planning relating to a charitable gift, and ethics.

Part (a) covers three separate areas. The first requires comparison of the tax implications for both the individual and the company of extracting funds as either dividends or payment to a pension. The next section requires consideration of whether or not private fuel provided by the company should be reimbursed, to avoid a fuel benefit. The final section requires tax planning for a sale of shares by the couple, to minimise the capital gains tax paid. Much of the technical content in part (a) of the question is from TX, but is tested here in a more challenging way.

Part (b) covers the regularly tested area of inheritance tax for lifetime giving versus transfer on death; here, in relation to a gift to charity.

Part (c) covers ethical concerns relating to accepting a new client who is related to existing clients.

The highlighted words in the written sections are key phrases that markers are looking for in your answer.

(a)   Florina and Kanzi

Florina's remuneration from Flight Hip Ltd

Tutor's top tips

When you are asked to calculate tax costs or savings, think about whether it will be possible to work 'in the margin' rather than preparing full income tax or corporation tax computations. There are only 4.5 marks available for this first part of (a), so you do not have much time.

It is clear that Florina will be a higher rate taxpayer based on her current salary and benefits, and her other dividends will have used part of her dividend nil rate band (DNRB). Accordingly, you can calculate the tax due on the dividend from Flight Hip Ltd very quickly using 0% for the part falling into the DNRB, and 32.5% for the balance.

Any tax allowable payments by the company (i.e. the pension contribution) will save corporation tax at 19%.

There is a mixture of numerical and discursive requirements in this question, be sure to use the most appropriate response option in the exam for each part of your answer. The spreadsheet is more appropriate for detailed calculations, whereas the word processor is more appropriate for the discursive parts.

Payment of dividend of £20,000

	£
Income tax:	
£500 (£2,000 – £1,500) × 0%	0
£19,500 × 32.5%	6,338
	–––––
Tax cost (equal to the tax saving if the dividend is not paid)	6,338
	–––––

Payment of pension contributions of £20,000

	£	£
Corporation tax saving (£20,000 × 19%)		3,800
Income tax:		
On the employer pension contributions	0	
On future pension withdrawal		
Tax free lump sum (£20,000 × 25% × 0%)	0	
Balance of pension (£20,000 × 75% × 20%)	3,000	
	–––––	(3,000)
		–––––
Net tax saving		800
		–––––

The total tax saving would be £7,138 (£6,338 + £800).

Provision of free petrol

Tutor's top tips

The free petrol provided by Flight Hip Ltd is for company cars, so the cost to the employee will be the income tax payable on the fuel benefit. The statutory mileage allowance is only relevant for employees using their own cars for business purposes, so does not apply here.

	Florina	Kanzi
	£	£
Income tax payable by Florina on the fuel benefit (Note):		
Car used by Florina (£24,600 × 26% × 40%)	2,558	
Car used by Kanzi (£24,600 × 23% × 40%)		2,263
Cost of private petrol:		
Florina (£3,000 × 17,000/19,000)	(2,684)	
Kanzi		(800)
Financial benefit/cost of the free petrol:		
	–––––	
Florina – income tax is less than cost	(126)	
	–––––	–––––
Kanzi – income tax is more than cost		1,463
		–––––

It would be financially beneficial for Kanzi to stop receiving free petrol from Flight Hip Ltd, as Florina's tax liability in respect of the benefit exceeds the cost of the petrol.

Tutorial note

The provision of the car and free petrol to Kanzi will give rise to a taxable benefit for Florina. This is because Kanzi is not an employee of Flight Hip Ltd but is a member of Florina's household.

Sale of shares in Landing Properties Ltd

Tutor's top tips

*Read the question carefully! Florina and Kanzi are **not** married, so a gift of shares from Florina to Kanzi will **not** take place at no gain, no loss, but will instead be treated as a disposal at market value.*

However, as the shares are a qualifying asset, gift holdover relief may be claimed to defer the gain until the shares are sold by Kanzi.

This means that you can still consider the usual tax planning points for the couple, i.e. use both annual exempt amounts and ensure that gains are taxed at basic rates rather than higher rates.

Gift from Florina to Kanzi – gift holdover relief

Landing Properties Ltd is an unquoted company. However, for gift holdover relief to be available, it must also be a trading company.

On the assumption that gift holdover relief is available, Florina should sell sufficient shares to realise a chargeable gain equal to her annual exempt amount of £12,300.

The total chargeable gain is as follows:

	£
Proceeds = MV	40,000
Less: Cost	(8,000)
Gain on shares	32,000

This gives a gain per share of £8 (£32,000/4,000), so Florina should sell 1,537 shares (£12,300 ÷ £8).

The remaining 2,463 (4,000 – 1,537) shares should be given to Kanzi in order to use his annual exempt amount and to take advantage of the fact that he is a basic rate taxpayer as opposed to a higher rate taxpayer. Florina's chargeable gain in respect of this gift will be held over against Kanzi's base cost in the shares.

Sale of 2,463 shares by Kanzi

	£	£
Proceeds (£40,000 × 2,463/4,000)		24,630
Less: Cost:		
Market value of gift from Florina	24,630	
Less: Gain held over		
((£40,000 – £8,000) × 2,463/4,000)	(19,704)	
	———	(4,926)
Chargeable gain		19,704
Less: Annual exempt amount		(12,300)
Taxable gain – falls within basic rate band		7,404
Capital gains tax (£7,404 × 10%)		740
Capital gains tax saving (£3,940 – £740)		3,200

Tutorial note

Kanzi's gain can be calculated more simply as £32,000 × 2,463/4,000 = £19,704.

(b) **Winston's charitable donation**

Tutor's top tips

Make sure that your answer is clearly labelled here, so that the marker can see whether you are considering the donation to charity as a lifetime gift or a transfer on death. The key difference between the lifetime gift and the transfer on death is the availability of the reduced rate of inheritance tax of 36%, which only applies for transfers on death.

In either case the residence nil rate band (RNRB) will be available since the chargeable death estate will include Winston's main residence and the property is inherited by his direct descendants (in this case his children). The available RNRB is the lower of £175,000 (given in the tax tables in the exam) and the value of the property (which is clearly higher in this case).

Lifetime gift – inheritance tax on death estate

Gifts to charity are exempt from inheritance tax.

Tutor's top tips

Note that if the donation is made during lifetime, it will reduce the assets remaining in Winston's death estate.

	£
Death estate (£1,500,000 – £150,000)	1,350,000
Less: Residence nil rate band	(175,000)
Less: Nil rate band (£325,000 – £225,000)	(100,000)
Taxable estate	1,075,000
Inheritance tax at 40%	430,000

Gift via Winston's will – inheritance tax on death estate

	£
Death estate	1,500,000
Less: Exempt legacy	(150,000)
Less: Residence nil rate band	(175,000)
Less: Nil rate band	(100,000)
Taxable estate	1,075,000
Inheritance tax at 36% (Note)	387,000

It is more tax-efficient for Winston to make the charitable donation via his will.

Tutorial note

The reduced rate of 36% is applicable because the charitable legacy of £150,000 exceeds 10% of Winston's death estate before deduction of the charitable legacy and the residence nil rate band but after deduction of the nil rate band, i.e. £1,400,000 (£1,500,000 – £100,000).

(c)   **Becoming Winston's tax adviser**

Tutor's top tips

There will be five marks on ethical issues in Section A of every exam. These can be very easy marks to score, as long as you have revised the commonly tested ethical scenarios and apply your knowledge to the scenario.

Always make sure that you read the requirement carefully: this question specifically asked for threats to the fundamental principles of professional ethics so you should have restricted your answer to those principles rather than general ethical issues around 'sophisticated tax planning'.

Professional competence

We must ensure that we have access to the appropriate expertise to carry out the sophisticated tax planning required by Winston.

Objectivity

It is possible that providing advice to Winston in connection with his estate planning could give rise to a conflict of interest, because a course of action which reduces Winston's total inheritance tax liability may not necessarily be beneficial for Florina.

We should obtain permission from both Florina and Winston to act for both of them and should consider making a different member of the firm responsible for each of them.

Confidentiality

Winston and Florina have attended a tax-planning meeting together and so do not appear to require their affairs to be kept confidential from each other. However, we should ensure that we have clear guidelines in place in order to maintain confidentiality where necessary and we should obtain written permission to discuss the affairs of one of them with the other when it is appropriate to do so.

Examiner's report

The first part of the question concerned income tax and capital gains tax issues for an individual and was not well done.

Extraction of profits by an individual from a company is another frequently tested topic. Candidates essentially had to compare the tax implications, for both the individual and the company, of two alternative ways of extracting profits from the company. An appropriate first step in such a question is to determine the current income tax position of the individual in terms of their marginal rate of tax, to ascertain whether a marginal approach can be taken. Despite the fact that this approach has been used in several past exam questions, very few candidates adopted this approach here, which was very surprising. The majority of candidates wasted a considerable amount of time calculating the individual's total income tax liability under both options, involving lengthy, detailed computations. Although, on occasion, detailed computations may be needed, candidates would be advised to ensure that they are able to identify when a marginal approach is appropriate, and able to calculate the relevant tax liabilities using this method.

The decision of whether or not it is beneficial to reimburse fuel provided by the company for private travel in a company car, is a very practical one. Taxable benefits are covered in depth at TX, and candidates should expect to see further testing of this knowledge at ATX, albeit in more practical scenarios. Many candidates produced very muddled answers here, in particular confusing application of the fuel benefit, which is relevant where the individual has a company car, with the tax-free statutory mileage allowance, which is used where an individual uses their own car for business journeys. Although this technical knowledge is not new at ATX, candidates should ensure they have practised past ATX exam questions so they are familiar with the ATX exam approach.

Finally, in this first part candidates had to advise on the availability of gift holdover relief, and calculate the number of shares to be gifted, using gift holdover relief, to obtain the maximum tax saving for the couple in question. Once again, many candidates' knowledge of this capital gains tax relief was rather vague and many barely attempted the planning point. Candidates need to be familiar with the conditions for, and implications of, capital gains tax reliefs such as this.

The second part of the question related to the different implications for inheritance tax of an individual making a charitable gift now, or leaving the same amount to the charity in their will. The majority of candidates were able to identify that a key point here was the availability of the reduced rate of inheritance tax available in a situation where the donation is made via the will and it represents at least 10% of the chargeable estate. However, apart from this, answers were very mixed, with the better answers clearly explaining and calculating the inheritance tax in both scenarios, while a common issue among weaker answers was a failure to provide any explanations, or even to label the computations – whether it related to the lifetime gift, or donation via the will – which caused unnecessary confusion and inevitably restricted the marks available. Candidates must clearly label their computations, and should take note of how this is done in model answers to past exam questions.

The final part of the question concerned ethical issues in relation to acting for a new client and answers were somewhat disappointing. In particular, a reference to 'sophisticated tax planning' required by the client (to elicit discussion of whether the firm had the necessary expertise), appeared to be regarded by a good number of candidates as alluding to possible tax evasion, and this was followed by a discussion of evasion, money laundering etc., a topic which the candidates had no doubt revised, but candidates should generally take the information provided in a question at face value, unless there is a clear indication that for some reason it is not to be relied upon.

ACCA marking scheme		Marks
(a) Dividend or pension		
Dividend		1.5
Pension contributions		4.0
Free petrol		
Florina		2.0
Kanzi		2.5
Sale of shares in Landing Properties Ltd		
Availability of gift holdover relief		1.5
Strategy		
Florina's chargeable gain		2.0
Kanzi's tax liability		3.5
		———
		17.0
	Maximum	14.0
		———
(b) Residence nil rate band		1.0
Nil rate band		1.0
Lifetime gift		2.0
Gift via will		3.5
		———
		7.5
	Maximum	6.0
		———
(c) Competence		1.0
Objectivity		3.0
Confidentiality		2.0
		———
		6.0
	Maximum	5.0
		———
Total		**25.0**
		———

52   JESSICA *Walk in the footsteps of a top tutor*

Key answer tips

The first part of the question focuses on the tax treatment of a redundancy package with a small income tax calculation. This offers easy marks if you have learnt the rules.

The second part of the question is a common requirement to see in ATX of discussing loss relief options and calculating tax savings. You should ensure you are well prepared to deal with the tax saving calculations.

The final part of the question covers the maximum contribution that can be made into a pension scheme without an annual allowance charge. Care should be taken around the level of relevant earnings and also the level of annual allowance.

The highlighted words in the written sections are key phrases that markers are looking for in your answer.

(a) **Income tax implications of the redundancy package**

The statutory redundancy pay is fully exempt from income tax. However, it reduces the £30,000 exemption available for the ex-gratia payment.

The taxable amount of the ex-gratia payment is therefore £20,000 (£37,000 – (£30,000 – £13,000)).

The cash equivalent of the gift of the laptop computer must also be included. This is the higher of:

1　　the market value at 31 March 2022, i.e. £540; and

2　　the value of the laptop computer at the date it was first provided to Jessica, less the amounts subsequently taxed on her as a benefit, i.e. £680 (£850 – £170 (20% × £850))

The total taxable amount of the package is therefore £20,680 (£20,000 + £680).

The package is taxed as the top slice of Jessica's income for the tax year 2021/22, so the income tax payable on the redundancy package will be £9,306 (£20,680 × 45%).

Tutorial note

Jessica's taxable income for the tax year 2021/22 already exceeds £150,000 (salary £145,000 + rental income £6,000; no personal allowance is available). Jessica is therefore an additional rate taxpayer.

(b) **(i)** **Reliefs available for Jessica's share of the partnership loss**

The trading loss for tax purposes has arisen in the tax year 2022/23.

It can be relieved against Jessica's total income for 2022/23, the tax year of the loss, and/or 2021/22, the previous tax year.

Alternatively, because the loss has arisen in one of the first four tax years in which Jessica will be a partner, it can be relieved against her total income of the three years prior to the year of the loss starting with the earliest year (i.e. 2019/20).

(ii) **Strategy for loss relief to maximise Jessica's income tax savings**

Tutor's top tips

It is important to consider each of the loss relief options in turn. You should consider Jessica's income for the year to determine what rate of tax she would pay so that the tax saving can be calculated.

Jessica will join the Langley Partnership on 1 July 2022. Accordingly, her share of the partnership loss for the year ending 31 March 2023 will be £48,000 (£160,000 × 9/12 × 40%).

In 2022/23, Jessica's only source of income will be rental income of £6,000. As this will be covered by her personal allowance, relieving the loss in this year will not result in any tax saving.

In 2021/22, Jessica's taxable income before loss relief will be £171,850 (£145,000 + £6,000 + £170 + £20,680).

As Jessica is an additional rate taxpayer, the loss of £48,000 will generate a tax saving of £20,293 ((£21,850 (£171,850 − £150,000) × 45%) + (£26,150 (£48,000 − £21,850) × 40%)).

If, alternatively, Jessica carries the loss back to the tax year 2019/20 it will be relieved against her total income of that year of £145,000. As the resulting total income of £97,000 (£145,000 − £48,000) is below £100,000, the personal allowance will become available. Accordingly, the total income tax saving will be £24,228 ((£48,000 × 40%) + (£12,570 × 40%)).

Therefore, the most beneficial claim is to carry back the loss and offset it in the tax year 2019/20 as this results in the highest tax saving, of £24,228.

(c) Jessica – maximum pension contributions 2022/23 and 2023/24

The maximum gross contribution which Jessica can make attracting tax relief each tax year is the higher of

1   Jessica's relevant earnings in the tax year; and

2   the basic amount of £3,600.

Jessica has no relevant earnings in the tax year 2022/23 as the Langley Partnership has made a loss in that year, and she has no other source of earned income. So the maximum contribution she can make in the tax year 2022/23 is £3,600.

In 2023/24, Jessica has relevant earnings of £82,000 (£205,000 × 40%) comprising her share of the partnership profit for the year ending 31 March 2024. Accordingly, she can make a contribution into the scheme of up to £82,000. This exceeds the annual allowance available of £40,000, but as she was a member of a pension scheme in 2022/23 she can bring forward her unused allowance from that tax year of £36,400 (£40,000 − £3,600).

Therefore, the total amount of annual allowance available is £76,400 (£40,000 + £36,400), so this is the maximum gross contribution which Jessica can make without incurring an annual allowance charge.

Tutorial note

No unused relief can be brought forward from years prior to the tax year 2022/23 as Jessica was not a member of a pension scheme until 1 May 2022.

Jessica's level of income is quite clearly low enough to ensure the full £40,000 annual allowance is available. You should not waste time doing lengthy calculations around this.

Examiner's report

This question concerned the receipt of a redundancy package on leaving employment, the reliefs available for an individual's share of a partnership trading loss, and the payment of contributions into a personal pension scheme.

The first part concerned the income tax implications of the receipt of a redundancy package comprising a statutory redundancy payment, an ex-gratia payment, and retention of a company provided laptop computer. Most candidates were clearly very comfortable with the availability of the £30,000 exemption in respect of the ex-gratia payment, and the fact that this would be reduced by the amount of the statutory redundancy payment. However, relatively few appeared to realise that the statutory redundancy pay is always exempt, irrespective of this, as this statement was rarely made. The majority of candidates included the laptop computer in their calculation, but did not know how to calculate its value, being an asset transferred to an employee who has previously been taxed on the provision of the benefit under the '20% × market value rule'. Termination payments are regularly tested at ATX, and should provide an opportunity for candidates to score well if they have practised these, and taken note of what has been required in previous model answers.

The second part of this question required candidates to state the loss reliefs available to a partner who has just joined a loss making partnership. On the whole, candidates scored well on this part. The main issue seen was a lack of accuracy in identifying the available reliefs. The rules relating to trading losses are frequently examined, and candidates are expected to be precise in this sort of question. Candidates would do well to invest time at the revision stage of their studies memorising the rules concerning relief for trading losses, and ensuring that they are able to recognise those rules which apply in a given scenario. In particular, they should be able to identify those which apply in certain situations only, such as the opening years of a business, as here. It was disappointing to see that a number of candidates included consideration of the relief available by carrying the loss forward, when the requirement had specifically stated that the taxpayer did not want to do this. This wasted time, particularly if the candidate then went on to consider the tax savings in the next part.

The third part of the question required a calculation of the loss available to the partner, and determination of the loss relief strategy which would provide the highest income tax saving for the taxpayer.

Those candidates who scored well on this particular part:

– adopted a structured, methodical approach to considering in turn each of the reliefs for the trading loss which they had identified in the previous part, stating the taxpayer's total income in each year, and hence being able to identify the rate of tax which would be saved.

– Didn't waste time considering irrelevant reliefs.

In order to gain a good mark in this type of question it is vital that candidates attempt past exam questions. Reading through model answers, while providing useful information, is often of limited help in these cases; candidates need to practise the structured approach necessary to produce a good, coherent answer.

The final part of the question concerned an explanation and calculation of the maximum amount of contributions which could be paid into the taxpayer's personal pension scheme without incurring an annual allowance charge. The majority of candidates were aware of the £40,000 allowance and the ability to bring forward unused allowances. However, a significant number failed to relate their knowledge to the scenario, bringing forward several years' worth of unused allowance, despite the fact that the taxpayer had not previously been in any pension scheme, and spending a considerable amount of time calculating whether or not the maximum amount of allowance would be restricted, when a quick calculation would have revealed that the taxpayer's income fell well below the income limits. At the ATX level, general rules are rarely required; candidates will invariably be asked to apply rules to a given scenario, so they must ensure they have taken this into consideration at every stage of their answer, to avoid wasting time.

		ACCA marking scheme		Marks
(a)		Cash amounts received		2.5
		Laptop computer		2.0
		Calculation of income tax payable		1.5
				6.0
			Maximum	5.0
(b)	(i)	Options for relief of Jessica's share of the partnership loss		3.0
	(ii)	Share of partnership loss year ending 31 March 2023		1.0
		Relief in 2022/23		1.5
		Relief in 2021/22		3.0
		Relief in 2019/20		2.5
		Conclusion		0.5
				8.5
			Maximum	7.0
(c)		Maximum contribution 2022/23		2.5
		Maximum contribution 2023/24		4.0
				6.5
			Maximum	5.0
Total				**20.0**

53   DEE   *Walk in the footsteps of a top tutor*

Key answer tips

This question tests a variety of different income tax and capital tax aspects. Some of the areas being tested are brought forward knowledge from TX but here they are tested in a more advanced way.

Part (a) looks at income tax savings on different investment options. It is important to read the question carefully so that you don't do any unnecessary calculations – income tax if Dee invests all the money herself was given to you so don't recalculate it! You need to ensure that you don't just focus on the calculations. You are also asked to explain how a more tax efficient split could be obtained as well as the consequences of a gift to a minor child. Over half the marks available are for this part.

Part (b) tests giving to a non-domiciled spouse. You need to appreciate that the usual spouse exemption will not be applicable here and explain ways to mitigate the IHT.

Finally, part (c) looks at tax efficient investments, EIS and VCT in particular. If you have learnt the tax implications surrounding these then it should be easy to score well on this final part. Keep your answer brief and to the point.

The highlighted words in the written sections are key phrases that markers are looking for.

(a)   Minimising income tax on investment income

Tutor's top tips

There is a lot to do in part (a) and it is easy to get overwhelmed by all the information.

Firstly, you need to calculate the income tax saving if Dee were to give Cam £150,000 to invest. The requirement gives you lots of guidance so ensure you follow it! You are told not to complete whole computations but just to work out the extra tax. It is clear from the income levels that Dee is an additional rate tax payer and Cam is a basic rate tax payer. You can use this information to calculate the tax just on the extra interest and dividends they will each received, rather than doing complete computations.

Gift of £150,000 to Cam – income tax saving

	£
Total income tax	
If Dee invests the whole of the £450,000	4,485
If Dee gives £150,000 to Cam (£2,736 + £150) (below)	(2,886)
	———
Income tax saving	1,599
	———

Dee – investing £300,000

Interest income
(£1,000 (£300,000 × 1/3 × 1%) × 45%)   450

Dividend income
((£8,000 (£300,000 × 2/3 × 4%) – £2,000) × 38.1%)   2,286

                                                                                                                  ─────
                                                                                                                  2,736
                                                                                                                  ─────

Cam – investing £150,000

Interest income
(£500 (£150,000 × 1/3 × 1%) × 0%) (savings income nil rate band)   0

Dividend income
((£4,000 (£150,000 × 2/3 × 4%) – £2,000) × 7.5%) (dividend nil rate
band)   150
                                                                                                                  ─────
                                                                                                                  150
                                                                                                                  ─────

Tutorial note

The interest and dividends in respect of funds held within ISAs are exempt from income tax. Accordingly, they do not reduce the savings income nil rate band or the dividend nil rate band.

As Dee is an additional rate taxpayer she does not have a savings nil rate band. Cam is a basic rate taxpayer therefore will have a £1,000 savings nil rate band.

Tutor's top tips

As well as the calculations you are also asked to consider what factors would be relevant to consider in obtaining a more tax efficient split of income.

Here you should consider the fact that Cam has not utilised all of his savings income nil rate band, and he also pays tax at a much lower rate than Dee. Therefore, it may be worthwhile giving more income to him where possible.

Factors relevant to obtaining a more income tax-efficient split of the total investment

Tax allowances

Cam has £500 (£1,000 – £500) of the savings income nil rate band remaining.

Income tax rates

Even if he were to have to pay income tax on his investment income, Cam's tax rates would be considerably lower than those of Dee.

Accordingly, it makes sense for Cam's income to be maximised and Dee's income to be minimised.

Yields on the investments

The greatest change in their income levels would be achieved by Cam investing more in shares and Dee investing less in shares. This is because the yield from shares is four times the yield on cash deposits.

Tutor's top tips

The final bit of this requirement is looking at the income tax treatment of the gift of cash to a minor. The gift in itself does not create an income tax liability but the money will be placed on deposit which is going to generate interest.

Where a child is under 18 and a parental settlement results in income of over £100 per tax year this can cause a problem in that the income get taxed on the parent instead of the child. Remember that this rule only applies where the child is under 18.

Gift to Oder

The interest income in respect of Dee's proposed gift to Oder would exceed £100 (£20,000 × 1% = £200). Accordingly, until Oder is 18 years old, all of the interest income (i.e. not just the excess over £100) would be taxed as if it were Dee's income. Accordingly, no tax saving would arise.

Once Oder is 18, the interest income would be treated as his income. Oder is unlikely to be an additional rate taxpayer, such that the interest income would be taxed at a lower rate than if it were received by Dee. This would then reduce the total income tax liability of the family.

(b) Gift to Cam Inheritance tax

Tutor's top tips

In part (b) you first of all need to explain why the gift to Cam could result in an IHT liability. Remember that as Cam is a non-UK domiciled spouse so only £325,000 can be given exempt from IHT, and there has already been a gift to him. You should also discuss how the liability could be avoided. Here you may think about the election to treat Cam as UK domiciled for IHT, but also consider how Dee received the money in the first place and if anything different could be done there.

For the second part you will need two CGT computations: one for Dee disposing of the whole house herself and another where she disposes of two thirds and Cam one third. Work out the difference between the two total liabilities to find the saving.

Cam is non-UK domiciled, such that the spouse exemption, which applies to gifts between spouses, is limited to a lifetime maximum of £325,000. This limit has already been exceeded due to the gift made by Dee to Cam on 1 August 2018, which was valued at £600,000.

Accordingly, Dee's gift of £150,000 to Cam would be a potentially exempt transfer, which could give rise to an inheritance tax liability if Dee were to die within seven years of the gift.

This potential liability could be avoided in either of the following ways:

–   The terms of Dee's father's will could be altered via a deed of variation; such that one-third of the London house is left directly to Cam. This would avoid the need for Dee to make a potentially exempt transfer to Cam.

–   Cam could elect to be treated as UK domiciled for the purposes of inheritance tax. This would mean that all gifts from Dee would be exempt under the spouse exemption with no upper limit.

Tutorial note

1   The deed of variation would have to be signed by Dee and be executed within two years of Dee's father's death. It should state that it is intended to be effective for both inheritance tax and capital gains tax purposes.

2   The downside of Cam electing to be treated as UK domiciled would be that any non-UK assets owned by Cam would cease to be outside UK inheritance tax and so would become taxable.

Capital gains tax (CGT) saving if Dee were to give Cam a one-third interest in the London house

	Dee	Cam
	£	£
Sale of the house by Dee as planned		
Chargeable gain (£450,000 – £390,000)	60,000	
Less: Annual exempt amount	(12,300)	
	————	
	47,700	
	————	
CGT at 28%	13,356	
	————	
Gift of one-third of the house to Cam		
Chargeable gain 2/3:1/3	40,000	20,000
Less: Annual exempt amount	(12,300)	(12,300)
	————	————
	27,700	7,700
	————	————
CGT at 28%/18%	7,756	1,386
	————	————

CGT saving of £4,214 (£13,356 – (£7,756 + £1,386))

Tutorial note

The gift of one-third of the house to Cam would take place at no gain, no loss because Dee and Cam are married. As a result, the gain of £60,000 would be split between them in the ratio 2/3:1/3.

(c) Tax-efficient investments

Tutor's top tips

You are asked to discuss income tax implications of investing in either EIS or VCT shares. Note that only income tax is required so don't waste time talking about CGT implications.

Think about any income tax relief available and the situations in which it may be withdrawn.

Also consider how any dividends received would be dealt with.

Income tax relief

Dee's income tax liability would be reduced by 30% of the amount invested in venture capital trust (VCT) shares, i.e. £15,000 (£50,000 × 30%).

The tax relief in respect of an investment in enterprise investment scheme (EIS) shares would be the same.

Withdrawal of income tax relief

The relief would be withdrawn if Dee were to sell the VCT shares within five years.

Dee would only need to retain the EIS shares for three years for the relief not to be withdrawn.

Dividends received in respect of the investments

Dividend income in respect of VCT shares is not subject to income tax.

Dividend income in respect of EIS shares is taxable.

Examiner's report

This question concerned income tax, capital gains tax (CGT) and inheritance tax (IHT) planning for a UK resident married couple, one of whom was not UK domiciled.

The first part of the question, which was worth 11 marks, concerned proposals to minimise the overall income tax liabilities of the couple. Performance on this question part was polarised, with a good number of candidates scoring 8+ marks, but equally, a large number scored fewer than 4 marks. Those candidates who scored well on this particular part:

- clearly spent time carefully reading and thinking about the requirements, so that they were able to adopt a structured, methodical approach to calculating the tax liabilities for each individual if the proposed strategy was followed.

- didn't waste time writing out facts from the question or suggesting alternative strategies which did not satisfy the stated requirements for the couple.

Many of those who scored low marks had attempted this question last, and appeared to have run out of time. The requirements may have appeared a little daunting in length, but those candidates who read through them carefully, and followed the very detailed guidance they contained, were rewarded with high marks. For these candidates, the standard of the calculations of the tax savings was very high, and most were able to recognise and explain the benefit of standard income tax planning measures for a married couple, such as using the savings and dividend nil rate bands, and taking advantage of the lower rate of tax paid by one of the couple. The most surprising aspect of candidates' answers related to the requirement to discuss the income tax implications of a parent providing an income-generating investment for a minor child. Not only did very few candidates recognise that the income from this investment would be taxed on the parent, but a significant number did not discuss any income tax implications at all. Despite the clear instruction in the requirement for discussion of income tax matters, an overwhelming majority of candidates (perhaps having seen the word 'gift'), discussed the inheritance tax implications, in some cases in quite some detail. Candidates are once again reminded of the importance of reading the question carefully; writing about the wrong tax clearly scores no marks.

The second part of the question related to the IHT implications of a UK domiciled spouse gifting cash from the sale of a property to their non-UK domiciled spouse, and the CGT saving from gifting a share of the property prior to sale, rather than cash following the sale. Although many candidates were not aware of the precise restriction on the spouse exemption in respect of a non-UK domiciled spouse, it was pleasing to see that the majority realised that the full spouse exemption was not likely to be available, so were able to score marks from recognising that there would only be a liability to IHT if the donor spouse died within seven years, and that a non-UK domiciled spouse is able to change their domicile on election.

In calculating the CGT saving as a result of transferring a share in the house to a spouse prior to sale, the majority of candidates adopted a full 'before and after' calculation in this case, calculating the total tax payable by the wife if she sold the house before giving her husband a share of the proceeds, with the total payable by the husband and wife together if she gave him a share of the house prior to sale. This latter strategy enabled the couple to take advantage of the husband's available annual exempt amount (AEA), and lower rate of CGT. This was an entirely reasonable approach to take in this scenario, as the calculation of the liability was quite straightforward. The main errors in this part were, firstly, not recognising that, as this was a sale of a private residence, the higher rates of CGT will apply, and secondly, focusing only on the reduction in the CGT payable by the wife, without taking in to account that there would also be a small liability for the husband in the latter strategy. A minority of candidates used a marginal approach to directly identify the amount of tax which would be saved. This proved to be very efficient if done correctly, but was quite tricky, and several candidates just provided a lot of numbers, without adequate labelling, which made it difficult to award marks in some cases.

The third part of the question required a comparison of the income tax implications of investing in enterprise investment scheme (EIS) or venture capital trust (VCT) shares. Overall, knowledge of these two types of investment was good, with the majority of candidates scoring at least three of the available five marks. However, a significant number of candidates wasted time by apparently discussing everything they knew about these schemes, including the CGT exemption, and the general requirements on the company in order for investors to qualify. Once again, the question was very specific in stipulating that only the income tax implications were required, and careful reading of the question might have prevented these candidates from producing fairly lengthy explanations, which attracted no marks.

	ACCA marking scheme		Marks
(a)	Income tax saving if gift made to Cam		5.5
	Factors relevant to obtaining a more income tax-efficient split of the total investment		4.0
	Gift to Oder		3.0
			12.5
		Maximum	11.0
(b)	Inheritance tax		
	Potential liability		3.0
	Advice		3.0
	Capital gains tax		
	Dee owns the whole of the house		2.0
	Transfer of one-third of the house to Cam		2.0
			10.0
		Maximum	9.0
(c)	EIS versus VCT investment		6.0
		Maximum	5.0
Total			**25.0**

54 PEDRO

> **Key answer tips**
>
> This question covers personal tax aspects including inheritance tax, furnished holiday lets and pensions.
>
> In the first part of the question you are asked to explain the IHT implications of a gift which happened many years ago. Firstly, consider the treatment in lifetime, and then on death. This is worth five marks so it may not be as straight forward as it appears!
>
> The second part of the question tests furnished holiday letting. This is an area that does not come up very often in ATX, but offers some easy marks if you have learnt the rules.
>
> The final part of the question tests pensions. Pedro is looking to make a large pension contribution, so you should consider whether all of this would receive tax relief or if there would be an annual allowance charge. You are told about his previous pension arrangements so bear this in mind when considering the available annual allowance.

(a) **Inheritance tax (IHT) implications of the gift of the holiday cottage to Pedro**

The gift of the holiday cottage was a potentially exempt transfer (PET), and therefore no tax was payable in Marina's lifetime. Although Marina died more than seven years after making this gift, IHT was payable as a result of her death as the gift constituted a gift with reservation. This is because Marina continued to derive benefit from the use of the holiday cottage following the gift, and she did not pay a market rent for staying in the cottage.

As the reservation was not lifted prior to her death, the IHT payable would have been calculated as the higher of (1) the total IHT payable if the cottage was included in her death estate at its value on death, and (2) the total IHT payable, if the cottage was taxed as a PET made in March 2012. As the latter liability is £nil, due to the date of the PET being more than seven years before Marina's death, the cottage would have been included in Marina's death estate. As the value of her death estate exceeded the nil rate band of £325,000 (as it included a portfolio of properties valued at £670,000), IHT was payable on the estate. The IHT attributable to the cottage, being a gift with reservation, was payable by the recipient of the gift, which, in this case, was Pedro.

(b) **Why the holiday cottage will qualify as a furnished holiday letting**

The letting of the holiday cottage satisfies all the conditions to qualify as a furnished holiday letting:

Availability – the cottage is available continuously for commercial letting from 1 July 2022 onwards, so will meet the condition to be available for at least 210 days in the first 12-month period.

Actual letting – the cottage will have a 70% occupancy rate throughout the period it is available for letting, such that it will be let for at least 105 days in the first 12-month period.

Pattern of occupation – no tenant will stay in the cottage for more than 14 consecutive days during the first year for which it will be available for letting, so there is no possibility of the number of days of 'longer term occupation' (more than 31 consecutive days) exceeding 155 in the first 12-month period.

The cottage is situated in the UK, has been let furnished, and on a commercial basis.

(c) **Reduction in Pedro's income tax liability for the tax year 2022/23 as result of making the planned contribution of £85,000 (gross) to a personal pension scheme**

Income tax liability with the pension contribution

		£
Employment income (£75,000 + £0)		75,000
Property income (£14,500 + £32,000)		46,500
		_____
Total/net income		121,500
Less: Personal allowance (see note below)		(12,570)
		_____
Taxable income		108,930
		_____
Income tax liability (W1)		
£108,930 × 20%		21,786
Add: Pension contribution additional charge (W2)		
£13,770 × 20%	2,754	
£7,230 × 40%	2,892	5,646
	_____	_____
£21,000		
	_____	
Income tax liability		27,432
		_____

Payment of the pension contribution leads to a reduction of £12,900 (£40,332 – £27,432) in Pedro's income tax liability for 2022/23.

Personal allowance

The pension contributions which qualify for tax relief cannot exceed Pedro's relevant earnings for the tax year. Pedro's relevant earnings for 2022/23 are £89,500 (employment income of £75,000, plus income from furnished holiday lettings of £14,500). The whole of the £85,000 contribution is therefore eligible for tax relief.

Adjusted net income is £36,500 (£121,500 – £85,000), so there is no restriction of the personal allowance.

Workings

(W1) Increase in basic rate band

The basic rate band threshold is increased to £122,700 (£37,700 + £85,000).

(W2) Annual allowance charge

	£
Contribution by Pedro (gross)	85,000
Contribution by Loule Ltd to occupational scheme	8,000
Total contributions 2022/23	93,000
Less: Annual allowance available – 2022/23 (W3)	(40,000)
2021/22 (W4)	(32,000)
Annual allowance charge	21,000

(W3) Annual allowance available 2022/23

Threshold income

	£
Net income	121,500
Less: Personal pension contributions (gross)	(85,000)
Threshold income	36,500

As Pedro's threshold income does not exceed £200,000, the annual allowance for 2022/23 is not restricted. It is not necessary to calculate Pedro's adjusted income for the year.

(W4) Unused annual allowance brought forward

The annual allowance brought forward from 2021/22 is £32,000 (£40,000 – £8,000).

The annual allowance is not available to bring forward from 2019/20 or 2020/21 as Pedro was not a member of a pension scheme in those years.

Examiner's report

This question concerned the IHT implications of a gift with reservation, a furnished holiday letting, and a calculation of the impact on an individual's income tax liability of them making a substantial contribution to their personal pension scheme.

The first part of the question required candidates to advise the client of the IHT implications of having received a lifetime gift following the death of the donor. Most candidates recognised that the lifetime gift was a potentially exempt transfer (PET) and also a gift with reservation. Significantly fewer knew the consequences of this as a result of the death of the donor, which was disappointing.

The second part of this question related to the holiday cottage referred to in the first part, requiring candidates to explain why this cottage would qualify as a furnished holiday letting. The majority of candidates demonstrated good knowledge of these rules and applied them correctly to the information given in the question. As a result, a good number were able to score at least four of the five available marks.

The third part of this question was worth ten marks and involved a detailed income tax computation including both occupational and personal pension scheme contributions. There were few very good answers to this question part, although many managed to score half marks. Weaker candidates were clearly very confused about the rules for pension contributions relief and produced some very muddled answers. It appeared that quite a few candidates adopted a 'scattergun' approach, including parts of calculations, presumably as they occurred to them, which proved difficult to follow, and to mark, in some cases. It is important to adopt a logical approach to this sort of question, working through the income tax computation line by line, thinking through one stage at a time. Question practice, once again, is invaluable for this. Additionally, some candidates wasted time by calculating the individual's income tax liability prior to making the personal pension contribution, when this was given in the question. Others wrote a detailed explanation of some of the rules, instead of, or as well as, calculations. The only explanation required was in respect of the amount of personal allowance available to the taxpayer. Other explanations, sadly, didn't score marks.

ACCA marking scheme

			Marks
(a)	Gift treated as a PET		1.0
	Recognition of gift with reservation		2.0
	Implications of gift with reservation		3.0
			6.0
		Maximum	5.0
(b)	Availability		1.5
	Actual days let		1.5
	Pattern of occupancy		2.0
	Furnished/commercial basis/UK		1.0
			6.0
		Maximum	5.0
(c)	With pension contribution		
	Total income		2.0
	Personal allowance note		3.0
	Tax calculation		1.0
	Annual allowance charge		4.0
	Tax on annual allowance charge		1.0
	Impact on tax liability		0.5
			11.5
		Maximum	10.0
Total			20.0

TAXATION OF CORPORATE BUSINESSES

FAMILY COMPANY ISSUES

55 TRIFLES LTD (ADAPTED) *Walk in the footsteps of a top tutor*

Key answer tips

This section B question covers two different areas: purchase of own shares by a company, and the tax implications of a close company. Whilst these areas tend not to appear in every exam, they are tested every few sittings.

Part (a) requires a discussion of the conditions for purchase of own shares, but focuses on just two conditions.

Part (b) requires the calculation of after-tax proceeds for both the income and the capital treatment but for the purchase of Victoria's shares only. This section should provide some easy marks.

Part (c) is trickier. It appears to cover loans to participators due to the wording of the information in the question (i.e. 'loan of a motorcycle'), but actually covers the provision of benefits to participators (i.e. 'use of asset' benefit).

The highlighted words in the written sections are key phrases that markers are looking for.

(a) **Purchase of own shares: Conditions for capital treatment**

Tutor's top tips

Read the requirement carefully. You are not required to consider all of the conditions for capital treatment, just the period of ownership and reduction in shareholding.

There will be no marks available for discussing any other conditions.

*To score marks here you must **apply** these conditions to Victoria and to Melba.*

Victoria

Ownership period

As Victoria inherited the shares from her husband, the required ownership period is reduced from five years to three years.

Victoria can include her husband's ownership as well as her own, giving a total ownership period from 1 February 2019 to 28 February 2023.

This is more than three years; therefore, Victoria satisfies this condition.

Tutorial note

Even if you did not know that the ownership period was reduced to three years for inherited shares, you could still score some marks here for applying the condition to the facts.

Reduction in level of shareholding

Victoria sells all her shares, and therefore satisfies the 'substantial reduction' in her shareholding test as she disposes of all of her shares.

Tutorial note

Victoria also has a lack of 'connection' to the company after the disposal as she no longer holds any shares in the company. However, the requirement was only to discuss the reduction in holding condition.

Melba

Ownership period

Melba has owned her shares since 1 February 2015. This is longer than the required five years, therefore Melba satisfies this condition.

Reduction in level of shareholding

Tutor's top tips

This is tricky! Remember that once shares are sold back to the company, they will be cancelled, so the total number of shares will be reduced.

*Victoria will sell her shares back to the company **before** Melba, so these shares will have already been cancelled.*

Before the buy back

Melba will have 1,700 shares from a total of 8,500 (10,000 – 1,500).

This represents a 20% share (1,700/8,500) in the company.

After the buy back

Melba will have 1,250 shares (1,700 – 450) from a total of 8,050 (8,500 – 450).

This represents a 15.5% share (1,250/8,050) in the company.

Melba's new percentage share in the company must be no more than 75% of her old share (i.e. no more than 15% (75% × 20%)).

15.5% is more than 15%, therefore this test is **not** satisfied.

Tutorial note

The 75% (or 25% substantial reduction) test must be applied to the **percentage** shareholding, not the number of shares.

If you got this wrong, or if you missed the fact that Victoria's shares had already been cancelled, you could still score follow-through marks here for applying the 75% test and for coming to a conclusion.

As well as the 75% test, Melba must also own no more than 30% of the remaining shares after the repurchase. There were no marks for discussing this, as the requirement was only to discuss the reduction in holding condition.

(b) **Victoria: after-tax proceeds from purchase of shares**

Capital treatment

Gain qualifying for business asset disposal relief (Note 1)

	£
Proceeds (1,500 × £30)	45,000
Less: Cost (probate value) (Note 2)	(16,000)
	29,000
Less: Annual exempt amount	(12,300)
	16,700
Less: Capital loss brought forward	(3,500)
Taxable gains	13,200
Capital gains tax (£13,200 × 10%)	1,320
After-tax proceeds (£45,000 – £1,320)	43,680

Tutorial note

1   Victoria will have been a director of the company and held at least 5% of the shares for the two years prior to the disposal, and will therefore qualify for business asset disposal relief.

2   Where shares are inherited from a spouse, the deemed cost to the recipient for capital gains tax purposes is the probate value.

If the shares were transferred during lifetime, the transfer would be at no gain, no loss and the recipient would take over the original cost.

Income treatment

	£
Proceeds (1,500 × £30)	45,000
Less: Original subscription price (1,500 × £2)	(3,000)
Distribution (Note 1)	42,000
Income tax ((£42,000 – £2,000) × 32.5%) (Note 2)	13,000
After-tax proceeds (£45,000 – £13,000)	32,000

Tutorial note

1   *Remember that to calculate the deemed dividend income (i.e. distribution), you must deduct the original subscription price from the payment irrespective of who subscribed for the shares, and regardless of any price actually paid for the shares.*

2   *The first £2,000 of the deemed dividend (i.e. distribution) will fall into the nil rate band. As Victoria is a higher rate taxpayer, the rate of tax suffered on the balance will be 32.5%.*

There would be no withdrawal of the personal allowance, as Victoria's total taxable income would be less than £100,000 (£55,000 + £42,000 = £97,000).

3   *A capital loss of £13,000 (£3,000 – £16,000) will also arise. Victoria cannot claim to offset this capital loss against income as she did not subscribe for the shares. This loss therefore has no effect on the current period's after-tax proceeds but may reduce tax on a future capital gain.*

(c)   Tax implications of the loan of the motorcycle

Tutor's top tips

The key to success here was to spot that Trifles Ltd is a close company.

Look out for this as many 'Ltd' companies are owned by only a few shareholders and are therefore close companies.

Remember that there are special rules governing the provision of loans and benefits to participators in a close company.

Trifles Ltd is controlled by five or fewer shareholders (participators), and is therefore a close company.

Implications for Melba

The provision of the motorcycle to Melba will be treated as a distribution, as Melba will not be an employee of Trifles Ltd after the sale of her shares.

The value of the benefit, calculated using the income tax rules, will be treated as a net dividend:

	£
Use of asset (£9,000 × 20%) (Note 1)	1,800
Less: Contribution (£30 × 12)	(360)
	———
Distribution	1,440
	———
Income tax (£1,440 × 32.5%) (Note 2)	468
	———

Tutorial note

1   The loan of the motorcycle will be treated as a 'use of asset' benefit each year Melba has the use of the motorcycle.

2   As Melba is a higher rate taxpayer with dividends in excess of the £2,000 nil rate band, the rate of tax suffered on the deemed dividend (i.e. distribution) is 32.5%.

If Melba was still an employee, the motorcycle would be treated as a normal employment benefit, and would be taxed at 40% in the normal way.

Implications for Trifles Ltd

Tutor's top tips

You will be given marks here for consistency!

Remember that dividends are not allowable expenses for companies, so it follows that if the loan of the motorcycle is to be treated as a dividend, none of the associated expenses are deductible.

However, if you missed the fact that Trifles Ltd is a close company and that Melba will no longer be an employee, you may have treated the motorcycle as a normal employment benefit. In this case, you will be given marks here for saying that costs will be allowable and employer's class 1A NIC will be due.

Trifles Ltd will not be able to claim capital allowances on the motorcycle, and there will be no allowable deduction for any running costs.

Examiner's report

Many candidates answered part (a) well but others, with similar knowledge levels, did not perform well because they failed to answer the question. Rather than addressing the two particular conditions set out in the question, this latter group attempted to address all of the conditions despite the majority of them being irrelevant.

Candidates had a good knowledge of the five-year rule and the 30% rule but were much less comfortable with the condition relating to the shareholder's interest in the company following the purchase. The rules require the shareholder's interest to be no more than 75% of the interest prior to the purchase – this is not the same as the shareholder selling 25% of his shares because the shares sold are cancelled thus reducing the number of issued shares.

Only a minority of candidates were aware that the ownership period of the husband could be added to that of the wife. Even fewer knew that the usual five-year ownership period is reduced to three where the shares are inherited.

Part (b) was answered well by the vast majority of candidates. The only point that many candidates missed was the availability of business asset disposal relief. It was particularly pleasing to see the majority of candidates correctly identify the after-tax proceeds as the amount received less the tax liability (as opposed to the taxable amount less the tax liability).

The final part of the question was more difficult and, unsurprisingly, caused more problems. The question concerned the loan of a motorcycle to a shareholder in a close company who was not an employee. Candidates had no problem recognising that the company was a close company but many then decided that this was a loan to a participator as opposed to the loan of an asset.

Another relatively common error was to state, correctly, that the benefit would be treated as a distribution but to then give an incorrect tax rate of 40%. Candidates would benefit from slowing down and ensuring that they apply their basic tax knowledge correctly in the exam.

ACCA marking scheme

		Marks
(a)	Victoria	
	Period of ownership	2.5
	Reduction in level of shareholding	0.5
	Melba	
	Period of ownership	1.0
	Reduction in level of shareholding	3.0
		7.0
(b)	Capital receipt	4.0
	Income receipt	3.0
		7.0
(c)	Close company	1.5
	Melba	
	Recognition of distribution	1.5
	Supporting calculations	2.0
	Trifles Ltd	1.0
		6.0
Total		**20.0**

56   NOCTURNE LTD (ADAPTED)   *Walk in the footsteps of a top tutor*

Key answer tips

This section B question has three separate requirements which can be attempted in any order.

The first two parts relate to Nocturne being a close company:

Part (a) is about the gift of an asset to a participator who is not an employee or a director.

Part (b) is about a loan made to the company by a participator who is also a director.

Part (c) is about the partial exemption for VAT.

The highlighted words in the written sections are key phrases that markers are looking for.

(a)   Provision of a laptop computer for Jed

Tutor's top tips

Read the question carefully: you are only asked to consider the after-tax cost for the company, Nocturne Ltd, not the impact on Jed.

Option 1: Purchase of a new laptop computer

Nocturne Ltd is a close company as it is controlled by any three of its four shareholders. As Jed is not a director or employee of Nocturne Ltd, the provision of the laptop computer will not be treated as a taxable benefit, but as a distribution.

Nocturne Ltd will not be able to claim capital allowances in respect of the new laptop computer and there will be no national insurance contribution implications.

No further capital allowances are available to Nocturne Ltd in respect of the existing laptop computer as its tax written down value is already £Nil.

Option 2: Transfer of an existing laptop computer

The disposal of the laptop computer to Jed will give rise to a balancing charge in Nocturne Ltd (W). The laptop computer is an exempt asset for capital gains tax purposes, as it is a chattel which cost and is worth no more than £6,000.

The new laptop computer to be used in the business will be eligible for capital allowances. The super deduction is available for 130% of the amount of the expenditure.

The corporation tax relief in the year ending 31 March 2023 due to capital allowances will be £416 (19% × £2,190 (W)).

Working: Capital allowances for year ended 31 March 2023

Balancing charge: £150

Super deduction: £1,800 × 130% = £2,340

Total allowances: £2,340 – £150 = £2,190

Tutorial note

The super deduction is available on plant and machinery purchased by companies between 1 April 2021 and 31 March 2023, therefore the laptop qualifies. An allowance of 130% is available for assets that would ordinarily go into the main pool (except cars and second-hand assets).

Summary of after-tax costs

Tutor's top tips

When considering two possible courses of action it is useful to summarise the tax implications of the two options in a table.

To calculate the after-tax costs, take account of all costs to the company and any corporation tax relief available for that expenditure.

	Option 1	Option 2
	£	£
Amount paid for new laptop	1,800	1,800
Less: Corporation tax saving (above)	0	(416)
	———	———
After-tax cost	1,800	1,384
	———	———

Conclusion

Option 2 is therefore the preferable option for Nocturne Ltd.

(b)   Provision of loan finance by Siglio

Tutor's top tips

*Make sure you are clear about the situation being described in the scenario: this is a loan **from** a participator, not **to** a participator.*

Explaining how savings income is taxed on an individual and the tax relief available for eligible interest on qualifying loans draws on pure TX knowledge and should have provided easy marks.

Interest received by Siglio

Siglio will receive interest on the loan from Nocturne Ltd net of a 20% income tax deduction. It will be taxed as savings income in Siglio's income tax computation. If Siglio is a basic rate taxpayer, the first £1,000 will be taxed at 0%. If he is a higher rate taxpayer this reduces to £500 and if he is an additional taxpayer, there will be no savings income nil rate band. Any interest in excess of the nil rate band (if available) will be taxed at his marginal rate of tax, but with credit given for the tax deducted at source.

Interest paid by Siglio

As Siglio has taken out a loan to provide the loan finance to Nocturne Ltd, he will be able to obtain tax relief on the interest paid on the loan because the following conditions are satisfied:

– Nocturne Ltd is a close company; and

– Siglio owns at least 5% of the shares in Nocturne Ltd.

Also, as he is the company's managing director, it is highly likely that he works full time for Nocturne Ltd. Therefore, Siglio will be able to deduct the interest paid on the bank loan in calculating his taxable income each year.

(c) (i) Recoverable input VAT for the year ended 31 March 2022

Tutor's top tips

All input tax (including that relating wholly or partly to exempt supplies) may be recovered if a business is below the de minimis limits. There are three tests to see whether a business is de minimis; the business need only meet one of them.

Test 1

Total input tax ≤ £625 per month on average, and value of exempt supplies ≤ 50% of value of total supplies.

Test 2

Total input tax less input tax directly attributable to taxable supplies ≤ £625 per month on average, and value of exempt supplies ≤ 50% of value of total supplies.

Test 3

Input tax relating to exempt supplies ≤ £625 per month on average, and input tax relating to exempt supplies ≤ 50% of total input VAT.

In this question you are only required to consider tests 1 and 2.

Applying the de minimis tests to the annual figures provided:

Test 1

Although the value of the exempt supplies is less than 50% of the total supplies, the total input VAT of £13,132 (£7,920 + £1,062 + £4,150) is above the de minimis limit of £7,500 (£625 × 12) so test 1 is not satisfied.

Test 2

Total input VAT less input VAT directly attributed to taxable supplies is £5,212 (£13,132 – £7,920).

This is below the de minimis limit of £7,500 and the value of exempt supplies is less than 50% of the total supplies so test 2 is satisfied and all the input VAT incurred of £13,132 is reclaimable.

Tutorial note

As test 2 is satisfied and all of the input tax is reclaimable, there is no need to apportion the unattributable input VAT.

Had both tests 1 and 2 been failed, the following working would have been required in order to carry out test 3:

Recoverable input VAT for the year ended 31 March 2022:

	Total	Recover	Disallow
	£	£	£
Wholly attributable to taxable supplies	*7,920*	*7,920*	
Wholly attributable to exempt supplies	*1,062*		*1,062*
Unattributable (£4,150 × 86%/14%)	*4,150*	*3,569*	*581*
Total	*13,132*	*11,489*	*1,643*

(ii) Annual test

Tutor's top tips

This part of the question covers the annual test for partially exempt businesses, and has nothing to do with the annual accounting scheme for VAT!

Nocturne Ltd's eligibility for the annual test

The annual test allows a business to apply the de minimis tests once a year instead of for every VAT return period.

The conditions to be satisfied are:

1   The business must have been de minimis in the previous partial exemption year

2   The business will consistently apply the annual test throughout any given partial exemption year; and

3   There are reasonable grounds to expect that the input tax incurred by the business in the current partial exemption year will not exceed £1 million.

Nocturne Ltd satisfied the de minimis condition in respect of the partial exemption year ended 31 March 2022 (condition 1) and there is no reason to believe that conditions 2 and 3 will not be met in relation to the partial exemption year ending 31 March 2023.

Potential benefits to be gained from use of the annual test

The benefits for Nocturne Ltd result from a provisional recovery of all input tax during the partial exemption year ending 31 March 2023 as the company can recover the full amount of input tax suffered in each return period without performing calculations to see if the de minimis tests are satisfied each time.

This will provide a cash flow benefit and an administrative time saving. This administrative time saving is particularly useful as Nocturne Ltd's turnover and associated costs are expected to increase in the year ended 31 March 2023, such that the simplified de minimis tests 1 and 2 may not be satisfied and the more complicated de minimis test 3 might otherwise be required.

Notwithstanding these benefits, an annual adjustment will have to be performed at the end of the year using the de minimis limits for the year as a whole, which may result in the need to repay part of the VAT previously recovered in full.

Examiner's report

The first part concerned two alternative ways in which a computer was to be provided to a shareholder who was not employed by the company. Despite knowing the relevant rules, candidates did not perform as well as they could have done in this part for two reasons. Firstly, they failed to consider all of the aspects of the situation and secondly, they did not answer the question set.

Most candidates appreciated that the provision of the computer would give rise to a distribution but many failed to address the capital allowances position of the company. This was important because it differed in the two alternative situations. Similarly, many candidates failed to address the tax treatment of the loss on the transfer of the existing computer in the second alternative. Candidates will benefit if they think before they write and identify all the different aspects of the transaction. They should then address each of the aspects in a concise manner.

The failure to answer the question set related to the need to determine the after-tax cost for the company. Most candidates focused on the tax treatment for the individual, which meant that they missed out on some of the available marks.

Part (b) concerned Siglio, the company's managing director, who was going to borrow money from a bank and then lend it to the company. Many candidates provided unsatisfactory answers to this question part because they wanted the question to deal with a loan from a close company to a participator in that company – but it wasn't. It was also important to deal with the two loans separately.

The loan to the company was a normal commercial loan. The company would obtain a tax deduction for the interest paid and Siglio would pay income tax on the interest income in the normal way. It was no more complicated than that.

The loan from the bank to Siglio was more interesting in that in that it would be a qualifying loan, such that the interest paid by Siglio would be tax deductible. Some candidates were aware of this point but very few stated the detailed reasons for the tax deduction being available.

The final part of the question concerned VAT and was in two parts.

Part (i) concerned the partial exemption de minimis tests. It was a straight forward test of the rules and was done well by those candidates who knew them. As always, it was important to read the question carefully and to address the requirement and nothing more; some candidates wasted time by addressing other aspects of VAT that were not required. Candidates should recognise that VAT is tested at every sitting and that the partial exemption rules are tested regularly.

Part (ii) concerned the annual test for computing recoverable input tax and was not done well. The problem here was that the majority of candidates addressed the annual accounting scheme rather than the subject of the question. This was unfortunate and meant that very few candidates did well on this part of the question. Candidates should always try to be sure as to what the question is about; both parts of part (b) related to partial exemption.

ACCA marking scheme				Marks
(a)		Close company		1.0
		Purchase of new computer for Jed		2.5
		Transfer of existing computer to Jed		3.5
		Conclusion		0.5
				7.5
			Maximum	7.0
(b)		Treatment of interest received		2.0
		Conditions for income tax deduction		2.5
		Conclusion re Siglio		0.5
				5.0
			Maximum	4.0
(c)	(i)	De minimis test 1		2.0
		De minimis test 2		2.0
		Conclusion		0.5
				4.5
			Maximum	4.0
	(ii)	Annual test – conditions		2.0
		– Application to Nocturne		1.0
		– Implications		3.0
				6.0
			Maximum	5.0
Total				20.0

57   GAIL (ADAPTED) *Walk in the footsteps of a top tutor*

Key answer tips

This section A question comprises corporation tax groups with a particular focus on capital gains groups, the withdrawal of company profits via bonus or dividend and some ethics.

Part (a) requires candidates to identify errors made in a schedule prepared on group transactions including a number of asset disposals.

Part (b) is a comparison of whether it is more tax efficient to take funds out of the company via a bonus or dividend, considering the income tax, NIC and corporation tax implications.

Part (c) offers easy marks relating to the disclosure of an error and potential tax evasion. This is an area that is regularly tested and could have been attempted first as a standalone question.

In section A questions the information needed to answer the question will often be split into at least two exhibits. It is important that you read through each exhibit available in the exam to obtain all relevant information.

The highlighted words in the written sections are key phrases that markers are looking for in your letter.

Tutor's top tips

The formal requirements at the end of the question serve only to highlight the number of marks available for each section. The detailed requirements are in the email from your manager.

As you come across the requirements copy them into the answer space so that you can type your answer below and ensure it is focused.

With questions that involve groups of companies it can be helpful to draw a group structure diagram before you start, and include on the diagram the transactions that have happened between the group companies. This will be easier than repeatedly having to refer back to the detailed information.

(a)   Schedule prepared by Mill

Tutor's top tips

Any time that a company sells shares you need to be thinking about the substantial shareholding exemption (SSE) and will always pick up marks for stating the conditions, and whether or not they have been met.

With regard to the capital gains group element of the question remember that an intangibles degrouping charge will arise if a company leaves a group still owning an asset that it received from another gains group company on a tax neutral basis within the last six years.

The computation

– The chargeable gain on the sale of the Simpson Building is incorrect. The sale of the building on 1 October 2018 will have taken place at no gain, no loss because Aero Ltd (A Ltd) and Zephyr Ltd (Z Ltd) were in a capital gains group (A Ltd owns at least 75% of Z Ltd). Accordingly, Z Ltd's base cost in the building is the amount paid for the building by A Ltd plus indexation allowance up to December 2017 since this is earlier than the no gain, no loss transfer.

– The post-tax proceeds on the sale of the Simpson Building will be the sale proceeds (not the chargeable gain) less the related corporation tax liability.

– Dividend income received by UK companies is generally not subject to corporation tax. Accordingly, A Ltd will not have a corporation tax liability in respect of the dividend received from Z Ltd.

The notes

1   The substantial shareholding exemption is available where a company sells shares in a trading company out of a substantial shareholding (a shareholding of at least 10%) of that company's ordinary share capital. The substantial shareholding must have been owned for a continuous period of at least 12 months in the six years prior to the sale.

   Accordingly, the SSE will be available on the sale.

2   An intangible asset (the brand) has been transferred to Z Ltd on a tax neutral basis within six years of the sale of Z Ltd. This would normally give rise to a degrouping charge in Z Ltd but this will not arise because the SSE applies to the sale of shares.

Cash available to pay to Gail as a result of transactions 1 and 2

	£	£
Sale of the Simpson Building by Z Ltd		
Sale proceeds		140,000
Less: Cost		
Cost to A Ltd	75,000	
Indexation allowance (December 2010 to December 2017) (£75,000 × 0.218)	16,350	
		(91,350)
Chargeable gain		48,650
		£
Corporation tax (£48,650 × 19%)		9,244
Dividend paid to A Ltd (£140,000 – £9,244)		130,756
Sale of Z Ltd		
Sale proceeds in respect of Z Ltd		250,000
Total cash available for Gail		380,756

Tutorial note

Indexation allowance is not permitted after December 2017. Therefore, in the above calculation no further indexation allowance is needed from the no gain, no loss transfer date to the date of eventual sale.

(b)   Payment to Gail

Tutor's top tips

The computations for bonus versus dividend are fairly straightforward in each case, but don't forget to take account of the fact that a bonus but not a dividend gives rise to a corporation tax deduction, and so this needs to be factored in.

With regard to the dividend calculations, remember to apply the dividend nil rate band and then the correct dividend rates for the parts of the dividend falling into the higher rate and additional rate bands.

Payment of a bonus of £380,756 – total additional taxes

	£
Annual employment income	85,000
Bonus	380,756
Net income	465,756
Less: Personal allowance	(0)
Taxable income	465,756

£	
37,700 × 20%	7,540
112,300 × 40%	44,920
150,000	
315,756 × 45%	142,090
465,756	194,550

	£
Recurring income tax liability on £85,000 of taxable income	(21,432)
Additional income tax	173,118
Additional employee's Class 1 national insurance contributions (£380,756 × 2%)	7,615
Additional employer's Class 1 national insurance contributions (£380,756 × 13.8%)	52,544
Reduction in A Ltd's corporation tax liability ((£380,756 + £52,544) × 19%)	(82,327)
Total additional taxes where a bonus is paid	150,950

Tutorial note

The reduction in the corporation tax liability will be dependent on there being sufficient taxable profits to absorb the tax deductions.

Payment of a dividend of £380,756 – total additional taxes

	£
Annual employment income	85,000
Dividend income	380,756
Personal allowance	0
	————
Taxable income	465,756
	————

£	
37,700 × 20%	7,540
47,300 × 40%	18,920
————	
85,000	
2,000 × 0%	0
63,000 × 32.5%	20,475
————	
150,000	
315,756 × 38.1%	120,303
————	
465,756	
————	
	————
	167,238
Recurring income tax liability on £85,000 of taxable income	(21,432)
	————
Total additional taxes where a dividend is paid	145,806
	————

There will be no national insurance contribution or corporation tax implications as a result of the payment of the dividend.

(c)   Disclosure of error

Tutor's top tips

Ethical issues will always appear in section A of the ATX examination for five marks, and these can be relatively easy marks to obtain.

Write in short paragraphs and try to make sure that you have at least five separately identifiable points in your answer.

The error made by Gail must be disclosed to HM Revenue and Customs (HMRC).

Gail can inform HMRC herself or she may authorise us to do so. However, we must not disclose the error to HMRC unless we have her permission.

We cannot continue to act for Gail unless this disclosure is made.

We should ascertain how the error arose in order to determine whether or not there are further errors to disclose. We should inform the firm's money laundering officer of the situation.

We should notify Gail of the following consequences of not informing HMRC of her error:

– If she refuses to disclose the error, we will advise HMRC that we no longer act for her. We would not, however, give any reason for our actions.

– Non-disclosure of the error would also amount to tax evasion. This could result in criminal proceedings under both the tax and money laundering legislation.

Examiner's report

Note that this part of the question has been adapted since it was originally set.

Part (a) required candidates to review a schedule which had been prepared by a junior member of the tax department. Candidates had to identify any technical errors in the schedule and explain whether or not the notes to the schedule were correct.

There were three errors to spot and candidates did well.

The first error related to the sale of a building. The point here was that the building had been acquired from a group company at no gain, no loss, such that its base cost was the original cost to the group. The majority of candidates identified this point.

The second error was that, in calculating post-tax proceeds, the junior member had deducted the tax from the gain rather than the sales proceeds. This has been a very common error in previous sittings when candidates are asked to calculate post-tax proceeds; very few candidates identified this as an error.

The final error was that the junior member had treated a dividend from a subsidiary as being subject to corporation tax. The majority of candidates identified this error.

The notes to the schedule related to degrouping charges and the substantial shareholding exemption.

Degrouping charges are not so easy to explain and candidates found it difficult to articulate precisely what had been transferred at no gain, no loss, and which company was leaving the group.

Many candidates would have benefited from stating clearly the circumstances in which a degrouping charge arises before trying to work out what would happen in relation to the particular facts of the question. This would have earned a mark and would have clarified the candidates' thinking.

Candidates' knowledge of the substantial shareholding exemption was good with many candidates scoring high marks on this aspect of the question.

Part (b) concerned the payment of a bonus or a dividend. This was more straightforward and was done quite well.

As far as the bonus was concerned, the only common error was a failure to consider the corporation tax savings, as requested by the manager in the question. Often, the candidates who missed this also failed to consider the NIC implications for the company of the method of remuneration used.

The payment of the dividend was also handled pretty well. *This part of the examiner's report has been amended following changes in tax treatment.*

The final part of the question concerned the need for the client to disclose income in respect of an earlier tax year. This was straightforward and was done well. Having said that, a minority of candidates had not prepared for this aspect of the exam and so did not attempt this part of the question. One common error was to describe the potential interest and penalties implications in great detail despite the question stating that these matters had already been explained to the client.

ACCA marking scheme		
		Marks
(a)	Explanations	
	Chargeable gain on the sale of the Simpson Building	1.5
	Post-tax proceeds on the sale of the Simpson Building	1.0
	Taxation of dividend from Zephyr Ltd	1.0
	Substantial shareholding exemption	2.5
	Degrouping charge	2.0
	No non-errors identified	1.0
	Calculation	
	Chargeable gain on the sale of the Simpson Building	1.5
	Other matters	1.5
		──
		12.0
	Maximum	11.0
		──
(b)	Payment of bonus	
	Taxable income	1.5
	Income tax liability	1.5
	National insurance contributions	1.5
	Reduction in corporation tax	1.5
	Payment of dividend	
	Calculation	2.5
	No NIC liability or CT deduction	1.0
		──
		9.5
	Maximum	9.0
		──
(c)	Necessary to disclose	2.5
	Implications of failing to disclose	3.0
	Consider possibility of further errors	1.0
		──
		6.5
	Maximum	5.0
		──
Total		**25.0**
		──

58   MARIA AND GRANADA LTD (ADAPTED) *Walk in the footsteps of a top tutor*

Key answer tips

This section B question covers company repurchase of shares, and aspects of the corporation tax and VAT implications of a company acquiring an unincorporated business.

Part (a)(i) requires an understanding of the rules which determine whether the capital (CGT) or income (dividend) treatment will apply to a shareholder's sale of shares back to the company. However, the question focuses specifically on one of the tests required for capital treatment namely that the shareholder's holding must be 'substantially reduced'. This is a new area in ATX and so you should ensure you learn the conditions!

Part (a)(ii) requires calculations for both alternatives. These calculations should have been straightforward even if you were not able to attempt part (a)(i), as you are told in the question to apply each set of rules.

Part (b)(i) requires an explanation of the corporation tax treatment of the acquisition of a brand (i.e. an intangible asset).

Part (b)(ii) focuses on the options and rules for using any losses that the new unincorporated business makes.

Part (c) deals with the VAT implications of the acquisition and the transfer of going concern rules, including the transfer of a property. These rules are some of the most commonly tested from the VAT section of the syllabus.

This question is mostly discursive so lends itself well to the word processor in the exam.

The highlighted words in the written sections are key phrases that markers are looking for in your letter.

(a)   (i)   Sale of 2,700 shares back to Granada Ltd

Tutor's top tips

This part of the question only requires you to consider the substantial reduction test for a purchase of own shares.

There are no marks for writing about the other conditions that must be satisfied for the capital treatment to apply, so confine your answer to the specific requirement.

For capital gains tax treatment to apply, Maria's shareholding in Granada Ltd must be reduced to no more than 75% of her pre-sale holding.

Maria has a 25% shareholding before the sale. Therefore, after the sale her shareholding must be reduced to no more than 18.75% (75% × 25%).

The total number of shares in issue after the sale will be reduced as the shares repurchased by the company are cancelled.

Maria will hold 7,300 (10,000 – 2,700) shares out of 37,300 ((10,000 × 4) – 2,700) total shares in issue. This is a 19.6% (7,300/37,300 × 100%) holding, i.e. greater than 18.75%, so that the condition relating to the reduction in the level of shareholding will not be met.

Sale of 3,200 shares back to Granada Ltd

Maria will now hold 6,800 (10,000 – 3,200) shares out of 36,800 (40,000 – 3,200) total shares in issue. This is an 18.5% (6,800/36,800 × 100%) holding, i.e. less than 18.75%, so that the condition relating to the reduction in the level of shareholding will be met.

(ii)   Sale of 2,700 shares back to Granada Ltd

Tutor's top tips

Remember that whenever an individual sells shares in a company, when dealing with the CGT implications you are likely to be given credit for advising whether business asset disposal relief (BADR) does/does not apply and why.

The income tax payable in respect of each share is £3.84 ((£12.80 – £1.00) × 32.5%). The post-tax proceeds per share are therefore £8.96 (£12.80 – £3.84).

Tutorial note

1   *As Maria does not satisfy all of the conditions for this sale to be dealt with under the capital gains tax rules, the disposal will be treated as an income distribution and Maria will have an income tax liability.*

2   *The net dividend is the difference between the sale proceeds and the amount originally subscribed.*

3   *As Maria is a higher rate taxpayer and has used her £2,000 dividend nil rate band, the rate of tax payable on dividends is 32.5%.*

Sale of 3,200 shares back to Granada Ltd

The capital gains tax payable in respect of each share is £1.18 ((£12.80 – £1.00) × 10%).

The post-tax proceeds per share are therefore £11.62 (£12.80 – £1.18).

Tutorial note

The disposal will qualify for BADR as Maria has owned at least 5% of the ordinary shares of Granada Ltd (a trading company) and has been director of the company for the two years before the disposal. The capital gain arising will therefore be taxed at 10%.

(b) **(i)** **Acquisition of the 'Starling' brand**

Tutor's top tips

Although intangibles are treated as trading assets and it is usual, therefore, to simply follow the accounting amortisation deductions for tax, the question requires you to be aware that if no amortisation charges have been made in the accounts it is possible to instead claim a straight line 4% deduction for tax purposes.

As the brand is an intangible asset which has been acquired as part of the 'Starling' trade, it will be treated as a trading asset by Granada Ltd and an allowable deduction will be available in calculating the taxable trading income for each accounting period.

Although Granada Ltd has not made any charge for amortisation in its statement of profit or loss, it may take an annual writing down allowance for tax purposes equal to 4% of the cost of the brand, on a straight line basis. This would be £1,600 (£40,000 × 4%) per year.

If an election is made to claim the 4% writing down allowance, any accounting debits for impairment would be disallowable for tax purposes. Such an election would be irrevocable.

(ii) **Relief for the expected loss from the former Starling Partners' trade**

Tutor's top tips

*Note that the 'major change in nature or conduct of trade' rules only apply to stop the carry forward of trading losses where there has been a change in ownership of a **company**, not a change in the ownership of an unincorporated business.*

As Starling Partners is an unincorporated business, Granada Ltd took over ownership of the assets and responsibility for the trade following its acquisition on 1 January 2022.

The forecast trading loss of £130,000 from Starling Partners' handbag trade could be offset against Granada Ltd's total income for the year ending 31 December 2022, comprising the trading profit from the knitwear business of £100,000 and the chargeable gain of £10,000.

So a loss of £20,000 (£130,000 – £110,000) will be left unrelieved.

As Granada Ltd does not want to carry any of the loss back, the unrelieved loss of £20,000 will be carried forward for relief against future total profits.

Granada Ltd wishes to change the nature of the Starling Partners' trade, by starting to sell to the export market from 1 January 2023. Although this may be seen as a major change in the nature of the trade, it should not serve to prevent the loss incurred in the year ended 31 December 2022 from being carried forward. The impact of a major change in the nature or conduct of a trade in restricting loss relief is only relevant where it precedes or follows a change in ownership of a company, not the acquisition of the trade and assets from an unincorporated business.

Accordingly, based on the expected total profit, all £20,000 of the carried forward loss may be relieved in the year ending 31 December 2023, although Granada Ltd does not have to make a claim to set off the loss in that year.

(c) **Value added tax (VAT) implications following the acquisition of the trade and assets of Starling Partners**

For VAT purposes, the transfer of Starling Partners' trade and assets qualified as a transfer of a going concern (TOGC). Therefore, no VAT will have been charged on the transfer of the assets generally, and so there will have been no input VAT for Granada Ltd to reclaim.

However, additional information is needed in respect of the building, as its treatment will depend on its age and whether or not the option to tax has been exercised.

Age of the building: If the building was less than three years old at 1 January 2022, its sale would have been a taxable supply, chargeable to VAT at the standard rate.

Option to tax: If the building was at least three years old, its sale would have been exempt from VAT, unless Starling Partners exercised the option to tax.

If the building was less than three years old or Starling Partners had opted to tax the building, then the transfer would have been a taxable supply, chargeable to VAT at the standard-rate. In either case, to bring the transfer of the building within the TOGC regime, so that no VAT is charged, Granada Ltd must also have opted to tax the building, prior to the date of transfer. Alternatively, if Granada Ltd did not opt to tax the building, but uses the building in its business, it may obtain an input credit for the VAT charged.

Examiner's report

Part (a)(i) of this question focused on the requirement for the sale of shares by an individual shareholder to the company to result in a 'substantial reduction' in their shareholding in order to receive capital treatment on the disposal. Unfortunately, it would appear that this is an aspect of a company purchasing its own shares which many candidates are not comfortable with. A small number of candidates just reproduced the conditions to be satisfied in order to obtain capital treatment, which was not required and so scored no marks. Of those candidates who did try to answer this part of the question, the most common mistake was to forget that when a company repurchases shares from a shareholder, the shares are cancelled so that the total issued share capital of the company is reduced as a consequence.

Part (a)(ii) of this question required the calculation of after-tax proceeds on the disposal of two alternative numbers of shares from a shareholding, one of which did qualify for capital treatment and one of which didn't. This information was given in the requirements. In spite of this, a lack of technical knowledge or inadequate reading of the question meant that a significant number of candidates did not apply this and treated both disposals as giving rise to chargeable gains, rather than correctly treating one of them as a distribution. Additionally, many candidates failed to recognise that the disposal which attracted capital treatment would also qualify for business asset disposal relief. In any question regarding the disposal of shares by an individual, candidates should automatically consider the application of business asset disposal relief. This is an area where it is very important to know the precise conditions, to be able to state definitively whether or not the relief applies, and the reasons why, or why not. Candidates who went on to calculate the after-tax proceeds generally identified the correct starting point on this occasion, which was pleasing.

Part (b)(i) concerned the tax deductions available to a company on the acquisition of an intangible asset. There were very few good answers to this part of the question. Intangible assets are examined frequently at ATX, so candidates need to be aware of their tax treatment as trading assets, rather than capital assets, for companies, and the consequential tax treatment of these for corporation tax purposes.

Part (b)(ii) required candidates to explain how the company could get tax relief for a loss incurred by a recently acquired trade. Several candidates incorrectly discussed group relief here. This was not the acquisition of shares in a company, which would have created a group, but the acquisition of trade and assets from a partnership. The two situations are completely different, and candidates must take care to ensure that they read and interpret the facts in this type of question correctly. It appeared that many candidates would have benefited from pausing and thinking more before they started to write. It is important in any question dealing with relief for losses that a well- considered and logical approach is taken. Well-prepared candidates were able to identify that at least part of the trading loss would have to be carried forward.

Note that this part of the question has been adapted since it was originally set.

Part (c) required an explanation of the VAT implications of the acquisition of the business and additional information needed to fully clarify the VAT position in relation to a building. The majority of candidates were able to identify that the transaction would not be liable to VAT as it concerned the transfer of a going concern. Candidates who performed less well on this part, however, then went on to explain why the going concern rules applied, stating all the conditions, but reasons why a particular treatment applies aren't required in a discussion of the VAT implications of that treatment. The VAT rules relating to property are very frequently tested at ATX and it was good to see that the majority of candidates were aware of the main facts here in relation to the age of the building and the existence, or otherwise of an option to tax.

					Marks
(a)	(i)	Sale of 2,700 shares			3.5
		Sale of 3,200 shares			1.0
					───
					4.5
				Maximum	4.0
					───
	(ii)	Sale of 2,700 shares			2.5
		Sale of 3,200 shares			2.0
					───
					4.5
				Maximum	4.0
					───
(b)	(i)	Entitled to deduction			1.0
		Writing down allowance			1.0
		Impairment/consistent treatment			1.0
					───
					3.0
					───
	(ii)	Current year relief			2.0
		Carry forward			1.5
		No relevance of change in nature of trade			2.0
					───
					5.5
				Maximum	5.0
					───
(c)		General implications of going concern transfer			1.0
		Additional information			4.0
					───
					5.0
				Maximum	4.0
					───
Total					**20.0**
					───

ACCA marking scheme

59   ACRYL LTD AND CRESCO LTD (ADAPTED)   *Walk in the footsteps of a top tutor*

Key answer tips

This is a two-part company-focused section B question.

Requirement (a) tests liquidations, specifically the effect of the timing of distributions on their corporation tax and income tax treatment.

Requirement (b) tests terminal loss relief for a company.

The highlighted words in the written sections are key phrases that markers are looking for in your answer.

(a)   Acryl Ltd

Tutor's top tips

Liquidations are not often tested in the exam, and this question requires precise knowledge of the tax treatment of distributions so you may have struggled here. Note however that as long as you knew that a pre-liquidation dividend was treated as an income distribution and a post-liquidation dividend as a capital distribution, there were straightforward marks available for explaining the income/capital gains tax due!

(i)   Implications of the commencement of winding up

The commencement of winding up will lead to the end of an accounting period on 31 December 2022 and the commencement of a new accounting period on 1 January 2023.

Acryl Ltd will remain liable to corporation tax until the winding up is completed. Accordingly, a corporation tax computation is required for each of the two accounting periods: the first from 1 July 2022 to 31 December 2022, and the second from 1 January 2023 to 31 March 2023.

(ii)   Distribution on 31 December 2022

In this case the distribution will be made prior to the commencement of winding up and therefore will be treated as an income distribution (i.e. a normal dividend) for tax purposes for both shareholders.

Mambo Ltd will not be subject to corporation tax on this dividend as companies are not subject to corporation tax on dividends.

Alan will be subject to income tax on the dividend. The first £2,000 will be subject to income tax at 0% as it is covered by the dividend nil rate band. The excess above £2,000 will be subject to income tax at 38.1% as Alan is an additional rate taxpayer.

Tutorial note

The question states that Alan's only income in the tax year 2022/23 will be a salary from Acryl Ltd. This information is included so you know that the dividend nil rate band is available to set against a distribution from Acryl Ltd that is treated as a dividend.

*Remember, the dividend nil rate band of £2,000 is available to taxpayers **regardless** of their taxable income. In contrast, the amount of savings income nil rate band available is different depending on whether you are a basic rate taxpayer (£1,000), a higher rate tax payer (£500) or an additional rate taxpayer (£nil).*

Distribution on 31 March 2023

As the distribution will be made while the company is in liquidation, it will be treated as a capital receipt on disposal of the shares in Acryl Ltd for both shareholders.

Mambo Ltd should not be subject to corporation tax on the disposal as it should qualify as a disposal out of a substantial shareholding. Mambo Ltd will have held at least 10% of the shares in Acryl Ltd for more than 12 continuous months out of the six years preceding the disposal and Acryl Ltd is a trading company.

Alan will be subject to capital gains tax on any gain arising. As Alan is eligible for business asset disposal relief on the disposal of his Acryl Ltd shares, capital gains tax will be charged at 10% on the taxable gain.

Conclusion

Mambo Ltd will not be subject to corporation tax under either alternative but Alan would probably prefer 31 March 2023 as he is likely to suffer a lower rate of tax if the distribution is made on this date.

Tutorial note

It is not necessary to consider the possibility of a capital loss on receipt of the distribution on 31 March 2023. Mambo Ltd and Alan subscribed for the shares at par, so they will have a very low base cost and Acryl Ltd has substantial distributable profits.

(b) (i)   Cresco Ltd – relief for trading losses

Tutor's top tips

Losses tend to appear in every exam, typically in a sole trader/partnership question or a corporation tax question, so you need to be ready for them!

In this question there were three losses to deal with which you may have found daunting. Remember to consider them in chronological order, the 2019 loss first, and then the two losses arising in the final two periods. Terminal loss relief only applies to losses generated in the final twelve months of trading, so you will need to apportion the loss for the year ended 31 May 2022.

You may find it easiest to set out the loss workings in the spreadsheet response option in the exam, with any notes produced in the word processor. Where using both response options ensure it is clear which part of your answer is in which response option.

	Year ended 31 May 2019	Year ended 31 May 2020	Year ended 31 May 2021	Year ended 31 May 2022	Period ended 31 December 2022
	£	£	£	£	£
Trading income	0	17,000	8,000	0	0
Bank interest receivable	5,000	3,000	3,000	0	0
	5,000	20,000	11,000		
Less:					
Loss for y/e 31 May 2019 (Note 1)	(5,000)				
Loss for y/e 31 May 2022 (Note 2)			(11,000)		
Loss for the 12 m/e 31 December 2022 (Note 3)		(20,000)			
	0	0	0	0	0

Losses unrelieved:

	£
Year ended 31 May 2022:	
(£24,000 – £11,000 – £10,000)	3,000
Terminal loss: (£50,000 – £20,000)	30,000
Total unrelieved:	33,000

Tutorial note

£10,000 of the trading loss in the year ended 31 May 2022 is included as part of the terminal loss and used against the profits of the year ended 31 May 2020 (see note 3 below).

Notes:

1   The trading loss for the year ended 31 May 2019 of £5,000 will have been relieved against the £5,000 of bank interest (total profits) in the year.

2   As there is no other income or gains in the year ended 31 May 2022, the trading loss of £24,000 will have been carried back and offset against the total profits in the year ended 31 May 2021 of £11,000 (£8,000 + 3,000). £13,000 of the loss remains unrelieved. However, £10,000 of this forms part of the terminal loss (see note 3).

3   As Cresco Ltd has ceased to trade on 31 December 2022, the loss of the last 12 months of trading is a terminal loss which is eligible to be carried back up to 36 months. The loss available for such relief is £50,000 (£40,000 + (£24,000 × 5/12), including the five months of loss for the period from 1 January 2022 to 31 May 2022. As there are no profits remaining in the years ended 31 May 2022 or 2021, the loss can be offset against the total profits of £20,000 (£17,000 + £3,000) in the year ended 31 May 2020.

(ii)   Value added tax (VAT) implications of the cessation of trade

Tutor's top tips

VAT implications of cessation of trade is a commonly tested topic so make sure you learn the rules.

Cresco Ltd must notify HM Revenue and Customs of the cessation of its business within 30 days of ceasing to make taxable supplies.

Output tax must be accounted for on any business assets it still holds at the date of cessation of trade in respect of which input tax was previously recovered. However, there is no need to account for this output tax if it is less than £1,000.

Examiner's report

Part (a)(i) required candidates to state the corporation tax implications arising for a company as a result of the appointment of a liquidator. The commencement of winding up/appointment of a liquidator is one of the factors which will bring a company's accounting period for corporation tax purposes to an end. This was worth only two marks, but most candidates appeared to not be aware of the impact on a company's accounting periods and so scored zero on this question part.

Part (a)(ii) was a 'textbook' question requiring an explanation of the tax implications for both an individual and a corporate shareholder of a distribution being made alternatively before the commencement of liquidation or on completion of the winding up. Answers were very mixed. A good number of candidates realised that the distribution would be taxed as a dividend prior to commencement of liquidation, but as a capital receipt once liquidation had commenced, although a surprising number were not aware of this distinction. For those candidates who realised this, the majority were able to go on and correctly identify the tax implications for the individual shareholder, but, disappointingly, not for the corporate shareholder. Many candidates referred to the corporate shareholder paying corporation tax on both of these, thereby failing to recognise that dividends are not taxable on corporate shareholders, and that the substantial shareholding exemption would apply in the case of the capital receipt. These are both fundamental points which candidates at ATX need to be very familiar with, as they can be tested in a variety of different scenarios.

In part (b)(i) candidates were required to show how a company could relieve trading losses incurred in its last few periods of account. This involved consideration of loss relief in an ongoing company, in addition to the availability of terminal loss relief. It is important in any question dealing with relief for losses that a well-considered and chronological approach is taken. Precise explanations of the reliefs are required in these sorts of questions. Well-prepared candidates were able to deal correctly with the earlier losses in accounting periods prior to the final period, and were aware that, on cessation, an extended three year carry back is available, but almost all neglected to correctly calculate the loss which was available for this terminal loss relief. Nevertheless, those who adopted a sensible, logical approach scored well on this question part.

Part (b)(ii) required candidates to explain the VAT implications for the company of ceasing to trade. Many candidates were clearly confident with this situation and scored the full three marks available.

		ACCA marking scheme		
				Marks
(a)	(i)	Effect on accounting periods		1.0
		Two computations required		1.0
				2.0
	(ii)	Distribution 31 December 2022		3.0
		Distribution 31 March 2023		5.0
		Recommendation with reason		1.0
				9.0
			Maximum	7.0
(b)	(i)	Loss year ended 31 May 2019		0.5
		Loss year ended 31 May 2022		1.5
		Terminal loss		5.0
		Loss unrelieved		1.0
				8.0
	(ii)	Notify HMRC		1.0
		Output tax on assets held on cessation		2.0
				3.0
Total				**20.0**

60   TRAISTE LTD *Walk in the footsteps of a top tutor*

Key answer tips

This question covers the tax implications of making an employee redundant, the post-tax proceeds on a sale of shares and the extraction of profits from a company by a director shareholder.

Requirement (a) tests redundancy payments, which regularly feature in the exam.

Requirement (b) tests the sale of shares by an individual, either to another individual or back to the company.

Requirement (c) covers payment of a bonus versus a dividend, but in terms of the payments made by the company to HMRC.

These three parts could be answered in any order.

The highlighted words in the written sections are key phrases that markers are looking for in your answer.

(a)   Redundancy package provided to Esta

Tutor's top tips

The car benefit received by Esta after she is made redundant is treated in the same way as the ex gratia payment.

    (i)   Income tax implications for Esta

The statutory redundancy pay is exempt from income tax. However, it reduces the £30,000 exemption available for ex-gratia payments.

To the extent that the ex-gratia payment exceeds the remainder of the £30,000 exemption, the excess will be charged to income tax at Esta's highest marginal rate of income tax.

The continuing use of the company car will be valued according to the normal rules for calculating the cash equivalent of this taxable benefit. It will be wholly taxable as the £30,000 exemption is initially allocated, and has already been applied, to the cash receipts.

(ii)   **Corporation tax deductions for Traiste Ltd**

Tutor's top tips

Be careful here! The amount deductible for Traiste Ltd will not be the same as the amount taxable on Esta.

The amount deductible by Traiste Ltd in respect of the redundancy package for Esta is as follows:

	£
Statutory redundancy	12,000
Ex-gratia payment	36,000
Lease payments: ((£420 × 6) × 85%)	2,142
Class 1A national insurance contributions ((£18,000 (W1) + £2,944 (W2)) × 13.8%)	2,890
	———
	53,032
	———

Workings

(W1) Ex-gratia payment

Class 1A national insurance is payable on the excess of the ex-gratia payment: £36,000 – (£30,000 – £12,000) = £18,000

(W2) Car benefit

The car benefit for Esta is £2,944 (£18,400 × 32% (15% + (140 – 55)/5) × 6/12).

(b)   Kat – proposed sale of shares

Tutor's top tips

The sale of shares to Jordi is a simple sale of shares to another individual, requiring a standard capital gains tax computation.

However, the sale of shares to Traiste Ltd would be a purchase of own shares, for which there are two possible tax treatments:

–   *Income treatment*

–   *Capital treatment (if conditions are satisfied).*

To Jordi

On the sale of the shares to Jordi, a chargeable gain will arise, calculated by reference to the market value of the shares as Kat and Jordi are connected persons. A chargeable gain of £25,500 (500 × (£52 − £1) will therefore arise on the disposal.

As Kat has held at least 5% of the shares in Traiste Ltd for at least than two years, and works for the company, business asset disposal relief applies.

As Kat has already used her annual exempt amount for the tax year 2022/23, there will be a capital gains tax liability of £2,550 (£25,500 × 10%).

Kat's after-tax proceeds will be £20,950 ((500 × £47) − £2,550).

To Traiste Ltd

As Kat wishes to sell her shares before the end of 2022, the disposal will not qualify for capital treatment as she will not have owned the shares for the requisite five years until 1 March 2023. She will therefore be taxed on the receipt as a dividend.

She will be treated as receiving a dividend of £25,500 (500 × (£52 − £1)). This will be taxed as follows:

	£
Balance of the nil rate band for dividends:	
£1,000 (£2,000 − £1,000) at 0%	0
Balance of the basic rate band (W):	
£7,920 (£8,920 − £1,000) at 7.5%	594
Balance of the dividend:	
£16,580 (£25,500 − £1,000 − £7,920) at 32.5%	5,389
	———
Income tax on dividend	5,983
	———

Working: Basic rate band remaining

	£
Employment income	40,350
Dividend	1,000
Less: Personal allowance	(12,570)
	———
Taxable income	28,780
Basic rate band	(37,700)
	———
Basic rate band remaining	8,920
	———

Tutorial note

The dividend income taxed at the nil rate reduces the remaining basic rate band.

After-tax proceeds are £20,017 ((500 × £52) − £5,983).

The sale of the shares to Jordi will therefore be preferable as it will leave Kat with the higher after-tax proceeds.

(c) Jordi – extraction of profits

Tutor's top tips

*The requirement is to explain the payments made by Traiste Ltd to HMRC in respect of the bonus or dividend, **not** to calculate the tax suffered by Jordi.*

However, you still need to consider the tax suffered by Jordi on the bonus in order to work out the gross bonus paid and the amounts deducted by the company under PAYE.

Payment of bonus

Traiste Ltd will have to account for income tax and class 1 employee's and employer's national insurance contributions (NICs), under the PAYE regulations.

Jordi will suffer deduction of income tax at the rate of 40%, and employee's NICs at the rate of 2% on the gross amount of the bonus. The gross amount payable will therefore need to be £34,483 (£20,000/0.58).

The total amount payable to HM Revenue and Customs (HMRC) by Traiste Ltd will be:

	£
Income tax on £34,483 at 40%	13,793
Employee's NICs on £34,483 at 2%	690
Employer's NICs on £34,483 at 13.8%	4,759
	19,242

This is due for payment by 22 April 2023.

Payment of dividend

No payments to HMRC will be required from Traiste Ltd.

Examiner's report

The first part concerned the redundancy of an employee. This part of the question consisted of two tasks.

Candidates did not have any particular difficulties with the first task which required them to explain the income tax implications of the redundancy package. Many answers were pleasingly concise and the relevant rules were well known by the majority of candidates.

However, candidates did not fare so well with the second task which required them to calculate the corporation tax deductions in respect of the redundancy package.

The main problem was that many candidates were unable to think in terms of 'allowable cost' as opposed to 'tax'. This led to candidates identifying the employment income benefit as the cost to the company as opposed to the cost of leasing the vehicle.

The second part of the question required candidates to explain the post-tax proceeds on a sale of shares. This is a part of the syllabus which candidates tend to be familiar with, such that most candidates should be able to do well. However, although this part was done very well by some candidates it was done poorly by others. The problem was that candidates did not spend sufficient time thinking about what was going on in the question. The shareholder was either going to sell the shares to an individual or was going to sell them back to the company. This latter disposal was, of course, a purchase of own shares by the company, but this was missed by many candidates.

Other common errors included; failing to recognise that the sale to the individual would be deemed to take place at market value because the vendor and the purchaser were connected persons and failing to identify the availability of business asset disposal relief.

On the plus side, the majority of candidates handled the concept of post-tax proceeds well in that they correctly deducted the tax liability from the proceeds received.

The final part of the question concerned the extraction of profits from a company by a director shareholder. The question required candidates to explain the payments to be made by the **employing company** to HM Revenue and Customs.

Unfortunately, many candidates failed to notice this precise aspect of the requirement, such that they simply focused on the recipient individual's tax liabilities in respect of the amounts received as opposed to the amounts which would be paid by the company in respect of the payments made. As a result, many candidates did not do as well as they could have in this part.

Candidates who did well in this question:

- had a precise knowledge of the various detailed rules

- read the requirements carefully and ensured that they answered the question set.

		ACCA marking scheme		Marks
(a)	(i)	Income tax implications for Esta		4.0
			Maximum	3.0
	(ii)	Cash payments deductible		1.0
		Car lease		1.5
		Class 1A national insurance contributions		3.0
				5.5
			Maximum	4.0
(b)		Sale of shares to Jordi		4.5
		Sale of shares to Traiste Ltd		5.0
				9.5
			Maximum	8.0
(c)		Payment of bonus		4.0
		Payment of dividend		1.0
				5.0
Total				**20.0**

61   DENT LTD (ADAPTED)

Key answer tips

This question is made up of three separate requirements which could be attempted in any order.

Part (a) covers VAT registration and requires you to consider the input VAT recovery implications of registering for VAT as well as explaining why voluntary registration would be beneficial. There are six marks for this requirement so you need to ensure you consider all aspects of input VAT and not just that incurred after registration.

Part (b) asks you to explain the corporation tax treatment of the R&D expenditure and calculate the allowable deduction for corporation tax purposes. There are four different costs incurred so you need to ensure you explain the treatment of each of them, as some of them may be treated differently. Once you have done this you can summarise your findings with the calculation.

In the final part of the question you need to explain the income tax treatment of a lump sum and calculate after tax employment costs for the company. In these calculations it is important that you think about any associated employer's NIC costs for the income and benefits provided, as well as what corporation tax saving will be available. Remember that Alina is working on the R&D project so some of the costs may be eligible for extra relief.

(a)   Compulsory registration for value added tax (VAT) and why voluntary registration is beneficial

If Dent Ltd registers for VAT on 1 April 2023, it can make a claim to recover input tax suffered on goods and services purchased prior to registration as follows:

Input tax may be recovered on assets which have been purchased for the purpose of the business in the four years prior to registration, provided they are still held by Dent Ltd on 1 April 2023. Thus, Dent Ltd will be able to recover the VAT paid on the purchase of the specialist equipment. However, VAT will not be recoverable on the cost of the consumables which have been consumed prior to 1 April 2023.

Input tax may be recovered on the supply of services for the purpose of the business, which were supplied within the six months prior to registration. Accordingly, Dent Ltd will not be able to recover input VAT on a proportion of the property costs and the agency fees which relate to the period from 1 July 2022 to 30 September 2022.

If Dent Ltd registers for VAT on 1 July 2022, all the VAT suffered on the goods and services supplied from commencement of the business will be recoverable. Additionally, there will be a cash flow advantage for Dent Ltd as it is likely to be in a repayment position in at least the first of its VAT returns.

Although Dent Ltd will have to charge VAT on its taxable supplies from 1 July 2022, this will not be a problem for its customers, as they will all be VAT registered and therefore able to reclaim any VAT charged.

(b) **Corporation tax relief available in respect of the research and development (R&D) expenditure**

The expenditure on the specialist equipment qualifies for a 100% capital allowance as it is capital expenditure on an asset to be used for R&D purposes.

Tutorial note

The specialist equipment will not be eligible for the 130% super deduction as it is not new.

As Dent Ltd is a small enterprise for the purposes of R&D expenditure, an additional 130% deduction is available in calculating the company's taxable trading income in respect of qualifying revenue expenditure which is directly related to the R&D activities. In this case, this will apply to the property costs (as they comprise only heat, light and water charges), consumables and the staff costs (including the pension contributions). However, this additional relief is restricted in respect of the contractor supplied by the agency (as an unconnected third party) to 65% of the cost, i.e. £16,250 (65% × £25,000).

Therefore, the total deduction available to Dent Ltd in the year ending 30 June 2023 is £657,525 (£353,000 + (130% × (£46,000 + £12,000 + (£185,000 – £25,000 + £16,250)))).

(c) **Lump sum payment and provision of computer and temporary living accommodation to Alina**

Income tax implications for Alina of receiving the lump sum payment

The lump sum payment is fully taxable on Alina in the tax year 2022/23 as it relates to future services to be performed by her.

Tutorial note

This sort of lump sum payment given to induce employment is often referred to as a 'golden hello'. It is taxable when it is received as it relates to future services to be provided by the employee.

After-tax cost to Dent Ltd

Lump sum payment

	£
Amount of payment	10,000
Class 1 employer national insurance contributions (NIC) (£10,000 × 13.8%)	1,380
Pre-tax cost of lump sum payment	11,380

This is eligible for the additional 130% deduction as it is qualifying R&D expenditure, so the tax-deductible amount for Dent Ltd is £26,174 (£11,380 × 230%).

Provision of computer and temporary living accommodation

	£
Rent paid (£660 × 6)	3,960
Class 1A NICs (£4,110 (W) × 13.8%)	567
	———
Pre-tax cost of the temporary living accommodation	4,527
Cost of computer	1,000
	———
Pre-tax cost of the provision of computer and temporary living accommodation	5,527
	———

The total tax-deductible amount is £31,701 (£26,174 + £4,527 + £1,000)

	£
Total pre-tax cost to Dent Ltd (£11,380 + £5,527)	16,907
Less: Corporation tax relief: (£31,701 × 19%)	(6,023)
	———
After-tax cost	10,884
	———

Working

	£
Taxable benefits for Alina in the tax year 2022/23:	
Computer (£1,000 × 20% × 9/12)	150
Accommodation benefit: Higher of	
(i) annual value = £1,400 (£2,800 × 6/12)	
(ii) rent paid by Dent Ltd = £3,960 (£660 × 6)	3,960
	———
Taxable benefit	4,110
	———

Tutorial note

1   *The provision of taxable benefits to an employee is not qualifying expenditure for the purpose of the additional 130% deduction for R&D expenditure.*

2   *Dent Ltd can claim AIA on the cost of the computer, but not super deduction as it is second-hand.*

Examiner's report

This question was in three main parts, dealing with VAT, research and development (R&D) expenditure and income tax and national insurance. The first part of the question asked for two VAT scenarios to be discussed. The first scenario concerned the implications of compulsory registration and the second scenario concerned the benefits of an earlier voluntary registration. Many candidates did not deal with these two scenarios separately and answered generally about VAT registration and so did not achieve all of the available marks. Some candidates gave detailed rules regarding when VAT registration would become compulsory, which was not asked for and earned no marks. A number of candidates were clear on the rules for input tax recovery on pre-registration expenditure but unfortunately did not apply the rules to the facts of the question.

The second part of the question required an explanation of the tax treatment of the R&D expenditure incurred and a calculation of the available R&D deduction relating to this expenditure. The question specifically stated that the company was a small enterprise for the purposes of R&D expenditure and yet a number of candidates discussed R&D tax relief in a large company as well as a small company. These candidates spent time providing explanations for which although correct, there were no marks awarded. Unfortunately, many candidates appeared to be unsure of the tax relief available for R&D capital expenditure but seemed to have a much better understanding of the basics of tax relief for R&D revenue expenditure.

The third part of the question concerned a lump sum payment and the provision of benefits-in-kind by a company to an employee. Candidates were required to state the income tax implications of the lump sum payment for the employee and to calculate the after-tax cost for the company of providing the payment and the benefits-in-kind. Initially candidates needed to calculate the value of the lump sum payment and each benefit-in-kind and then calculate the employers' national insurance contributions. They then needed to add the actual cost of the payment and the benefits-in-kind to the employers' national insurance contributions and deduct the corporation tax saving from the total. It was pleasing to see that many candidates were able to deal well with these requirements. However, some candidates did not recognise the difference between the actual cost to the employer of providing the benefits-in-kind and the taxable value of the benefits-in-kind in the hands of the employee.

	ACCA marking scheme		
			Marks
(a)	Pre-registration expenditure – goods		3.0
	Pre-registration expenditure – services		1.5
	Benefits of voluntary registration		2.5
			———
			7.0
		Maximum	6.0
			———
(b)	Capital expenditure – explanation		1.0
	Additional deduction for revenue expenditure – explanation		3.5
	Total deduction – calculation		2.0
			———
			6.5
		Maximum	6.0
			———
(c)	Income tax implications for Alina		1.0
	Pre-tax cost of lump sum payment		2.5
	Pre-tax cost of computer and living accommodation		4.0
	Total pre-tax expenditure		0.5
	Corporation tax saving		0.5
			———
			8.5
		Maximum	8.0
			———
Total			**20.0**
			———

62 DORIAN

Key answer tips

This question focuses on a close company, its transactions with one of the directors and the late filing of its corporation tax return.

In part (a), although the question states that the company is a close company, the requirement specifically asks for an explanation as to why the company is close. It is worth learning the definition as being able to identify a close company is a common requirement in the exam.

Part (b) moves on from the definition of a close company to the implications. Another expectation of the ATX exam is the ability to explain the consequences of close company status in respect of loans made, and benefits provided, to shareholders.

In part (c) a comparison is required of two alternative ways of the company providing assistance with travel costs to the employee, and then a determination of which of the two would be better for the employee. Here computations are required; remember to provide clear, professional looking and sufficiently labelled numerical answers with accompanying explanations. It would be useful to use the spreadsheet for this part of your answer.

Part (d) requires a brief explanation of the implications for a company of the late filing of its corporation tax return. Administration will be tested at some point in the exam, and learning the key areas should provide some easy marks.

(a)   Reason for close company status

A company is a close company if it is controlled by:

–   Any number of shareholders who are also directors, or

–   The five largest shareholders in the company.

Control is exercised by shareholders who own more than half of the company's issued share capital.

For the purpose of determining control, a shareholder is regarded as owning any shares owned by their associates, in addition to the shares which they own personally. Associates include direct relatives, so Dorian is associated with his father.

Dorian is regarded as owning 28% of the shares (his own 5% plus his father's 23%). The remaining five directors own a total of 25%, so that overall the six directors own 53% of the issued share capital, and control the company.

Tutorial note

There are additional complexities when determining whether or not a company is a close company, but the above points were sufficient to score full marks.

(b)   Tax implications for Dorian and Taupe Ltd of early repayment of Dorian's £7,500 loan

There will be no tax implications for Dorian. This will be the only loan outstanding in 2024/25, so there will be no loan interest benefit arising as it does not exceed £10,000.

As Taupe Ltd is a close company, it will have paid notional tax of £2,438 (£7,500 × 32.5%) to HM Revenue and Customs (HMRC) in respect of the loan to Dorian, who is a participator in the company.

HMRC will repay the £2,438 to Taupe Ltd nine months and one day after the end of the accounting period in which the loan is repaid.

Accordingly, if Dorian repays the loan on 30 April 2024, Taupe Ltd will receive the repayment by 1 February 2025, one year earlier than it would if the loan were repaid on 30 June 2024.

Tutorial note

Where the total loans to the employee do not exceed £10,000, at any point in the tax year, they are an exempt benefit, and therefore no preferential interest benefit will arise.

The company is exempt from paying notional tax where the loan satisfies three requirements:

–   The loan does not exceed £15,000, and

–   The individual is a full-time working employee, and

–   The individual (including associates' interests) owns 5% of the shares or less.

Notional tax will have been payable in respect of the £7,500 loan made to Dorian, because Dorian (including his associate Basil) owns more than 5% of the shares in Taupe Ltd.

(c)   The cost to Dorian of the two alternative travel assistance proposals

Alternative 1: Provision of an interest-free loan to purchase a season ticket

Dorian already has an existing interest-free loan from Taupe Ltd of £7,500. If he receives a further loan from Taupe Ltd of £4,800, the total amount outstanding will exceed £10,000, such that a taxable benefit will arise in respect of the whole of these loans.

Both of the loans are interest-free, so there will be a taxable benefit, calculated by reference to the official rate of interest, of £246 ((£7,500 + £4,800) × 2%). This will be subject to income tax at 40%, as Dorian will be a higher rate taxpayer in 2023/24, but the loans will not result in a liability to class 1 national insurance contributions (NICs) for Dorian. The income tax payable would be £98 (£246 × 40%).

When the loan is written off on 5 April 2024, the amount written off will be treated as a distribution, and therefore liable to income tax at the rate of 32.5%. As Dorian has no other dividend income, the dividend nil rate band would be available, such that Dorian would incur an income tax liability of £910 ((£4,800 – £2,000) × 32.5%)).

The cost to Dorian of this alternative will be £1,008 (£98 + £910).

Tutorial note

Where a close company makes a loan to a shareholder, and that loan (or part of it) is later written off, for IT purposes it will be treated as a distribution (a dividend) in the hands of the shareholder. This treatment is the same regardless of whether the shareholder is, or is not, an employee.

For the purposes of NIC, if the shareholder is also an employee, class 1 NIC will be due on the loan written off. Candidates who were aware of this were awarded credit in their answers.

Alternative 2: Payment of a mileage allowance and provision of a free car-parking space

The mileage allowance will be subject to income tax at 40% and class 1 NIC at 2%. This will give rise to a total tax cost of £1,512 (£3,600 × 42%).

Dorian will have additional travel costs, not covered by the mileage allowance of £300 ((£5,220 – £1,320) – £3,600).

Provision of a car parking space at, or near, an employee's normal place of work is an exempt benefit for income tax and NIC.

The total cost to Dorian of this alternative is therefore £1,812 (£1,512 + £300).

Provision of the interest-free loan to purchase a season ticket results in the lower overall cost for Dorian.

Tutorial note

The approved mileage rates are not relevant in this case as the driving costs are not related to journeys made in the course of Dorian carrying out his duties of employment.

(d)   Implications for Taupe Ltd of the late filing of its corporation tax return

Taupe Ltd's corporation tax return for the year ended 30 April 2021 should have been filed by 30 April 2022 (12 months after the end of the period of account), as the notice requiring the filing of this return was issued before 1 February 2022.

As the return was filed more than three months late, a fixed late filing penalty of £200 will arise. Although the return for the year ended 30 April 2020 was also filed late, the penalty will not be increased to £1,000 as the return for the year ended 30 April 2019 was filed on time.

Examiner's report

This question focused on a close company, its transactions with one of the directors and the late filing of its corporation tax return.

This question was not at all well attempted by candidates, as there appeared to be a considerable lack of knowledge of close company legislation. In ATX-UK candidates are expected to be able to accurately define a close company and be able to explain the consequences of close company status in respect of loans made, and benefits provided, to participators. Candidates would be well advised to learn these rules, and practise questions in relation to their application in any given scenario.

Part (a) required candidates to explain why the company in the scenario was classed as a close company.

Nearly all candidates knew that it was something to do with the number of directors and shareholders, but relatively few were able to correctly state the rules, relating to the need for control, the relevance of associates, and concluding on the reason why this company fell within the definition. Candidates therefore struggled to score any marks on this question part or scored only one mark out of a possible four.

Part (b) related to the repayment of a loan made by the company to a participator, and the implications for both the participator and the company of it being repaid early.

Despite being told in the question that notional tax was payable by the company on this loan, a number of candidates discussed why the loan would be exempt from this notional tax charge, which clearly could not be relevant here. A reasonable number of candidates recognised that the notional tax would be repayable to the company when the participator repaid the loan, but were not able to elaborate on this, and, in particular, to recognise that early repayment would mean that the repayment would fall into an earlier accounting period for the company, and therefore bring forward the repayment of the notional tax by 12 months. Many answers were extremely brief and rather general.

Part (c) involved a comparison of two alternative ways of the company providing the participator with assistance with travel costs, to determine which of the two would result in the lower cost for the participator.

Alternative 1 comprised the provision of an interest-free loan to purchase a season ticket. Candidates needed to pause and think about this in context. The original loan to this participator was still outstanding, so the total loans would exceed £10,000, and there would be a taxable benefit, calculated by reference to the official rate of interest. Also, as this loan was to be written off at the end of the tax year, candidates had to consider the income tax implications of this write off. The majority of candidates identified either the beneficial interest implications, or the implications arising from the write off, but only a minority identified and dealt with both. Fewer still appeared to realise that the loans needed to be considered in total, not individually.

Alternative 2 included the payment of a mileage allowance and provision of a free car-parking space. Many candidates recognised that the provision of the car-parking space would be an exempt benefit, but fewer identified that the mileage allowance would be fully taxable as it related wholly to non-business (home to work) travel. Workings to calculate the additional costs to be borne by the participator were often muddled, and insufficiently explained. In particular, a number of CBE candidates who chose to use the spreadsheet response option for this question part – which was fine – just provided numbers with no accompanying labels or explanations. Candidates are reminded that their workings should be clearly presented and explained, in order that a marker can follow them.

Finally, the majority of candidates did provide a sensible conclusion re the lower cost for the participator, which was pleasing to see.

Part (d) required a brief explanation of the implications for the company of the late filing of its corporation tax return.

A significant number of candidates did not know that the normal filing date for a company's corporation tax return is 12 months after the end of its accounting period. The most popular incorrect answer was nine months and one day after the end of this period, which is, of course the due date for payment of tax by non-large companies. Additionally, many appeared to guess at the late filing penalty which would apply, without giving a reason.

	ACCA marking scheme		Marks
(a)	General definition		2.0
	Associates		1.0
	Application to scenario		1.5
			4.5
		Maximum	4.0
(b)	Tax implications for Dorian		1.0
	Tax implications for Taupe Ltd		4.5
			5.5
		Maximum	5.0
(c)	Interest benefit		3.5
	Loan written off		2.0
	Mileage allowance alternative		4.0
			9.5
		Maximum	8.0
(d)	Filing date		1.5
	Penalty		2.0
			3.5
		Maximum	3.0
Total			20.0

63   SAMPHIRE LTD AND KELP LTD

Key answer tips

This question covers the provision of benefits to a director/shareholder, which incorporates assumed knowledge from the TX exam as well as dealing with the close company rules. There is also the disposal of a leased factory, which triggers a chargeable gain, and the purchase of a new factory and warehouse which enables a rollover relief claim.

Part (a) requires in-depth knowledge of the close company rules and the impact of providing either an asset or a loan to a director who is also a participator. You are told in the question that Samphire Ltd is a close company and this is a key hint in the scenario which will help you to approach this part of the question. You also need to be confident about how to establish whether a company is a close company, as this information may not always be provided in the question.

Note that for both sub-parts of part (a) you are required to explain as well as performing the calculations. This means that you should have some writing to support your figures, and you will not be able to score well without this.

Part (b) is a chargeable gains question covering the disposal of a lease on a factory and the outright purchase of a new factory and warehouse. The question is split into two sub requirements Part (b)(i) is purely computational and requires the use of lease percentages provided in the question. This is worth three marks and should be straightforward to calculate. Part (b)(ii) requires an explanation, along with supporting calculations, of the gain left chargeable after the consideration of rollover relief. However, you need to read the scenario carefully as full rollover relief is not available. There are seven marks available for this part of the requirement; with so many marks available this is unlikely to be a straightforward rollover relief question.

(a)   (i)   Alternative 1: Gift of a computer to Nori

The transfer of the computer to Nori will not result in a balancing charge on the main pool, as the proceeds will be £nil.

The transfer of the computer will also be a disposal of a chattel by Samphire Ltd, but this will be an exempt disposal as both cost and deemed proceeds are less than £6,000.

As Nori is a director of Samphire Ltd, the gift of the computer will give rise to a taxable benefit of £1,500, i.e. the market value of the computer at the date of the gift. Accordingly, there will be a Class 1A national insurance contributions (NIC) liability for Samphire Ltd of £207 (£1,500 × 13.8%). Corporation tax relief of £39 (£207 × 19%) will be available in respect of this.

Therefore, the total additional taxes payable in respect of this alternative for Samphire Ltd are £168 (£207 – £39).

(ii) **Alternative 2: Make a loan to Nori**

Samphire Ltd is a close company. Accordingly, on making a loan to Nori, a participator, it must make a payment of notional tax of £488 (£1,500 × 32.5%) to HM Revenue and Customs (HMRC). This payment will be due by 1 January 2025. Following the write off of the loan (on 6 April 2025), HMRC will repay all the notional tax to Samphire Ltd (by 1 January 2027).

Writing off the loan is treated as a distribution, so there will be no corporation tax implications for Samphire Ltd.

Although the loan is interest-free, it will not give rise to a taxable benefit for Nori. This is because the total amount of the loan will not exceed £10,000 at any time. Accordingly, Samphire Ltd will not have any liability to Class 1A NIC.

However, a liability to Class 1 NIC will arise on writing off the loan on 6 April 2025, as Nori is also an employee of the company. Accordingly, Samphire Ltd will have a Class 1 NIC liability of £207 (£1,500 × 13.8%) and corporation tax relief in respect of this of £39 (£207 × 19%).

Therefore, the total additional taxes payable in respect of this alternative for Samphire Ltd is also £168 (£207 – £39).

(b) **(i)** **Gain on the sale of the lease**

	£
Proceeds	206,000
Less: Cost (£165,000 × 96.593/99.289)	(160,520)
Unindexed gain	45,480
Less: Indexation allowance (0.047 × £160,520)	(7,544)
Chargeable gain	37,936

Tutorial note

This requirement was to calculate the gain on the sale of the lease of Factory 1. Technically this is an 'assignment of a short lease'. The cost figure needs to be restricted by reference to the lease percentages provided in the question but you also need to remember to apply the indexation allowance, as this is a disposal by a company.

(ii) **Gain remaining chargeable after claiming the maximum amount of rollover relief.**

Kelp Ltd owned the lease on Factory 1 for six years from 1 November 2016 to 1 November 2022. However, it did not occupy the building for trading purposes during the last six months of ownership from 1 May 2022 to 1 November 2022. Accordingly, only £34,775 (£37,936 × 5.5/6) of the gain is eligible for rollover relief.

In order to relieve the whole of this eligible gain, Kelp Ltd must reinvest £188,833 (£206,000 × 5.5/6) in qualifying business assets within the four-year period commencing one year before the disposal of Factory 1.

The factory acquired from Samphire Ltd (Factory 2) is a qualifying business asset, acquired within the year prior to the disposal of Factory 1. Kelp Ltd and Samphire Ltd are not in a gains group, as they are owned by an individual, not a company. Accordingly, the price paid by Kelp Ltd of £138,000 is its relevant acquisition cost. As Kelp Ltd will use Factory2 wholly for trading purposes, the full amount of £138,000 is the qualifying cost for rollover relief purposes.

The warehouse to be acquired by Kelp Ltd is also a qualifying business asset, and it will be acquired within the three years following the disposal of Factory 1. However, as only 70% of the warehouse will be used by Kelp Ltd in its trade, only £54,600 (£78,000 × 70%) of its cost will be a qualifying acquisition for rollover relief purposes.

Accordingly, £192,600 (£138,000 + £54,600) has been reinvested in qualifying business assets. As this exceeds £188,833, the whole of the eligible gain of £34,775 can be deferred, leaving an immediately chargeable gain of £3,161 (£37,936 − £34,775).

Examiner's report

Requirement (a)

This part of the question concerned a UK resident close trading company which was looking to either make a gift of a computer to a director of the company or a loan to the same director to allow him to purchase the computer himself.

Requirement (a)(i) – 4 marks

The requirement here was to explain, with supporting calculations, the total additional taxes payable by Samphire Ltd if the company gifts the computer to the director.

It is important to focus on the requirement here and to break it down – first of all, 'explain, with supporting calculations' means providing a combination of words and numbers in the answer. Secondly, the reference to 'total' additional taxes implies that there will be more than one additional tax which is relevant and that therefore the sum of all of them should eventually be provided. Thirdly, the question refers to the total additional taxes 'payable by Samphire Ltd', and not by the director. Some candidates discussed the additional taxes payable by the latter; this did not earn credit because it was not what was required. It is always worth double checking a requirement to ensure that it is fully understood, perhaps by highlighting the key words in order to ensure that candidates are doing exactly what it is they are being asked to do.

The question stated that the written down value of the main pool, where the computer would originally have been allocated, was £nil and that the sale proceeds for the purpose of capital allowances were also £nil. This therefore indicated that there would be no balancing charge on the main pool as a result of the gift.

The gift of a capital asset should also lead to a consideration of the capital gains consequences for the company although on this occasion this was an exempt disposal, the cost and sale proceeds of the computer both being less than £6,000.

Since the gift of the computer was to a director of the company, this would also constitute a taxable benefit for the individual. However, it was only the tax implications for the company of making the gift which were relevant on this occasion. The provision of the asset by way of gift will mean that the company will have to pay class 1A national insurance contributions (NIC) on the taxable benefit amount, which will then be tax deductible for the company when calculating its corporation tax liability.

Thus the total additional taxes payable by the company are the class 1A NIC cost less the 19% corporation tax relief thereon.

Requirement (a)(ii) – 6 marks

This part of the question required an explanation, together with supporting calculations, of the total additional taxes payable by Samphire Ltd if the company were to make a £1,500 loan to the director, and then to write off that loan two years later.

Once again, it is advisable to break down the requirement and highlight the key words. Candidates were being asked to explain and give supporting calculations, so both did need to be provided here. They were asked for total additional taxes, implying once again the need to consider more than one tax, and then total them all up. And finally, they were being asked for additional taxes payable by the company, not the director, so this should be kept in mind when preparing the answer.

Many candidates correctly identified that, since this was a loan from a close company to a director who is also a shareholder, this would result in a notional tax charge being payable by the company. Several then went on to discuss what would have happened if the loan was repaid, but in doing so failed to pick up on the facts of the question where they were specifically told that the loan would be written off in two years' time.

This write-off would lead to repayment of the notional tax, meaning that the overall tax cost to the company will be £nil.

There would however be a cashflow impact because, having paid the notional tax, the company would have to wait two years for its repayment from HMRC. The write-off of the loan itself would be classified as a distribution so there would be no corporation tax implications from the company's perspective. There were however some further consequences which needed to be considered and many candidates did not go on to think about these. These involved the national insurance cost to the company.

The loan would not give rise to a taxable benefit for the director because, although interest free, it was below the £10,000 threshold. This means there will be no class 1A NIC liability for Samphire Ltd.

However, when a loan to a director gets written off, class 1 NICs will be payable by the company on the amount of the write-off; this will then be tax deductible for the company when calculating its corporation tax liability.

Therefore, in conclusion, the total additional taxes payable by the company under this alternative scenario are the class 1 NIC cost of the write-off as reduced by the 19% corporation tax saving on that amount.

Requirement (b)

This part of the question involved a different company, Kelp Ltd, which was disposing of a lease on a building and acquiring a factory and a warehouse.

Requirement (b)(i) – 3 marks

This requirement was to calculate the gain on the sale of the lease of Factory 1. Technically this is an 'assignment of a short lease'. The calculation of the chargeable gain involves the usual 'Sale proceeds less cost and (this being a company making the disposal) less indexation allowance' but, in view of the wasting nature of the asset involved, the cost figure needs to be restricted by reference to the lease percentages provided in the question.

A significant number of candidates didn't go on to calculate the indexation allowance; despite being given relevant indexation factors in the question.

Requirement (b)(ii) – 7 marks

This part of the question required an explanation, with supporting calculations, of the amount of the chargeable gain calculated in part (b)(i) remaining liable to corporation tax, after taking advantage of maximum rollover relief claims

Once again, a full analysis of the requirement is important before starting to work on the answer. Explanations and calculations need to be provided. Having worked out the maximum rollover relief, it is then necessary to go to state how much of the gain will remain liable to corporation tax after the rollover relief claim has been made

Firstly, before even considering the replacement assets acquired, it is necessary to consider how much of the gain arising on the disposal of the lease on Factory 1 is eligible for rollover relief.

The question states that Factory 1 was owned for 6 years but only used for trading purposes for 5 years and 6 months, having been rented out for the final six months of ownership. Consequently, only 5.5/6 of the gain is eligible for rollover relief i.e. £37,936 × 5.5/6 = £34,775.

This also means that Kelp Ltd must reinvest 5.5/6 of the sale proceeds from Factory 1, if this gain is to be rolled over in full i.e. £206,000 × 5.5/6 = £188,833.

So to summarise, with regard to the asset being disposed of, there are two items which have to be pro-rated for non-trade use; namely the gain and the amount of sale proceeds which need to be reinvested.

Looking now at the assets in which Kelp Ltd has reinvested, these must be qualifying business assets purchased within the four-year period commencing one year before the disposal of Factory 1.

In the scenario Kelp Ltd acquires Factory 2 from Samphire Ltd. Kelp Ltd and Samphire Ltd are both owned by the same individual, Nori. Many candidates thought that this therefore meant that they were in a single gains group but this would only have been correct if they had been owned by a company, and not an individual. As such, since Factory 2 is to be wholly used for trading purposes, its full cost of £138,000 counts as qualifying expenditure for rollover relief purposes.

Kelp also acquires a second property within the relevant four-year time-frame, namely the warehouse. But this is only to be used 70% for trade purposes. Therefore, only 70% of the cost of the warehouse counts as qualifying expenditure for rollover relief purposes i.e. 70% × £78,000 = £54,600.

All of the above figures now need to be brought together in order to answer the question. The total qualifying acquisition cost of Factory 2 and the warehouse comes to £138,000 + £54,600 = £192,600. Since this amount is greater than the relevant sale proceeds from the sale of Factory 1 i.e. £188,833, it means that the whole of the eligible gain of £34,775 can be rolled over. However, it should be noted that the question actually asks for the amount of chargeable gain remaining liable to corporation tax, after a maximum rollover claim; given that £34,775 of the total gain of £37,936 is being rolled over, this leaves an amount of gain of £3,161 which is left in charge. This amount needed to be stated in order to answer the question fully

		ACCA marking scheme		Marks
(a)	(i)	Tax implications of transfer		1.5
		Class 1A national insurance contributions (NIC)		2.0
		Tax cost		1.0
				4.5
			Maximum	4.0
	(ii)	Loan to participator		4.5
		NIC implications		3.0
		Tax cost		1.0
				8.5
			Maximum	6.0
(b)	(i)	Calculation of chargeable gain		3.0
	(ii)	Gain eligible for rollover relief		1.5
		Reinvestment required		2.0
		Qualifying expenditure – factory 2		2.0
		– warehouse		1.5
		Conclusion		1.0
				8.0
			Maximum	7.0
Total				20.0

GROUPS, CONSORTIA AND OVERSEAS COMPANY ASPECTS

64   DAUBE GROUP (ADAPTED) *Walk in the footsteps of a top tutor*

Key answer tips

Part (a) is a typical corporation tax groups question covering: trading losses, capital gains aspects, VAT and stamp duty land tax.

The key to success is applying your knowledge to the scenario given and making sure that your answer only deals with the required issues; otherwise you are likely to run out of time.

Part (b) is a totally separate stand-alone section on the professional and ethical issues to consider before taking on a new client. Remember there will always be five marks in each exam on ethics.

There are easy marks available here, and it may therefore be a good idea to start with this part of the question just in case you run out of time on part (a).

The highlighted words in the written sections are key phrases that markers are looking for.

Tutor's top tips

As is usual for Section A questions, the formal requirements at the end of the question really just tell you how many marks are available for each section. The detailed requirements can all be found in the information provided in the question. Remember that in the exam the requirements you see at the end of the question in this exam kit will be on a separate button. The detailed information and requirements will be located in exhibits which you can click into to view.

As you read through, highlight any requirements and instructions that you find. Copy these into the answer space to help you keep your answer focused. The requirements in this question are all in the email from the manager.

Make sure that you set out your answer to part (a) as a report, as there are marks available for this. You need to write in full sentences, but don't waste time preparing a lengthy introduction.

(a)   **Report**

    To   Mr Daube

    From   Tax advisers

    Date   6 December 2022

    Subject   Various corporate matters

(i)   **Sale of Shank Ltd**

    Use of trading losses

Tutor's top tips

There are two different trading losses to consider here:

- The loss brought forward from the year ended 31 March 2022
- The current year loss for the year ended 31 March 2023.

You will need to deal with each of these separately in your answer, and clearly label them.

The examining team asks you to consider all possibilities, so make sure that you do that. However, you must ensure that you apply your knowledge to the scenario: there is no point in spending time discussing reliefs that are not actually possible.

Loss brought forward

The loss brought forward of £35,000 can be set against future total profits within Shank Ltd. As there are no profits available in the current year, the unrelieved loss would be available for surrender as group relief along with the current year loss (see below).

Any excess loss after group relief claims would be carried forward against future total profits in Shank Ltd.

However, there is a possible restriction on the use of this loss as Shank Ltd will change its owners when it is sold to Raymond Ltd on 1 February 2023.

If there is a major change in the nature or conduct of trade within five years of this change in ownership, the loss will not be allowed to be carried forward past 1 February 2023.

A major change would include a change in products or services offered, markets or customers.

As Mr Daube is of the opinion that the company will only become profitable if there are fundamental changes to its commercial operations, it seems likely that the restriction will apply.

Tutor's top tips

Look for clues in the question – you are specifically asked to consider any anti-avoidance legislation that may restrict the use of the losses. This is a big hint that there is some relevant anti-avoidance legislation here!

Make sure that you apply the rules to the scenario: there will be 'fundamental changes' to the company's commercial operations.

Tutorial note

A 'change in ownership' occurs when more than 50% of the share capital in the company changes ownership. As Hock Ltd is disposing of all of the share capital in Shank Ltd, there clearly is a change in ownership.

*However, for the restriction in use of losses to apply, there must be **both** a change in ownership and a major change in the nature and conduct of trade.*

Current year loss

Tutor's top tips

Read the question carefully. The statement that Shank Ltd has surrendered the maximum possible losses to group companies applies to the losses in the past pre-31 March 2022, not the loss for the year ended 31 March 2023.

Therefore, you need to include group relief as a key option available in your answer for the use of the loss in the year ended 31 March 2023.

The loss for the year ended 31 March 2023 cannot be set against current year profits or previous year profits of Shank Ltd, as there are none available. Shank Ltd has no other source of income.

All or part of this loss and the £35,000 excess brought forward loss could be surrendered to other companies within Shank Ltd's 75% losses group. This group contains Hock Ltd, Shank Ltd, Rump Ltd and Brisket Ltd, but **not** Knuckle Ltd.

The loss available for surrender must be time apportioned, as Shank Ltd will only be part of the losses group for part of the year. For the purposes of group relief, Shank Ltd is deemed to leave the group once 'arrangements' for sale are in place. The contract for sale will represent such an 'arrangement', therefore Shank Ltd can only surrender losses up to 1 November 2022.

The maximum loss available for surrender to Hock Ltd and Rump Ltd is therefore £31,500 (7/12 × (£19,000 + £35,000)) from 1 April 2022 to 31 October 2022.

Brisket Ltd has only been part of the losses group since 1 May 2022, therefore the maximum loss available for surrender to Brisket Ltd is £27,000 (6/12 × (£19,000 + £35,000), from 1 May 2022 to 31 October 2022.

The maximum loss that can be claimed by group companies will be limited to their taxable total profits for the corresponding period.

Any remaining losses will be carried forward by Shank Ltd along with its loss incurred between 1 November 2022 and 31 January 2023, as described above.

Tutor's top tips

This part of the question is all about explaining the reliefs available, not about giving advice on which relief might be best.

There is no information given about the profits of the other group companies for you to offer such advice.

Tutorial note

The requirement is to give advice to Mr Daube about the options for the use of the trading losses within his group of companies, and so marks in the answer are going for advising on the loss incurred up to 31 January 2023 only, when Shank Ltd leaves the group.

There are therefore no marks for commenting on what can happen with the loss after Shank Ltd left Mr Daube's control.

However, were this a requirement, the loss for the year ended 31 March 2023 is actually divided into three parts:

- *1 April 2022 to 31 October 2022 (seven months loss): group relief possible within Hock Ltd group for this loss and the excess brought forward trading loss, any excess carried forward.*

- *1 November 2022 to 31 January 2023 (three months loss): can only be used within Shank Ltd and as it has no other income, will be carried forward.*

  Losses carried forward cannot be surrendered to the new group for a period of five years after the change in ownership.

- *1 February 2023 to 31 March 2023 (two months loss): can be group relieved within the new group.*

Loss on sale of Shank Ltd

The sale of Shank Ltd will be covered by the substantial shareholding exemption, as Hock Ltd is disposing of shares and has held at least 10% of the shares in Shank Ltd for 12 months in the six years before the sale, and Shank Ltd is a trading company.

Accordingly, there will be no relief for the capital loss on the disposal of the shares.

Tutorial note

You are probably aware that gains on the sale of shares are covered by the substantial shareholding exemption. However, remember that the 'exemption' means that not only are there no chargeable gains, there are no allowable losses either!

Threshold for payment of corporation tax by instalment

Tutor's top tips

*Make sure that you read the verb in the question. You are asked to 'explain' the threshold for **all** of the companies. Just calculating the threshold is not enough here.*

Also, remember that not all companies will necessarily have the same limits. Check the dates carefully to see which companies have joined or left during the year, as these may be related to old or new groups too.

Companies are 51% group companies where one company controls another, or where companies are under the common control of another company.

Companies that join during the accounting period are deemed to be part of the group from the beginning of the following accounting period. Companies that leave during the accounting period are deemed to still be part of the group until the end of the current accounting period.

Knuckle Ltd has no related 51% group companies, so the threshold for Knuckle Ltd will be £1,500,000.

All of the Hock Ltd group companies except Brisket Ltd are 51% group companies for the year ended 31 March 2023.

Accordingly, the threshold for Hock Ltd, Shank Ltd and Rump Ltd for the year ended 31 March 2023 is £500,000 (£1,500,000 ÷ 3).

Brisket Ltd will be related to its previous owner and any other companies related to its previous owner. The threshold for Brisket Ltd could therefore be different from that shown above.

Tutorial note

A company is a 51% group company in the year that it leaves a group, but not in the year that it joins.

Shank Ltd will not be related to its new owner until the following year.

Brisket Ltd, however, will be related to its previous owners, and if applicable, other related companies in that group.

There is not enough information in the question, to specifically calculate the number of 51% group companies and therefore the threshold for Brisket Ltd.

(ii) Sales of buildings

Gains/losses on sale

Gar building

The sale of the Gar building to Hock Ltd will be at no gain, no loss, as Shank Ltd and Hock Ltd are part of the same 75% capital gains group.

Tutor's top tips

There is no need to do a calculation here, it is enough to just state that the transfer will be at no gain, no loss and explain why.

There were no extra marks available for any calculations of the base cost of the deemed transfer.

Tutorial note

Although Shank Ltd is deemed to leave the 75% losses group on 1 November 2022, it is still part of the 75% capital gains group until the sale is completed on 1 February 2023.

Had the base cost been requested, the transfer would have occurred at the base cost of £283,500 (£210,000 + IA (£210,000 × 0.350)). The estimated proceeds given in the question are irrelevant.

*There will be no degrouping charge in respect of the Gar building when Shank Ltd leaves the group. A degrouping charge only arises if the **recipient** company leaves the group less than six years after a no gain, no loss transfer, with the asset acquired.*

Cray building

	£
Proceeds	42,000,000
Less: Cost	(24,000,000)
Unindexed gain	18,000,000
Less: Indexation allowance (£24,000,000 × 0.250)	(6,000,000)
Chargeable gain	12,000,000

Monk building

	£
Proceeds	290,000
Less: Cost	(380,000)
Capital loss	(90,000)

Sword building

Tutor's top tips

Be very careful here!

Before you can work out the gain on the Sword building, you need to calculate the allowable cost. There has been a rollover relief claim, but only part of the proceeds was reinvested, so only part of the gain on the Pilot building will have been rolled over.

	£
Proceeds	460,000
Less: Deemed cost (W1)	(210,000)
Unindexed gain	250,000
Less: Indexation allowance (£210,000 × 0.168)	(35,280)
Chargeable gain	214,720

Workings

(W1) Deemed cost of Sword building

	£
Original cost	255,000
Less: Rollover relief (W2)	(45,000)
Deemed cost	210,000

(W2) Rollover relief in respect of Sword building

	£
Gain on sale of the Pilot building	60,000
Less: Sale proceeds not reinvested in the Sword building (£270,000 – £255,000)	(15,000)
Rollover relief claimed	45,000

Tutorial note

The chargeable gains will arise in the company that made the disposal.

The chargeable gain arising in Knuckle Ltd's corporation tax computation cannot be moved to any other company as Knuckle Ltd is not in a capital gains group.

However, the chargeable gain arising in Rump Ltd can be moved within the capital gains group, for example to utilise capital losses brought forward.

Explaining this, however, is not mark earning as it is not specifically required in the question.

Use of capital losses

Tutor's top tips

Make sure that you provide the detailed explanations requested, and remember that capital losses are more restricted than trading losses.

The examining team is kind here, and tells you to watch out for the pre-entry loss on the Monk building. Even if you were unsure about the rules regarding pre-entry capital losses, you could still score some marks for a sensible attempt at describing its possible use.

Brought forward capital losses

Rump Ltd has brought forward capital losses which can be offset against the £12 million gain on the Cray building.

However, as the brought forward capital losses exceed £5 million, they will be subject to restriction. The amount that can be offset against the gain on the Cray building is restricted to £5 million plus 50% of the excess gains over £5 million.

The remaining capital losses continue to be carried forward against future capital gains in Rump Ltd and cannot be reallocated in the gains group.

Tutorial note

The £5 million deductions allowance is not examinable in detail, so you would not be expected to do any calculations with regards to this.

In this instance, if you were to do calculations, the amount of the gain which could be offset by the brought forward capital losses is £8.5 million (£5 million + 50% × (£12 million − £5 million)).

Remember that brought forward capital losses cannot be reallocated in a gains group, so these will be carried forwards in Rump Ltd.

Pre-entry loss

The Monk building was sold by Brisket Ltd before it joined the Hock Ltd group. Accordingly, the capital loss that arose before 1 May 2022 when Brisket Ltd joined the group is a restricted pre-entry loss.

It can only be set-off against gains on disposals made by Brisket Ltd on assets that it owned before it joined the group, or bought subsequently from unconnected persons for use in its own business.

Tutorial note

The question asks for the options available for the use of the loss only.

It does not ask for discussions re tax planning.

Therefore, no marks would be allocated to making such comments.

VAT on sale of buildings

Tutor's top tips

VAT on land and buildings and the option to tax are regularly tested in the exam. You must make sure that you learn the rules!

Inter-group transfer

Provided Hock Ltd and Shank Ltd are members of a VAT group; VAT should not be charged on the inter-group sale of the Gar building.

Other sales

VAT should only be charged on the sale of commercial buildings if:

- they are less than three years old; or
- the owner has opted to tax the building.

Stamp duty land tax

Tutor's top tips

The stamp duty rates and thresholds are given in the tax tables provided in the examination. To score marks here, you must make sure that you apply these rates to the buildings in the question.

Inter group transfer

There will be no stamp duty land tax payable on the transfer of the Gar building, as Shank Ltd and Hock Ltd are within the same 75% group.

Other sales

Stamp duty land tax will be payable at 0% on the first £150,000, then 2% on the next £100,000, then at 5% above £250,000 on the sale price of other buildings, and will be payable by the purchaser.

Tutorial note

Even though Shank Ltd leaves the 75% group within three years of the transfer of the Gar building, there is still no stamp duty land tax payable.

*Stamp duty land tax is only payable where the **transferee** company leaves the group within three years.*

(iii) **Sales by Knuckle Ltd to overseas customers**

VAT implications

Tutor's top tips

Consideration of the VAT implications of imports and exports is another popular area in the exam.

There are only two marks available here, so you should try to make two succinct points in your answer.

Sales to customers outside the UK are zero-rated.

The exports will not affect Knuckle Ltd's ability to reclaim input VAT, as all sales will still be taxable sales.

(b)   Before agreeing to become tax advisers to Mr Daube and his companies

Tutor's top tips

There are five marks available for this section, so try to make sure that you have at least five separately identifiable points available and address each of the requirements: information needed and actions to take!

Information needed:

- Proof of identity for Mr Daube (e.g. passport), and proof of address (e.g. utility bill)
- Proof of incorporation, primary business address and registered office for each company
- The structure, directors and shareholders of the companies
- The identities of those persons instructing the firm on behalf of the company and those persons that are authorised to do so.

Action to take:

Consider whether becoming tax advisers to Mr Daube and his companies would create any threats to compliance with the fundamental principles of professional ethics, for example integrity and professional competence.

Where such threats exist, we should not accept the appointment unless the threats can be reduced to an acceptable level via the implementation of safeguards.

Contact the existing tax adviser in order to ensure that there has been no action by Mr Daube or his companies that would, on ethical grounds, preclude us from accepting appointment.

Examiner's report

Part (a) was in three parts and, on the whole, was done well by many candidates. The vast majority of candidates prepared their answer in the correct report format although a minority wasted time producing a long and unnecessary introduction.

Candidates' knowledge of the reliefs available in respect of trading losses was often very good but many let themselves down by addressing the issue in the abstract rather than in relation to the companies in the question.

This resulted in detailed explanations of reliefs that were simply not applicable (in particular the offset of losses against current and previous years' profits) such that candidates then had too little time to explain the relevant points properly.

As always, candidates benefited if they paused to allow themselves to identify the issues within the question.

There was to be a change of ownership of the loss making company and an apparent major change in the manner in which it would carry on its activities going forward. Accordingly, it is likely that it would be unable to carry forward its losses beyond the date of the change of ownership. There were also arrangements in force for the company to be sold such that it would leave the group relief group prior to the legal transfer of the shares.

Many candidates spotted both of these points but those that did not need to think about how they would do things differently such that they would spot them in the future. Finally, a surprising number of candidates thought, incorrectly, that Knuckle Ltd was a member of the group relief group.

The capital loss on the sale of the company was not available for offset due to the substantial shareholding exemption. Somewhat surprisingly, many candidates missed this and, of those that spotted the point, many thought that whilst a gain would not be subject to tax, a loss would still be allowable.

For the final element of this part of the question candidates were asked to explain the corporation tax threshold of the companies. Many candidates simply stated the number of 51% group companies and the consequent thresholds; but that was not an explanation. What was needed were the reasons for the limits being what they were including references to the companies being controlled by the same company and the effect of companies joining and leaving the group. The threshold was not the same for each of the companies. Candidates needed to consider each of the companies and apply their knowledge of the rules to that company's particular circumstances.

Note that this part of the question has been amended since it was originally set.

Part (ii) concerned the planned disposal of a number of buildings. The capital gains were reasonably straightforward with just an added complication of a gain rolled over into the cost of one of the buildings.

However, many candidates missed the fact that one of the buildings would be transferred at no gain, no loss as the vendor and the purchaser were in a capital gains group. Others made errors in connection with the indexation allowance (applying the indexation factor to the unindexed gain rather than the cost) and the treatment of the held over gain. There was a sense here that some candidates had switched off in that some of the errors were very basic and were perhaps an indication of not paying sufficient attention as opposed to a lack of knowledge.

Candidates were told in the question that there was a pre-entry capital loss arising on the sale of one of the buildings. Only a small minority had a clear understanding of the manner in which the pre-entry loss could be used.

A minority of candidates wasted time on this part of the question explaining, often in some detail, how the gains and losses should be offset. This was not part of the requirements and there was insufficient information in the question to arrive at sensible conclusions. Candidates will always benefit from taking the time to read each requirement carefully and then taking care not to deviate from the tasks set.

The VAT and stamp duty land tax elements were handled well by many candidates. Those who did not do so well need to apply their knowledge to the facts as opposed to simply writing what they know. For example, the prices at which the buildings were to be sold meant that, where duty was payable, the rate would be 0%, 2% then 5%. Yet some candidates answered in the abstract and gave the various rates of duty for all possible prices that could be charged. Only a small number of candidates considered the possibility of there being a VAT group; slightly more identified that there would be no stamp duty land tax on the property transferred within the group.

Note that this part of the question has been amended since it was originally set.

Part (iii) concerned the VAT implications of selling goods overseas. There were many excellent answers to this part that, whilst being brief, often scored almost full marks. Weaker candidates either had not learned the rules or confused their terminology using the phrase 'no VAT will be charged' as opposed to 'zero rated'; the two terms do not mean the same thing.

The majority of candidates scored well in part (b). Many took the sensible approach of starting the question with this part in order to ensure that they had sufficient time available to prepare an appropriate answer. A minority had not taken the time to learn this area of the syllabus with the result that they were unable to obtain some very straightforward marks.

ACCA marking scheme				
				Marks
(a)	(i)	Use of trading losses		
		Losses carried forward		3.5
		Current year loss		5.5
		Loss on sale of Shank Ltd		2.0
		Corporation tax threshold		3.5
				————
				14.5
			Maximum	12.0
				————
	(ii)	Gar building		2.0
		Cray building		1.0
		Rump Ltd brought forward losses		2.5
		Sword building		2.5
		Monk building		
		Capital loss		0.5
		Use of pre-entry loss		2.0
		VAT		3.0
		Stamp duty land tax		2.0
				————
				15.5
			Maximum	12.0
				————
	(iii)	Customers situated outside the UK		1.0
		Recoverability of input tax		1.0
				————
				2.0
				————
		Appropriate style and presentation		2.0
		Effectiveness of communication		2.0
				————
				4.0
				————
(b)		Information needed		3.0
		Action to take		3.0
				————
				6.0
			Maximum	5.0
				————
Total				**35.0**
				————

65   DRENCH, HAIL LTD AND RAIN LTD (ADAPTED)

  Online question assistance and Walk in the footsteps of a top tutor

Key answer tips

This is really four separate questions.

Part (a)(i) covers the acquisition of a subsidiary, with or without losses, by either an individual or a company, and is the hardest part of the question.

Part (a)(ii) is really two written questions: one on close company loans to participators and one on the cash accounting scheme for VAT. These questions should have been very straightforward if you have learnt the rules, and could be attempted before (a)(i).

Part (b) deals with the ethical issue of confidentiality. Again, this part is very straightforward and could be attempted before the other parts of the question, in order to gain some easy marks.

The highlighted words in the written sections are key phrases that markers are looking for.

Tutor's top tips

The formal requirements at the end of the question just tell you how many marks are available for each section. The detailed requirements are all in the email from your manager.

(a) **MEMORANDUM**

To	The files
From	Tax assistant
Date	9 December 2022
Subject	Acquisition of Rain Ltd and other matters

(i) Acquisition of Rain Ltd

Tutor's top tips

There are four alternatives to consider here:

*1 Drench acquires Rain Ltd personally and Rain Ltd **does not** obtain the new contracts.*

*2 Drench acquires Rain Ltd personally and Rain Ltd **does** obtain the new contracts.*

*3 Hail Ltd acquires Rain Ltd and Rain Ltd **does not** obtain the new contracts.*

*4 Hail Ltd acquires Rain Ltd and Rain Ltd **does** obtain the new contracts.*

In order to score well on this part of the question, you must consider all four options. It is very important that you label your answer clearly, so that the marker can see which option you are dealing with.

Rain Ltd acquired by Drench personally

Tutor's top tips

Think carefully about the group relationships that exist here.

Drench is an individual, not a company.

Companies controlled by the same individual will not be 51% group companies for corporation tax purposes and cannot form a 75% group relief group.

Therefore, the companies cannot transfer losses and will not affect the payment dates for corporation tax purposes.

Rain Ltd does not obtain the new contracts

The only option available for relief of the £110,000 trading loss will be to set it against Rain Ltd's own profits.

An amount of £50,750 can be set against total profits (i.e. the chargeable gain) for the period ending 30 June 2023.

The remaining loss of £59,250 (£110,000 – £50,750) will then be carried forward for offset against Rain Ltd's future total profits.

There is no possibility of carrying back the remaining loss, as Rain Ltd had no taxable income or gains in the previous accounting period.

Tutor's top tips

Be very specific when writing about loss reliefs. For example, just saying that the remaining loss will be carried forward is not enough. You must also state that it will be set against future total profits.

Rain Ltd does obtain the new contracts

The corporation tax liability of Rain Ltd will be as follows:

Corporation tax – nine months ending 30 June 2023

	£
Trading profit	285,000
Chargeable gain	50,750
Taxable total profits	335,750
Corporation tax at 19%	63,793

Corporation tax payment date

If Rain Ltd is acquired by Drench personally, Rain Ltd will not be related to Hail Ltd as both companies will not be under common control of the same company.

Rain Ltd, Flake Ltd and Mist Ltd will be 51% group companies for the period ending 30 June 2023, giving three related companies in total.

As Rain Ltd prepares accounts for a nine-month period, the threshold must also be time apportioned.

Rain Ltd's threshold for corporation tax purposes for the nine months ending 30 June 2023 is, therefore £375,000 (£1,500,000 × 1/3 × 9/12).

Tutorial note

Remember that when a company leaves a group part way through the accounting period, it is taken into account in determining the payment dates of the old group and its payment date is affected by the other companies in the old group, as it was a 51% group company at the end of the previous AP.

Rain Ltd will not need to pay its corporation tax in quarterly instalments, as it does not have profits above this threshold.

The corporation tax will be due by 1 April 2024 (i.e. nine months and one day after the end of the accounting period).

Rain Ltd acquired by Hail Ltd

Tutor's top tips

Again, think carefully about the group relationships that exist here.

*Hail Ltd is a company, so this time, Rain Ltd and Hail Ltd **can** form a 75% group relief group, and therefore **can** transfer losses.*

Rain Ltd does not obtain the new contracts

This time, there are several options for relief of the £110,000 loss, and Rain Ltd should choose the option that gives the earliest tax saving, as all options will save tax at the same rate of 19%.

Rain Ltd could again claim relief for the loss against its own profits, as set out above where Drench acquires Rain Ltd.

Group relief

Hail Ltd and Rain Ltd will form a 75% group relief group.

Rain Ltd could, therefore, surrender its current period loss against Hail Ltd's taxable total profits for the same period.

Losses arising before Rain Ltd is acquired by Hail Ltd cannot be surrendered against group profits arising within five years of the acquisition.

As Rain Ltd only joins the Hail Ltd group on 1 January 2023, the maximum loss available for surrender must be time apportioned as follows:

$(£110,000 \times 6/9) = £73,333$ available

The maximum loss claimed by Hail Ltd would be restricted to its taxable total profits for the corresponding period:

$(£100,000 \times 6/12) = £50,000$

As the available loss is more than the maximum claim, the maximum group relief would be restricted to £50,000.

Accordingly, in order to obtain relief as early as possible, the loss should be utilised as follows:

	Loss used	Tax saved
	£	£
Set against Rain Ltd taxable total profits	50,750	
Surrender to Hail Ltd	50,000	
	———	
	100,750	
	———	
Total tax saved (£100,750 × 19%)		19,143
		———

Payment for group relief

Amounts paid for group relief are ignored for corporation tax purposes, as long as the amount paid is no more than the amount of loss surrendered.

Rain Ltd does obtain the new contracts

Rain Ltd will still have the same corporation tax as when acquired by Drench (i.e. £63,793).

As Rain Ltd will now be controlled by Hail Ltd, Hail Ltd will be a 51% group company. However, this will not affect the threshold for payment of corporation tax by instalment until the following accounting period.

Therefore, the payment date will be exactly the same as before (i.e. 1 April 2024).

Tutorial note

Remember that when a company joins a group part way through the accounting period, it is not taken into account in determining the payment dates of the new group and the new group companies are not taken into account in determining its payment date, as it was not a 51% company at the end of the previous AP. It will be related in the following AP.

This means that when a company moves from one group to another, it is related to the old group in the year of change and the new group in the following AP.

Tax treatment of Rain Ltd's building

Potential tax liabilities: Degrouping charge

The transfer of the building from Mist Ltd to Rain Ltd would have been at no gain, no loss, as Mist Ltd and Rain Ltd were part of a 75% gains group at the time.

Whether Rain Ltd is purchased by Drench or Hail Ltd, it will be leaving the Flake Ltd group within six years of the no gain, no loss transfer whilst still owning the building.

This will result in a degrouping charge in the nine months ending 30 June 2023 as set out below.

	£
Market value on 1 July 2019 (date of the no gain/no loss transfer)	260,000
Less: Cost to Mist Ltd	(170,000)
Less: Indexation allowance (January 2010 to December 2017) (0.276 × £170,000)	(46,920)
Degrouping charge	43,080

Tutorial note

There is no indexation allowance post December 2017.

The degrouping charge will be added to Flake Ltd's proceeds for the sale of the shares in Rain Ltd, and may increase the gain on disposal of the shares.

However, the disposal of shares will be covered by the substantial shareholding exemption, as Rain Ltd is a trading company, and Flake Ltd will have held at least 10% of the shares for at least 12 months in the six years before the disposal.

Base cost of the building

The base cost of the building for Rain Ltd will now be £260,000 as at 1 July 2019 (i.e. the market value at the date of the no gain, no loss transfer).

Tutorial note

If Rain Ltd did not leave the Flake Ltd group, the base cost of the building would be the original cost to the group of £170,000 plus indexation allowance to the earlier of the date of the transfer (1 July 2019) or December 2017.

(ii)   **Loan to Drench and value added tax (VAT) cash accounting scheme**

        Loan from Hail Ltd to Drench

Tutor's top tips

The requirement asks for the tax implications for Hail Ltd (i.e. the employer) only, so don't waste time writing at length about the implications for Drench.

However, you do need to consider the taxable benefit for Drench, as employer's class 1A national insurance contributions will be based on this.

Hail Ltd is a close company, as it is controlled by one shareholder (participator): Drench.

Accordingly, this will be a loan from a close company to a participator, and Hail Ltd must pay a tax charge to HMRC of £5,850 (32.5% × £18,000).

This tax charge should be paid with the corporation tax liability, by 1 April 2024.

When the loan is repaid by Drench, HMRC will repay the £5,850 tax charge to Hail Ltd within nine months and one day from the end of the accounting period of repayment.

Tutorial note

Watch out for close companies in the exam, as they regularly feature in questions.

A company is close if it is controlled by its directors (any number), or if it is controlled by five or fewer shareholders.

Hail Ltd must also pay employer's class 1A national insurance contributions, as the loan will give rise to a taxable employment benefit for Drench.

The benefit will be based on the official rate of interest of 2%, and the NICs payable will be calculated at 13.8% as follows:

$$(£18,000 \times 2\%) = £360 \times 13.8\% = £50.$$

The NICs will be deductible when computing the company's taxable trading profits.

Hail Ltd should include the loan on Drench's Form P11D in order to report it to HMRC.

VAT cash accounting scheme

Tutor's top tips

The cash accounting scheme for VAT is a topic that was tested at TX.

It is important that you retain your TX knowledge, as the examining team frequently tests TX topics in the ATX exam.

There are two specific aspects to write about here:

1   The advantages of the scheme

2   Whether it will be possible for Rain Ltd to operate the scheme.

Advantages

The advantages of the scheme are:

- Improved cash flow, as output VAT in respect of credit sales is only paid to HMRC when cash is received from the customer.
- Automatic relief for irrecoverable debts. If the customer does not pay, no output VAT is paid to HMRC.

Tutor's top tips

*Don't just describe how the scheme works. You need to say **why** it is advantageous for VAT to be accounted for when cash is received from a customer.*

Availability to Rain Ltd

A business can only join the cash accounting scheme if it has annual taxable sales revenue of no more than £1,350,000.

If Rain Ltd acquires the new contracts, it will have sales revenue of £1,425,000 for the nine months ending 30 June 2023, and so will not be able to join the scheme.

If Rain Ltd does not acquire the new contracts, it will be able to join the scheme, as long as its VAT returns and payments are up to date and it has had no convictions for VAT offences or penalties for dishonest conduct.

Tutor's top tips

Even if you could not remember the limits applicable to the scheme, you could still score marks here for knowing that there were limits, and for attempting to apply the rules to the scenario.

(b)   Briefing note – use of knowledge

Tutor's top tips

Ethical issues appear in every ATX exam, for five marks. It is worth learning the key principles, as these are often easy marks that can be scored very quickly.

However, you must make sure that you apply the principles to the scenario and don't just list them.

Try to make sure that you have at least five separate points in your answer, as you will probably score one mark per relevant point.

- As members of the ACCA, we must comply with the ACCA Professional Code of Ethics.
- One of the fundamental principles of this code is confidentiality.
- We must not disclose confidential information to other parties without our client's permission.
- This restriction continues to apply even if we no longer act for the client.
- Accordingly, we should not use confidential information acquired from our ex-client to assist Rain Ltd.
- However, it is acceptable to use our general experience and expertise gained from advising our ex-client.

Examiner's report

In part (a)(i) there were four possibilities to consider.

The question asked for the tax implications to be compared such that numbers should have been produced for each of the four possible situations. The question also stated that Drench was aware of the general implications of forming a group and that the comparison should focus on certain specific issues. It was important for candidates to be clear as to what they had been asked to do and also what they had been asked not to do. The answers to this question were not as good as expected.

The following general mistakes were made by many candidates:

- Many candidates did not structure their answers to this part particularly well such that it was not always clear which of the four possible situations was being addressed.

- Despite the question instructing candidates to focus on specific issues, many candidates wasted time by addressing general issues. Accordingly, a considerable amount of unnecessary information was provided in connection with groups generally and the extraction of profits from companies.

- A minority of candidates reached an initial conclusion that Rain Ltd should be acquired by Hail Ltd such that numbers were only prepared for that eventuality.

- When addressing the purchase of Rain Ltd by Drench, a minority of candidates erroneously relieved the company's losses against the income of Drench.

In addition to the general mistakes set out above, many candidates stated that the losses of Rain Ltd would have to be carried forward if the company were purchased by Drench due to the unavailability of group relief. This omitted the possibility of a current year offset against the chargeable gains in Rain Ltd. The other specific common error related to the effect of the acquisition on the accounting periods of Rain Ltd with many candidates confusing the need to time apportion losses for the purposes of group relief with the need to prepare tax computations for separate accounting periods.

Matters done well included the identification of the degrouping charge, the corporation tax payment dates and the calculations of the maximum possible group relief.

Part (a)(ii) concerned a loan from Hail Ltd to Drench and the VAT cash accounting scheme. This part was done reasonably well with many candidates demonstrating a good knowledge of the technical areas.

The question asked for the tax implications **for Hail Ltd** of the loan. Almost all candidates recognised that Hail Ltd was a close company such that a 32.5% charge would be payable to H M Revenue and Customs. However, very few candidates identified that Hail Ltd would have to pay class 1A national insurance contributions in respect of the benefit relating to the loan. This is not an obscure point and would have been known to almost all candidates. It may be candidates need to think about the requirement and identify all of the possible issues before commencing writing in order to identify as many relevant points as possible.

The majority of candidates were able to identify the advantages of using the VAT cash accounting scheme and to link the facts in the question to the scheme's limit in respect of annual taxable supplies; this part of the question was answered well.

The final part of the question concerned the ethical considerations relating to confidentiality and was done well by the majority of candidates.

		ACCA marking scheme	
			Marks
(a)	(i)	Rain Ltd acquired by Drench personally	
		Rain Ltd makes tax adjusted loss	
		Use of losses	2.5
		Rain Ltd makes tax adjusted profit	
		Corporation tax liability	1.0
		Corporation tax threshold	1.5
		Corporation tax payment date	2.0
		Rain Ltd acquired by Hail Ltd	
		Rain Ltd makes tax adjusted loss	3.5
		Rain Ltd makes tax adjusted profit	1.5
		Rain Ltd building	
		Degrouping charge and tax treatment	3.5
		Base cost to Rain Ltd	1.0
			———
			16.5
		Maximum	15.0
			———
	(ii)	Loan to Drench	
		Close company loan to participator	1.0
		Payment to HMRC	2.0
		Employment income benefit	2.5
		Cash accounting scheme	
		Advantages	2.0
		Conditions	2.0
			———
			9.5
		Maximum	8.0
			———
		Appropriate style and presentation	1.0
		Effectiveness of communication	1.0
			———
			2.0
			———
(b)		Confidentiality, 1 mark per relevant point	5.0
			———
Total			**30.0**
			———

66 JANUS PLC GROUP (ADAPTED) *Walk in the footsteps of a top tutor*

Key answer tips

This question mainly covers corporation tax groups but also examines the capital goods scheme, intangible assets (patent rights), VAT on the import of services and the substantial shareholding exemption.

The groups section tests whether you understand the different types of groups that exist for corporation tax purposes. If you were not able to distinguish between the different groups you would struggle to score high marks here.

The highlighted words in the written sections are key phrases that markers are looking for.

Tutor's top tips

Before answering the groups part of the question you should take some time to decide which companies form a group relief group and identify the consortium. It is also important to realise which companies have joined or left the group in the year as this will affect the loss claims.

Remember that Castor Ltd is not a consortium owned company because the remaining 30% is owned by individuals.

(a) Use of the trading loss of Janus plc

(i) Alternative reliefs available

Tutor's top tips

To score the marks available for explaining the reliefs you need to apply your knowledge to the facts in the scenario. Don't just list all of the possible options; be specific.

Janus plc can use the trading loss itself and/or surrender the loss as group/consortium relief. Make sure that you state clearly:

- *which profits the loss can be set against, and*
- *for which period.*

Utilising the loss themselves

Janus plc can relieve the trading loss against its chargeable gain of £44,500 in the year ended 31 March 2022. Once this current period claim has been made, the loss can then be relieved against the company's total profits of the previous accounting period of £95,000.

Group relief

Janus plc can surrender trading losses to its 75% subsidiaries. For a company to be a 75% subsidiary, Janus plc must have an effective 75% interest in the company's ordinary share capital, its distributable income and its net assets were it to be wound up. Accordingly, Janus plc is in a group relief group with Seb Ltd and Viola Ltd only (Tutorial note).

Any amount of losses can be surrendered up to the level of the group member's taxable total profits for the corresponding accounting period. Seb Ltd and Viola Ltd did not become members of the group until 1 December 2021. Accordingly, only 4/12 of each of these companies' taxable total profits can be relieved via group relief.

Tutorial note

Castor Ltd (and therefore Pollux Ltd also) is not in a group relief group with Janus plc as Janus plc owns < 75% in Castor Ltd. There is no need to mention this specifically in the answer as once the definition is given, it is sufficient to demonstrate the application of the rules by just concluding which companies are in the group relief group.

Similarly, Duet Ltd is not in a group relief group with Janus plc as Janus plc owns < 75%, but it is a consortia company as explained below.

Consortium relief

Duet Ltd is a consortium company as at least 75% of its share capital is owned by companies, each of which own at least 5%. Accordingly, £110,000 (£200,000 × 55%) of its taxable total profits can be relieved via consortium relief.

Tutorial note

The maximum consortium relief is always based on the % share of the results in the consortium company.

If the consortium company makes a loss, the members can each claim their % of that loss.

If the consortium company makes a profit (as is the case here), the members can each surrender losses against their % of the consortium company's profit.

Castor Ltd is not a consortium company as the minority interest shareholding is owned by an individual rather than a company.

(ii)   Strategy in order to maximise the loss utilised

Tutor's top tips

Having set out the reliefs available in (a) (i) you then need to apply those reliefs in this part of the question.

The trading loss of Janus plc should therefore be relieved as follows:

		Loss utilised £	Loss available £
Total loss			330,000
Janus plc:	Current year	44,500	
	Prior year	95,000	
Seb Ltd (maximum = 4/12 × £37,000)		12,333	
Viola Ltd (maximum = 4/12 × £86,000)		28,667	
Duet Ltd (maximum = 55% × £200,000)		110,000	
		———	(290,500)
Loss carried forward			39,500

(b) Assets to be sold

(i) P HQ

Tutor's Top Tips

Castor Ltd owns 80% of Pollux Ltd which is at least 75% thus the two companies are in the same capital gains group, so when Pollux Ltd acquired the building from Castor Ltd the transfer took place at no gain/no loss.

The transfer value of the building would be original cost plus indexation allowance.

However, Janus plc only owns 70% of Castor Ltd which is less than 75% so when Pollux Ltd sells the building to Janus plc the transfer must take place at market value which will result in a capital gain arising.

*The examining team has asked you to **explain** how to compute this.*

Pollux Ltd and Janus plc are not in a capital gains group as Castor Ltd is not a 75% subsidiary of Janus plc.

The sale of the building will result in a chargeable gain equal to the excess of the proceeds, £285,000, over the building's base cost.

Tutorial note

There is no degrouping charge here, as such a charge can only occur when a company leaves a capital gains group (i.e. when there is a sale of shares).

This question involved the sale of a building, not a sale of shares.

Pollux Ltd acquired the building from Castor Ltd. The two companies are in a capital gains group as Pollux Ltd is a 75% subsidiary of Castor Ltd.

Accordingly, the building would have been transferred at no gain, no loss.

The base cost of the building to Pollux Ltd is the original cost when it was acquired by Castor Ltd (assuming Castor Ltd did not acquire it via a no gain, no loss transfer), together with indexation allowance from the date the building was acquired by Castor Ltd until December 2017 (as this is earlier than the date it was sold to Pollux Ltd).

The indexation allowance reflects the movement in the retail prices index for the relevant period (rounded to three decimal places) multiplied by the relevant cost of the building.

Information required – the date the building was acquired by Castor Ltd and the price paid.

(ii)   Warehouse

Tutor's top tips

A good knowledge of the capital goods scheme for VAT is required in order to answer this part of the question.

The requirement is to 'calculate', so there is no need to provide any explanation.

Year ended 31 March 2021
£64,000 × 70%   £44,800 recoverable from HMRC

Year ended 31 March 2022
£64,000 × 15% (70% – 55%) × 1/10   £960 repayable to HMRC

Year ended 31 March 2023
£64,000 × 20% (70% – 50%) × 1/10   £1,280 repayable to HMRC
£64,000 × 30% (100% – 70%) × 7/10   £13,440 recoverable from HMRC

Tutorial note

The capital goods scheme is relevant where a partially exempt business buys a building for more than £250,000 and there is a change in the partial exemption % during the ten-year adjustment period.

Here the recoverable input VAT drops from 70% to 55% then 50%, so Viola Ltd has to pay back some of the input VAT initially reclaimed.

There is also a final adjustment in the year of disposal for the remainder of the ten-year adjustment period.

The % used for the final adjustment on the sale of the building will always be either:

- *100% taxable (if the sale of the building is subject to VAT, as it is here), or*
- *0% taxable (if the sale of the building is an exempt supply).*

(iii) Patent rights

Tutor's top tips

Patent rights are an intangible non-current asset.

For intangibles other than goodwill, the tax treatment generally follows the accounting treatment with the effect that:

- *amortisation of an intangible asset is an allowable expense (or, if preferred, a writing down allowance of 4% straight line can be claimed instead of amortisation)*
- *the taxable profit on disposal is calculated as the sale proceeds less the net book value (i.e. amortised cost) if no election has been made (or, if the election is made, the sale proceeds less the tax written down value).*

As the patent rights relate to the company's trade, both the amortisation and the profit on disposal are included in taxable trading profits.

The patent rights are an intangible non-current asset. On a disposal of the rights, the sales proceeds will be compared with the amortised cost.

	£	£
Proceeds		41,000
Cost	45,000	
Less: Amortisation (£45,000 × 10% × 4)	(18,000)	
Amortised cost		(27,000)
Profit on sale		14,000

The profit on sale will be included as part of Castor Ltd's trading income because the patent rights were purchased for the purposes of the trade.

(c) Investment in Kupple Inc

(i) Value added tax (VAT) on the import of consultancy services

Tutor's top tips

The VAT implications for purchasing consultancy services from overseas are very similar to the implications for importing goods.

The VAT treatment of imports and exports is regularly tested in the ATX exam.

When services are provided to a business, the place of supply is the place where the customer's business is established.

Accordingly, the consultancy services provided by Kupple Inc to Janus plc will be treated as being made in the UK.

Janus plc will be required to account for output tax in respect of the supply under the reverse charge procedure. It will then be able to recover the output tax as input tax in the normal way.

(ii)   Sale of the shares

Tutor's top tips

Knowledge of the substantial shareholding exemption for companies – particularly the 12-month ownership requirement – is the key to success in this part.

The examining team deliberately leaves the disposal date vague, and does not say whether the shares will be sold at a profit or loss.

This means that you need to consider all possibilities:

- *Sale within 12 months at a gain*
- *Sale within 12 months at a loss*
- *Sale after more than 12 months at a gain*
- *Sale after more than 12 months at a loss.*

The tax treatment of the profit or loss on the sale of the shares will depend on when the sale occurs.

Sale within 12 months

If the shares are sold during the first 12 months of ownership, the sale will result in a chargeable gain (proceeds less cost) or an allowable loss (proceeds less cost).

An allowable loss could be offset against the chargeable gains of Janus plc or of the other companies in its chargeable gains group (Seb Ltd and Viola Ltd).

Sale after more than 12 months

However, as Janus plc will hold at least 10% of Kupple Inc's shares, once the shares have been held for 12 months, the substantial shareholding exemption will apply.

As a result of this exemption, any profit would not be taxable and any loss would not be allowable.

Examiner's report

Some candidates spent too long on part (a) and provided very detailed explanations of group relief and consortium relief; the amount of detail provided must relate to the number of marks on offer. Also, there was a tendency to repeat things, for example stating that Janus plc is in a loss group with Seb Ltd and Viola Ltd followed by a statement that it was not in a loss group with Castor Ltd. Candidates should identify the points they intend to make and then make them as concisely as possible. They will find this more efficient than making it up as they go along.

Note that this part of the question has been adapted since the question was originally set.

For part (b)(i) those candidates, who knew their stuff, slowed down, thought more and wrote less did well. This question demanded a clear understanding of the conditions necessary for a chargeable gains group to exist.

Unfortunately, many candidates thought that Janus plc and Pollux Ltd were members of a chargeable gains group; this was not the case because Janus plc does not own at least 75% of Castor Ltd. Other candidates failed to notice that Castor Ltd and Pollux Ltd were members of such a group.

The other technical problem that candidates had with this question was that many thought it included a degrouping charge. However, a degrouping charge can only occur when a company leaves a chargeable gains group, i.e. there needs to be a sale of shares, and this question involved the sale of a building. Accordingly, time spent writing about degrouping charges was wasted.

In part (b)(ii) applying the capital goods scheme to the purchase, use and subsequent sale of a building was done well by those candidates who both knew what to do and had practised applying the rules prior to the exam. Weaker candidates had a vague, confused knowledge of the rules or simply tried to describe them as opposed to apply them to the specific circumstances of the question. Very few candidates knew how to handle the adjustment following the sale of the building.

Part (b)(iii) the sale of an intangible asset and was done reasonably well by the majority of candidates.

In part (c)(i) the purchase of services from overseas to which the reverse charge applied was not answered particularly well; very few candidates had a clear understanding of the VAT treatment of the transaction.

Part (c)(ii) concerned the sale of shares in a company and was answered well. It required candidates to recognise that the substantial shareholding exemption might apply to the sale provided the conditions were satisfied. This question illustrated the need for candidates to be methodical as, if maximum marks were to be obtained, candidates needed to consider four situations; sale at a profit and sale at a loss with the substantial shareholding exemption either applying or not applying in each case.

				Marks
		ACCA marking scheme		*Marks*
(a)	(i)	Alternative reliefs		
		Against total profits of Janus plc		1.5
		Group relief		
		Identification of group		1.5
		Amount of loss		1.0
		Consortium relief		2.0
	(ii)	Advice and summary		2.5
				8.5
			Maximum	8.0
(b)	(i)	Administrative premises		
		There will be a gain on the disposal		1.5
		Indexed base cost		3.5
		Information required		0.5
				5.5
			Maximum	5.0
	(ii)	Warehouse		4.0
	(iii)	Patent rights		
		Calculation		1.5
		Explanation		1.5
				3.0
(c)	(i)	VAT on consultancy services		2.5
			Maximum	2.0
	(ii)	Sale of shares		4.0
Total				**26.0**

67   LIZA *Walk in the footsteps of a top tutor*

Key answer tips

This section B question addresses three unrelated issues:

Part (a)(i) requires a calculation of the chargeable gain on the sale of a building and the correct treatment of expenses incurred in acquiring, enhancing and maintaining the property. This is a straightforward part of the question based on TX knowledge so should be a good opportunity to pick up marks.

Part (a)(ii) covers group rollover relief, a commonly tested syllabus area.

Part (a)(iii) is a tricky part of the question that requires you to calculate the additional expenditure required such that the chargeable gain calculated in (a)(i) can be fully deferred. The complication is that the asset owned by Bar Ltd was not used in the trade for the entire period of ownership and the new asset acquired is only partly used for trade purposes.

Part (b) tests capital allowances, which is another TX topic and is tested in a straightforward manner. SBAs are dealt with differently to capital allowances on plant and machinery, so ensure you know the differences in the rules.

Part (c) tests the rules on companies joining a VAT group and the advantages of registering companies as a single VAT group. This is a very commonly tested area in the ATX exam and usually a good opportunity to score some easier marks.

The highlighted words in the written sections are key phrases that markers are looking for.

(a)   (i)   Chargeable gain – Sale of Building I

Tutor's top tips

Don't forget that expenditure on an asset to make it fit for use is capital expenditure and is therefore allowable expenditure for chargeable gains purposes.

	£	£
Net sales proceeds		860,000
Less: Purchase price	315,000	
Legal fees	9,000	
Work on roof to make fit for use	38,000	
	———	(362,000)
Unindexed gain		498,000
Less: Indexation allowance (June 2016 to December 2017)		
(0.057 × £362,000)		(20,634)
Chargeable gain		477,366

Tutorial note

A deduction is available for the legal fees incurred in acquiring the building and the costs incurred shortly afterwards to make the building fit for use.

The cost of repainting the building would have been an allowable deduction in calculating the company's trading profits and would not be allowable when computing the chargeable gain.

Indexation allowance is frozen at December 2017.

    (ii)   Acquisition of qualifying assets for the purposes of rollover relief

Tutor's top tips

You need to explain which companies in the group are part of the 75% chargeable gains group and therefore can purchase replacement assets for rollover relief purposes. Don't forget to include the time limit for claiming rollover relief. This is easily missed, but an easy mark if you have learned the rule.

The assets can be purchased by companies within the Bar Ltd chargeable gains group.

A chargeable gains group consists of a principal company, Bar Ltd, its 75% subsidiaries, the 75% subsidiaries of those subsidiaries and so on.

Bar Ltd must have an effective interest of more than 50% in all of the companies in the group.

Accordingly, the only companies able to purchase qualifying replacement assets are Bar Ltd and Pommel Ltd.

Ring Ltd is not a 75% subsidiary of Bar Ltd, such that it and Vault Ltd cannot be members of the Bar Ltd chargeable gains group.

The Hoop Ltd group is a separate group.

The qualifying replacement assets must be purchased in the period from 1 June 2021 to 31 May 2025.

    (iii)   The additional amount that would need to be spent on qualifying assets

Tutor's top tips

Don't forget that rollover relief is only available if the asset has been used in the trade.

Bar Ltd owned the building from 1 June 2016 to 31 May 2022, a period of 72 months. The building was not used for trading purposes from 1 January 2018 to 30 June 2019, a period of 18 months.

Accordingly, the building was used for the purposes of the trade for a period of 54 (72 – 18) months, such that only 54/72 of the gain can be relieved via rollover relief.

Therefore, qualifying business assets costing £645,000 (£860,000 × 54/72) will need to be acquired in order to relieve the whole of the gain qualifying for rollover relief.

Only two-thirds of the new building is to be used for trading purposes, such that only £480,000 (£720,000 × 2/3) of its cost will be a qualifying acquisition for the purposes of rollover relief.

Accordingly, the additional amount that would need to be spent on qualifying acquisitions in order to relieve the whole of the gain that qualifies for rollover relief would be £165,000 (£645,000 – £480,000).

(b)   Capital allowances available in respect of the new building

Tutor's top tips

FYA at a rate of 50% is available on special rate pool additions such as integral features. 6% WDA can then be claimed from the following accounting period.

Where the AIA is available, it is preferable to claim this instead, since this allows quicker relief for the assets.

Integral features

Electrical, water and heating systems qualify for plant and machinery capital allowances on the price of £150,000.

They are classified as integral features, such that they are included in the special rate pool where a 50% first year allowance is available.

The annual investment allowance available to the Bar Ltd group should be set against these additions in preference to the 50% first year allowance and in priority to those assets which qualify for the 18% writing down allowance.

Structures and buildings allowances (SBAs)

The cost of the building less the value of the land and integral features of £370,000 (£720,000 – £200,000 – £150,000) qualifies for SBAs at the rate of 3%.

SBAs can be claimed from the date the building is brought into qualifying use (1 May 2022).

The annual investment allowance is not available to offset against the £370,000 which qualifies for SBA.

Tutorial note

Qualifying use for SBAs includes use in the trade and for property letting.

(c)   Group registration for the purposes of Value Added Tax (VAT)

Tutor's top tips

This section also covers material from the TX syllabus.

VAT groups are frequently tested so make sure you can demonstrate a good knowledge of VAT groups and be specific to the question.

A sole trader can be included in a VAT group if he or she is the controller of a group of companies. As Liza is not a sole trader she cannot be a member of the VAT group.

Note that zero-rated companies should not be included in the VAT group as they can reclaim any VAT charged by the other group companies on a monthly basis. This is a cash flow advantage to the group.

The companies able to register as a group

Two or more companies may register as a group provided they are established in the UK, or have a fixed establishment in the UK, and they are controlled by the same person. The person can be an individual, a company, or a partnership.

Accordingly, all of the companies in the Bar Ltd and Hoop Ltd groups can register as a single group for the purposes of VAT.

The potential advantages of registering as a group

The advantage of a group registration would be that there would be no need to charge VAT on the transactions between the group companies. This would reduce administration and improve the group's cash flow.

Whether companies would benefit from joining the group

Vault Ltd makes zero-rated supplies and will therefore be in a repayment position, such that it can improve its cash flow by accounting for VAT on a monthly basis. However, if it were registered as part of a VAT group, it would not be able to do this as the group, as a single entity, is very unlikely to be in a regular repayment position. Accordingly, if a group registration is to be entered into, consideration should be given to excluding Vault Ltd from that registration.

Examiner's report

Part (a)(i) was a gentle introduction to the question and was done well.

Part (a)(ii) was done well by those candidates who knew the rules for group rollover relief and who expressed themselves carefully.

This part required candidates to know three things: that rollover relief can be claimed where one company in a gains group sells a qualifying business asset and another company in the group buys one, the definition of a gains group, and the time period in which a replacement asset needs to be purchased in order for rollover relief to be available.

The majority of candidates knew the first and third points although a small minority failed to address the third point despite, probably, knowing the rule. The difficulty came in dealing with the second point and the definition of a gains group where a minority of candidates revealed a level of confusion. This stemmed from a problem in distinguishing the 75% aspect of the rule from the 51% aspect and led to some candidates concluding erroneously that Vault Ltd and Bar Ltd were in a gains group. For there to be a chargeable gains group, the direct holding between each company in the chain must be at least 75%; if it isn't, the two companies cannot be in a group regardless of the level of the indirect holding.

The final part of part (a) was the hardest part of the question and was not done particularly well.

It required candidates to know the basic rule whereby the whole of the relevant proceeds has to be spent on replacement assets in order for the maximum gain to be rolled over, whilst recognising the relevance of the non-business use of both the asset sold and the asset acquired. Almost all candidates knew the basic rule but the majority struggled to apply it in these particular circumstances.

The following part of the question has been amended to test a new syllabus area (SBAs)

Part (b) concerned the availability of capital allowances in respect of electrical, water and heating systems acquired as part of a building and was done well.

The following section of the examiner's report has been amended following adaptations made to the original question.

In the final part of the question the majority of candidates made a reasonable job of discussing the advantages of registering as a VAT group and made a series of concise points. However, the definition of a group for the purposes of VAT was not handled particularly well. In particular, a sizable minority of candidates thought that the required holding was 75% as opposed to control. In addition, many candidates did not appreciate that control could be exercised by an individual (i.e. Liza), as well as by a company, such that all of the companies in the question were able to register as a single group.

As always, a minority of candidates wrote in general terms, for example, about partial exemption, rather than addressing the specifics of the question, such that they wasted time.

ACCA marking scheme				*Marks*
(a)	(i)	Chargeable gain		3.5
			Maximum	3.0
	(ii)	Chargeable gains group		2.0
		Identification of relevant companies		1.5
		Qualifying period		1.0
				4.5
			Maximum	4.0
	(iii)	Amount relievable via rollover relief		2.0
		Total acquisitions necessary		1.0
		Further acquisitions necessary		1.5
				4.5
			Maximum	4.0

(b)	Integral features		
	Plant and machinery as integral feature		1.0
	Special rate pool		0.5
	50% FYA		1.0
	Use of AIA		1.0
	Structures and buildings allowances		
	Available allowances		1.0
	Date brought into qualifying use		0.5
	No AIA		0.5
			────
			5.5
		Maximum	4.0
			────
(c)	Ability to register as a group		2.0
	Discussion		4.0
			────
			6.0
		Maximum	5.0
			────
Total			**20.0**
			────

68 SPETZ LTD GROUP (ADAPTED) *Walk in the footsteps of a top tutor*

Key answer tips

The section B question concerns VAT and overseas issues in relation to corporation tax, and was the least popular of the section B questions in this exam. This is probably because it requires detailed knowledge of some smaller topics in the syllabus and involved some overseas aspects!

Part (a) requires a calculation of the VAT partial exemption annual adjustment in respect of a company and should have been straightforward, although remembering all the detail of the three de minimis tests is demanding.

The first part of (b) requires an explanation of how to determine whether or not the company was resident in the UK which is worth only three marks. It is testing TX knowledge which should be easy if you have learnt the rules, but difficult if you have not.

The second part of (b) requires an explanation of the company's corporation tax liability together with the advantages and disadvantages of making an election to exempt the profits of an overseas permanent establishment (branch) from UK tax.

There was a third part to the original question, but this has been removed as it is no longer examinable.

The highlighted words in the written sections are key phrases that markers are looking for.

Tutor's top tips

The VAT requirement is a standalone part and asks for a calculation, a due date and an explanation of reasons as to whether the de minimis limits apply.

Make sure that you address all three elements of the requirement.

Note that partial exemption is regularly examined in the ATX exam.

When a business sells both taxable and exempt sales it is necessary to apportion input VAT on overheads between taxable sales and exempt sales. If the input VAT attributable to exempt sales exceeds the de minimis amount, then it cannot be claimed back.

(a)   **Novak Ltd**

Value added tax – partial exemption annual adjustment

	Total	Recoverable	Irrecoverable
	£	£	£
Input tax			
– attributed to taxable supplies	12,200	12,200	
– attributed to exempt supplies	4,900		4,900
Unattributed input tax (W1)	16,100	11,914	4,186
	33,200	24,114	9,086

To determine whether or not the £9,086 irrecoverable input VAT is in fact recoverable, the three de minimis tests must be considered:

*   De minimis test 1 is not satisfied, as the total input tax (£33,200) exceeds an average of £625 per month (£625 × 12 = £7,500).

*   De minimis test 2 is not satisfied, as the total input tax less that directly attributed to taxable supplies (£33,200 – £12,200 = £21,000) exceeds an average of £625 per month (£21,000 ÷ 12 = £1,750).

*   De minimis test 3 is also not satisfied, as exempt input tax of £9,086 exceeds the de minimis limit of £625 per month.

Accordingly, in total for the year, only £24,114 is recoverable.

The £9,086 input VAT is not de minimis and is therefore irrecoverable.

	£
Recoverable input VAT for the year	24,114
Less: Input tax recovered on quarterly returns	(23,200)
Annual adjustment = Additional input tax recoverable	914

The annual adjustment must be made on:

- the final VAT return of the year

    (i.e. the return for the period ended 30 September 2022), or

- the first VAT return after the end of the year.

Working: Recoverable unattributed input tax

(Taxable supplies/Total supplies) × 100

= (£1,190,000 ÷ (£1,190,000 + £430,000)) × 100 = 73.4%

This is rounded up to 74%.

(b)   (i)   Residence status of Kraus Co

Tutor's top tips

With only three marks available, three short succinct points need to be made and applied to the scenario given.

The key point to make is that overseas incorporated companies such as Kraus Co are treated as UK resident if they are controlled and managed from the UK.

- A company is regarded as resident in the UK if it is incorporated in the UK or if its central management and control is exercised in the UK.
- Kraus Co was incorporated in the country of Mersano. Accordingly, it will only be resident in the UK if its central management and control is exercised in the UK.
- The central management and control of a company is usually regarded as being exercised in the place where the key operational and financial decisions are made (e.g. where meetings of the board of directors are held).

(ii)   Kraus Co

Tutor's top tips

The calculation required is very simple as Kraus Co has no other income or gains other than trading income.

However, the majority of the marks are available for explaining the branch profits exemption and consequences.

UK resident companies are subject to corporation tax on their worldwide income, with DTR available if applicable.

	£
UK corporation tax (£520,000 × 19%)	98,800
Less: Unilateral double tax relief	
Lower of UK rate and overseas rate	
(£520,000 × 17%)	(88,400)
UK corporation tax liability	10,400

Tutorial note

The profits will be subject to UK tax because no election has been made to exempt the profits and losses of the overseas permanent establishment from UK corporation tax.

Note that the branch election is irrevocable and applies to all current and future overseas branches of the company. It is therefore important to carefully consider if an election will be beneficial, as once it is made overseas branch profits will not be subject to UK corporation tax, but losses of overseas branches could not be set off against UK profits and UK capital allowances would not be available in respect of the overseas branches' plant and machinery.

Election to exempt the overseas profits from UK tax

The advantage of making such an election would be that the profits made in Mersano would not be subject to UK corporation tax. Based on the current rates of corporation tax in the two countries, this would save corporation tax at the rate of 2% (19% – 17%).

When considering this election, it should be recognised that it is irrevocable and would apply to all future overseas permanent establishments of Kraus Co. Accordingly, there would be no relief in the UK for any losses incurred in the trade in Mersano in the future or for any other losses incurred in any additional overseas trades operated by Kraus Co.

Examiner's report

Part (a) was done reasonably well by those candidates who had a working knowledge of the de minimis rules. A minority of candidates had very little awareness of the rules, such that their performance was poor. Candidates who did not have a precise knowledge of the rules were able to score reasonably well provided they satisfied the requirement and attempted to address all three de minimis tests.

Part (b)(i) simply required a statement of the rules regarding country of incorporation and place of management and control but the majority of candidates were unable to state these fundamental rules.

Part (b)(ii) was done well. The majority of candidates prepared a short accurate calculation and were able to state the particular disadvantages of making such an election.

Note that part of this examiner's report has been deleted, as it relates to part of the question that has been removed.

		ACCA marking scheme		Marks
(a)		Input tax attributed to taxable supplies and unattributed input tax		1.5
		Test 1		1.0
		Test 2		1.5
		Test 3		1.5
		Adjustment and date		1.5
				―――
				7.0
				―――
(b)	(i)	Not incorporated in the UK		1.0
		Central management and control		2.0
				―――
				3.0
				―――
	(ii)	Calculation of liability		1.5
		Taxation of worldwide profits		1.0
		Discussion of election		
		Advantage		1.5
		Disadvantages		2.0
				―――
				6.0
			Maximum	5.0
				―――
	Total			**15.0**
				―――

69 KLUBB PLC *Walk in the footsteps of a top tutor*

Key answer tips

This section B question covers three areas: corporation tax administration; a comparison of share schemes: SIP versus CSOP, and the CFC rules.

Part (a) is TX revision of filing dates for a long period of account and basic corporation tax penalties. This should offer easy marks if you remember the rules.

Part (b) tests your knowledge of the conditions for two tax advantaged share schemes, SIPs and CSOPs. Share schemes are a new topic at ATX level and are regularly tested.

Part (c) covers another new topic at the ATX level – CFCs. If you have not learnt the detailed rules you may struggle with this part of the question.

The highlighted words in the written sections are key phrases that markers are looking for.

Tutor's top tips

This is really three separate, standalone questions and you can attempt them in any order as long as you clearly label your answer.

(a) **Late submission of corporation tax returns**

Tutor's top tips

You are not asked to identify corporation tax payment dates or the penalties for late payment of tax, so there would be no marks for doing so.

Corporation tax returns are required for the two accounting periods within the long period of account: the 12 months ended 30 November 2020 and the four months ended 31 March 2021.

The returns should have been filed by 31 March 2022 (12 months after the end of the 16-month period of account).

There will be a late filing penalty of £100 in respect of each of the returns because they were filed within three months of the filing date.

However, this £100 penalty is increased to £500 where the returns for the two preceding accounting periods were also submitted late.

Tutorial note

It has been assumed that HM Revenue and Customs (HMRC) issued notices prior to 1 January 2022 requiring the returns to be made.

(b) **Comparison of a share incentive plan (SIP) with a company share option plan (CSOP)**

Tutor's top tips

This part of the question does not ask you to write everything you know about SIPs and CSOPs. The client is specifically interested in the flexibility each scheme offers and the tax implications.

You are required to compare three specific areas:

- *Employees who can/must be included in the scheme*
- *Number or value of shares which can be acquired*
- *Income tax and CGT implications of acquiring and selling shares.*

Use these as headings in your answer to help you to focus, and make sure that you clearly state which scheme you are referring to and which tax – income tax or CGT.

Employees who must be included in the plan

A CSOP is significantly more flexible than a SIP.

Klubb plc would be able to select particular employees to join a CSOP whereas, under the rules for SIPs, Klubb plc would be required to offer shares to all of its full time and part time employees, although a minimum qualifying period of employment may be specified.

The number or value of shares which can be acquired by each plan member

Again, a CSOP is more flexible than a SIP.

Klubb plc can choose to award options to purchase different numbers of shares to each member of a CSOP. The options awarded are simply at the discretion of Klubb plc. However, the award is subject to a maximum whereby a member is only allowed to hold options to purchase shares with a maximum value (at the time the options were granted) of £30,000.

Under the rules for SIPs, free shares up to a maximum value of £3,600 can be given to each member of the plan each tax year. These free shares must be awarded on similar terms to all of the plan members. This means that any variation in the number of free shares awarded must be by reference to objective criteria, for example, length of service or performance targets.

In addition, a member of a SIP can purchase partnership shares (at market value) up to a maximum value of the lower of £1,800 and 10% of salary each tax year. Klubb plc could then give the plan members up to two further free shares (known as matching shares), in respect of each partnership share purchased. This represents additional free shares with a maximum value of £3,600.

Tax implications of acquiring and selling the shares

Under the rules for SIPs, there are no income tax implications when free shares or matching shares are awarded to scheme members. Similarly, there are no income tax implications when shares are withdrawn from the plan if they have been held within the plan for five years. There will be no capital gains tax on the immediate sale of the shares because their base cost is equal to their market value at the time they are withdrawn from the SIP.

The rules for a CSOP are not as generous as those for a SIP.

There would be no tax charged on the grant and exercise of the options.

However, there would be a chargeable gain on the sale of the shares equal to the proceeds received less the amount paid for them.

Tutorial note

It was not necessary to make all of the above points in order to score full marks for this question.

(c) **(i)** **Status of Hartz Co and availability of the low profits exemption**

Tutor's top tips

The controlled foreign company rules are complex, and there are several exemptions that could apply.

However, this part of the question just requires you to know – and apply:

- *the definition, and*
- *the low profits exemption.*

There are no marks available for discussing other aspects of CFCs.

Hartz Co is a non-UK resident company.

It will be a controlled foreign company (CFC) if it is controlled by UK resident persons.

Accordingly, its status depends on the residency of Mr Deck. If he is a UK resident, Hartz Co will be a CFC.

Hartz Co is not expected to satisfy either of the conditions for the low profits exemption. This is because:

- its profits are expected to exceed £50,000; and
- although its profits are expected to be less than £500,000, it will have chargeable gains (non-trading profits) of more than £50,000.

(ii) **CFC charge**

	£
Chargeable profits of Hartz Co	330,000
Chargeable profits apportioned to Klubb plc (30% × £330,000)	99,000
Corporation tax at 19%	18,810
Less: Creditable tax (£330,000 × 11% × 30%)	(10,890)
CFC charge	7,920

Tutorial note

Chargeable gains are not part of chargeable profits and thus are not included in the calculation of the CFC charge.

Examiner's report

In part (a) the first thing candidates had to point out was the need to split the long period of account into two accounting periods. Unfortunately, many candidates failed to identify this point. Candidates then had to know the filing dates and the penalty rules. However, many candidates wrote about the dates on which corporation tax has to be paid as opposed to the filing dates of the returns, such that they did not answer the requirement set.

Part (b) of the question was more substantial. It was very important to identify clearly the particular areas that needed to be addressed, and to stick to them. Failure to do this could result in irrelevant parts of an answer that would score no marks, despite being technically accurate. Unfortunately, many candidates were insufficiently disciplined in their approach and regarded the question as being about the two share schemes generally as opposed to being about certain aspects of the two schemes.

Generally, candidates' knowledge of this area was good with many candidates providing satisfactory answers. The candidates who did best were those who structured their answer in a very clear manner so that it was always clear which aspect of which scheme was being addressed. This clear structure enabled candidates to keep their answers relatively brief whilst addressing all of the precise requirements of the question.

However, a minority of candidates appeared to be making up their answer as they went along, such that they were setting out each thought as it occurred to them. The problem with this approach was that some points were repeated, other points were made which were not relevant and some aspects of the requirement were omitted altogether.

Most candidates knew that under a share incentive plan, shares need to be offered to, broadly, all employees whereas, under a company share option plan, the employer can choose certain employees to join the scheme. Candidates' knowledge of the number or value of shares that could be offered under each scheme was also satisfactory notwithstanding that some candidates confused the two schemes or confused the different categories of shares that can be offered under a share incentive plan.

When it came to the tax implications of acquiring and selling the shares it was important for candidates to stick to the facts of the question. It was clear from the question how long the shares would be held for and when they would be sold. Accordingly, there was no need to address all of the different tax implications that could occur if the shares were sold at other times. Candidates who failed to realise this wasted time writing lengthy answers that were not addressing the requirements of the question.

When explaining the tax implications, stronger candidates were clear as to which scheme they were writing about and which tax (income tax or capital gains tax) they were addressing. The answers of other candidates were more confused and used the general term 'tax' as opposed to the specific tax concerned.

Part (c)(i) was done reasonably well by many candidates.

Candidates had two main problems when answering this first part of the question. First, they confused the definition of a controlled foreign company with the exemptions that are available. Secondly, there was a tendency to write about all of the available exemptions as opposed to the particular one in the question requirement; this resulted in irrelevant parts of answers.

For part (c)(ii) candidates had to remember to exclude the gains from the calculation of a CFC charge, bring in only 30% of the trading profits, and deduct an appropriate amount of creditable tax. Answers here were generally not as accurate as might have been hoped.

ACCA marking scheme				
				Marks
(a)		Two accounting periods		1.0
		Filing date		1.0
		Penalty		2.0
				———
				4.0
				———
(b)		Employees		2.0
		Value		
			SIP	4.0
			CSOP	2.0
		Tax on realisation of value		
			SIP	2.0
			CSOP	2.0
				———
				12.0
			Maximum	9.0
				———
(c)	(i)	Status of Hartz Co		2.5
		Low profits exemption		2.0
				———
				4.5
			Maximum	4.0
				———
	(ii)	Profits apportioned		1.5
		Calculation of charge		1.5
				———
				3.0
				———
Total				**20.0**
				———

70 SPRINT LTD AND IRON LTD (ADAPTED) *Walk in the footsteps of a top tutor*

Key answer tips

This section A question covers three separate areas: corporation tax for a long period of account, the differences between purchase of shares by an individual or by another company and registration for VAT.

Part (a) requires calculation of tax for a 16-month period of account, which is mainly revision of TX. Once again, this reinforces the importance of retaining basic TX knowledge.

Part (b) is a written section that requires a clear explanation of the differences between a company being held directly by an individual or as part of a corporate group. Think carefully before answering this section.

Part (c) covers registration for VAT – another TX topic that should have offered easy marks. You could have answered this part first before tackling the trickier parts of the question.

The highlighted words in the written sections are key phrases that markers are looking for.

(a) **Iron Ltd – corporation tax payable for the period ending 30 June 2023**

Tutor's top tips

Remember that a long accounting period must be split into the first 12 months and the balance, with two corporation tax computations prepared.

The indexation factor provided in the requirement should have given a hint that there were some gains to calculate here.

Rollover relief is often tested in corporation tax questions, so you should make sure you learn the rules. Watch out for depreciating assets, as they are treated differently for rollover relief purposes.

There are easy marks available for stating the due dates for payment of the corporation tax.

Year ending	Year ending 28 February 2023 £	4 months ending 30 June 2023 £
Trading income		
£30,000 × 12/16	22,500	
£30,000 × 4/16		7,500
Chargeable gains (below)		
Industrial building	90,368	
Fixed machinery	0	
Crystallisation of deferred gain re sale of fixed machinery	3,200	
Taxable total profits	116,068	7,500
Corporation tax payable		
£116,068/£7,500 × 19%	22,053	1,425
Due date (W)	1 December 2023	1 April 2024

Chargeable gains

	Industrial building £	Fixed machinery £
Proceeds	160,000	13,700
Less: Cost (£100,000 – £31,800)	(68,200)	(13,500)
Indexation allowance (June 2017 to December 2017) (0.021 × £68,200)	(1,432)	
(0.021 × £13,500 – but restricted because indexation allowance cannot create a loss)		(200)
Chargeable gain	90,368	0

Working: Due date

The threshold for payment of corporation tax by instalment is as follows:

Year ending 28 February 2023	£1,500,000
Four months ending 30 June 2023 (£1,500,000 × 4/12)	£500,000

As Iron Ltd's taxable total profits are below the threshold, quarterly instalment payments are not required.

Tutorial note

Iron Ltd is not related to Sprint Ltd (or Olympic Ltd) for the purposes of establishing the corporation tax threshold, as they are not 51% subsidiaries of a third company. Christina is an individual, not a company.

(b)   Ownership of Iron Ltd

Tutor's top tips

There are four different aspects to consider in this part of the question: ownership of shares by the company (with group implications); ownership of shares by the individual; sale of shares by the company (with substantial shareholding exemption); sale of shares by the individual (with business asset disposal relief).

A logical structure and use of headings to deal with each aspect in turn is important here.

Where possible, try to refer to facts from the scenario such as the potential trading loss in Iron Ltd. This will gain more marks than simply writing about general tax implications.

Ongoing ownership of Iron Ltd

Corporation tax

It would be advantageous for Sprint Ltd, rather than Christina, to purchase Iron Ltd for the following reasons.

–   It is possible that Iron Ltd will make a trade loss for the period ending 30 June 2023. If this were to occur, a proportion of the loss could be surrendered by way of group relief to Sprint Ltd and/or Olympic Ltd and be deducted in arriving at the taxable total profits of the recipient company. Whilst all three companies remain in the group, group relief would also be available between them in respect of any losses in future periods.

–   Iron Ltd will join Sprint Ltd's capital gains group on 1 November 2022. The capital loss to be made by Sprint Ltd on the sale of the warehouse could therefore be relieved against the chargeable gains to be realised by Iron Ltd on the sale of the industrial building and the fixed machinery. This would reduce the corporation tax liability of Iron Ltd by £7,220 (£22,053 – ((£116,068 – £38,000) × 19%)).

- A gain made by one of the companies in the group on the disposal of a qualifying business asset (land, buildings or fixed machinery used in the business) could be deferred if a qualifying business asset is purchased by any other company in the group during the qualifying period.
- Any future transfers of assets from one group company to another would take place on a no gain, no loss basis.

There is a possible disadvantage in Iron Ltd joining the Sprint Ltd group of companies in relation to capital allowances. The annual investment allowance will be split between the three companies if they are members of a group, whereas an additional full annual investment allowance would be available to Iron Ltd if Christina were to own Iron Ltd personally (unless Iron Ltd were to share premises or carry on activities similar to those of Sprint Ltd or Olympic Ltd).

Another disadvantage in Iron Ltd being purchased by Sprint Ltd is that Iron Ltd will be a 51% group company with Sprint Ltd (and consequently Olympic Ltd) for the purposes of determining the threshold for payment of corporation tax by instalment. Accordingly, the corporation threshold will be divided by three, making it more likely that one or all of the companies may have to pay tax by quarterly instalment.

Value added tax (VAT)

It may be beneficial for Sprint Ltd and Iron Ltd (and possibly Olympic Ltd) to register as a group for the purposes of VAT. This is because it would remove the need for Iron Ltd to charge VAT on the sales it makes to Sprint Ltd. This will, however, be possible regardless of who owns Iron Ltd because Christina will have effective control of all three companies in both situations.

Sale of Iron Ltd

Sprint Ltd owns Iron Ltd

Any chargeable gain (or loss) on the sale of the shares will be exempt due to the substantial shareholding exemption (SSE). This exemption will be available because Sprint Ltd will have owned at least 10% of the ordinary share capital of Iron Ltd for more than a year and Iron Ltd is a trading company.

Although the existence of the SSE would appear to be a significant advantage, it should be recognised that the proceeds on sale will then need to be transferred to Christina. This could be carried out via, for example, the payment of a dividend to Christina. As Christina is a higher rate taxpayer with a substantial amount of investment income, she is likely to have used her dividend nil rate band. Therefore, she would have an income tax liability of 32.5% or even 38.1% of the dividend received.

Tutorial note

Credit was also available for reference to other ways in which the proceeds of sale could be transferred to Christina, for example, via the payment of a bonus.

Christina owns Iron Ltd personally

On a sale by Christina of the shares in Iron Ltd, there will be a chargeable gain equal to the excess of the sales proceeds over the price paid for the shares. This gain, after the deduction of any annual exempt amount not used against any other gains, will be subject to capital gains tax at 10% due to the availability of business asset disposal relief (BADR).

BADR will be available because Iron Ltd is a trading company and Christina will have owned at least 5% of its shares for at least two years, and Christina will be a director of Iron Ltd.

Tutorial note

It can be seen from the marking scheme that it was not necessary to make all of the above points in order to score full marks.

(c)   VAT registration

Tutor's top tips

This looks like a fairly standard section on VAT registration and penalties. The twist here was to spot that the client should be monitoring taxable sales, not cash receipts.

Iron Ltd should be monitoring the level of its taxable supplies (excluding sales of capital assets), as opposed to its cash receipts, in order to determine when it needs to register for VAT.

The implications of registering late are:

–   Iron Ltd will be required to account for output tax on the sales it has made after the date on which it should have been registered. This will be a cost to Iron Ltd unless it is able to recover the VAT from its customers.

–   A penalty may be charged for failing to register by the appropriate date. This penalty would be a percentage of the potential lost revenue where the percentage depends on the reason for the late registration.

–   Interest may be charged in respect of the VAT paid late.

Examiner's report

Part (a) required a calculation of the corporation tax payable for a company in respect of a 16-month set of accounts, including consideration of two asset disposals where rollover relief had been claimed previously. It was surprising, and indeed disappointing, to see that the majority of candidates calculated the corporation tax payable for the 16-month period as a whole, rather than recognising the need to split this into two separate accounting periods, the first covering the first 12 months and the second covering the remaining four months. This led to the loss of a number of what should have been easy marks. Candidates are reminded that a good level of familiarity with the TX syllabus is required for ATX; it is not enough to just focus on the new areas, candidates must ensure that they are also confident in dealing with more basic issues.

The majority of candidates recognised that the sale of the two business assets would cause the gain rolled over on the acquisition of these assets to become chargeable. However, the different treatments in respect of the depreciating asset (fixed machinery) and non-depreciating asset (building) was identified by only a small number of candidates.

Part (b) was for 13 marks and was the largest part of the question. It required a comparison of the tax implications of a company being acquired by an individual as opposed to by another company. Candidates who did well had a good knowledge of the subject, adopted a sensible, logical approach and addressed all of the issues briefly, as instructed in the question. Weaker candidates fell down in at least one of these areas.

The adoption of a logical approach in this sort of question requiring a comparison of two alternatives can save considerable confusion and avoid wasting time due to needless repetition. Candidates should pause and think before they start writing. Dealing fully with the implications of one of the alternatives first, and then the other, tended to provide a much clearer answer than those who adopted a less logical approach, apparently writing points as they occurred to them, without making it clear which alternative they were dealing with, constantly swapping between the two, and leading to a confusing answer.

Candidates should avoid repetition, including making the same point from different angles. An example in this case would be where a candidate has stated that if the company is acquired by another company, they would form a group for group relief purposes. Stating separately at a later point that if acquired by an individual there will not be a group for group relief purposes, scored no additional marks.

Part (c) concerned the often-tested area of registration for VAT, an area which the vast majority of candidates are very technically comfortable with. However, all but a handful failed to read the question in sufficient detail, and provided a very detailed account of the tests applied to determine whether compulsory registration is required, but this did not address the question and wasted a good deal of time. Where the subject coverage is very familiar it is particularly important to understand the context in which it is being tested. In this case, the key issue was recognition that monitoring the level of cash receipts is not relevant, it is the level of taxable supplies, i.e. the invoiced value of taxable sales which is relevant.

		Marks
	ACCA marking scheme	
(a)	Trading income	*Marks* 1.0
	Chargeable gains	
	Industrial building	2.0
	Machinery	1.5
	Crystallisation of deferred gain	1.0
	Chargeable gains in correct period	0.5
	Corporation tax payable	1.0
	Due dates	2.5
		――
		9.5
	Maximum	9.0
		――
(b)	Ongoing	
	Group relief	2.0
	Relief for capital losses	2.0
	Rollover relief	1.0
	No gain, no loss transfers	1.0
	Annual investment allowance	1.0
	51% group companies	1.0
	VAT group registration	2.0
	Sale of Iron Ltd	
	Sprint Ltd owns Iron Ltd	3.5
	Christina owns Iron Ltd	2.0
		――
		15.5
	Maximum	13.0
		――
(c)	Taxable supplies as monitoring basis	1.0
	Implications of late registration	2.5
		――
		3.5
	Maximum	3.0
		――
Total		**25.0**
		――

71 HAHN LTD GROUP (ADAPTED) *Walk in the footsteps of a top tutor*

Key answer tips

This is a classic Section A corporation tax groups question with a mix of technical marks on corporation tax and VAT, ethical marks on HMRC errors and presentation marks.

There are four requirements, all of which can be answered independently, so careful thought should be given to the order in which you attempt the question. Identify the parts that you think you can answer quickly and attempt these first, leaving parts of the question that you think you will be tempted to spend too long on until last.

Make sure that you set out the question as a memorandum with an appropriate heading, set out your answer neatly and express yourself clearly in order to score the presentation marks available. You should also try to answer the question succinctly; this will save you time and help with the professional marks!

Requirement (a)(i) tests the common exam topic of group rollover relief. Requirement (a)(ii) tests group relief, focusing on cash flow issues.

Requirement (b) tests group VAT registration, another often tested area of the syllabus.

Requirement (c) tests the ethical implications of a client not reporting an HMRC error.

The highlighted words in the written sections are key phrases that markers are looking for in your memorandum.

(a) Memorandum

> **Client:** Hahn Ltd group
>
> **Subject:** Group loss planning and other matters
>
> **Prepared by:** Tax senior
>
> **Date:** 8 September 2022

Tutor's top tips

Group rollover relief is often tested in the exam. However, there is an unusual twist here as you are asked to calculate the amount of proceeds to reinvest to leave a specific amount of the gain chargeable after rollover relief. In order to score well here you need to have a good knowledge of how to calculate rollover relief where proceeds are only partially reinvested.

(i) **Chargeable gain of Frit Ltd**

The additional qualifying assets which would need to be purchased in order for the chargeable gain realised by Frit Ltd to be fully relieved by its capital losses brought forward is calculated as follows:

	£
Sales proceeds of asset sold by Frit Ltd	125,000
Less: Capital losses brought forward (Note 1)	(31,000)
Proceeds to be spent on qualifying assets	94,000
Less: Qualifying assets already purchased by group companies (£14,000 + £10,000)(Note 2)	(24,000)
Additional amount to be spent on qualifying assets	70,000

Tutorial note

1   *Any amount of the proceeds from the sale of the building by Frit Ltd not reinvested in qualifying assets within the time limit will remain chargeable in year ended 31 March 2023. Therefore, in order for the chargeable gain after rollover relief to be equal to the capital loss brought forward in Frit Ltd, an amount of £31,000 should not be reinvested, such that only £34,000 of the £65,000 gain will be rolled over and the remaining £31,000 of the gain will be relieved by the capital losses brought forward.*

2   *The additional qualifying assets can be purchased by any member of the capital gains group. The group consists of all of the companies apart from Joli Ltd (not a 75% subsidiary of Hahn Ltd) and Ruth Ltd (not a 75% subsidiary of Lise Ltd). Therefore, the £6,000 spent on qualifying assets by Ruth Ltd cannot be utilised as reinvestment of the Frit Ltd proceeds.*

(ii)   **Relieving the trading loss of Frit Ltd Intercompany trading**

Tutor's top tips

Group relief has always been a popular topic in the exam. Historically, there were three different rates of corporation tax that applied to companies depending on their profits, and therefore achieving the maximum tax saving was a key issue in group relief questions. Now that there is a single rate of corporation tax, the tax saving in the year of the loss will generally be the same regardless of which group company uses the losses. Group relief questions are now likely to focus on other objectives such as preserving QCD relief and cash flow. You should therefore make sure you are prepared to answer questions on this.

Note that as the rate of corporation tax was the same in previous years there is a timing advantage to carrying back the loss within the loss-making company to generate a repayment of tax. However, this question states that Frit Ltd will not be able to carry its loss back.

The focus in this requirement is cash flow, and using the group losses to reduce augmented profits below the profit threshold where instalments need to be made.

Intra-group sales

A transfer pricing adjustment will be required in respect of the sales at undervalue from Hahn Ltd to Stra Ltd. This is because Hahn Ltd controls Stra Ltd, and the group is large for the purposes of the transfer pricing rules. Accordingly, the trading profit of Hahn Ltd must be increased by £10,000 (£104,000 – £94,000), the excess of the arm's length price over the price charged for the intra-group sales. As Stra Ltd is also within the charge to UK corporation tax, its trading profits can be reduced by the same amount.

Rationale for the allocation of the trading loss

In order to maximise the benefit to the group's cash flow position, Frit Ltd's trading loss should be surrendered to those companies paying corporation tax by quarterly instalments.

–   Firstly to any company whose profits can be reduced to the payment by instalments threshold, such that instalments will no longer be required

–   then to any other company with profits in excess of the payment by instalments threshold, such that their instalments will be reduced

–   finally, to any other company.

The payment by instalments threshold for the Hahn Ltd group companies (excluding Chad Ltd) for the year ending 31 March 2023 is £300,000. This is the threshold of £1,500,000 divided by five (the number of 51% group companies as at 31 March 2022 being Hahn Ltd, Frit Ltd, Lise Ltd, Ruth Ltd and Stra Ltd).

The threshold for Chad Ltd for the year ending 31 March 2023 is £187,500. This is the threshold of £1,500,000 divided by eight (the number of 51% group companies in the Zeno Ltd group as at 31 March 2022, being Zeno Ltd and its effective 51% subsidiaries).

Tutorial note

The instalments threshold is divided by the number of 51% group companies as at the end of the previous accounting period. Therefore, Chad Ltd will not be included in the Hahn Ltd group for these purposes until the year ended 31 March 2024.

Allocation of the loss

	Note	£
Frit Ltd trading loss		540,000
Surrender to:		
Lise Ltd (£375,000 – £300,000)	1	(75,000)
Chad Ltd	2	(315,000)
Hahn Ltd (balance)	3, 4	150,000

Notes

1   The taxable total profits of Lise Ltd should be reduced to no more than £300,000 so that the company will not have to pay corporation tax by instalments.

2   Chad Ltd will have been a member of the group relief group for only seven months of the accounting period. Accordingly, the maximum loss which can be surrendered by Frit Ltd to Chad Ltd is £315,000, i.e. the lower of:

   • Frit Ltd loss for the corresponding seven-month period of £315,000 (£540,000 × 7/12); and

   • Chad Ltd profit for the corresponding seven-month period of £393,750 (£675,000 × 7/12).

   This is not sufficient to reduce the taxable total profits of Chad Ltd to £187,500 but it will reduce the company's corporation tax liability and therefore the instalments due.

3   The trading profit of Stra Ltd will be £28,000 (£38,000 – £10,000 transfer pricing adjustment). Stra Ltd must assume set off of its own trading loss brought forward against its total profits, before claiming group relief. This will reduce its TTP to £nil as Stra Ltd has no other income or gains. On this basis, no losses can be transferred from Frit Ltd to Stra Ltd.

4   Joli Ltd is not an effective 75% subsidiary of Hahn Ltd and is therefore not in the group relief group.

   Ruth Ltd is neither a direct 75% subsidiary of Lise Ltd nor an effective subsidiary of Hahn Ltd and is therefore not in the group relief group.

Tutorial note

It would be equally acceptable to surrender the balance of the loss of £150,000 to Lise Ltd rather than Hahn Ltd because the corporation tax liability of both companies is due on 1 January 2024 rather than by quarterly instalments.

Although it is possible to surrender trading losses brought forward as group relief, this surrender is only available for excess losses after set off against the surrendering company's own total profits. As Stra Ltd does not have any excess trading losses brought forward, there is no possibility of surrender from Stra Ltd.

Corporation tax liabilities for the year ending 31 March 2023

	Hahn Ltd	Chad Ltd	Lise Ltd	Ruth Ltd
	£	£	£	£
Taxable total profit	180,000	675,000	375,000	320,000
Transfer pricing adjustment	10,000			
Group relief	(150,000)	(315,000)	(75,000)	0
	40,000	360,000	300,000	320,000
Corporation tax at 19%:				
Due in instalments		68,400		60,800
Due on 1 January 2024	7,600		57,000	

Frit Ltd and Stra Ltd will have no taxable total profits and therefore will not have a corporation tax liability.

Payment schedule

	£
Instalments ((68,400 + 60,800)/4):	
14 October 2022	32,300
14 January 2023	32,300
14 April 2023	32,300
14 July 2023	32,300
Nine months and one day (7,600 + 57,000):	
1 January 2024	64,600

(b) Group registration for the purposes of value added tax (VAT)

Tutor's top tips

Group VAT registration is a commonly tested topic in the exam. It is important to learn the requirements for a group of companies to form a VAT group, the consequences of doing so, and also the reasons why some companies may be better left outside of the group. However, to score well you must make sure you link your answer to the scenario.

There were some tricky marks here, testing the interaction of the cash accounting and annual accounting schemes with VAT groups. However, four out of the five marks available could be scored without mentioning these!

A group registration could be made in respect of all of the companies in the Hahn Ltd group with the exception of Joli Ltd (because this company is not controlled by Hahn Ltd). However, it is not necessary to include all of the qualifying companies within the group registration.

Sales from one company in the VAT group to another would be disregarded for the purposes of VAT. Therefore, there would be no requirement to charge VAT on the sales made by Hahn Ltd to Stra Ltd.

The annual accounting scheme is not available where companies are registered as a group. The cash accounting scheme would be available but only if the group's taxable turnover was less than £1,350,000. These matters should be considered before deciding whether or not Stra Ltd should be included in the group registration.

The inclusion of Frit Ltd in the group registration would result in the group being partially exempt. This could increase the total input tax recovered by the group, for example, if the results of the group as a whole satisfy the partial exemption de minimis limits. Alternatively, the calculation of the recoverable input tax for the group as a whole could result in a reduction in the total input tax recovered. Accordingly, further consideration is required before deciding whether or not Frit Ltd should be included in the group registration.

(c) Chad Ltd – refund of VAT

Tutor's top tips

Ethical issues will appear in every exam as part of section A for five marks. This is 10% of the marks you need to pass the exam! Provided you have revised the commonly tested ethical scenarios these marks should be relatively easy to score.

Here you needed to consider the ethical implications of a potential HMRC error. Don't forget to consider the possibility that it may not be an error!

We should investigate the VAT reporting of Chad Ltd in order to determine whether or not there is a valid reason for the refund.

If we are unable to identify a valid reason, we would have to conclude that the refund was made as a result of error on the part of HM Revenue and Customs (HMRC), in which case it should be repaid immediately. We should inform Chad Ltd that failing to return the money in these circumstances may well be a civil and/or a criminal offence.

We should also advise Chad Ltd to inform HMRC of their error as soon as possible in order to minimise any interest and penalties which may otherwise become payable.

If Chad Ltd is unwilling to return the money, we would have to consider ceasing to act as advisers to the company. We would then have to notify the tax authorities that we no longer act for Chad Ltd, although we would not provide them with any reason for our action. We should also consider whether or not it is necessary to make a report under the money laundering rules.

Examiner's report

Part (a), which was in two parts, related to a group of UK resident companies. The first of these parts required candidates to calculate the amount to be reinvested in qualifying assets in order to leave no gain on the disposal of a building chargeable to corporation tax. Most candidates made a reasonable attempt at this, but a very significant proportion also included detailed explanations to accompany their calculations, despite these clearly not being required. The fact that this question part was worth only three marks should have led candidates to realise that a lengthy discussion was not required. Accordingly, these candidates wasted time, which could have beneficially been spent elsewhere. Candidates would be advised to double check what is required by each question before making a start. The main technical error was a failure to realise that the total investment needed must equal the sale proceeds of the building, not the chargeable gain.

The second part of part (a) required candidates to relieve a trading loss within a group so as to minimise the amount of corporation tax payable by the group companies in instalments. Clearly, the majority of candidates were not aware of how this could be achieved, and therefore did not state a strategy for relieving the loss. The loss was therefore relieved in a somewhat random manner within the group. With the introduction of a unified rate of corporation tax, cashflow issues such as this are going to be more important for groups of companies and are therefore likely to appear in future questions. It was, however, pleasing to see that almost all candidates were aware that all the companies would pay tax at the same rate, so they didn't try to relieve the loss so as to save the maximum amount of tax, which has, in previous years, been a major planning point.

There were a good number of easy marks in this part for calculating the amount of corporation tax payable by each company, which most candidates achieved, but a few didn't appear to have read this part of the requirements and so failed to produce the necessary schedule. The answers to the requirement to state the due dates for payment of the instalments, where necessary, elicited a significant number of incorrect answers in relation to the starting date as many candidates thought that this was after the end of the accounting period, rather than within it. Practical issues such as due dates for payment of tax by both companies and individuals are essential knowledge within many tax planning scenarios at ATX.

Overall, group aspects of corporation tax remain a key topic at ATX and candidates should endeavour to practise a wide range of questions on these to ensure that they are confident in dealing with different aspects of this area.

Part (b) of this question related to the consideration of specific matters relating to the group of companies when deciding which companies should be included in a group registration for value added tax (VAT) purposes. Despite the requirement stating that candidates were to refer only to the specific matters within the memorandum provided, a significant number wrote in detail about the general advantages and disadvantages of registering as a group, which was not relevant, and so wasted time. However, many candidates did identify the specific issues – one of the companies being partially exempt, and another using the annual accounting scheme and the cash accounting scheme – but then discussed what this meant for the relevant companies themselves, rather than the implications of including that company within a group registration. Unfortunately, though, having identified the issues, they didn't go on to score as many marks as they could have done by answering the precise requirement.

Part (c) of this question concerned an unexpected refund of tax from HM Revenue and Customs (HMRC), and the actions to be undertaken by the firm in respect of this. This is a frequently tested area of ethics, and on the whole, candidates' performance was good, with clear explanations of the advice to be given to the client, and the consequences of the client not following this advice. Candidates generally appeared to have practised this type of question, and a good number scored full marks.

					Marks
			ACCA marking scheme		
(a)	(i)	Calculation			3.5
					———
					3.5
				Maximum	3.0
					———
	(ii)	Transfer pricing			3.5
		Rationale for loss planning			2.0
		Threshold for payment by instalments			2.5
		Members of group relief group			1.0
		Allocation of loss between group companies			4.0
		Corporation tax liabilities			5.0
		Payment schedule			4.0
					———
					22.0
				Maximum	18.0
					———
(b)		Companies to be included			2.0
		Sales between members of the VAT group			1.0
		VAT schemes			2.0
		Frit Ltd			1.0
					———
					6.0
				Maximum	5.0
					———

		Marks
(c)	The need to repay the tax	3.0
	Ceasing to act	3.0
		6.0
	Maximum	5.0
	Problem solving	1.0
	Clarity of explanations and calculations	1.0
	Effectiveness of communication	1.0
	Overall presentation	1.0
		4.0
Total		**35.0**

72 HEYER LTD GROUP *Walk in the footsteps of a top tutor*

Key answer tips

This 25 mark section A question tests corporation tax groups, VAT and ethical issues.

There are four requirements that could be answered in any order, so you should think carefully about which part you answer first, in order to maximise your score in the time available.

Requirement (a) tests group planning within a capital gains group, which is an important topic in the exam.

Part (b) covers the transfer of trade and assets within a group, which is not often tested.

Requirement (c) tests the basic level topic of VAT registration.

Requirement (d) is possibly the most straightforward part of this question, and tests the ethical implications of non-disclosure of information to HMRC.

The highlighted words in the written sections are key phrases that markers are looking for in your answer.

(a) Group planning

Tutor's top tips

The email from your manager sets out four sub-requirements for this part of the question, so you should make sure that you address all of these.

You could use the key words from these sub-requirements as headings in your answer, to help to give structure.

Requirement to pay corporation tax by instalments

In respect of the year ending 31 December 2022, a company in the Heyer Ltd group will be required to pay corporation tax in instalments if its taxable total profits (TTP) exceed £83,333 (£1,500,000/18) and either:

– it had TTP of more than £83,333 in the year ended 31 December 2021; or

– its TTP for the year ended 31 December 2022 are more than £555,556 (£10,000,000/18).

Tutorial note

Companies which have a corporation tax liability of less than £10,000 are not required to pay tax in instalments. This point is not referred to in the answer as none of the companies fall within this definition.

Strictly, the requirement to pay instalments is based on a company's augmented profits (TTP plus non group dividends received). However, we are told in the question that no company receives any dividends from outside the group.

The Heyer Ltd capital gains group

The Heyer Ltd capital gains group consists of Heyer Ltd, its 75% subsidiaries and their 75% subsidiaries. In addition, Heyer Ltd must have an effective interest of more than 50% in any company which it does not own directly.

Accordingly, all of the group companies are in a single capital gains group with the exception of Orin Hod Ltd.

Amount of chargeable gains and capital losses to transfer between group companies

You should aim to:

1   Reduce the TTP of as many companies as possible to £83,333, such that they are no longer required to pay corporation tax in instalments.

2   Reduce the TTP of those companies which are still required to pay corporation tax in instalments, as this will reduce the amount of each instalment.

3   The whole or part of any current period chargeable gain and/or capital loss can be transferred between companies in a capital gains group.

– Gains and losses should be transferred in order to match them against each other.

– Gains should be transferred from a company which has TTP in excess of the £83,333 threshold to a company which has TTP below the threshold.

Relevance of the specific information

Tutor's top tips

To score well in this question, it is important that you not only set out the general objectives, but also apply these to the companies in the scenario.

Companies do not need to pay by instalments if they were not large in the previous accounting period unless their augmented profits exceed £10 million. This limit is shared by 51% related companies and so is £555,556 for the Heyer Ltd group.

Mantet Ltd

Mantet Ltd had TTP for the year ended 31 December 2021 of less than £83,333. Accordingly, it will not be required to pay its corporation tax liability for the year ended 31 December 2022 in instalments unless its TTP for that year are more than £555,556. With this in mind, chargeable gains should be transferred to Mantet Ltd from other companies in the Heyer Ltd capital gains group provided its TTP are kept below £555,556.

Newell Rap Ltd

Newell Rap Ltd's capital losses are pre-entry capital losses because they were realised before Newell Rap Ltd was acquired by Heyer Ltd. These losses cannot be used to relieve gains on assets realised by other members of the Heyer Ltd capital gains group.

Orin Hod Ltd

Orin Hod Ltd's TTP exceed £83,333. However, it is not a member of the Heyer Ltd capital gains group because it is not a 75% subsidiary of Heyer Ltd. Accordingly, it is not possible to reduce its TTP by, for example, transferring its chargeable gains to other companies.

Other 100% owned companies

All of these companies are required to pay corporation tax in instalments.

Current period chargeable gains and capital losses realised by these companies should be transferred to other companies in the Heyer Ltd capital gains group in accordance with the guidance set out above.

(b)   Group restructuring

Tutor's top tips

Even if you were not sure about the special rules that apply when there is a transfer of trade and assets between companies under 75% common control, you could have picked up some marks for explaining the implications of a transfer of assets within a 75% gains group.

Chargeable gains

Chargeable assets, including the business premises, will be transferred at no gain, no loss automatically, because all of the companies are 75% subsidiaries of Heyer Ltd. Accordingly, no chargeable gains will arise.

Stamp duty land tax (SDLT)

No SDLT will be due in respect of the sale of the business premises because Heyer Ltd owns at least 75% of the ordinary share capital of all of the companies.

Capital allowances

Machinery and equipment will be automatically transferred at tax written down value, rather than market value, because Heyer Ltd controls at least 75% of each of the companies. Accordingly, no balancing charges will arise.

Capital losses

The unused capital losses of Newell Rap Ltd, and any other company whose trade and assets will be transferred, will not be transferred to Lodi Ltd, but current period capital losses can be transferred to companies in the same capital gains group, as set out above.

(c)   Pink Time Ltd

Tutor's top tips

Although this question covers the basic level topic of compulsory VAT registration, the key to scoring well was to identify that Pink Time Ltd makes zero-rated supplies, and will not have to charge output VAT even if it does register.

The taxable supplies of Pink Time Ltd will exceed the registration threshold of £85,000 by the end of November 2022 (£35,000 × 3 = £105,000). However, the company may apply to be exempt from registration because it only makes zero-rated supplies.

It would be beneficial for Pink Time Ltd to register for value added tax (VAT) because it would then be able to recover its input tax. The fact that its customers are members of the public is irrelevant because Pink Time Ltd makes zero-rated supplies and therefore will not be charging any VAT.

Pink Time Ltd would be in a VAT repayment position if it were to register for VAT because it only makes zero-rated supplies.

It could improve its cash flow position by making its VAT returns monthly rather than quarterly.

(d)   Disclosure of transfer pricing

Tutor's top tips

There will always be five marks on ethical issues in section A of the exam, and these can be easy marks to obtain.

This requirement covers the implications of a client not disclosing information to HMRC, and is similar to requirements seen in past exams.

It is more than 12 months since the return filing date, and therefore too late to amend the corporation tax returns. Accordingly, this information must be disclosed to HM Revenue and Customs (HMRC). We should encourage Heyer Ltd to make this disclosure.

The management of the Heyer Ltd group can inform HMRC or may authorise us to do so. However, we must not disclose the error to HMRC without permission.

We cannot continue to act for the companies unless this disclosure is made.

We should notify the group of the following consequences of not providing this information to HMRC:

–   If they refuse to disclose the error, we will advise HMRC that we no longer act for them. We would not, however, give any reason for our actions.

–   Non-disclosure of the error would also amount to tax evasion. This could result in criminal proceedings under both the tax and money laundering legislation.

We should inform our firm's money laundering officer of the situation.

We should ascertain how the non-disclosure occurred in order to determine whether or not there may be other matters which have been omitted from the group companies' corporation tax returns.

Examiner's report

The first part required candidates to prepare guidance for a tax assistant on how to minimise the corporation tax payable in instalments by the group companies by transferring chargeable gains and capital losses between them.

This was a slightly unusual requirement. It was vital that candidates spent some time thinking about how **they** would carry out the assistant's task before they started trying to explain to the assistant how to do it.

Candidates needed to think in terms of what needed to be done (objectives), and how it was to be achieved (strategies). The objectives were

•   where possible, to reduce the taxable total profits (TTP) of each company below the limit of £1,500,000 (divided by the 18 companies in the group)

•   to reduce the TTP of any company required to pay tax in instalments.

These objectives can be achieved by:

- matching gains and losses in a particular company
- transferring gains from a company with TTP above the threshold to one with TTP below the threshold.

As expected, candidates found this task difficult and there was a tendency to fall back on describing the rules in general terms as opposed to trying to address the specific requirement.

The second part of the question concerned the proposal to transfer the trades and assets of five of the group companies to another of the group companies and was also challenging. The challenge here was to address all of the issues set out in the manager's email in the time available. Only four points needed to be made but there was only one mark for each point.

Having said that this was a challenging question, many candidates made a good job of it. In particular, they kept their answers brief and tried to address all of the issues raised. Weaker candidates focused on only one or two of the manager's issues which restricted the number of marks which could be obtained.

The one common technical error concerned the capital allowances treatment. The point here is that the assets would be automatically transferred at tax written down value because the companies are all under 75% common control both before and after the transfer of the trades.

The third part of the question concerned a whether a company making zero-rated supplies was required to register for VAT and the benefits of registering. This part was not done particularly well. This was partly due to candidates writing standard answers to the whether or not to register question without focusing on the fact that the company was making zero-rated supplies.

This meant that the following two points were often missed:

- the company could apply to be exempt from registration even if its supplies exceeded the registration limit
- if the company were to register, there would be no effect on its customers, even though they are members of the public.

The final part of the question concerned the disclosure of information to HM Revenue and Customs and was done well by the vast majority of candidates.

<table>
<tr><th colspan="3">ACCA marking scheme</th></tr>
<tr><td></td><td></td><td>Marks</td></tr>
<tr><td>(a)</td><td>Requirement to pay by instalments</td><td>3.5</td></tr>
<tr><td></td><td>Definition of capital gains group</td><td>2.0</td></tr>
<tr><td></td><td>Amount to transfer</td><td>4.0</td></tr>
<tr><td></td><td>Specific information</td><td></td></tr>
<tr><td></td><td>   Mantet Ltd</td><td>2.0</td></tr>
<tr><td></td><td>   Newell Rap Ltd</td><td>2.0</td></tr>
<tr><td></td><td>   Orin Hod Ltd</td><td>1.0</td></tr>
<tr><td></td><td>   Other 100% companies</td><td>0.5</td></tr>
<tr><td></td><td></td><td>―――</td></tr>
<tr><td></td><td></td><td>15.0</td></tr>
<tr><td></td><td>**Maximum**</td><td>11.0</td></tr>
<tr><td></td><td></td><td>―――</td></tr>
<tr><td>(b)</td><td>One mark for each relevant point (maximum of 4 marks)</td><td>4.0</td></tr>
<tr><td></td><td></td><td>―――</td></tr>
<tr><td>(c)</td><td>One mark for each relevant point (maximum of 5 marks)</td><td>5.0</td></tr>
<tr><td></td><td></td><td>―――</td></tr>
<tr><td>(d)</td><td>The need to disclose</td><td>4.0</td></tr>
<tr><td></td><td>Other matters</td><td>3.0</td></tr>
<tr><td></td><td></td><td>―――</td></tr>
<tr><td></td><td></td><td>7.0</td></tr>
<tr><td></td><td>**Maximum**</td><td>5.0</td></tr>
<tr><td></td><td></td><td>―――</td></tr>
<tr><td>Total</td><td></td><td>**25.0**</td></tr>
<tr><td></td><td></td><td>―――</td></tr>
</table>

73 ACHIOTE LTD *Walk in the footsteps of a top tutor*

Key answer tips

This is a four-part company-focused section B question covering intangible fixed assets, transfer pricing, gains groups and VAT in respect of a commercial building.

The four parts could be attempted in any order. As they are mostly discursive they lend themselves well to being completed in the word processor response option in the exam. Any small calculations can be completed in tables.

The highlighted words in the written sections are key phrases that markers are looking for in your answer.

(a)   Goodwill

Tutor's top tips

The intangible fixed asset rules for companies are often tested in the exam. Remember that the rules that apply to goodwill and other intangibles are not the same.

No amortisation in respect of goodwill is deductible for corporation tax purposes, so the amortisation charged in the accounts for the year ended 31 March 2022 must be added back for tax purposes.

Patent

As the patent is transferred between two members of a capital gains group, it will be transferred at a price which is tax neutral.

The written down value of the patent in Achiote Ltd at the date of its sale to Borage Ltd was £26,600 (£38,000 – (3 × 10% × £38,000)). Accordingly, this will be the deemed acquisition price for Borage Ltd.

Borage Ltd will continue to amortise the patent over the remainder of its ten-year life.

In the year ended 31 March 2022 amortisation charged in its accounts will be £950 (£26,600/7 × 3/12).

This amount is allowable for corporation tax purposes.

(b) Loan to Caraway Inc

Tutor's top tips

Exam questions often test the transfer pricing rules applicable to the sale of goods between connected companies.

The principles are the same for a loan: if the amount received by the UK company is less than the market rate, an adjustment must be made.

Note that there are five marks available for this part of the question, so you should try to write at least five separate points in your answer.

It would appear that an arm's length rate of interest on the loan would be 8% as this is the rate at which Caraway Inc could have obtained an equivalent loan from an unrelated party. As Achiote Ltd controls Caraway Inc, they are connected companies and so the transfer pricing rules apply.

The interest receivable by Achiote Ltd is £2,000 (£100,000 × 2%) less than it would be under an arm's length agreement.

This means that Achiote Ltd's non-trading loan relationship income is reduced by this amount, such that less tax is payable in the UK. Therefore, Achiote Ltd must adjust the figures within its corporation tax return to reflect the arm's length price.

As there is no double tax treaty between the UK and Nuxabar, Nuxabar will be regarded as a non-qualifying territory. As a result, the exemption which might otherwise have been available if a group is not large will not be available to the Achiote Ltd group.

Achiote Ltd can seek advance approval from HM Revenue and Customs (HMRC) in respect of any intra-group pricing arrangements, including the rate of interest to be charged on a loan.

(c) **Transfer of the item of equipment and the sale of shares in Caraway Inc**

Sale of item of equipment

Tutor's top tips

Think before you answer this part of the question!

*An overseas resident company **cannot** transfer assets at no gain, no loss within a capital gains group.*

The intra-group transfer of the item of equipment by Achiote Ltd to Caraway Inc will not be treated as a no gain, no loss transfer, because even though Achiote Ltd owns 80% of the company, such that the companies are in a capital gains group, the fact that Caraway Inc is not a UK resident company means that the asset will no longer be within the charge to UK taxation.

This is therefore a chargeable disposal for Achiote Ltd at 1 March 2022.

Although the equipment has fallen in value, no capital loss will arise as the asset qualified for capital allowances as it was used in Achiote Ltd's trade.

Sale of shares in Caraway Inc

Tutor's top tips

The substantial shareholding exemption is regularly tested in the exam, so you must learn and apply the conditions.

In this scenario, the exemption does not apply and a gain must be calculated.

The sale of the 8% holding in Caraway Inc will not be exempt from corporation tax under the substantial shareholding exemption (SSE) rules. This is because Achiote Ltd will only have held its shares in Caraway Inc for nine months prior to the proposed disposal date and so will not meet the criteria to have owned at least 10% of the shares in Caraway Inc for a continuous 12-month period out of the six years prior to disposal.

Accordingly, a chargeable gain will arise on the disposal, calculated as follows:

	£
Disposal proceeds	66,000
Less: Cost (£258,000 × 8/80)	(25,800)
Chargeable gain	40,200

There will be no indexation allowance, as the shares were acquired after December 2017.

Tutorial note

The equipment is not exempt as a wasting asset as it qualified for capital allowances due to being used in a business.

(d)   (i)   Reasons why Rye Ltd might not charge value added tax (VAT) on its sales to Achiote Ltd

Tutor's top tips

Read the question carefully: the first part of this requirement concerns Rye Ltd, a company that supplies goods to Achiote Ltd. It is not about the commercial building.

Rye Ltd is a small company, and its taxable supplies may not yet have reached the registration threshold.

Rye Ltd's taxable supplies have reached the registration threshold, but its supplies to Achiote Ltd are zero-rated.

(ii)   Option to tax the commercial building

Tutor's top tips

VAT on land and buildings and the implications of opting to tax often feature in the exam, so you should be prepared to answer questions on these rules.

As the building purchased by Achiote Ltd was less than three years old, and a commercial building, it would have been a standard-rated supply. So Achiote Ltd will have incurred a significant amount of input value added tax (VAT) in relation to this expenditure.

For this reason, it will be financially beneficial (at least in the short term), for Achiote Ltd to opt to tax the building in order to be able to reclaim this tax.

This will also enable Achiote Ltd to recover the input tax in respect of the building's running costs.

However, VAT must then be added to the rent charged by Achiote Ltd to Rye Ltd. The impact of this on Rye Ltd will depend on its size and the nature of its supplies.

–   If its taxable supplies are currently below the registration limit, Rye Ltd could voluntarily register for VAT purposes and reclaim the input VAT charged on the rent payments.

–   If Rye Ltd's taxable supplies have reached the registration threshold, but its supplies are wholly or partially zero-rated, provided it has registered for VAT purposes, the input VAT charged on the rent payments will, again, be reclaimable, and may lead to a (higher) repayment of VAT from HMRC.

Tutorial note

In order to determine whether or not opting to tax the commercial building would be commercially beneficial, longer term implications, such as the impact on the building's future marketability, would also need to be considered. Credit was also available for candidates who made reference to partial exemption.

Examiner's report

The first part required an explanation of the corporation tax implications of acquiring goodwill and a patent. The goodwill was a minor point and was handled well by the majority of candidates. The patent, however, was not handled so well. Many candidates treated it as a standard asset as opposed to being part of the intangible assets regime. As a result, the inter-group transfer was treated as a no gain, no loss transfer as opposed to a tax neutral transfer. This, in turn, caused problems when calculating the tax deductions available in the future.

The second part concerned transfer pricing. This part was not done particularly well because many candidates did not identify sufficient mark-scoring points.

It was important to start the explanation at the beginning by identifying why the transfer pricing rules applied. This required a reference to the fact that one of the companies controlled the other and the lack of an arms' length price. Many candidates did not do this but simply took it for granted that the regime applied.

Once the relevance of the rules had been established, candidates should then have explained the effect of the rules by reference to the need to increase the company's taxable profit and the amount of the increase. It was this part which most candidates focused on.

It was then necessary to consider any other relevant matters including the availability of the exemption where a group is not large and the possibility of obtaining advance approval of the arrangements from HM Revenue and Customs.

The third part concerned the chargeable gains implications of the sale of an item of equipment and of some shares. Candidates needed to concentrate and take care in order to score well.

The equipment was being transferred between two companies in a chargeable gains group. However, the company acquiring the property was not resident in the UK, such that the no gain/no loss treatment would not apply to the transaction. In addition, due to the availability of capital allowances, the loss arising on the disposal would not be available.

When dealing with the sale of the shares, it was important to recognise that the substantial shareholder exemption would not be available because the vendor would not have owned the shares for a 12-month period in the six years prior to the sale.

The final part concerned various aspects of VAT.

The aspects of this part relating to the option to tax a commercial building were generally handled well. However, candidates found the other aspect of this part more difficult.

Candidates were asked to suggest reasons why a company which made taxable supplies did not charge VAT on sales made to an unconnected party. Stronger candidates stopped for a moment to gather their thoughts and then wrote about the registration limit and/or the making of zero rated supplies. Weaker candidates simply wrote about registration in general and often lengthy terms. Candidates need to be in a rhythm throughout the exam of reading, thinking and then writing.

ACCA marking scheme			
			Marks
(a)	Goodwill		1.0
	Patent		4.0
			5.0
		Maximum	4.0
(b)	Transfer pricing – reason why it applies		1.0
	– implications and action		5.0
			6.0
		Maximum	5.0
(c)	Transfer of equipment		2.5
	Sale of shares		3.5
			6.0
		Maximum	5.0
(d)	(i) Reasons why VAT is not charged		2.0
	(ii) Beneficial due to input VAT incurred		1.5
	Implications of option to tax for Rye Ltd		3.0
			4.5
		Maximum	4.0
Total			**20.0**

74 HARROW TAN LTD *Walk in the footsteps of a top tutor*

Key answer tips

This is a typical Section A scenario question covering various group corporation tax issues, stamp duty land tax and VAT.

The first part of the question covers a sale of shares, including discussion of the regularly-tested substantial shareholding exemption and degrouping charges.

Requirement (ii) tests group relief for trading losses, another key area.

Requirement (iii) covers rollover relief, with gains group aspects.

The final part tests some basic-level areas of VAT: annual accounting, entertaining and gifts. You could have attempted this part before tackling the corporation tax issues.

The highlighted words in the written sections are key phrases that markers are looking for in your memorandum.

Tutor's top tips

You are asked to prepare notes for a meeting, so make sure that you do this to gain the marks for presentation.

Use the headings from the manager's email to help to give you answer structure, and note the instruction to EXPLAIN the matters, which requires a written answer. However, you should keep your answer brief and to the point, using short paragraphs or bullets.

Meeting notes

Client	**Harrow Tan Ltd group**
Subject	**Various group matters**
Prepared by	**Tax senior**
Date	**7 September 2022**

(i) Sale of shares in Rocha Ltd

Tutor's top tips

There is a note in the question that states that 'there may be three or four issues which need to be brought to Corella's attention'. This is a useful clue, so think carefully before you start writing and try to come up with at least three different issues to cover in your answer.

Watch out for the degrouping charge, as this is easily missed!

Substantial shareholding exemption

The gain on the sale of the shares in Rocha Ltd will not be subject to tax if the conditions of the substantial shareholding exemption (SSE) are satisfied.

The conditions are:

– Rocha Ltd must be a trading company – this condition is satisfied.
– At least 10% of the ordinary share capital must have been held for 12 months during the six years prior to the sale.

Accordingly, in order for the SSE to be available, the sale would need to be delayed until 1 December 2022.

Taxable gain

If the sale takes place on 1 October 2022 the SSE **will not** be available, and the taxable gain will be calculated as follows:

	Notes	£
Gain per company		3,476,500
Add: Indexation allowance	1	133,500
Degrouping charge	2	294,440
Rollover relief	3	1,350,000
Taxable gain		5,254,440

This taxable gain would result in a substantial corporation tax liability. Accordingly, it is important that the SSE conditions are satisfied.

Tutorial note

Alternatively, you could have recalculated the taxable gain as follows:

	£
Sale proceeds	*10,300,000*
Add: Degrouping charge	*294,440*
Less: Cost (per question)	*(5,340,000)*
Taxable gain	*5,254,440*

Either approach would score the same marks in the exam.

Notes

1 Indexation allowance

Indexation is frozen at December 2017. As the shares were acquired after December 2017, there is no indexation allowance available on the sale of the shares.

2   Degrouping charge

A degrouping charge will arise in respect of the building which was sold to Rocha Ltd by Seckel Ltd.

This is because:

–   Rocha Ltd and Seckel Ltd are members of the Harrow Tan Ltd capital gains group (they are both 75% subsidiaries of Harrow Tan Ltd).

–   The building would have been transferred automatically at no gain, no loss.

–   Rocha Ltd will leave the Harrow Tan Ltd capital gains group when it ceases to be a 75% subsidiary on the sale of the shares. This will occur within six years of the acquisition of the building.

–   Rocha Ltd will still own the building when it leaves the group.

The degrouping charge will be calculated as follows:

	£
Market value on 1 January 2022	800,000
Less: Cost	(330,000)
Indexation allowance May 2003 to December 2017 (£330,000 × 0.532)	(175,560)
Degrouping charge	294,440

3   Rollover relief

–   Company shares are not qualifying assets for the purposes of rollover relief.

–   Accordingly, it will not be possible to roll over any of the gain on the sale of the shares.

Stamp duty land tax

Tutor's top tips

Remember that the rates of stamp duty land tax are provided in the tax tables in the exam.

Stamp duty land tax (SDLT) will not have been payable by Rocha Ltd in respect of the purchase of the building from Seckel Ltd because both companies were 75% subsidiaries of Harrow Tan Ltd at that time.

However, because Rocha Ltd will cease to be a 75% subsidiary of Harrow Tan Ltd within three years of purchasing the building, it will have to pay SDLT of £29,500.

£			£
150,000	× 0%		0
100,000	× 2%		2,000
———			
250,000			
550,000	× 5%		27,500
———			———
800,000			29,500
———			———

(ii) Group relief – year ending 31 December 2022

Tutor's top tips

*Read the requirement carefully here: you are asked to explain the **maximum** amount of Seckel Ltd's trading loss which can be surrendered to the other companies, so there is no need to consider any tax planning points.*

Harrow Tan Ltd

A company can claim available group losses up to a maximum of its taxable total profits (TTP).

For Harrow Tan Ltd, this will be £40,000 plus the chargeable gain on the sale of the shares in Rocha Ltd (if the SSE is not available).

Rocha Ltd

For the purposes of group relief, Rocha Ltd left the group on 31 July 2022, when the agreement was signed to sell 60,000 of the company's shares.

The maximum surrender to Rocha Ltd will therefore be £35,000 (£60,000 × 7/12), as this is less than the loss available for this period.

Tosca Ltd

The maximum surrender to Tosca Ltd will be its TTP for the year of £70,000.

Uta Far Ltd

The effective interest of Harrow Tan Ltd in Uta Far Ltd is less than 75% (80% × 90% = 72%).

Accordingly, Uta Far Ltd is not in a group relief group with Seckel Ltd and cannot receive any losses.

However, it is possible to transfer some or all of Uta Far Ltd's chargeable gain on the sale of the building to another group company, such that it could then be relieved by group relief from Seckel Ltd.

(iii)   Rollover relief

Tutor's top tips

Don't forget that the definition of a gains group is different from the definition of a group relief group.

It is important that you learn these definitions and are able to apply them to a scenario.

Rollover relief is tested regularly in the exam, so you must learn the qualifying assets, the qualifying time period, and the rules regarding the operation of the relief. Be prepared to explain and apply these rules.

Relief potentially available to the group

Rollover relief

Since the building sold by Uta Far Ltd on 1 May 2022 was used in its trade, rollover relief is available in respect of the gain on the building.

The whole of the gain can be rolled over if there are qualifying additions in the qualifying period of at least £1,800,000. Any amount of the sales proceeds which has not been used to acquire qualifying business assets cannot be relieved and will be subject to corporation tax up to a maximum of the gain of £85,000.

The qualifying period is the four-year period starting one year prior to the date on which the disposal of a qualifying business asset occurred (1 May 2022).

Capital gains group

For the purposes of rollover relief, a capital gains group is treated as a single entity.

This means that qualifying business assets can be acquired by any company in the same capital gains group as the company which has sold a qualifying business asset.

The Harrow Tan Ltd capital gains group consists of:

–   Harrow Tan Ltd
–   its 75% subsidiaries
–   and their 75% subsidiaries
–   Harrow Tan Ltd must have an effective interest of more than 50% in any non-directly held companies.

Harrow Tan Ltd's interest in Uta Far Ltd is 72% (80% × 90%), such that all five companies are in the Harrow Tan Ltd capital gains group.

Rocha Ltd is only in the group until Harrow Tan Ltd sells the 60,000 shares (at which point Rocha Ltd will no longer be a 75% subsidiary).

Part C of Corella's schedule

The land and building qualify for rollover relief.

Further information is needed in respect of the machinery; it must be fixed, rather than movable, if it is to qualify for rollover relief.

Patents and trademarks are intangible assets which are not qualifying additions for the purposes of chargeable gains rollover relief.

Conclusion

Based on the information provided, there has been insufficient reinvestment of the proceeds on the disposal by Uta Far Ltd to obtain rollover relief. However, there may be other qualifying additions.

(iv)   Tosca Ltd – promotion of new product

Increase in turnover

Tutor's top tips

There are three special VAT schemes for small businesses that you saw in your earlier studies and are still tested in the ATX exam:

- *the annual accounting scheme*
- *the cash accounting scheme*
- *the flat rate scheme.*

There is no information on these schemes in the tax tables provided in the exam, so make sure that you remember the key conditions.

Tosca Ltd should notify HM Revenue and Customs (HMRC) that it expects its turnover to exceed the annual accounting turnover limit of £1,600,000. The company may then be required to leave the scheme. Once its turnover for an accounting year does exceed this limit, it will be required to leave the scheme.

Once the company is no longer in the annual accounting scheme, it will have to submit four VAT returns a year rather than one.

Its VAT payments will then fluctuate because they will be calculated by reference to its outputs and inputs in the quarter rather than being based on its VAT liability for the previous year.

Entertainment and gifts

Tutor's top tips

Take care in this section. You are not asked to discuss the corporation tax implications of expenditure on entertainment and gifts, just the VAT implications.

Tosca Ltd will not be able to recover the input tax in respect of the cost of entertaining its customers.

It will not be necessary to account for output tax on the gifts of the pens, provided the total cost of any gifts made to the same person does not exceed £50 in a year. The related input tax will be recoverable in full.

It will also not be necessary to account for output tax on the gifts of the new product, even though its value exceeds £50, because it is a sample of the company's own products. Again, the related input tax will be recoverable in full.

Examiner's report

This question concerned a variety of corporation tax issues facing different members of a group of companies. It was quite a challenging question, but some good answers were provided by candidates who read the question carefully, and followed the detailed guidance. The use of subheadings, taken from the issues in the manager's email, provides a useful structure in this type of question, which all candidates should consider adopting.

The first part of the question, which was worth 12 marks, related to the sale of shares in one of the group companies. For 12 marks, a candidate should expect to have to identify several different issues, and in this case, the examiner indicated that there were three or four issues to be considered here. Many candidates managed to identify one or two, but relatively few were able to produce a comprehensive answer to this part. Candidates who had practised past exam questions in this subject area would have been able to identify and discuss the key issues of substantial shareholding exemption, degrouping charge, and withdrawal of the stamp duty land tax exemption, and consequently scored well. These are key elements of knowledge at ATX and are tested frequently in a variety of different ways.

The second part of the question concerned group relief available for the trading loss of one of the group companies. It was pleasing to see that many candidates were able to accurately define a group for group relief purposes, and to apply this to the group in the scenario. The question required candidates to state the maximum loss which could be surrendered to each of the group companies. However, a significant number of candidates appeared to misread this, and introduced a planning element, discussing in some detail, the optimum relief available to the group, taking into consideration whether or not each company would pay corporation tax in instalments. Candidates are strongly advised to spend a little time reading the detail of the requirements very carefully, to ensure that they focus their efforts in the right direction. Time spent in this way should help to ensure that candidates focus their answer on what is required, and do not go off at a tangent, providing irrelevant information or computations, which waste time.

The third part of the question related to the availability of rollover relief within the group, and, again, it was pleasing that most candidates were able to correctly define a group for this purpose and apply this to the group in the scenario. However, knowledge of the assets which qualify for rollover relief was rather more vague, with many candidates failing to recognise that a share disposal does not qualify. Whereas many candidates were aware that the gain eligible to be rolled over might be restricted, very few could accurately explain the restriction. Candidates sitting ATX will frequently be tested on the capital gains reliefs available for both companies and individuals, and would be well advised to ensure that they spend some time learning the details of these.

The final part of the question concerned VAT implications of using the annual accounting scheme and of incurring expenditure on promotional activities. The majority of candidates were familiar with the terms of the annual accounting scheme. However, many answers relating to the expenditure on entertainment, gifts and samples, related to the corporation tax implications of these not being allowable, with no reference at all to VAT. Although some candidates did appreciate the VAT implications with regard to input VAT on each of these, very few identified the correct output VAT implications.

Overall, candidates who prepared satisfactory answers to the question:

- clearly addressed each of the three issues set out in the manager's email
- read the requirements very carefully and followed the guidance provided
- did not waste time including irrelevant material
- produced clearly laid out and labelled computations.

	ACCA marking scheme		
			Marks
(i)	Substantial shareholding exemption		3.5
	Degrouping charge		
	Explanation		4.0
	Calculation		1.5
	Rollover relief		1.0
	Calculation and taxable gain		2.0
	Stamp duty land tax		2.5
			————
			14.5
		Maximum	12.0
			————
(ii)	Harrow Tan Ltd		2.0
	Rocha Ltd		2.0
	Tosca Ltd		1.0
	Uta Far Ltd		3.0
			————
			8.0
		Maximum	6.0
			————
(iii)	Capital gains group		3.0
	Implications		3.0
	Part C of the schedule		2.0
			————
			8.0
		Maximum	7.0
			————
(iv)	Increase in turnover		3.5
	Entertainment and gifts		3.0
			————
			6.5
		Maximum	6.0
			————
	Ability to follow instructions		1.0
	Clarity of explanations and calculations		1.0
	Effectiveness of communication		1.0
	Overall presentation and style		1.0
			————
			4.0
			————
	Total		**35.0**
			————

75   SET LTD GROUP (ADAPTED) *Walk in the footsteps of a top tutor*

Key answer tips

This question covers various aspects of corporation tax and VAT and is broken down into different sections relating to different companies. There are several different areas to consider so it is important to ensure time is allocated appropriately between the different requirements.

Part (a) looks at use of capital and trading losses within a group as well as payment of corporation tax by instalments. This topic is fairly regularly tested at ATX.

Part (b) looks at two different aspects of overseas VAT. There is no longer any difference between the treatment inside and outside the EU, so try not to get confused with the old rules if your earlier studies were under a different finance act.

The third part of the question tests knowledge of the CFC exemptions with application to two companies.

The final part of the question asks for different methods in which a trading loss can be relieved and the factors to consider when choosing the method of relief. This is another commonly tested area and something you should be well prepared for.

The highlighted words in the written sections are key phrases that markers are looking for in your answer.

(a)   Ghost Ltd – corporation tax payments

Steam Ltd capital loss

Ghost Ltd and Steam Ltd are members of a capital gains group because Set Ltd owns at least 75% of the ordinary share capital of both companies.

Accordingly, the capital loss in respect of the disposal of the building by Steam Ltd could be transferred to Ghost Ltd. However, the loss could only be offset against chargeable gains (i.e. not trading profit or other income) realised by Ghost Ltd after it became a member of the Set Ltd capital gains group on 1 June 2022.

Wagon Ltd trading losses

Ghost Ltd and Wagon Ltd are members of a group relief group because Set Ltd owns at least 75% of the ordinary share capital of both companies. Trading losses made whilst the companies are members of the group can be transferred from one company to the other.

Ghost Ltd became a member of the Set Ltd group relief group on 1 June 2022. Its eight-month accounting period ending on 31 December 2022 will have seven months in common with the 12-month accounting period of Wagon Ltd ending on 31 December 2022. Accordingly, the maximum trading loss which can be transferred from Wagon Ltd to Ghost Ltd is the lower of:

–   7/12 of the trading loss of Wagon Ltd available for surrender (see below), and

–   7/8 of the taxable total profits of Ghost Ltd for the eight-month period ending 31 December 2022.

The trading loss of Wagon Ltd available for surrender as group relief is:

– the trading loss for the year ending 31 December 2022

– the excess trading loss brought forward, to the extent that Wagon Ltd cannot set this loss against its own total profits in the year ending 31 December 2022. If Wagon Ltd has no other income, this will be the whole of the £31,500 loss brought forward.

Tutorial note

Ghost Ltd changed ownership when it became a member of the Set Ltd group. Accordingly, if Ghost Ltd had a trading loss brought forward at the time that it joined the Set Ltd group, it would not be available to surrender this loss to the Set Ltd group for five years following the change in ownership.

However, there is no such restriction on the loss brought forward in Wagon Ltd, as Wagon Ltd has not changed its owners. This loss is available for surrender to Ghost Ltd, subject to the overlapping period adjustment set out above.

Payments of corporation tax

Tutor's top tips

Payment of corporation tax in instalments is brought forward knowledge from TX but can often be tested in ATX. You must ensure that you consider all relevant accounting periods as well as any payments already made.

In respect of the year ended 30 April 2022

14 August 2022

The final payment for this accounting period will be due. The amount due is £597,500 (the total liability for the accounting period), less all the instalment payments already made in respect of the period.

In respect of the eight-month period ended 31 December 2022

14 November 2022

The first payment for this accounting period will be due. The amount due will be 3/8 of the estimated corporation tax liability for the eight-month period, i.e. £172,500 (3/8 × £460,000).

(b) **Wagon Ltd – value added tax (VAT)**

Purchases from Line Co

The purchases of components will be dealt with under postponed VAT accounting. Wagon Ltd will record import VAT as output VAT on its VAT return in the VAT quarter covering the date of importation.

Provided the components are used to make taxable supplies, the VAT paid can be reclaimed by Wagon Ltd as input tax on the same VAT return.

Sales to Signal Co

The sales to Signal Co will be treated as zero-rated supplies.

Zero-rated supplies are treated as taxable supplies, so this will not impact Wagon Ltd's ability to recover input VAT.

(c) **Dee Co and En Co – controlled foreign company (CFC) charge**

Dee Co

No CFC charge can arise in respect of Dee Co because Set Ltd owns less than 25% of Dee Co's ordinary share capital.

En Co

Low profits exemption

The low profits exemption does not apply even though En Co has taxable total profits of less than £500,000. This is because the company's non-trading income exceeds £50,000.

Low profit margin exemption

The low profit margin exemption applies because En Co's accounting profit of £280,000 does not exceed 10% of its operating expenditure of £3,200,000.

Tutor's top tips

The question stated that the only exemptions that needed consideration were those for low profits and low profit margin. Ensure that you don't waste time going through the other exemptions as this will score no marks!

(d)   Steam Ltd – Project Whistle

Tutor's top tips

This part of the question was worth eight marks and so you should be looking to discuss several loss reliefs here in order to score well.

Loss reliefs available

A trading loss made by Steam Ltd in the year ending 31 December 2023 can be relieved, broadly speaking, in two ways:

(i)   It can be offset against the income and gains of Steam Ltd and/or the taxable total profits of other companies in the Set Ltd group relief group.

–   Steam Ltd could offset the loss against its total income and gains of the loss-making accounting period, and then against its total income and gains of the previous 12 months.

–   The loss could also be offset against the current period taxable total profits of Set Ltd and any other company which is an effective 75% subsidiary of Set Ltd.

–   Any loss remaining will be carried forward by Steam Ltd for relief against its future total profits, with group relief possible for any excess.

(ii)   Any amount of the loss up to a maximum of 230% of the qualifying research and development expenditure can be surrendered in exchange for a cash payment of 14.5% of the surrendered amount.

Factors to consider when choosing between the available reliefs

Relief under (i) above will result in a corporation tax saving of 19% of the loss relieved. This equates to a saving of 43.7% (230% × 19%) of the cost incurred in respect of the research and development.

Relief under (ii) above equates to a corporation tax saving of only 33.35% (230% × 14.5%) of the cost incurred.

Accordingly, a greater tax saving will be achieved by relieving the loss against taxable profits (under (i)) rather than surrendering it in exchange for a cash payment (under (ii)).

However, if there are insufficient profits to relieve all of the trading loss, any loss remaining will have to be carried forward unless it is surrendered in exchange for the 14.5% cash payment.

From a cash flow point, it will be better to claim the cash payment rather than to carry the loss forward. The cash payment option is also beneficial if it transpires that Steam Ltd or the Set Ltd group will not make sufficient profits in the future to relieve the losses carried forward.

Examiner's report

This question concerned various corporation tax and VAT issues for a group of companies. Each part related to a different group company and different tax aspects.

The first part of the question concerned a newly acquired, wholly owned subsidiary company, and its ability to receive a capital loss or trading loss from other group companies, and, separately, the corporation tax instalments which will fall due in the next six months.

In relation to the losses, many answers were disappointingly vague, in particular not stating whether the candidate was considering the capital loss or the trading loss in their discussion, or implying that the rules were the same for both, which is not the case. Dates were given in the question, so candidates were expected to refer to these in their answers.

The identification of the amounts and due dates for payment of the company's corporation tax instalments was, surprisingly, not well done. Virtually no candidate recognised that the final instalment for payment of a company's corporation tax liability was going to be the balance of the final corporation tax liability for the year i.e. the final liability less the three instalments paid previously, which is extremely unlikely to be the same as one quarter of the final liability, as the previous instalments have been based on estimates. A good number of candidates correctly calculated the amount of the first instalment for the subsequent short accounting period, but in both cases, application of knowledge of the due dates was weak. These must be accurately stated in order to score the marks.

The second part of the question related to the VAT implications of importing and exporting to non-UK resident companies, neither of which are registered for VAT. Answers were very mixed; again several answers were very vague, and future candidates should take note of how this has been addressed in the model answer. In particular, with imports, candidates must be precise as to how UK VAT will be paid/accounted for on the purchases.

This part of the question has been amended to remove the VAT treatment of goods outside/within the EU following changes to legislation.

The third part of the question concerned the application of two specific controlled foreign company (CFC) exemptions – the low profits exemption and low profit margin exemption. Overall, knowledge of these two exemptions was good, with a significant number of candidates scoring full, or almost full marks. The most common errors were to use the wrong figures to calculate the profit margin, and to fail to recognise that for one of the companies, no CFC charge would arise due to the UK company holding less than 25% of the shares in that company. A small number of candidates wasted time by considering other exemptions from CFC status, despite being clearly instructed in the requirement to consider just these two.

The fourth part of the question concerned the trading loss relief available to a company which qualifies for the additional 130% deduction available for qualifying research and development expenditure. Overall, this question part was quite well attempted, with the majority of candidates being able to explain the cashflow implications of the 'surrenderable loss' in this case, but in some instances candidates focused entirely on this and failed to take a broad enough approach, not considering in equal detail the 'normal' loss reliefs available to a company and their implications, in order to be able to fully discuss the factors to consider when choosing between the available reliefs. The question clearly implied that more than one relief would be available, and there were eight marks *(seven in the original question)* for this requirement, so this should have prompted candidates that a broader approach was needed.

			Marks
	ACCA marking scheme		*Marks*
(a)	Steam Ltd capital loss		2.0
	Wagon Ltd trading losses		
	Loss brought forward		1.0
	Current period loss		3.0
	Payments of corporation tax		
	In respect of the year ended 30 April 2022		2.5
	In respect of the eight-month period ended 31 December 2022		2.0
			10.5
		Maximum	9.0
(b)	Purchases from Line Co		
	Postponed VAT accounting		0.5
	Record output VAT		1.0
	Recover input VAT		1.0
	Sales to Signal Co		
	Zero-rated		1.0
	Input VAT recovery		1.0
			4.5
		Maximum	4.0
(c)	Dee Co		1.0
	En Co		3.0
			4.0
(d)	Loss reliefs available		
	Relief against profits		4.0
	Surrendered for cash payment		1.0
	Evaluation of the reliefs		4.0
			9.0
		Maximum	8.0
Total			**25.0**

76 GRAND LTD GROUP *Walk in the footsteps of a top tutor*

Key answer tips

This long section A question tests many core aspects of corporation tax along with some VAT and ethics. There is a lot of information to take on board so it is important to read through it carefully and pick out the key points.

Part (a) looks at the classic scenario of a sale of shares versus a sale of trade and assets. You need to appreciate that with a sale of shares SSE is going to be key so it is important to identify early on if this will be relevant and explain why. With the sale of trade and assets it's important to take a logical approach dealing with one asset at a time and then bring this all together at the end to see the corporation tax impact.

Part (b) is a short section dealing with tax evasion v avoidance. This is completely standalone and could be attempted first. This is often a good tactic in the exam as the ethics requirement can offer some easy marks, so ensure you get them!

The highlighted words in the written sections are key phrases that markers are looking for.

(a)   **Memorandum**

   Client Grand Ltd group

   Subject   **Sale of Colca Ltd**

   Prepared by   **Tax senior**

   Date   **4 September 2022**

   (i)   **Offer A – in respect of a sale of the company's shares**

Tutor's top tips

This part of the question is made up of three areas.

Firstly, you must consider whether tax relief will be available for the loss on the sale of the shares. This is testing the substantial shareholding exemption. You must explain whether or not the criteria are met, and if so this means that the loss is not allowable.

You then need to go on to consider the tax implications of Colca Ltd leaving the group still owning the Atuel building. The obvious thing to discuss here is a potential degrouping charge as they are leaving the group within six years of a no gain no loss transfer. However, you should also think about whether there are any stamp tax implications.

Finally, you need to calculate post tax proceeds.

   Tax relief available in respect of the capital loss on the sale of the shares

   –   The capital loss on the sale of the shares will not be allowable for tax purposes due to the automatic application of the substantial shareholding exemption (SSE).

–   The SSE applies because:

  –   Colca Ltd is a trading company; and

  –   Grand Ltd will have owned at least 10% of the ordinary share capital of Colca Ltd for at least 12 months in the six years prior to the sale of the company.

The tax implications of Colca Ltd leaving the Grand Ltd group whilst owning the Atuel building

Degrouping charge

–   The sale of the Atuel building by Sautso Ltd to Colca Ltd took place at no gain, no loss because the two companies were members of a capital gains group. This resulted in a base cost in the building for Colca Ltd equal to Sautso Ltd's cost.

–   Colca Ltd will leave the Grand Ltd group within six years of purchasing the building from Sautso Ltd, such that a degrouping charge will arise. Colca Ltd will be deemed to have sold the building for £255,000, its market value as at 1 April 2020.

    This deemed disposal results in a capital loss. However, this loss merely reduces Grand Ltd's proceeds for the shares in Colca Ltd. This in turn will increase the capital loss on the sale of the shares, which is exempt due to the SSE (as noted above).

Tutorial note

1   *There was no need to calculate the capital loss in respect of the degrouping charge because it merely increases the capital loss on the sale of Colca Ltd, which is exempt under the SSE.*

2   *Colca Ltd will also be deemed to have purchased the building for £255,000, such that this will be its base cost in the building when calculating the chargeable gain or allowable loss arising on any future disposal of the building.*

Stamp duty land tax (SDLT)

–   There was no SDLT liability when Colca Ltd purchased the Atuel building from Sautso Ltd because both companies were 75% subsidiaries of Grand Ltd.

–   However, Colca Ltd will leave the Grand Ltd group within three years of purchasing the building, such that it will have to pay the SDLT which would have been due at the time of purchase if the group exemption had not been available.

Post-tax proceeds

	£
Sale proceeds	730,000
Less: SDLT payable by Colca Ltd in respect of the Atuel building	(2,250)
Post-tax proceeds	727,750

Working

SDLT payable by Colca Ltd in respect of the Atuel building

	£
150,000 × 0%	0
100,000 × 2%	2,000
5,000 × 5%	250
255,000	2,250

(ii)   **Offer B – in respect of a sale of the company's trade and assets**

Tutor's top tips

The first part of this requirement asks for post-tax proceeds. You are given proceeds in the question so set up a table starting with this and slot in the tax on the various disposals as you calculate it.

You need to consider the following:

1   Tax on any gain from the Oribi building

2   Tax on any balancing adjustments in capital allowances in respect of the machinery (you're told to ignore any gains or losses on this in your calculation)

3   Tax saved in respect of any loss on the sale of the Atuel building.

Post-tax proceeds

	£
Sale proceeds	
Trade and assets	695,000
Tax liability/credit in respect of:	
Chargeable gain on the Oribi building (£85,790 (W1) × 19%)	(16,300)
Plant and machinery balancing charge (£12,100 × 19%)	(2,299)
Allowable loss on the Atuel building (£110,000 (W2) × 19%)	20,900
Post-tax proceeds	697,301

Workings

(W1) Sale of the Oribi building

	£
Proceeds	410,000
Less: Cost (£320,000 – £17,000)	(303,000)
Less: Indexation allowance (£303,000 × 0.070)	(21,210)
	———
Chargeable gain	85,790
	———

(W2) Sale of the Atuel building

	£
Proceeds	230,000
Less: Cost (original cost to Sautso Ltd)	(340,000)
	———
Allowable loss	(110,000)
	———

Tutor's top tips

Next you are asked to discuss the chargeable gains treatment of the machinery.

You are told that most of the items are worth less than their original cost, which would mean they would give rise to a capital loss. Consider what the treatment of this should be given that capital allowances have been claimed on the machinery.

There are also a small number of items worth more than their cost, so ensure you also explain the treatment of those.

You are told that the machinery is movable. Think about what this means in terms of eligibility for rollover relief.

In the final part of the requirement you need to explain which companies Colca Ltd can transfer capital losses to. This is basically asking you to discuss which companies are in a chargeable gains group with Colca Ltd. Make sure you discuss the rules that determine which companies should be included.

Chargeable gains and allowable capital losses on the sale of the machinery

- The items of machinery will not be exempt under the wasting chattels rule because they qualify for capital allowances.
- However, any item where both the cost and the proceeds are less than £6,000 will be exempt.
- In respect of the chargeable items of machinery (where the cost or the proceeds is at least £6,000):
  - An item sold at a loss will not result in an allowable capital loss. This is because Colca Ltd will have received capital allowances equal to the fall in value of the item.
  - An item sold at a profit will result in a chargeable gain. Rollover relief will not be available because the items are movable as opposed to fixed.

Transfer of capital losses to group members

–   The whole or part of any capital loss can be transferred to Grand Ltd, Sautso Ltd and any other member of the Grand Ltd capital gains group.

–   This group consists of Grand Ltd, its directly held 75% subsidiaries, their directly held 75% subsidiaries and so on

–   Where each company is an effective 51% subsidiary of Grand Ltd.

(iii)   Offer B – value added tax (VAT)

Tutor's top tips

In part (iii) you are asked to discuss VAT on the transfer of trade and assets. This is testing the transfer of a going concern (TOGC) rules. Ensure you list out the conditions for this treatment in order to score some easy marks.

Note that there are land and buildings included in the transfer. Remember that if they would be taxable at the point of the transfer then the purchaser would need to opt to tax them. Think about the situations in which a building may be taxable at the point of transfer.

Colca Ltd should not charge VAT on the sale of its business if the sale is a transfer of a going concern (TOGC). This requires all of the following conditions to be satisfied:

–   the business of Colca Ltd is transferred as a going concern

–   the purchaser will use the assets to carry on the same kind of business as Colca Ltd

–   there is no significant break in trading

–   the purchaser is VAT registered or will become registrable as a result of the purchase.

However, even where the sale of the business qualifies as a TOGC, VAT must still be charged on the sale of any building included as part of the sale if either:

–   an option to tax has been made in respect of the building; or

–   the building is a commercial building which is less than three years old.

No option to tax has been made in respect of either of the buildings to be sold by Colca Ltd.

However, the Atuel building is a commercial building which will be less than three years old on 1 December 2022, such that the sale of this building will be a standard-rated supply and VAT must be charged unless the purchaser opts to tax the building.

(b)   Tax evasion and tax avoidance

Tutor's top tips

The final requirement offers five marks on ethical issues, specifically the quite topical area of tax evasion v avoidance. You are asked firstly to distinguish between tax evasion and avoidance which should present some easy marks.

You then need to state the purpose of the general anti-abuse rule and explain why it is likely to apply to the plan in question. Make sure you relate this back to the facts in the question to score well.

Tax evasion, tax avoidance, and the purpose of the general anti-abuse rule (GAAR)

Tax evasion is unlawful. It involves the provision of false information or the withholding of information in order to evade tax. Tax avoidance involves the use of legal methods in order to reduce the amount of tax payable.

The GAAR is intended to counteract tax advantages, obtained via what would otherwise be legal tax avoidance methods, where the arrangements can be considered to be abusive.

Why the GAAR is likely to apply to the plan drawn up by Bryce and his daughter

– the tax advantage obtained would be a tax deduction in excess of the cost of the machinery

– the tax arrangements would be the formation of the subsidiary and the series of leasing contracts which are intended to obtain the tax advantage

– the arrangements are likely to be regarded as abusive because they appear to have been designed to give rise to additional tax deductions rather than for genuine commercial reasons.

Examiner's report

This question required advice on the corporation tax consequences of disposing of a wholly-owned subsidiary company by either selling all of the shares, or, alternatively, selling the trade and assets, together with the value added tax (VAT) implications if the sale of trade and assets route is chosen. There was also an ethics requirement to discuss tax evasion, tax avoidance and the purpose of the general anti-abuse rule (GAAR), and its application to a proposed plan to claim extensive capital allowances. The sale of shares versus sale of trade and assets decision is one which is regularly tested, so a well-prepared candidate should have been familiar with the main issues which they needed to discuss. Additionally, there are significant differences, practically and commercially, between selling shares in a company, and selling its trade and assets, which are reflected in the approach taken for tax purposes. If candidates are not familiar with a scenario, they should take time to think about the reality of the situation, which will often give them pointers as to the tax treatment. More generally, many candidates need to spend more time ensuring they are familiar with key areas relating to chargeable gains for companies – the substantial shareholding exemption (SSE), calculation of indexation, conditions for rollover relief and chattel exemptions in particular.

The use of subheadings, taken from the issues in the manager's email, provides a useful structure in this type of question, which all candidates should consider adopting.

The first part of the question, which was worth 8 marks, required candidates to explain whether or not tax relief would be available for a loss on the sale of the shares, the implications of the subsidiary leaving the group with a building which had recently been transferred to it by another group member, and a calculation of the after-tax proceeds. It was disappointing to see that a significant number of candidates did not mention that the SSE applied in this case, and so wasted time describing reliefs for the capital loss which were not relevant. Awareness of SSE, and when it applies is fundamental at ATX. In any question concerning a corporate disposal of shares, the candidate's first thought should be to consider the application of SSE. There will be marks for considering this, and for demonstrating knowledge of the conditions, which will allow a decision to be made as to whether or not it applies. A few candidates did consider it, but concluded that it did not, or need not, apply where there is a loss, so, again wasted time with unnecessary calculations and discussion of reliefs.

The majority of candidates recognised that the company leaving the group with an asset that had been transferred to it within the last three years would give rise to a degrouping charge (and cited the six-year time limit), but only very few also recognised that there would also be stamp duty land tax implications. A small minority of candidates confused the implications of a share sale with those of a trade and asset sale, and so included calculations of the gains/losses on the individual assets in addition to, or instead of, the shares. This confusion then continued into the second part of the question, meaning that relatively few marks were available. As stated above, a few moments spent thinking about the reality of the different scenarios should have enabled a candidate to at least set off in the right direction.

The second part of the question concerned the disposal of the trade and assets of the company, as an alternative to the sale of shares. This part was worth 11 marks and, on the whole, was done better than the sale of shares, with the majority of candidates calculating a correct, or nearly correct, gain/loss on the two buildings, and, pleasingly, identifying the balancing charge on the machinery. The most common errors in this part were to treat the whole business as a single asset, and calculate just a single gain/loss by reference to the total costs and proceeds. It was also pleasing to see that most candidates did try and address all parts of this requirement, but in a significant number of cases were let down by their lack of detailed knowledge in relation to capital gains tax exemptions and reliefs, in this case the chattels exemptions (wasting chattels and £6,000 rule), and the precise requirements for rollover relief (movable plant and machinery doesn't qualify).

The third part of the question concerned charging VAT on the sale of the building and machinery if the company decides to sell the trade and assets. This was worth 7 marks. Most candidates picked up a few marks here in relation to the buildings, and consideration of their age and the option to tax. However, very few picked up a key issue, embedded in the facts of this scenario, that transferring the trade and assets would constitute the transfer of a going concern, such that the transaction would be outside the scope of VAT, apart from, potentially, the buildings. Candidates at ATX should not rely on always been prompted in relation to the issues being tested, with a direct reference to the issue. They are encouraged to spend a little time thinking about the reality of the situation, so as to be able to identify the aspect(s) of a tax which may be relevant.

The final part of the question required candidates to distinguish between tax evasion and tax avoidance, to state the purpose of the general anti-abuse rule (GAAR), and to explain its application to the plan proposed by the client. This was clearly an area candidates were prepared for, and was generally done very well, with most candidates scoring at least four of the five available marks. A few candidates produced an exceptionally long answer, and, while they probably scored full marks, these could also have been obtained with a much more concise answer, leaving more time for other parts of the exam. It may be tempting to write at length on a topic with which a candidate is very familiar, and confident, but attention should always be paid to the maximum number of marks available.

Overall, candidates who prepared satisfactory answers to this question:

- appeared to have practised similar questions
- read the requirements very carefully
- applied their knowledge well to the scenario
- produced concise explanations and clearly laid out computations.

ACCA marking scheme				Marks
(a)	(i)	Offer A		
		Calculation of post-tax proceeds		1.0
		Loss on the sale of the shares		3.0
		Leaving the Grand Ltd group		
		Degrouping charge		2.5
		Stamp duty land tax		3.5
				10.0
			Maximum	8.0
	(ii)	Offer B		
		Calculation of post-tax proceeds		1.5
		Oribi building chargeable gain		2.0
		Plant and machinery balancing charge		1.0
		Atuel building allowable loss		1.5
		Plant and machinery chargeable gains/allowable losses		4.0
		Capital gains group		2.0
				12.0
			Maximum	11.0
	(iii)	Transfer of a going concern		4.0
		Rules in relation to buildings		4.0
				8.0
			Maximum	7.0

(b)	Tax evasion, tax avoidance and the purpose of the GAAR	4.0
	Application to plan	3.0
		———
		7.0
	Maximum	5.0
	Problem solving	1.0
	Clarity of explanations and calculations	1.0
	Effectiveness of communication	1.0
	Overall presentation and style	1.0
		———
		4.0
		———
	Total	**35.0**
		———

77 PLAD LTD AND QUIL LTD (ADAPTED) *Walk in the footsteps of a top tutor*

Key answer tips

This question covers loss relief including group relief, capital allowances, VAT groups and ethics.

Each of the three requirements are independent of one another so you could attempt them in any order. The ethics requirement is one where some easy marks could be earned so it may be a good idea to start with that one first.

The sub requirements in part (a) follow on from one another so you need to ensure you finish the first before moving on to the second. Time management is important here to make sure you have enough time to attempt all parts. If you need to, make up an answer for the first requirement so you can then do the second which has some easier marks in!

The highlighted words in the written sections are key phrases that markers are looking for.

(a) Group relief

Tutor's top tips

You may find the calculation in this part of the question a little bit tricky. You can still score some easy marks by explaining the basis of what you are trying to do.

Remember that the liability in respect of the UK trading profit will not receive any DTR so this profit should be covered in full. For the overseas income the overseas tax rate is clearly lower than in the UK, so DTR will be for the overseas tax. You don't want to waste the DTR so you need an amount of group relief that will bring profits down to a level where the tax will equal that paid overseas.

(i)   **Maximum group relief**

- The whole of Plad Ltd's UK trading profit of £58,000 should be covered by group relief. However, in order not to waste double tax relief (DTR), an amount of Plad Ltd's Chekkan profits should remain subject to corporation tax.

- The amount of Chekkan profits which should remain subject to corporation tax is £5,158 (£7,000 × 14%/19%), being the amount on which the UK corporation tax (£5,158 × 19% = £980) equals the whole of the Chekkan tax paid by Plad Ltd (£7,000 × 14% = £980).

- In this situation, the Chekkan tax suffered will be fully relieved as DTR (being the lower of the UK tax on the Chekkan income and the Chekkan tax suffered).

- Accordingly, the group relief should be the UK profits of £58,000 plus the balance of the Chekkan profits of £1,842 (£7,000 – £5,158), i.e. £59,842. With group relief of this amount, Plad Ltd's UK corporation tax liability will be fully covered by DTR, such that there will be no UK corporation tax payable.

Tutorial note

The following calculation demonstrates that where the group relief is £59,842, as calculated above, none of the DTR will be wasted and the corporation tax liability will be zero.

	£	£
Taxable total profits before group relief		65,000
Group relief		(59,842)
Taxable total profits		5,158
Corporation tax at 19%		980
Double tax relief – the lower of:		
UK tax on overseas profits (£5,158 × 19%)	980	
Overseas tax (£7,000 × 14%)	980	
		(980)
Corporation tax liability		0

(ii)   **Corporation tax liabilities**

Tutor's top tips

You have two companies to calculate corporation tax for in this requirement, assuming losses are used as soon as possible. Quil Ltd is the loss making company so it would be useful to calculate its results first so you can see what the losses are. Remember that there are easy marks to be obtained for a simple capital allowances calculation.

Remember to reduce the loss by your group relief claim from part (i), it doesn't matter if this is wrong as you will get follow through marks!

The email from your manager mentions that the loss should be used as soon as possible, this means avoid carrying it forward where you can. Bear this in mind when you are using the loss.

Plad Ltd

Year ending 31 March 2023

The corporation tax liability of Plad Ltd for the first year will be £nil, as explained above.

Year ending 31 March 2024

	£
Taxable total profit pre group relief	65,000
Less: Group relief (W3)	(43,308)
	————
Taxable total profit	21,692
	————
Corporation tax at 19%	4,121
Less: DTR	
The lower of:	
UK tax on the Chekkan profits of £1,330 (£7,000 × 19%)	
Chekkan tax of £980	(980)
	————
Corporation tax liability	3,141
	————

Quil Ltd

	Year ending 31 March	
	2023	**2024**
	£	£
Trading profit/(loss) before capital allowances	(5,000)	162,000
Capital allowances (W1)	(267,000)	(900)
Structures and buildings allowances (W2)	(1,650)	(6,600)
	————	————
Trading loss	(273,650)	
	————	————
Trading profit	0	154,500
Chargeable gain	–	16,000
	————	————
	0	170,500
Loss brought forward (W3)	–	(170,500)
	————	————
Taxable total profit	0	0
	————	————
Corporation tax liability at 19%	0	0
	————	————

(iii)   Conclusion

Tutor's top tips

Here you just need to summarise your earlier findings. There are easy marks here so don't miss out on them!

Bring in your loss figures from the earlier parts of the question and don't forget to quantify the tax benefit.

- Where the two companies are in a group relief group (as opposed to being owned personally by Claire) trading losses of £103,150 (£59,842 + £43,308) would be relieved by group relief in the two-year period rather than being carried forward.

- At the least, this is advantageous from the point of view of cash flow, as it delays total tax payments of £19,599 (£103,150 × 19%).

- In addition, if group relief were not available, such that Quil Ltd had to carry forward unused losses, there is no certainty that the losses would ever be relieved.

Tutorial note

Quil Ltd is required to use its losses brought forward against its own total profits before it can surrender losses to Plad Ltd as group relief.

Workings

(W1) Capital allowances

	AIA	FYA	Special rate pool	Allowances
	£	£	£	£
Year ending 31 March 2023				
Additions qualifying for super deduction				
£40,000 × 130%		52,000		
Super deduction 130%		(52,000)		52,000
		―――		
		0		
Additions qualifying for AIA	230,000			
AIA	(200,000)			200,000
	―――	30,000		
First year allowance				
£30,000 × 50%		(15,000)		15,000
		―――	15,000	
				―――
				267,000
			―――	―――
TWDV carried forward			15,000	
Year ending 31 March 2024				
WDA at 6%			(900)	900
			―――	―――
TWDV carried forward			14,100	
			―――	

Tutorial note

The super deduction of 130% is available for plant and machinery purchased by companies between 1 April 2021 and 31 March 2023 that would ordinarily go into the main pool (except cars and second-hand assets).

50% FYA is available to special rate pool additions purchased between the same dates. AIA would also be available and should be claimed first, with the balance attracting 50% FYA.

No WDA is available on the balance until the following accounting period.

(W2) Structures and buildings allowances

Year ending 31 March 2023

(£600,000 – £230,000 – £150,000) = £220,000 × 3% × 3/12 = £1,650

Year ending 31 March 2024

£220,000 × 3% = £6,600

(W3) Quil Ltd – loss memorandum

	Year ending 31 March	
	2023	**2024**
	£	£
Trading loss brought forward	0	213,808
Trading loss for the current year	273,650	
Offset against total profits of Quil Ltd	0	(170,500)
Surrender to Plad Ltd	(59,842)	(43,308)
Trading loss carried forward	213,808	0

(b) Group registration for value added tax (VAT) purposes

Tutor's top tips

When you read the schedule from Claire you will see that she already knows some of the implications of being in a VAT group. When you are drafting your answer ensure you do not cover any of these as you will not score any marks for that.

You need to focus on any aspects that Claire is not aware of.

Two companies can register as a group for the purposes of VAT provided they are established in the UK and one controls the other or they are both controlled by the same person. Accordingly, Plad Ltd and Quil Ltd will be able to register as a group regardless of whether Plad Ltd owns Quil Ltd or they are both owned personally by Claire.

Claire should be aware that the annual accounting scheme will not be available if the two companies are registered as a group.

Tutorial note

If Claire was a sole trader then she would be able to join to VAT group as well, as she is the controller of a group of companies.

(c)   Plad Ltd – unreported chargeable gain

Tutor's top tips

There is always an ethics requirement in Section A for five marks and they can often be the easiest marks to achieve, so ensure you have left adequate time for this.

Ensure you cover both the implications for Plad Ltd and your firm, as requested in the email from your manager. They also noted that you shouldn't address any money laundering requirements or penalties so make sure you don't waste time discussing these.

Plad Ltd

- The company has a responsibility to report this omission to HM Revenue and Customs (HMRC) and to pay the outstanding corporation tax. It will be committing tax evasion, a criminal offence, if it fails to do so.
- HMRC will charge Plad Ltd interest on any tax which becomes payable.

Our firm

- We should investigate how this error arose and consider whether or not there are likely to be further errors.
- We will not retain a client which is engaged in deliberate tax evasion, as this poses a threat to the fundamental principles of integrity and professional behaviour. Accordingly, we could not continue to act for Plad Ltd unless the chargeable gain is disclosed to HMRC.
- If we were to cease to act for Plad Ltd, we would notify HMRC, although we would not provide them with any reason for our action.

Examiner's report

This question was split into three distinct parts looking at corporation tax, value added tax (VAT) and ethics respectively.

The first part of the question asked candidates to explain, with supporting calculations, the maximum amount of group relief which could be transferred between two group companies, whilst preserving double tax relief in the recipient company. A number of candidates were able to produce the calculations but did not offer any explanation, thereby not achieving full marks. As previously mentioned, future candidates should focus on the 'command' words in the requirement to ensure they are answering all parts of the requirement.

Note that the next section of the question has been amended since it was originally set, to test structures and buildings allowances and enhanced capital allowances.

The next element in this part of the question required candidates to calculate the corporation tax liabilities of two group companies assuming the available trading loss was used as soon as possible. Most candidates answered well in respect of the capital allowances part of this question but performed less well at group relieving the loss, where many candidates appeared to lack a clear understanding of the technical rules. To succeed in the ATX-UK exam, both a detailed knowledge of the technical areas of the syllabus is required as well as the ability to apply that knowledge to a given scenario.

Many candidates were able to conclude correctly on the advantage of a particular group holding structure.

The second part of the question required candidates to advise on matters the client should be aware of in relation to group registration for VAT purposes. The client was already aware of certain issues stated in the question but needed advice on additional issues. A large number of candidates simply repeated the issues already stated in the question and were unable to discuss any additional matters, which was not an effective use of time and earned no marks.

The final part of the question concerned the ethical issues arising from an unreported chargeable gain. It was pleasing to see most candidates answering well on this issue. However, the requirement specifically asked candidates not to address money laundering or penalties and yet many candidates went on to discuss these matters, which again, was not an effective use of their valuable time and earned them no marks. Once again these candidates would have benefitted from spending time ensuring they fully understood the requirement and planning their answer, before beginning to write.

	ACCA marking scheme		
			Marks
(a)	Tax-efficient group relief		5.0
	Plad Ltd corporation tax liabilities		
	Year ending 31 March 2023		1.0
	Year ending 31 March 2024		3.5
	Quil Ltd corporation tax liabilities		
	Capital allowances		4.0
	Structures and buildings allowances		1.5
	Two years ending 31 March 2024		3.5
	Conclusion		2.0
			20.5
		Maximum	17.0
(b)	Conditions for group registration		2.0
	Annual accounting scheme		1.0
			3.0
(c)	Plad Ltd		2.5
	Our firm		4.0
			6.5
		Maximum	5.0
Total			**25.0**

78 KITZ LTD

Key answer tips

This corporation tax focused section B question looks at degrouping charges, transfer pricing and intangible fixed assets.

In part (a) you are asked to explain the chargeable gains implications arising from a sale of shares. You are told that an asset has been transferred to the company being sold several years ago, so should consider the possibility of a degrouping charge. Note that the question states no calculations are needed so ensure you don't waste time preparing any.

Part (b) asks for the corporation tax implications of a loan from both the perspective of the lender and the borrower – make sure you cover both to score well. You're told about how much the borrower was offered by a bank and at what interest rate, think about why you're being told this. Could there be transfer pricing issues?

The final part of the question looks at intangible fixed assets and the associated rollover relief. Here you need to think about the information from other parts of the question- remember what Feld Ltd was going to use the loan for. You should always be prepared to join information together from different parts of the question, it won't always be kept in discrete parts.

(a) **Chargeable gains implications for Kitz Ltd arising from the sale of the shares in Mayr Ltd on 1 July 2022**

The sale of the 75% shareholding in Mayr Ltd on 1 July 2022 will be exempt from corporation tax under the substantial shareholding exemption (SSE). This is because Kitz Ltd owned more than 10% of the shares in Mayr Ltd for a continuous 12-month period out of the six years prior to sale, and Mayr Ltd is a trading company.

The sale of the warehouse to Mayr Ltd on 8 April 2017 was originally a no gain no loss transfer, because Kitz Ltd and Mayr Ltd were in a capital gains group, as Kitz Ltd owned 75% of Mayr Ltd. As Mayr Ltd left the group within six years of this transfer, still owning the warehouse, a degrouping charge will arise. This is added to the consideration received by Kitz Ltd on the sale of the Mayr Ltd shares. However, the SSE, which applies to sale of the shares, will also apply to the degrouping charge, such that this will also be exempt.

(b) **Corporation tax implications of the interest charged on the loan by Kitz Ltd to Feld Ltd for the year ending 31 March 2024**

Tutorial note

There are clues in the question that transfer pricing could be applicable here. Though this is often tested involving an overseas company the rules can still apply to transactions between two UK companies, as is the case here.

Feld Ltd has been offered an interest rate of 10% per annum from a bank (which is an unrelated party), so this would appear to be an arm's length rate of interest.

As Kitz Ltd controls Feld Ltd, they are connected companies for the purpose of transfer pricing. No exemption is available as the companies are not small or medium-sized enterprises (SMEs).

As the interest receivable by Kitz Ltd is 7% per annum, i.e. lower than the arm's length rate, Kitz Ltd must make a transfer pricing adjustment, and include interest receivable in its corporation tax computation calculated at the rate of 10%. This will be an addition of £13,500 (£450,000 × (10% − 7%)) for the year ending 31 March 2024. Interest receivable of £45,000 (£450,000 × 10%) will be included as non-trading loan relationship (NTLR) income.

As Feld Ltd is also within the charge to UK corporation tax, it can make a claim to amend its computation to an arm's length basis, and deduct a total of £45,000 in respect of the interest payable on the loan.

The interest payable in respect of the proportion of the loan used to acquire assets for use in Feld Ltd's business will be deducted from trading income; the interest payable in respect of the proportion of the loan used to acquire shares in Durn Ltd will be deducted from NTLR income.

Accordingly, for the year ending 31 March 2024, £20,500 (£45,000 × 205/450) is deductible from Feld Ltd's trading income of £587,000, and £24,500 (£45,000 × 245/450) is deductible from its NTLR income of £48,100.

(c) **(i)** **Corporation tax implications for Kitz Ltd of the sale of the patent to Durn Ltd**

Durn Ltd will not be in a capital gains group with Kitz Ltd and Feld Ltd, as Feld Ltd will not have the minimum 75% holding in Durn Ltd which is required for this. Accordingly, the sale of the patent, which is an intangible asset, will give rise to a trading profit for Kitz Ltd, equal to the excess of the sale proceeds over the tax written down value of the patent at the date of sale. The profit on sale of the patent will therefore be £42,000 (£72,000 − £30,000). This will be included in Kitz Ltd's taxable trading profit for the year ending 31 March 2024.

(ii) **Impact on Kitz Ltd's corporation tax liability for the year ending 31 March 2024 if the maximum rollover relief claim is made**

As Feld Ltd is a UK resident, wholly owned subsidiary of Kitz Ltd, the two companies are in a capital gains group.

Feld Ltd will acquire an intangible fixed asset (goodwill of an unincorporated business) on 1 April 2023, which is within the 12 months prior to the sale of the patent by Kitz Ltd.

Accordingly, rollover relief will be available for part of the profit on the sale of the patent to be deferred against the cost of the goodwill. As the cost of the goodwill is less than the sale proceeds for the patent, the maximum profit which can be deferred is restricted to the excess of the amount invested in the goodwill over the original cost of the patent.

Therefore, the maximum profit which can be deferred is £8,000 (£68,000 − £60,000).

This would lead to a reduction in Kitz Ltd's corporation tax liability of £1,520 (£8,000 × 19%).

Tutorial note

Where intangibles rollover relief is claimed a gain should be left chargeable equal to the proceeds not reinvested (£72,000 – £68,000 = £4,000) plus any amortisation claimed on the old asset (£60,000 – £30,000 = £30,000).

Examiner's report

This question was in three main parts, dealing with a company selling shares in a subsidiary, transfer pricing and the sale of an intangible fixed asset.

The first part of the question asked for an explanation of the implications of a sale of shares in a subsidiary and many candidates were able to identify the availability of the substantial shareholding exemption and the associated conditions for this exemption. However, a substantial number of candidates missed the further point regarding a degrouping charge arising, despite clues in the question pointing towards this. Candidates should practise as many questions as they can before sitting the ATX-UK exam so that they become accustomed to picking up relevant information given in exam questions.

This question part specifically asked for no calculations and yet a significant number of candidates gave calculations. Even if candidates' workings were correct, there were no marks awarded for calculations when they have been specifically asked not to provide them. Once again, the candidates are wasting their limited exam time and earning no marks. Candidates should read the requirement carefully and only answer what is being asked for.

The second part of the question dealt with the transfer pricing consequences for two group companies making an intra-group loan at an interest rate below market rate. This part of the question was generally very poorly answered. Many candidates were not aware of the most basic elements of the transfer pricing rules and very few could apply the rules to the facts of the question. The ATX-UK exams will seek to examine all areas of the syllabus and candidates need to have a solid understanding of all aspects of the syllabus.

The third part of the question dealt with the sale of an intangible fixed asset (IFA) and subsequent rollover relief. It was clear that very few candidates understood the detailed IFA rules and even less understood the IFA rollover relief and this part of the question was very poorly answered. Once again, candidates should be aware that any part of the syllabus can be tested and given that all questions are compulsory, candidates should aim to be prepared to answer questions on any topic.

	ACCA marking scheme		
			Marks
(a)	Availability of substantial shareholding exemption		3.0
	Implications re degrouping charge		4.0
			7.0
		Maximum	6.0
(b)	Implications for Kitz Ltd		4.0
	Implications for Feld Ltd		3.5
			7.5
		Maximum	7.0
(c) (i)	Implications of the sale of the patent		2.5
	Calculation of trading profit		1.0
			3.5
		Maximum	3.0
(ii)	Reason for availability of rollover relief		2.0
	Maximum rollover relief available		2.5
	Calculation of reduction in corporation tax liability		0.5
			5.0
		Maximum	4.0
Total			20.0

79 MITA *Walk in the footsteps of a top tutor*

Key answer tips

This question covers capital gains tax reliefs, R&D, intangibles, consortium relief, VAT and overseas aspects of corporation tax. Most of these are new areas at ATX so it should not be a surprise to see these tested.

The first part of the question looks at capital gains tax reliefs. These are commonly tested but the examining team continue to comment on the fact that candidates don't seem to know them well enough. Make sure you spend some time going over these.

Part (b) covers various areas of corporation tax and VAT. Make sure you give yourself enough time to have a go at each of the areas so you can pick up some of the easier marks.

The final part of the question focuses on the overseas aspects of corporation tax. This is a new area at ATX, so you should be prepared for this to be tested. Make sure you are happy with the consequences of the permanent establishment (PE) exemption. This is often tested when PEs come up!

The highlighted words in the written sections are key phrases that markers are looking for in your answer.

(a) **Sale of 4,000 shares in Porth Ltd on 1 May 2023**

Mita – capital gains tax (CGT) liability

	£	£
Proceeds at market value		260,000
Less: Cost		
Market value of assets sold to Porth Ltd	120,000	
Less: Incorporation relief	(37,400)	
	———	
	82,600	
	———	
£82,600 × 4,000/10,000		(33,040)
		———
		226,960
Less: Gift holdover relief (balancing figure)		(60,000)
		———
Gain chargeable (£200,000 – £33,040)		166,960
		———
CGT at 10% (business asset disposal relief)		16,696
		———

Tutor's top tips

Capital gains tax reliefs are commonly tested in ATX so ensure you know the qualifying conditions for each relief as well as how they operate, so you can answer questions like the one above.

(b) **Quod Ltd**

Tax deduction available in respect of the scientific research costs

Tutor's top tips

Research and development expenditure is one of the new topics tested at ATX and is commonly examined. Ensure you are comfortable with how the relief works depending on the size of the company, and also depending on the nature of the expenditure.

– The equipment and computer hardware will qualify for a 100% capital allowance as capital expenditure incurred for the purpose of research and development.

Accordingly, the total cost incurred of £102,000 will be deductible for the purposes of corporation tax.

– As Quod Ltd will be a small enterprise for research and development purposes, certain categories of revenue expenditure which are directly related to research and development activities will qualify for an additional 130% deduction when calculating the company's taxable trading income.

This additional deduction is not available in respect of the capital expenditure or the rental costs.

Only 65% of amounts paid to external contractors qualify for this additional deduction.

– Tax deduction available:

	£	£
Total research costs	102,000	102,000
Less:		
Equipment and computer hardware (capital)	(27,500)	
Rent	(17,400)	
Staff costs (£7,000 × 35% (100% – 65%))	(2,450)	
Amount qualifying for additional deduction	54,650	
Additional deduction (£54,650 × 130%)		71,045
Tax deduction available		173,045

Tutorial note

The equipment and computer hardware will not be eligible for the super deduction since it is acquired after 31 March 2023.

Tax treatment of the purchase of the Cloque brand

– The amount of £1,000 charged to the statement of profit or loss in respect of this expenditure would be allowable for the purposes of calculating taxable trading profit.

– Alternatively, for the purpose of calculating the company's taxable trading profit, Quod Ltd could elect to write off £1,400 (£35,000 × 4%) per year, which would clearly be beneficial.

Amended tax adjusted trading loss for the year ending 31 March 2024

	£
Budgeted tax adjusted trading loss	(44,000)
Additional deduction in respect of research costs	(71,045)
Amortisation of Cloque brand (£1,400 (£35,000 × 4%) – £1,000)	(400)
Amended tax adjusted trading loss	(115,445)

Amount of trading loss available for use by Porth Ltd

–   Porth Ltd will not be able to use the trading loss of Quod Ltd unless Quod Ltd is a consortium company. Quod Ltd will be a consortium company if at least 75% of its ordinary share capital is owned by companies, each of which own at least 5% but less than 75%.

–   Accordingly, for consortium relief to be available, BJB Ltd must own the 30% holding rather than Mr Berm.

–   The maximum amount which could be surrendered to Porth Ltd as consortium relief is £69,267 (£115,445 × 60%), reflecting Porth Ltd's holding of 60% of the ordinary share capital of Quod Ltd.

Value added tax (VAT) implications of purchasing advice from the overseas supplier

Tutor's top tips

When dealing with VAT on services it is important to ascertain whether the transaction is between two businesses (B2B) or between a business and a consumer (B2C). Make sure you clearly state which type of transaction you are dealing with and what the VAT treatment would be for the relevant party you are asked about.

–   The provision of this advice will be a business to business (B2B) service. It will be treated as supplied in the UK, because that is where Quod Ltd is established.

–   Quod Ltd will be required to pay VAT at the UK standard rate of 20% to HM Revenue and Customs (HMRC) under the 'reverse charge' principle. The rate of VAT in the overseas country is irrelevant.

–   The input VAT can be reclaimed on this expense in the same way as any other input tax incurred by the company.

–   Accordingly, Quod Ltd's VAT position will be the same as if the services had been purchased from the UK supplier.

(c)   Ryb Ltd

UK corporation tax on the profits of Ryb Ltd

Ryb Ltd is subject to UK corporation tax on the profits of its permanent establishment (PE) in Tirona because a PE is not a separate legal entity and UK resident companies are subject to corporation tax on their worldwide income.

	£
UK corporation tax (£75,000 × 19%)	14,250
Less: Unilateral double tax relief (£75,000 × 14%)	(10,500)
	———
UK corporation tax liability	3,750
	———

Election to exempt the profits of the PE from UK tax

– The advantage of making such an election would be that the profits made in Tirona would not be subject to UK corporation tax.

Based on the current rates of corporation tax in the two countries, this would save corporation tax at the rate of 5% (19% – 14%).

– However, it should be recognised that there would be no relief in the UK in the event of any losses being incurred in the trade in Tirona in the future.

– Once made, the election is irrevocable and would apply to all future overseas permanent establishments of Ryb Ltd.

Accordingly, there would be no relief in the UK for any losses incurred in any new overseas trades operated by Ryb Ltd.

Tutor's top tips

The question mentioned plans to create more PEs in other countries. This was a clue to discuss the fact that the PE exemption would apply to future PEs as well. Make sure you consider all information given in the question and think about why you have been given it.

Examiner's report

This question concerned an individual's sale of shares in a recently incorporated company, various corporation tax issues in relation to a newly set up joint venture company, and the acquisition of a new subsidiary company which trades wholly through an overseas permanent establishment. Overall, this question was not done well, which was surprising.

The first part of the question required candidates to calculate the CGT payable on the sale of shares in a newly incorporated company, in respect of which incorporation relief had been claimed. Despite the requirement being only to calculate the liability, a significant number of candidates also included explanations, which did not score marks. This was particularly noticeable among those candidates who sat computer-based exams (CBE). Many included calculations in the spreadsheet, then explained the calculations in the word processing document, which was totally unnecessary, and just wasted time. The majority of candidates omitted to deal with the previously claimed incorporation relief, despite it being clearly flagged up in the question. It was also disappointing that many candidates did not include gift holdover relief, or business asset disposal relief, both of which were relevant here. The different reliefs available to reduce, eliminate or defer capital gains are very frequently examined at ATX, and are regarded by the examining team as an extremely important part of the syllabus. It is therefore strongly recommended that candidates take time within their revision to ensure that they are familiar with the conditions required for the different reliefs, and then, precisely how they operate.

Going forward, candidates would be well advised to ensure that they practise a wide variety of questions involving capital gains tax reliefs, to improve their knowledge and application of these.

The second part of the question was worth 15 marks and comprised five tasks. In the first two tasks relating to the explanation of the tax treatment of research and development expenditure incurred by a small enterprise, and the acquisition of an intangible asset, many candidates displayed a surprising lack of technical knowledge, despite both being frequently tested areas. Fortunately, many were able to gain follow through marks in their calculation of the effect of these on the company's budgeted trading loss for the period. It was good to see that a majority of candidates recognised that the lossmaking company would be a consortium company such that proportionate loss relief would be available to the parent company. Finally, in this part, the fifth task, relating to application of the reverse charge principle in respect of services received by a UK company from an overseas company again demonstrated a lack of knowledge, or of understanding of this process by very many candidates.

The final part of the question was essentially a classic textbook question requiring discussion of the advantages and disadvantages of making an election to exempt the profits of an overseas PE from UK corporation tax. Most candidates were able to list two or three of these, but very few got all four. However, the first part of this requirement, requiring candidates to state why the company in question was liable to corporation tax in the UK (all its profits were generated in the PE overseas), elicited some intriguing answers. The company was clearly stated as being UK resident, and the overseas PE as being just that i.e. not a subsidiary, yet a significant minority of candidates thought the company was a controlled foreign company (CFC), which was clearly incorrect, and then went on to waste time talking about the exemptions. A good number of others thought that the company would be liable to UK tax because its parent company was UK resident. Clearly there appeared to be significant misunderstanding of these overseas issues. Questions have been frequently set on corporate overseas issues in the past, and candidates would be well advised to practise a broad range of these.

ACCA marking scheme			Marks
(a)	Chargeable gain		2.0
	Gift holdover relief		1.5
	Capital gains tax		1.0
			4.5
		Maximum	4.0
(b)	Research costs		
	Notes		4.5
	Calculation		1.5
	Amortisation of brand		2.0
	Calculation of available loss		3.0
	Consortium relief		4.0
	Value added tax		3.0
			18.0
		Maximum	15.0
(c)	UK corporation tax liability		3.0
	Effect of making election		4.5
			7.5
		Maximum	6.0
Total			**25.0**

80   REP LTD *Walk in the footsteps of a top tutor*

Key answer tips

This question covers ethics, establishing a company with overseas activities, controlled foreign companies, VAT on land and buildings and IHT on lifetime gifts. There is a lot to cover, so it is important that you allocate your time carefully between the different requirements to ensure that you don't run out of time.

The first part on ethics covers whether the firm is able to use knowledge acquired from working with other clients to assist this client. The key principle to identify here was confidentiality! Ethics will always offer some easy marks and this topic is tested on a reasonably regular basis.

Part (b) covers three main areas to do with establishing the new company. Part (i) requires explanations on corporate residency. Make sure you follow a logical approach covering UK residency issues and overseas residency issues separately. Part (ii) asks for a list of the implications of making an election to exempt profits of an overseas permanent establishment. This is a frequently examined topic and should provide easy marks. Finally, part (iii) requires an explanation of the purpose of the CFC rules and the CFC charge that can arise. Make sure that you only mention the relevant points and don't waste your time covering the CFC exemptions as this is not part of the requirement and will not score any marks. You need to manage your time efficiently, so that you have enough time to answer all three sub requirements.

You are also asked for explanations in part (c) about whether the input VAT suffered on the purchase of an investment property can be recovered. VAT on land and buildings is a common exam topic and should provide some easy marks. Make sure you remember to cover all of the basic points to score maximum marks.

Part (d) requires the calculation of lifetime inheritance tax on a gift into a trust. Make sure you set out your calculations in a clearly labelled pro forma. There are other lifetime gifts in the question but don't waste your time with any unnecessary calculations; the question asks for the lifetime IHT on just one of the gifts!

The highlighted words in the written sections are key phrases that markers are looking for in your answer.

Notes for meeting

Client REP LTD and Lamar

Purpose **Discussion of corporate and personal matters**

Prepared by **Tax senior**

Date **8 September 2022**

(a) **Knowledge obtained from advising other clients**

– We have experience of advising clients trading from permanent establishments situated overseas.

– We have also advised on trading in the country of Garia.

– We will be able to use this general experience and expertise for the benefit of REP Ltd.

– However, we must not use any confidential information obtained as a result of our professional and business relationships for the benefit of REP Ltd (or any other client).

– Confidentiality is one of the fundamental principles of ethics within ACCA's Code of Ethics and Conduct.

– This principle of confidentiality applies to confidential information obtained in respect of both ex-clients and continuing clients.

Tutorial note

Candidates who mentioned the fundamental principle of professional competence and due care were also awarded credit

(b) **Investment in JAY Ltd**

(i) **Residency of JAY Ltd**

Taxation of profits

The profits of the business will be generated in Garia regardless of where JAY Ltd is resident.

Accordingly, the profits will always be subject to business tax at 13% in Garia.

Tutorial note

Companies suffer tax on their worldwide profits in the country in which they are resident, therefore if JAY Ltd is resident in Garia it will suffer Garian tax on the profits.

Profits of overseas permanent establishments are taxed in the country in which they are located. If JAY Ltd is not resident in Garia it will still have an overseas permanent establishment in Garia.

So either way Garian tax of 13% will be suffered on the profits.

If JAY Ltd is resident in the UK

The profits would be subject to UK corporation tax because the permanent establishment (PE) in Garia is not a separate legal entity and UK resident companies are subject to corporation tax on their worldwide profits.

However, double tax relief would be available in the UK: the amount payable in the UK would be 6% (19% – 13%) of the profits, as set out below:

	£
UK corporation tax (£135,000 × 19%)	25,650
Less: Double tax relief (£135,000 × 13%)	(17,550)
UK corporation tax payable	8,100

Tutorial note

Double tax relief is available at the lower of UK corporation tax due (£25,650) and overseas tax suffered (£17,550)

If JAY Ltd is resident in Garia

The profits will only be subject to tax in Garia at the rate of 13%, as noted above.

JAY Ltd would not have a UK corporation tax liability in respect of these profits.

Any dividends received by REP Ltd and CRO Ltd from JAY Ltd would be exempt from corporation tax.

Relief available in respect of trading loss

If JAY Ltd is resident in the UK

If REP Ltd owns 30% of JAY Ltd:

- JAY Ltd would be a consortium company because at least 75% of JAY Ltd would be owned by companies, each of which own at least 5%, and less than 75%, of the company.
- In these circumstances, REP Ltd would be able to offset up to 30% of JAY Ltd's trading loss against its taxable total profits.

Tutorial note

A consortium exists where two or more companies each own at least 5%, collectively own at least 75% but do not individually own at least 75% of the shares in a UK resident company.

Consortium relief allows the surrender of trading losses between the consortium company and the consortium members.

Where the loss is in the consortium company, the members (such as REP Ltd) can claim their proportionate ownership of the loss; so here REP Ltd can claim a maximum of 30% of the trading loss (restricted to the TTP in REP Ltd).

If REP Ltd owns 20% of JAY Ltd:

– No relief would be available to REP Ltd in respect of any trading loss of JAY Ltd because CRO Ltd would own more than 75% of JAY Ltd.

Tutorial note

There would be no consortium relief available if REP Ltd were to only own 20%. This is because CRO Ltd would own 80%, which is at least 75%, and therefore a normal 75% loss relief group would exist between JAY Ltd and CRO Ltd, which REP Ltd would not be part of.

If JAY Ltd is resident in Garia

No relief would be available in the UK for REP Ltd in respect of any trading losses realised by JAY Ltd in Garia.

Tutorial note

Consortium relief and group relief are only available between UK resident companies.

(ii)   **Election to exempt the profits of JAY Ltd's overseas PE from UK tax**

This election is available to UK resident companies which generate profits from PEs situated overseas. If JAY Ltd were to make this election:

– its profits in Garia would no longer be subject to corporation tax in the UK. If no election is made, UK corporation tax would be payable on the profits in Garia at the rate of 6% (19% – 13%) after double tax relief

– no relief would be available in the UK in respect of any losses generated by the activities in Garia

– it would be irrevocable

– it would apply to all future overseas PEs of JAY Ltd.

Tutorial note

The election to exempt the profits from overseas permanent establishments of UK resident companies is a blanket election. It therefore applies to all of a company's overseas permanent establishments that exist at the date of making the election and all of its overseas permanent establishments that may exist in the future.

(iii)   Controlled foreign company (CFC) rules

The UK tax system charges corporation tax on the worldwide profits of UK resident companies. However, it does not charge corporation tax on the profits earned overseas by a non-UK resident company.

A UK resident company could seek to exploit the latter rule by establishing a non-UK resident subsidiary in which to generate its overseas profits. The CFC legislation is designed to prevent overseas subsidiaries being used to avoid tax in this way.

Where the rules apply (and no exemption is available), UK resident companies owning at least 25% of a CFC are charged UK corporation tax on their proportionate share of the CFC's chargeable profits.

(c)   Purchase of investment property

When REP Ltd grants a lease of the building to a tenant, it will be making an exempt supply.

REP Ltd will not be able to recover any value added tax (VAT) in relation to the purchase of the building unless it makes an election opting to tax it.

Opting to tax the building would have the following additional implications:

–   REP Ltd would be required to charge VAT on the monthly rental payments due from the tenant.

This will not be a problem where the tenant is able to recover all of the VAT charged. However, any irrecoverable VAT will represent an additional cost to a potential tenant.

–   Apart from an initial cooling-off period of six months, an option to tax a building cannot be withdrawn until 20 years have elapsed.

–   Whilst the option to tax remains in place, REP Ltd would be required to charge VAT on a sale of the building.

Tutorial note

The sale of a new (less than three years old) commercial building is standard-rated for VAT. REP Ltd will therefore suffer input tax on the purchase price.

The input tax is only recoverable if REP Ltd uses the building to make taxable supplies. It is worth noting here that the capital goods scheme would not apply as the building did not cost at least £250,000 exclusive of VAT – the question also makes it clear that it does not apply!

Leasing of land and buildings is exempt from VAT unless the building is opted to tax. If the building is opted, then VAT must be charged on all future supplies of the building – including leasing and the eventual sale (if within 20 years). Leasing then becomes a taxable supply, therefore the input tax suffered on the purchase would be recoverable.

(d) **Proposed gift of shares to trust on 1 November 2022**

Inheritance tax (IHT) payable

	£	£	£
Transfer of value (W)			900,000
Less: Annual exemptions 2022/23 and 2021/22 (used by PET on 1 July 2022)			0
Chargeable amount			900,000
Nil rate band at gift		325,000	
Less: Gross chargeable transfers (CLTS only) in 7 years pre gift (1.11.2015 – 1.11.2022)			
CLT 1 May 2018	170,000		
Less: Annual exemption 2018/19	(3,000)		
2017/18 (used by PET on 1 February 2018)	0		
		(167,000)	
			(158,000)
Taxable amount			742,000
IHT payable (£742,000 × 25%)			185,500

Working: Transfer of value

	£
Value of shares held prior to the gift: (80,000 × £24 (80%))	1,920,000
Value of shares held after the gift: (60,000 × £17 (60%))	(1,020,000)
Transfer of value	900,000

Tutorial note

1   *Annual exemptions are allocated to lifetime gifts in a strict chronological order:*

CLT 1 August 2012   *uses the annual exemptions for 2012/13 and 2011/12*

PET 1 February 2018 *uses the annual exemptions for 2017/18 and 2016/17*

CLT 1 May 2018   *uses the annual exemption for 2018/19; the annual exemption for 2017/18 has already been used by the PET on 1 February 2018*

PET July 2022   *uses the annual exemptions for 2022/23 and 2021/22*

> 2 When calculating the lifetime tax on a CLT the nil rate band in force at the date of the gift is used, less the gross chargeable value of any CLTs that fall within the seven years prior to the date of the gift (PETS are ignored in nil rate band calculations for lifetime tax).
>
> 3 The rate of IHT use for lifetime gifts depends on who is paying the tax.
>
> If the donor pays, the rate is 25%.
>
> If the trustees pay, the rate is 20%.

Examiner's report

This question related to a corporate client which required advice on various aspects of establishing a new company which will operate wholly overseas, the value added tax (VAT) implications of purchasing and leasing a new commercial building, and the inheritance tax (IHT) implications of a proposed gift by the managing director into a discretionary trust.

Candidates should note that the requirements for this question were clearly set out, using a series of subheadings, and the use of these subheadings in their answer, provides a useful structure in this type of question, which all candidates should consider adopting.

Part (a) focused on the firm's ability to use knowledge which it has gained from working with other clients to assist this company.

The majority of candidates were able to recognise the ethical principles concerned here and apply them correctly to this scenario. Answers to this part were generally good.

Part (b) comprised three parts, each relating to specific aspects of establishing the new company.

Candidates who scored well on this question part showed evidence of having carefully read each of the requirements and spent time thinking and planning their answer, which was then well structured and easy to follow. All candidates would be advised to do this in a question part like this, which was worth a significant proportion of the marks (15 marks), to demonstrate a well thought out and professional approach

Part (b)(i) required candidates to consider the different UK tax implications of the new company being UK resident (and therefore operating through a permanent establishment overseas), or alternatively being an overseas resident company.

Additionally, candidates had to consider the loss relief which would be available to the UK investing company in each of these situations.

High scoring candidates adopted a logical approach to discussing the general UK tax implications of the new company being UK resident, or overseas resident, and then going on to address the relief available for trading losses in each of those situations.

Use of several subheadings served to break up the information and make it easier for the reader to follow. Weaker answers tended to be more jumbled, so it was sometimes difficult to grasp which particular situation a candidate was talking about.

Part (b)(ii) required an explanation of the implications of making an election to exempt the profits of the overseas permanent establishment from UK tax.

Answers to this part tended to polarise; some candidates were obviously very familiar with this area and appeared to easily score full marks. Others unfortunately didn't seem to be prepared for this and so were able to make no, or very little attempt at this part. Overseas aspects of taxation are very frequently tested areas in relation to both companies and individuals, and candidates would be well advised to spend time learning and practising these rules in quite some detail.

Part (b)(iii) related to controlled foreign company (CFC) legislation. The client specifically wanted an explanation of the purpose of the CFC rules, and the charge which can be levied under them.

A majority of candidates were able to identify that the CFC rules comprise anti avoidance legislation to prevent overseas subsidiaries being used to avoid UK taxation on profits earned by the company. However, a great many then went on to detail the exemptions from CFC status – which they were able to reproduce quite precisely – but were not relevant to what the client wanted to know. This wasted valuable time, for no marks. Candidates are once again reminded of the need to read the requirements very carefully, and to confine their answers to what is specifically being asked for in this particular question – which may not be the same as a past question which they have recently practised.

Part (c) concerned the recovery of input VAT in respect of the purchase of a commercial building which is to be immediately leased to a trader.

Most candidates discussed the relevance of the option to tax the building in order to recover the input VAT, but relatively few referred to this being necessary on the grant of the lease, which would otherwise be an exempt supply. A minority of candidates confined their answers to this aspect of the requirement only, and did not fully address the requirement in the manager's email to explain more generally matters which the client should be aware of, which included the ramifications of opting to tax the building for both the company and the tenants of the building.

Part (d) required a calculation of the immediate IHT payable by the managing director on a proposed gift of shares into a discretionary trust.

On the whole, this question part was done well. Many candidates recognised the need for application of the diminution in value approach and performed this correctly. The main issue was confusion over which of the previous lifetime gifts – which included both chargeable lifetime transfers (CLTs) and potentially exempt transfers (PETs) – to take into account in calculating the remaining nil rate band available to set against this lifetime gift. This is a fundamental concept, which is tested at TX-UK, but ATX-UK candidates must revise the rules and ensure they are confident with the principle of accumulation in calculating IHT payable on CLTs in lifetime, as well as IHT payable as a result of the donor's death. A few candidates spent a considerable amount of time producing a table of all the lifetime gifts, deducting annual exemptions where appropriate. Such an approach is unlikely to be required in ATX UK. Candidates are advised to carefully read and think about requirements such as this to ensure that they focus on the relevant gifts which need to be considered, and not just take a blanket approach, by including all of them.

Professional skills

Marks were available for professional skills in question 1.

In this case candidates were required to prepare notes for use at a meeting with the client in relation to a number of different tax issues. Candidates should keep two things at the back of their minds while addressing this type of requirement: First, that explanations provided must be concise, but comprehensive enough to form the basis of the discussion with the client. Second, the notes should be presented in a logical, structured way, such that they will be easy to follow in the meeting. Candidates who scored well addressed all parts of the requirements, structured their answer according to the matters to be addressed (which were clearly spelled out in the manager's email), wrote concisely in short, clear paragraphs, provided easy to follow calculations and demonstrated a logical thought process in addressing each of the issues.

Overall, candidates who prepared satisfactory answers to question 1:

- directly addressed each of the tasks within the manager's email.

- had good knowledge of the UK residence status rules for companies.

- applied their knowledge well to the scenario and provided concise explanations where required.

- produced a clearly labelled and laid out IHT computation.

			ACCA marking scheme		
					Marks
(a)		One mark for each relevant point			5.0
					5.0
(b)	(i)	Taxation of profits			
		Subject to tax in Garia			1.0
		If JAY Ltd is UK resident			3.0
		If JAY Ltd is resident in Garia			2.0
		Relief for losses			
		If JAY Ltd is UK resident			4.0
		If JAY Ltd is resident in Garia			1.0
					11.0
				Maximum	9.0
	(ii)	One mark for each relevant point			4.0
					4.0
				Maximum	3.0
	(iii)	One mark for each relevant point			4.0
					4.0
				Maximum	3.0

(c)			
	Granting of lease		2.0
	Implications for the tenant		2.0
	Implications for the future		2.0
			⎯⎯
			6.0
		Maximum	5.0
			⎯⎯
(d)			
	Taxable amount of transfer to trust		2.5
	Nil rate band		2.5
	IHT liability		1.0
			⎯⎯
			6.0
			⎯⎯
	Problem solving		1.0
	Clarity of explanations and calculations		1.0
	Effectiveness of communication		1.0
	Overall presentation and style		1.0
			⎯⎯
			4.0
			⎯⎯
Total			**35.0**
			⎯⎯

Section 3

SPECIMEN EXAM QUESTIONS

SECTION A

BOTH questions are compulsory and MUST be attempted

1   **FARINA AND LAUDA**   *Walk in the footsteps of a top tutor*

You should assume that today's date is 7 December 2022.

Your manager has had a meeting with Farina and Lauda, potential new clients, who are partners in the FL Partnership.

The memorandum recording the matters discussed, together with an email from your manager, is set out below.

MEMORANDUM

To   The files

From   Tax manager

Date   6 December 2022

Subject   FL Partnership

Background

Farina and Lauda began trading as the FL Partnership on 1 May 2017. Accounts have always been prepared to 31 March each year. They are each entitled to 50% of the revenue profits and capital profits of the business.

On 1 March 2023, the whole of the FL Partnership business will be sold as a going concern to JH plc, a quoted trading company. The consideration for the sale will be a mixture of cash and shares. Capital gains tax relief on the transfer of a business to a company (incorporation relief) will be available in respect of the sale.

Farina and Lauda will both pay income tax at the additional rate in the tax year 2022/23 and anticipate continuing to do so in future years. They are very wealthy individuals, who use their capital gains tax annual exempt amounts every year. Both of them are resident and domiciled in the UK.

The sale of the business on 1 March 2023

The assets of the FL Partnership business have been valued as set out below. All of the equipment qualified for capital allowances.

	Value	Cost
	£	£
Goodwill	1,300,000	0
Inventory and receivables	30,000	30,000
Equipment (no item to be sold for more than cost)	150,000	200,000
Total	1,480,000	

The total value of the consideration will be equal to the value of the assets sold. Farina and Lauda will each receive consideration of £740,000; £140,000 in cash and 200,000 shares (a 2.4% holding) in JH plc.

Future transactions

Farina:

On 1 August 2023, Farina will make a gift of 15,000 of her shares in JH plc to the trustees of a discretionary (relevant property) trust for the benefit of her nieces and nephews. Farina will pay any inheritance tax liability in respect of this gift. The trustees will transfer the shares to the beneficiaries over the life of the trust.

Farina has already made the following gifts:

| 1 May 2021 | Cash of £300,000 to a discretionary (relevant property) trust |
| 1 July 2022 | Cash of £40,000 to one of her nephews |

Lauda:

On 1 June 2024, Lauda will give 40,000 of her shares in JH plc to her son.

For the purposes of giving our advice, the value of a share in JH plc can be assumed to be:

	£
On 1 March 2023	3
On 1 August 2023	4
On 1 June 2024	5

Email from your manager – dated 7 December 2022

I want you to prepare a memorandum for the client file in respect of the following:

(i) **Capital allowances**

A **detailed** explanation of the calculation of the capital allowances of the FL Partnership for its final trading period ending with the sale of its equipment to JH plc for £150,000 on 1 March 2023.

(ii) **Farina**

1   A calculation of the inheritance tax payable by Farina in her lifetime in respect of the gift of the shares to the trustees of the discretionary (relevant property) trust on 1 August 2023 and the date on which the tax would be payable. You should note that this gift will not qualify for business property relief.

2   A brief explanation of the availability of capital gains tax gift holdover relief in respect of the transfer of the shares to the trustees of the discretionary (relevant property) trust and the subsequent transfers of shares from the trustees to the beneficiaries.

(iii) **Lauda**

A review of whether or not Lauda should disclaim incorporation relief.

The review should encompass the sale of the FL Partnership business, the gift of the shares to Lauda's son and the effect of incorporation relief on the base cost of the remaining shares owned by Lauda, as she intends to sell all of her shares in JH plc in the next few years.

You should include a summary of your calculations and a statement of the key issues for me to discuss with Lauda. You should also include BRIEF explanations of the amount of incorporation relief available, the availability of any additional or alternative reliefs, and the date(s) on which any capital gains tax will be payable.

Tax manager

Required:

(a) It is anticipated that Farina and Lauda will require some highly sophisticated and specialised tax planning work in the future.

Set out the information that would be required, and the action(s) that should be taken by the firm before it agrees to become the tax advisers to Farina and Lauda.

(5 marks)

(b) Prepare the memorandum requested in the email from your manager. The following marks are available.

(i)   Capital allowances. (5 marks)

(ii)   Farina. (7 marks)

(iii) Lauda. (14 marks)

Ignore value added tax (VAT).

Professional marks will be awarded in part (b) for the overall presentation of the memorandum, the provision of relevant advice and the effectiveness with which the information is communicated. (4 marks)

(Total: 35 marks)

2 FORTI LTD GROUP

You should assume that today's date is 7 December 2022.

You have received an email from your manager with an attached schedule in connection with the Forti Ltd group of companies. The schedule and the email are set out below.

Email from your manager – dated 7 December 2022

The Forti Ltd group

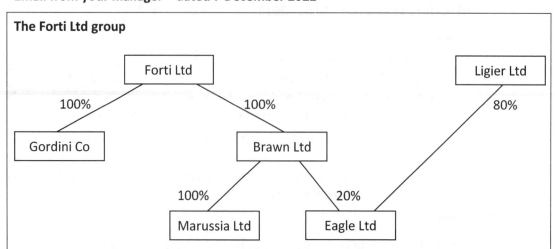

Forti Ltd has an issued share capital of 120,000 ordinary shares. It is owned by 12 shareholders, each of whom owns 10,000 ordinary shares.

All six of the companies are trading companies. Gordini Co is resident in and trades in the country of Arrowsia; it does not carry out any activities in the UK. The other five companies are all resident in the UK. There is no double tax treaty between Arrowsia and the UK.

The only changes to the group structure in recent years relate to the purchase and subsequent sale of Marussia Ltd by Brawn Ltd as set out in note 3 to the attached schedule.

Ligier Ltd has no links to the Forti Ltd group other than its shareholding in Eagle Ltd.

The work I require you to do is as follows:

(a)   Brawn Ltd – Review of the corporation tax computation

I attach a schedule detailing the corporation tax computation for Brawn Ltd for the year ended 31 March 2022. This schedule has been prepared by an inexperienced tax assistant.

Brawn Ltd is a medium-sized enterprise for the purposes of tax relief on research and development expenditure. I can confirm that the substantial shareholding exemption is not available in respect of the disposal of Marussia Ltd and that the figures given for the indexed cost of Marussia Ltd in the schedule, the degrouping charge in note 3, and the tax adjusted trading losses referred to in notes 4 and 5 have all been calculated correctly.

Please review the computation and related notes in order to identify any errors and prepare a revised schedule showing calculations of the correct taxable total profits and corporation tax liability. You should include notes explaining the errors you have identified and the changes you have made.

(b) **Other corporate matters**

  (i)   Brawn Ltd will only be a close company if Forti Ltd is a close company.

    Set out the matters that need to be considered in order to determine whether or not Forti Ltd is a close company.

  (ii)   Set out the matters which need to be considered in connection with the sale of components to Gordini Co referred to in note 6 to the schedule.

(c) **Value added tax (VAT) annual accounting scheme**

  The management of the Forti Ltd group have asked for advice on the annual accounting scheme.

  State the conditions which must be satisfied by any company wishing to operate the annual accounting scheme and explain the operation of the scheme.

Tax manager

Schedule prepared by a tax assistant

Brawn Ltd – Corporation tax computation for the year ended 31 March 2022

	Notes	£	£
Tax adjusted trading income	1, 2		240,800
Sale of Marussia Ltd – Proceeds	3	484,000	
Less: Indexed cost		(390,000)	
Annual exempt amount		(12,300)	
		———	81,700
			———
			322,500
Less losses transferred from:			
Marussia Ltd (£60,000 × 5/12)	4		(25,000)
Eagle Ltd (£52,500 × 20%)	5		(10,500)
			———
Taxable total profits			287,000
			———
Corporation tax at 19%			54,530
			———

Notes

1   The treatment of the following items of expenditure needs to be checked.

	£	
The cost of establishing a company share option plan (CSOP)	6,000	Disallowed
The cost of entertaining overseas customers	4,000	Disallowed
Accrued management bonuses to be paid on 1 February 2023	7,000	Allowed

2   The tax adjusted trading income is after deducting a total of £120,000 (£48,000 × 250%) in respect of research and development expenditure. The expenditure consisted of salaries paid to Brawn Ltd staff of £21,000 and payments for subcontracted labour of £27,000.

3	Marussia Ltd was purchased on 1 August 2021. On 1 November 2021, Brawn Ltd signed a contract to sell Marussia Ltd for £484,000, and the sale took place on 31 December 2021. Accordingly, the substantial shareholding exemption was not available. The sale of Marussia Ltd resulted in a degrouping charge of £21,500. This has been included as a chargeable gain in the corporation tax computation of Marussia Ltd.
4	Marussia Ltd made a tax adjusted trading loss of £60,000 in the year ended 31 March 2022.
5	Eagle Ltd made a tax adjusted trading loss of £52,500 in the year ended 31 March 2022 and did not pay a dividend.
6	During the year ended 31 March 2022, Brawn Ltd began selling components to Gordini Co. Are there any issues which need to be considered in respect of this in relation to Brawn Ltd's corporation tax liability?

Required:

Carry out the work required as set out in the email from your manager. The following marks are available:

(a) **Brawn Ltd – Review of the corporation tax computation.**

      Note: Ignore value added tax (VAT).   **(12 marks)**

(b) **Other corporate matters.**

    (i)   **Close companies.**   **(5 marks)**

    (ii)   **Note 6 to the schedule.**   **(3 marks)**

(c) **Value added tax (VAT) annual accounting scheme.**   **(5 marks)**

                                                (Total: 25 marks)

SECTION B

BOTH questions are compulsory and MUST be attempted

3 KESME AND SOBA

You should assume that today's date is 7 December 2022.

Kesme and Soba, a married couple, require advice on Kesme's taxable income and rent-a-room relief, the letting exemption available on a future sale of the family home, the remittance basis, and the assets which will be received by Soba under Kesme's will.

Kesme:

- Has been UK resident since the tax year 2018/19.
- Is deemed non-UK domiciled.
- Is married to Soba.
- Has not made any lifetime gifts for the purposes of inheritance tax.

Soba:

- Has been UK resident since the tax year 2008/09.
- Is deemed non-UK domiciled.

Kesme's income for the tax year 2021/22:

- Salary (gross) and benefits from Noodle plc, his current employer, of £48,500.
- Pension from a former employer of £24,100 (gross).
- Kesme and Soba rent out a furnished room in their jointly-owned family home for £17,650 per year.
- There are allowable expenses in respect of the rental income of £1,600.

Share-based remuneration provided to Kesme by Noodle plc in the tax year 2021/22:

- 400 shares in Noodle plc were issued to Kesme for £2,500.
- Kesme was granted non-tax advantaged share options to purchase 300 shares for £4 per share.
- Kesme exercised non-tax advantaged share options and purchased 250 shares for £3 per share. Kesme had paid 50 pence for each of these options.
- A share in Noodle plc can be assumed to be worth £12 throughout the tax year 2021/22.
- Noodle plc does not operate any HM Revenue and Customs (HMRC) tax advantaged share schemes.

Income to be received in the tax year 2022/23 in respect of investments in the country of Penne:

- Kesme will receive £1,400.
- Soba will receive £19,500.
- Neither Kesme nor Soba plan to remit any of this income into the UK.
- There is no income tax in the country of Penne.

Kesme's estate and his will:

- Kesme's gross chargeable estate has a current value of £1,280,000.
- This value includes a plot of land situated in the UK worth £370,000.
- In his will, Kesme has left the plot of land to his daughter and the residue of his estate to his wife, Soba.

Required:

(a) Explain the availability and operation of rent-a-room relief in relation to Kesme and calculate his taxable income for the tax year 2021/22 on the assumption that the relief is claimed.

(8 marks)

(b) State, with reasons, whether or not the remittance basis is available to Kesme and/or Soba and, on the assumption that it is available to both of them, explain whether or not it is likely to be beneficial for each of them.

Note: No calculations are required for this part. (6 marks)

(c) Calculate the value of the residue of the estate that Soba would receive under Kesme's will if Kesme were to die today. (4 marks)

(d) Explain how the spouse exemption available in respect of transfers from Soba to Kesme would be different if Soba were domiciled in the UK. (2 marks)

(Total: 20 marks)

4 SPIKE

You should assume that today's date is 7 December 2022.

Spike requires advice on the loss relief available and the value added tax (VAT) position following the cessation of his business and on the tax implications of a relocation payment provided by his new employer.

Spike:

- Ceased to trade on 30 September 2021 and sold the assets used in his unincorporated business.
- Sold his house, 'Sea View', on 1 March 2022 for £125,000 more than he had paid for it.
- Began working for Set Ltd on 1 May 2022.
- Has no income or chargeable gains other than the amounts referred to in the information below.

Spike's unincorporated business:

- There are overlap profits from the commencement of the business of £8,300.
- The sale of the business assets resulted in net chargeable gains of £78,000.
- The tax adjusted profits/(loss) of the business have been:

		£
Year ended 31 December 2017	Profit	52,500
Year ended 31 December 2018	Profit	68,000
Year ended 31 December 2019	Profit	54,000
Year ended 31 December 2020	Profit	22,850
Nine months ending 30 September 2021	Loss	(13,500)

Sale of the business:

- The majority of the business assets were sold to unrelated purchasers during September and October 2021.
- Spike retained some of his business assets for his own use.

Remuneration from Set Ltd:

–   Spike is being paid a gross salary of £65,000 per year.

–   On 1 July 2022, Set Ltd paid Spike a relocation payment of £33,500.

The relocation payment of £33,500:

–   Spike sold 'Sea View', and purchased a new house, in order to live near the premises of Set Ltd.

–   £22,000 of the relocation payment is to compensate Spike for having to sell his house at short notice at a low price.

–   £11,500 of the relocation payment is in respect of the costs incurred by Spike in relation to moving house.

Required:

(a)   (i)   Calculate the trading loss for the tax year 2021/22, and the terminal loss on the cessation of Spike's unincorporated business.   **(4 marks)**

        (ii)   Explain the reliefs available in respect of the losses calculated in part (a)(i) and quantify the potential tax savings for each of them.   **(10 marks)**

(b)   State the value added tax (VAT) implications of the cessation of the business and the sale of the business assets.   **(4 marks)**

(c)   Explain the income tax implications for Spike of the relocation payment.   **(2 marks)**

Notes

1   You should assume that the tax rates and allowances for the tax year 2021/22 apply to all tax years.

2   Ignore national insurance contributions throughout this question.

                                                          (Total: 20 marks)

Section 4

ANSWERS TO SPECIMEN EXAM

1   FARINA AND LAUDA   *Walk in the footsteps of a top tutor*

Key answer tips

This question is in two main parts: two partners in a partnership planning to sell their business to a company in exchange for cash and shares, and then planning to make disposals of the shares acquired on incorporation.

Part (a) was the guaranteed five marks on ethics which tests the information required and action to be taken before becoming tax advisers to two partners. This part is usually at the end of the question, but as it is an independent part it can be attempted at any point. The topic is straightforward and should provide easy marks. However, you need to make sure that you make reference in your answer to the partnership scenario given.

Part (b) firstly requires the capital allowances on the sale of the business to the company and should also provide five easy marks for TX knowledge. However, detailed explanations (not computations) are required, but only in relation to the final trading period.

Secondly, the IHT and CGT implications of the transfer of shares into a discretionary (relevant property) trust are covered for seven marks. The majority of the marks in this part are for the calculation of an IHT liability although the consideration of CGT implications and gift holdover relief are also required.

The last part of this question was the trickiest part as it requires a review of whether or not one of the partners should disclaim incorporation relief for 14 marks. A methodical approach and good use of headings and sub-headings to break your answer down is needed. It is important to deal with each step in turn – the sale of the business followed by a gift of shares, and then subsequent sale of shares in the future.

The question states that incorporation relief is available on the sale of the business, but you need to calculate the tax that would be charged in respect of these transactions both with and without incorporation relief and then make some sensible comments regarding your findings.

The highlighted words in the written sections are key phrases that markers are looking for.

Tutor's top tips

As is the norm for Section A questions in recent sittings, the formal requirements for part (b) that appear at the end of the question only tell you how many marks are available for each section of the memorandum. The detailed requirements can be found in the information provided.

As you read through the information highlight any requirements and instructions that you find. The requirements in this question are all in the email from the manager.

In part (b) the examining team has asked for a memorandum which addresses certain issues and you may find it useful to number these requirements so that you can tick them off as you attempt them.

Make sure you set out your answer in the required format. For a memorandum you need a suitable heading which will identify to whom it is addressed. Numbered headings which agree to the numbered points in the manager's email will make your answer easier to mark. Section A will always have four professional marks to cover presentation, relevant advice and quality of communication.

(a)   Becoming tax advisers to Farina and Lauda

Tutor's top tips

Be careful to answer the specific question here and address the facts of the scenario.

*The question does not ask for lists of information needed in order to be able to give advice once they are clients – it wants information required **before** becoming advisers.*

*Also note that the partners will want the provision of **specialised** tax advice – a hint that you need consider if the firm has the expertise to provide the advice needed.*

Information required in respect of Farina and Lauda:

- evidence of their identities; and
- their addresses.

Action to be taken by the firm:

- The firm should contact their existing tax advisers. This is to ensure that there has been no action by either Farina or Lauda which would, on ethical grounds, preclude the acceptance of the appointment.

- The firm should consider whether becoming tax advisers to Farina and Lauda would create any threats to compliance with the fundamental principles of professional ethics. Where such threats exist, the appointment should not be accepted unless the threats can be reduced to an acceptable level via the implementation of safeguards.

- With this in mind, the firm must ensure that it has sufficient competence to carry out the sophisticated tax planning required by Farina and Lauda.

- In addition, it is possible that providing advice to Farina and Lauda on the sale of their business could give rise to a conflict of interest, as a course of action (for example, the timing of the sale) which is beneficial for one of them may not be beneficial for the other. The firm should obtain permission from both Farina and Lauda to act for both of them and should consider making a different member of the firm responsible for each of them.

(b)   **MEMORANDUM**

To	The files
From	Tax senior
Date	7 December 2022
Subject	The FL Partnership

The purpose of this memorandum is to advise Farina and Lauda, the partners in the FL Partnership, on the sale of the business to JH plc and on the proposed disposals of shares in JH plc in the future.

(i)   Capital allowances of the FL Partnership for its final trading period

Tutor's top tips

Detailed explanations are required, not numbers.

Remember that only five marks are available and only the final period of trading needs to be considered.

There will be no annual investment allowance, first year allowances or writing down allowances in the period in which the business ceases.

Instead, there will be a balancing adjustment; either a balancing allowance or a balancing charge.

The balancing adjustment will be calculated as follows:

		£
TWDV b/f at the start of the period		X
Add: Additions in the period		X
Less: Disposals during the period		
Lower of cost and sales proceeds		(X)
		X
Less: Proceeds on the sale of the equipment (1 March 2023)		(150,000)
Balancing allowance/(balancing charge)		X/(X)

It will not be possible to elect to transfer the equipment to JH plc at its tax written down value because Farina and Lauda will not be connected with JH plc. This is because they will not control the company.

Tutorial note

On incorporation, if the previous owners of the business control the company incorporating the business, a succession election can be made to transfer the assets at TWDV instead of market value. As a result, balancing adjustments can be avoided on incorporation, but this will affect the base cost of the assets taken over by the company.

(ii)   Farina

1   Inheritance tax

Tutor's top tips

A calculation of IHT is required, so there is no need to provide explanations in this part of your answer.

Don't forget the easy mark for stating the due date of payment which is easily gained, but easily lost if you do not remember to write it down.

	£	£	£
Value of shares (15,000 × £4)			60,000
Less: Annual exemption 2023/24 (Note)			(3,000)
Chargeable lifetime transfer			57,000
Nil rate band at time of gift		325,000	
Less: Chargeable transfers in the previous seven years (Note)	300,000		
Less: Annual exemptions for 2021/22 and 2020/21	(6,000)		
		(294,000)	
Available nil rate band			(31,000)
Taxable transfer			26,000
IHT at 25% (Note)			6,500

The inheritance tax due will be payable on 30 April 2024 (Note).

Tutorial note

The gift on 1 July 2022 is a potentially exempt transfer. This gift uses the annual exemption for 2022/23, but has no effect on the nil rate band as it is not yet chargeable.

The lifetime IHT on the chargeable lifetime transfer is at 25% as the tax will be paid by Farina, the donor.

The gift is on 1 August 2023 which is in the first half of the tax year 2023/24 (i.e. up to and including 30 September).

The lifetime IHT is therefore due on the following 30 April (i.e. 30 April 2024).

If the gift had fallen into the second half of the tax year (i.e. after 30 September) the IHT would be due six months after the end of month in which the gift took place.

2   Capital gains tax gift holdover relief

Tutor's top tips

Although it is not clear from the requirement, there are only 1.5 marks for this part. Therefore, it is important to be follow the examining team's instructions and be brief and to the point.

Gift holdover relief will be available in respect of the transfer of the shares to the trustees because the transfer is immediately subject to inheritance tax.

For the same reason, gift holdover relief will also be available in respect of any subsequent transfers of shares from the trustees to the beneficiaries.

Tutorial note

Gift holdover relief is available where there is an immediate charge to IHT, even if the gift is covered by the nil rate band.

When the shares are put into the trust it is a CLT for IHT purposes, and therefore there is an immediate charge to IHT. This would be the case even if the gift is covered by the nil rate band.

When the shares are distributed out of the trust there will also be an immediate charge to IHT (known as an exit charge).

Accordingly, as there is an immediate charge to IHT, gift holdover relief is available both when the shares are put into the trust and when they are distributed.

(iii)   **Lauda**

Tutor's top tips

With many things to consider it is important to break down the answer and to think through each stage carefully:

- *The sale of the business – with and without incorporation relief.*

- *The gift of the shares.*

- *The subsequent sale of shares.*

Make sure you address all of the requirements, including a statement of key issues to discuss, brief explanations, availability of alternative reliefs and the due date of payment.

The sale of the business will result in a chargeable gain in respect of the goodwill.

The gain, equal to the market value of the goodwill of £1,300,000, will be split equally between Farina and Lauda, such that Lauda's chargeable gain will be £650,000.

As all of the equipment qualified for capital allowances, no capital losses will arise on its sale.

Tutorial note

The only chargeable asset is goodwill and therefore there is only one gain to consider.

Inventory and receivables are not chargeable as they are working capital, not capital assets.

Note that if the equipment was sold at a profit then there would a chargeable gain arising, unless the examining team specifically stated that they were all small items with cost and market values that did not exceed £6,000.

Tutor's top tips

Incorporation relief defers the gain on incorporation until the later disposal of shares. It is therefore necessary to consider all the series of events both with, and without, using incorporation relief.

If the relevant conditions are satisfied, then incorporation relief is automatically applied to the gain.

For incorporation relief to be disapplied the taxpayer must make an election within two years from the 31 January following the end of the tax year in which the transfer took place.

With incorporation relief

The sale of the business – 1 March 2023

	£
Capital gain on the sale of the goodwill	650,000
Less: Incorporation relief	
£650,000 × (£600,000/£740,000) (Note 1)	(527,027)
Taxable gain	122,973
Capital gains tax at 10% (Note 2)	12,297

The tax will be payable on 31 January 2024.

Lauda's base cost in the shares in JH plc

	£
Market value of the shares received (200,000 × £3)	600,000
Less: Incorporation relief	(527,027)
Base cost	72,973

The gift of 40,000 shares on 1 June 2024 (Note 3)

	£
Proceeds at market value (40,000 × £5)	200,000
Less: Cost (£72,973 × (40,000/200,000))	(14,595)
Taxable gain	185,405
Capital gains tax at 20% (Note 4)	37,081

The tax will be payable on 31 January 2026.

Explanatory notes

1 The relief is restricted by reference to the value of the shares divided by the value of the total consideration received. Lauda will receive a total of £740,000, consisting of cash of £140,000 and shares worth £600,000 (200,000 × £3).

2 Capital gains tax will be charged at 10% because business asset disposal relief will be available. This relief is available because the business is a trading business, it is to be sold as a going concern, has been owned for at least two years and JH plc is not a close company. It is assumed that Lauda has not exceeded the lifetime limit of £1,000,000 and will claim this relief.

3 Gift holdover relief will not be available in respect of this gift because the shares are quoted and Lauda will hold less than 5% of the company.

4 Capital gains tax will be charged at 20% because Lauda pays income tax at the additional rate. Business asset disposal relief will not be available because Lauda will hold less than 5% of JH plc.

Tutorial note

Business asset disposal relief (BADR) may be denied on chargeable gains relating to goodwill where the goodwill is acquired by a close company and the individual making the disposal becomes a shareholder in the company.

However, in this scenario the acquiring company is a plc which is likely to have many shareholders, and is therefore not a close company so the restriction does not apply and BADR is available.

Even if JH plc was a close company, BADR would still be available on gains relating to goodwill as Lauda will own less than 5% of the shares in JH plc.

In order for BADR to be available in respect of the gift of the shares, Lauda would also need to be an employee of JH plc on a part time or full time basis.

Investors' relief cannot be available as JH plc is a quoted (listed) company.

Without incorporation relief

Tutor's top tips

Consideration is needed of the same three events without incorporation relief, followed by a summary of findings and comments arising from the comparison.

The sale of the business on 1 March 2023

	£
Capital gain on the sale of the goodwill	650,000
Capital gains tax at 10% (Note 1 below)	65,000

The tax will be payable on 31 January 2024.

Lauda's base cost in the shares in JH plc

	£
Market value of the shares received (200,000 × £3)	600,000

The gift of 40,000 shares on 1 June 2024 (Note 2 below)

	£
Proceeds at market value (40,000 × £5)	200,000
Less: Cost (£600,000 × 40,000/200,000)	(120,000)
Taxable gain	80,000
Capital gains tax at 20% (Note 2 below)	16,000

The tax will be payable on 31 January 2026.

Explanatory notes

1   BADR will still be available if incorporation relief is disapplied in this scenario.

2   Capital gains tax will be charged at 20% because Lauda pays income tax at the additional rate. BADR will not be available because Lauda will hold less than 5% of JH plc.

Summary

	With incorporation relief	Without incorporation relief
	£	£
CGT on:		
Sale of the business	12,297	65,000
Gift of the shares on 1 June 2024	37,081	16,000
	─────	─────
	49,378	81,000
	─────	─────

The effect of incorporation relief on the base cost of the shares

	£	£
Reduction in base cost due to incorporation relief		527,027
Base cost re: gift of the shares on 1 June 2024		
Without incorporation relief	120,000	
With incorporation relief	(14,595)	
	─────	
Increase in the base cost of the gift		(105,405)
		─────
Overall reduction in base cost		421,622
		─────
Additional tax at 20%		84,324
		─────

Tutorial note

The model answer above could be simplified as shown below.

The base cost of the remaining 160,000 shares would be as follows:

If incorporation relief is claimed: £72,973 × (160,000/200,000) = £58,378

If incorporation relief is not claimed: £600,000 × (160,000/200,000) = £480,000

Reduction in base cost = (£480,000 – £58,378) = £421,622 as above

Key issues

Tutor's top tips

As a result of your calculation, consider what issues you need to bring to Lauda's attention.

If Lauda were to disclaim incorporation relief, she would have higher initial capital gains tax liabilities.

However, disclaiming incorporation relief will result in a higher base cost in the shares, such that on a sale of the shares in the future, there will be tax savings which will exceed the increased initial liability.

Tutorial note

1   *Incorporation relief reduces the capital gains tax payable on the sale of the business and the gift of the shares by £31,622 (£81,000 – £49,378). When this amount is deducted from the additional tax due because of the reduced base cost, we arrive at an overall increase in the capital gains tax liability of £52,702 (£84,324 – £31,622).*

   This overall increase in the capital gains tax liability is simply the tax on the deferred gain of £527,027 at 20% in the future rather than at 10%, due to the availability of BADR, now:

   £527,027 × (20% – 10%) = £52,703 (and a rounding difference of £1).

2   *Capital gains tax gift holdover relief in respect of gifts of business assets will not be available on the sale of the business to JH plc, because Farina and Lauda are not going to gift the business to the company; they are going to sell the business at market value, which will be received in the form of cash and shares.*

		ACCA marking scheme		
				Marks
(a)		Information required		1.0
		Contact existing tax adviser		1.0
		Fundamental principles		1.0
		Competence		1.0
		Conflict of interest		2.0
				───
				6.0
			Maximum	5.0
				───
(b)	(i)	Allowances available		1.5
		Calculation of balancing adjustment		2.0
		Consideration of transfer at tax written down value		1.5
				───
				5.0
				───
	(ii)	Inheritance tax		
		Chargeable lifetime transfer		2.0
		Inheritance tax liability		3.0
		Due date		1.0
		Gift holdover relief		1.5
				───
				7.5
			Maximum	7.0
				───
	(iii)	Capital gain on sale of business		1.5
		With incorporation relief		
		Incorporation relief		1.5
		Capital gains tax and due date		1.0
		Chargeable gain on gift of shares		2.0
		Capital gains tax and due date		1.0
		Without incorporation relief		
		Capital gains tax on sale of business		1.0
		Capital gains tax on gift of shares		1.5
		Explanations		4.0
		Summary and key issues		4.0
				───
				17.5
			Maximum	14.0
				───
		Overall presentation and style		1.0
		Provision of relevant advice		1.0
		Clarity of explanations and calculations		1.0
		Effectiveness of communication		1.0
				───
				4.0
				───
Total				**35.0**
				───

2   **FORTI LTD GROUP**

    (a)   **Brawn Ltd – Corporation tax computation for the year ended 31 March 2022**

	Notes	£
Tax adjusted trading income per original schedule		240,800
Costs relating to company share option plan	1	(6,000)
Accrued management bonuses	2	7,000
Research and development expenditure (£120,000 – £98,115)	3	21,885
		263,685
Sale of Marussia Ltd – Chargeable gain (£81,700 + £21,500 + £12,300)	4, 5	115,500
		379,185
Less losses transferred from:		
Marussia Ltd (£60,000 × 3/12)	6	(15,000)
Eagle Ltd	7	–
Taxable total profits		364,185
Corporation tax at 19%		69,195

Notes

1   The cost of establishing a company share option plan is an allowable deduction when computing tax adjusted trading income.

2   The management bonuses are not an allowable cost as they have not been paid within nine months of the end of the accounting period.

3   The additional tax deduction in respect of research and development expenditure is 130%, not 150%. In relation to payments for subcontracted labour, this additional deduction is only available in respect of 65% of the amount paid. Accordingly, the total deduction is £98,115 (£21,000 + (£21,000 × 130%) + £27,000 + (£27,000 × 65% × 130%)).

4   The degrouping charge should be added to the sales proceeds on the sale of Marussia Ltd, such that it increases the chargeable gain arising.

5   The capital gains tax annual exempt amount of £12,300 is not available to companies.

6   For the purposes of group relief, Marussia Ltd is regarded as having left the group once there were arrangements in force for it to leave the group. The signing of the contract on 1 November 2021 amounts to such arrangements, such that the company is only a member of the group relief group for the three months from 1 August 2021 until 31 October 2021.

7   Eagle Ltd is not a consortium company because it is in a group relief group with Ligier Ltd. Accordingly, it is not possible for any of Eagle Ltd's trading losses to be transferred to Brawn Ltd.

(b)   **Other corporate matters**

(i)   **Close companies**

Forti Ltd will be a close company if it is controlled by:

– any number of directors who are shareholders, or

– its five largest shareholders.

A company is controlled by those shareholders who own more than half of the company's share capital.

When determining whether or not a company is close within this definition, each shareholder is regarded as owning any shares owned by their associates as well as the shares owned personally. A person's associates include their direct relatives, business partners and the trustees of certain trusts set up by the shareholder or their direct relatives.

Control of Forti Ltd can be exercised by seven shareholders holding 58.3% (7/12) of the shares.

Accordingly, unless Forti Ltd is controlled by shareholder directors, it will only be close if some of its shareholders are associated with each other.

Tutorial note

There are further complexities when determining whether or not a company is close but the points set out above were sufficient to score full marks.

(ii)   **Transfer pricing (note 6 to the schedule)**

The transfer pricing rules will apply to the sale of components by Brawn Ltd to Gordini Co because these two companies are both controlled by Forti Ltd. The exemption for small and medium-sized enterprises is unlikely to be available, regardless of the size of the Forti Ltd group, as there is no double tax treaty between the UK and the country of Arrowsia.

Under the transfer pricing rules, if Brawn Ltd has sold components to Gordini Co for less than an arm's length price, it is required to increase its taxable profits by the excess of the arm's length price over the price charged.

(c)   **Value added tax (VAT) annual accounting scheme**

Conditions

– The company's VAT reporting and payments must be up to date, such that its VAT debt is not increasing.

– Taxable supplies (excluding VAT) must not be expected to exceed £1,350,000 in the following 12 months.

– The company must notify HM Revenue and Customs (HMRC) if it expects its taxable supplies for a year to exceed £1,600,000. The company must leave the scheme if its taxable supplies for a year exceed £1,600,000.

– The scheme is not available where registration is in the name of a group.

Tutorial note

Companies which are normally in a repayment situation can account for VAT annually if they wish, but this would not be advisable from a cash flow point of view as they would only receive one repayment for the whole year.

Operation of the scheme

– The company will be required to make nine monthly payments starting at the end of the fourth month of the year.

– Each payment is equal to 10% of the company's liability for the previous year as adjusted for any additional information provided to HMRC.

– Alternatively, a company can choose to make three larger interim payments equal to 25% of its liability for the previous year.

– The company must submit its VAT return within two months of the end of the year together with any final balancing payment.

ACCA marking scheme			Marks
(a)	Notes		
		Tax adjusted trading income – other matters	2.0
		Research and development	2.0
		Chargeable gains	2.0
		Losses transferred from Marussia Ltd	1.5
		Losses transferred from Eagle Ltd	2.0
	Calculation		5.0
			14.5
		Maximum	12.0
(b)	(i)	Definition of close company	2.5
		Associates	1.5
		Application	2.0
			6.0
		Maximum	5.0
	(ii)	Reasons why transfer pricing rules apply	2.5
		Adjustment required	1.0
			3.5
		Maximum	3.0
(c)	Conditions		3.0
	Operation of the scheme		3.0
			6.0
		Maximum	5.0
Total			**25.0**

3   KESME AND SOBA

(a)   Income tax

Availability and operation of rent-a-room relief

Rent-a-room relief is available because Kesme and Soba are letting a furnished room in their main residence.

Claiming the relief will allow each of them to deduct £3,750 (£7,500/2), rather than their share of the allowable expenses (a smaller figure), from their share of the gross rental income.

This relief must be claimed by 31 January 2024 (22 months after the end of the tax year 2021/22). The claim will then continue to apply until it is withdrawn.

Tutorial note

The election would also cease to apply in the unlikely event that the gross annual rent fell below £7,500.

Taxable income for the tax year 2021/22

	£
Salary and benefits	48,500
Pension from former employer	24,100
Property business income ((£17,650/2) − £3,750)	5,075
Shares acquired ((400 × £12) − £2,500)	2,300
Grant of non-tax advantaged share options – no tax on grant	0
Exercise of non-tax advantaged options (250 × (£12 − £0.5 − £3))	2,125
	────
	82,100
Less: Personal allowance	(12,570)
	────
Taxable income	69,530
	────

(b)   The remittance basis

The remittance basis is available to UK resident individuals who are neither domiciled nor deemed domiciled in the UK. Accordingly, it is available to both Kesme and Soba.

Kesme will have unremitted overseas income of less than £2,000. Accordingly, the remittance basis will apply automatically, such that there will be no loss of his personal allowance, and the unremitted income will not be subject to income tax in the UK. There will also not be a remittance basis charge. This is clearly beneficial for Kesme, as the income will also not be subject to tax in the country of Penne.

Soba will have unremitted overseas income of more than £2,000, such that the remittance basis will not apply automatically. In addition, because she has been resident in the UK for 12 of the 14 tax years prior to 2022/23, if Soba were able to claim the remittance basis there would be a remittance basis charge of £60,000 as well as the loss of her personal allowance. This is clearly not beneficial for Soba as it exceeds the amount of income which she would be sheltering from UK tax.

(c)   Soba

Value of the residue of the estate

Soba will receive the residue of the estate, i.e. the estate less the gift to the daughter and the inheritance tax on that gift.

	£
Kesme's gross chargeable estate	1,280,000
Less: Gross gift to daughter (W)	(400,000)
Residue of the estate received by Soba	880,000

Working

	£
Legacy to daughter	370,000
Less: Nil rate band	(325,000)
	45,000
Inheritance tax at 40/60 (Note)	30,000
Gross gift (£370,000 + £30,000)	400,000

Tutorial notes

1   Although Kesme is non-UK domiciled, the specific legacy to his daughter will be chargeable to UK IHT because it is a UK asset.

2   The inheritance tax due on the specific gift to the daughter will be paid out of the residue of the estate, such that it will be borne by Soba. Because the residue of the estate is exempt, due to the spouse exemption, the gift must be grossed up.

3   Proof of Kesme's IHT liability

	£
Kesme's estate	*1,280,000*
Less: Legacy to Soba (above) – spouse exemption	*(880,000)*
Gross chargeable estate	*400,000*
Less: Nil rate band	*(325,000)*
Taxable estate	*75,000*
Inheritance tax at 40%	*30,000*

(d) **The spouse exemption available to Soba**

There is no limit on the 100% spouse exemption available to Soba where both Soba and Kesme are non-UK domiciled.

However, if Soba were domiciled in the UK, the 100% spouse exemption in respect of transfers from her to Kesme would be restricted to the first £325,000 of total assets transferred.

	ACCA marking scheme		Marks
(a)	Rent-a-room relief		
	Availability		1.0
	Operation		1.5
	Claim		1.5
	Employment income		1.0
	Property business income		0.5
	Share options		3.0
	Personal allowance		0.5
			9.0
		Maximum	8.0
(b)	Availability of remittance basis		1.0
	Kesme		3.0
	Soba		3.0
			7.0
		Maximum	6.0
(c)	Value of the residue of the estate		
	Calculation of amount received by Soba		2.0
	Inheritance tax liability		2.0
			4.0
(d)	Spouse exemption available to Soba		
	No limit if both Kesme and Soba non-UK domiciled		1.0
	Restriction if Soba UK domiciled		1.0
			2.0
Total			20.0

4   SPIKE

(a)   (i)   Loss relief available on the cessation of the trade

Trading loss for the tax year 2021/22

	£
Loss for the period from 1 January 2021 to 30 September 2021	13,500
Add: Overlap profits	8,300
	21,800

Tutorial note

The basis period for the tax year 2021/22 runs from 1 January 2021 (the end of the basis period for the previous year) until 30 September 2021 (the cessation of trade).

Terminal loss

	£	£
6 April 2021 to 30 September 2021:		
Loss (£13,500 × 6/9)		9,000
Add: Overlap profits		8,300
		17,300
1 October 2020 to 5 April 2021:		
1 October 2020 to 31 December 2020 profit (£22,850 × 3/12)	5,713	
1 January 2021 to 5 April 2021 loss (£13,500 × 3/9)	(4,500)	
Net profit ignored for the purposes of the terminal loss	1,213	–
Terminal loss		17,300

(ii)   The reliefs available in respect of the trading loss and the terminal loss

Relief of the loss for the tax year 2021/22.

The loss for the tax year 2021/22 can be offset against Spike's total income of 2021/22 and/or 2020/21.

Once the loss has been offset against the total income of a particular tax year, it can also be offset against the chargeable gains of that same year.

Spike has no income in the tax year 2021/22. But, a claim can be made for the whole of the loss to be relieved against his 2021/22 chargeable gains.

Relieving the loss against the gains on the sale of the business assets would save capital gains tax at the rate of 10% due to the availability of business asset disposal relief. The tax saved would be £2,180 (£21,800 × 10%).

Spike's sale of his house will be an exempt disposal of his private residence if he has always occupied it, or is deemed to have always occupied it. If part of the gain on the house is taxable, capital gains tax will be payable at 28% because the gains on the business assets will have used the basic rate band. Accordingly, if this is the case, the loss should be offset against any gain on the house in priority to the gain on the business assets.

In the tax year 2020/21, the loss would be offset against the total income of £22,850. The claim cannot be restricted in order to obtain relief for the personal allowance of that year. The tax saved would be £2,056 (£10,280 (£22,850 – £12,570) × 20%).

Relief of the terminal loss

The terminal loss can be offset against the trading profit of the business for 2021/22 and the three preceding tax years, starting with the latest year.

The trading profit in the tax year 2021/22 is nil, such that the terminal loss will be relieved in the tax year 2020/21. This would save tax of £2,056 (£10,280 (£22,850 – £12,570) × 20%).

The excess of the trading loss of 2021/22 over the terminal loss is £4,500 (£21,800 – £17,300). This amount can be offset against total income and chargeable gains in 2021/22 and 2020/21 as set out above. However, once the terminal loss has been relieved in the tax year 2020/21, Spike's remaining total income of £5,550 (£22,850 – £17,300) is less than the personal allowance, thus there is no taxable income and therefore, no further tax saving to be achieved in either of the two relevant years. Accordingly, the remaining loss should be relieved against the chargeable gains of 2021/22. This would save tax of £450 (£4,500 × 10%) if the loss is relieved against the gains on the sale of the business assets, or £1,260 (£4,500 × 28%) if it is relieved against a non-exempt gain arising on the sale of the house.

(b) Value added tax (VAT)

Spike should have notified HM Revenue and Customs of the cessation of his business within 30 days of ceasing to make taxable supplies, i.e. by 30 October 2021.

He may be liable to a penalty if he failed to do so.

Spike should have charged VAT on any machinery and inventory which he sold whilst he was still registered for VAT.

When Spike deregistered, he should have accounted for output tax on all business assets which he still owned in respect of which he had previously recovered input tax. There was no need to account for this output tax if it was less than £1,000.

(c) The relocation payment

The compensation in respect of the sale of the house at short notice at a low price will be regarded as having been derived from employment, such that it will be taxable in full.

£8,000 of the payment in respect of the costs of moving house will be exempt; the remaining £3,500 (£11,500 – £8,000) of the payment will be taxable.

			Marks
ACCA marking scheme			*Marks*
(a)	(i)	Loss for the tax year 2021/22	1.0
		Terminal loss	3.0
			4.0
	(ii)	Relief of the loss for the tax year 2021/22	
		The reliefs available	2.0
		Tax savings – 2021/22	
		Business assets	1.5
		House	2.0
		Tax savings – 2020/21	1.0
		Relief of the terminal loss	
		The reliefs available	3.0
		Tax savings – terminal loss	1.0
		Tax savings – excess of trading loss over terminal loss	1.5
			12.0
		Maximum	10.0
(b)		Requirement to deregister	2.0
		Output tax	2.0
			4.0
(c)		Relocation payment	2.0
Total			**20.0**